The 479th Fighter Group in World War II

The 479th Fighter Group in World War II

in Action over Europe with the P-38 and P-51

Terry A. Fairfield

Schiffer Military History
Atglen, PA

Dustjacket and color aircraft profile artwork by Steve Ferguson, Colorado Springs, CO

On the dustjaket: Lieutenant Berkley E. Hollister, flying the 434th Fighter Squadron P-38 he named "Little Edris" to honor of his wife, is shown attacking a train parked at a railway station. Aircraft from the 434th FS took part in the attack, which occurred on 22 June 1944 at the railway station south of St. Quentin, France. Lt. Hollister made two strafing runs on the train. On his second pass, he dropped two 250-lb. bombs, but they both overshot and missed the train. After the war it was reported that 380 German troops were killed in the attack. They had been passengers on the train.

Dedication

This book is gratefully dedicated to preserving the memory of the men who served with the 479th Fighter Group during World War II and who through the blessings of the Living God above, helped preserve the freedoms we enjoy today. I also want to dedicate this effort to my father, Paul W. Fairfield, who set me on the beginnings of this journey many years ago. Thanks Dad, you did just fine.

Book design by Robert Biondi.

Library of Congress Catalog Number: 2004105449.

Printed in China.
ISBN: 0-7643-2056-4

We are always looking for people to write books on new and related subjects. If you have an idea for a book, please contact us at the address below.

Published by Schiffer Publishing Ltd.
4880 Lower Valley Road
Atglen, PA 19310
Phone: (610) 593-1777
FAX: (610) 593-2002
E-mail: Info@schifferbooks.com.
Visit our web site at: www.schifferbooks.com
Please write for a free catalog.
This book may be purchased from the publisher.
Please include $3.95 postage.
Try your bookstore first.

In Europe, Schiffer books are distributed by:
Bushwood Books
6 Marksbury Ave.
Kew Gardens
Surrey TW9 4JF
England
Phone: 44 (0)20 8392-8585
FAX: 44 (0)20 8392-9876
E-mail: Bushwd@aol.com.
Free postage in the UK. Europe: air mail at cost.
Try your bookstore first.

CONTENTS

Foreword ... 6
Prologue ... 7
Introduction ... 10
Acknowledgements ... 12

Chapter 1 479th Fighter Group (TE): August 1943 to May 1944 ... 14
Chapter 2 May 1944 ... 30
Chapter 3 Wattisham AAF Station F-377 ... 36
Chapter 4 June 1944 ... 54
Chapter 5 July 1944 ... 88
Chapter 6 August 1944 ... 118
Chapter 7 September 1944 ... 161
Chapter 8 October 1944 ... 201
Chapter 9 The Seven Dogs Pub ... 227
Chapter 10 November 1944 ... 232
Chapter 11 December 1944 ... 251
Chapter 12 January 1945 ... 288
Chapter 13 February 1945 ... 307
Chapter 14 March 1945 ... 344
Chapter 15 April 1945 ... 378
Chapter 16 Finis 1945 ... 423

Book Closing: *by Coburn T. Palmer* ... 451
Appendices ... 452
Color Aircraft Profiles ... 481
Bibliography ... 497
Index ... 499

FOREWORD

The 4th Air Force authorized the activation of the 479th Fighter Group (twin engine) 21 October 1943; consisting of the 434th Fighter Squadron, the 435th Fighter Squadron and the 436th Fighter Squadron 28 October 1943. Lieutenant Colonel Leo F. Dusard, Jr., assumed command of the 479th Fighter Group with Major Joseph A. Shurlmistras commanding the 434th Squadron, Captain John A. Glover the 435th Squadron and Captain William R. Walker the 436th Squadron. Lt. Col. Leo Dusard very quickly was removed from command of the 479th Fighter Group and sent overseas on a personnel replacement assignment. Major Francis J. Pope temporarily took Lt. Col. Dusard's duties. Lieutenant Colonel William E. Dyess was assigned to take command of the 479th Fighter Group, but before he assumed command, he was killed while checking out in a P-38 aircraft. I, Kyle L. Riddle, then a Lieutenant Colonel, was assigned and took command of the 479th Fighter Group on 23 December 1943, assuming direct command 26 December 1943.

After approximately three months of combat training, the 479th Fighter Group crossed the U.S. continent by rail and embarked for England by convoy to report to the U.S. Eighth Army Air Force and our operational base at Wattisham Royal Air Force Base on 15 May 1944.

We flew our first two combat missions for practice, on 25 May 1944. Our third combat mission was a sweep over Holland and Belgium looking for enemy aircraft. None were spotted but we were introduced to flak from enemy ground positions.

Our primary combat mission assignments throughout the war were escorting daylight bombing missions by the Eighth Air Force against targets on the continent of Europe; protecting the bomber aircraft from any enemy aircraft attacks. Secondary missions were "seek and destroy." These missions were flown at lower altitudes. We were constantly alert for enemy aircraft assembling or en route to attack our friendly air forces or friendly ground troops. Other targets on these missions were ground traffic of trains, military vehicles on roads and highways, enemy troop concentrations, etc. We received frequent assignments of these secondary missions just prior to and following D-Day.

In this history book, all ranks and grades from within the 479th Fighter Group were asked to relate some experience(s) involved in their separate efforts, however small or large, direct or indirect, that contributed to accomplishing our mission assignments in support of the Eighth Air Force as well as other U.S. Army Air Forces, other Allied Air Forces and Allied Ground Forces, all who sought to liberate occupied Europe from the Axis Forces.

Each pilot should and surely each of us does, pause frequently now when some current happening causes us to remember a wartime incident and think how fortunate we were to have the ground support we did that provided us with a very reliable instrument, machine or tool (viz. the aircraft we flew) that enabled us to perform our combat missions. Yes, I include the person that performed the most insignificantly indirect work to properly maintain the aircraft we flew.

The 479th Fighter Group established an enviable combat record during the approximate one year we were in combat. I am proud to have had a part in its formation and subsequent wartime efforts.

BG Kyle L. Riddle
USAF (Ret.)

PROLOGUE

On Saturday, 10 May 2003, I had the honor of attending a sixtieth anniversary commemoration of the date that the Royal Air Force turned Wattisham Airfield over to the Americans for their use during World War II. My wife and I had gone to England and traveled there to the former United States Army Air Force station so that we might join a group of 479th Fighter Group veterans who had returned to take part in the event. Maggie Aggiss, chairperson of the Wattisham Airfield Museum, and her co-workers, having extended an invitation to all of the group's veterans to attend, had worked diligently to assemble a wonderful program for them and their families. The daylong festivity bore witness to their successful efforts and through the gracious courtesy of the Royal Army, whose forces now occupy the airfield and utilize it as a base for helicopters, we all were able to enjoy the celebration at its proper location. The Royal Army in the spirit of the occasion even permitted an honorary return of the base to American hands for a few hours.

The following day, Sunday 11 May 2003, the veterans, their families, members of the Wattisham Airfield Museum and members of the East Essex Aviation Society spent several pleasant hours at the Nettlestead Chace residence of Mrs. Nell Bloor, a historic estate located near Wattisham Airfield. (Mrs. Bloor was married to Stephen Fuller and bore that married name until she remarried later after his death in 1964. Mrs. Fuller then took the surname of Bloor from her second husband.) We all had been invited to her home where our hostess entertained us during a fashionable garden party. Mrs. Bloor is a very likable and lively ninety-seven year-old lady who with her former husband, had made friends with many officers from the RAF as well as the 479th Fighter Group and had often invited them to her home during and after the war. She provided a haven and place of rest for them to escape the stress if even only for a short while. There, after the war, Mrs. Bloor established and still maintains a small garden of remembrance dedicated to her friends who had been lost keeping freedom alive. Her kindness in opening her home to the group during those times is still remembered and stands a fine example of Anglo-American friendship.

Above: Former Bison Squadron pilot (First Lieutenant) James E. Frolking who represented the group, is pictured during a short speech in which he accepted command of the airfield. *Courtesy of the author.*

Below: The house, all that remains of the original built during the mid-1550s, and garden at Nettlestead Chace. *Courtesy R. D. "Chris" Stone, Air Cdre. RAF (Ret.)*

A portrait done of Mrs. Nell Fuller (Bloor) showing her as she would have appeared during the time the group was present at Wattisham Airfield. *Courtesy of the artist, R. D. "Chris" Stone, Air Cdre. RAF (Ret.)*

A portion of the memorial garden. The large stone at the head of the garden reads: "At the going down of the Sun, and in the Morning too, we shall remember them" *Courtesy of the author.*

Some of the garden stonework upon which various names are inscribed. Note the center one that bears the name of Pigg (First Lieutenant Robert N.), a pilot who was lost during the war. *Courtesy of the author.*

INTRODUCTION

"Mr. Vice President, and Mr. Speaker, and members of the Senate and House of Representatives: Yesterday, December 7, 1941 – A date which will live in infamy – the United States of America was suddenly and deliberately attacked by naval and air forces of the Empire of Japan." Words spoken by then President of the United States, Franklin Delano Roosevelt in his December 8, 1941 address to Congress requesting a Declaration of War with Japan.

The full-scale war in Europe had been in progress for over two years and Japan had been at war, expanding its empire in Asia and the South Pacific for nearly ten years when, at 7:55 AM Sunday morning, December 7, 1941, the false veil of isolationism, with which many in the United States had sought to surround the country with, was finally wrenched away. The Japanese surprise attack on the U.S. Navy's Pacific Fleet at Pearl Harbor and other nearby U.S. Army military facilities drew America into an inevitable war with the Axis Powers.

Fortunately, prior to the Japanese attack, some of our nation's leaders, both civilian and military, foresaw the time when we would be involved in war and steps were taken toward preparedness. Previously, the nation's attitude was one of defensiveness only, relying upon the U.S. Navy. Gradually however, because of events taking place within and outside of the United States, thoughts of changing this policy came to the forefront. An offensive structure through the use of air power was one of these developments and that doctrine had a strong proponent in an army flyer named William (Billy) Mitchell. As a colonel in charge of America's air support in France during World War I, he had witnessed the effectiveness of aircraft in warfare. As early as 1924, Mitchell, now a Brigadier General and the United States Assistant Chief of Air Service, had issued a "Report of Inspection of United States Possessions in the Pacific and Java, Singapore, India, Siam, China & Japan." In his report, General Mitchell warned that the Japanese would be our next enemy and that a 7:30 A.M. air attack on our Navy at Pearl Harbor would produce excellent results against our vulnerable battleships. Scoffed at by many, throughout his life General Mitchell remained steadfast to his vision of the airplanes domination of future warfare and the need for the creation of a Department of the Air Force as a separate branch of service equal to the already existing Departments of the Army and Navy. During 1937, United States Navy Lieutenant Commander Logan Ramsey published an article in which he stated that our fleet would be attacked first in order to leave us defenseless against further attacks. Ironically, Lt. Commander Ramsey gained a measure of fame later at Pearl Harbor when he broadcast the first alert on December 7, 1941: "AIR RAID PEARL HARBOR ... This is no drill."

President Franklin D. Roosevelt recognized the need to rebuild the U.S. military and through his administration, planed for, among other things, the expansion of the Army Air Corps and encouraged American aircraft manufacturing in the late 1930's. Heavy bombers such as the Boeing B-17, first flown in July of 1935 and later Consolidated Aircraft Corporation's B-24 became the vogue. Thought to be able to fly fast and high enough to limit vulnerability to fighter attack and antiaircraft artillery, they were to strike the offensive death dealing blows to the enemy. Medium bombers like the Douglas produced A-20, North American's B-25 "Mitchell" (so named to honor General William Mitchell) and Martin's B-26 were also conceived and built. Fighter development was not lacking though, for it would have been unwise to neglect such matters. Lockheed's P-38, Bell Aircraft's P-39, the Curtiss P-40, Republic's P-47 and North American's P-51 saw their genesis during this period. In an effort to unify elements of the rapidly expanding service branch, the Army Air Corps became The Army Air Force on June 20, 1941, through the War Department's issuance of Army Regulation 95-5. General H. H. Arnold continued as its leader, overseeing its growth from 14 groups as of late 1938, to 67 groups by late 1941.

During this time the United States was divided into four geographical regions, each assigned an air force, numbered one through four. A fifth air force was needed once United States entered the war since the Roosevelt administration, during the course of the American-Britain Conversations (ABC-1) in late 1941, had committed to Great Britain to be its chief ally. The Fifth Air Force, was created January 2, 1942 to be the air element in an invasion of Axis occupied Africa, but on January 6, 1942 the fledgling air force being developed was renumbered under revised plans. Officially activated on January 28, 1942, the Eighth Air Force, as it became, was stationed at Savannah Army Air Base in Savannah, Georgia. The Fifth, Sixth and Seventh Air Forces being activated and assigned to duties in other regions outside of the United States.

Colonel Asa N. Duncan led the Eighth Air Force from its beginnings in a National Guard Armory on Bull Street in Savannah, Georgia. Once in England, the Eighth was led by Major General Carl A. Spaatz, with Brigadier General Ira Eaker heading VIII Bomber Command and a short while later, Brigadier General Frank O'D. Hunter heading VIII Fighter Command. In addition to the above named commands, the "Mighty Eighth", the name by which it has grown to be known as, included an air force support command, a service command, a composite command and all the men and material involved.

The strength of the Eighth Air Force waxed and waned in time with development and implementations of the various wartime conferences, operations and plans. The first of the great wartime conferences, the Arcadia Conference held in Washington, D.C. from December 24, 1941 to January 14, 1942 and attended by President Roosevelt and Prime Minister Winston Churchill, wrought forth the establishment of the Eighth Air Force in Great Britain. The Air War Plans Division Plan (AWPD-1) drafted in January of 1942, set the original strength. The Air War Plans Division Plan of 1942 (AWPD-42), a September revision of AWPD-1, increased its strength. And so it went, the Peabody Plan, then the Bradley Plan, which was to be the final plan for the Eighth Air Force buildup for the invasion of Hitler's "Festung Europa." Then along came the Trident Combined Chiefs of Staff (CCS) Conference in Washington during May of 1943, the Quadrant CCS Conference at Quebec, Canada during August 1943 and the Sextant CCS Conference at Cairo, Egypt meeting November through December 1943. Final strength was at last decided and achieved just prior to the invasion of France, D-Day, June 6, 1944.

It was during one of those planning sessions that the seeds of the 479th Fighter Group were sown. The last of the great fighter groups to join the Mighty Eighth, the 479th's beginnings can be traced to General Order 166, Headquarters Fourth Air Force, which on October 21, 1943 authorized its activation. Assigned to IV Fighter Command, the 479th Fighter Group and its subordinate units, the 434th Fighter Squadron, the 435th Fighter Squadron and the 436th Fighter Squadron were assembled at Grand Central Air Terminal (GCAT), Glendale, California. Los Angeles Fighter Wing Special Order No. 257 authorized the assignment of 38 officers and 162 enlisted men. In preparation for activation, certain key personnel from the 329th Fighter Group based nearby were ordered to the Army Air Forces School of Applied Tactics (AAFSAT) at Orlando, Florida to study and learn the latest information and methods of operation for fighter groups in combat.

In the pages that follow, an attempt has been made to record just how the 479th Fighter Group, "Riddle's Raiders", lived and fought while in Europe until the final victory was won and VE-Day was declared. Each and every man played his part and an effort has been made to show at some point in this volume, a part of the picture of how those members participated in one of the Eighth Air Force's great fighter groups of World War II.

Regarding the particular jargon found throughout this text, the author chose to write in the vernacular of the era to preserve a feeling of the time. The idioms used were those spoken by the men and included within their records.

ACKNOWLEDGEMENTS

At the top of my list, I wish to cite my wife, who suffered long as I spent the countless hours necessary to the production of this volume. She has been both patient and helpful, serving as my editor-in-residence. I could not have asked for a better helpmate. Thank you Bonnie.

I am indebted to Mike O'Connor, who unselfishly relinquished his desires to write this volume in the first place and who gave me the information he had gained from the Air Force Historical Research Agency at Maxwell Air Force Base, Alabama. The journey began here.

A debt of gratitude also is due my mentor and guide, Steve Blake, whose friendship and advice have been invaluable.

During the course of my early struggling with the sheer weight of the project, Dwayne Tabatt supplied me with additional information that added to the nucleus of my database. Thank you, Dwayne. Your help was greatly appreciated.

Many thanks go to the supplier of a huge amount of data on P-51's, Ted Damick, a good brother in Christ.

Finally, I want to thank those men who served with the 479th Fighter Group, as well as their wives, all who unselfishly took me in as a friend, gave their time and lent me their resources in order that this work might reach completion. It has been my very great honor to know and to have known many of those who gave so much to our country in order that we might enjoy the freedoms we have today. This great generation is rapidly fading as time takes its toll upon them, but through the efforts of this book, it is hoped that the memory of them and of their achievements will be preserved for future generations to know and appreciate. Their sacrifices must not be forgotten. Thank you good friends. You have become like family to me and as each of you passes, I hurt, but I take comfort in the truth that someday, we will all be together again in that great family above.

Special mention goes to close friends now departed, Fred Hayner from the 434th Fighter Squadron and John Sipek from the 436th Fighter Squadron. I miss you guys.

Those persons or group members who contributed time and material are as follows: The 434th Fighter Squadron Association, The 436th Fighter Squadron Association, Maggie Aggiss, Edward L. Akin, Themis N. Anastos, Kenneth D. Axt, Eugene W. Bailey, Roger H. Barrell, Charles L. Beatty, Stephanie A. Benoit, David L. Born, Clifford W. Bowers, Kermit A. Brickson, Robert I. Bromschwig, Calvin J. Butler, Jack M. Clark, George H. Cooper, William S. Culbertson, Charles H. Darling, William H. Daudistel, Wilmer D. Davis, Stephen Decker, Johnny M. Deetjen, Stanley E. Derby, Albert R. DiPaola, Gordon L. Doolittle, Carol Donaldson, Walter M. Drake, Charles B. Elmgren, George E. Falkner, Edwin J. Fillipow, Cheri Fleming, Kathy Grdenich Fleming, Roger A. Freeman, Ray K. Friend, James E. Frolking, Kevin Gallagher, William M. Gates, Robert Gerrard, George S. Gleason, Travis M. Greenwood, Harold F. Grenning, Kenneth J. Hansen, Flamm D. Harper, Frederick C. Hayner, Clarence G. Haynes, Frederick L. Hart, John W. Hedenberg, William H. Hehn, Albert S. Heigh, Arnold G. Helding, James R. Helms, George D. Hendrix, Leslie L. Heuman, Howard G. Hightower, Oranne (Sowerby) Hilgerman, Thomas A. Hollingsworth, Berkley E. Hollister, Verne E. Hooker, Robert H. Horman, Herman E. Hoversten, William Hugill, Arthur F. Jeffrey, Herbert R. Jordan, Stanley Kellett, Robert B. Kleinman, James H. Koerber, Gerald V. Landreth, Marie H. Lewis, Ernest S. Lundstrom, Richard

M. Lunstrum, Ronald L. Maley, Alton A. Massey, Allen J. Moon, William M. Morgan, Arlett G. Mosier, Jr., Sally Mulvany, John N. Murr, Albert M. Myers, Louis K. Nesselbush, Raymond Niekamp, Robin Olds, Victor R. Plassenthal, Henry P. Plunk, Mario V. Prevosti, Guy M. Purdy, Bernard J. Reilly, Edwin G. Richards, J.T. Richardson, Donald Riddle, Kyle L. Riddle, Charles F. Schlitz, Eugene E. Sears, James J. Shuttleworth, John Shuttleworth, Richard G. Simpson, Edward H. Sims, John J. Sipek, James W. Smart, Theo J. Sowerby, Milan J. Stanovich, Stanley L. Steele, R. D. "Chris" Stone, Harold L. Stotts, Clarence M. Surges, Loetta Taylor (Kennedy), Thomas H. Thompson, John T. Tipps, Albert S. J. Tucker, Eugene V. Venezia, Frank W. Watkins, John E. Wendt, Lewis J. West, Arthur H. Wilcox, Roy A. Wiley, Alvin R. Wilhite, Glen A. Wold, Ruth Zemke and The Wings of Freedom Museum in Huntington, Indiana.

I sincerely apologize to any person or organization who has rendered aid in any form and whom I have missed mentioning. My intent was to cite all those who have helped.

Terry A. Fairfield
April, 2004

CHAPTER ONE

479TH FIGHTER GROUP (TE) AUGUST 1943 TO MAY 1944

During August of 1943, Lieutenant Colonel Leo F. Dusard, Jr., who was to become the 479th Fighter Group's first commanding officer, began the process of the group's formation. Drawing personnel from the 329th Fighter Group Headquarters, the embryonic 479th FG began development in a headquarters building across the street from its parent, the 329th FG Headquarters, a part of the 329th FG located at Santa Ana Army Air Base, Santa Ana, California. One of Lt.Col. Dusard's first duties was to pick certain key personnel from the 329th FG who would be sent for training at the Army Air Forces School of Applied Tactics (AAFSAT) at Orlando, Florida. The officers and enlisted men sent were to study and learn the latest information and methods of operation for fighter groups in combat. Once trained, they were to return to California and begin formation of a new Fighter Group, the 479th. On 28 August 1943, the hand picked personnel left for AAFSAT in Florida. While training there, the as yet unformed fighter group suffered its first loss when Captain W.H. Brooks lost his life when he crashed in a P-47 at Zephyrhills, Florida. Upon the men's return, the 479th Fighter Group was activated 28 October 1943, per General Order 166 dated 21 October 1943. The order that emanated from Headquarters, Fourth Air Force, was backdated to be effective 15 October 1943. Additionally, per General Order 166, the new fighter group was assigned the 434th, the 435th and the 436th Fighter Squadrons (TE) as subordinate units and they were activated on the same 28 October 1943 date. The group was to draw its cadre from the 329th FG and was given the mission of an Operational Training Unit flying the Lockheed twin-engine (thus the TE appendage on the group's title) P-38 Lightning.

Lt.Col. Dusard was officially authorized command of the 479th FG on 15 October 1943. With the official assumption of that command on 28 October 1943, Lt.Col. Dusard began assembling the group, starting with the 38 officers and 162 enlisted men he was first allotted. From that allotment came the 479 FG Headquarters Commanding Officer, Major Francis J. Pope and the three commanding officers for the squadrons: Major Joseph A. Shurlmistras, 434th FS; Captain John G. Glover, 435th FS; and Captain William R. Walker, 436th FS. The fighter group moved and began organizing at Grand Central Air Terminal, (GCAT) Glendale, California and was assigned to the Los Angeles Fighter Wing per Headquarters, Fourth Air Force General Order 20 dated 1 November 1943.

Lt.Col. Dusard almost became the group's second casualty when he landed a P-38. He overshot the runway at GCAT and ended up almost in the concrete lined Glendale Wash, a huge drainage ditch. When the damaged aircraft was reached, he was emerging from the plane's cockpit and muttered to one of his men, Master Sergeant Arthur H. Wilcox, "That's a hell of a thing for a group commander to do." M/Sgt. Wilcox had been one of the AAFSAT attendees and was currently serving as one of the group headquarters' armorers. He was one of the first on the scene, having witnessed the accident and gone to disarm the plane's guns.

The Lieutenant Colonel was well liked by his men, but unfortunately his tenure with the group was short lived, for he received orders relieving him of his command, effective 11 November 1943 and sending him overseas. Maj. Francis J. Pope became Lt.Col. Dusard's temporary replacement and he took over the helm that same date until a replacement could be found for the Lt.Col. Barely had Maj. Pope assumed his duties when once again, tragedy struck the fledgling group. This time it came in the form of an automobile accident in southern California on 13 November 1943. The accident took the life of First Lieutenant Charles D. Stansbury from the 436th FS.

Lt.Col. Dusard's replacement was to be Lieutenant Colonel William E. Dyess, a hero of the American defense forces in the Philippines. Lt.Col. Dyess, for whom Dyess Air Force Base at Abilene, Texas is named, was a First Lieutenant commanding the 21st Pursuit Squadron of the 24th Pursuit Group in the Philippines when the Japanese attacked that country on 8 December 1941. The squadron had been there for only 18 days when the attack began. As fighting continued, combat losses and Japanese strafing gradually cut the group's strength to the point that the group was ordered to move its remaining resources to the Bataan Peninsula. Fighting a losing battle there with the better equipped Japanese forces, Lt. Dyess distinguished himself both through his leadership and valor in maintaining a fighting force with which to continue attacking the invaders. Attrition took its toll though and on 3 April 1942, after giving his chance of escape to another, recently promoted Major Dyess was captured by the Japanese and made a prisoner. Suffering through the infamous Bataan Death March and the hardships of being a prisoner of the Japanese, one year later, Maj. Dyess, along with eleven other men, made a successful escape from the prison camp where they were being held. Eventually able to link up with guerrilla forces, Maj. Dyess and others finally were able to return home and regain their health.

Promoted to Lieutenant Colonel and rehabilitated, Lt.Col. Dyess spent a good deal of time with the group and was to assume command of the 479th, but once more, fate dealt the group a bad card. On 22 December 1943, Lt.Col. Dyess was killed while checking out in a P-38. During his take off roll, the aircraft developed a malfunctioning engine that could be heard detonating by those nearby as he attempted to get airborne. Without full power and lacking sufficient experience in emergency procedures for the situation, (he had waved training in the twin engine fighter, apparently having felt he had sufficient skill) he crashed and the group was once again without a leader. The officer who replaced Lt.Col. Dyess was the man who was to lead the group for the majority of its time, Lieutenant Colonel Kyle L. Riddle, the man for whom the group is named "Riddles Raiders". Lt.Col. Riddle assumed command on 26 December 1943.

From the time of the group's formation, until early February 1944, the 479th and its component squadrons were stationed at GCAT. There the group grew in manpower, organized and trained to become a cohesive fighting unit for the combat to come. Examples of activities that took place during these days are found in the following entries to the group's historical chronology:

<u>1 November 1943</u>: A meeting of all 434th FS officers was held at 1000 hours for the purpose of setting up each section and planning a ground school for the enlisted men.
<u>3 November 1943</u>: Capt. William T. McElhinney was assigned to the group and appointed Group Flight Surgeon.
<u>4 November 1943</u>: All officers and enlisted men fired the Qualifications Course with the Caliber 30, M1- Carbine.
<u>6 November 1943</u>: All officers and enlisted men participated in a personal inspection and parade. An inspection of the barracks and barracks area was also made.
<u>8 November 1943</u>: Ground training began in the morning. During the afternoon, the 479th FG played the 329th FG in a game of softball. The 479th lost.
<u>11 November 1943</u>: Officers were appointed Class A Finance Officers for the purpose of paying the regular monthly payroll for their respective organizations, i.e., Group Headquarters and the three squadrons.
<u>13 November 1943</u>: Major Pope, Capt. Walker and First Lt. Turner received orders to ferry three P-38s from Albuquerque, New Mexico to San Bernadino, California.
<u>16 November 1943</u>: First Lt. Joseph F. Schneider was assigned to the group and further assigned as Flight Surgeon for the 434th FS. First Lt. Clifford J. Moore was assigned to the group and further assigned to the 436th FS.
<u>18 November 1943</u>: During the morning, all officers and enlisted men fired the Qualifications Course with the Thompson Submachine Gun. The afternoon brought another softball match between the 479th and the 329th FG's, the losers to buy the beer. The 479th lost again.
<u>18 November 1943</u>: Captains Jackson and McElhinney, plus First Lt. Patterson were detailed to attend the Oxygen Training School at March Field, California.
<u>19 November 1943</u>: Lieutenants Harris and Horton were detailed to attend a two-week Camouflage School at March Field, California.

20 November 1943: All officers and enlisted men participated in a personal inspection and parade. An inspection of the barracks and barracks area was also made.

22 November 1943: First Lt. Clarence O. Johnson and Second Lt. Gilbert L. Miller were assigned to the group and further assigned to their respective squadrons, with Lt. Johnson going to the 436th FS and Lt. Miller going to the 435th FS. Second Lt. John J. Benson was detailed to attend a four-week course in aircraft maintenance at the Lockheed-Vega Aircraft Factory, Burbank, California.

25 November 1943: Thanksgiving Day.

27 November 1943: All officers and enlisted men participated in a personal inspection and parade. An inspection of the barracks and barracks area was also made.

1 December 1943: Special Order #16 authorized enlisted men's promotions.

2 December 1943: First Lt. Keith E. Canella received orders to attend Fixed Gunnery School at Foster Field, Texas.

3 December 1943: First Lt. Thomas R. Brown was assigned to the group and appointed Group Chaplain.

8 December 1943: Capt. Trout and First Lt. John J. Courtney, Jr. were assigned temporary duty as test pilots at the Long Beach, California 58th sub-depot.

10 December 1943: Several of the officers had been planning a so-called bivouac, but the continual rains the area had been experiencing seemed to have kept a "damper" on that so far. The "liquid sunshine" was bringing a variety of ailments to many others, perhaps a harbinger of things to come.

11 December 1943: The Deerslayer Bivouac Saturday Afternoon Club finally got underway. Composed of Maj. Mercready, Capt. Stoops, Lts. Duffié, Grossenbacher, Turner, Schneider, Leeds and Horton, along with Sgt.'s Hicks and Lemke; the men hiked and camped about in some of the nearby areas. Lt. Turner, hailing from Tampa, Florida, apparently saw snow for the first time and had an encounter with a vicious 60-year-old burro.

12 December 1943: Captain Edward F. Stoops, Jr. as well as First Lieutenants Claire A.P. Duffié and George K. Sykes were granted leave of absence.

18 December 1943: Parade and review rained out.

20 December 1943: Capt. John D. Monahan received orders temporarily assigning him to the 58th sub-depot at Long Beach, California for the purpose of testing aircraft. Rains and wind threatened the Christmas Carol Sing. Held in an auditorium, floods still kept the bulk of the audience away.

332nd Fighter Squadron
329th Fighter Group AAF
Army Aidrome, Santa Ana, California
Thanksgiving Day — November 26, 1942

MENU

Cream of Mushroom Soup
Oyster Crackers
* * * *
Fruit Cocktail
* * * *
Roast Tom Turkey — Virginia Baked Ham
* * * *
Oyster Dressing — Cranberry Sauce
Snowflake Potatoes — Candied Yams
Giblet Gravy — Raisin Sauce
Buttered Peas — Whole Kernel Corn
* * * *
Hot Parkerhouse Rolls — Hot Butter Rolls
* * * *
Celery Hearts — Carrot Sticks
Fresh Vegetable Salad — French Dressing
Stuffed Olives — Ripe Olives — Green Queen Olives
Sweet Pickle Chips
* * * *
White Bread — Rye Bread — Wheat Bread — French Bread
* * * *
Fresh Milk — Chocolate Milk — Lemonade — Coffee
* * * *
Chocolate Cake — Devils Food Cake — White Layer Cake
Apple Pie — Pumpkin Pie — Lemon Pie — Mince Meat Pie
Ice Cream and Cookies
* * * *
Apples — Oranges — Grapes — Bananas — Assorted Nuts
* * * *
Butter — Peanut Butter — Jam — Sugar
* * * *
Assorted Candy — Cigars — Cigarettes
* * * *
Claret Wine

A copy of the Thanksgiving Day menu from the previous year at Santa Ana Army Airfield. *Courtesy of James W. Smart.*

24 December 1943: Bing Crosby sang before midnight services at the Casino.

25 December 1943: Christmas Day was enjoyed by all, despite the fact it was not a white Christmas. It was most of the men's last spent in the ZOI (Zone of the Interior – the U.S.) until after VE Day and for others, their last ever.

28 December 1943: More rain.

29 December 1943: Pistol Qualifications were shot using the U.S. Pistol, Caliber .45, despite more rain.

31 December 1943: New Years – everyone was off to celebrate the passing of 1943 and the beginning of 1944.

17 January 1944: Maj. James M. Herren is assigned to the 434th FS, replacing Maj. Shurlmistras as C.O.

And so it went, each day filled with duties, boredom, sports, promotions, (and an obligatory passing out of 6-cent cigars by the recipient of the promotion) rain, cold and what so many times was listed in the history as "the usual organizational activities". Sometimes the activities weren't so usual though. On 18 January 1944, the P-40F that was assigned to the 436th FS, the only plane it had at the time, was demolished in a landing accident at GCAT. The squadron had just received the plane a few weeks earlier. The pilot was the 436th FS's First Lieutenant Clarence O. Johnson, already a veteran of service in the MTO. He was not injured despite the P-40 winding up on its back. The wrecked ship was transferred to the 58th sub-depot for repair or salvage. (Note above, that is where several of the group's pilots had been temporarily assigned to test aircraft.) Happily, the month of January also saw delivery of the first six stateside P-38s to be assigned to the group. Two each of the H models were divided amongst the three squadrons and the ships were immediately put to use. Flying was somewhat curtailed though, due to the excessant rains. Oh, yes, the 479th finally managed to at least tie the 329th in a softball game!

Married men were permitted to live off base with their wives and Clarence (Clancy) M. Surges, who was a sergeant in the 434th FS's Operations at the time, remembers living with his wife, Lila, in Costa Mesa until he shipped overseas. She had come out to visit him while he was stationed with the 329th FG and wound up staying for a year-and-a-half. She worked at the Newport Harbor Yacht Club where Clancy met a number of movie stars, including Humphrey Bogart, Andy Devine and Richard Arlen. Clancy had three cars during that time, a '35 Graham-Page, a '36 Plymouth and a '37 Studebaker. He'd sell one, then get another each time he was transferred to another airfield. He thought it was like having a paid vacation there. He and Lila would bike ride to Laguna Beach and when at home, their door was always open to visitors. An occasional over-night guest needed a ride back to the field, but that was okay. What a life, he thought. That all changed dramatically for Clancy, as it did for most others, while they were in the ETO.

As time passed, manpower increased. On 31 December 1943, the group had 57 officers or 36% of its authorized strength and 278 enlisted men or 31% of its authorized strength. By 31 January 1944, strength had increased to 138 officers or 87% of its authorized strength and 723 enlisted men or 81% of its authorized strength.

Robin Olds from the 434th FS had a talent for humor and drawing cartoons. This one depicts the growing pains the newly formed fighter group was suffering at GCAT. Notice the building shown under the windmill – the Elbow Room, a nightclub the men thought well of. *Courtesy of George E. Falkner.*

The beginning of February brought about a change of duty station for the group and each of its squadrons. Grand Central Air Terminal had a short runway and population was heavy nearby. The airport simply could not handle all of the air traffic and byproducts of the training that was occurring there. Thus, the lights and glitter of nearby Hollywood, as well as the Elbow Room, a local "watering hole", were to become a memory after the 6th. Before leaving though, there was a big party in the new Glendale Officer's Club, the evening of the 5th. Brigadier General Russell Randell, C.O. of Fourth Fighter Command, introduced Sophie Tucker who sang a number of songs for the crowd. She had a hard time leaving the stage because of the enthusiastic audience. Maj. James "The Masher" Herren, the 434th's new squadron C.O., was present with "all flags flying" and going great guns with a very beautiful blonde who was dressed in green. Major Herren came with quite a reputation as a ladies man.

Departing from Glendale on Sunday, the 6th of February, the squadrons went their respective ways for a while. The 434th FS relocated about 20 miles south at Lomita Flight Strip. Their move was accomplished by a convoy of about thirty vehicles sent from March Field. Loading began at 0830 hours and the trucks left with sirens screaming at 1000 hours. After laboring up the surrounding hills, the squadron arrived at Lomita an hour-and-a-half later, had lunch and then began unpacking. The 435th FS headed about 50 miles west to Oxnard Flight Strip. Their journey began a little later, at 1245 hours. The convoy ride was uneventful and the squadron arrived a couple of hours later to begin settling in. The 436th FS went about 35

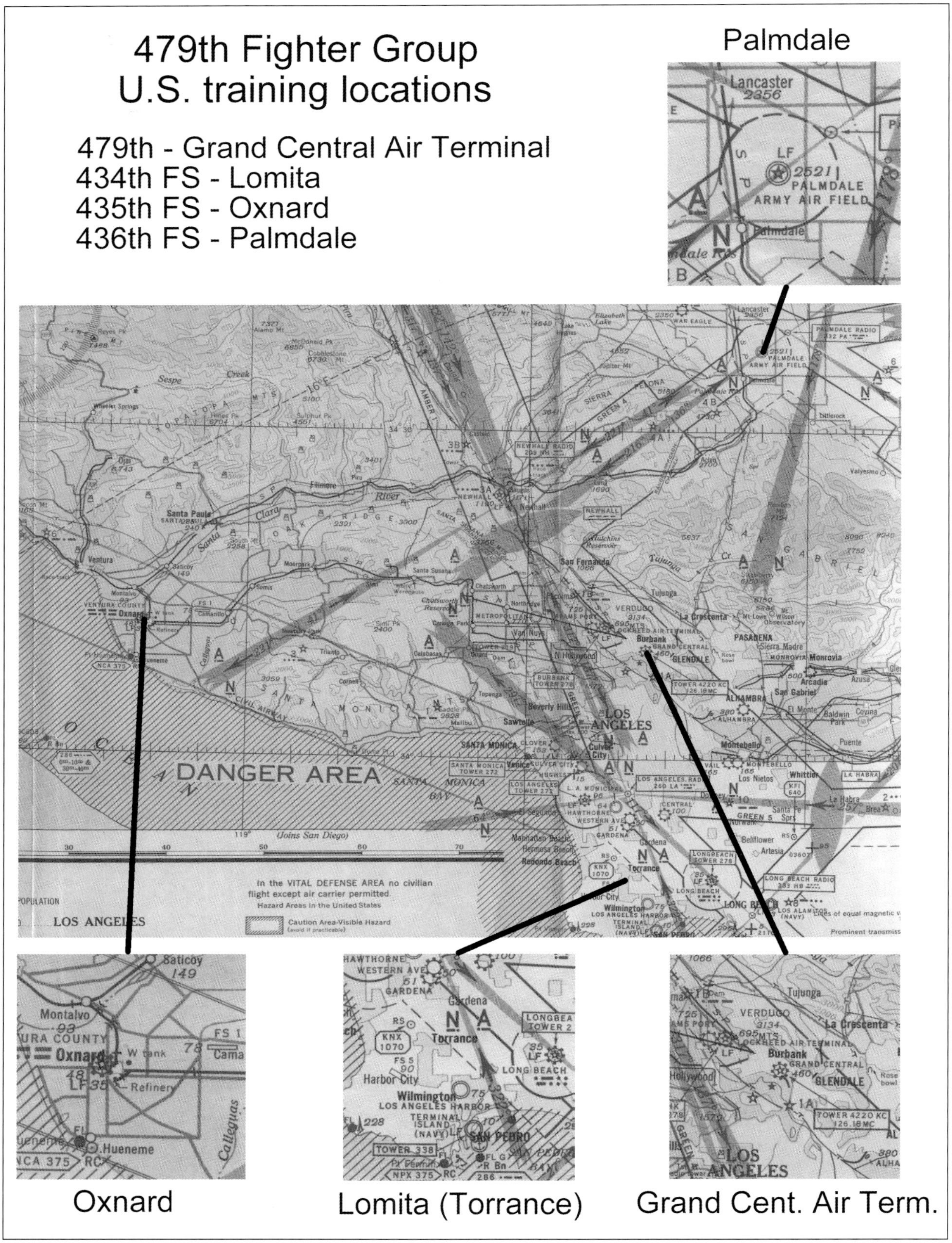

Airfields that the 479th Fighter Group occupied during its stay in the United States.

miles north to Palmdale Army Airfield. Once the location their move was to take them was known, the men of the 436th "began looking forward to a pleasant and inexpensive stay in the desert". Leaving at 0930 hours, a convoy of trucks from Muroc Air Field moved the squadron. They arrived in time for chow at noon. Then the work began, as the previous occupants had left the area in a sorry condition. 479th FG HQ moved to Lomita the following day, 7 February. Their short journeys completed, each of the squadrons and the group headquarters then spent time in the "usual organizational activities", setting up in their respective new homes and gaining more personnel. The group lost an enlisted man, though. Corporal Thomas D. Griffin, assigned to group headquarters, had an interest in becoming a pilot. He once had aspirations to be a glider pilot, but since he had joined the 479th, his desire had become to get into a P-38 with its two Allison engines to keep him up. As he stated, he was almost certain that a glider didn't have two Allison engines. He passed his examinations for acceptance into the aviation cadet program and was transferred out of the group, pending his appointment to aviation cadet training.

Established in their new settings, the squadrons and group headquarters trained in earnest for what was to come. Each of the squadrons found they had aircraft at their duty stations and more flying could be accomplished. At Palmdale though, the rains while still present, mostly gave way to dust storms, which driven by high winds, made life most unpleasant. Lomita had its drawbacks also; as probably did Oxnard, but at Palmdale, when the sun went down in the evening, the temperatures dropped considerably and the oil heaters the men had to keep them warm were a sorry lot. Tongue-in-cheek threats were made to build a big bonfire in the center of the BOQ (Bachelor Officers Quarters) if someone didn't do something about the heaters. Again, a harbinger of things to come. Perhaps a wise person in charge foresaw this all as proper training for the English climate?

Additional men were assigned to the group and personnel were exchanged amongst the squadrons, as those in charge sought the best fit for a position. The "usual organizational activities" took place as well as the not so usual. On 9 February, First Lieutenant John J. Courtney, an experienced Flight Leader from the 435th FS, was forced to bail out of the P-38 he was flying, just southeast of the field at Oxnard. His parachute opened at a very low altitude, but he escaped with only a shoulder injury. The occurrence would serve him well at a later date when he would be once again forced to "take to the silk" over enemy-held territory. The early to mid-month weather having held back the rains with a few sunny days, presented the pilots at Lomita with much needed time to fly. The men at Oxnard, however, were experiencing high winds in the range of 35-40 MPH. That was okay, though, because all personnel were going through a series of immunization shots, preparatory for their shipment overseas. Needless to say, there were a lot of sore arms and posteriors. The men at Palmdale had a bit of excitement when Captain Thomas T. Galloway, A Flight's leader, brought his damaged P-38 back for a landing after his plane's left engine had its supercharger explode during a training flight. The explosion sent fragments of the supercharger and its protective armor plate in all directions, embedding many in the aircraft's tail boom and wing. Extensive damage was done, necessitating a lot of sheet metal repairs.

Technical Sergeants Herbert J. Schlaffman, James W. Smart and William A. Haas in a Jeep named "Rose". The 434th FS crew chiefs were parked beside one of the squadron's tarpaper covered buildings at Lomita. *Courtesy of James W. Smart.*

Sunday morning, 13 February saw Chaplain Thomas R. Brown a busy man, as he had to cover all three squadron locations that day. It was the first Sunday since the group's separation and the Chaplain would experience the travel until the group left for overseas. On the less spiritual side, the next day, in addition to the physical training the men at Lomita underwent in the morning, the evening boasted a USO show that was presented in the mess hall. Among other things, there was an acrobatic dancer, a hip-swinger that told stories with her hands, an accordionist and finally, a Master of Ceremonies who had a bulldog. The best part of the show though, was the mess sergeant, who ran about pulling the flypaper off the ceiling during the acts.

Training continued and no one escaped that. The enlisted men received a refresher course in basic training as well as additional instruction on new material including demonstrations on camouflage, chemical warfare and booby-traps. The last subject was the direct cause of many mysterious explosions on and about Lomita Flight Strip for the next two weeks. Some of the men there including Technical Sergeant Earl L. Hicks, got hold of some push-pull whistle bombs and fastened them where they would do the least damage and cause the most fright. It got so that the men there were afraid to open a door lest they would hear a shrill whistle and a loud explosion right under their feet.

The middle of the month also saw the first issue of the long-awaited group newspaper appear in print. The paper called "Kontak" was four pages in length and was (and still is) very enjoyable reading. It contained personal notes about people in the group as well as news of sports programming. Personnel demanding to know where he obtained his scoops besieged the editor, Sergeant Neal Russo, but he always managed to escape answering those questions. The 15th also saw the handiwork of "Mr. Jack Frost" at Palmdale. All in the squadron awoke that morning to be treated to the sight of the normally brown and sandy desert, covered with a carpet of white snow. Many were curious and the weather officer, Lieutenant Church, wandered about all that day in a state of astonishment, trying to figure out and explain the phenomenon.

Personnel continued to flow into the group and on the 16th, the 479th at Lomita received 108 armorers. What must have been the better part of a whole graduating class was assigned to the new fighter group. Those in charge at Lomita experienced the usual SNAFU (Situation Normal, All Fouled Up) for the new men's arrival. Every step had been taken to insure a smooth and rapid expedition of them when they got to the group in the morning. Arrangements had been made for the trucks necessary to their movement and those had arrived the night before. The mess hall was all prepared for an "additional army" for breakfast and finally, a team had been assembled for the speedy assignment and handling of all the records. The plans went haywire when the men finally pulled into the Wilmington Train Station toward noon. The armorers were to have arrived at the field, so frantic calls were made for the transportation. The chow line that day was the longest in the organization's history. As the group's diarist noted, the new men must have known that fried chicken was on the lunch menu. Finally, by mid-afternoon, the men were on their way to their assigned squadrons.

The 17th of February was a day of note for both the 435th and 436th FS's. The 435th men at Oxnard almost had an early Fourth of July fireworks display when a tent covering a large supply of ammunition caught fire. The quick thinking of several enlisted men saved the ammunition. They dragged the blazing tent off the cache and fortunately, nothing more than the tent burned. The 436th's Captain Thomas T. Galloway had another in-flight emergency when the P-38 he was flying had a supercharger failure. This time his aircraft lost the right engine when the supercharger's impeller was blown out in an explosion caused by a backfire. It was believed that the unit's regulator failed and caused the problem. At 25,000 feet at the time, Capt. Galloway returned to make a successful single-engine landing that would have made the best pilots envious.

The BIG news for all of group HQ was the arrival of doughnuts on a daily basis in the S-2 intelligence room. Beginning Friday, 18 February there were donuts to go with the coffee already there. Six dozen of the tasty treats arrived and disappeared within an hour. Thus was the case, henceforth.

The 18th was also the date of a squadron dance at Palmdale. Invitations went out to the surrounding area and seventy-five girls showed up to give the place some life and take the monotony away for a short time. A GI orchestra from nearby Muroc was provided and everyone had a great time.

Rains, mixed with snow, made an appearance at Lomita and Oxnard this date.

20th of February: the rains were still present and, in fact, the night before, a regular deluge had begun, accompanied by thunder and lightning at Oxnard. At Lomita, five or six inches of water coursed through the operations building and more was coming in from all directions, including through the roof! The men there all swore that Noah could have learned an additional thing or two had he been there. Operations, Engineering and Intelligence personnel, taking up mops and brooms, acted with vigor to make the place fairly hospitable, but made little headway against the onrushing torrents. Since the day was Sunday, church was scheduled in the schoolroom, but Chaplain Brown took one look at the water there and decided that since the Chaplain's Kit didn't include an ark, the day's service had to be called off. He had better luck at Oxnard and Palmdale, even though it had begun raining on the 436th, also.

All of the dampness was again having an effect on the health of the men at Lomita and "Doc" Joseph F. Schneider had his hands full. In addition to the many immunization shots being given, sick call was keeping him busy. There was one

Left: First Lieutenant Robin Olds, a 434th FS pilot, by one of the training P-38s at Lomita. *Courtesy of Frederick C. Hayner.* Right: Second Lieutenants Berkley E. Hollister, Themis N. Anastos, James L. Wallace and William H. Hehn after a successful hunting trip at Lomita. Utilizing skeet shotguns, the men brought back a few jackrabbits. Note the many oil wells that appear in the background. The area was heavily dotted with them. *Courtesy of Berkley E. Hollister.*

customer he nearly didn't get though. Technical Sergeant James W. Smart had to be dragged to the dispensary for treatment of a cold that had him down for the past several days.

The foul weather continued until Wednesday 23 February. During that time the men attended ground schools and worked on various projects including digging ditches around buildings to divert the waters and laying 2x4 plank walkways. The weather was so fickle at early-week, that it actually hailed at Lomita and the men there read in the newspaper that Los Angles had seven inches of snow! Some of the men were beginning to have their own ideas about California as the land of sunshine. Fact is that some wag at the 436th suggested the squadron requisition an aircraft carrier from the Navy so that the pilots would not lose so much precious flying time. Finally, the rains let up somewhat and flying became the order of the day.

Another issue of the group newspaper "Kontak" came out and again people were chasing the culprit, this time Sergeant Joseph W. Donohue, who filled in for Sgt. Russo. Everyone wanted to know where he got all the "stuff" he published.

The 435th FS lost a P-38 to an accident on the 24th of the month. One of the newer pilots, Lieutenant Charles T. Stayley, misjudged his height above the runway while he was taking off and retracted his landing gear too soon. The ship, failing to have sufficient speed for flight, settled on the runway in a belly slide. The lieutenant involved was not injured by the accident, but certainly had a strip torn off his backside later.

The 435th FS sent a drawing of their proposed squadron insignia through channels to Washington for approval. The insignia featured the cartoon character Bugs Bunny riding a winged cannon that had bolts of lightning replacing the usual P-38 twin-booms.

The remainder of the month consisted of rain, flying, ground training, physical training, a dance and floor show at the 435th's Oxnard home, inspections and "the usual organizational activities". Many long hours of labor were put in as the men drew ever closer to their final date with the POM (Post Overseas Movement) Inspectors who would check everything to ensure men and material were ready for overseas movement.

March definitely came in like a lion as per the old adage. Once more the men had to endure abnormal weather conditions in "sunny" California, all of which would have just seemed normal if they had known where they were going and what life was going to be like there. The first few days consisted of ground training because there was no flying anywhere. Winds, rain, sand and even snow greeted the men as they tried to go about their duties. In preparation for eventual departure overseas, the men of the group were issued M1 Carbines and were trained in the care and use of them. Later in the month, the squad leaders were told to turn in their carbines and were in turn issued M3 submachine guns, which the men said, looked very much like a Buck Rogers Rocket Gun.

On the 6th of the month, Second Lieutenant Chester W. Granville, a pilot from the 435th FS became a member of the Caterpillar Club through no desires of his own. It seems that during an aerial gunnery mission out over the Pacific Ocean, the target tow cable was shot and severed from the tow plane.

Lt. Granville just happened to be in the correct position to snare the falling cable in his plane's propellers. The plane immediately became uncontrollable and Lt. Granville "hit the silk". After he had spent an uncomfortable half-hour in the cold waters of the Pacific, a Navy Catalina landed nearby and loaded the wet Lieutenant onboard. He was taken to a hospital where he quickly recovered.

The next day, First Lieutenant Donald D. McClure from the 435th FS was forced to make a belly landing on a plowed field that ran parallel to the runway at Oxnard Flight Strip. One of his plane's engines had quit completely and his landing gear would not go down into its proper position. He had no choice but to set the ship down on her underside. Lt. McClure did a beautiful job of landing and escaped uninjured from the washed out airplane.

Other events on the calendar included the building of crates for the packing and shipment of the group's and the three squadron's equipment. Classes in booby traps and camouflage were taken.

Gerald (Jerry) R. Landreth, then a corporal, was assigned to the 434th FS as a part of the squadron's radio control network. At Wattisham he would become a part of the group's CNS (Control Network System) crew, the men who among other things, when the weather was bad and the pilots couldn't find their way back home, gave them directions to the airfield. (AKA: "Heater Homer") He later was transferred out of the group to join a signal group that formed the basis of the forward controllers collectively known as "Nuthouse". However for this moment, Jerry was still at Lomita, sitting in a radio direction-finding truck that was parked on top of a hill located near Highway 1. He had recently been issued an M1 Carbine and he was wondering just how well it shot. He was all by himself, so when he happened to look out and see a bird's head bobbing along in the weeds, he thought he had spotted a pheasant and an opportunity to try out his carbine. He got ready, took aim and squeezed off a shot. His aim was true and the grass where the bird had been seen, exploded. Sure enough, he had gotten himself a pheasant! At least that is what he thought. When he jumped down out of the truck and went over to where the bird was, five or six more *peacocks* jumped up out of the grass and flew down to a farm below. Jerry said that surprised him because he didn't know there were any farms within 50 miles of where he was. He quickly decided he had better get rid of the bird, so he began digging a hole in which to bury the bird. The hole wasn't quite large enough and he had some difficulty stuffing the big bird with its long tail feathers into the hole he had prepared. He was successful though and never heard anything about the incident.

The second week saw each of the squadrons as well as the group HQ out for bivouacs in their surrounding countryside. During the bivouacs, the men attended more training lectures. Perhaps to soften the rustic element of the campsites, the special services department provided beer to wet the men's whistles. Then, of course, along came the singing. Among the many groups, which had turned their talents to that venue, perhaps the Lomita crew provides some good insight to the evening's fun. Groups of men, scattered about the wooded area in which they were settled down, made the best of the circumstances. One could hear many colorful voices, some thick with the effects of malt and hops. From the tearful cowboy ballads of the western boys to the popular songs of the day, one could choose some rung of the ladder for selections to suit his fancy, his pitch or his memory. The rhythm section was afforded by a quaint group of enlisted men, who seemed to be keeping time by enclosing two primitive-looking, bone-like cubes in their fists and shaking them in a menacing manner above their heads, but close enough to their ears that they seemed to be listening intently to the quality of the rattle. T/5 Guisiano seemed to be the best performer, for his companions paid him numerous amounts of money to rattle over and over again. Sergeants Wilcox, Banks, Meek and Nesemeier were successful in their efforts as commandos. They slipped past the guards in an attempt to sneak out of camp, but they only walked a short distance before they were caught and returned. The men broke camp the next morning and made the long march back to the flight strip.

On 12 March, the 479th FG was shocked to learn that Major Robert C. Twyman, the Deputy Group Commander, suffered fatal injuries when he was forced to parachute out of the P-38 he was flying in an acrobatic mission.

Shortly after that loss, another P-38 crashed, this time in the drink. Second Lieutenant Carl L. Peterson from the 434th FS had to bail out of his burning plane while he was over water. When on the way down in his parachute, he happened to look down and as he told it: "I saw a great big shark, right about where I was due to hit the water. I thought to myself, 'Pete, after all that you've been through, jumping out of a burning airplane and now I'm going to be eaten by a shark!' So I took off my flying boots and threw them down at him. I must have scared him away, too, because he didn't bother me when I was in the water." A Coast Guard crashboat picked up Lt. Peterson within 15 minutes.

During mid-month, the group was to participate in an Army maneuver to Paine Field in Washington State, but the planes only got as far as Hamilton Field near San Rafael, California before the exercise was cancelled due to bad weather.

The 14th and the 19th, depending on the location, presented the men with something new: censorship was instituted, another step toward overseas movement.

On the 24th of March, men and planes from the 434th and the 435th FS's relocated to the 436th FS's Palmdale base for the forthcoming Combined Training Maneuvers to be held at Muroc Army Air Field. Late that morning, Second Lieutenant William E. Henderson of the 436th FS crashed in his P-38 while on a gunnery mission over Little Rock, California. The lieutenant lost control of his plane after he flew into the target tow cable. The next day, another of the 436th's P-38s was lost when Captain Jules D. Biscayart was forced to bail out of his aircraft after completing an aerial gunnery mission. His egress at 1,000 feet from the disabled plane was textbook perfect and Capt. Biscayart parachuted safely down to earth eight miles southwest of Van Nuys, California. The P-38 he was flying crashed in an orange grove and was completely destroyed. A number of years ago, Mr. Biscayart (now a civilian) wrote of his experience that day. He stated:

> "I had ten or so in-flight engine failures during my year-and-a-half as a P-38 pilot and instructor in the U.S. The last one occurred just a few weeks before I left with my new squadron for overseas. I was called upon to take a flight of four trainees on a last minute, late afternoon, aerial gunnery training mission over San Nicholas Island, which is about 65 miles off the coast of California. While we were there, my right engine gave out a couple of puffs of smoke. A loud bang followed and the engine caught fire. I immediately turned toward shore, hoping at least to be able to belly in on the beach, as I knew there were sharks in the waters below. I knew also that since it was late in the day, the rescue people wouldn't be able to find me right away if I had to go down in the water. I continued on, with my mates telling me my engine was smoking badly and urging me to bail out. I made it to within gliding distance of the beach, then realized that Van Nuys Airport was only a few miles farther, so I attempted to get in there. I was cleared in, but about a mile out on final approach, my engine exploded and I had to bail out. I landed in an orange tree."

Second Lieutenant Travis M. Greenwood, a 436th FS pilot shown beside one of the squadron's P-38s at Palmdale. *Courtesy of Travis M. Greenwood.*

Captain John W. Harrell, the pilot of the target tow plane reported that Capt. Biscayart did a beautiful job of attempting to save himself and the ship, but in the end, only the most important thing, the pilot, survived.

The maneuvers commenced on the 25th and lasted five days during which crews represented the group from most every section and department. The combat simulation pitted the Red Forces (the enemy) against the Blue Forces (friendly) of which the group was a part. The Red Forces "held" the state of California, but the Blue Forces had advanced up the state as far as a line extending approximately from Santa Maria to Death Valley. Blue Forces had established a beachhead on Monterey Bay and had pushed inland. The group's mission was to repulse all ground and aerial attacks of the Red Army, attack enemy forces in the air and on the ground as the Blue

Lieutenant John G. Glenn, A pilot from the 436th FS, is shown beside one of the squadron's P-38 at Palmdale. *Courtesy of Travis M. Greenwood.*

Army advanced and to serve as escort for the Blue bombers invading the Red territories. Palmdale Army Air Field was successfully defended the several times it was attacked. Additionally, scrambles, air alerts and patrols were constantly being directed during the exercise. Many interceptions were made, which resulted in the "loss" of numerous Navy F-4U Corsairs and enemy bombers. The most spectacular attack took place when Captains Thomas T. Galloway and John D. Monahan led their flights against 16 enemy Corsairs and accounted for four of them. The maneuvers were considered a success and the situation was to be replicated for real and on a much larger scale in a few months.

The men from the 434th and 435th FS's were happy to return to their Lomita and Oxnard homes after the maneuvers and leave the cold nights and windy, dusty days of Palmdale behind. Returning, the P-38 Lieutenant Martin G. Gorian from the 435th FS was flying, developed engine trouble. Because of this as well as other difficulties, he had to bail out of the ship and parachute down to safety.

While the men who participated in the maneuvers were gone from their home bases, those left behind busied themselves for the POM inspectors, who arrived one last time to check up on things.

The month was closed out with several parties and celebrations, for the time had come for the group to begin its move toward overseas.

The beginning of April saw the men of the 479th Fighter Group preparing to leave their homes at Lomita, Oxnard and Palmdale. Training was temporarily waived as final details, both military and at home, were attended to during the first week of the month. Last minute packing became the order of the day. In the case of the 434th FS, the last of the shipping crates were packed at night by light from the headlamps of Jeeps and trucks in front of supply. During the 7th and 8th, the group headquarters and the squadrons boarded busses and trucks headed for Santa Maria Army Air Field, their point of departure from the West Coast. The men had worked hard to bring the group to this point and felt proud to be members of the organization. Roy A. Wiley, Jr. was one of the 434th FS's technicians who specialized in working on fighter communications equipment. He is a good example of the type of men who made up the group. Just before the squadron was to begin deployment, he injured his knee at Lomita and had to be hospitalized at Long Beach. Because of that injury, it looked like a medical discharge for the Technical Sergeant. Roy Wiley wasn't having any of that; he wanted to stay with the squadron. He pleaded his desires to his commanding officer Major James M. Herren, who was able to convince the right people that T/Sgt. Wiley was needed in his job and would be able to perform his duties. Wearing a full leg cast, Roy Wiley rejoined his squadron at Santa Maria. From there he stayed with the squadron throughout their deployment move and service overseas. His knee probably never properly healed and shortly after the war ended, he had to be hospitalized again because of it. This time the knee problem led to a medical discharge.

Jack M. Clark was a Chief Warrant Officer at the time, first with Group Headquarters, then after movement to England, the 435th FS. He was their Armament and Chemical Officer during the war. Prior to coming to the group/squadron, he had risen through the enlisted men's ranks and had been promoted to Warrant Officer because of his talents and abilities. He rose to the rank of First Lieutenant while with the squadron. In 1987, he wrote of his experiences during his time with the 435th, a part of which is reproduced here:

> "During our preparation for shipment overseas, Second Lieutenant Frank P. (Lindy) Linduska and Chief Warrant Officer Herbert Plemens and I were assembling things we needed that we thought would be hard to get overseas. Lindy thought the most useless thing that we would need would be a skate key, and so he bought one for each of us as a joke. In our fashion to never lose our sense of humor, we each attached them to our dog tag chains. When we were at any gathering, we would expose the 'key' and sure enough, someone would ask, 'What is that?' Our routine was to give this skit: 'It's a skate key.' Then the person asking would usually say. 'I know it's a skate key, but what's it for?' We would then say, 'This end is to tighten the clamps, this end is to adjust the length of the skates and the slot in the middle is to put a strap through so you can hang it around your neck. If the asker said he knew all of that and persisted asking 'But what is it for?' we would repeat the whole routine. By this time, frustration and indignation usually were on the rise in the asker. That was the point and it was our little joke. There was no symbolism to the key other than a means of having a bit of fun or so the three of thought – wrong!
>
> "Some people, especially those high level intelligent types in group headquarters tried to make some mysterious symbol of it and word got around that if you did not have a skate key, you were not in the 'Skate Key Club' and you were not on the 'inside'. Keys began to show up in great numbers and Lindy, Herb and I viewed all of this nonsense with great amusement. In fact, we found out at a later

date that one of our pilots who had been shot down and captured by the Germans had his key with him at the time. He told us that during interrogation the Germans asked him the question 'What is that?' The poor pilot went through the routine and got the hell beat out of him for being a wise ass."

While at Santa Maria, the group's activities were confined to calisthenics, inspections, sports, clothing exchanges and a general raiding of all the Post Exchanges. The comment was made in one of the squadron's records that one would have thought that the men were going to be away for ten years, the way they cleaned out the PXs. Saturday, 15 April, to the accompaniment of the Santa Maria Air Field Band, group headquarters and the squadrons marched in full field gear to the three trains that would transport them to Camp Kilmer, New Jersey. Passing through California, Nevada, Utah, Wyoming, Colorado, Kansas, Missouri, Illinois, Indiana, Ohio, Pennsylvania, Washington D.C., Maryland and finally New Jersey, the train rides were uneventful. Relief from boredom came from daily stops for physical exercise and the "card and dice games" that took place onboard the trains. The train the 435th FS traveled on stopped in Wyoming to hospitalize one of its enlisted men who had become ill. He was left behind as the squadron proceeded on. Passing through Mount Sterling, Ohio the 435th's train struck an automobile at a crossing, killing the auto's driver. The incident was not publicized due to the secrecy of the group's movement. In the case of the 434th FS, various unnamed participants were letting off excess energy by shooting at western wildlife from the moving train. Jerry Landreth shot at a few more pheasants while he was on the train, but this time he didn't hit anything. At other times, the squadron's train moved slowly enough climbing hills, that men were able to get off at the beginning of the train, do some shooting, then re-board near the end of the train as it passed on by them. This continued until while in Nebraska they were caught, reprimanded and the ammunition was taken away from everyone. George D. (Dan) Hendrix remembers this well. As he tells it:

"It took five days to cross the country and of course we 20 to 25 year old hot blooded fighter pilots were getting bored. On about the third day, as we were crossing Nebraska, some of us noticed that there were a lot of pheasants in the cornfields near the tracks. Somebody suggested that it would be fun to shoot at the birds from the train, so about a half dozen of us headed for the caboose with our .45 cal. pistols strapped to our hips. We proceeded to have a great time shooting at the pheasants from the rear of the train that afternoon. I don't think we hit anything because that side arm just wasn't made for hunting. After a while, everyone except Bud [Harold F.] Grenning and I tired of the sport and left. Somehow, word of what we were doing got to Col. Riddle, our group commander. Bud and I were told to report to the commander's compartment immediately. We got there and reported in with the crispest possible salutes as we stood at ramrod straight attention before him. We were given the most thorough ass chewing I for one, have ever experienced or witnessed. All the while he was giving us our dressing down, the Colonel's face was a deep purple. The reprimand ended with Col. Riddle telling us: 'If I ever hear of either one of you screwing up ever the slightest, I'll throw the book at you!' Our only response as we were dismissed was, Yes Sir!"

The boys continued to be boys, however, and when the train stopped at a snow-covered location, a few snowball fights broke out, relieving some of their bottled up energy. Finally, five days later, the group arrived and moved into their temporary quarters.

While at Camp Kilmer, their staging area for shipment overseas, the men once again attended training programs. Lectures were given on chemical warfare, first aid, sex hygiene, physical examinations, lifeboat discipline, how to embark and disembark in case of an emergency, clothing inspections, etc. The fifth day there, 12-hour passes were issued and all took advantage of them to see the sights of New York City. Allen J. Moon, then a private and a radio maintenance man with the 434th FS, utilized his time by visiting the Stage Door Canteen. He said the place was a mob scene adrift with a sea of olive drab with some sailors stirred in. He soon tired of it and returned early, just in time to be assigned the duty of keeping the latrine clean in the officer's quarters. There he determined that all men were created equal because officers returning from a night on the town could be just as sick as were some of the returning enlisted men. He mopped the floors more than a few times. The last day of the month, the group received alert orders and all made ready to move again.

May of 1944 began the combat life of the 479th Fighter Group. Departing Camp Kilmer by trains on 2 May, the men first went to Jersey City or Hoboken, (depending which squadron a man was in) New Jersey, then continued up the Hudson River by ferry to pier 49 at Brooklyn, New York. There, to the accompaniment of a marching band, the men loaded down with all of their equipment, marched to the gangplank and boarded the ship that was to take them overseas, the USS *Argentina*. Technical Sergeant Roy A. Wiley, (see above) still in a full leg cast and carrying his duffel bags, helmet, rifle, gas mask, etc., went up that gangplank too. The former luxury liner from the American Republic Lines was one of the best and most active troopships that served during the war. Her former glory was masked by her present duties, however. The converted ocean liner left its berth in the wee hours of the following morning and joined a convoy, destination unknown. She sailed on the southern edge of the convoy and the men of the group said that even on clear days, neither the front nor the end of the convoy could be seen.

Private Allen J. Moon, shown seated in the right foreground, was amongst new friends at the Canteen. *Courtesy of Allen J. Moon.*

Onboard ship, the men had a space six-ft. long by one-and-one-half feet high to call their own. Then a Corporal and an armorer with the 436th FS, Stanley (Stan) Kellett recalled how the group of enlisted men he was with there were bunked eight men high in a hallway that led to one of the ship's bathrooms. They had no extra room for themselves beyond the small space where they bedded down. Furthermore, the men occupied that cramped space with all their clothing and equipment, including their rifles. Men passing by on the way to or from the toilet, or "head' as it is called, were always brushing against the bunks as the ship swayed and rolled. Corporal Kellett tired of that the second night out and went up on deck where he found some space under the bridge. Using his gas mask for a pillow, he went to sleep there. He discovered the next morning that he had to be up by six o'clock because the decks were hosed off at that time. As the days passed, more and more men discovered Stan's "stateroom" and joined him there. By the end of the voyage, Stan said there were about forty men sleeping there.

The officers were confined also; many were crowded 16 to a stateroom designed originally for one or two passengers, but some were packed in up to as many as 32 men in larger rooms. They bunked in tiers of hammocks strung four high from the floor to the ceiling. In addition, the officers were required to be in Class "A" uniform during meals so there was considerable jostling in the rooms when time came to dress for a meal. The Army didn't like idle minds so the men were kept busy with make work tasks such as this.

All available space onboard was utilized toward the goal of moving large groups of personnel over the oceans and as a consequence, the men on board were packed in the ship like sardines in a can. Even the former swimming pools were converted and pressed into service as communal toilets where privacy was nonexistent. There were two meals a day, but the men had the use of the ship's PX where they could purchase snacks. On the sixth day out, the men were permitted to take their first shower. They each had six minutes worth of luxury.

During one of the days at sea, volunteers were sought for a work detail. The job was to bring fresh fruit and potatoes up to the galley from the ship's stores down in a lower hold.

The troopship that the men sailed on, the former luxury liner USS *Argentina*. *Courtesy of William M. Morgan.*

Sergeants Clarence (Clancy) M. Surges, Alvin (Al) R. Willhite and William (Bill) M. Morgan from the 434th FS jumped at the chance and went down for a load of fruit and vegetables. While Sgts. Surges and Willhite were down in the hold, they began to hear sounds like explosions reverberating through the hull of the ship. Suddenly, the ship's watertight doors closed and the lights went out! Talk about dark! Sgts. Surges and Willhite thought they were probably goners and began to reconcile themselves to their fate. Fortunately, that was not to be the case. The lights came back on after a period of time and the doors opened. Clancy and his friend grabbed their loads of oranges, put a few extra in their pockets and sped back up to the galley. They never went back down there again. Sgt. Morgan felt the same way too. He had been similarly trapped on the stairs leading up to the galley. With that exception, what was thought to be a submarine attack on the convoy, the trip was slow and monotonous. At least the weather was nice for most of the trip and things such as the general quarters drills, the abandon ship drills, two boxing bouts and a movie helped to spell boredom. Additionally, the ship's public address system broadcast popular radio programs such as The Jack Benny Show and Bob Hope as well as the Special Service's daily live talent shows. Finally, there were a number of amateur shows with two local talent bands that performed and those "card and dice games". Strictly forbidden, the dice were confiscated every time a game was found. It gradually became a contest as to which would win out, the ban or the dice supply.

One of the topics of conversation had always been the group's final destination and certainly it was one of the main subjects of speculation during the voyage. That secret was never fully learned by most until the last moments of their journey. The convoy had split up the night before the *Argentina*'s arrival at port and when land was finally sighted, the men's anticipation was undoubtedly high. Where were they? Some thought it was Africa; others said it was Italy. The grapevine rumors placed them at Ireland. Some suspicions were confirmed when the Transport Commander gave an orientation lecture on the United Kingdom. The answer was forthcoming. Arriving just before noon on 14 May at Gourock, Scotland, the men were moved, first by harbor steamer from the ship to the shore, then by train down through Scotland and into England. Private Allen J. Moon in talking about the train ride down said:

A view of wartime Scotland. *Carroll C. Sprague Collection, courtesy of the East Essex Aviation Society.*

> "It had been some 15 hours since we had subjected ourselves to the shipboard powdered eggs, but we were now on our way to our new home and had a sit down meal – as opposed to the stand up meal ritual we had on the fantail of the *Argentina*. No, there was not a diner car on the troop train, but our train made a brief stop in the northern England city of Leeds where the British Red Cross met our train with welcome sack lunches filled with homemade baked goods including cookies, strawberry tarts and strange offerings called meat pies. The pies were smallish things, which were quickly discovered to be stuffed with kidneys, brains and mutton. A quick-thinking American officer came running through the cars warning us to 'Wait 'till we have cleared the town before you salvo the pies!' Thus we averted an early rupture of Anglo-American relations as the Brits had given of their meager meat ration to aid our plight."

Unfortunately, after having traveled some 6,500 miles, as the group moved ever closer to its destination, the men, in the trucks they had switched to, became lost in the night around 4:00 AM and spent a number of hours roaming the countryside. They arrived well after daybreak. The tired men had a good breakfast and went to bed at their new home, Army Air Force Station 377, Wattisham, Suffolk County, England. The men of the group finally knew the secret. Ironically, the Germans were probably aware of the newly-arrived group before many of its men really understood just where they were. The first night they spent there, the German radio broadcasting personality Lord Haw-Haw was heard over the airwaves welcoming the 479th Fighter Group to England and to Wattisham. The Nazi radio broadcaster even gave the names of the group's commanding officers and said the Luftwaffe would be visiting the base soon. As promised, a few days later a lone bomber came over during the night and dropped a load of bombs. Fortunately, they all missed.

Wattisham was (and still is, but now utilized by the Royal Army as a helicopter base) a permanent airfield, originally belonging to the RAF. Built in 1938 as a part of the pre-war expansion program, it is located about nine miles northwest of Ipswich, in an isolated rural area. The first tenants were of course, RAF personnel and aircraft, but in August 1942, plans called for the field to be turned over to the US Army Air Force. The USAAF was to use the field as an air depot for the repair and servicing of a B-17 bomb wing scheduled to arrive the following year. Shortly afterward, work began on the construction of concrete surface runways for the bombers to use and more buildings to facilitate expansion of the depot. Restructuring and reorganization took place during which time it was determined that there would be sufficient depots for the bombers without the addition of Wattisham. Therefore, in mid-1943, before the full use of the Wattisham facility was realized, it was decided that the base would remain an air depot, but that it should service fighter aircraft. Additionally, it was decided to house a fighter group there in the future. Work was halted on the paved runways that would have been needed by the heavy bombers, leaving the length running east/west, the only portion completed. A concrete taxiway that ran around the perimeter and some additional hardstands had also been constructed during this time. An application of steel matting over the grass surface southwest-northeast main runway was all that was added after the concrete work ceased. The buildings had been completed.

The air depot was redesignated as the 4th Strategic Air Depot and subsequently grew in size to a population of about 4,000 men. The 4th SAD expanded to include the technical area and engineering area built to the south of Wattisham and the entire airfield complex was renamed Hitcham, the name Wattisham being dropped. The air depot's occupancy of the entire airfield was short-lived, however, and the Wattisham name came to be restored upon its original facilities shortly after the airfield was divided between the 4th SAD and the incoming 479th FG. The Hitcham name remained applicable to the southern portion of the airfield where the depot finally became consolidated, having had to move from the Wattisham portion of the field in order to make room for the incoming fighter group.

The mosaic pieces were coming together. During the period of late March and early April 1944, the various support units that would serve with the 479th FG during its tour of duty in England were assembled from personnel drawn from existing units throughout the United Kingdom. Brought together at each of the parent unit's locations, the men were trained and preparations for their next moves were made. By the second week of April 1944, the 4th SAD had completed vacating Wattisham's premises and work had begun to prepare for the 479th's arrival. The 15th of April became moving day for most of the newly-assembled supporting units and the station's main gate must have seen quite a lot of traffic that date as they all arrived. Detachment "A" from the 1177th Quartermaster Company Service Group (AVN) arrived around 1100 hours and began setting up their work areas for supplying the incoming fighter group with everything from clothing to gasoline. Men from the 331st Service Group arrived mid-afternoon and began moving supplies to the airfield and setting up facilities, while Detachment "A" of the 1063rd Military Police Company (AVN), having arrived there earlier, provided security at the base. The MPs moved into the former RAF Guard House. The Chemical Section of the 331st SG found excellent gas defense facilities there that lacked only an overhaul and a thorough cleaning. The 1447th Ordnance Supply and Maintenance Company (AVN) arrived for duty at 1130 hours. The 364th Service Squadron entered onto the base at 1730 hours and secured their billets, the former RAF Married Quarters. The men assigned to the squadron would take care of such things as carpentry, sheet metal work, PX clerks, parachute-riggers and general utility men. The 2123rd Engineering Firefighting Platoon (AVN) arrived and moved into a centrally located building that provided the necessary living quarters, office and fire station combined in a single location. On 16 April, the 1054th Signal Company's Detachment "A" arrived to take over the duties of establishing and maintaining base communications. Their activities included from staffing the base Tannoy system and getting cryptographers ready, to setting up a VHF radio station and putting up antennas for the base radio direction finding station, the all important "Heater Homer" station. The irony of that situation was at the time the efforts were being made to string and raise the antennas, various visiting 8th Air Force personnel felt that the homing system was not a necessary adjunct to the operation of a fighter group on the airfield! Fortunately, the British Air Ministry prevailed; sending three representatives to ensure the antennas went up. The 77th Station Complement Squadron arrived on 23 April, prepared to man the various organizations as they reported. By the month's end, the 331st Service Group, Headquarters and Headquarters Squadron had completed its establishment of a headquarters section and direct contact via TWX, (teletype) telephone, mail and courier service with Saffron Walden (65th Fighter Wing Headquarters) had begun. A PX had been set up and was operating and various recreational facilities were made available to the officers and enlisted men. Policies, pending the arriving group's approval, were also in place. Preparations for housing the officers and enlisted men of the soon to arrive fighter group were still under way though. The Military Police were ready; the Quartermasters were nearly ready; the fire fighters were ready, but still undergoing training; communications were still being prepared and the ordnance section was ready. Let it be known here that much of the work done in the way of setting up and repairing facilities and equipment was accomplished through the men's creative ingenuity, as many of the parts needed were not yet available. All of the supporting unit's personnel deserve a great deal of credit for a job well done.

Early May saw much continued activity as those at AAF Station F-377 made final preparations for the arrival of "Riddle's Raiders". The wait was not long.

CHAPTER TWO

MAY 1944

The airfield that the men of the 479th FG arrived at and found to be their home that 15 May 1944, was in essence, ready for their occupancy. AAF Station F-377 had large hangars (albeit, the middle two had been burned out during the Blitz of 1941), brick buildings and central heating which served many of the buildings including the Bachelor Enlisted Quarters (BEQ), and the Bachelor officer Quarters (BOQ). The living quarters featured tiled bathrooms with hot and cold running water, bathtubs and showers. The enlisted men shared open bay type quarters while the officers were assigned two or sometimes three men to a room depending on size and location. There were EM and O clubs, a movie theater, tennis courts, etc. All a far cry from the Nissen huts and primitive conditions normally envisioned with a wartime airbase. Granted some of that did exist on the base but the norm was as told above. The only thing missing was some furniture such as desks, partitions and filing cases and those were quickly made as the group settled into their work areas and quarters. Other amenities such as snack bars were also added as time permitted.

They also found four of their own waiting for the group's arrival. Major Sidney S. Woods, Captain A. B. Parsons, Captain Evan S. Pillsbury II and First Lieutenant Morris W. McGee, members of an advance party who had gone ahead of the main body of troops in order to help work out details for a smooth transition, were there to greet them. The members had secured much needed equipment and thirty-seven of the group's beloved P-38s to start with. Many of the planes were old and worn out, but the pilots were anxious to get back into the air. Instead of going through the customary several weeks of pre-combat training, the group made do with only two training missions before going on operational status, May 26 – just eleven days after having arrived in the UK. This feat would later earn them a commendation from 65th Fighter Wing. (The very first person to fly a combat mission as a member of the 479th FG was Major Woods, who flew a mission with another group on 9 May. Additionally, Lieutenant Colonel Kyle L. Riddle, the group's commander, took seven of the group's pilots along when he joined the 55th FG on two bomber escort missions, 23 and 25 May. They came back, able to provide some valuable pointers for the rest of the pilots.)

The task now at hand was to wage war on the enemy, but the exuberance of the group's youthful pilots after having been cooped up traveling to England was too much to be contained. Joyful to be flying once again, many were feeling the heady effects described by John Gillespie Magee, Jr. in his immortal sonnet "High Flight" as they slipped the surly bonds of earth. On 24 May, First Lieutenant Keith E. Canella from the 434th FS, made a low north to south pass over the flying field at Wattisham in an effort to "cut the grass" with his P-38. Probably lacking familiarity with the field, he failed to negotiate the slight rise in ground near center field. His propeller blades bit into the turf, cutting slices in the rise as he tried to pull the big bird up from the ground. Unable to wrestle the damaged plane into the air once more, he bounced over the ground and wound up striking one of the hangars at the Hitcham Air Depot and finally coming to rest in the midst of some stacked up construction materials nearby. His plane was totally demolished and began to burn. Lt. Canella escaped with minor injuries, perhaps later wishing he had not escaped so lightly for he received a severe dressing down by the group CO, Lieutenant Colonel Riddle.

25 May 1944

65th FW FO Unk.

No. 1 Thursday. Major John H. Lowell was the group's leader. Maj. Lowell was on loan to the 479th FG for these first introductory missions because of his long experience in England, serving with the 364th Fighter Group. (He was Squadron Commander of that fighter group's 384th FS at the time of his transfer and served with the squadron from June 1943 to late July 1944.) He led a total of 34 P-38s, ten from the 434th FS, 12 from the 435th FS and 12 from the 436th FS on the group's first formal mission. The pilots took off in the morning for a practice sweep over England. One of the group's P-38s was forced to return early. They received their first taste of English weather, as the clouds were very thick, with ceilings beginning as low as 100 feet in some places and at best, 1000 feet in others. The weather, in fact, forced the planned course of Oxford, Bristol, Nottingham, Boston, then home, to be abandoned. Instead, they flew south to Beachy Head and made R/V (*Rendez-Vous*) with a flight of B-24s that they escorted north across the Thames Estuary.

25 May 1944

65th FW FO Unk.

No. 2 Thursday. Maj. Lowell led the group, which consisted of 34 P-38s, (10-434th, 12-435th & 12-436th). The pilots took off in the afternoon, again for a practice sweep over England. One of the group's P-38s was forced to return early. Again, the weather over England was very thick, with ceilings beginning as low as 100 feet in some places and at best, 1000 feet in others. Their planned route was to take them over Grimsby, Liverpool, Bristol and Birmingham, but the weather was closing so fast that Maj. Lowell brought his charges back home after just an hour aloft.

On this date, the group suffered its first loss in the ETO. Captain William A. Walker, the popular commanding officer of Bison Squadron (436th FS) was killed in a crash of his P-38 while alone on a gunnery practice mission. His left engine caught fire and as he was attempting to land, he crashed near Rattlesden. Capt. Walker was an experienced combat pilot, having fought the Japanese in the Southwest Pacific. After having brought the squadron through its teething stages of organization, training and processing for combat, it was ironic that he should be lost without having seen the coastline of the continent.

A view of First Lieutenant Keith E. Canella's P-38 after having come to rest near the hangar it struck. Note the damaged upper right corner of the building. *Courtesy of Clarence M. Surges.*

26 May 1944

65th FW FO 100

No. 3 Friday. Maj. Lowell led the group, which consisted of 34 P-38s (11-434th, 12-435th & 11-436th). Their assignment was a fighter sweep over Holland and Belgium, giving the pilots their first look at enemy territory. Four of the group's P-38s were forced to return early. Weather was 10/10ths overcast upon entering over the continent, but thinned out to 3/10ths cloud coverage near the end of the trip. The course included Aldeburgh, England, L/F (Landfall In) over Katwijk-An-Zee, Holland at 1526 hrs./20,000 feet, then on to Tilburg, Holland. From there, they passed into Belgium, rounding the points of Charleroi, Mons and making L/O (Landfall Out) over Blankenberghe, at 1616 hrs./18,000 ft. They had high hopes of finding some enemy aircraft to shoot at, but the only plane seen in the skies was one lone plane, south of Mons that didn't stay around long enough to be identified. The Germans were active on the ground though, as the group received flak from

Major John H. Lowell is shown seated and ready to go in a P-38. Note the rear-view mirror mounted on the right hand side of the plane's windshield. *From original 479th FG history.*

Katwijk-An-Zee and Blankenberghe. No one was hit, however, and the trip was relegated to the group's history as another "first".

Flamm D. (Dee) Harper, then a Second Lieutenant pilot with the 434th FS said:

> "On most missions, the enemy welcomed us to the continental coastline with bursts of anti-aircraft fire – big German 88mm guns. I will never forget my first combat mission. The first bursts of flak shocked me. I could not believe it! They were shooting at me! They were really shooting at me! They were trying to kill me. My shock immediately turned to anger and at this point, a warrior was born. Here I had spent a year in flight training learning to be a combat fighter pilot, but up until now, the reality of it all had never settled into my brain."

26 May 1944

65th FW FO 101

No. 4 Friday. Maj. Lowell led the group, which consisted of 30 P-38s (10-434th, 11-435th & 9-436th) on a fighter sweep over Holland, Belgium and France, the group's second outing for the day. Two of the group's P-38s were forced to return early. The skies were still clouded over, with a low overcast beginning at mid-channel and extending to the Paris, France area, apparently the result of a front located north and east of Brussels, Belgium L/F for the group was over St Valery, France at 1958 hrs./19,000 ft. Passing near Paris, the group swept northward through the areas of St. Quentin and Cambrai, into Belgium, passing Charleroi there and then on into Holland, making L/O west of Schouwen Island, Holland at 2047 hrs./ 19,000 ft. Two P-51s were seen headed west at 17,000 ft. in the vicinity of Achlet, Belgium.

27 May 1944

VIII FC FO 351

No. 5 Saturday. Maj. Lowell led the group, which consisted of 36 P-38s (12-434th, 11-435th & 13-436th) on a withdrawal escort for 1st BD (Bomb Division) B-17s attacking their 8th AF Mission 373 primary targets in Germany. Five of the group's P-38s were forced to return early. The weather ranged from 3/10ths cloud coverage to CAVU (Ceiling And Visibility Unlimited). L/F for the group was in the vicinity of Blankenberghe, Belgium at 1253 hrs./16,000 ft. They made R/V with the bombers near Vielsalm, Belgium at 1336 hrs./ 21-26,000 ft. Twenty miles east of there, an unidentified A/C was seen to explode. An enemy aircraft was observed southeast of Lille, France, but it was being chased by about 15 P-51s so that one was left alone. A bit later the group was ordered to Lille to check on bandits, but none were observed. On the way out stragglers were picked up and escorted to the channel. L/O was over Coxyde, Belgium at 1500 hrs./16,000 ft.

28 May 1944

VIII FC FO 352

No. 6 Sunday. Maj. Lowell led the group, which consisted of 42 P-38s (14-434th, 12-435th & 16-436th) on a penetration escort for 3rd BD B-24s attacking their 8th AF Mission 376 primary target, the POL (petroleum/oil/lubricant) facilities at Halle, Germany. Up: 1128 hrs., down: 1539 hrs. with four early returns. The weather was CAVU over the North Sea and for most of the trip. R/V with the bombers was 60 miles east of Great Yarmouth, England at 1300 hrs./22,000 ft. Prior to R/V, the group had made a sweep over the Zuider Zee, Holland. Once over Germany, the 339th FG joined in escort west of Dümmer Lake. There was no fighter opposition and the escort was uneventful.

John W. Hedenberg was a pilot with the 436th FS. He joined the squadron in Palmdale and flew missions in Europe from the beginning of the 479th's entry into the war until his last on 18 October. He kept a diary in which he made brief entries regarding each mission that he went on. The diary represents, in many cases a wonderful window providing insights to both the mission and the men who flew them. Excerpts from that diary are included periodically in each of the following chapters until the diary entries end in October 1944, at which time John completed his combat tour and rotated back to the U.S. While it may seem to the reader that too many of John's experiences have been placed into this book, it is the author's intent that they each serve as examples of the kinds of events that most men went through during their tours as fighter pilots in the 8th Air Force during World War II. On this date he recorded:

> "Group made another B.E. [Bomber Escort] mission today. Escorted on penetration to Dummer Lake. I went

Lieutenant John W. Hedenberg and Technical Sergeant Frank W. Watkins the crew chief of Pretty Gal, the P-38 Lt. Hedenberg usually flew. *Courtesy of John W. Hedenberg.*

along as a spare, turned back over the North Sea, promptly got thoroughly lost over England. After 2 hours of stooging around, finally landed at Horham (B-17 base) to find out where I was. Took off and got back to Wattisham in 3 minutes! Moral – Always carry a map! …Hope better luck tomorrow." In an explanation he later added to each of the diary entries, he wrote this: "It took surprisingly little time to develop an intuitive feel for the English and European countryside as seen from 18,000 to as much as 28,000 feet altitude. After a dozen missions or so, most of us were capable of flying above solid overcast for several hours, then ducking down below for a quick look at the ground. Recognizing approximately where in Western Europe we were, we then could set a course that would take us back over England, the shortest way."

29 May 1944

VIII FC FO 353

No. 7 Monday. Lieutenant Colonel Kyle L. Riddle was the group's leader. It was time for the Group Commander to take charge and lead his "Raiders" into battle. He led a total of 45 P-38s, 12 from the 434th FS, 16 from the 435th FS and 17 from the 436th FS. Their assignment was a penetration escort for 3rd BD B-17s attacking their 8th AF Mission 379 primary target, the aircraft industry at Leipzig, Germany. Up: 0932 hrs., down 1351 hrs. with seven early returns. Once again, the weather was CAVU, except for a light haze over the continent. The group made R/V with their assigned bombers over Ijmuiden, Holland at 1032 hrs./20,000 ft. Heading east into Germany, the group passed Bremen and Hanover, noting that each was surrounded by smoke pots. Escort was continued until Stendal, at which point the group broke away at 1200 hrs./28,000 ft. and returned home.

Observations made during the mission included: The marshalling yards at Hamm were seen to be packed with goods trains and shuttle engines. The Dortmund-Elms Canal was thick with barges 23 miles west of Hamm and there was also barge activity at Nijmegen, Holland.

30 May 1944

VIII FC FO 354

No. 8 Tuesday. Major Sidney S. Woods led the group, which consisted of 45 P-38s (12-434th, 16-435th & 17-436th) on a penetration to target and withdrawal escort for 2nd BD B-24s attacking their 8th AF Mission 380 primary target, the airdrome at Oldenburg, Germany. Up: 0913 hrs., down 1341 hrs. with two early returns. R/V with the assigned bombers was over the Zuider Zee at 1021 hrs./20,000 ft. The Big Friends were escorted to the target and back for an uneventful mission. Bombing results looked good with fires and columns of smoke in the target area. The group broke escort 20 miles east of Cromer, England at 1304 hrs./6,000 ft.

Observations made during the mission included: An Me 109 was seen flying near the deck near Schillig, Germany. Smoke pots were operating in the Wilhelmshaven harbor area. There were seven flak boats noted at the Bremerhaven waterfront, but none of them fired on the force. There were also seven or eight naval vessels under way southeast of the mouth to the Elbe River.

31 May 1944

VIII FC FO 355

No. 9 Wednesday. Lt. Col. Riddle led the group, which consisted of 49 P-38s (17-434th, 16-435th & 16-436th) on a target withdrawal escort for 3rd BD B-17s attacking their 8th AF Mission 382 primary target, the marshalling yards at Osnabrück, Germany. Five of the group's P-38s were forced to return early for various reasons.

Passing into Germany, the weather consisted of clouds in the Ruhr area with persistent haze the entire route. R/V with the proper bombers was made prior to the target and they were escorted through and back home. The bombing results appeared to be good, with fires and smoke seen coming from the target area. There were eight single-engine enemy aircraft following the bomber course from Melle, Belgium to Lissendorf,

Captain Frank J. Keller is shown standing beside his P-38 while his wingman for this mission, Second Lieutenant Arnold G. Helding, joking around for the camera shot, holds his hand over Capt. Keller's victory marking. *Courtesy of Arnold G. Helding.*

Germany, but they were beyond reach at 35,000 ft. and did not bother with the B-17s. Flak however claimed seven B-17s, two at Osnabrück, two at Münster and three at Hamm. No 'chutes were reported as having been seen. Another B-17 was seen gradually going down, so a flight from Newcross Squadron (434th FS) gave the bomber cover, but it subsequently crashed. Following that, Newcross Squadron tallied the first German aircraft credited as destroyed by that squadron and also by the group. That honor went to Captain Frank J. Keller, who destroyed a Ju 88 on the ground in the Humfeld area at 1230 hrs. His encounter report reads as follows:

> "During bomber escort on FO 355, a B-17 was seen struggling after leaving the target area and began to lose altitude as it fell behind the main formation. Our flight followed it down and gave cover. Seven chutes from the bomber were seen to open and when they reached the ground, the airmen ran into nearby woods. The B-17 veered as though to land on a nearby A/F, but went into an abrupt turn, crashed on an open field and burst into flames some distance from the A/F. Our flight returned to the south end area of the A/F to carry out a low, tree-top level strafing attack. Several dummies and one Ju 88 were seen on the field. Having the Ju 88 in range, I fired a short burst from 300 yards and the plane exploded, bursting into flames. We then proceeded on our course home. I claim one Ju 88 destroyed on the ground."

The claim was confirmed by Capt. Keller's wingman, Second Lieutenant Arnold G. Helding, who said they came out low over the woods as they approached the airfield. The dummy planes were sighted as well as the single Ju 88. When Capt. Keller fired his short burst, the Ju 88 exploded almost immediately and was practically right under the two P-38s when it did so. The captain's plane sustained damage to one of its props as he passed through the exploding Ju 88 and was struck by debris. Capt. Keller's gunnery was an excellent piece of work as he only fired 100 rounds of .50 cal. API and 17 rounds of 20mm HEI ammunition.

The only observation recorded from the mission was the note that eight to ten barges were seen on the Ems Weser Canal between Alswede and Hille.

Closing out the month is this note from John W. Hedenberg's diary for this date:

> "We escorted bombers all the way around. Osnabruck and Hamm thoroughly plastered. Moderate to heavy flak over target, light from there, all the way back to coast. At one point I happened to glance back and saw bursts of flak following right up my behind. Changed course and altitude – NOT SLOWLY! Put hole in my flap when dropped [external fuel] tanks. Hope we get displacing struts soon – Too much flap repair this way. Saw no E/A to shoot at, though they were up above at about 35,000 to 40,000 feet, spotting. Group drew first blood today. Man in another squadron destroyed a Ju 88 on the ground near Osnabruck."

While the 479th FG began their efforts in the air war, men on the ground had been working very hard to complete the group's transition and occupancy of their new home. All of the forementioned detachments, groups, squadrons, platoons and sections continued toward making Wattisham a suitable place to live and fight from.

The Special Services Section began showing movies twice a night, seven days a week at the Post Theater for the enlisted men and four nights a week for the officers in their BOQ. Station and squadron parties were scheduled at both the Red Cross Aero Club and the Victory Theater. USO shows began to play on the base. The section also saw to it that there was regular entertainment in each of the squadron ready rooms as well as out on the line for those who could not enjoy the regularly scheduled fare. Sports programs such as hardball and softball leagues were started, a track team was organized and volleyball courts were constructed. Tourneys were established and competition was strong. A required physical training program was also begun. Other sporting events like basketball and football later fell into place as the seasons changed. Special Services also had the responsibility of providing orientation, advanced education, newspapers and magazines for the men.

The Personnel Section began handling the routine of record keeping, transmitting allotments, making payrolls, deposits to the soldier's accounts and monthly reports such as insurance, War Bonds, personnel rosters, etc.

The Station Photographic Laboratory, located on the second floor of the Station Ordnance Building, began unpacking its equipment and installing it as soon as they could evict the 4th SAD men. The latter were loath to give up their well-appointed location and drug their heels while being moved out. Once in, the men discovered there was a difference in voltages between what their equipment used and what the British supplied. The problems were ironed out and the lab made ready to process film.

The Station's Medical Section set up the dispensary, which consisted of a twenty-five-bed facility located in a two-story, concrete structure that also housed the station dental facility. In addition, each of the squadrons set up their own small dispensary in their respective dispersal areas.

The Base Motor Pool "rolled" into action as the number of vehicles assigned to it rapidly increased as the month progressed.

Last, but certainly not least, Station Engineering began unpacking and setting up what equipment that had thus far arrived. The total lack of their machine shop was a severe handicap until it finally arrived the 1st of June. In the meantime, the men did the best they could with repairs, the first of which was a P-38 that had a nose wheel collapse on 25 May. The ship required sheet metal repairs of its nose, wheel well and wheel well door. The engineering section also set up workshops for welding, batteries, propellers, hydraulics, radiators, electrical, instruments, parachutes, and a mobile repair/retrieval unit.

CHAPTER THREE

WATTISHAM AAF STATION F-377

The following pages of this chapter contain a photographic tour of Army Air Force Station F-377, Wattisham Airfield. All photos were taken during the period 1944 through 1945 and serve to illustrate where the men of the 479th Fighter Group and its ancillary units lived, worked and what they saw during the majority of their time in England. Unlike most war time airfields, Wattisham still exists and today serves as home for Britain's 3 and 4 Regiments Army Air Corps, a part of 16 Air Assault Brigade. Currently flying Lynx and Gazelle helicopters, the two regiments will soon be taking delivery of new Apache Attack Helicopters. Located there also is 7 Air Assault Battalion REME, a helicopter repair facility, 132 Aviation Supply Unit, a Royal Logistics Corps, Brigade Parachute Squadron (RAF), B Flight Search and Rescue (22 Squadron Royal Air Force) and an Air Training Corps for youth 13 to 18 years old.

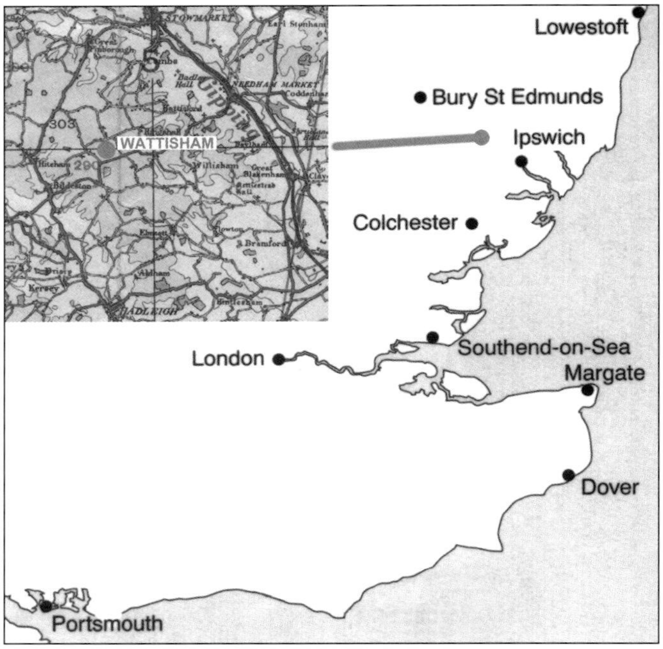

This map locates Wattisham airfield, Suffolk County, in the country of England. Located approximately nine miles northwest of Ipswich, Wattisham as an airfield was brought into existence during 1938. It was built as part of the Royal Air Forces' pre-war expansion and was originally a grass-surfaced flying field that was home to a number of RAF medium bomber squadrons. It was a permanent station with buildings constructed primarily of brick and featured central heating. The station was turned over to the USAAF in 1942 for use as an air depot as the Army Air Force began its buildup in England. At that time, work began on three concrete runways, one of which was finished before the work was halted. Another was completed during the early part of 1945. In addition, there was a concrete perimeter track around the flying field and a total of seventy-one hardstands. When the 479th Fighter Group occupied the station, some Nissen type buildings and later tents were utilized to house the nearly 2,000 personnel that made up the fighter group and its subsidiary units.

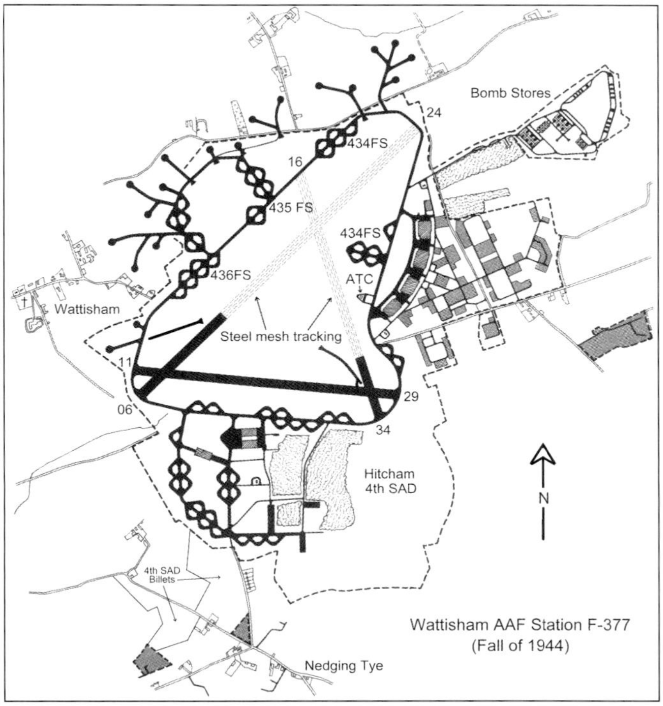

Wattisham airfield. This map is adapted from a reproduction of the original through the courtesy and kind permission of Roger A. Freeman and comes from his book "The Mighty Eighth War Manual" published by Motorbooks International, Publishers and Wholesalers, Inc. *Courtesy of Roger A. Freeman.*

An oblique aerial photo of Wattisham airfield taken from the south and looking northwest. *Carroll C. Sprague Collection, courtesy of the East Essex Aviation Society.*

An oblique aerial photo of Wattisham airfield taken from the southeast and looking northwest. *Carroll C. Sprague Collection, courtesy of the East Essex Aviation Society.*

An oblique aerial photo of Wattisham airfield taken from the south and looking north. *Carroll C. Sprague Collection, courtesy of the East Essex Aviation Society.*

An oblique aerial photo of Wattisham airfield taken from the east and looking west. *Carroll C. Sprague Collection, courtesy of the East Essex Aviation Society.*

This photo which shows Wattisham's boiler plant in the foreground and billeting beyond, was taken from the top of the station's water tower which is located slightly east of a point midway between the middle two hangars. *Courtesy of Loetta Taylor (Kennedy).*

Taken from the station water tower, the view is toward hangar one and the 434th FS area. *Courtesy of Loetta Taylor (Kennedy).*

A higher oblique aerial view of Wattisham and Hitcham, looking southeast. The photograph was taken mid-1945. *Courtesy of Harold L. Stotts.*

A southeast facing low aerial oblique view of the 434th FS hardstands (left side) and the 435th FS hardstands (right side). *Courtesy of Clarence G. Haynes.*

A southeastern looking low oblique angle view showing the 434th FS hardstands and the start of Runway 24. Note that the runway is just beginning to be surfaced. *Courtesy of Davis L. Born.*

Above: The set of 434th FS hardstands located adjacent to those of the 435th FS. They were opposite hangar one and across Runway 24. *Courtesy of the Wings of Freedom Museum.*

Below: The other set of hardstands used by the 434th FS. These were located just in front of the hangar line. *Courtesy of the Wings of Freedom Museum.*

A view looking across the hangar side hardstands used by the 434th FS and toward hangars one, two and three. *Courtesy of Arnold G. Helding.*

The first of four photographs showing the line shacks that ground crewmembers constructed in order to be near the aircraft they maintained. Constructed from the packing crates that belly tanks were shipped in, the rudimentary shelters gave some measure of comfort to the men who worked very long hours to keep their ships available for missions. Men from the 434th FS used this shack. *Courtesy of Loetta Taylor (Kennedy).*

A line shack from the 436th FS. This squadron was located the farthest away from the main portion of the station and therefore somewhat isolated. *Courtesy of Kenneth D. Axt.*

Another of the 436th FS line shacks. Because of the home made and many times crude heating systems employed in these shacks, they were considered fire traps and the British who ultimately had control over the base, sometimes made fire inspections and then issued orders to demolish the shacks. Usually the shacks stayed in place though. *Courtesy of Kenneth D. Axt.*

Corporal Stanley Kellett from the 436th FS is behind this .50 cal. near the Bison Squadron dispersal area. Note the tents in the background. *Courtesy of Stanley Kellett.*

A 436th FS line shack. Interestingly enough, despite the warnings by the British to remove the shacks, after the war was over and the 479th FG was leaving Wattisham, the shacks could not be torn down because they were then considered property of the RAF. *Courtesy of Kenneth D. Axt.*

Technical Sergeant Phillip Ortega who was a radar mechanic and Corporal Charles Pasternack, a radio mechanic, are seen here with a stack of practice bombs in their Bison Squadron area. Note the Blister Hangar behind them. *Courtesy of Raymond Niekamp.*

One of the many defensive anti-aircraft positions found around the station. This .50 cal. position is shown being manned by Sgts. Harold L. Greenlee, Jack E. Gowan and William M. Morgan from the 434th FS. *Courtesy of William M. Morgan.*

Sergeant William E. Shaw, a 436th FS armorer, is manning this AA position. *Carroll C. Sprague Collection, courtesy of the East Essex Aviation Society.*

The hangar line from front to rear in the photo – hangars one, two, three and four. *Carroll C. Sprague Collection, courtesy of the East Essex Aviation Society.*

Another view of the hangar line. © *2000 Elmo Sears, courtesy of Elmo Sears.*

Hangars two and three. Note the station water tower, which can be seen between the two hangars and also the stockpiled steel belly tanks in the left foreground. There are some of the paper tanks that can be seen further back and on the right. © *2000 Elmo Sears, courtesy of Elmo Sears.*

Hangar two, damaged by the Blitz in 1941, was used for storage. *Courtesy of John J. Sipek.*

Hangar two and a fire station, both damaged during the Blitz of 1941. *Courtesy of Clarence M. Surges.*

A fire station was located between hangars one and two. Note the damage to the side of the building that was done during the Blitz of 1941. *Courtesy of John J. Sipek.*

The next five photos are laid out in sequence to make up a walk around tour of Wattisham's Control Tower. This view looks nearly east toward the front of the building. © *2000 Elmo Sears, courtesy of Elmo Sears.*

The next view is also toward the east and the front of the building, but shows more of the side. Upon enlargement of the photograph, a number of aerial rockets can be seen leaning on the upper railing. These were used to signal the pilots. Large yellow signs that give the number of the runway being used can also be seen near the top of the tower. *Courtesy of Clarence G. Haynes.*

Looking northeast, hangars (left to right) one, two and three can be seen in the background. *Courtesy of Arnold G. Helding.*

The view is now looking to the northwest. The day this photo was taken, the planes were using Runway 29/11 as can be seen on the large signs near the top of the tower. *Courtesy of Harold L. Stotts.*

Facing southwest, the back of the Control Tower can be seen. Runway 29/11 was again in use. © *2000 Elmo Sears, courtesy of Elmo Sears.*

Big Friends over Wattisham. *Courtesy of Arnold G. Helding.*

This group of buildings, located off the north end of hangar one, was used by the 434th FS for Operations, S-2 Engineering and the pilots Ready Rooms. *Courtesy of Arnold G. Helding.*

Another view of the same buildings. Staff Sergeant Frederic (Fred) C. Hayner, the squadron painter for the 434th FS utilized the small building in the foreground. He secured permission to live in the small paint building and thus be closer to his work area. A P-51 canopy can be seen on some benches to the right of the building. Fred once commented that that canopy could have been from one of the Mustangs that Robin Olds had flown because it was off of the plane more than it was on. Fred said it seemed like he was always painting another victory symbol or two on the canopy railing. *Courtesy of David L. Born.*

An early photo of the 434th FS Operations Room. *Courtesy of Clarence M. Surges.*

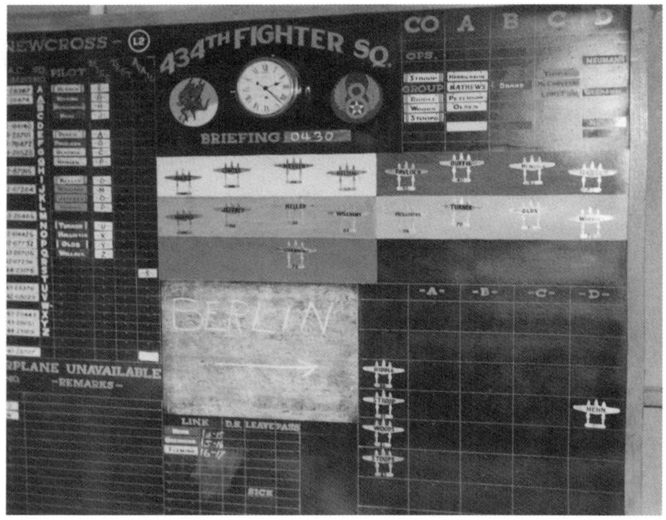

This photograph was taken either 4 or 5 July 1944. It shows the Operations Status Board found in the 434th FS S-3 Room. Among other things, on the board can be seen the P-38s assigned to the squadron, who the planes were to be flown by that day, what flights the pilots were assigned to and the position they were to fly in their flight. *Courtesy of Arnold G. Helding.*

This is the 434th FS Ready Room where the pilots went to await the mission they were to fly or just plain relax if they weren't flying that day. Note the snack bar in the background. *Courtesy of Arnold G. Helding.*

The 435th FS Ready Room. *Courtesy of James H. Koerber.*

The 436th FS S-2 room, front of the room. *Courtesy of the 436th Fighter Squadron Association.*

The 436th FS S-2 room, rear of the room. *Courtesy of the 436th Fighter Squadron Association.*

An enlargement of the pilot's roster board found in the rear of the S-2 room. The board lists many of the pilots who flew for the 436th FS and the missions they flew. *Courtesy of Herman E. Hoversten.*

A picture of the fireplace in the 436th FS S-2 room where according to Lieutenant Herman E. Hoversten, one of the squadron's early pilots, it was the warmest place in England. *Courtesy of Herman E. Hoversten.*

Officer's Quarters housing (primarily non-flying) was arranged in the shape of an upside down "U" with the Commanding Officer's quarters located at the top center of the complex. This view shows the CO's house and the right side row of houses. *Courtesy of Albert M. Myers.*

The left side of the Officer's Quarters complex is shown as two officers bicycle past on their way to work. *Courtesy of Albert M. Myers.*

A front view of the BOQ (Bachelor Officers Quarters) where the pilots from all three squadrons lived. The small complex housed the pilots, their mess and the Officer's Club. Quarters were in the left and right wings and the mess occupied the middle section behind the club, which was to the front. The 434th FS occupied the lower portion of the left wing while the 435th was in the upper story. The 436th was in the right wing. Some additional non-flying personnel were also billeted here. *Carroll C. Sprague Collection, courtesy of the East Essex Aviation Society.*

A slightly different view of the same BOQ. *Courtesy of David L. Born.*

A view of the backside of the BOQ's right wing. *Courtesy of Robert H. Horman.*

Another view of the BOQ's front. © *2000 Elmo Sears, courtesy of Elmo Sears.*

A small bar at the BOQ. *Courtesy of George D. Hendrix.*

A look around the room that Lts. David L. Born and Clifford W. Bowers occupied during their time with the 434th FS. Their room was on the ground floor of the BOQ's left wing. These pilots liked their pin ups! *Courtesy of David L. Born.*

View #2. *Courtesy of David L. Born.*

View #3. *Courtesy of David L. Born.*

An aerial view of the BOQ. *Courtesy of David L. Born.*

Some of the Enlisted Men's Barracks buildings. *Courtesy of Loetta Taylor (Kennedy).*

A closer view of one of the barracks buildings. *Courtesy of the Wings of Freedom Museum.*

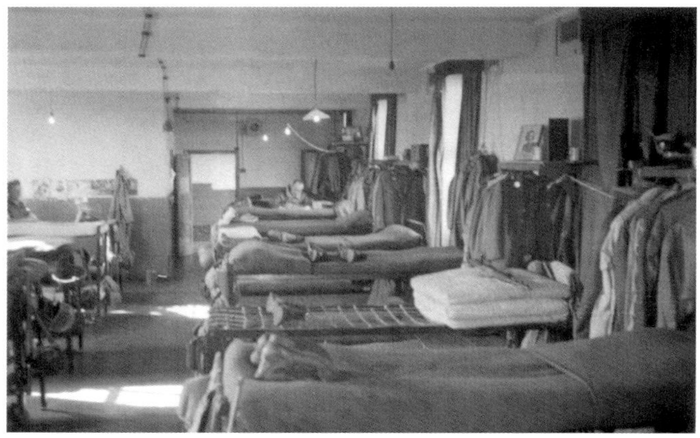

A look into Enlisted Men's Quarters, this one belonging to the armorers of D Flight, 434th FS. The men assigned here also spent a great deal of time in the line shacks near their assigned aircraft. *Courtesy of Loetta Taylor (Kennedy).*

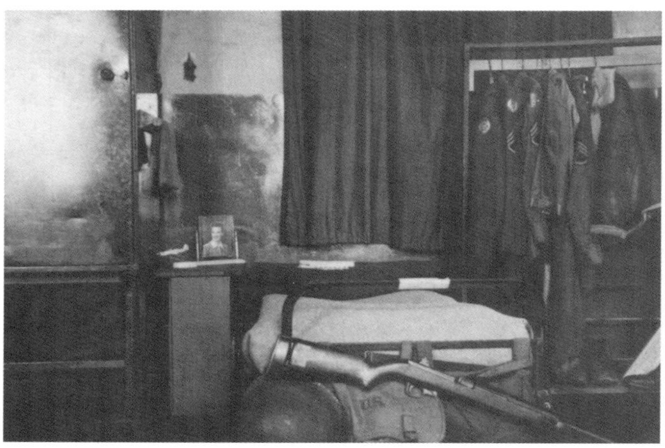

A bunk in Enlisted Men's Quarters, home to Raymond Niekamp of the 436th FS Communications Section. Note that all of the men were issued arms and kept them where they were billeted. *Courtesy of Raymond Niekamp.*

The Enlisted Men's Mess. As usual, there was a line out front. *Courtesy of the 436th Fighter Squadron Association.*

The head of the chow line in the EM Mess. *Courtesy of the 436th Fighter Squadron Association.*

Sitting down for a meal at the EM Mess. *Courtesy of the 436th Fighter Squadron Association.*

The cooks worked all night making these donuts in the Enlisted Men's Mess. Enlargement of the photo reveals there were at least 1,800 donuts in the trays on the counter. *Courtesy of Loetta Taylor (Kennedy).*

The station flag flying at half-mast at HQ in mourning the death of President Franklin D. Roosevelt. © *2000 Elmo Sears, courtesy of Elmo Sears.*

Station/Group Headquarters. *Carroll C. Sprague Collection, courtesy of the East Essex Aviation Society.*

A firehouse located across the street from the station headquarters. *Carroll C. Sprague Collection, courtesy of the East Essex Aviation Society.*

The station Guard House. *Courtesy of David L. Born.*

Another view of the Guard House. *Carroll C. Sprague Collection, courtesy of the East Essex Aviation Society.*

The Little Wheels Club, a meeting place for lower ranking enlisted men to go and relax. *Carroll C. Sprague Collection, courtesy of the East Essex Aviation Society.*

The Rocker Club. The upper ranking NCOs enjoyed their time relaxing here. *Courtesy of the Wings of Freedom Museum.*

The Station Motor Pool. *Courtesy of the 436th Fighter Squadron Association.*

The Station Ordnance, Armament and Lab building that was located between hangars two and three. *Carroll C. Sprague Collection, courtesy of the East Essex Aviation Society.*

This sign was located at the Motor Pool and was a bit of humor created by several of the men who worked in the Fuel and POL Section there, Pvt. John A. Zoost and Pfc. Donald R. McMullen. *Courtesy of David L. Born.*

A view inside the Heater Homer Direction Finding Station. Sgt. Aloysius G. Warth is seen operating the radio direction finder. The small facility was not located on the airfield proper, but in fact southeast of there, about a half mile away and near the village of Great Bricett. *Courtesy of Lewis J. West.*

The Prop Shop where propellers for the group's aircraft were repaired. *Courtesy of David L. Born.*

The station radio transmission station. *Courtesy of Lewis J. West.*

The Red Cross Aero Club. *Carroll C. Sprague Collection, courtesy of the East Essex Aviation Society.*

Another view of the Red Cross Aero Club. *Courtesy of Clarence M. Surges.*

Miscellaneous buildings near the Officers Quarters. *Courtesy of Harold L. Stotts.*

A view of the station looking north toward the water tower. *Courtesy of Harold L. Stotts.*

The Station Hospital. *Carroll C. Sprague Collection, courtesy of the East Essex Aviation Society.*

An unknown soldier guarding a machine gun post. *Courtesy of the 436th Fighter Squadron Association.*

The volleyball courts. *Courtesy of David L. Born.*

The Firing Range where Newcross Squadron pilot Lieutenant David L. Born is seen practicing and sharpening his aim with his issued Colt .45 Automatic. *Courtesy of David L. Born.*

The station Post Office and Exchange. *Courtesy of David L. Born.*

Parade Grounds located near some of the Enlisted Men's Quarters. It was then being used as parking for some of the Motor Pool vehicles. *Courtesy of Raymond Niekamp.*

A line up at the newly installed Coca-Cola dispenser in the PX. The dispenser was put into operation the second week of July 1944 and thereafter, the popular ICE COLD beverage was available at all times to the men. *Courtesy of Eugene W. Bailey.*

The Special Services Bulletin Board where information concerning all of the activities available on the airfield. Current movies being shown, dances, plays, lectures and transportation schedules were all posted here. *Courtesy of Loetta Taylor (Kennedy).*

CHAPTER FOUR

JUNE 1944

The 434th Fighter Squadron is the only squadron represented in the group's Mission Summary records for the month of June. Records for the other two squadrons were not found among those preserved. Unfortunately, because of this lack of information, the all-important month of June 1944 and its historical significance is presented in a somewhat lop-sided manner. Whenever possible, the author has supplied pertinent data that attempts to fill in the gaps, but no amount of patchwork can make up for what is missing. The author asks for the reader's understanding concerning this matter.

2 June 1944

VIII FC FO 358

No. 10 Friday. The group put up 42 P-38s for a fighter sweep in support of 1st, 2nd and 3rd BD bombers attacking their 8th AF Mission 384 primary NOBALL (V1 buzz bomb launch sites) targets in the Pas de Calais area of France. Approximate time up: 1100 hrs., down: 1400 hrs. The weather presented the attacking force with 10/10ths cloud coverage, but the war went on. L/F for the group was near the Cape Gris-Nez area at 1145hrs./20,000 ft. The patrol was uneventful. Even flak at Cape Gris-Nez and along the coast down to Boulogne was inconsequential, being recorded as heavy, meager and inaccurate. The heavies arrived in the area at 1230 hrs. and bombed through the clouds. The results were unobserved. The group drifted south in the overcast to the vicinity of Dieppe. They broke from the continent in that area at 1335 hours and arrived back at England in the vicinity of Dungeness at 1345 hrs.

2 June 1944

VIII FC FO 359

No. 11 Friday. This afternoon's fighter sweep of the Évreux area, was in support of bombers attacking their 8th AF Mission 385 targets in France, a part of the cover up operation designed to deceive the Germans into believing the forth coming invasion would occur in the Pas de Calais area. Approximate time up: 1820 hrs., down: 2215 hrs. L/F in the area of Dieppe was as scheduled. Flak in that area was heavy, intense and accurate. The squadrons were being vectored by their controller over the entire area and through the fair weather, the bombing results of an attack on an air field by their assigned bombers was observed to be excellent. No enemy aircraft were seen, but Lieutenant Robin Olds from Newcross Squadron spotted a train in the area just north of Rouen. He attacked it in a strafing run and destroyed the locomotive. L/O was in the area of St. Valery-en-Caux at 2140 hrs./10,000 ft.

Technical Sergeant Glen A. Wold was the crew chief for all of the "Scat" airplanes that Robin Olds flew during his time at Wattisham. Glen remembers the squadron's arrival there with a certain fondness and that applies especially to the time he first met then Lieutenant Olds and learned Robin was to fly his airplane, a P-38 and the first of the Scat lineage. As Glen puts it:

> "It is my understanding that the pilots were permitted to choose the mechanic who would crew the plane that they would fly. Senior officers had first choice of course. My first meeting with Lt. Olds occurred on the 434th's flight line. He introduced himself and we began talking about the airplane. He outlined the things he hoped would

be accomplished on the plane he would be flying, things like filling in the export screw heads on the wing surfaces and waxing the entire aircraft. I was beginning to wonder to myself, 'What have I got here?' Lt. Olds explained that these things would lessen air resistance and increase airspeed. He also insisted on helping in these endeavors. We talked about aircraft and engine maintenance where once more, Lt. Olds let me know that he intended to spend any available time that he had with me during our periodic inspections of the plane. He wanted to learn as much as he could about its maintenance and things he might be able to service in an emergency. (This knowledge paid off at a later date when the P-51 he was flying had a magneto failure over France and he was forced to land at an airfield there. The mechanics at the French airfield were unfamiliar with the P-51, but Lieutenant or probably Captain by then, Olds was able to guide a mechanic in the removal of a magneto from a wrecked P-51 and its replacement of the malfunctioning one in his aircraft. This was no small feat, but everything worked and he soon returned back to our base.)

"All of the men who worked on the planes put a lot of effort into their job. The crew chiefs, the armorers, the specialists such as radio men, electrical, sheet metal and instrument men, the men in the hangars, the inspectors and the personal equipment men all worked long, hard hours to provide the pilots with airplanes and equipment in the best possible condition. We knew that it was up to us to ensure that the men flying the ships that we worked on had the best chance of survival that we could provide. We all worked as a team and when our planes and pilots went out on a mission, we sweated out their return. If all went well and our prayers were answered in the affirmative, we were rewarded with their safe return and could start breathing normally again. It was truly icing on the cake for us when our pilot did a victory roll over the field. We all shared in that bit of glory, knowing that our many hours had paid off. Once the planes were back on the ground, we started the process all over again in preparation for the next mission."

A later photo ofTechnical Sergeant Glen A. Wold, who is shown standing next to one of his P-51s, Scat #5 or VI. *Courtesy of Glen A. Wold.*

3 June 1944

VIII FC FO 365

No. 12 Saturday. This morning's patrol of the area south of Boulogne, was in support of bombers attacking their 8th AF Mission 388 tactical targets in the Pas de Calais area of France. Approximate time up: 0950 hrs., down: 1245 hrs. L/F was in the area of Berck at 1045 hrs./21,000 ft. The cloud coverage of 5/10ths caused the cancellation of some of the bombing attacks, but others pressed on. The squadrons patrolled the area bounded by le Crotoy on the coast of France, southeast to Abbeville, north to Frévent and northwest to le Crotoy again. Heavy, meager, but accurate flak was encountered at Abbeville. While in the Frévent area, the 434th FS was vectored east to investigate bandits, but nothing was found. They returned to the patrol area. The patrol was uneventful and the group made L/O in the vicinity of Cayeux-Sur-Mer at 1200 hrs./22,000 ft.

From John W. Hedenberg's diary, the following two entries help to shed some light on what was happening during this time. For 3 June:

> "Same thing as yesterday morning, patrolled Calais area. Still nothing doing. Weather man full of bull. Told us would be about 1/2 cloud cover when we got back, but it turned out all of England solid overcast. The group played hell getting down through the stuff and dodging barrage balloons finding the field." John later added: "The above description was a considerable understatement. In

these situations, we found the vicinity of the base on return by asking for steering courses from the radio direction finding station [Heater Homer] that was at the airfield. The station would ask us for a "long count" radio transmission and use their rotatable loop antenna to find us. This was done while we were flying tight formation in the gloomy, half-dark between two layers of overcast. Then, when ordered by the tower, two of us at a time would duck, leader flying on instruments and wingman snuggled up close in formation, down below the lowest cloud layer. (Where the ceiling was about 100 feet, it was even darker and pouring rain.) Each two-plane element would then search about at tree top level until the field was found and landed upon. Then the control tower would call the group to send down another element. There were no crashes this day, but a lot of us added a few gray hairs." For 5 June: "Started squadron [instead of group] missions today. At briefing we were told our job for a while would be patrolling shipping in the channel. No doubt what is coming. This is it – what the whole world is waiting for. I didn't get to go, but the boys say there were thousands of boats – landing craft, DDs [destroyers] BBs [battleships] cruisers, carriers, etc., all steaming south from the Isle of Wight area, toward France."

This photograph was taken by Bison Squadron pilot John W. Hedenberg. Shot while he was flying his P-38, it shows accompanying 436th FS P-38s forming up over Wattisham for a mission. *Courtesy of John W. Hedenberg.*

Another picture of 436th FS P-38s forming up over Wattisham for a mission. *Courtesy of John W. Hedenberg.*

5 June 1944

VIII FC FO Unk.

No. 13 Monday. This was the one everyone had been waiting for, the one that the 479th Fighter Group had been specifically sent to participate in, the beginning of the invasion of France. Starting in the afternoon, the pilots of the 479th FG would be patrolling the area between England and the French coast, helping, along with other P-38 groups, to provide an impenetrable umbrella of cover for the invasion forces streaming across the English Channel and into France. Operation NEPTUNE had begun. Briefed by their leaders, pilots from the three squadrons were told only that they would be flying an area patrol over the English Channel, between the Isle of Wight on the coast of England and Cherbourg on the coast of France. Security regarding observations was stressed, but it was made known that more information about the mission would be forthcoming. Thus, the pilots went out on what they thought was to be a routine mission. Upon return, the air was electric, but cautioned not to speak of what they might have seen, the men strictly adhered to this admonition. However, during interrogation, the whole story came out. The invasion was on! The pilots said they had never seen so many ships and furthermore, they didn't know there were so many on any one spot in the world!

The previous day, 4 June 1944, all 8th AF P-38 groups had stood down in order that the alternating bands of white and black paint might be applied to the aircraft wings and tail booms. The P-38 with its easily recognizable shape was the logical plane to provide the top cover so necessary to the operation. It was thought that nervous gunners on board the many vessels crossing the channel, would be able to distinguish its shape more readily than any other Allied A/C and not shoot at their own cover.

Frederick (Fred) C. Hayner, then a Staff Sergeant, was the 434th Fighter Squadron's painter ("Hayner the Painter, Best in the West" was the nickname given him during the time the squadron spent organizing in California.) and he remembers painting some of those stripes. In 1998, he told about that day:

"An order came down that required all aircraft to be marked with so-called 'Invasion Stripes'. The stripes were to be applied around both wings and in our case, around both tail booms. They were to be five alternating bands of white, black, white, black and white, 18" in width. With 18 P-38s to be painted, terror arose in my heart! How was I ever going to accomplish this in two days? I started masking and spraying. What I saw next was both welcome and upsetting. There were the ground crews, armed with six-inch paintbrushes, slopping the paint onto those beautiful aircraft! Some were taking the time to mask at the edges, but some weren't even bothering to do that. It broke my heart, even though I had come to the realization that this was the only way the job would get done in time. When it was all done, I think that I can only claim about four aircraft that had my spray application on."

"Hayner the Painter" – Staff Sergeant Frederick C. Hayner. *Courtesy of Frederick C. Hayner.*

A former lieutenant and Bison Squadron pilot, Howard G. Hightower, described in a 1994 letter, some of his experiences from those preparatory 4th and 5th June days, prior to the invasion. What follows is adapted from that letter:

"I believe June 4th was a Sunday. About mid-morning someone came into our ready room and said the flight crews were painting white and black stripes all over our planes. Well, we all went out, got on our bicycles and rode over to where the planes were parked. I found my crew chief and asked him what was up. He stated 'Beats the hell out of me Lieutenant! They said to paint them like this and that's what we are doing.'

"My flight was scheduled to fly the next day, June 5th. The weather was bad so we played poker throughout the morning and into the afternoon. About mid-afternoon we got a call to attend a briefing. As we all entered the briefing room, there was an air of excitement because we had suspicions of what was happening. At the front of the room, the group's C.O., Lieutenant Colonel Kyle Riddle, pulled the curtain back that was covering a large map. On the map was a box that was drawn from the shores of England to the coasts of France. The box had 479th written in it and we were briefed on an area patrol we were to fly that covered that box. We went out to discover that the invasion was on.

"We flew in a southwest direction, heading to the east of London and turned south in the vicinity of Brighton. The ceiling was low, about 500 to 600 feet, with haze and scud [ragged storm clouds] that yielded one to one-and-a-half miles of visibility. We continued in a southerly direction for about three to four minutes and started seeing what we learned was the invasion fleet. It was a hell of a sight and I knew I was personally witnessing a great moment in history. I knew I had a small part in a time of great historical significance, best of all, I had one of the best seats in the house! [Many of the group's pilots have made the same or similar statements, noting their front row seats to this thrilling sight.] Lieutenant Clarence O. Johnson, who had previously flown a tour with the 82nd Fighter Group in the Mediterranean, was our flight leader and he was eager. He started us off on a southeasterly course, angling across the path of the boats to our east, toward the French coast. He was feeling for the left flank. In a short time, there were no more boats, just ocean and in a short distance, the veil of mist and fog. I remember we flew cover over a group of small landing craft. They appeared to be 12-14 feet wide, 40-50 feet long, square-nosed, low-sided and filled with men. The boats were in excellent formation with several boats abreast and stretched out for a fair distance. We stayed with the boats, patrolling, just we four P-38s and the boats.

"We had split into elements, Lt. Johnson and his wingman Lieutenant Victor C. Wolski forming one plus myself and Lieutenant George Straub forming the other. We flew 800-1,000 feet apart on each side of the boats. When we got to the front of the boat procession, Lt.'s Johnson and Wolski would turn into our element and we would turn into theirs, each of us doing a 180-degree turn and heading back down the column toward the rear. When we got there, we would turn around and do it again. This gave good cover for the men and boats.

"As I flew over the gray water this fog and scud shrouded dull day, I looked down at the men huddled together in their boats and they in turn watched us, turning their faces upward as we passed near. When they did this, you could see a solid patch of white faces in the dullness that surrounded them. Each group of boats was like that as we passed by.

"At one point, we flew forward toward the front and saw what appeared to be tug boats lined up abreast, from east to west. They seemed to be pulling nets, sweeping for mines. A couple of miles behind them were a number of small destroyer-like vessels darting about maybe checking for submarines.

"When time came for us to return to our base, we headed back, passing hundreds of vessels on the waters below. Once back and all excited, we found our names on the mission board, scheduled for tomorrow. We learned later that was to be the big day.

"Reflecting back on what I saw and what I've learned since that date, I have to believe the troops we covered that day were first wave assault troops. They were on the extreme left flank going down and they would have been the extreme left flank going in. There were no boats in front of these troops because we flew to the absolute front and saw only the minesweepers. We then returned and resumed our patrol. The beach they were headed for must have been Sword. Every year on June 6th, I think of them and D-Day. I always wander about those unknown men. Who were they, where were they from and how did they fare? It has always bothered me when I think about having to leave them because we were running low on fuel. I wish that we had been able to carry belly tanks for that mission, but I suppose the invasion planners didn't want the tanks falling on the troops below should we have had to drop them."

When the flash came over the Teletype: "Execute Plan NEPTUNE", the group was ready. For the next ten days, all day long, from sun-up until after dark, the P-38 pilots cruised high over the channel, preventing German aircraft from getting at the endless stream of surface craft that shuttled back and forth between England and the Normandy coast. The 479th FG patrol was executed by squadrons and comprised some eight "missions" a day. Two squadrons flew three "missions" each and the third flew two. When time came for one squadron to return to base, it was relieved by a second and the second was relieved by the third and the third by the first again. In this way, a constant search was maintained for enemy planes that might slip through similar patrols to the north.

That is how it went for the next fifty-seven "missions" which covered the dates 5 June through 15 June 1944. Separating them by squadron, the 434th FS flew 21, the 435th FS flew 18 and the 436th also flew 18. Rather than list and detail each and every one of them, an abbreviated listing is provided in order that the repetitions not become laborious and loose meaning. By far, the greatest portion of the "missions" that the group flew during those key days, were uneventful, with nothing to report, but that was good for those on the seas and ground. The areas patrolled by the 479th FG were listed as "Victor" and "X-ray". "Victor" was the Cherbourg Peninsula side of the invasion area and "X-ray" was the Le Havre area:

Date	**Patrol areas**	**Observations**
5 June	Area Patrol	Weather bad with about 9/10ths coverage.
6 June	"Victor" & "X-ray"	Weather fair.
7 June	"Victor" & "X-ray"	Weather overcast. One C-47 in water, called Mayday, two A/C left upstairs to get fix and to investigate at lower altitude. Two dinghies in water, one with two men and the other with three. Fix was obtained. (Prob. 9th AF 313th TG A/C.)
8 June	"Victor" & "X-ray"	Weather very poor, one "mission" unable to penetrate it.
9 June	"Victor" & "X-ray"	Weather very poor, most "missions" scrubbed. The group suffered a casualty while enroute home when Lieutenant Edward J. Spillane from the 436th FS became engaged in rat-racing with a P-47 from the 353rd FG over their base. He failed to pull out of a maneuver and crashed fatally at Raydon.
10 June	"Victor" & "X-ray"	Weather over areas good with broken clouds. Five Fw 190s sighted at 8,000 ft. Derelict watercraft were seen floating. Flak encountered at Cherbourg. Huge fire seen at Valognes.
11 June	"Victor" & "X-ray"	Weather closing in again.

12 June	"Victor" & "X-ray"	Weather clearing to CAVU. Lt. Flamm D. Harper lost a belly tank over channel, forcing him to land early for gas.
13 June	"Victor" & "X-ray"	Weather good except for some clouds.
14 June	"Victor" & "X-ray"	Weather thickened from 2/10ths to 4/10ths, then again cleared.
15 June	"Victor" & "X-ray"	Weather 7/10ths. The 434th FS joined with the 435th FS on a patrol/sweep of France. L/F over Deauville at 1915 hrs./8,000 ft. Course: Liseux, Le Neubourg, Gournay, then vectored by controller to Beauvais to intercept six bogies, but not able to make contact. Flak heavy, moderate and accurate in Poix-Horny area. L/O over Ault at 2015 hrs./8,000 ft.

6 June, from the diary of John W. Hedenberg:

"Today is the day. Ran two missions same as yesterday's. I was spare on both – Both times got as far as Beachy Head and had to come back because no aborts. We now have 1,000 lb. bombs waiting by each ship. Will probably use them in a few days. The news [that the long-awaited second front had a last started] came over the radio this morning, but we pilots knew about it a day before that. The boys say the traffic across the channel is as thick as ever, but no one has had a look at the beachhead yet. These patrols are low-altitude, 2,500-3,000 feet and visibility is not good, of course. The weather is perfect for the invasion. Apparently, the Germans were fooled by our plastering of the Calais area, then striking lower down between Le Havre and Cherbourg. As far as we know now, everything is going well. Today no E/A to speak of sighted, but I imagine tomorrow, all hell will break loose. It remains to be seen."

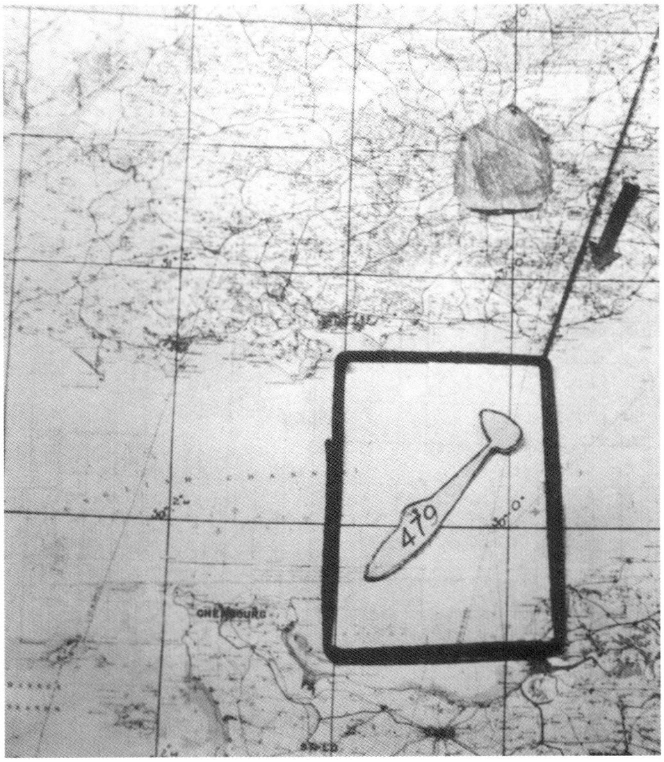

Above: A photo of a map that was located in one of the group's briefing rooms. It shows the overall area patrolled by the pilots of the 479th FG. *From original 479th FG history.* Below: D-Day patrol map showing fighter patrol areas – not drawn to scale. Patrol areas shown are Victor, William and X-Ray. The remainders shown are patrol lines.

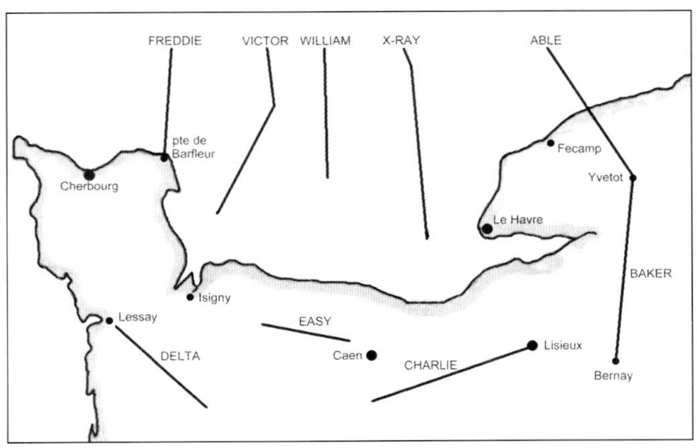

George D. (Dan) Hendrix flew three missions as a young 434th FS second lieutenant that first day of the invasion:

"On D-Day, we were in an all-out effort. I logged 12 hours for the three missions I flew that day. The biggest hazard then was the possibility of colliding with another Allied aircraft. I understood at times that day, there were over a thousand aircraft flying over that small strip of channel water between the English coast and that of France. Making that worse, there was an overcast that began at around 1,500 feet most of the day, so all of those aircraft were compressed into that small piece of airspace. No German pilot with any sense would have stuck his nose into that melee for fear of running into one of those planes. From that aspect, our air cover was very successful and our troops did not have to suffer enemy air attacks while landing at Normandy. One of my most vivid memories of this day is that of the channel covered with landing craft and the almost overcast-like masses of C-47s hauling paratroopers and towing gliders."

At 2300 hrs. on the night of 7 June, an alert was sounded and Wattisham's AAF Station F-377 was confronted with the horrifying spectacle of a 34th BG B-24 being shot down by a German night intruder from II/KG 51. It was one of three shot down by intruders that night. This one crashed and burned some distance from the field, but the explosion and flames were clearly visible to the men on guard duty and to those clustered about the entrances to air raid shelters. All of the bomber's crew were able to parachute to safety except for the unfortunate tail gunner who was killed. William (Bill) S. Culbertson, then a Corporal with the 436th FS, was on guard duty that night and recalls one of his friends firing at a low flying night fighter with his Thompson submachine gun.

Alerts followed quite regularly for the next few nights and on 10 June, the field received the attention of a few bombers who dropped their loads on Wattisham. The bombs hit toward the southwest end of the field, close to the Fourth Strategic Air Depot at Hitcham, but did little damage. After this incident, the men were more inclined to head to the air raid shelters when the alert sounded. (At least for awhile.)

The C-47 reported as down in the channel waters 7 June, was probably one of two lost by the 9th AF, 313th Transport Group between England and France that day. A pilot from the 434th FS, Lieutenant George W. Gleason, told later about seeing a C-47 ditched in those waters. He said that while flying the squadron's "Racetrack Pattern" as he called it, they saw a C-47 in the water with about 40 men struggling to stay afloat next to it. By the squadron's next circuit, the Gooney Bird had sunk and there appeared to be only about 20 or so men, still afloat. On the third pass over the area, there were less than ten still above water. Sadly, their fourth time around bore witness to what appeared to be no survivors. Gleason could not help, but feel badly about the lost of life, but the men above could do nothing for them except call for help. He felt it was such a waste that the men never had a chance to help fulfill what they were intended to do. In fact, they never had a chance to survive at all. Another of the 434th FS's pilots, Lieutenant George Hendrix (see above) told a similar story of seeing C-47s skimming the channel water's surface as they hauled troops and towed gliders to France. He said that several times he saw one hit the water and go into the drink, but he assumed that since the C-47 seemed to float for a while, that everyone had a chance of getting rescued.

Lieutenant George D. Hendrix with his crew chief Staff Sergeant Henry J. Robitz to his left and the assistant crew chief to his right. *Courtesy of George D. Hendrix.*

The following excerpts from John W. Hedenberg's diary help to illustrate the group's efforts during the times its pilots were on patrol, providing air cover for the invasion:

7 June "Went on mission similar to yesterday. What's wrong with the Germans? Still no Luftwaffe. Flew protective umbrella at low altitude – 0 to 1,000 feet. Several times went up and down beach of Cherbourg Peninsula and almost over the town at 300 feet. Beach deserted, not a soul in sight, no flak, though Grasshoff and Hartnett both say saw tracers go by. Every now and then battleships standing offshore fired a few rounds – probably counter battery. Constant stream of ships and landing craft crossing channel. Dinghies and damaged landing craft drifting here and there. Everything has a deceptively quiet look."

8 June "Down to the beachhead again today. Still no enemy air activity. Weather terrible, flying in the rain most of the time. I'll bet the poor infantry is cussing the weather, but it's their best protection from the German Luftwaffe. Got a good look at Le Havre, which is still in enemy hands. Place appeared deserted, no shipping in the harbor. Only sign of life I saw was a pair of possible E boats making knots in the basin. Reported them to S-2. Too close to our landing forces to be up to any good. What a day! I'm dead tired. Flying in this weather is no joke. We'll be the hottest damn instrument pilots in the world when this is over."

9 June "Spillane killed today in accident – Rat-racing on the deck. Too bad, really a swell Joe." John further explained: " I liked Jim Spillane very much. There were many hours of shared bull-sessions, poker playing, flying and other enjoyable activities lots of us had done together during our training and living as a unit. Most of the time we managed to keep our sanity when people were getting killed, by repressing our feelings. Life would have been impossible otherwise.

"The term rat-racing on the deck referred to a dangerous game, which we all never the less enjoyed greatly, of playing follow-the-leader across the countryside at as close to zero altitude above ground as we could get, at speeds of 250-300 miles an hour. This meant ducking down into valleys, hopping over tree lines, etc., to the maximum degree possible without hitting anything. Needless to say, it was highly risky and sometimes someone would make a tiny, but fatal mistake or fail to see some obstacle. At such times, that someone usually got killed rather instantly in an explosion of flames."

Lieutenant George W. Gleason with the plane's crew chief Staff Sergeant Alfred M. Perdue and assistant crew chief Sergeant Stephen O. Coakley on their P-38. *Courtesy of Frederick C. Hayner.*

10 June "Another patrol over the channel. Still no enemy activity."

11 June "Same. Hell of a lot of our ships. No enemy."

12 June "Likewise. A jillion Allied planes, nothing else. Getting damned boring, especially since only a few miles south, over the beachhead itself, there is plenty of action. According to a report, the Abbeville Kids are back in circulation there. Forgot to mention yesterday that the mission was very long – no belly tanks. I ran too short to get all the way back. Landed at West Malling (south of Gravesend) with a total of 25 gallons. Cutting it pretty close. West Malling is a Spitfire and Mosquito base. Those Englishmen certainly turned out en mass to get a look at a Lightning. Treated me swell, insisted on my drinking a cup of tea with them – Nice people." John further added: "The RAF people were indeed open-heartedly friendly, the tea I was given, however, was more hostile. It was so strong that it was as black as the strongest coffee, resembling in flavor to my unacclimated taste, nothing so much as battery acid. I couldn't manage more than a few sips, which amused my hosts very much."

13 June "Started out for the channel again this morning in terrible weather. We got about as far as The Naze, [On the coast of England, just below Ipswich.] had to turn back. Visibility about a mile, ceiling very low. Had to come back on the deck – Never more than 100 feet above the ground. Had a close call – Visibility so poor in heavy rain at the field, that misjudged distance from runway. Didn't know it till dragged wheels through barbed

wire fence 100 yards short of runway. Goosed it and managed to stagger that far before touching down. Close, but made it – Damn good ship!"

14 June "Started out this morning on another milk run, but came back on account of left intercooler went out. Stayed long enough to count as an early return instead of an abort. Flew again in the afternoon, still no Luftwaffe."

15 June "Wasn't on morning mission, but went in the evening again. The morning job was our first strafing sweep. The boys got a train, but no E/A seen. They went in at Le Havre after completing regular two-hour patrol over the channel, flew a semi-circular course down over Evreux and came out by Le Treport. The job I went on in the evening was the same old patrol. That patrol is certainly useless. The Germans haven't even come near the channel once. They tell us we're through with it tomorrow, though."

Miss Angeline (Angie) Sampson began her assignment as Program Director for the Red Cross Aero Club this date, much to the delight of the men. *Carroll C. Sprague Collection, courtesy of the East Essex Aviation Society.*

Referring back up to the patrol/sweep that is listed as having occurred on 15 June and to J. Hedenberg's diary entry for same, the group having patrolled for some two to three hours was released from duty over the channel and headed inland following the above-described route. Dropping their dry belly tanks, the 436th FS headed in and up toward Gournay. Former Bison Squadron pilot, Howard G. Hightower described in a 1995 letter, part of what happened during that flight:

"Having passed Lisieux and heading for Le Neubourg, the group was flying a line abreast formation with the 436th on the right and Lieutenant Clarence O. Johnson leading our flight on the extreme right of the squadron. We were flying over patches of low cumulus clouds and through one of the holes, Lt. Johnson spotted a small village with a railroad siding. The siding was loaded with a solid train of tank cars, but there was no engine in sight. Lt. Johnson requested permission to take our flight down. Permission was given and we dropped under the clouds and headed for the train. The signal was given for a right echelon turn and we headed west so that we would strafe across the cars and not down the track. We made one pass, pulled up with each plane doing a 180-degree turn and headed back for a second pass. Lt. Johnson was on the extreme right with Lieutenants Victor C. Wolski, George Straub and myself following in echelon. Just before I fired at the train on our second pass, I glanced to the right. I saw that Lt. Johnson had finished firing and was at the cars, Lt. Wolski was just about finished shooting and Lt. Straub was about at the mid-point of his firing pass. I glanced to the left for some reason and low and behold, there were two or three flights starting to strafe down the track toward us. I pulled up, for either they would have been in my fire or I would have been in theirs. The low scattered clouds had created a problem, concealing us when the whole group showed up. There could have been planes coming in from several directions at once to shoot up those tank cars. A prime example of this was that on this mission, one of our pilots, Lt. Thomas T. Galloway, came home with a hole in one of his props. The hole was out near the propeller's tip. It was about 5/8 of an inch in diameter, about the size for a .50 cal. bullet."

All was not daring and glory for the men of the 479th FG. Many men remained on the ground in support of the pilots who took the risks during those history-making days of the invasion. Men like Corporal Allen J. Moon who was asked many years later by his grandchildren: "What did you do during D-Day, Granddad?" His response:

"I described the intense effort of all the forces on that awesome day. I told them the sky was virtually a cloud of aircraft and the channel, a near-carpet of invasion craft. I went on about how the invasion was the magnificent culmination of preparation and planning and that the beaches of Normandy were stained red with the blood of many brave Allied men. Persisting, the grandchildren asked, 'But, Granddad, where were you?' My reply: 'They also serve, who stand and wait.' I was on K.P. in the Officer's Mess, washing pots and pans, watching it all happen and muttering: 'Go get 'em!' from the security of my position on the 'China Clipper'."

This photograph shows part of the damage done to the P-38 Second Lieutenant Richard M. Lunstrum was flying when he struck a drop tank accidentally released by a P-38 flying ahead of him. The accident occurred just after his squadron had crossed the channel and passed into France. The damage forced Lt. Lunstrum to abort the mission. *Courtesy of William M. Morgan.*

16 June 1944

VIII FC FO 393

No. 70 Friday. This was a late afternoon, early evening escort for bombers attacking their 8th AF Mission 416 target, an airfield in France. The cross channel patrols and beachhead sweeps had come to an end. The 479th FG was back on regular ops. Approximate time up: 1700 hrs., down: 2000 hrs. L/F and R/V with the Big Friends were in the area of Schouwen, Holland at 1730 hrs. The proper bombers were escorted to the target airfield near Signy-L'Abbaye where they unloaded through heavy overcast. The results were not observed. Flak over the target was heavy, intense and accurate while over Schouwen it had been heavy, meager and inaccurate. Pilots of the 435th FS encountered the first damage to their planes done by the enemy during this mission. Flak had punctured a number of the squadron's P-38s, although none seriously. The pilots were somewhat excited as they felt they had finally attracted the attention of the Germans. So far they had flown nearly seventy missions without getting a scratch on their aircraft. A mad scramble took place to recover the numerous pieces of flak that had lodged in the planes. Naturally the pilots had first choice in the matter, but a few of the enlisted men managed to carry away a small fragment or two for a souvenir. Returning, the group broke with the bombers at an undetermined point due to weather, but it was close to home as the time was 1940 hours, forty minutes before touching down at Wattisham.

17 June 1944

VIII FC FO 394

No. 71 Saturday. One of several missions this day, the first, utilizing 43 P-38s, was a late morning escort for 1st BD B-17s attacking their 8th AF Mission 418 target, the airfield at Breteuil, France. Approximate time up: 1100 hrs., down: 1400 hrs. L/F and R/V with the Big Friends were in the area of Coxyde, Belgium at 1145 hrs. Providing both top and bottom cover for the bombers, they were taken to the target area, but due to bad weather with 10/10ths cloud coverage, the field was not found and an unknown target of opportunity was attacked. The results were unobserved. The mission was uneventful with no enemy aircraft nor flak present. Escort was broken over the channel, northwest of Le Tréport, France at 1315 hrs.

17 June 1944

VIII FC FO 395

No. 72 Saturday. The group put up 49 P-38s for this, another mission for the day. Their assignment was an evening fighter-bomber attack on bridges in France in support of 8th AF Mission 418. The 434th FS provided escort for the other two squadrons. Approximate time up: 1939 hrs., down: 2245 hrs. The weather was overcast for the entire trip, from the English coast through landfall in to landfall out. The group made L/F in the vicinity of Dunkerque where they received a peppering of light, meager and inaccurate flak. Visibility above and below the layer of overcast was fine, but it was a definite factor in what targets were struck and who came back home. As the squadrons let down through the clouds near the primary target at Crécy-la-Chapelle, they became somewhat separated, breaking up into individual flights and in some cases, elements. The resulting consequence was that now the attack on the primary target became a search for targets of opportunity. Bridges and the approaches to bridges as well as a railroad yard, steam engines and goods wagons were damaged. Generally speaking, the 434th FS attacked tactical targets near Crécy, the 435th FS went to Clastras and the 436th tackled targets in the vicinity of Louviers. These are only approximate locations, however, as the A/C were scattered. Still though, the squadrons maintained radio contact with each other, but in some instances, transmission became difficult because of the excessive calls made necessary by the many separations.

Newcross Squadron suffered the loss of one of their pilots in a mid-air collision which occurred as they let down through the cloud layer. Second Lieutenant Frank Grdenich described the accident:

> "I was leading the Fourth Flight [Blue] in the squadron with Lt. Ohligschlager [Second Lieutenant James K. Ohligschlager] on my left and Lt. Williams [Lieutenant Bailey A. Williams] on my right. The overcast extended approximately from 3,500 feet to 7,000 feet in two layers. The order was given to descend through the overcast, flights in trail with a throttle setting of 25 inches Hg. I followed the squadron down through the first layer of clouds. When I last saw Lt. Ohligschlager, he was on my left wing, in the normal position for a wingman, fairly close. We began descent through the main part of the overcast. The accident occurred at approximately 5,500 feet Visibility was nil, as we were in solid cumulus. Lt. Ohligschlager apparently passed me in the clouds as his plane suddenly came up under the nose of my ship, slightly off to the left. The visibility was such, that the accident occurred at practically the same instant that I caught sight of him. There was no time to avoid contact, although I pulled up as quickly as I could. The damage to my airplane was mainly near the left wing tip where the outer fuel tank was ripped open. The propeller blades on that side were slightly bent and the engine began throwing oil. I am quite certain the damage to Lt. Ohligschlager's plane was not such that he could not have gotten out safely, as we had sufficient altitude and our airspeed was only 250 mph during the descent. I'm sure my left wing struck his right rudder and my left propeller nicked his right tail boom. The accident must have jammed his controls as I know the collision wasn't violent and I was able to maintain control of my ship, although I had to feather my left engine on the way home due to oil pressure failure. There were three squadrons in the area and in the radio confusion while joining up beneath the overcast, I was unable to find out whom I had collided with. I continued home alone, above the overcast. This accident was purely the result of attempting to go through a solid cumulus overcast in close formation. The visibility was very bad."

Sadly, two days later, the day after Lt. Grdenich filed this report, he himself, would be lost in France, the result of another mid-air collision.

Second Lieutenant James K. Ohligschlager was in fact able to escape his damaged A/C and parachuted down to become a POW. He was captured by the Germans at a point about a mile north of Montge, and 18 miles southeast of Creil.

Lakeside Squadron (435th FS) lost a pilot on this mission also. Captain Calvin (Cal) J. Butler was hit by flak and went down northwest of Paris. Second Lieutenant Rayne B. Fairchild gave this report:

> "Captain Butler and I broke out of the overcast at about 4,000 feet. We circled to pick up the squadron and flight, but not seeing them or the target, made a run on a bridge. After bombing the bridge, we flew through some flak and made a pass at a train in a yard. Captain Butler probably got hit then. He climbed, zigzagging and turning as he went and flew into the overcast at the northwest side of Paris. I went up through the overcast and circled, but he did not come through. I returned home alone."

That only tells a small part of the adventure though. Cal Butler shared the complete story with me and has graciously agreed to allow me to quote from his autobiographical memoirs entitled "My Struggle". Reproduced in part here, it begins:

> "On June 17, 1944, my day started off with a daylight mission. I can't recall where, but it evidently was of little significance. We returned by around 06:30 AM and Maj. Glover [Major John G. Glover was the 435 Fighter Squadron's commanding officer.] led the next mission. I led the following one, then again at about 04:30 PM, I flew off for my third mission of the day. It was short, only lasting till about 06:30 PM. Not a whole bunch of flying time, but from 04:30 AM to 06:30 PM makes a long day, even for a young person. I had gone to the barracks after debriefing and was in the shower when John Glover interrupted the nice warm water by turning it off. He said,

'Cal you've got to take the mission for me.' My retort was 'What mission and why? You certainly realize I flew my first of three missions at daylight. I am tired!' John looked at me with a forlorn look and said, 'I'm sick.' I was upset to hear this. We all flew occasionally when we didn't feel good. My next question was, 'What's the matter, John, did they load bombs on the airplane?' John replied, 'Yes they did and it is a full size effort to bomb a bridge just inside France, ahead of our lines. Forty-eight aircraft. You will be leading the second squadron.' I could see now why John had gotten sick. I had felt all along that he did not belong in combat, now it was more evident than ever. I said, 'Okay John, I'll take your mission. Brief me!' As he was giving me the details of the important mission, I was putting back on my sweaty clothing. I asked John to return my clean clothing to my room. Here I was, going back to the line, beat, getting into my aircraft and trying to get into position for takeoff. I fired up and began to taxi. I got to the end of the runway as Col. Riddle was taking off. It was hot so I had cracked the left window for some ventilation. As the last bird from the 434th headed down the runway, I taxied out and began my take off for the mission. When I thought the aircraft should be flying, even with its extra load of 2000 pounds of bombs, it was not getting airborne. My wingman was flying over me, when I caught a breeze on my face and realized the left window was still cracked. When flying overloaded aircraft, you want everything to be as normal as possible. The P-38 needed the lift created by the perfect shape of the cockpit area. The partially open window spoiled that. I turned the crank that raised the window and flew off at the end of the runway, better late than never. As you can see, I was never with it on this mission. When we got to our altitude, I formed on Col. Riddle's right flank as the 436th formed behind and to the left.

"The weather had been predicted to be scattered to broken, however, the weather at the target was solid overcast with an occasional hole, a change for the worst. We could not see the target area and since I had not been to a briefing, I had no idea what the target was to be, except that it was a heavily defended bridge. Col. Riddle found a small hole and proceeded to let down through it. I led my squadron closely behind Riddle. The overcast hole closed and it was IFR from the start. The clouds were thick, like wet fog. I lost all contact with the balance of my squadron. I established a let down rate of 700 to 1000 feet per minute. I was hoping my squadron would appear. As I reached the bottom, I spotted a P-38. It was Rayne Fairchild from my squadron, the 435th. We got in formation, then saw four other P-38s. I wagged my wing for them to join. Instead, they headed back into the overcast. This upset me also. Now we were alone, seeking a target with no description. I felt we had better find a place to unload our bombs and get the hell out of there. I could not understand then and can't to this day, how 48 aircraft can let down through an overcast and only 6 find the base and or the target area. Then, to have those other four leave and go back home really set me off. Weren't we there to fight a war or were we back to fun, games and bad excuses. Out of 48 aircraft, two only got to a target! The other 46 had returned to the base and proceeded to the first party since arriving in England. [This is not an entirely accurate statement, as other A/C found targets and succeeded in inflicting damage to the enemy. As a point of further information, Station F-377 held its first Officer's party at the Officer's Club that evening. It included lunch, drinks, a band and women to dance with.] What the hell did we come over here for? I could not believe what was happening. It was raining hard. Below the overcast, visibility was not over 1/4 to 1/2 mile. It was difficult to see a target of any kind. We could not see anything recognizable. Actually we were on the north side of Paris, but at the time, we did not know that. As the first bridge appeared, we began our dive. The flak came up in mass. I got a bad hit on the left engine and it caught fire. We kicked off our bombs, I feathered the left engine and shut-off all the flammable fluids. The fire went out slowly. We were flaring out from our dive, still with plenty of speed, when I spotted a locomotive just building up steam outside of a marshalling yard. I turned about 10 degrees to the right, which put us dead on for the locomotive. We had our speed coming off the target and by now my bird was perfectly trimmed. Rayne could see what I intended and as I fired a range burst, he followed. We were just out of range. I waited for the target to come in range, then gave it another burst, which was dead on the boiler. Then we both gave it a long burst. With the API ammunition, it began to shed steam, then blew. We avoided the fragments, but to the north of the engine was what seemed like about 2000 troops, all waiting for us. They started shooting, using a pattern fire. As we went through their fire, everything broke. The small arms fire littered the entire aircraft. It was devastating. I looked at Rayne. He appeared terrified. We had to head for home. We climbed to the base of the overcast and took our safe course home.

"As we climbed into the base of the overcast I noticed my engine temperatures rising. At first I thought it was because I was using a bit more power than normal. However, as we leveled off and reduced power, the temperature on my remaining engine continued to rise. It was at this point, I realized I might not get back to Wattisham that evening. The right engine was now pumping some smoke. The temperature gauges were off the dial. Fairchild hovered over me like a mother hen. It appeared as though he was trying to hold me up. I knew we were close to our lines, but not how close. As it turned out, I went down about 35 kilometers from our friendlies. Rayne was close enough that I could see the hair on his face and his ragged teeth. The airspeed was diminishing rapidly as the good engine began to falter. I had ridden as far as could be expected. Now I had to choose between a bailout and a belly landing. Finally, I called Rayne and told him to head for home, I was going to bail out. My last look at Fairchild was frightful. He looked like the one bailing rather than me. He had been very protective ever since I began to have trouble. To this day, I have never had another aircraft hover over me such as Rayne did. His look was that of terror. [Cal was heard to say over the radio, 'This is Captain Butler, I'm gonna bail out. Both engines on fire. Good luck, Cal.'] From this point on, I did everything by the book. I slowed the aircraft, dropped my seat, popped the canopy, rolled it to the inverted position and gave a big shove with my legs. The big shove only moved my body about 18 inches. I had thought I would be free of the bird immediately, but think again! A shell had exploded behind the seat and left fragments of jagged metal that had snagged me. I was half way out, could go no further and could not get back into the cockpit. I struggled to free the chute from the metal with no success. I cursed like I have never cursed before or since. I was diving straight to the ground with no hope of a release from the aircraft. Speed built rapidly and my position looked hopeless. I was in a corner and there was no way out. I was trapped. By now, my back was bent streamlined on the fuselage with the wind ripping me apart. The rest of me as well as my parachute were still in the cockpit. I knew I was rapidly running out of time. Basically though, I wasn't giving up. I had not yet accepted my demise, but had done everything within my power to escape. (That is except, pray. At this point in my life, I was unaware of that power.) Suddenly and with no help from me, I was free. The freedom was momentary, then I hit the tail of the aircraft with my back. The blow was devastating, like being hit by a giant with a 2x12. Then it was quiet. I don't recall opening the chute, yet there I was, about ten feet off the ground, above a plowed field with the chute fully open. The bottom of the canopy was nearly touching the ground. I knew my back was injured, so I reached as high as possible on the shroud lines to soften the blow when I hit. As the chute began to oscillate, I neared the ground. Pulling as hard as possible, I succeeded in softening my contact with the ground. Once down, I saw there was a huge hole about 15 feet away. Fire was coming out of the hole and shells were exploding. I guess this is really where I belonged, but I had beat the system. I have no idea how or why.

"It was nearly dark, but there was a French farm worker hoeing weeds in a fence row 200 yards away. He motioned to the forest. I knew if I could hide till dark, I might get away. From the waist down I had no feeling. I tried to stand, but failed. I began moving toward the forest, but found I was making little or no progress. I looked behind me and discovered my chute and dinghy were both being towed. I got out of the chute and drug the dinghy to me. I got my escape kit and emptied all the valuables into my pockets. The map, money, and other escape items would be invaluable if I got away. Had I been more mobile and thinking a little better, I would have thrown the evidence into the blazing hole and let them think I was there too. Thinking seemed to be the last thing I did that night. Before the mission began, I should have called Glover's hand and told him I was too sick to fly also. He was, after all, the CO.

"I hid the chute and dingy the best I could and crawled my way about 150 feet inside the forest. I heard the Germans coming and covered up with brush. I laid very still. It was nearly dark and if they missed me, I had a chance of the Frenchman finding me. Until now, I had failed to assess my personal injuries. My shoes were gone; they had been GI boots. They must have been blown off. My Gabardine flying suit was shredded in one-inch strips, from the bottom of the legs to the belt. It looked like a hula skirt. All the pockets were gone unless they were zipped to an inside pocket. I was a bloody mess. Otherwise

I appeared to be intact. I had failed to realize my legs left drag marks, which loomed out like a signal. 'Follow these,' they said. The enemy troops found the site of the crash by the fire in the hole and the noise of exploding 50 caliber and 20mm shells. It didn't take them long to see my drag marks, which were obvious. I was quiet and well covered with brush. The strange language and shouting of the troops was a fearful sound. I could not see anyone and was still hoping that darkness would be my ally. It was getting close. Finally the troops headed directly toward me. They were stomping the brush as they came. On their first pass through, they missed me. They went about 100 yard beyond my position, had conference and then came stomping back. As they approached, I knew the game was up. A soldier was heading directly toward me. I would be very fortunate if they missed me this time. The soldier came directly to my location and stomped on me. Stepping on me frightened him. He stepped back and began to uncover me, then leaned over to pick me up. As he did, his machine gun fell into my hands. Momentarily, I had delusions of a giant escape, but then I came to my senses and handed back his gun. If I could have run, it might have been a different story. At any rate, one near prisoner against 20 soldiers armed with machine pistols wouldn't have much of a chance. It was a smart move to return his gun. He kept yelling *'Roust! Roust! Roust!'* I learned later; this meant get up and out of there. I laid there and pointed to my back. By now, all the soldiers had gathered and all were yelling *'Roust!'* They motioned for me to get up. I declined and stayed put. Finally two of them reached down and picked me up. Before they did, each gave his gun to one of his partners. They carried me to their headquarters, which was a farmhouse surrounded by a high rock wall. They took me inside and laid me on the kitchen table face up. One by one they began stripping me of anything that they could take as a souvenir, my watch, rank and insignia of any type. They even cut off pieces of my uniform. Later that night, a higher-ranking soldier arrived and asked me some questions in English. He accused me of being a spy since they had uncovered all the material that was in the dinghy. It was our escape package, but I could not deny it was mine. I gave him my name, rank, and serial number. That was all. It made him mad, but so what. I wasn't expecting to be popular. Finally they decided to take me to a hospital. They loaded me into weapons carrier of some type. They made me set up in the back. I was riding on an iron bed and there were no springs. It was bumpy and very painful. By now I wondered if my back had been broken. I was still pretty numb from the waist down. On top of all that, I was now suffering the results of the crash. I was sick all the way around. Along the way to the hospital they stopped at a fighter base. I think it was Abbeville, but I was never sure. [Probably not, as the distance was too great from the crash site.] They carried me into the officer's barracks and put me on display for the pilots. Spit and polish such as I have never seen before. These pilots looked like they had just stepped out of Vogue with their shined boots and bellowed pants all neatly pressed. It was obvious they were special. Some of the pilots sneered at me. None offered conversation. I was their hated enemy. I was a bloody mess, wearing a hula skirt and in my bare feet. They called the pilots from upstairs. As they filed down, it became apparent they might be hurting worse than we had suspected. The older officers may have been as old as 25 to 35. They were in the minority. The younger pilots could not have been over 15 years old. All were *Feldwebel* rank or what we would call sergeant pilots. They were still children. There was nothing in-between. I knew now, that if we had been lucky enough to find 100 German aircraft together, we could have had a ball. Not too many of this crew would be experienced. I have looked back on my statement at Glovers meeting and often thought how we would have been able to fight the masses with only 16 aircraft. How could we loose? The meeting with the German pilots was an experience that I would never forget. We continued on to the hospital, Cliche Hospital, in northern Paris. The prison ward was the 18th floor. They gave me a bed and I fell to sleep immediately. I was in a state of shock.

"This was the beginning of another era, the one where the enemy gives the order and you obey or else. The following morning one of the German doctors came near my bed and stared at me then made this upsetting statement. *'Likning, nix goot.'* (Lighting, no good). Then he left the room. That was the extent of my medical care at Cliche Hospital. Nurses would come no closer than 10 feet or so. They would stare and say something in German, then leave. I had no idea what was going on. That morning, the fellow in my adjoining bed asked if I knew what was going on. My answer was a distinct 'No.' He then introduced himself as being Sergeant Polkerswinski. He was from Chicago. Later he told me if I ever got to

Chicago, to look in the phone book. Any Polkerswinski I called, would remember him. He was a tail gunner on a B-26. He had been shot down and seriously injured in the interim. At that point I was reluctant to talk to him, as I considered any other patient could be a plant. However, 'Polker' had a problem that he might not live through. About 2 inches of bone in his left arm had been destroyed when he went down. The German doctors had decided to graft a bone in its place. The only problem was, he had developed a case of gangrene which was rapidly spreading. Twice a day the nurse would come in, lance and drain his wound. He wanted them to cut off his arm before it was too late, but he continued to only receive the twice-daily treatments. When I left, it was worse, with no sign of stopping. As we conversed, I was very careful not to reveal anything, even of my identity. One day, out of the clear, he made the statement that he had seen me get hit and assumed I went down. Remember that it was raining so hard, our flight visibility was less than 1/2 mile. He said that when the air raid siren blew, he had pulled his bed to a position near the window, where he could see the bridge and marshalling yard. He watched as we dive-bombed the bridge and said he saw three hits on the bridge. One of the bombs must not have been armed, as we had dropped four. He saw my aircraft get hit hard and catch fire. He watched me feather the engine and the fire go out, but asked the big question: 'Why in hell did you later strafe the locomotive with one engine out?' That was a good question! I've asked myself that one, many a time. I guess at the time, I felt I was impervious to all major harm. [Perhaps this is part of the answer, but in recent conversations with Cal, he told me several times, that really, he was so mad at the Germans for hitting the brand new P-38 that he had just gotten, that he was going to get even.] It was stupid and I put my wingman in jeopardy. We should have gotten into the overcast and returned to Wattisham. After hearing this story, I began to trust 'Polker'. He told me the story so I could understand the attitude of the doctors and nurses on that floor. I had no idea there was a hospital so close to the target. So by now, I was classified by the enemy, as being a real war criminal. They did not understand that you could not see the hospital signs from the cockpit in the driving rain, even though I was visible to them! I knew now why I got no treatment. I guess they were entitled! I had inadvertently bombed a bridge four blocks from the hospital I was now lying in. Had I realized the hospital was there I would have chosen some other target. Maybe even the one we were after, if I had any idea where it was!"

Captain Calvin J. Butler gained the dubious honor of becoming the first member of the 479th FG to be questioned by the Luftwaffe's master interrogator, Hanns-Joachim Scharff at the Luftwaffe Intelligence and Evaluation Center, Auswertestelle West. Captain Butler eventually wound up spending the remainder of his wartime days as a POW in Stalag Luft III, Sagan, Poland. Second Lieutenant James K. Ohligschlager, also captured this day, was the second member of the group to be questioned by the famous German interrogator.

The squadrons also flew spotter missions during the day, but these were not summarized nor recorded in the histories.

18 June 1944

VIII FC FO 396

No. 73 Sunday. Lt. Col. Riddle was the group's leader. His force of P-38s was assigned a penetration to target and withdrawal escort for 3rd BD B-17s attacking their 8th AF Mission 421 target at Bremen, Germany. Approximate time up: 0700 hrs., down: 1130 hrs. The weather was overcast during the entire trip, but visibility above the clouds was good. This morning's P-38 escorts arrived near the Heligoland body of water located off the Schleswig-Holstein area of northern Germany for a 0845 hrs./21,000 ft. R/V with their assigned bombers. They circled for thirty minutes, but none appeared. The group continued on to the target area where they picked up some 1st BD B-17s and escorted them home. There was no flak or enemy aircraft sighted during the mission.

18 June 1944

VIII FC FO 397

No. 74 Sunday. The group was part of a force tasked for fighter-bomber attacks on railroad bridges in the St. Quentin area of France. Approximate time up: 1645 hrs., down: 1850 hrs. They flew the routed course, making L/F over Dunkerque at 12,000 ft. Continuing in; the area was covered by solid overcast. At 1755 hours, the group did a 180-degree turn and returned to home base, passing out over Dunkerque again at 1815 hrs./ 12,000 ft. There was no flak nor enemy aircraft to report.

Left: Fighter pilot to be, Cadet Frank Grdenich. *Courtesy of Kathy Grdenich Fleming.* Right: This plaque was recently placed by the French at the sight of Lt. Frank Grdenich's crash to memorialize his loss in the effort to free that country from the Nazis. *Courtesy of Kathy Grdenich Fleming.*

19 June 1944

VIII FC FO 398

No. 75 Monday. The group was part of a force whose assignment was a bomber escort for B-17s attacking their 8th AF Mission 423 target, the airfield at Cognac/Chateaubernard, France. Approximate time up: 0745 hrs. down: 1130 hrs. Approaching the French coast, the group encountered a huge mass of clouds comprised of two layers that extended from 2,000 to 29,000 ft. Above that, there was haze at 30,000 ft. The P-38s were to R/V with the bombers in the vicinity of La Rochelle, but failed to make contact with them. They steered the scheduled course until 0935 hours, but only saw some bomber boxes that immediately merged into the overcast and were lost to vision. Radio contact was made, but the bombers were never found, nor was the airfield. It was doubtful that the bombers found the target either. The escort was abandoned and the group returned home minus four of its planes.

The 434th FS lost two of its pilots in the vicinity of Rennes. First Lieutenant Ward A. Kuentzel and Second Lieutenant Frank Grdenich were last seen by the other two pilots in their flight, around 0920 hours, just as they broke out above the overcast at about 27,000 feet. Second Lieutenants Richard G. McChrystal, who was flying as number two on Lt. Kuentzel's wing and John T. Tipps, who was number four, gave the following reports – Lt. McChrystal:

"I was flying on Lt. Kuentzel's wing as we broke through the overcast at 27,000 feet. We were flying straight in a gentle climb when Lt. Kuentzel started into a right turn and then started into a dive. I stayed on his wing until my ship began to buffet and I lost sight of him. I recovered and let down through the overcast, breaking through at 1,500 feet over the Cherbourg Peninsula. I came home immediately."

Lt. Tipps:

"We had climbed up through the overcast to about 27,000 feet and were flying along straight and level when we started into a slight turn to the right and going down. I closed in on Lt. Grdenich's wing and continuing, made about a 280-degree turn to the right that became an almost straight down dive. I broke away and went on instruments somewhere near 22,000 feet. The last I saw of the flight, there were three ships, in tight, going almost straight down. I climbed back up to 28,000 feet and headed home without further delay."

It is theorized that Lt. Kuentzel became a victim of Anoxia (oxygen want or in other words, a lack of oxygen) and passed out. He had been using an English flying helmet that he adapted an American oxygen mask to and the suspicion was that he was not getting a good fit and therefore failed to get enough oxygen. It was additionally felt that Lt. Grdenich had stayed with Lt. Kuentzel to the end. The mystery would have gone unsolved had it not been for the dogged efforts of Kathy Grdenich Fleming, Lt. Grdenich's niece. During the years 2000-2001, she put forth a great effort to uncover the facts surrounding the loss of the two pilots. The crux of her research has been the discovery through French eyewitnesses, that as the two planes, still in their dive, came out beneath the clouds they had been passing through, Lt. Kuentzel's P-38 rolled over that of Lt. Grdenich and cut the empennage off the plane Lt. Grdenich was flying. Uncontrollable, the tailless plane crashed into the ground near Pointe de Vere. Lt. Kuentzel's plane was seen to somehow level off near the ground and continue on for about two miles, but then his Lightning exploded as it crossed over a row of trees. Both pilots were killed.

While the 435th FS was making a turn over the R/V point, two of the pilots from that squadron collided at 29,000 ft. First Lieutenant Donald D. McClure and Second Lieutenant Leland K. Horne were killed as a result of another mid-air collision at about 0930 hrs. After the collision, in which the propellers of one plane cut the tail empennage of the other off, both planes immediately went into spins that continued down into the overcast. Neither pilot was seen to bail out. Again, through the efforts of Kathy Grdenich Fleming, it has been tentatively determined that the two pilots and their planes plunged into the Bay of Biscay, as no evidence or eyewitnesses to their final moments have ever been found.

Verne E. Hooker, a former pilot with the 435th FS witnessed the above-described tragedy and recently wrote this about it:

> "A large personal loss to me occurred on this date. My roommate and my former flight instructor collided right in front of me at about 29,000 feet. To see the two aircraft go down and disappear into the huge cloud bank below was a sad sight. In my opinion, a faulty oxygen mask caused one of them to lose consciousness and this resulted in the accident."

"Ain't Misbehavin' II". The 452nd BG B-17 is shown bellied in just before it exploded near the group CO's quarters and nearby BOQ. The fire had just begun to take hold of the number two engine area. *From original 479th FG history.*

One of the B-17s sent out to bomb an airfield in France that day, returned to England and was forced to crash land at Wattisham. B-17G BO, serial number 42-102541, "Ain't Misbehavin' II", assigned to the 452nd BG/728th BS had suffered flak hit over its target and was not able to open its bomb bay doors. Returning on two engines, the bomber lost a third just before making Wattisham. Bellying in on the southeast part of the station, the plane's left wing tip clipped a treetop before it settled to the ground. Sliding and kicking up lots of dust, the big bird came to a stop in the general vicinity of the station's Officer Quarters and the Group Commander's house. At that point, number two engine caught fire as the bomber's crew came tumbling out. Fire fighters and base personnel from Wattisham began making their way toward

A frontal view of the group commander's quarters after the B-17 exploded. Note all of the windows that were broken out as well as the damage to the roof, which was missing many tiles. *Courtesy of Eugene W. Bailey.*

The backside of the group CO's quarters received the brunt of the damage as it faced the explosion. *Carroll C. Sprague Collection, courtesy of the East Essex Aviation Society.*

the scene as the crew was running from it. The crew made it be known that there were still twenty 250-pound bombs on board the burning aircraft and most everyone headed for cover. The bomb load exploded and the concussion wave knocked everyone down, where they were showered with debris and fragments from the disintegrated B-17. Lt. Thomas R. Brown, the group's chaplain and Maj. Albert B. Parsons, Group Operations Officer, were in House Number One where they had been watching the action. They each received bits of flying glass from the windows through which they had been watching. Others were cut or bruised as well, but all injuries were minor and the station hospital patched everyone up. The station received a number of well-ventilated buildings and the explosion left a large crater. The tennis court in front of the Officer's Quarters sported a piece of wing spar as well as a propeller blade sticking out of the ground.

John W. Hedenberg described the incident in his diary:

> "Was sitting in the lounge, smoking and reading the paper (Cherbourg Peninsula now cut off, it said) after lunch when men suddenly started rushing out the door like mad. Jumped up, went out and climbed on my bike to go see what was up. A B-17 had come in for emergency landing – Almost out of gas – and was about 10 feet off the ground with three engines cut out. The remaining one pulled the ship around, dug in a wing and the ship hit flat and spun around 180 degrees. The crew got out like lightning and ran like hell. We, not knowing any better, stood watching. The ship started burning slightly along the wing behind No. 2 engine. The fire trucks couldn't get to it and after about five minutes, the ship and its bombs suddenly blew up with the most tremendous noise I have ever heard. I was only 100 yards away! Felt no concussion, but instinctively hit the ground – But fast! For a minute it rained aircraft pieces – where the ship had been, there was nothing. A smoking turbo lit about ten feet from me. Close. The blast had a funny effect. Blew out all the windows of a hangar much farther away than me. Knocked Capt. Harrell off the toilet where he was at the moment in the operations building (also farther away), blew out a door in the S-2 room and blew a truck off the road into a ditch – driver unhurt. Yet, a couple of dozen other men and I were practically alongside and only had ringing ears."

The left side of the BOQ Club received some damage also. *Carroll C. Sprague Collection, courtesy of the East Essex Aviation Society.*

A view of the inside of the group CO's house. *Carroll C. Sprague Collection, courtesy of the East Essex Aviation Society.*

Right: An inside view of the damaged BOQ Club with its broken windows and debris lying about. *Courtesy of Eugene W. Bailey.*

Allen J. Moon, always the wit, was nearly a hero that day. As he told it:

> "On rare instances we were cast in situations that bordered on foolish bravery. This was the case when I returned to the radio shack from the mess hall in the early afternoon to find a B-17 afire just off the runway and quite close to the shack. The flames were licking up from the wing and scorching the cockpit. I bounded through the weeds and over some barbed wire to aid any of the crew I might, when I heard a faint voice from the far side of the burning craft telling me to 'Get the Hell outa there, it's loaded with bombs!' I quickly retraced my steps over the barbed wire after I saw a few heads peering from a ditch on the far side of the 17. They belonged to the plane's crew, who had sought refuge as they waited for the thing to blow.
>
> "I ran back to the radio shack where I alerted my captain as to the gravity of the situation and suggested we might do well to evacuate the building. I was directed to return to work, which I did. All was normal for about ten minutes, then a flash of red, black, yellow and white put all of us on the floor and split the building apart at the corners. The captain emerged from his office holding a handkerchief to his head as blood ran down his neck. Discretion is the better part of valor so I did not say 'I told you so.' I was promoted to sergeant shortly thereafter."

20 June 1944

VIII FC FO 402

No. 76 Tuesday. Lt. Col. Riddle led the group's 49 P-38s on a bomber escort in support of 8th AF Mission 425, an attack on an oil refinery in Germany. Approximate time up: 0630 hrs., down: 1145 hrs. The weather was overcast over the channel, but CAVU over the continent. The Big Friends made a long loop up over the North Sea and came into Germany over the vicinity of Cuxhaven. The group arrived southeast of Bremerhaven at the scheduled R/V point at 0830 hrs./25,000 feet, but was unable to contact the proper bombers. A wide orbit was made, including over Cuxhaven in hopes of finding them, but the effort was fruitless. The group then took a heading of approximately 130 degrees and made R/V with some other 3rd BD B-24s over Ahnsen, ten miles from Gifhorn at 0900 hrs./26,000 ft. just as the bombers were making their bomb run. The primary target at Misburg was a mass of orange flames with black smoke reaching to 15,000 ft. when they left. One B-24 was seen to explode over the target. No chutes were seen from the bomber. The B-24s were escorted back to within 20 miles of Lowestoft, England.

First Lieutenant Louis K. Nesselbush from the 436th FS was lost between Bremen and Nienburg when his P-38 had an engine failure. Lt. Nesselbush called over the radio stating that his right engine had a piston rod fail. His cockpit was seen to be filled with smoke and then his airplane began to smoke. The smoke cleared temporarily when he feathered his right propeller, but a few seconds later, the right engine burst into violent flame. Lt. Nesslebush's plane yawed twice to the right, but he brought it back under control. Then it yawed and went over into a spin. After five or six turns, Lt. Nesselbush bailed out of the stricken aircraft and his parachute was seen to open. The other flights stayed above to provide cover while his flight leader and two others from the flight circled him on the way down as he descended. He landed on the edge of a wood near Verden, southeast of Bremen. Lt. Nesselbush was captured about five hours later, north of where he first landed. He too became a visitor to Auswertestelle West and a brief guest of Hanns Scharff before he was shipped off to a POW camp.

Observations made during the mission included: Four to eight cargo ships were sighted leaving the harbor at Wesermunde. There were smoke screens that ran on a north to south line placed east and west of Emden. Flak over Emsede and Hannover was heavy, intense and accurate.

21 June 1944

VIII FC FO 407

No. 77 Wednesday. This was a long trip and the furthest into Germany that the group had traveled thus far. Their assignment was a target withdrawal escort for 3rd BD B-24s returning from out of the German heartland and their 8th AF Mission 428 attack on the capital of Berlin. Approximate time up: 0815 hrs., down: 1315 hrs. The group made R/V with the B-24s near Brandenburg at 1030 hrs./22,000 ft. after traveling across the continent. Coming out, one flight from the 434th FS escorted a Big Friend, who was low on gas, from the Neumünster area to the coastline. The pilot of the bomber then radioed that they were going to Sweden. The flight broke with them at 1150 hrs./20,000 feet, turned back on course and ran into some heavy, meager, but accurate flak over Kiel at 1240 hrs. The group continued escort with the rest of the bombers and they all ran into heavy, intense and accurate flak just before leaving the continent. The group broke from the bombers over the North Sea at 1230 hrs. No enemy aircraft were sighted.

22 June 1944

VIII FC FO 411

No. 78 Thursday. The group put up 49 P-38s for this mission. It was a fighter-bomber attack on a railroad bridge near the town of La Fère, which is south of St. Quentin, France. The attack on the bridge was to take place using 250-lb. GP, as well as 1,000-lb. bombs and continue on by strafing of rail transportation southeast, between Soissons and Rheims. Approximate time up: 1350 hrs., down: 1700 hrs.

L/F was in the vicinity of Blankenberghe, Belgium at 1450 hrs./16,000 ft. Heading southeast to the target, the 435th and 436th FS's attacked the bridge first using a glide-bombing technique while the 434th FS provided top cover for them. They failed to destroy it so the 434th FS followed up with a dive-bombing run, but they also failed to destroy it. There were near misses, but the bridge still stood when it was all over. The squadrons continued on to strafe targets of opportunity in the area and laid claim to a generator station, a locomotive, 20 boxcars, three tank cars, two switch houses, two water towers, a canal barge, nine trucks and two personnel carriers destroyed. Additional damage was done to a factory, a radar station, a gun emplacement and two other tank cars. A lone Fw 190 made several weak passes at a 434th FS P-38, but broke away without firing when it was turned into. The 436th FS got on the scoreboard when one of their pilots, First Lieutenant Clarence O. Johnson, pounced on a lone low-flying Fi 156 Storch and downed it with a short burst. This happened in the area of Reims. Lt. Johnson was a seasoned fighter pilot who had already completed one tour in the Mediterranean Theater of Operations during 1943. There, he had accumulated four victories, so the Storch added a fifth and made Lt. Johnson an ace.

William (Bill) S. Culbertson, the above-mentioned Corporal with the 436th FS, was classified at the time as a draftsman and had the duties of ordering and taking care of the squadron's maps. Among other things, he marked the pilot's maps with courses for missions and kept up the flak maps. He also helped in briefings, made graphic training aids, gave recognition training, edited the gun camera film and placed it on personal reels for the pilots. He recently told of one such film clip that he remembered vividly. The film showed Lt. Johnson's Storch kill. The Lieutenant's flight had been flying low as they returned to Wattisham. As the flight came up over a hill, they happened across the lone German observation plane, nearly right in front of them. Bill Culbertson described the short encounter: "Lt. Johnson immediately got his sights on the German, fired a short burst and exploded the Storch. The Lieutenant was so close to his slow-flying victim that the film

Gun camera film taken of the factory 434th FS pilot Lieutenant Berkley E. Hollister was strafing. *Courtesy of Berkley E. Hollister.*

First Lieutenant Clarence O. Johnson. *Courtesy of Steve Blake.*

showed him passing through the debris almost instantly. There was no time nor room to avoid it." Culbertson marvels that Lt. Johnson lived to tell about his success.

No amount of success could make up for the loss the 434th FS felt when this day was done, however. The squadron lost four pilots during the mission. Two of the four fell, one directly and one indirectly, as a result of the attack on the railroad bridge by La Fère. First Lieutenant Keith E. Canella was hit by flak during the dive-bomb attack on the bridge as was First Lieutenant Albert S. J. Tucker, Jr. Second Lieutenant Leroy Lutz was hit by flak during a subsequent attack on a train as possibly was First Lieutenant Dwight F. Ilsley. Three of the four men, along with Second Lieutenant Quentin S. Pavlock, made up the second flight that left Wattisham early in the afternoon. Lt. Pavlock gives some insight into what happened to his wingmen:

> "We were called down from our position as top cover by the group leader. We were to dive-bomb the bridge. Lts. Canella, Ilsley, Lutz and I started down from 13,000 feet, the second flight to go down. Up till about 10,000 feet, the dive was shallow. Then, seeing that we would overrun the target, Lt. Canella pushed over into a steep angle dive. Until that steep dive, Lts. Ilsley and Lutz were in position, but at about 8,000 feet, I looked and could not see either of them. I did not see them again throughout the rest of the mission. My airspeed was over 450 mph at this time. Lt. Canella released his bombs, then I did. I was to his right so I had picked a factory as my target. As I started to pull out, the following events happened almost simultaneously: Lt. Canella's bombs burst in the river just short of the bridge. His plane was hit by ground fire in the right engine, which immediately poured out black smoke. I felt my plane hit also and start to skid. I proceeded to pull out, then looked over to Lt. Canella's ship, which was now approximately in a 45-degree dive, and going slightly to the left. I observed more hits on the center nacelle of his plane after which his plane, still in a dive, crashed into the ground on the river's left bank, about 100 yards ahead of the bridge and immediately exploded. I did not see Lt. Canella bail out and I am positive he was in the airplane when it crashed. I pulled out on the deck and looked for the rest of the flight, but could not see them. I continued on a strafing run for twelve minutes, then climbed to 16,000 feet and came home."

First Lieutenant Keith E. Canella beside the P-38 he flew, Sweet Mary. *Courtesy of Arnold G. Helding.*

Alvin (Al) R. Willhite served as one of the 434th's squadron inspectors. As a Master Sergeant, he oversaw major maintenance on the aircraft, received the all Tech Orders calling for updates, ordered the kits to complete the updates and saw that they were installed correctly. A few years ago, Al told about the closeness between the ground crew and the pilots. He said those fliers put their lives on the line every time they went out on a mission and when they didn't come back, it really affected the guys who made up their crews. He recalled one very specific instance of this and even now, fifty some years later, he still got emotional about remembering what happened. He told:

> "One of the pilots, Lieutenant Keith E. Canella stopped by my desk one day and wanted to know how long he could stay in a P-38 with an engine on fire. I told him that I would show him what the specifications said, then he could decide for himself. We reviewed the specs, then went out to one of B Flight's planes to look at what we had been talking about. I removed the cowling and we looked at the firewall then went back to the engineering office to discuss the matter further. I asked him why he wanted to know all this and he said he had witnessed a

pilot who had bailed out of his plane getting shot at by soldiers on the ground as he descended in his parachute. He further stated that he would consider staying in a damaged airplane as long as possible because of what he had seen. That was pretty much the end of the conversation, but it wasn't very long after that, Lt. Canella was lost on a fighter-bomber mission. He had been hit by flak and his plane began smoking. He was not seen to leave his plane and after being hit several more times, the plane dove into the ground."

Second Lieutenant Berkley E. Hollister tells what probably happened to Lt. Ilsley:

"I was flying number two position in the lead flight. We were assigned as top cover for the other two squadrons, who were to bomb a bridge. After they had finished their bomb run, our squadron leader called the group leader for permission to go down and dive-bomb the bridge because it was still standing. We peeled off from approximately 12,000 feet and made our pass on the bridge by elements and flights, as best we could. Being in the lead flight, the results of our squadron's attack were unknown to me. Flak and tracer bullets were heavy in the target area. In the excitement of our dive-bombing run, I pushed the wrong button and did not drop my 250-lb. bombs. So, after flying low over a given strafing course for approximately ten minutes and not seeing anything to shoot at, our squadron leader called a 90-degree turn to the left to go after trains in the depot of a small village. We made one pass at the trains, strafing them without much noticeable damage. We then turned and came around for a second strafing pass, after which there was still little apparent damage. I dropped my bombs on this pass, but I was told by another witness that they went over the train I was after and exploded beyond it. It was just after pulling up to 200-300 feet from this pass, that I saw, in a split second glance, another P-38 below me, cartwheeling, upside down. Its center section was on fire and I believe the tail section was off. I couldn't see it hit the ground as my wing passed over it and we were heading home. I could not identify the P-38 that crashed."

Berkley Hollister in recently writing about the mission, gave further details concerning the events of that day. He stated:

"In the mission briefing, my squadron, the 434th FS, was assigned as top cover for the 435th and 436th FS's, who were to bomb a small bridge south of St. Quentin, France. The trip to the target was uneventful as I recall. When we arrived in the area, we took up our positions and circled above at what was probably 13,000 feet while the other two squadrons attacked the target. We watched as each of their P-38s made a pass at the bridge. Afterwards, it appeared that the bridge had received no hits and was still standing. Amazing!

"The leader of our squadron, Captain Frank J. Keller called the group leader, who was flying with another of the squadrons and requested permission to go down after the bridge. Now, I do not mean to criticize our leaders and never did officially, but I did not like the idea of us going down on that bridge after there had been lots of planes past it already. We knew by experience now, that the Germans had anti-aircraft guns almost everywhere and this bridge was no exception. They would certainly be ready and waiting for us when we came. They were! When we attacked, the leader of our second flight, Lieutenant Keith Canella received direct hits in his cockpit and dove straight into the ground. Two other pilots, Lieutenants Dwight Ilsley and Albert Tucker were hit also and went down past the target area. We heard later that Lt. Tucker was a POW. With Lieutenant Robin Olds leading our flight, we made our pass at a lower altitude and one of our bombs hit the bridge. I did not see the hit because I was busy following and staying with our flight.

"According to our mission plan, we were to fly low and be looking for strafing targets after the attack on the bridge. It did not take long before we found a train trying to leave a small town. We circled and strafed the train from low altitude. I made my passes from 100-200 feet, diving to almost ground level and getting good hits. During one pass, while I was watching the target and shooting, I caught a quick glimpse of a P-38 passing quickly under me as I glanced down between my nose and right engine nacelle. It was upside down and had major flames coming from its center section. I instantly realized that nobody was going to get out of that alive, but my concentration had to stay on the target, as the train was struggling to get moving. I also noticed something that we had been warned about previously. One of the boxcars in the train had its sides folded down and there was an anti-aircraft gun mounted on it. I do not recall if the gun crew was firing at

A view of the rail bridge (center bridge) near La Fére, taken from the gun camera film shot by Lt. Hollister as he began his attack on the bridge. *Courtesy of Berkley E. Hollister.*

Gun camera film taken of the switchyard that Lt. Berkley E. Hollister was strafing. Note the small black diagonal line located in the upper left corner of the frame. This was a marker that the plane's gun camera placed on the individual frames of film as they were exposed. Its purpose was to indicate that the guns were being fired at that moment and it only appeared while the guns were being fired. Unfortunately, many of the P-38s that the 479th FG used were older models that had their gun cameras mounted in the nose. This of course was the same location as the aircraft's armament and resulted in blurry images from the vibration that occurred when the four .50 cal. machine guns and the 20mm cannon were being fired. However, when the pilot released the firing button, the camera would continue to run for a few more frames and those pictures would be somewhat clearer. Considering the conditions that these photos were taken under, the images are good. *Courtesy of Berkley E. Hollister.*

> the time, everything happened in a flash. I do know that we did a lot of damage to that train and in fact I learned from a former French citizen now living in the US, that our squadron killed about 380 German soldiers and wounded many more, all of whom were train passengers that day. As a teenager, the man had lived near the town that the train was leaving.
>
> "The remainder of the mission was more or less uneventful. We somehow got scattered while looking for other targets and I remember attacking a radar station and another train. I also remember that I apparently passed very near a flak tower while at low level and saw tracer bullets from the gun located there, passing over the center section of my plane. It seemed as though I could reach out my window and touch them as they went whizzing past. All in all, it was a day that I'll never forget."

There were no AAF reports concerning what happened to Lt. Lutz, only some notes and a photo of his grave in France that came to the group after the liberation of that country. However, a French eyewitness recently gave an account of what happened to Lt. Lutz that day. Andre Mathy, then a 13 year old resident of Mardeuil, a small town located several miles northwest of Épernay, witnessed the crash of Lt. Lutz's P-38. According to Mathy, Lt. Lutz had attacked a train carrying German armored vehicles on their way to reinforce troops at Normandy. After making two passes and dropping his two bombs, Lt. Lutz's P-38 was hit in the right engine on his third pass. The plane was dropping down for a crash, heading straight for Mardeuil according to Mathy and other eyewitnesses. Lt. Lutz, apparently recognizing the impending disaster, somehow managed to apply full power and veer right, crashing instead, in a nearby field. Lt. Leroy Lutz was killed in the crash, his body discovered close to the plane. His parachute was partially opened. He must have started to bail out of the crippled aircraft, but got back in when he recognized where the plane was headed. He chose to stay with it, steering away from the town and undoubtedly saved lives. After the crash, the Germans stripped the body of all identification and later placed it in a German casket, which was turned over to the townspeople.

The French built a special casket and in accordance with their law, kept the body in a vault until it could be identified. On the third of July, the Germans sent a package to the mayor of Mardeuil. It contained Lt. Lutz's billfold and dogtags. They now had the name of their hero. The townspeople turned out in huge numbers to honor him with a flower-laden funeral. The ceremony included full military honors provided by the Germans, who also left a palm leaf upon the tomb to recognize the courage and valor of the brave pilot who gave his life to save others.

Lieutenant Lutz was flying a P-38 named Lucky Lady this day. Named and flown by Lieutenant Arnold G. Helding, the artwork on the plane had an interesting origin. The idea came from a cocktail napkin and was transferred from the napkin to the P-38's nose by the squadron's painter/artist, Frederick (Fred) C. Hayner, also known as "Hayner the Painter". Shortly after the Lucky Lady went down, a resident of the town went to the crash site and salvaged a portion of the nose art to keep as a remembrance. Many years later that piece was given to the Lutz family and exists today.

The fourth 434th FS pilot to go down in France that day was First Lieutenant Albert S.J. Tucker, Jr. Second Lieutenant Harold E. (Smiley) Mathews was flying with Lt. Tucker at the time and described what happened:

Servicing the nose camera in a P-38. *Courtesy of Frederick C. Hayner.*

> "First Lt. Albert Tucker was hit over the target, a railroad bridge at La Fère. A piece from his right engine flew back and hit my left wing. Lt. Tucker reported that he was unable to feather his right prop more than 60 degrees and that it was windmilling [continuing to turn because of the force of air passing by it]. He made a gradual right turn to the approximate safe course home. His altitude at the time was about 150 feet and I was above, providing top cover. I endeavored to lead him out of the area by avoiding the airdromes and villages. Lt. Tucker's plane would not respond to his attempts for altitude, so I

Gun camera film taken of the radar station Lt. Hollister had just strafed. *Courtesy of Berkley E. Hollister.*

Gun camera film taken of the train Lt. Hollister was strafing. *Courtesy of Berkley E. Hollister.*

kept up top cover by flying a series of lazy eights between 1800 and 3600 feet. We proceeded on in that manner until we were in the vicinity of Cambrai. At that time, coolant smoke began pouring from Lt. Tucker's right engine and small licks of flame appeared around its supercharger. At the same time, we began getting some AA fire. My ship was hit in the left tail boom, causing the plane to skid and requiring heavy trim to keep it straight. I looked back and saw Lt. Tucker's left engine catch fire. His ship veered from course and crashed, apparently under control, at about 1500 hrs. When I left the area, I noticed Lt. Tucker's right wing some distance from his ship. The wing was on fire. I did not see him leave the plane. I took evasive action from the area, got up into the overcast and headed for home."

Lt. Tucker had successfully bellied in less than a mile west of the airfield at Wizernes and gotten out of his aircraft. He was captured and became a POW for the duration of the war. Lt. Mathews made it back to England, where he ran out of gas and crash-landed near Sudbury.

Second Lieutenant Berkley E. Hollister beside the P-38 he flew, Little Edris. *Courtesy of Frederick C. Hayner.*

Lieutenant Arnold G. Helding by "his" Lucky Lady. *Courtesy of Frederick C. Hayner.*

Second Lieutenant Leroy F. Lutz. *Courtesy of George D. Hendrix.*

23 June 1944

VIII FC FO 413

No. 79 Friday. The group went after another railroad bridge in France on this dive-bombing mission. Their target was in the vicinity of Soissons. Approximate time up: 1130 hrs., down: 1510 hrs. The weather was overcast with tops up to 7-10,000 ft. for the entire trip. Because of the cloud coverage, L/F and L/O could not be determined. The target area was covered by 2-4/10ths clouds with tops up to 8,000 ft. Most of the ordnance

Right: Second Lieutenant Leroy F. Lutz's grave in France. *From original 479th FG history.*

Far right: The actual cocktail napkin from which Staff Sergeant Frederick C. Hayner produced the Lucky Lady nose art. *Courtesy of Frederick C. Hayner.*

Below: The existing piece of Lucky Lady nose art. *Courtesy of Frederick C. Hayner.*

Lt. Lutz' grave.

was expended, but again, the bridge withstood the attack because the bulk of the bombs fell short. There was light, moderate, but inaccurate flak in the target area. Coming home, the group received heavy, moderate and accurate flak in the vicinity of St. Omer.

It was on exactly this type of mission that the following incident occurred and in fact, it could be this very mission. Themis (Ted) N. Anastos, then, First Lieutenant Anastos, in charge of the 434th FS armament section, detailed what happened that day: The group had been assigned a dive-bombing mission and the P-38s were loaded with two 1000-lb. HE bombs. Second Lieutenant John T. (Tom) Tipps of the 434th FS had taken off with the rest of the squadron for a mission. As he began climbing up to meet with his flight and the rest of the squadron, one of his engines failed. Now on one engine with a fighter heavily loaded with gas, ammunition and 2,000-lbs. of bombs, Lt. Tipps started around, back towards the field to land. Fortunate to still be flying at this point, Lt. Tipps needed to get rid of the extra weight of the bombs. He tried to salvo them over a safe area, but the release mechanism malfunctioned and only released the front two shackles. The rear two shackles remained secure, thus allowing the two 1,000-lb. bombs to pitch down nose first and dangle in that position. What a predicament! To make matters worse, by the nose dropping downward, the safety wires attached to each bomb's fuse went taut, pulling out the pin which held the fuse safe. The arming propellers spun off and the bombs became ready to do their job! Lt. Tipps did not recognize that problem until later because he was too busy trying to control the big fighter and keep it in the air. He successfully came back, made his approach and landed. Fortunately, the bombs did not fall off or explode during the landing. They were dangling with their noses about a foot above the runway and taxiway as he returned to his area. Personnel on the field and in the tower had immediately seen the danger and warned everyone away from the hazard. Lt. Tipps had already left, needing no warning, as his mother had not raised a dummy! The call went out for Armament to come deal with the bombs. Lt. Anastos took his Master Sergeant, Jack E. Lemke, over to look at the situation. The first thing that needed to be done was to remove the bomb fuses. Lt. Anastos told M/Sgt. Lemke to stay clear because he was going to defuse the bombs. Lt. Anastos thoughts were that he was a single person with no family to be responsible for and that M/Sgt. Lemke was a married man. M/Sgt. Lemke refused, so Lt. Anastos took one bomb and the M/Sgt. took the other. Lt. Anastos told his M/Sgt. that if anything went wrong, to let him know. Fortunately, the fuses came right out with no difficulties. That was a blessing because sometimes the fuses had to be installed and tightened with a monkey wrench, but these were easily screwed out. The other bit of good fortune was that despite the landing and handling, the fuses did not set the bombs off. As Ted explained, sometimes fuse/bomb combinations were sensitive enough that once they were armed, something as minor as hitting a raindrop could set them off, while other times, a bomb could hit concrete and fail to explode.

The P-38 that Lieutenant Mathews bellied in is shown in this photograph that was taken about two weeks later. Parts have been salvaged for use on other aircraft. *Courtesy of Clarence M. Surges.*

24 June 1944

VIII FC FO 415

No. 80 Saturday. Today's mission was an escort for both 1st and 3rd BD B-17s attacking their 8th AF Mission 438 primary target at Bremen, Germany. Approximate time up: 1100 hrs., down: 1545 hrs. The group made R/V with their assigned B-17s, the 434th FS joining two combat wings from the 1st BD 40 miles northwest of Borkum in the East Friesian Islands at 1210 hrs, 24,000 ft. That squadron escorted the bombers to a point where the Big Friends split their course and the fighters continued on with the first two boxes to the vicinity of Wesermünde, Germany at which point, P-47s took over. The 434th FS returned to the vicinity of Scharhörn Island, Germany and orbited at 23,000 ft. There they picked up two combat wings of 3rd BD B-17s at 1316 hrs. and escorted those to the Bremen target. Taking the bombers through the target and back out to L/O, the squadron broke from escort near the center of the North Sea.

Observations made during the mission included: An early returning P-38 pilot from the 434th FS sighted four suspicious bogies, possibly enemy aircraft at 1335 hours, 25 miles north of Borkum Island. Flak was heavy, moderate and inaccurate over Scharhörn Island and Bremen. It was noted that there were many vessels in the harbor at Hamburg despite the city having put up a smoke screen.

John W. Hedenberg had this note in his diary for this date:

> "Started another escort mission to Bremen, but aborted over the North Sea on account of turboregulators way out of adjustment. To keep equal manifold pressure at altitude on both engines, throttles were so far apart couldn't handle them with one hand. Impossible to fly formation that way, so came back. In evening, after regulators changed, test-hopped ship. Took her up to 30,000 and does she stagger and buffet up there with two belly tanks! Ship okay now."

25 June 1944

VIII FC FO 417

No. 81 Sunday. This morning's mission was an escort for 3rd BD B-24s attacking their 8th AF Mission 441 primary target, an airfield at Bourges, France. Approximate time up: 0640 hrs., down: 1030 hrs. R/V was in the area of Aubigny at 0817

Lieutenant John T. Tipps beside a P-38. *Courtesy of Frederick C. Hayner.*

hrs./21,000 ft. Passing Rouen, the flak was light, meager and inaccurate. Over the target, the bombing results looked good with smoke on the area. The bombers were escorted to mid-channel where the group broke away at 0950 hrs. The mission was uneventful.

25 June 1944

VIII FC FO 418

No. 82 Sunday. The mission late this afternoon was another escort, this time for 1st BD B-17s attacking their 8th AF Mission 442 primary target, the marshalling yards and a railroad bridge over the canal north of Auxerre, France. R/V was made at 1919 hrs./20,000 ft. and the Big Friends were taken over the target where a number of direct hits were observed. Flak there was heavy, moderate and inaccurate. The 434th FS observed two large black puffs of smoke, each trailing a black streamer, appear immediately behind two B-17s at 20,000 ft. Red Flight from the same squadron escorted a straggler B-17 with one wheel hanging down, to ten miles off Hythe, England.

From the diary of John W. Hedenberg:

> "Got up at 0415 this morning to go on another escort job, but was going as a spare and at the last moment there were no spare ships, so went back and hit the sack. The mission was to bomb an airfield south of Paris. They ran another one of the same in the afternoon and I managed to go on that one.... We ran into some really wicked flak down there – Thought I'd had it a couple of times. When they put shells between Biscy [Capt. Jules Biscayart] and me while I was flying on his wing, I began to get mad. Those gunners were just too damned sharp! On the way out, Biscy went on single engine, so Teeter [Lt. Robert Teeter] and I escorted him back. He wade a good landing at Manston."

Armorer Corporal James B. Dillon, assistant crew chief Corporal Guy M. Purdy and crew chief Staff Sergeant John E. Gilchrist by their 434th FS P-38, No Guts? The pilot who named the plane and who also regularly flew it was Lieutenant Harold F. (Bud) Grenning, Jr. Bud Grenning wrote this in early 1998 about the planes he flew:

> "The first airplane assigned to me at Wattisham as my very own was a P-38J model. I chose No Guts? as the name I wanted painted on the nose. We each had chosen a name and or nose art for the squadron painter Sergeant Fred Hayner to apply on our ships. Fred wasn't sure he liked that name and I'm quite certain that my crew chief, Staff Sergeant Gilchrist, his assistant Corporal Purdy and the plane's armorer Corporal Dillon didn't care for it either. That's the name that went on her though.
>
> "The name came from an expression I used while we were still training at Lomita. I often used it on our D Flight leader, First Lieutenant and later Captain, Hiram G. (Satch) Turner in certain situations. I would say to him, 'Whatsamatter, no guts?' I guess I said it enough times that he started calling me No Guts? instead of my name. He'd say something like, 'Okay, No Guts, what should we do now?'
>
> "Sometime later, someone else was to fly No Guts? on one of my days off and wound up putting it into a ditch. [See 15 July 1944.] By that time Satch and quite a few others from our batch of original pilots were killed or missing so the expression didn't have any fun or humorous connotation to it anymore. I decided not to give my replacement P-38 any name."

As an aside, Staff Sergeant Gilchrist came to his duties as a crew chief via a round about way. He had been trained as a paratrooper and was on his way to combat in the South Pacific. The ship he and his outfit were being transported on was attacked and sunk by the Japanese Navy. The survivors were picked up and S/Sgt. Gilchrist was among them. His injuries were such that his jumping out of airplanes was over though. He underwent retraining and became an airplane mechanic. His reintroduction to combat was as an Eighth Air Force crew chief. *Courtesy of Frederick C. Hayner.*

27 June 1944

VIII FC FO 419

No. 83 Tuesday. This was a fighter-bomber attack on rail and transportation targets in France, southeast of Paris. Melun, Fontainebleau, Sens and Troyes set the boundaries for the general area attacked. The group's P-38s were loaded up with one each fragmentation bomb and belly tank. The idea was to drop the bomb on one target and to toss the belly tank at another likely target, then set the gasoline on fire by strafing it. Approximate time up: 1820 hrs., down: 2140 hrs.

The group crossed in near Calais around 1900 hrs./12,000 ft. and was in the general target area an hour later. The weather consisted of 4-6/10ths cumulus clouds with a 2,500 ft. base and topped out at 6-7,000 ft. Visibility was good. The 434th FS started at Montereau at 2005 hrs./4,000 ft. and worked their way through Sens to Troyes, bombing and strafing. The other squadrons did similarly. The grand total of damage and destruction included power stations, oil tanks, switch towers, railroad bridges, various sections of track, a large quantity of goods wagons, heavy trucks, staff cars and flak emplacements.

The pilots had been receiving some light flak throughout the area, but when Second Lieutenant Burton S. Gross from the 435 FS called his flight leader to report that he had an engine on fire, the flight he was with had received none. Lt. Gross was flying number four in the 435th FS's White Flight and was pulling up just after having completed a strafing run. He told his flight leader he was going to belly in. Two pilots from the 434th FS saw his P-38 trailing smoke and flame from the right engine. At that time Lt. Gross was about 50 feet above the ground and headed down. He succeeded in bellying in the fighter, putting it down in a cultivated field about five miles northeast of Troyes. One of the two 434th FS pilots who saw the landing, Second Lieutenant Harold E. Mathews made a 180-degree turn over Lt. Gross as he was setting the plane down. Lt. Mathews reported that Lt. Gross hit all right, but at a high speed. He said that dust, smoke and flame covered the immediate area and that flak and small arms fire prevented him from staying and observing more. Both 434th FS pilots stated that they doubted Lt. Gross had much of a chance of surviving the landing. They were correct, for German records indicate Lt. Gross died in the wreckage of his burned aircraft.

Herman E. Hoversten recalled a mission like that when he was a Lieutenant flying with the 436th FS. As he told it during March of 2002:

> "The most dramatic mission from my standpoint was one of our first group strafing missions somewhere south in the peaceful part of France. For the mission, our group leader had decided that we would fly the strafing run wide open. After taking off, I quickly discovered that my airplane had somehow had its trim tabs cross-rigged and as a result I was having difficulty maintaining the speed that the rest of the group was flying. During the full speed strafing run, I started out in my assigned spot well to the front, but the resultant drag from the miss rigged trim tabs and the rudder I had to apply to counteract the effect of the trim tabs caused me to fall behind. Most of those behind me overtook and passed me by. Somewhere along the run down on the deck we began taking fire from what seem to me like German 88s. We had been told that the 88s could not be fired that low, but believe me, they can! I guess though it was really light anti-aircraft fire, but it seemed pretty heavy at the time.
>
> "Just as I was about to be overtaken by what seem to be the very last plane in the group, another P-38 passed me on the right. It was about 75 feet off my right wing. Suddenly, what seemed to have been a direct flak hit caused that plane to explode. All I could see was that P-38 instantly changed into a ball of fire and then it fell to the ground.
>
> "Shortly thereafter, our group leader called for us to ascend and 'Form up over that city with the tower in the middle of it'. The tower was the Eiffel and the city, Paris. Lots of heavy flak there. As we spiraled up, we came under fairly heavy fire from the German 88s. At about 7,500 feet, I heard a tremendous crash, felt my plane stagger and the cockpit began filling with black smoke. It got so thick I couldn't even see anything on the instrument panel. I radioed that I had been hit and was bailing out. Somebody replied 'Good luck' for which I devoutly hoped.
>
> "I had practiced how to feather a prop many times in local flights over England and during that short conversation, I shut down the right engine and feathered its prop. When the prop quit rotating, the smoke cleared from the cockpit. When I could see, I let go of my grip on the canopy release and settled down to take stock of my situation. When I began to think clearly, I found my engine rpms were still at 3,000 from out wide open strafing run. My manifold pressure was probably in the neighborhood of 35 inches, but who was keeping track?
>
> "At any rate, I proceeded on a course for England, all the while trailing thick black smoke. Everything went well until I noticed my left knee was bouncing up and down. I had overlooked trimming to counteract the drag from the dead right engine. After trimming for straight and level flight, I settled back to enjoy myself. However, about then, I became slightly sick to my stomach. I mistakenly felt that a bite from the candy bar I had in my flight suit would settle my stomach. Not so. I became more nauseated. Then I lit a cigarette. It totally calmed my nerves. That's the only good thing that I can say for smoking though.
>
> "During my journey home, my two roommates, Hans Grasshoff and Price Henry took up positions, one on each

wing. I appreciated their company immensely. I even appreciated their humor. Grasshoff started it by calling to ask me if he could have my boots if I didn't make it back. Then Henry wanted my civilian sunglasses.

"About half way across the channel, the fire went out and the trail of black smoke stopped. Coming into Wattisham, I made my usual extra hot landing because of the mistaken certainty that a 'go around' was impossible on one engine. (Tony LeVier had never put on his famous P-38 demonstration at our base.)

"When I dismounted from the cockpit, I was very surprised to find no holes in the engine cowling. It turned out that the engine had thrown a rod, which in turn had cut the engine in half. It was almost as though a huge power saw had done the job. The front few cylinders and propeller were supported only by the crankshaft."

Landfall out for the group was in the vicinity of Boulogne at 2100 hrs./10,000 ft.

28 June 1944

VIII FC FO 421

No. 84 Wednesday. The group's assignment was an escort for 3rd BD B-24s attacking their 8th AF Mission 445 primary target, a marshalling yard near Saarbrücken, Germany and a target of opportunity, an airfield northeast of Brussels, Belgium. Approximate time up: 0650 hrs., down: 1115 hrs. L/F was in the vicinity of Blankenberghe at 0735 hrs./19,000 ft. R/V with the assigned bombers was over Saarbrücken, Germany at 0835 hrs./22,000 ft. The bombers were ten minutes late. Heading back into Belgium, the Big Friends attacked an airfield ten miles northeast of Brussels. The results were partially obscured by overcast, but hits on a barracks were noted. The bombers and some stragglers were escorted to about mid-point over the North Sea where the group broke escort at 1045 hrs.

Observations made during the mission included: What was possibly a long-nose Fw 190, was seen about 30 miles southwest of Koblenz at 0835 hours. Five freight trains heading northwest towards Koblenz were spotted about the same time. There was possible enemy voice jamming on the VHF channels. Flak was heavy, moderate and inaccurate at Saarbrücken, but both light and heavy as well as intense at Zeebrugge, Belgium.

Captain Jules D. Biscayart in a P-38. *Courtesy of Steve Blake.*

29 June 1944

VIII FC FO Unk.

No. 85 Thursday. The group flew a bomber escort in support of 8th AF Mission 447. The R/V point for the 436th FS was listed as Wahrenholz, Germany, but unfortunately, that is all the record to be found for the mission.

Fortunately, John W. Hedenberg recorded some information about the mission in his diary:

> "Another escort job today. Covered bombers on withdrawal from raid on Leipzig. Got to within 20 minutes of Berlin, but still haven't seen it. Don't know where the Luftwaffe is hiding – 74 combat hours and I still haven't seen an enemy plane for sure over the continent and haven't fired my guns at anything. Capt. Biscayart aborted over the North Sea, leaving us to carry on. Over the German-Dutch border on the way out, Teeter and I picked up a straggler [crippled heavy bomber] and escorted him out, getting down to 15,000 feet in the process. He had one engine out and was throwing everything moveable overboard. Guess he was glad enough to see us. Lots of flak over Hanover, a little over Den Helder at the north end of the Zuider Zee. On the whole, a very quiet mission."

The above-cited report gives ample proof as to the reason the following poem was written by T/Sgt. Robert H. Bryson, a bomber crewmember:

"Lightnings in the Sky"

"Oh, Hedy Lamarr is a beautiful girl
And Madeleine Carroll is, too
But you'll find, if you query, a different theory
Amongst any bomber crew.
For the loveliest thing of which one could sing
(This side of the Heavenly gates)
Is no blonde or brunette of the Hollywood set –
But an escort of P-38s.

"Yes, in days that have passed when the tables were massed
With glasses of Scotch or Champagne,
It's quite true, that the sight was a thing to delight
Us, intent upon feeling no pain.
But no longer the same, nowadays, in this game,
When we head North from Messina Straights,
Take the sparkling wine – every time, just make mine
An escort of P-38s.

"Byron, Shelley and Keats ran a dozen dead heats
Describing the view from the hills,
Of the valleys in May when the winds gently sway
An army of bright daffodils.
Take the daffodils, Byron – the wild flowers, Shelley –
Yours is the Myrtle, Friend Keats;
Just reserve me those cuties – American Beauties –
An escort of P-38s.

"Sure we're braver than Hell; on the ground all is swell
in the air it's a different story:
We sweat out our track through the fighters and flak;
We're willing to split up the glory.
Well, they wouldn't reject us, so Heaven protect us
And, until all this shooting abates,
Give us courage to fight 'em and – one other small item –
An escort of P-38s."

30 June 1944

VIII FC FO 424

No. 86 Friday. Closing out the month was a fighter-bomber attack on a marshalling yard at Nevers, France. Approximate time up: 1830 hrs., down: 2130 hrs. L/F was over Gravelines

Crew chief Staff Sergeant Louis Kortis, Lieutenant Herman E. Hoversten and assistant crew chief Corporal Thomas J. Dasta by their P-38, the Virgin. *Courtesy of Herman E. Hoversten.*

and the group arrived in the target area at 2010 hrs. They bombed and strafed targets of opportunity for about twenty minutes and headed out, making L/O in the vicinity of Boulogne. The group's damaged and destroyed tally for the mission included locomotives, freight cars, switch houses, water towers, a station house, an oil dump, a radar station, barracks, a staff car, flak towers, high-tension lines and heavy trucks.

Danger for the pilots was not always found while flying combat missions as is shown by the following two illustrations. The first is from John W. Hedenberg:

> "No early mission today, but group went on a strafing mission about the time Teeter, Frolking [Lt.'s Robert Teeter and James Frolking] and I left for London. [48-hour pass.] Slow-timed Grasshoff's [Lt. Hans Grasshoff] ship in the morning – Had an amusing time flying close formation with a B-17 and steeple chasing over clouds. 5/10ths fair-weather cumulus – Lots of fun. Got to London about 2130 in the middle of an alert, took the underground to Picadilly Circus and started hunting a hotel. People have started sleeping in the underground stations again, quite a few of them. Found that the hotel we had stayed at last time [the Regency Palace] had been badly damaged by one of the buzz bombs – Finally ended up at the Savoy. Did we get taken to the cleaners! Marvelous, palatial hotel, but we paid!"

Two pilots from Newcross Squadron were also on 48-hour passes. The exact date is uncertain, but on or within a day or so of this date, Second Lieutenants Flamm D. Harper and

Bailey A. Williams also went on leave to London. Their experience, documented by Lt. Harper is as follows:

> "I had started to enclose newspaper clippings in my letters home to my wife Mary, particularly those covering air raids in which I participated, whenever articles were available. I began doing this regularly, starting with an air raid on July 4, 1944. This method of keeping Mary advised as to where I was and what I was doing did not last long. I was reported as MIA on July 15, 1944.
>
> "One of the news articles that I had sent bore the headline: 'ROBOT FALLS ON HOTEL'. The brief article that followed told of a V1 Buzz Bomb that hit a hotel near west central London. In part, it stated, 'Residents in a hotel in southern England had remarkable escapes when a buzz bomb fell on the roof of an annex. There were no fatal casualties, but members of the staff, visitors and people in the street were injured. A waitress in the hotel said that some people ran out and others couched beneath tables. 'I had just time to dive for shelter,' she said. 'I saw one man with his eyes gashed by splinters and others were cut about their faces'.
>
> "I believe the date of that was late June 1944. It was when Bailey 'Willie' Williams and I took a rest and recuperation leave in London. The city had been living under a constant Red Air Raid Alert for several weeks because of Buzz Bomb attacks, but this did not deter the two of us from heading to London where the parties were. We checked into the St. Regis Hotel located in the Piccadilly Circus area.
>
> "We were awakened the next morning at about 9 AM by the motor of a buzz bomb. I walked to the window; spotted the buzz bomb and saw its engine cut off. It then entered about a 60-degree dive. It impacted a couple of blocks from us in major department store on Oxford Street. I turned to Bailey and said, 'That one was pretty close. The next one will be on the other side of town.' Then I walked to the wash basin (located on the same wall as the window) and started to rinse my face off with cold water. The next thing I knew, I was picking myself off of the floor and had a small cut on my hand. My blouse, which had been hung over the back of a nearby chair, looked like it had 2,000 holes in it from the splintered window glass that had gone flying. The whole window frame had been blown out of the wall and was draped around Bailey.

What the well-dressed fighter pilot wore as demonstrated by Captain Bailey A. Williams from the 434th FS. *Courtesy of Berkley E. Hollister.*

The beloved P-38. *Courtesy of Frederick C. Hayner.*

He was momentarily knocked out. The buzz bomb had apparently hit the annex on the roof housing the elevator for the hotel and blew most of the two top stories of the hotel away. Major parts of the buzz bomb fell into the street in front of the hotel. For all practical purposes, we were now on the top floor. The elevator was out, the stair well was blocked with debris, and several small fires were burning. Once out in the hallway, we encountered two Canadians. It took about 30 minutes before we, with the help of rescuers working their way up the stairs, could extract ourselves from the mess.

"Once out of the hotel we walked across the street to a sidewalk café, ordered two beers and sat down at a table with several ATS girls (British Air Transport Service). Watching the rescuers clean up the debris in the street, we made small talk for a couple of hours. Willie and I also discussed whether we should stay in London or finish our leave in Glasgow, Scotland. During this time several more buzz bombs flew nearby on to their unknown destinations. Willie and I became more mentally uneasy with each bomb. We had entered London with the 'Bravado' of young fighter pilots knowing the city was under constant attack. Our close call had destroyed the mental block that protects us all – 'It will happen to the other guy'. Suddenly we both recognized London was not the place to be. We grabbed our bags, hailed a taxi and headed for the U.S. Military Clothing Sales Store to buy me a new blouse. While I was involved with this task, Willie was checking transportation to Glasgow. It turned out, as I recall, suitable transportation arrangements to Glasgow were not feasible. Our discomfort from the constant bombardment continued to build. As I remember, we just cancelled out and returned to duty at Wattisham. Sixty years later, I still carry a small scar on my left hand from the cut that I received when the buzz bomb exploded."

CHAPTER FIVE

JULY 1944

1 July 1944

VIII FC FO (Unk.)

No. 86 Saturday. Maj. Glover led the 435th FS, which consisted of 15 P-38s in a fighter-bomber attack against rail and tactical targets in France. Squadron up: 1830 hrs., down: 1935 hrs. with no early returns. The mission was recalled at 1858 hrs. by 65th FW due to deteriorating weather conditions over the continent. The P-38s had just "gotten their feet wet" over the channel. The other two squadrons never even got off the ground.

About this time, Allen J. Moon, then a sergeant in the communications section, suffered an amusing experience. As he told it:

> "GIs from the Midwest generally had basic driving skills that had been developed on maybe a tractor or a friend's Model-T, this all being in place well before their 16th birthday. These skills were seldom known to the young men cast into uniform from the cities of New York, Boston or Philadelphia. One of the 479th's sergeants was a victim of having grown up in this puberty, auto-sterile landscape, but had, however, managed to pass the driving test after having had all his training on a powerful 6x6 truck. His actual driver's license was being issued from 65th Fighter Wing HQ and had not yet arrived at the base as promptly as the newly-qualified driver had hoped for. To further his competence, our communications officer agreed to let him gain added 'stick-time' in our jeep while delivering VHF radio sets to the flight line. I was asked to assume the co-pilot position and let the sergeant pilot the diminutive vehicle on its appointed rounds.
>
> "The first turn was executed around the radio shack with much jerking, engine-racing and clutch-slippage. Second gear was engaged with a resultant powerful lurch forward as we approached a 90-degree turn that ended up as being a 180-degree turn at full throttle into and through the double doors of our shack. We crashed into the potbelly stove in the center of the room, knocked it over and finally came to rest against a brick support for the far workbench.
>
> "I suffered a bruised knee and the sergeant suffered a much-depleted ego plus court marshal charges of 35 bucks for damages to the 'trainer'." Allen said, "I guess jeeps are a bit different from 6x6s."

4 July 1944

VIII FC FO 427

No. 87 Tuesday. Lt. Col. Riddle was the group's leader and he also led the 434th FS, which consisted of 17 P-38s. Lt. Courtney led the 435th FS, which consisted of 15 P-38s and Maj. Monahan led the 436th FS, which consisted of 17 P-38s. Their assignment, the first of two for the day, was a bomber escort for 3rd BD B-17s attacking their 8th AF Mission 451 primary target, a bridge at Saumur, France. 434th FS up: 0605 hrs., down: 1049 hrs. with two early returns. 435th FS up: 0625 hrs., down: 1053 hrs. with three early returns plus two escorts for them. 436th FS up: 0600 hrs., down: 1100 hrs. with four early returns plus two escorts for them.

The group passed over Selsey Bill on the south coast of England about 0710 hours, flew south over the channel and made L/F at France in the vicinity of Cabourg, about 0730 hrs./22-23,000 ft. The 435th FS, having left later and following the same route, made these points correspondingly later. Proceeding down to R/V, the 436th FS encountered two unidentified enemy aircraft diving at them at 0740 hrs. Two of the squadron's pilots turned into the E/A, hoping to engage them, but instead the single-engine A/C retreated. Bison Squadron spent much of its time flying back and forth between Le Havre and Barfleur. With not much to do, the pilots noticed the bitter cold at the altitude they were flying. (Despite the fact it was summer and warm on the ground, the air temperatures at the 23-27,000 ft. altitudes the men were flying could range between minus ten to minus forty degrees. The poor heating system of the P-38 which ducted warm air from the aircraft's engines via a tube to the cockpit, served only to raise the temperature there to around freezing. A long, cold and uneventful high-altitude flight of five to six hours would often stiffen a pilot to the point that after he landed and parked his airplane, he then would need to be helped from his cockpit.) A flight of 435th FS P-38s picked up three boxes of 3rd BD B-17s just north of the R/V point and stayed with them as they flew due northeast to Bologne. The bombers then made a 180-degree turn and headed back southwest. Finally the P-38s had to break away and head for home. The assigned B-17s were joined by their escorts south of the target, in the vicinities of Buzancais and Pellevoisin at 0811 hrs./21-23,000 ft. At that time, the Big Friends seemed to be in good formation and none appeared to be in trouble. Two other 435th FS flights were not able to provide escort for the bombers at R/V. White Flight, from 435th left the bombers just west of the R/V point, and gave chase to two Fw 190s. The Focke-Wulfs were pursued north to Sillie, which is just northwest of Le Mans. The enemy aircraft were lost there in the overcast. At that point, the flight went down to strafe ground targets. Attacking a marshalling yard at Sillie, they shot up a locomotive, eight goods cars, three trucks and a water tower. They also observed a string of flat cars loaded with shot-up trucks there. A third 435th FS flight, failing to connect at all with the B-17s, left the R/V area, advising their squadron leader that they were going on to look for the bombers.

Following the mission course, the next transmission heard from them advised that, "Lakeside [435th FS] Yellow Two [Second Lieutenant Rayne B. Fairchild] on fire in engine area, pull up and bail out." They had joined White Flight and provided top cover for the strafing attack on the marshalling yard. Then, having lost White Flight in the clouds, Captain Robert D. Green, Yellow Flight Leader, took his flight down through a hole in the clouds and continued on down to strafe ground targets. At 0845 hours, Yellow Flight had been on the deck at 200 feet for about ten minutes when they flew over an automatic weapons position seven miles north of Laval. Lt. Fairchild was hit and his engine began to smoke. Capt. Green started to circle to the left and ordered Lt. Fairchild to bail out. The Lieutenant made a 90-degree left turn, lined up with the flak position and fired at it. He then made another 90-degree turn and bellied into a large flat field. He survived and became a POW. During this time, Capt. Green had completed his circle to the left. He radioed the rest of the squadron stating that they were going home. Moments later and heading in that direction, the three remaining Yellow Flight P-38s, still at 200 feet, passed over a hill and ran over another automatic weapons position. Now it was Capt. Green who was in trouble. His aircraft was hit in the right engine and it began to smoke. As he continued on, the P-38's engine and wing began to blaze. Another member of the flight, Second Lieutenant Everett P. Ford, who had closed up with the Captain, called him on the radio and advised him to bail out. No response was received and a few seconds later, the burning P-38 dipped down and crashed into the ground, exploding on impact. Capt. Green did not get out.

Sergeant Allen J. Moon in the jeep. *Courtesy of Allen J. Moon.*

P-38 L2-A, the plane that Second Lieutenant Jack S. Denny was flying this day is shown being serviced shortly after it was received by the squadron. Note that there are no squadron markings yet present on the aircraft. *Carroll C. Sprague Collection, courtesy of the East Essex Aviation Society.*

The bombers and their escorts reached the target at Saumur at 0837 hrs. where the B-17s bombed through 8-9/10ths cloud cover, those conditions having prevailed throughout most of the mission. No results were observed. Flak over the target was heavy, moderate, but inaccurate. The bombers were taken back out of France as various flights and squadrons broke away at different times and places. The 434th FS broke away west of Paris and went looking for targets of opportunity on the ground, but weather prevented any attacks. They did note that the Gise Canal between Noyon and Chauny was heavily laden with barge traffic. L/O for the squadron was over the Pas de Calais 1005 hrs. The remaining flight from the 435th FS, stayed with the bombers through L/O at St. Valery, which was at 1000 hrs./20,000 ft. The 436th FS escorted the Fortresses as far as mid-channel, finally breaking away at 1030 hrs.

4 July 1944

VIII FC FO 429

No. 88 Tuesday. Lt. Col. Riddle was the group's leader and he also led the 436th FS, which consisted of 16 P-38s. Capt. Jeffrey led the 434th FS, which consisted of 15 P-38s and Lt. Courtney led the 435th FS, which consisted of 14 P-38s. Their assignment, the second for the day, was a fighter sweep and strafing mission in southwest France. 434th FS up: 1553 hrs., down: 2017 hrs. with one early return. 435th FS up: 1549 hrs., down: 2009 hrs. with one early return. 436th FS up: 1640 hrs., down: 2050 hrs. with no early returns.

Crossing out of England along the southern coast and crossing the channel, L/F at France was near Pte. de la Pércée on the western side of Normandy's Omaha Beach at about 1705 hrs. Flying south, the group made its way past Laval and down to Saintes, arriving there about 1745 hrs. It was there that the strafing run was to begin. Attacking rail and tactical targets of opportunity, the squadrons worked their way north along the rail lines to Nantes. At this point, the time was 1805 hrs. and ammunition as well as gas was getting low so it was time to head home. The huge tally of destroyed and damaged was a yard long and included trains with associated locomotives, goods wagons, freight cars, oil tank cars, two freight cars "confirmed" (they blew sky-high when attacked) to be carrying ammunition, railroad switch houses, numerous flak towers, rail bridges, water towers, warehouses, factories, buildings, barracks, a power plant, power line towers and power lines, a mining operation, a radio station, trucks, troop trucks with occupants and a black sedan whose occupant flew the coop!

It was pretty much a good show, but unfortunately, Second Lieutenant Jack S. Denny from Newcross Squadron was hit by flak. He and Captain Jack G. Grossenbacher had been strafing on the deck. The two had lost sight of each other when Lt. Denny called stating that his P-38 had suffered a hit in the left engine and he would have to shut it down. In addition, Lt. Denny noted that he also had been hit. He was suffering a head wound that left him unable to see from his right eye. He was, however, able to keep his bird flying. Capt. Grossenbacher, already in a climb, began trying to locate Lt. Denny. He continued communication with Lt. Denny, telling him to set a climbing course for home. At 14,000 feet, Capt. Grossenbacher spotted Lt. Denny below him. He called to the lieutenant and went down to his altitude. Lt. Denny was flying

The flak damaged P-38 that Lieutenant Thomas H. Orrick bellied in at Wattisham gets all fluids, armament and camera removed prior to being taken away for salvage. *Courtesy of Eugene W. Bailey.*

Flak damage to Lieutenant Orrick's P-38 shows up on the trailing edge of the ship's right wing. *Courtesy of Eugene W. Bailey.*

on one engine and again communicated that he had a head injury and was only able to see with one eye. The two then arranged visual signals in order for Capt. Grossenbacher to get Lt. Denny on a course for home. About five minutes after that, Lt. Denny began to get into some clouds. Instead of circling to gain altitude and avoid them, he continued on into them and became lost from Capt. Grossenbacher's sight. That was about 1925 hrs. The captain searched above and below the clouds, but was unable to find Lt. Denny. At that point, he had to head for home. Fortunately, Lt. Denny was able to continue on by himself and eventually land behind allied lines at Normandy. Lt. Denny returned to Wattisham in August.

L/O was over Omaha Beach again, between 1845 and 1900 hrs.

Lieutenant Thomas H. Orrick was also shot up but managed to return to Wattisham where he bellied his P-38 in. He walked away from the damaged aircraft.

5 July 1944

VIII FC FO 430

No. 89 Wednesday. Maj. Glover was the group's leader and he also led the 435th FS, which consisted of 14 P-38s. Maj. Keller led the 434th FS, which consisted of 14 P-38s and Maj. Monahan led the 436th FS, which consisted of 17 P-38s, two of which were relays. Their assignment was the same as yesterday afternoon's fighter strafing mission to the Saintes/Nantes, France area. 434th FS up: 0657 hrs., down: 1105 hrs. with no early returns. 435th FS up: 0655 hrs., down: 1055 hrs. with one early return. 436th FS up: 0644 hrs., down: 1100 hrs. with two early returns. Second Lieutenant Carl L. Peterson from the 434th FS, crashed during take off, having run off the end of the runway. The P-38 he was assigned for the mission burst into flames, but Lt. Peterson was able to escape with minor burns.

Left: The remains of Scat II, a P-38 that Robin Olds had named, lay in a field after Second Lieutenant Carl L. Peterson crashed during take off. *Courtesy of Clarence M. Surges.* Right: Better times for Scat II. Lieutenant Robin Olds is shown standing beside the second mount he flew while in England. *Courtesy of Berkley E. Hollister.*

the Me 109 and in a dive. Looking up, I noticed Lt. Hass in a luftberry with another Me 109 and turned to help him. As I closed, the second 109 broke away from Lt. Hass and made a head-on pass at me, during which we each fired about a five second burst at each other. I saw several strikes on the Me 109 from my burst. Then we both turned and I followed him. I had completed my turn and had him lined up in my sights just as he was rolling out of his turn. He made a quick turn and came at me again in a head-on pass. We closed on each other and fired until the Me 109 had to pull up to avoid a collision. During the pass, I observed parts falling from both sides of the aircraft and it was smoking from the many strikes I had made upon it. I turned to get on his tail and with that, the German pilot bailed out and I saw his chute open. The Me 109 went down in flames. When I saw the German parachute, I also saw another chute, closer to the ground. I assume that Lt. Hass was in that one, since I had observed his ship burning and hadn't seen any other aircraft in trouble in the vicinity. During all this, I didn't observe any hits on my ship. I claim one Me 109 as destroyed."

Second Lieutenant Gerold M. Mulvany. *Courtesy of Sally Mulvany.*

Captain Thomas T. Galloway from the 436th FS confirmed the kill. Second Lt. Jene A. Hass landed near a wooded area and was taken prisoner by the Germans within a matter of minutes.

Gerold M. Mulvany in recalling an encounter he had while flying with the 436th FS, told about an event that probably gave him the jitters when all was said and done. The exact date is unknown, but the circumstances of the experience would seem to indicate it occurred on this date. Mulvany, then a Second Lieutenant stated:

"On one occasion we were involved in a sweep of the area known to be the home of the famed 'Abbeville Kids' a crack Luftwaffe fighter group. Sure enough, we became involved in a mix-up with some of them and I went after one of the leaders. I pulled a sucker turn under his nose, staying under him to catch which way he would break. He pulled up and I went with him. He snap-rolled and as we passed each other, it seemed like our canopies were less than three feet apart. Because he was in a high-speed stall, I slid past him and quickly split-essed. Then, looking up into my curved rear-view mirror, I spotted him big as life, sitting on my tail. Things became a blur for a moment right after that. I remember a sound like a sledgehammer hitting a can and it seemed as though I was in that can. When I regained a sense of what was happening, I found myself down on the deck, my right wing was flapping and popped rivets were sticking out everywhere. My helmet and mask were pulled down over my face and I saw bolt ends as well as other junk flying around in the cockpit. I yanked my mask off and regained control just in time to safely pass under some high-voltage wires I was about to hit. When I got home, my ground crew found grass and leaves in the intercoolers of both my P-38's engines. The plane was damaged and I found that I had broken through the copper wire that provided a stop for my right engine throttle. I evidentially had jammed it into the war emergency power setting while somehow pulling back on my left engine throttle as my wingman said he saw me began tumbling end for end. He said he lost sight of me when that happened. Chalk one up for the strength of the P-38."

Breaking up into individual squadrons and flights, the group continued on, strafing targets of opportunity. The 434th FS continued southwest and attacked an airdrome in the Laon/Couvron area. A radar station, with its supporting flak positions and barracks was damaged there. Turning back, the squadron found a marshalling yard near St. Omer and destroyed/damaged six trucks, three locomotives and twenty goods wagons there. The squadron crossed out by flights, between

Culiers and Dunkerque at 0945-1050 hrs. The 435th FS headed southwest also and found a 15-truck convoy, which they strafed and caused general havoc to. Returning, they crossed out in the vicinity of Dunkerque at 1040 hrs./10,000 ft. The 436th FS continued the sweep and in heading home, made L/O over Gravelines at 1045 hrs./10,000 ft.

Observations made during the mission included: A 50-vehicle convoy was spotted five to ten miles southeast of St. Omer, heading towards that location. Numerous other trucks heading in various directions were seen at different locations. Rail stock was seen parked on sidings. Flak at the airdrome in the Laon/Couvren area was both heavy and light, intense and accurate. At Calais, it was heavy and intense. At Dunkerque it was light to heavy, intense and accurate. At Cambrai it was heavy, intense and accurate. At St. Omer and at St Valenciennes it was heavy, moderate and accurate.

Loading belly tank bombs on a P-38. *Courtesy of Loetta Taylor (Kennedy).*

6 July 1944

VIII FC FO 434

No. 000 Thursday. Capt. Jeffrey led the 434th FS, which consisted of nine P-38s. Their assignment was to be a fighter-bomber mission in France. Time up: 1345 hrs., down: 1414 hrs. The attack was to be made using napalm bombs, but the mission was recalled by 65th FW because of deteriorating weather conditions. Specially adapted belly tanks were prepared for a twenty-five plane mission, but the group's records only indicate that the nine 434th FS P-38s participated. Ten thousand gallons of seventy-eight octane gasoline was thickened by the addition of a gelatinous agent and the mixture was used to fill some fifty 150/165 gallon capacity, steel belly tanks. The tanks were modified by the addition of a 2,000-pound GP bomb fin and a special fuse to ignite the mixture upon impact. After the recall, the tanks were dropped into the channel before the aircraft returned to Wattisham.

6 July 1944

VIII FC FO 435

No. 91 Thursday. Capt. Jeffrey led the 434th FS, which consisted of ten P-38s, Maj. Glover led the 435th FS, which consisted of 16 P-38s and Maj. Monahan led the 436th FS, which consisted of 16 P-38s. Their assignment in France was a bomber escort for 2nd BD B-24s attacking their 8th AF Mission 456 targets, bridges in the Saumur area. 434th FS up: 1718 hrs., down: 2133 hrs. with no early returns. 435th FS up: 1720 hrs., down: 2147 hrs. with two early returns. 436th FS up: 1721 hrs., down: 2130 hrs. with three early returns.

The records preserved for the 434th FS are illegible, but it can be assumed that the squadron took an active part in this mission, even though no account can be given for their activities. The 435th FS made L/F near St. Aubin at 1915 hrs./24,000 ft. Heading south, R/V with their assigned bombers was over Fontaine Milon, near Le Mans at 20,000 ft. The B-24s were escorted to Saumur to bomb a bridge there. The results were poor. The bombers continued on southeast to Menteoreau where another bridge was attacked. Here, the results were called fair. Returning north, an airfield at La Flèche was hit, but the results were unknown. The squadron broke away from the bombers over the channel at 2130 hrs./16,000 ft. The 436th FS crossed into France over Crepon at 1910 hrs./21,000 ft. They noted a flash that was believed to be an aircraft exploding,

A 434th FS bird taking off for mission form up. *Courtesy of the 436th Fighter Squadron Association.*

five miles northwest of the Bayeaux airfield. The squadron made R/V with their assigned B-24s from the 20th, 93rd and 448th BGs at Sable. The primary target at Saumur was not reached. The city hit near Saumur, was on the north side of the river. It had two bridges leading to it. The easterly bridge was of concrete construction with four or five columns. It received two or three hits on its north approach. The westerly bridge was steel construction and appeared to be hit in the center as smoke was seen at that place. The city proper was also well hit by the bombers. Returning, L/O was near St Valery at 2040 hrs./20,000 ft. The squadron broke from the bombers near Dungeness, England at 2100 hrs.

There were no observations reported. Flak at Caen, Rouen and Saumur was heavy, meager to intense and accurate.

Captain Hiram (Satch) G. Turner. *Courtesy of Berkley E. Hollister.*

7 July 1944

VIII FC FO 436

No. 92 Friday. Lt. Col. Sidney S. Woods was the group's leader and he also led the 435th FS, which consisted of 16 P-38s. Maj. Herren led the 434th FS, which consisted of 12 P-38s and Capt. Galloway led the 436th FS, which consisted of 16 P-38s plus two P-38 relays. Their assignment was bomber escort for withdrawing 1st and 3rd BD B-17s that had attacked their 8th AF Mission 458 primary targets at Leipzig, Germany. 434th FS up: 0825 hrs., down: 1400 hrs. with no early returns. 435th FS up: 0830 hrs., down: 1336 hrs. with no early returns. 436th FS up: 0835 hrs., down: 1340 hrs. with four early returns.

The records preserved for the 434th FS are nearly illegible, but some details were clear enough to be picked out. The squadron made L/F over Den Helder, Holland at 0932 hrs. Continuing east, the squadron made R/V with their assigned 1st BD B-17s south of Hanover, Germany at 1030 hrs. Taking their charges back, the squadron's flights broke up and escorted damaged B-17s towards home. Red Flight, led by Captain Hiram (Satch) G. Turner, Jr., picked up a crippled B-17 near Dümmer Lake in Germany and escorted it to just off the Dutch coast where the bomber was forced to ditch in the North Sea. Capt. Turner contacted Air/Sea Rescue and the flight circled the wreck until the crew was all safely in their dinghies. After circling for quite some time, Capt. Turner's three other flight members began getting low on gas so the Captain sent them home. He remained over the bomber crew to await rescue. Capt. Turner reported that every now and then he would buzz the bomber boys to let them know he was still there. He said they would stand up in their dinghies and wave until they almost fell in the water. The rescue boat got off course so Capt. Turner had to go searching for it and get it back on course. Finally the boat arrived for the pick up and hauled the crew on board. Capt. Turner returned to Wattisham and logged in a total of seven hours, forty-one minutes, a long time to be airborne. Capt. Turner said that he certainly lived up to his nickname and that one portion of his anatomy definitely ached. The squadron returned to base via different routes and arrived at different times due to the break up and various escorts.

The 435th FS made L/F over Ijmuiden, Holland at 0936 hrs./20,000 ft. The squadron R/V'd with their assigned 3rd BD Big Friends approximately 40 miles south of Hanover at 1030 hrs./24,000 ft. and escorted stragglers out to L/O. Heavy, dark smoke was seen in the direction of Leipzig. The mission for the squadron was recorded as uneventful and L/O was near Egmond, Holland at 1130 hrs./19,000 ft.

The 436th FS made L/F over Egmond at 0933 hrs./20,000 ft. and R/V with their B-17s near Northeim, Germany at 1030 hrs./24,000 ft. The escort was uneventful and the bombers were taken to north of Zwolle, Holland where they were left at 1145 hrs./20,000 ft. The squadron then turned back and spread out to look for stragglers. Finding none, they again returned to the coast, making a scattered L/O between Zandvoort and Den Helder, Holland at 1200 hrs.

There were no observations recorded from the mission. Flak over Hanover was heavy, intense and accurate while over Minden, it was heavy, meager and accurate.

8 July 1944

VIII FC FO 437

No. 93 Saturday. Lt. Col. Woods was the group's leader and he also led the 436th FS, which consisted of 16 P-38s. Maj. Keller led the 434th FS, which consisted of 11 P-38s and Capt. Carter led the 435th FS, which consisted of 14 P-38s. Their assignment was a fighter sweep in France, in support of 3rd BD B-17s attacking their 8th AF Mission 460 targets. 434th FS up: 0508 hrs., down: 0940 hrs. with one early return. 435th FS up: 0515 hrs., down: 0945 hrs. with no early returns. 436th FS up: 0500 hrs., down: 0950 hrs. with no early returns.

L/F for the group was over Gravelines between 0545 and 0556 hrs. at 12-18,000 ft. Flying southwest, the squadrons R/V'd with each other near Chartres about 0630 hrs. and headed west into their patrol area. They patrolled an area roughly bounded by Laval to the southeast, Pontivy to the southwest, St. Brieuc to the northwest and Domfront on the northeast. No enemy aircraft were sighted and the mission was uneventful except for Red Flight from the 436th. They found a train near Illiers to destroy. The patrol area was left between 0815 and 0830 hrs. L/O was over St. Valery at 0850 hrs. for the 434th FS, Le Havre at 0845 hrs. for the 435th FS and Trouville at 0900 hrs. for the 436th FS. Arriving at the coast of England, two planes from the 436th's Red Flight received AA fire from a battery at Clacton-on-Sea.

Observations made during the mission consisted of trains, marshalling yards and airfield sightings along the patrol route. All flak reported was heavy, moderate to meager and inaccurate to accurate. Locations were Calais, Evreus, Chaumont, Digny, Vernon, Les Andelys and southwest of Paris.

9 July 1944

Sunday. Led by First Lt. Clifford J. Moore, seven P-38s from the 436th FS flew a practice mission in the afternoon. They flew out on a course of 90 degrees from Wattisham in an attempt to avoid some bad weather. Out over the North Sea they climbed on a 270-degree course towards Thetford where they were supposed to R/V with some bombers. However, the bad weather prevented a link up. The seven P-38s continued on for several minutes beyond the R/V time and then turned on a course for home through the solid overcast. Arriving back some two hours after they had taken off, the pilots, as well as everyone else on the base, began a wait of several days for the weather to clear enough to begin flying missions again. In the meantime, training missions were flown to give new, incoming pilots some experience.

The ground crew is shown beside their charge, The Uninvited, flown by First Lieutenant Clifford J. Moore. Shown left to right are Corporal Kenneth D. Axt the assistant crew chief, Corporal Thomas E. O'Malley the armorer and Technical Sergeant Stanley M. Taydus, the crew chief. *Courtesy of Kenneth D. Axt.*

11 July 1944

VIII FC FO 441

No. 94 Tuesday. Lt. Col. Riddle was the group's leader and he also led the 434th FS, which consisted of 12 P-38s. Capt. Carter led the 435th FS, which consisted of 15 P-38s and Capt. Galloway led the 435th FS, which consisted of 18 P-38s. Their assignment was a bomber escort for withdrawing 2nd BD B-24s that had attacked their 8th AF Mission 466 targets in the Munich area of southern Germany. 434th FS up: 1140 hrs., down: 1650 hrs. with two early returns. 435th FS up: 1146 hrs., down: 1700 hrs. with no early returns. 436th FS up: 1135 hrs., down: 1700 hrs. with six early returns, three of which were escorts to the other three.

L/F was the vicinity of Ostend, Belgium between 1224 and 1234 hrs./18-20,000 ft. for all three squadrons. The mission was uneventful for the 434th FS, but not so for the other two squadrons. The 435th FS R/V'd with their assigned B-24s in the area of Haslach, Germany at 1323 hrs./22,000 ft. The bombers were escorted to L/O over Schouwen Island, Holland at 1520 hrs. and on out farther to over the North Sea, where the squadron broke away at 1620 hrs./15,000 ft. Shortly after break away, the squadron observed a B-24 ditched in the North Sea, about 30 miles east, northeast of Margate, England. Two dinghies were seen, but a count on occupants was not possible because four other B-24s and a flight of 55th Fighter Group P-38s had all begun to circle the area. "May Day" calls to Air-Sea Rescue were heard being given on "B" channel.The 436th FS made R/V with the proper bombers over Germany at 1335 hrs. The bombers were flying at 18-25,000 ft. One B-17 that was low on gas was picked up and escort begun, but that ended when the bomber's pilot indicated his intentions of landing in Switzerland. One of the Bison (436th FS) pilots escorted a B-24 flying on a single engine, all the way from the R/V area to the coast of France at Cayeux. The Big Friend gave out a "May-Day" call and ditched in the channel through the overcast at that point. The B-24 was from the 389th BG, squadron unknown, but squadron aircraft letter "T". L/O for the squadron was at 1600 hrs./18,000 ft. west of Schouwen Island. The remainder of the bombers were left over the North Sea. The mission was very dull and boring for most of the Bison Squadron pilots. They didn't even see any flak.

There were no observations recorded from the mission. Flak east of Antwerp, Belgium was heavy, moderate and inaccurate while at Lillie, France, it was heavy, moderate and accurate and at Le Tréport, France, it was heavy, meager and accurate.

After this date, the alternating black and white bands of paint, the so-called "Invasion Stripes", were removed from the group's planes. This was accomplished by means of the paint being stripped from the natural metal finish P-38s and painting over with a coat of olive drab in the case of painted aircraft.

12 July 1944

VIII FC FO 442

No. 95 Wednesday. Maj. James M. Herren led the group and he also led the 434th FS, which consisted of 16 P-38s. The records from the 435th FS are missing, but it can be assumed that the squadron took an active part in this mission, even though no account can be given for their activities. Capt. Biscayart led the 436th FS, which consisted of 17 P-38s. Their assignment was a bomber escort for withdrawing 1st BD B-17s that had attacked their 8th AF Mission 469 targets in the Munich, Germany area. 434th FS up: 1236 hrs., down: 1719 hrs. with no early returns. 436th FS up: 1230 hrs., down: 1730 hrs. with five early returns, two of which were escorts to the other three.

The weather was bad with 10/10ths overcast covering the continent. Only a few holes were seen. Approximate R/V was made by the squadrons near Schweighausen, Germany at 1425 hrs./20,000 ft. Returning, L/O was west of Schouwen Island at 1630 hrs./18,000 ft. The bombers were escorted to the English coast. Six or more single-engine A/C were seen to be taking off from an airfield located near Longuyon, France, but nothing evolved from that. The mission was uneventful and only one flak report gives any indication of activity. Flak over Brussels, Belgium was heavy, moderate and inaccurate.

This date, every man in the 479th Fighter Group received a copy of a commendation from Brigadier General Jesse Auton, a likeness of which is reproduced and follows here:

HEADQUARTERS
65TH FIGHTER WING
Office of the Commanding General
A.P.O. # 637 AAF STATION F-370

12 July 1944

SUBJECT: Commendation.
TO : _____[Name]_____

1. I desire to commend you and each member of every unit on AAF Station F-377, for the contribution you have made and the record you have established in aiding the 479th Fighter Group to become operational in eleven days after arrival at your station in this theater of operations.

2. No other fighter group has become operational and taken part in combat flying so soon after arrival. This record is worthy of note and emulation. You have brought credit to yourself and to the United States Army Air Forces.

/s/ Jesse Auton
/t/ JESSE AUTON
Brigadier General, U.S.A.
Commanding

13 July 1944

VIII FC FO 444

No. 96 Thursday. Lt. Col. Riddle was the group's leader and he also led the 436th FS, which consisted of 15 P-38s. The records preserved for the 434th FS are illegible, but it appears that the 434th FS put 17 P-38s into the air this day. It can be assumed that the squadron took an active part in this mission, even though no account can be given for their activities. Capt. Carter led the 435th FS, which consisted of 15 P-38s. Their assignment again was a bomber escort for withdrawing 1st BD B-17s that had attacked their 8th AF Mission 471 targets in the Munich, Germany area. 435th FS up: 0955 hrs., down: 1335 hrs. with one early return. 436th FS up: 0947 hrs., down: 1345 hrs. with two early returns.

The weather played a large part again in the mission, as there was a 10/10ths overcast covering the continent. The 435th FS made L/F over Ostend, Belgium at 1112 hrs./21,000 ft. and picked up their assigned B-17s ten minutes southwest of Metz, France. The 436th FS came in over Coxyde, Belgium at 1040 hrs./21,000 ft. and made R/V with their bombers at 1113 hrs./23,000 ft. and near the same place as did the 435th FS. The escort was uneventful except that the 435th FS noted a single, large burst of what they thought might be a new type of flak. Seen somewhere between Hirson and Mons, France, the difficulty in positively locating it being due to the overcast, it was described as a huge orange flash, followed by a great puff of black smoke with white streamers falling from the burst. The explosion was seen from about a mile away. (The possibility exists, that what they saw was not a flak burst, but in fact two fighters, a P-38 from the 55th FG and a P-47 from the 56th FG, which had collided south of Brussels.) The Big Friends were escorted out over the Dutch island of Schouwen, crossing out between 1233 and 1240 hrs./17-20,000 ft. They were taken home to near the English coast where the squadrons broke for home themselves. Flak was heavy, meager and inaccurate near Coxyde.

On 14 July 1944, every man in the 479th Fighter Group received a copy of a commendation from Brigadier General Jesse Auton, a likeness of which is reproduced and follows here:

HEADQUARTERS
65TH FIGHTER WING
Office of the Commanding General
A.P.O. # 637 AAF STATION F-370

A cartoon drawn by Robin Olds. *479th FG records.*

14 July 1944

SUBJECT: Commendation of AAF Station F-377.

TO : _____[Name]_____

1. I desire to commend you for your part in the activities of your station against the enemy during the critical period of the invasion of France from 6 June 1944 to 27 June 1944. The success of this operation depended a great deal upon the support given by the aircraft of your group. You performed your duty in such a zealous manner, working many hours a day beyond the normal amount, that your aircraft gave maximum support to our ground forces.

2. The continued success of our Armies culminating in the total defeat of the Hun necessitates the utmost attention to duty which I am sure you will continue to give.

/s/ Jesse Auton
/t/ JESSE AUTON
Brigadier General, U.S.A.
Commanding

15 July 1944

VIII FC FO 449

No. 97 Saturday. Lt. Col. Woods was the group's leader and he also led the 435th FS, which consisted of 16 P-38s. Maj. Herren led the 434th FS, which consisted of 18 P-38s. Capt. Galloway led the 436th FS, which consisted of 16 P-38s plus two P-38 relays. The squadron's assignment was a fighter-bomber attack in support of 8th AF Mission 474 against targets

Gun camera film showing part of the munitions site after the attack. *Robin Olds via Flamm D. Harper.*

One of the storage buildings. *Courtesy of Flamm D. Harper.*

of opportunity in France. 434th FS up: 1715 hrs., down: 2130 hrs. 435th FS up: 1725 hrs., down: 2140 hrs. with no early returns. 436th FS up: 1710 hrs., down: 2150 hrs. with one early return.

L/F was over the French coast between St. Valerie and Cap D'Antifer at about 1811 hrs./10-15,000 ft. Heading south, the squadrons R/V'd with other P-38 groups at 1900 hours, south of Tours. The 434th and 435th FSs dropped down on the deck while the 436th FS went down to 5,000 ft. and flew top cover for the two other squadrons. The weather was heavy, with 7-10/10ths cloud cover in the area, but lucrative targets were found and the 435th FS took the high road, strafing and bombing targets of opportunity along the railroad line from Tours to Bourges and then over to Sanceces. The 434th FS took the low road, following a more southeasterly route from Tours, down towards Montluçon. West of Montmorillon, Newcross (434th FS) Blue Flight found, as the squadron's records state, "...a particularly delicious ammunition dump and had a delightful time blowing it to h—l."

Led by First Lieutenant Robin Olds, the flight attacked the rectangular shaped, single story storage buildings, bombing and strafing the light colored storage facilities. There were 36 of them and it was later revealed that the explosive contained in the masonry buildings was old black powder, but it certainly was volatile. Lt. Olds, leading the attack, strafed some and then dropped his 250-lb. GP bomb on another, causing a tremendous explosion.

Continuing on, bombing and strafing, the flight managed to set 20-25 of the storage locations on fire, causing flames that went up to 1,500 feet and smoke that went up to 10,000 feet. The aircraft flown by both Lt. Olds and by Second Lieutenant George W. Gleason were damaged by the attack. Lt. Olds suffered quite a lot of flak damage, while Lt. Gleason came home with a number of rocks he had picked up. These were blown into the air by the large explosion caused by Lt. Olds. By far though, the pilot whose plane suffered the worst damage during the attack was Second Lieutenant Flamm D. (Dee) Harper. Lt. Harper, having previously been a spare at the start of the mission, had joined Blue Flight replacing Second Lieutenant Marden L. McArthur who suffered a mishap. Just prior to mission take off, Lt. McArthur had run off the perimeter taxiway and into a ditch when the right brake failed on the P-38 (L2-Y) he was to fly.

Lt. Harper was immediately behind Lt. Olds and in front of Lt. Gleason when Lt. Olds caused the large explosion with his 250-lb. bomb. Lt. Gleason described the moments during the attack and after, in his statement concerning the action:

The P-38 Second Lieutenant Marden L. McArthur went into a ditch with. The plane was the A/C that Lieutenant Harold F. (Bud) Grenning usually flew and had named No Guts? By now though, the artwork on the plane's nose had been worn off. *Courtesy of Clarence M. Surges.*

"Lt. Harper was in the middle of the explosion from the ammunition dump and I was immediately behind him. His right engine began to smoke and he feathered it up. He also was not getting any power from his left engine, but he had the airplane under perfect control and bellied it in a field. After the plane stopped, Lt. Harper jumped out of the cockpit and ran towards the nearest woods."

That simple version does not even begin to tell the whole story. For that, I turn to Flamm Harper, the Second Lieutenant whose P-38 was forced down by the explosion he flew through.

Flamm states that when the explosion occurred in front of his P-38, he could see chunks of concrete from the storage building flying 200-300 feet into the air. His low-flying airplane became a wreck, flying through the debris. The right engine must have been struck by a large chunk of something, as it was tilted upwards and was on fire. The cockpit heating system was damaged and directing smoke from the burning engine right into his face. The left engine was vibrating badly, probably because of a damaged propeller. The canopy, with its bulletproof windscreen, had been ripped from the fuselage pod. His leather flight helmet had been torn off and he had suffered head injuries caused by the flying pieces. At this point, other members of the flight described Flamm's P-38 as tumbling or porpoising through the air. Minus his helmet and goggles, the tearing wind from the slipstream plus the combined effects of shock, smoke and blood in his eyes left Flamm barely able to see his wing tips and thus he had no idea of his position relative to the ground. He was flying blind! All he could think of was getting out of the doomed aircraft. He unlatched his seat belt and started to bail out. As he began raising up and leaning his upper torso out towards a wing, preparatory to exiting the plane, he realized that just before the explosion, he had been flying only 100 feet above the ground. Hauling himself back in, Flamm began to try and regain control of the P-38. His thoughts were of returning back north towards Wattisham. Unfortunately, he was heading south, had only one ailing engine and little or no control over his airplane. Seconds later, he made out some trees looming up ahead. It would only be a matter of a heartbeat or two before he hit the ground. Bracing himself for the impact, he grabbed the control wheel with both hands and cradled his head in his arms to protect himself during the crash. He was whipped around in the cockpit by the forces of the impact and crash, but surprisingly, wound up still holding the wheel when the plane stopped moving. This is especially amazing because he had not refastened his seat belt and shoulder harness after the bail out attempt.

Lieutenant Flamm D. (Dee) Harper. *Courtesy of Flamm D. Harper.*

Flamm had come down, as he puts it, through no efforts of his own, on the only clear, flat area in the vicinity. His P-38, seemingly guided by divine hands, had rolled into a steep bank, turned to the left, away from a river ahead and then rolled out, bellying in on a meadow alongside the La Gartempe River, near the village of Concise. A high clay bank alongside the river would have made survival of the crash impossible, had Flamm's airplane continued flying in the direction in which it had been headed. The turn had saved his life.

He immediately got out of the aircraft because of the danger of fire or an explosion. A young French girl named Jacqueline Thomas was standing at the edge of the meadow and motioning him to follow her. He was taken to her family's house where they exchanged his pilot's gear for civilian

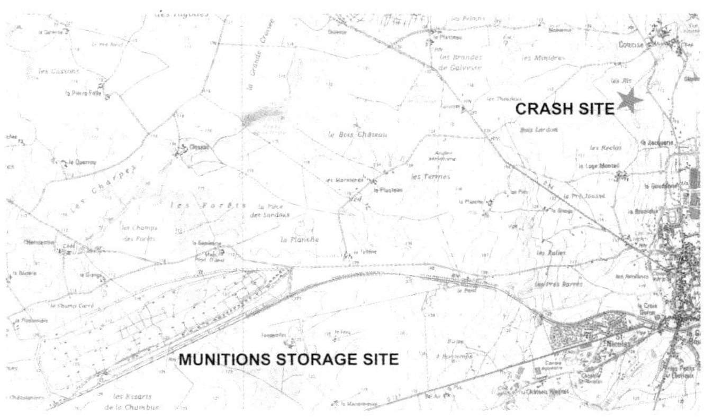

A map showing the locations of the munitions storage and Lieutenant Harper's crash site. *Courtesy of Flamm D. Harper.*

clothes. Her father Henri then took Flamm on a "little fishing trip" up the river. Carrying fishing poles, the two began to work their way upstream to a safe place by giving the appearance of being two fishermen out for the day on the river. Passing through and eluding both German troops and the French Vichy militia who were both looking for the pilot of the downed plane, the two arrived at a cave where Flamm was to hide. Meanwhile, Henri's wife drove to find some Maquis (French resistance fighters) to tell them where Flamm was to be hidden. Later that afternoon, he was met in the cave by a group of armed Frenchmen and taken to the village of Asnieres-sur-Blour and into a small café/bar where he spent the evening amidst total strangers who seemed to be having a great time. Not understanding why he was there, Flamm could not relax. Furthermore, he had very little comprehension of what was taking place due to the language barrier. He began to entertain the idea of escaping, feeling he had fallen into the wrong hands. Fortunately, no opportunity presented itself for him to run and later that evening he was taken to a large farmhouse where he was turned over to a English officer, a Captain Tonkin, who was the commander of a Special Air Service (SAS) detachment located in the area. The SAS detachment was operating behind enemy lines and had been parachuted in several weeks before the invasion at Normandy to disrupt German troop and supply movements toward the beachhead. During an intense grilling by Capt. Tonkin, it was determined through a Frenchman who had seen Flamm crash and leave his plane, that Flamm was who he said he was and not a German infiltrator. At Capt. Tonkin's request, Flamm remained at the farmhouse overnight. The next morning Flamm finally had a chance to clean up after a good night's sleep. His face was in bad shape from the ordeal and was still covered with blood. After doing the best he could with that, he was fed a good breakfast.

Shortly thereafter, the SAS officer returned by car and took Flamm with him, back to his camp, which was hidden in a forest. There were twenty men there, all a part of the detachment. They were well supplied and even had several civilian automobiles as well as four American jeeps. All sported Lewis .303 caliber machine guns protruding through the passenger's side of the windshield.

That afternoon, Capt. Tonkin explained to Flamm the nature of their operations. He also told Flamm that at the time there was no way to get him out of the country and back to his unit. Flamm was given a choice of going into hiding and waiting for the allies to overrun his location so that he might return safely, or remaining with the detachment strictly as a "guest" for as long as they remained in the area, or joining the SAS as a working member and participating in their activities. It was further explained to him, that as a member of the detachment, it was doubtful that the Geneva Convention agreements on the treatment of prisoners of warfare would apply to them and that members of the SAS had a price put upon their heads by the German leader Adolph Hitler. The fact was, they were wanted men, dead or alive. Hitler had issued orders that amongst other things, stated that "...all enemies on so-called commando missions, even if they are to all appearances, soldiers in uniform or demolition troops, whether armed or unarmed, in battle or in flight, are to be slaughtered to the last man." Flamm chose to become a full-fledged member and was issued a British uniform and weapons. Receiving treatment in the form of a French doctor pouring Schnapps over his head wounds the next day, life with the SAS began.

Lt. Harper standing on the right side of Captain Maingard's "commando car". Three of the SAS troopers are pictured with him. *Courtesy of Flamm D. Harper.*

An example of the type operation Flamm played a part in occurred the night of 20 July. Reports of a large number of locomotives stuck at the Poitiers railway yard were acted upon by the unit when pressure operated mines were placed upon the Poitiers to Bordeaux rails. The Germans were on to that little trick however, and the mines were brushed away by trains equipped with special sweepers mounted in front of the train engine. The next night, Flamm accompanied two other SAS troopers, Captain Ford and Sergeant Brown, as they went out to mine a rail bridge on the same line. They installed manually operated detonators and when a train approached the bridge, the men set the explosives off, destroying the bridge. They had hoped the train would not be able to stop in time and roll into the ravine below the bridge. Unfortunately, only the front part of the train plunged off the edge. The remainder of the

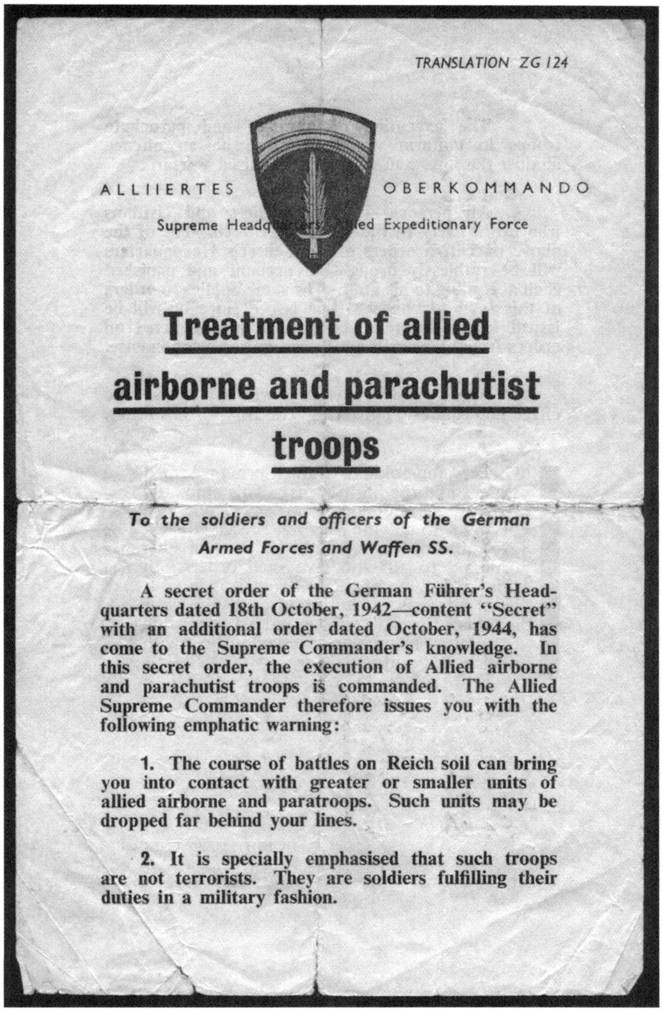

TRANSLATION ZG 124

ALLIIERTES OBERKOMMANDO

Supreme Headquarters Allied Expeditionary Force

Treatment of allied airborne and parachutist troops

To the soldiers and officers of the German Armed Forces and Waffen SS.

A secret order of the German Führer's Headquarters dated 18th October, 1942—content "Secret" with an additional order dated October, 1944, has come to the Supreme Commander's knowledge. In this secret order, the execution of Allied airborne and parachutist troops is commanded. The Allied Supreme Commander therefore issues you with the following emphatic warning:

1. The course of battles on Reich soil can bring you into contact with greater or smaller units of allied airborne and paratroops. Such units may be dropped far behind your lines.

2. It is specially emphasised that such troops are not terrorists. They are soldiers fulfilling their duties in a military fashion.

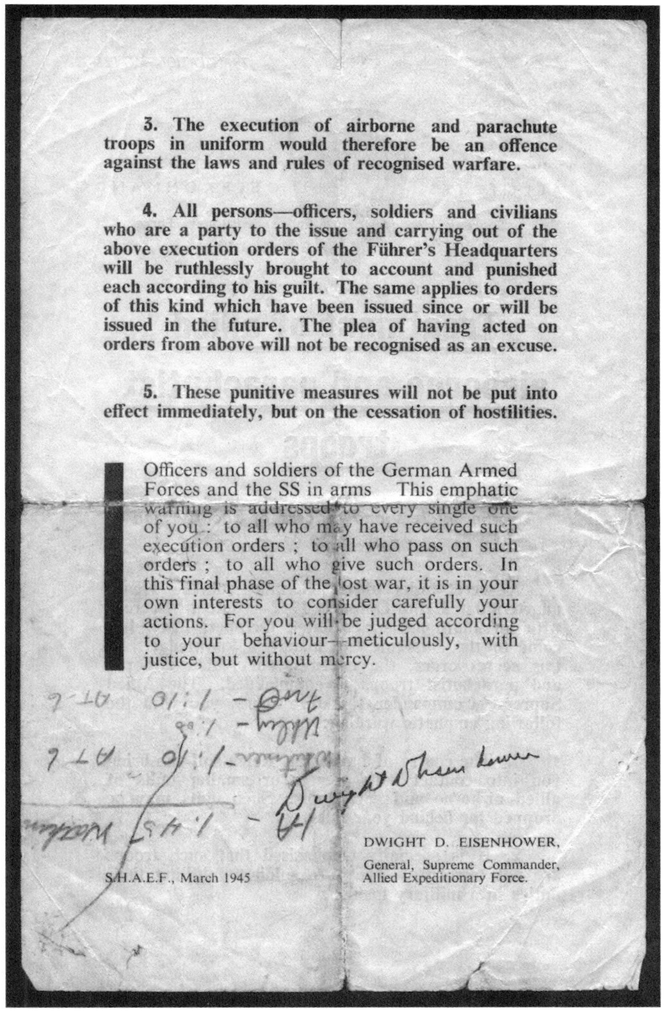

3. The execution of airborne and parachute troops in uniform would therefore be an offence against the laws and rules of recognised warfare.

4. All persons—officers, soldiers and civilians who are a party to the issue and carrying out of the above execution orders of the Führer's Headquarters will be ruthlessly brought to account and punished each according to his guilt. The same applies to orders of this kind which have been issued since or will be issued in the future. The plea of having acted on orders from above will not be recognised as an excuse.

5. These punitive measures will not be put into effect immediately, but on the cessation of hostilities.

Officers and soldiers of the German Armed Forces and the SS in arms This emphatic warning is addressed to every single one of you: to all who may have received such execution orders; to all who pass on such orders; to all who give such orders. In this final phase of the lost war, it is in your own interests to consider carefully your actions. For you will be judged according to your behaviour—meticulously, with justice, but without mercy.

DWIGHT D. EISENHOWER,
General, Supreme Commander,
Allied Expeditionary Force.

S.H.A.E.F., March 1945

Front and back of a leaflet dropped in occupied territories. One of many, its purpose was to counter Hitler's death order. *Courtesy of Robert H. Horman.*

train did not fall and the last coaches were full of German troops who swarmed out. An uneven firefight began and Flamm was introduced to night fighting. He found it very scary and decided that he would rather do his shooting from a nice cozy fighter cockpit. The three men rapidly exited the area and made good their escape.

He participated in their operations under the auspices of the British Army's Operation BULBASKET for a total of twenty-two days and his true story is rich in material that rivals the best fiction of similar genre. After his over three weeks in the field with the SAS detachment, Flamm Harper was returned to England, flying out the evening of August 6, 1944 with other allied personnel going back. They left from an airstrip that Flamm had recently helped gouge from the earth near Bon-Bon.

After a month of debriefings, Flamm eventually was able to return to the 479th Fighter Group. He arrived back in early September, but was not allowed to participate in combat. He later returned to the U.S.

The 434th FS tallied an impressive total of destroyed and damaged targets of a tactical nature. There were railroad cars, goods wagons, switch houses, railway stations, sections of rail line, an oil tank, a water tower, electric power stations, high-tension power lines, bridges, a dam, a flak tower, a mine and a factory that Lieutenant James E. Fleming caused a lot of destruction to. Lt. Fleming attacked an "L-shaped" factory that he said was six to eight stories high and had two wings that were 200-300 feet long. He strafed the factory and then dropped his 250-lb. GP bomb from about 25 feet above the factory. A high column of smoke arose from the exploding bomb and about three minutes later, the area of the hit was engulfed in flames and smoke. When last seen, flames had covered the junction of the two wings as well as a third of each wing.

The 435th FS fared well also, having destroyed and damaged targets that included a locomotive, bridges, a staff car, a power station, high-tension power lines, a mill, oil tanks, radio towers, a dam and a flak tower.

The squadrons reformed east of Sanceces at 1950 hrs./ 14,000 feet, to leave the area. According to First Lieutenant John W. Hedenberg, "The flak was wicked over Le Havre and Caen. They were shooting through the overcast with the aid of radar. Those gunners know their stuff!" L/O was over the Bayeaux area at 2000 hrs./10,000 ft. Arriving back home, the 436th FS suffered the loss of an aircraft. Second Lieutenant Frederick M. Mead had to crash-land his P-38 in a grain field. He came to rest near a wooded area, just a few miles southwest of Canterbury. The plane did not burn and Lt. Mead was out of the aircraft and walking away from it in a matter of moments. His generator had gone out while he was still over the continent and then his fuel gave out as he was trying to get home. The plane was demolished, but Lt. Mead only suffered minor cuts and bruises.

16 July 1944

VIII FC FO 450

No. 98 Sunday. Maj. Herren led the 434th FS, which consisted of 16 P-38s, four of which were relays, Maj. Glover led the 435th FS, which consisted of 15 P-38s and Maj. Monahan led the 436th FS, which consisted of 16 P-38s. Their assignment was a bomber escort for withdrawing 1st and 3rd BD B-17s that had attacked their 8th AF Mission 476 targets in the Stuttgart and Munich, Germany areas. 434th FS up: 0902 hrs., down: 1313 hrs. with three early returns. 435th FS up: 0914 hrs., down: 1335 hrs. with one early return and one escort for him. 436th FS up: 0910 hrs., down: 1345 hrs. with one early return.

L/F was in the Ostend, Belgium area at about 0950 hrs. Heading southeast into the lower Ruhr Valley area, the returning B-17s were picked up at various points by the different squadrons. The 434th FS made R/V with their assigned 3rd BD bombers 25 minutes early and north of their course, at 1024 hrs. in the vicinity of Saarlouis, Germany. One flight was dispatched to stay with them while the other two flights went on to R/V with the other 1st BD B-17s near

The work crew and one of the Jeeps used to clear airstrip. Lt. Harper is shown leaning on the right fender. *Courtesy of Flamm D. Harper.*

Haslach at 1050 hrs. The escorts went without a problem and the bombers were left over Schouwen Island, Holland. The 435th FS was also assigned to escort 3rd BD B-17s and met them early at 1035 hrs. in the same vicinity as the 434th met theirs. They had nine to twelve boxes of bombers to look after. At 1300 hours, bomber "F" for Frank was heard to say he was ditching off Schouwen Island. The location was unknown, but was believed to be along the course. One of the relays also heard the call and gave the "May Day" that went out. Relay "K" for King circled the location, but was unable to get Colgate (65th FW) on the radio at the time. The relay could not remain on station because his gas was getting low and one engine was out.

The 436th had an uneventful escort. R/V was near Schweighausen at 1044 hrs./20,000 ft. Most of their time was spent escorting stragglers back to the main formation. L/O and break away for them was over Schouwen Island at 1300 hrs./20,000 ft.

There were no observations from the mission reported and flak was only noted in the Antwerp and Brussels, Belgium areas where it was heavy, meager to intense and accurate. The 434th FS history records the mission as "a Milk Run".

17 July 1944

VIII FC FO 451

No. 99 Monday. Lt. Col. Riddle was the group's leader and he also led the 434th FS, which consisted of 16 P-38s. Maj. Glover led the 435th FS, which consisted of 16 P-38s. The 436th FS put up 17 P-38s, but the squadron's leader is unknown. Their assignment was a MEW controlled patrol in support of 8th AF Mission 478. 434th FS up: 1020 hrs., down: 1415 hrs. with one early return. 435th FS up: 1025 hrs., down: 1427 hrs. with no early returns. 436th FS up: 1015 hrs., down: 1430 hrs. with one early return.

The 434 and 436th FSs made L/F over Nieuport, Belgium about 1100 hrs./11,000 ft. The 435th FS came in over Ostend, Belgium at 1108 hrs. Heading to their assigned area in the vicinity of St. Pol, France, the squadrons patrolled from 1115 until 1330 hours, at which time they headed for L/O between Dunkerque, France and Ostend at 1345 hrs.

Observations made during the mission included: Noting the airfields and construction activity at those airfields located at Drucat and Criel in France. At Criel, it was noted there were approximately 50 camouflage nets that could have been hiding A/C. A possible V1 Buzz Bomb sight was spotted in the same vicinity. Flak over Nieuport was heavy, meager and inaccurate.

434th FS line chief Master Sergeant James W. Smart getting into the second P-38 Lieutenant Harold F. Grenning flew. *Courtesy of James W. Smart.*

18 July 1944

VIII FC FO 454

No. 100 Tuesday. Maj. Herren was the group's leader and he also led the 434th FS, which consisted of 15 P-38s. Capt. Carter led the 435th FS, which consisted of 16 P-38s and Capt. Galloway led the 436th FS, which consisted of 16 P-38s. Their assignment was a bomber escort for withdrawing 1st BD B-17s that had attacked their 8th AF Mission 481 targets at Peenemünde, Germany, the Baltic development and test site for rocket propelled weapons. 434th FS up: 0752 hrs., down: 1300 hrs. with one early return. 435th FS up: 0758 hrs., down: 1306 hrs. with three early returns. 436th FS up: 0752 hrs., down: 1315 hrs. with no early returns.

The squadrons left England behind at Great Yarmouth and proceeded up the North Sea, crossing into northern Germany over the Friesische Islands, in the vicinity of Amrum at 0935 hrs. Passing south of Flensburg and over Kiel, they headed east-southeast to R/V at 1030 hrs./20,000 ft. with the B-17s in the area between Dierhagen on the coast, to Demmin, southeast of that location. Their assigned Big Friends were picked up by each of the squadrons and were uneventfully shepherded back out, making L/O at 1115 hrs. The route home was similar to that taken in and the squadrons broke away from their charges approximately 80 miles northeast of Cromer, England at 1230 hrs. The mission itself was uneventful, but it was the group's longest mission so far and pilots logged in over five-and-a-half hours of flight time.

Overcast prevented any observations during the mission. Flak over the Flensburg, Kiel and Heide areas was heavy, intense and accurate, forcing evasive action in some cases.

Sustineo Alas – "I sustain the wings". The photographs above and on the next page serve to illustrate those great guys who kept 'em flying.

19 July 1944

VIII FC FO 456

No. 101 Wednesday. Lt. Col. Riddle was the group's leader and he also led the 435th FS, which consisted of 17 P-38s. Maj. Herren led the 434th FS, which consisted of 16 P-38s and Maj. Monahan led the 436th FS, which consisted of 17 P-38s. Their assignment was a penetration to target and withdrawal escort for B-24s attacking their 8th AF Mission 482 targets in western Germany. 434th FS up: 0746 hrs., down: 1310 hrs. with five early returns. 435th FS up: 0730 hrs., down: 1255 hrs. with three early returns plus one escort. 436th FS up: 0745 hrs., down: 1305 hrs. with one early return.

L/F for the squadrons was between Blankenberghe and Ostend, Belgium at 0822 hrs./20,000 ft. Beyond this point, no further report can be given for the activities of the 434th FS because the records are illegible. Heading in southeast, the 436th FS intercepted several calls in the vicinity of Saarbrücken

Left: 435th FS pilot Lieutenant Philip D. Gossard with his armorer Private First Class John P. Clodfelter, crew chief William M. Samples and assistant crew chief Corporal Sergeant Denver T. Susong. *Courtesy of Carol Donaldson*. Right: 436th FS crew chief J. T. Richardson by his charge. *Courtesy of J. T. Richardson*.

at 0912 hrs. There were reports that bombers were being bounced south of Schweinfurt and one call for the same, near their R/V point. All locations were searched, but the results were negative. The group made R/V with their assigned bombers over Babenhausen at 0945 hrs./20,000 ft. and watched the target being struck a few minutes later at 0949 hrs. Results were not observed due to heavy smoke and dust clouds covering the area. On the way out, the 436th FS observed a B-17 heading west and on the deck, make a sharp turn south while over Ulm. It was thought the bomber was heading for Switzerland. Continuing out, the Big Friends were left on their own over the Dutch Islands, near Schouwen at 1225 hrs./20,000 ft. The 436th FS did stay with one B-17 that was escorted to England.

Observations made during the mission included: Several camouflaged airfields were seen in Belgium. Flak over Namur, south of Aachen and at Karlshue was heavy, intense and accurate.

20 July 1944

VIII FC FO 457

No. 102 Thursday. Lt. Col. Woods was the group's leader and he also led the 434th FS, which consisted of 17 P-38s. Capt. Courtney led the 435th FS, which consisted of 16 P-38s and Capt. Galloway led the 436th FS, which consisted of 18 P-38s. Their assignment was a bomber escort for withdrawing 1st BD B-17s that had attacked their 8th AF Mission 484 targets at Leipzig, Germany. 434th FS up: 0930 hrs., down: 1457 hrs. with no early returns. 435th FS up: 0953 hrs., down: 1435 hrs. with two early returns. 436th FS up: 0940 hrs., down: 1510 hrs. with three early returns.

L/F for the 434th FS was south of Haarlem, Holland at 1030 hrs./20,000 ft. The squadron received heavy, moderate and inaccurate flak there. Traveling east, the weather was 3-5/10ths cloud coverage all the way to the target area at Leipzig, where the bombers were picked up at 1147 hrs. The bombing results looked good and heavy smoke and many fires were observed. The squadron saw a B-17 receive a direct flak hit in the target area and dive straight down out of sight. No parachutes were observed. P-51s were also seen in the area. Another B-17, with its right outboard engine on fire, was observed southeast of the target area. The bomber flew on as the fire burned for three or four minutes until the flames finally burned through the plane's wing and the B-17 exploded in mid-air. Again, no parachutes were seen to come from the aircraft. The Big Friends were scattered amongst the clouds and ranged in altitudes from 10,000 ft. to down on the deck, but the squadron escorted them all the way back to England.

The 435th crossed in over the Dutch town of Volkenburg at 1036 hrs./21,000 ft. Flying east into Germany and past Münster and Paderborn, they made R/V west of Leipzig, in the area of Artern, Germany at 1131 hrs./24,000 ft. Joining with at least six boxes of "Triangle First Division" B-17s, it was noted that the bomber's formation was good, with only a few stragglers. Flak was heavy, intense and accurate along the route, but the mission was uneventful for the squadron and their charges were brought through the target and out, passing over Schouwen Island, Holland at 1345 hrs./20,000 ft. Another bomber formation, Vinegrove 1-1, was heard calling for help, but they were north of Gotha, Germany and out of reach.

L/F for the 436th FS was over Katwijk aan Zee at 1040 hrs./18,000 ft. Following the same general route that the 435th flew, they also made R/V with their assigned bombers near Artern at 1135 hrs./23,000 ft. The bombers that the 436th FS was assigned to protect were scattered at R/V. One B-17 marked with the letter "K" inside the triangle on its tail and the letter "F" below the triangle (379th BG) was escorted from the R/V to Aldenhoven, near the German/Belgian border. The bomber was left there at 1330 hrs./17,000 feet, apparently alright. Another three B-17s with triangle markings on their tails were escorted from Treis, south of Koblenz, Germany to the Antwerp, Belgium area, where two of them were left. Escort of the third continued as one of its engines was shut down and had its prop feathered plus another engine/prop was "windmilling". The Big Friend was taken to Woodbridge, England where he was left at 1450 hrs./6,000 ft. This bomber was identified as having the letters "SCH" under the triangle. The rest of the bombers were taken to a point 35 miles east of Felixstowe, England where they were broken away from at 1335 hrs./17,000 ft.

The only observation made during the mission was the somber note of an empty dinghy sighted eight miles east of Oxford Ness, England.

A practice mission utilizing the group's newly acquired P-38 Droop Snoots was also run today. This version of the big Lockheed fighter involved removal of all weaponry and associated equipment found in the plane's nose section, removal of the forward section of the nose and its replacement with a Plexiglas nose similar to that of a B-17G bomber. Additional modifications allowed for a bombsight to be placed in the nose and an additional crewmember to operate it. The Droop Snoot flew as lead during a bombing run and all other aircraft dropped their bombs on its signal. The results of the practice mission were reported as excellent. While use of the modified P-38s enabled the regular P-38s to carry two 1,000-lb. bombs each and perform daylight precision bombing attacks similar to their Big Friends, the aircraft were also handy to take rides about the country in. They were much more comfortable than the "Piggy-Backs" the group already had.

One of the P-38 Droop Snoots that the group had.This NMF one was assigned to the 434th FS. *From original 479th FG history.*

This OD finished Droop Snoot belonged to either the 435th FS or the 436th FS. *From original 479th FG history.*

21 July 1944

VIII FC FO 458

No. 103 & 104 Friday. The group was divided into two forces, A and B groups. Lt. Col. Riddle led A group, which consisted of 24 P-38s (8-434th FS & 16-435th FS). Maj. John D. Monahan led B group, which consisted of 26 P-38s (8-434th FS & 18-436th FS). Their assignments were penetration to target and withdrawal escorts for 1st and 3rd BD B-17s attacking their 8th AF Mission 486 targets in Germany – the ball bearing and under carriage works at Schweinfurt, as well as the Kugelfischer Schweinfurt ball bearing works at Bamberg. A group up: 0805 hrs., down: 1329 hrs. with no early returns. B group up: 0813 hrs., down: 1400 hrs. with two early returns.

L/F for A group was over Ostend, Belgium at 0843 hrs./ 24,000 ft. Heading east, the group made R/V with their assigned three boxes of 1st BD B-17s near Homburg at 0945 hrs./24,000 ft. Turning southeast, A group escorted the bombers through the target at Schweinfurt where the bombing results were seen as excellent with a very good bombing pattern. The loss of one B-17 was observed as it was noted to spin down, then explode due to the heavy, intense and accurate flak over the city.

The flak continued to follow the fighter-bomber force as it withdrew from the target and headed back home. It had been the same going in, with both heavy and light flak present almost continually, the whole route. Two pilots from the 434th FS, Captain Jack G. Grossenbacher and his wingman, Second Lieutenant Richard G. Simpson, had left the formation and were escorting a crippled B-17 home. They were north west of Frankfurt, Germany when Capt. Grossenbacher noted his oxygen was growing low. Capt. Grossenbacher radioed Lt. Simpson, instructing him to join his wing and begin descending to a lower level. Lt. Simpson did so and on a course of 280-290 degrees, the two let down to 9,000 ft. They passed over the small town of Kindsbach, Germany, weaving as they went, because of the flak everyone had been receiving the entire trip. The hostile fire claimed another victim as Lt. Simpson saw Capt. Grossenbachers P-38 take what appeared to be a direct hit in the nose nacelle. Lt. Simpson pulled up and to the left of the Captain, where there were a few scattered clouds. Five or ten seconds later, Lt. Simpson rolled over on his side to check on Capt. Grossenbacher. He noted a parachute to partially open, then become hung up on the planes tail assembly. The flak was very hot in the area, forcing Lt. Simpson to leave. For this reason and the fact that visibility was bad, he was not able to determine if Capt. Grossenbacher got out of the damaged P-38. Lt. Simpson climbed to 19,000 ft. and began the long, lonely journey home, flying solo. He later reported that it might have been possible for Capt. Grossenbacher to have untangled himself from the tail, but very improbable. Unfortunately, Capt. Grossenbacher failed to free himself from his P-38. Some field workers recovered his body from a thorn bush on 15 August 1944, about a quarter mile from where his plane crashed. Evidence indicated he had been thrown from the plane as it crashed.

The remainder of A group finished escort of the bombers, crossing over the Dutch Isles at 1249 hrs./17,000 ft. The P-38s broke from the B-17s over the North Sea and went home.

After L/F over Ostend, Belgium at 0855 hrs./17,000 ft. B group found their assigned 1st and 3rd BD bombers, making R/V in the Mannheim, Germany area at 1015 hrs./26,000 ft. The group took their bombers to the Bamberg area, but scattered clouds covered the target, preventing the attack. Separating into smaller forces, the bomber boys said they would take targets of opportunity on the way back home. So it was and L/O was scattered from Ostend to Katwijk aan Zee, Holland between the hours of 1235 to 1310 and 10-15,000 ft. Break away was anywhere between Aachen, Germany to the English coast from 1200 to 1330 hrs.

Three P-38 Pathfinders possibly photographed at Wattisham, but the actual location is unknown. The picture is included because the specially modified Lightning was rarely seen in England. These three were part of only a hand full in the UK. The model, a P-38L with a H2X radarscope, was adapted to carry both a pilot and a radar operator. It was to be employed as the lead aircraft in any bomber or fighter-bomber formation attacking a target obscured by weather conditions. *Courtesy of Arnold G. Helding.*

Observations made during this portion of the mission included: Barges and freighters were sighted in the North Sea southeast of Walcheren Island and four red unidentified objects seen on an airdrome east of Antwerp, Belgium. Heavy, intense and accurate flak shot up through the overcast, followed this group.

24 July 1944

VIII FC FO 461

No. 105 Monday. Maj. Glover was the group's leader and he also led the 435th FS, which consisted of 15 P-38s. Maj. Jeffrey led the 434th FS, which consisted of 15 P-38s plus one P-38 relay. Capt. Galloway led the 436th FS, which consisted of 15 P-38s. Their assignment was an area patrol in support of bombers attacking their 8th AF Mission 492 tactical targets in the St. Lô area of France. The targets were German positions facing American troops near St. Lô. 434th FS up: 1041 hrs., down: 1416 hrs. with no early returns. 435th FS up: 1040 hrs., down: 1418 hrs. with two early returns. 436th FS up: 1033 hrs., down: 1410 hrs. with two early returns.

The weather did not cooperate during this mission. Clouds covered much of the area and prevented many of the bombers from striking their objectives. Undercast with tops reaching 6,900 ft. was reported. An accidental release by a lead bombardier caused another twelve aircraft to follow and drop their bombs off the target and on American ground forces nearby. Sixteen were killed and another sixty were wounded. L/F over France was between St. Valery-en-Caux and Dieppe for the squadrons. Crossing in between 1140-1145 hrs./17-20,000 ft. and continuing south, they reached their assigned patrol area at 1150 hrs./17-18,000 ft. Fanning out, the squadrons covered the area bounded by Rouen, Évreux, Verneuil and Lisieux, with the 435th going as far south as Chartres. The patrol was not uneventful, for Colgate (65th FW) vectored the 435th FS to bogies approximately 40 miles southwest of Évreux. There, the squadron was bounced by a single Me 109, as about 20 more 109s remained above. The Me 109 attacked the tail end man in the last flight, Second Lieutenant Alexander Evanenko. Captain William M. Gates saw the E/A on Lt. Evanenko's tail and told him twice to break to the left, but the Lieutenant failed to respond. Lt. Evanenko finally did roll over on his back and split-ess away, but by then his P-38 had suffered engine and instrument damage. He set a course for home on one engine. Capt. Gates followed in an attempt to join up, but never could pick Lt. Evanenko up on the designated safe course home. All attempts by the Captain to radio Lt. Evanenko were in vain. Air Sea Rescue later reported that Lt. Evanenko had been in contact with them, had crossed out over the channel at 1325 hrs. near Le Tréport, France and was vectored to Manston, England. A plot kept by A/S Rescue indicated that Lt. Evanenko kept bearing to the left of his course. When he was asked that if he wanted a land point closer, his response was yes, so he was vectored to Dungeness, Eng. He was above the overcast and when he was asked if he could orbit below the clouds, he replied he could not due to the loss of his instruments. He eventually did come out of the overcast at 2,500 feet, but kept bearing to the left, in the direction of Beachy Head, England. Lt. Evanenko's radio transmissions became weak with the last contact being made at 1343 hrs. He should have been over land at that point, but was never heard from again. It was believed he tried to orbit and spun into the channel just short of Beachy Head, England.

Captain William M. Gates by the P-38 he flew, Swanee Jr. *Courtesy of Clarence G. Haynes.*

Captain John A. Sullivan, a 436th pilot, was leading Lakeside (435th FS) Yellow Section when they were vectored to the area southwest of Évreux. In sending them, the controller stated that E/A were forming in the area. As the squadron arrived at the vectored location, the controller radioed again, notifying the squadron that the E/A had seen the oncoming fighters. The squadron's flights began circling and gaining altitude. The 436th FS flying as top cover, called the 435th pilots, telling them that an enemy fighter was bouncing Red Flight, the last flight in the Lakeside squadron. Lakeside Leader, Maj. Glover started a sharp turn to the left, but spotted 15-20 single-engine fighters above and to the right of the squadron. They were in a perfect position for attack if the squadron continued its turn. Therefore, Lakeside Leader deferred to Red Leader, depending on him to turn into the single enemy fighter while he, Lakeside Leader and the remainder of the squadron, kept the larger number covered. Red Leader did not turn into the oncoming fighter. When it got nearly within range, Capt. Sullivan made a sharp break inside White Leader to make a head-on pass at the Me 109. While he was about 500 yards from the E/A, which was still shooting at Red Four, Second Lt. Evanenko, the two planes broke apart. Lt. Evanenko spit-essed to the right (see above description of this action) and the E/A broke to the left, right into Capt. Sullivan's line of flight. In the sudden break, the Me 109 stalled out in a vertical bank, immediately in front of the Captain. He fired a short burst at about 200 yards and was about to get on the 109's tail when four P-38s dove through the formation and forced Capt. Sullivan to break off his attack in order to avoid a collision. The Me 109 had been hit, was smoking and had fallen off into a spin immediately after Capt. Sullivan's attack. He claimed one Me 109 damaged.

Two 436th FS P-38s became involved in a mid-air collision at this point. Captain Thomas T. Galloway, the B group leader had brought his flight up behind the attacking Me 109. Being directly astern of the E/A when it broke up and to the left, Capt. Galloway and his wingman, Second Lieutenant Neil W. Kemper collided in the confusion of too many planes after the lone Me 109. Both P-38s went spinning down, side by side in a flat spin. Capt. Galloway was killed, as a result of the collision while Lt. Kemper was able to bail out after a delayed jump. Upon landing, Lt. Kemper was immediately taken in by members of the French resistance. The Maquis kept him hidden from the Germans until he could be returned to allied forces in August.

Two other 436th pilots had joined in the attack on the Me 109 and between the two, the E/A was shot down. Second Lieutenants Hans J. Grasshoff and Henry P. (Porter) Plunk tackled the escaping E/A. Lt. Grasshoff got a deflection shot at the 109, seeing definite hits on the E/A's wing and fuselage, before the elusive enemy pilot split-essed away. Lt. Grasshoff caught up to the plane again, but by this time Lt. Plunk was on the Me 109's tail. Both began shooting at the E/A, Lt. Plunk from dead astern and Lt. Grasshoff from ten-degrees deflection. The enemy pilots auxiliary fuel tank on the belly of the plane finally exploded and at that point, the German pilot bailed out. The chase had begun around 1300 hrs. at 18,000 ft. and finished down at 8,000 ft. Oil from the damaged enemy fighter coated Lt. Plunk's windshield and obscured his vision for a while.

At a later date, former Lieutenant Porter Plunk supplied more details to his above-described combat with an Me 109. He recalled the enemy plane disintegrated in a mass of flame and oil from his victim covered his windshield. However, just before his vision was totally obscured, he saw the pilot emerge from the 109's cockpit and Lt. Plunk assumed the enemy pilot had successfully bailed out. Later intelligence reports noted that the pilot's body had been found in the area that the combat took place. The German pilot had never gotten the chance to open his parachute. He had left the protection of the armor plating behind his seat and jumped into the gunfire from Porter's P-38.

Oil, which coated Lt. Plunk's windshield, had cut off visibility from his cockpit and threatened to make the trip back to Wattisham difficult. He cut back on his engine throttles and reduced his airspeed to just above stalling. Rolling down one of his side windows, he reached out and wiped a small patch of his canopy, clearing it so he could see forward. That accomplished, and the side window back up, he advanced the throttles and headed out of the area, back to home base. He hoped there were none of the Me 109 pilot's friends around.

Having returned to England, Lt. Plunk decided to put down at the first airfield he could find and was directed to Manston, a huge emergency complex for damaged returning aircraft. The field had seen the landing and crash landing of a great many aircraft and was well equipped to handle any emergency. On this occasion however, no crash crew was required as Lt. Plunk made a safe landing. Having gotten his ship cleaned and gassed up, he continued on to Wattisham.

Captain Glenn Miller and his band at Wattisham/Hitcham. *Courtesy of Roger Barrell.*

L/O for the two groups occurred in the same general area as L/F. Time out was around 1330 hrs.

The only observation recorded from the mission was that of a B-24 seen to explode as the result of flak, approximately 25 miles southeast of Vire, France. The bomber was hit at 21,000 ft. Black smoke and flames were seen, but no chutes were noted. Other than this incident, flak was nil in the patrol area.

Late in the afternoon, the celebrated bandleader Captain Glenn Miller brought his band, minus the strings who stayed behind for their regular Monday evening "Strings With Wings" radio broadcast, to Wattisham/Hitcham for a concert. (The American Band of the AEF had arrived at Gourock, Scotland via the liner *Queen Elizabeth* on 28 June 1944 and was transported to southern England by an overnight troop train, which departed Glasgow at 10:00 PM. The band arrived in London at 7:00 AM the next day, and from Euston Station there, they were trucked to their billet. Their trip was much like that of the 479th FG in its travels from the U.S. to Wattisham.) The band flew sixty miles from Twinwood Farm in six B-17s, flying almost wing tip to wing tip. This was the largest base the band had performed at so far in their tour and the assemblage was recorded as being over 10,000 people. The concert was at the Hitcham engine hangar and after the performance, the band had dinner at the base. About an hour before dark, the Miller group left and flew back to Twinwood Farm.

25 July 1944

VIII FC FO 462

No. 106 Tuesday. Lt. Col. Woods was the group's leader and he also led the 436th FS, which consisted of 17 P-38s. Maj. Herren led the 434th FS, which consisted of 16 P-38s and Capt. Sullivan led the 435th FS, which consisted of 17 P-38s. Their assignments were area patrols of France's Brest Peninsula, in support of bombers attacking their 8th AF Mission 494 tactical targets in the St. Lô area. German defense positions were again the object of the attack. 434th FS up: 0827 hrs., down: 1241 hrs. with no early returns. 435th FS up: 0825 hrs., down: 1253 hrs. with two early returns. 436th FS up: 0820 hrs., down: 1235 hrs. with one early return. Tragedy struck this day also, but on a larger scale. Despite even more safety precautions having been taken to prevent a happening such as what had occurred the previous day, three separate errors in bombing brought about the loss of 102 U.S. Army personnel killed. Among those was a Lieutenant General. The errant bombs wounded another 380 soldiers.

L/F for the squadrons was the area of St. Malo, at which point they spread out to patrol their assigned, overlapping areas. The overall area was roughly bounded by Avranches to the east of St. Malo, south to Antrain, southwest to Monfort, west to Carhaix-Plouguec and north to the coast above Lannion. The patrol was uneventful and L/O was between St. Malo and Avranches at 1115-1140 hrs.

Observations made during the mission included a fully-operating marshalling yard with many goods wagons, a partially camouflaged ammo dump near a woods, airdromes at Moncontour and Guincamp and large as well as small vessels anchored in the harbor at Grandville. The 435th FS reported seeing a P-47 that appeared to be in trouble, jettisoning its bomb load in the water between the Isle of Jersey and the Cherbourg Peninsula. Shortly afterwards the plane seemed okay. Both the 434th and the 436th FSs reported seeing explosions and smoke in the water at the same location that the bombs were dropped. Flak was heavy, intense and accurate over Alderney Island, while it was heavy moderate and inaccurate at Lamballe, 15 miles east of St. Brieuc.

26 July 1944

Wednesday. Capt. Benjamin H. King led two other P-38s from the 436th FS and a P-38 from the 434th FS on an Air Sea Rescue mission. Up: 1025 hrs., down: 1600 hrs. with one early return. They R/V'd with two RAF Warwicks over Cromer, England at 1045 hrs. Four P-51s accompanying another two Warwicks, also joined with them here. They flew northeast up the North Sea and searched an area off the western coast of Denmark. Fifteen fishing vessels flying the Danish flag were seen near Cromer, but nothing else was sighted.

27 July 1944

VIII FC FO 468

No. 107 Thursday. Maj. Herren was the group's leader and he also led the 434th FS, which consisted of 16 P-38s. Capt. Sykes led the 435th FS, which consisted of 18 P-38s and Capt. Harrell led the 436th FS, which consisted of 18 P-38s. Their assignment was a fighter-bomber attack on the rail system southeast to north of Paris, France in support of 8th AF Mission 499. 434th FS up: 1742 hrs., down: 1915 hrs. with no early returns. 435th FS up: 1745 hrs., down: 2050 hrs. with one early return. 436th FS up: 1741 hrs., down: 2030 hrs. with three early returns.

L/F for the squadrons was between Cayeux and a point east of Dieppe between 1835 and 1839 hrs./15-20,000 ft. The squadrons overshot their target area, which was bounded by Amiens, Compiègne and Mons. Recognizing the error, the 434th and 435th FSs went down on the deck at 1900 hrs. while the 436th attempted to provide top cover. The two attacking squadrons bombed and strafed targets of opportunity along rail lines, starting in the vicinity of Troyes and heading generally west and northwest to Amiens. Their 500-lb. GP bombs were put to good use as the list of destroyed and damaged is impressive. The destroyed tally ran: seven locomotives, 25 goods wagons, seven oil tank cars, a switch house, a rail junction, a factory, two high-tension towers and a truck. The damaged list included: an entire train, a flak train and its personnel, three passenger cars, a railroad station, a railroad watch tower, sections of track, four water towers, a building, two bridges, 27 flak towers and 17 high-tension towers. Along the route, some of the 434th FS pilots tried to work over an airdrome at Romilly. First Lieutenant Quentin S. Pavlock and his wingman, Second Lieutenant William H. Rodgers shared in a damaged claim for a Ju 88 they shot up at the drome. Flak was very intense so they did not stay around to finish it off. Flak from the same location accounted for the loss of Second Lieutenant Marden L. McArthur. His P-38 was hit in the left engine, which immediately caught fire. The plane began a slight climb, rolling to the right at the same time. Continuing the roll onto its back, the aircraft split-essed into the ground and exploded.

The 435th FS lost a pilot, too. Second Lieutenant William B. McKay was flying number three position in Red Flight, approximately 50 feet above the ground. His wingman, Second Lt. Ivan A. Ervin reported intermittent visual contact with his element leader, but stated that he had Lt. McKay in sight 12 of the 16 minutes that the squadron was on the deck. Weather was good and visibility was good, also. The terrain was hilly with many dips in it. The last time that Lt. Ervin saw his leader was in the vicinity of Ham. Second Lt. McKay was reported as missing, but in fact, the Germans claimed him as shot down by flak and killed in the crash of his P-38 near Ham.

The 436th FS was having such a difficult time providing top cover and keeping up with all the activity that they gave up and at 1910 hours, went down on the deck after targets for themselves. Starting about 20 miles east of Troyes and heading in a northwesterly direction, they attacked targets of opportunity for twenty minutes, finally climbing back up to altitude at Soissons. L/O was over Cayeux at 1955 hrs./17,000 ft.

The 434th FS made L/O at 1940 hrs. and the 435th FS crossed out near Calais at the same time, as did the 436th FS.

Observations made by the squadrons during the mission included: A camouflaged train was seen heading northwest from Melun as well as ten camouflaged trucks and a freight train with forty plus goods wagons were noted as parked on a siding near La Calle Sur Morin. Ten Me 109s attempted to engage a 434th FS P-38, eight to ten miles north of Paris, but the pilot, out of ammunition, avoided the attack by dodging into the clouds.

28 July 1944

VIII FC FO 469

No. 108 Friday. Lt. Col. Riddle was the group's leader and he also led the 434th FS, which consisted of 16 P-38s. Capt. Sykes led the 435th FS, which consisted of 12 P-38s and Maj. Monahan led the 436th FS, which consisted of 16 P-38s. Their assignment was a withdrawal escort for 1st BD B-17s having attacked their 8th AF Mission 501 primary target, the refineries at Merseburg/Luna, Germany. 434th FS up: 0854 hrs., down: 1304 hrs. with one early return. 435th FS up: 0845 hrs., down: 1315 hrs. with no early returns. 436th FS up: 0847 hrs., down: 1330 hrs. with no early returns.

L/F in for all three squadrons was near Ostend, Belgium between 0930 and 0935 hrs./16-19,000 ft. The predominant weather over the continent as well as in the R/V area was overcast with a few breaks through which the ground could be seen. The B-17s were on time, on course and their formation was reported as good. R/V occurred in the vicinity of Fulda, with the 434th FS picking up their assigned bombers at 1030 hrs./23,000 feet, the 435th getting to theirs at 1020 hrs./20,000 ft. and the 436th joining their Big Friends at 1025 hrs./21,000 ft. The escort was generally uneventful and once again, it was noted that the bomber formations were excellent with very few stragglers. Heading northwest and passing near Koblenz, Germany, between Liège, Belgium and Aachen, Germany, then into Holland, the escort continued. At 1210 hours, B-17 was seen to go down through the overcast in the Eindhoven, Holland area. It was later seen to be burning on the ground. No chutes were noted. L/O was over the Dutch islands of Overflakkee and Schouwen at 1220-1230 hrs./18-20,000 ft. Escort was broken at varying points along the way back, with the 436th persisting the longest. They broke away near Orford Ness, England at 1310 hrs./3,000 ft. They were almost to their own backyard!

While the group was away on this mission, the 436th FS suffered the loss of First Lieutenant Robert R. Teeter. As was most always the case, training was an ongoing process at Wattisham. On days when the group had no mission, training flights usually went out over England. The same was true for those days when there were missions to be flown. Those left behind often went out on training flights for various reasons. Lt. Teeter was killed making a transition flight in one of the group's newly acquired P-51s. After being in the air for about an hour, Lt. Teeter called for an emergency landing. Returning and lining up for landing, at about 300 feet in the air, he began lowering his landing gear. At this point his engine was heard to be running rough and missing. Continuing his approach, the engine lost most of its power and his aircraft began to stall out. The left wing caught the ground, causing the plane to cartwheel, catch fire and burn upon coming to rest.

Observations made by the squadrons during the mission included noting that the areas of Overflakkee as well as all, but the western tip of Schouwen were flooded. Eighty plus barges were seen in the Rhein River at Koblenz and ten plus barrage balloons were placed around a small lake near Koblenz. What appeared to be a landing strip that was being constructed

Right: Corporal Edward A. Tinker, Jr. beside Captain Arthur F. Jeffrey's regular mount, Boomerang, the aircraft he flew this day. *Courtesy of Frederick C. Hayner.*

Far right: Captain Arthur F. Jeffrey. *Courtesy of Clarence G. Haynes.*

was spotted on the beach ten miles northeast of Dunkerque, France. Flak was heavy, meager and inaccurate at Koblenz and at the Gilze Rijen Airdrome. It was heavy, intense and accurate at Liège and Aachen and heavy, moderate and inaccurate at Namur.

29 July 1944

VIII FC FO 470

No. 109 Saturday. Maj. Herren was the group's leader and he also led the 434th FS, which consisted of 17 P-38s. Maj. Glover led the 435th FS, which consisted of 11 P-38s and Capt. Biscayart led the 436th FS, which consisted of 18 P-38s. Their assignment was a penetration to target and withdrawal escort for 1st and 3rd BD B-17s attacking, for the second day in a row, their 8th AF Mission 503 primary target, the oil refineries at Merseburg/Luna, Germany. 434th FS up: 0735 hrs., down: 1304 hrs. with no early returns. 435th FS up: 0755 hrs., down: 1308 hrs. with two early returns. 436th FS up: 0740 hrs., down: 1250 hrs. with two early returns.

L/F for the squadrons was over the coast of Holland with the 434th FS taking a more northerly route, passing over Arnhem at 0837 hrs./18,000 ft. and the 435th FS plus the 436th FS, passing near Valkenburg about 0835 hrs./19-20,000 ft. Over Germany, the 434th FS picked up four or five boxes of 1st BD B-17s in the vicinity of the target at 0947 hrs./22,000 ft. The bomber boys were in good formation and happy, since they already had an escort of P-51s. The 435th FS R/V'd with their assigned 3rd BD B-17s east of Merseburg at 0935 hrs./22,000 ft. and the 436th FS got to their 3rd BD Big Friends over Sondershausen at 0943 hrs./23,000 ft. All three squadrons reported seeing B-17s being hit and going down near the target. The 435th FS saw three lost, with no chutes apparent from any of them. Bombing results were seen to be good, with large fires and towering columns of dense black smoke prevalent in the target area. The 436th observed a terrific flash within the target area at about 0955 hrs. One of their pilots stated that he even heard the sound of an explosion over the roar of his engine. This, from 21,000 feet!

On the return trip, Captain Arthur F. Jeffrey of the 434th FS, made history. He is given the credit for being the first pilot in the world to shoot down a rocket-propelled aircraft. The Allies had become aware of the existence of the German Me 163 Komet previously and had briefed their pilots to be alert to the fact that the rocket fighter would be making its presence known some time in the future. That time had come to pass on the previous day, 28 July 1944, when the first aircrew reports of the small fighters were received. ("*Wie ein Floh – aber oho*!" Just a Flea – but o-oh!) The very next day, Captain Jeffrey demonstrated that the speedy adversary was not invincible.

The following are reproduced reports concerning the historic event:

Combat report, 434th Fighter Squadron,
479th Fighter Group,
AAF, APO 657 Station F-977, 1 August 1944.

COMBAT REPORT

A. Type of action: aerial combat.

B. Date: 29 July 1944.
C. Unit: 434th Fighter Squadron, 479th Fighter Group (P-38).
D. Time of attack: 1145.
E. Location: over Wilhelmshaven, Germany.
F. Weather: Overcast, tops 3,000 feet, scattered high clouds.
G. Type of enemy aircraft: Me 163.
H. Enemy casualties: one Me 163.
I. Narrative:

I was leading Newcross Yellow Flight on a bomber escort mission under VIII Fighter Command Field Order Number 470. In the vicinity of the target area (Merseburg) the Group Leader dispatched my flight to escort a crippled Third Division B-17 home. My wingman and I acted as close cover, while Yellow Three and Four provided top cover. The B-17 plodded along at 11,000 feet, dodging holes in the overcast to keep out of flak, and at 1145, I observed an Me 163 in attack position behind it. Where the Me 163 came from, I don't know. I had been on "C" channel, trying to contact the bomber, so I didn't have time to call the bounce, but took out after him. The Me made a slight low side 5 o'clock pass on the B-17, followed through in slight dive, then leveled off. About this time the German must have seen me coming, because he made another slight dive, then started a very steep climb, weaving all the while, as though he were trying to see behind him. During this weaving, I closed with him, and opened fire, and observed strikes on the Me 163. At 15,000 feet the Me leveled off and started to circle to the left, as though positioning himself to attack me. I could turn tighter than he, as I got in a good deflection shot, with the closest range estimated to be 200-300 yards. Then the Me did a mild split-ess and spiraled off in an 80-90-degree dive. I followed, firing as long as I had him in range, observing strikes. During this dive the Me was pouring out smoke, but whether it was "Jet" propulsion or the result of my fire, I don't know. I had to gentle my dive out to about 70 degrees, but the Me continued straight down, in a dive, which approached the vertical. At 4,000 feet I was indicating 500 miles per hour, and the Me was pulling away from me, as I started my pull out. The Me 163 disappeared into the clouds at 3,000 feet, still in an almost vertical dive, and, in my opinion, could not have been indicating less than 550 miles per hour. I completed my pull out at 1,500 feet, blacking out momentarily in the process and ducked down out of the clouds to look for the Me. Not seeing him immediately, I went back into the clouds to avoid flak.

It is my opinion that no ship and no pilot could pull out of an 80 to 90-degree dive from 3,000 feet, indicating 550 miles per hour or better.

I claim one Me 163 destroyed.

J. Ammunition expended: 720 rounds 50 cal, A.P.I.; 145 rounds 20mm H.E.I.

Arthur F. Jeffrey,
Captain, A.C.

STATEMENT IN SUPPORT OF COMBAT CLAIM

On 29 July 1944, I was flying Number Two in Newcross Yellow Flight on a bomber escort mission under VIII Fighter Command Field Order Number 470. We were escorting a crippled bomber from the target area, with my Flight Leader, Captain Arthur F. Jeffrey and I providing close cover, while Numbers Three and Four acted as top cover. In the vicinity of Wilhelmshaven, Germany, at 11,000 feet, I observed an aircraft, later identified as an Me 163, closing in on the bomber dead astern. Captain Jeffrey took out after it, and the German went into a very steep, weaving climb, with Captain Jeffrey firing intermittently. After about 4,000 feet of climbing, the Me circled to the left, and Captain Jeffrey attacked again. I had one bad engine, and couldn't climb as fast as they, so I couldn't see if he was getting strikes or not. Then the Me split-essed and went down in very steep, almost vertical dive. Captain Jeffrey and I followed, but again I couldn't keep up with them. I started to pull out between 3,500 and 4,000 indicating a little over 400 miles per hour. The Me went into the clouds, which were around 3,000 feet, still in a dive of 80 degrees or better, and must have been indicating 550 or 600, and showed no signs of pulling out. I don't see how the German could have gotten out of that dive.

Richard G. Simpson,
2nd Lt., A.C.

MISSION SUMMARY REPORT

Hot stuff: Encounter with Me 163 Single-Jet job: Newcross Yellow Flight, Captain Arthur J. Jeffrey leading, escorted a straggler B-17, 3rd Div., last four numbers 7007, marked with "D" inside of square on tail, from target area. At 1145, 1,100 feet over Wesermünde, one Me 163 made a slightly low side 5 o'clock pass on the B-17, followed through in a slight dive, then leveled off. Captain Jeffrey and wingman took out after him, and the Me made another slight dive, climbed, weaving all the while. During this weaving, Capt. Jeffrey closed and opened fire, observing hits. The Me climbed to 15,000, giving off intermittent spurts of smoke, either from the exhaust or from strikes. At 15,000 the Me circled to the left, the P-38 turned tighter, getting a good deflection shot. Estimated closest range, 300 yards. The Me did a mild split ess and spiraled off into an 80 to 90-degree dive, giving off "jet" exhaust or smoke all during the dive. Capt. Jeffrey followed in a 90-degree dive, gentling to 70 degrees, firing and observing strikes until the Me began to pull away and he was forced to gentle his dive to 70 degrees. Capt. Jeffrey started to pull out of his dive at 4,000 or 3,500 feet, indicating a little over 500 mph. The Me still pulling away, went into the overcast at 3,000 feet, still in an 80-90-degree dive and was undoubtedly indicating 550-650 mph. Capt. Jeffrey pulled out at 1,500 feet, blacking out while doing so. He could see no immediate sign of the Me beneath the overcast, and then climbed back up through the overcast to avoid flak. The entire engagement lasted 3-4 minutes.

Newcross Yellow 3 and 4, flying top cover at 16,000 behind and above the bomber and Yellow 1 and 2, did not see the first jet attack, but at approximately 1148, an Me 163 made a 70-degree pass on the bomber from the sun. The flight had been keeping special watch to high rear and had seen no contrails. During the dive, the Me emitted blue spurts. Dive gentled to 60 degrees, then the Me went into a cloud deck at about 8,000 feet. No chance to follow.

Pilot's descriptions and sketches agree with poop in AIS No. 19. Me 163 climbs at very steep angle, much steeper than P-38, but P-38 could turn tighter.

Left bomber 1155, just off east Frisian Islands, 10,000 feet.

The B-17 involved was B-17G, EP-B, 42-107007, "She Hasta" belonging to the 100th Bomb Group and being flown by Lieutenant William Greiner, breaking in a new crew. It had suffered an engine out and other damage over the target. Forced to drop from their "B" Group formation, the struggling A/C was picked up by Newcross Yellow Flight and was being escorted back to England. After the attack by the Komet, the B-17 was forced to ditch in the North Sea off the coast of Ameland. Eight of its crew survived to become POW's while a ninth member, waist gunner Bernard Baumgarten who was severely wounded during the action above, went down with the aircraft. This was one of eight B-17s lost by the "Bloody Hundredth" that day.

In a subsequent interview, now just plain "Art" Jeffrey, told of an intelligence briefing received in July 1944 that warned pilots about the existence of a bat-like looking German rocket plane. This A/C was the one Art encountered while escorting the shot up B-17. According to Art, the B-17 was flying on about two and a half engines, had half its tail gone and was steadily loosing altitude. The worst thing, however, was that the bomber was on a northwest course that would cause it to miss England. Art described the day as gray with intermittent cloud layers when they picked the Big Friend up over Germany. Art said he instructed his second element leader to stay up and fly top cover while he took his wingman down to help. Not able to raise the crew by radio, Art went well over to the copilot's side, tipped his P-38 up so the bomber crew could identify him as friendly and not try to shoot at him. As luck would have it, when Art got in close enough for hand signals, a waist gunner opened up on him. Backing off, Art tried again to communicate, but had no success. It was at that time that Art noticed the Me 163 heading straight for the B-17. He went after the Komet at about 6,000 feet without his wingman, who had forgotten to switch his A/C fuel mixture from auto lean to rich.

Jeffrey described the Komet pilot as appearing to be inexperienced as he didn't seem to know what to do in a fight.

Later, upon returning to Wattisham, home to the 479th Fighter Group, Art was only going to claim a probable, but said that other pilots reported having seen the bat-like A/C dive into the ground. He was told to talk to nobody about this and that he was to be debriefed by General Jesse Auton, Commander of the 65th Fighter Wing. It so happened that the General was on his way from Wing HQ to preside over an awards ceremony to be held at the station. After the General arrived, Art recounted the entire sequence of events to him.

Members of the 479th Fighter Group assembled in hangar number one for an awards ceremony this date. The awards were presented by General Jesse Auton, commander of the 65th Fighter Wing and took place inside the hangar because of rain. *Courtesy of Edwin J. Fillipow.*

Gen. Auton turned to Lt. Col. Kyle Riddle, Commander of the 479th, who was also present and said, "Well, Kyle, it looks like we got our first rocket plane!"

Each of the squadrons continued escort of their assigned Big Friends out of Germany to a point where landfall out was made. L/O for the 434th FS was over the Frisian Islands at 1130 hrs./24,000 ft. They broke away from the B-17s over the North Sea about ten minutes later. The 435th made L/O over Ameland Island at 1130 hrs./20,000 ft. They also broke away over the North Sea. The 436th FS made L/O over the coast north of Groningen, Holland at 1130 hrs./20,000 feet at which point they also broke from the bombers.

The only observation made during the mission was the ineffective use of smoke pots in the target area. Flak at Münden, Groningen and Naumburg was heavy, moderate and accurate. The area from Merseburg to Halle, the flak was heavy, intense and accurate. The same was true at Hamm.

31 July 1944

VIII FC FO 472

No. 110 Monday. Lt. Col. Woods was the group's leader and he also led the 435th FS, which consisted of 16 P-38s. Capt. Jeffrey led the 434th FS, which consisted of 15 P-38s and Capt. Biscayart led the 436th FS, which consisted of 16 P-38s. Their assignment was a bomber escort for 2nd BD B-24s attacking their 8th AF Mission 507 primary target, chemical works at Ludwigshafen, Germany. 434th FS up: 1108 hrs., down: 1525 hrs. with one early return. 435th FS up: 1110 hrs., down: 1535 hrs. with one early return. 436th FS up: 1100 hrs., down: 1600 hrs. with one early return.

On this trip, the skies were overcast with cloud tops up to 18,000 ft. There were occasional breaks over the target area though. L/F for the 4534th FS was over Dunkerque, France at 1157 hrs./16,000 ft. L/F for the 436th FS was over Coxyde, Belgium at 1150 hrs./14,000 ft. Over Germany, the 434th FS made R/V with their B-24s in the vicinity of Kaiserslautern at 1220 hrs./23,000 ft. The 435th FS R/V'd with their bombers north of Meusenheim at 1220 hrs./24,000 ft. and the 436th FS R/V'd with their assigned bombers in the Buchenveuren area at 1230 hrs./21,000 ft. All three squadrons reported the B-24s to be in poor formation. The 436th FS added that the bombers were flying combat wings abreast and spread out. Due to the

Right: General Jesse Auton, shown at Wattisham this date. *From original 479th FG history.*

weather, the bombing results were unobserved although the 436th FS noted numerous hits within the industrial area. The escort was uneventful save for a few interesting events. Blue Flight from the 434th FS escorted an aborting B-24 all the way from Kaiserslautern back to Great Yarmouth. At 1230 hrs, the 434th FS heard a B-17, Vinegrove 5-1-3 give a distress call, stating that he had number four engine shot out, but the squadron could not render assistance as the bomber could not be found. In the Merzig area, about 1330 hours, the 436th FS saw a B-24 heading towards France. Shortly afterwards, seven chutes were seen to come from the bomber. The 434th FS made L/O over the Dutch Islands at 1425 hrs./17,000 ft. and broke from the bombers at mid-water over the North Sea at 1430 hrs./16,000 ft. The 435th and 436th FSs both made L/O over Overflakkee Island, at 1450 hrs./22,000 ft. and at 1500 hrs./ 18,000 feet, respectively. They also broke from the bombers at mid-water, although the 436th FS spent time picking up stragglers.

Observations made during the mission included barges seen in the canal near Bingen, Germany, an airfield with taxi strips running into the surrounding woods and what appeared to be fresh construction on a military camp five miles south of Bergen-op-Zoom, Holland. Flak was heavy, intense and accurate over Brussels, Belgium, as well as over Ludwigshafen and Speyer, in Germany. It was heavy moderate/meager and inaccurate over Antwerp, Coxyde, and Dunkerque.

An interesting fact concerns the replacement pilots received by the group during the months of June and July. The 479th FG received 47 new pilots during those two months. The group received the men in two batches, one came the second week of June, and the other arrived the second week of July. Of those 47 pilots, 35 came from graduating class 44-A, Williams Field. After graduation, the class was split with part going to the 329th FG at Van Nuys, California and the other part going to the 454th FS at Salinas, California. The first batch received during June came from those sent to Van Nuys. These pilots actually traveled with the 479th in the same trains that they took from California to Camp Kilmer, the same trains from Camp Kilmer to New Jersey, the same ferry boats to the same troop ship, the USS *Argentina* and over to England. However, once in the UK, the replacement pilots went on to the 496th Fighter Training Group at Goxhill, England for further training before assignment to the 479th. The pilots sent to Salinas followed a similar route about a month later and rejoined their classmates at Wattisham.

Above: Lieutenants Donald A. Dunn and Edwin J. Fillipow from the 436th FS, Everett P. Ford from the 435th FS and John G. Glenn from the 436th FS receive their Air Medals. The last individual is unfortunately unknown. *Courtesy of Edwin J. Fillipow.*

Right: Lieutenant Colonel Sidney S. Woods. *Courtesy of Clarence G. Haynes.*

CHAPTER SIX

AUGUST 1944

1 August 1944

VIII FC FO 473

No. 111 Tuesday. Lt. Col. Herren was the group's leader and he also led the 434th FS, which consisted of 17 P-38s. Capt. Courtney led the 435th FS, which consisted of 16 P-38s and Major Monahan led the 436th FS, which consisted of 16 P-38s. Their assignment in France was an area patrol and bomber withdrawal escort for 3rd BD B-24s attacking their 8th AF Mission 508 targets, airfields in the area south of Paris. 434th FS up: 1330 hrs., down: 1840 hrs. one early return. 435th FS up: 1340 hrs., down: 1810 hrs. with two early returns. 436th FS up: 1320 hrs., down: 1855 hrs. with no early returns.

L/F for the group was over le Tréport, between 1412 and 1429 hrs./15-18,000 ft. Heading southwest down to the Nantes area, the group spread out and patrolled an area of France known as H-6 for the period of about an hour and fifteen minutes. The patrol was uneventful. Heading northeast, R/V with the B-24s was at different points, both geographical and within the formations, by each squadron. The 434th FS made the first contact. The 435th FS picked the heavies up near Paris, escorting them through there and the 436th FS got to them near Malesherbes. Contacts were made between 1535 and 1600 hrs. at altitudes varying between 20,000 and 23,000 ft. Escorting the bombers, the 434th FS noted that the Big Friend's box formations were good, but that the boxes were strung out. One of the targets, the Mondesire airdrome was well covered with excellent bomb hits reported to be on the runways. Other bombing results were not observed. The bombers were escorted all the way out, making L/O in the vicinity of Cabourg at 1700 hrs. The group nearly took them home, with the 434th FS escorting a straggler as far as Beachy Head, the 435th FS going as far as Selsey Bill, near Portsmouth, both on the southern coast of England and the 436th FS breaking away at mid-channel.

Observations made during the mission included two trains seen, one with 50 cars and another with 50-75 cars. Flak in the patrol area was heavy, intense and accurate, as it was at Lisieux.

2 August 1944

VIII FC FO 474

No. 112 Wednesday. Lt. Col. Riddle was the group's leader and he also led the 436th FS, which consisted of 17 P-38s. Maj. Keller led the 434th FS, which consisted of 16 P-38s and Maj. Glover led the 435th FS, which consisted of 16 P-38s. Their assignment was a MEW controlled fighter-bomber attack on tactical targets. 434th FS up: 1800 hrs., down: 2030 hrs. with no early returns. 435th FS up: 1756 hrs., down: 2050 hrs. with no early returns. 436th FS up: 1750 hrs., down: 2059 hrs. with one early return.

L/F was made over Nieuport, Belgium by both the 434th FS at 1846 hrs./15,000 ft. and by the 436th FS at 1837 hrs./ 17,000 ft. The 435th FS crossed over the continent a little farther south, at Coxyde, Belgium 1845 hrs./17,000 ft. Heading east, the group attacked targets by squadrons, beginning with the 436th FS dropping thirty, 500-lb. General Purpose bombs at the Brussels, Belgium. Melsbroek airdrome. Results were not observed because of intense flak and extreme haze. The remaining bombs were expended on a railroad, a railroad bridge and a factory. The squadron also damaged and destroyed flak towers, high-tension electrical lines, water towers, observation towers, a gas storage tank, a fuel storage tank, a locomotive and a few goods wagons by strafing. The tally was paid for in advance by the loss of Second Lieutenant Fred A. Moser, Jr., who didn't even get a chance to drop his bombs. German flak hit the Bison Squadron pilot's P-38 in both engines, setting the left one on fire. His attempts to put the fire out failed. Hit at 1850 hrs./11,000 feet, ten miles north-north east of Brussels, the plane snapped twice, then went into a spin. Lt. Moser tried to pull out of the spin at 8,000 feet, but the A/C went into a slow spiral. Not able to recover, Lt. Moser bailed out, fractured his right ankle and wrenched his shoulder after a rough landing. An anti-aircraft gun crew captured him and he became a prisoner. Lt. Moser started his stay in a hospital where later he was to see one of his squadron mates, Lieutenant Thomas J. O'Holleran, who was shot down two weeks later. The other two squadrons, providing cover, each observed the loss.

The group continued on around the eastern side of Brussels and on down in a southwesterly direction along the Brussels-La Louvière-St. Quentin line where the 435th FS went on the attack this time. The squadron bombed and strafed two marshalling yards, railways, factories, a convoy of trucks, two locomotives and 12 goods cars, a freight house and a canal lock. Into France now, the 434th FS took over the duty, working over the Valenciennes area. Sweeping and hitting rail yards and facilities there and at Denain, Douai, Le Calean, Soignies, and another airfield at Cambrai, the squadron added to the Germans misery. More locomotives, goods wagons, rail lines and runways were put out of action.

Flak over Ostende, Belgium was heavy, meager and inaccurate. Over Coxyde and north of Brussels as well as in France, north of St. Quentin, east of Lens, at Clastres, Boulogne and St. Valery, it was heavy, intense and accurate. Flak at the marshalling yards and the airfields was light, intense and accurate.

L/O was north of St. Valery, France at about 1945 hrs. Bad weather back home forced some of the group's P-38s to land at other airfields. A two-plane relay flight from the 436th FS had covered the coastal area from Dunkirk to Cayeux, France. The weather and low fuel forced the two P-38s to land in England at Debden, in order to gas up and be able to continue on. One of the two, Second Lieutenant Howard G. Hightower, didn't make it back to Wattisham, however. Debden, then home to the 4th Fighter Group, logged this entry in their tower log:

A piece of art done of the 434th's Robin Olds. *Courtesy of George E. Falkner.*

> "After quite a few homings, we had (8) P-38s land here from Wattisham, also (26) P-47s from Martlesham. [Many aircraft were being diverted to Debden because home bases along the coast were closed in.] P-38 letter "7" [sic – should be squadron letter "T".] from 436 Squadron, Pilot Lt. Hightower, crashed on landing. He was very short of fuel and did not think he could make it around to the west end to come in west to east. I [the tower] told him to use any runway he wanted. He had one prop feathered and only five gallons of gas left so he came in south to north. His approach was very high and he did not touch down until he had only 300 yards of runway left. He started to use his brakes as soon as he touched down and after traveling the remaining 300 yards of the runway, his right landing gear collapsed. He continued on through the fence and across the road. The crash crew and ambulance were there immediately. The pilot was OK, however, the plane was washed out pretty bad. Arrangements have been made for a guard to remain with the A/C and all concerned were notified."

The tower log goes on to record the disposition of the remaining 479th FG P-38s, four of which left later in the evening and returned to Wattisham. The remaining three returned the following day.

3 August 1944

VIII FC FO 476

No. 113 Thursday. Lt. Col. Woods was the group's leader and he also led the 435th FS, which consisted of 15 P-38s. Maj. Herren led the 434th FS, which consisted of 16 P-38s and Capt. Sullivan led the 436th FS, which consisted of 16 P-38s. Their assignment was a fighter-strafing attack on rail and tactical targets in the Mulhouse, France area. 434th FS up: 1326 hrs., down: 1716 hrs. with five early returns. 435th FS up: 1335 hrs., down: 1719 hrs. with one early return. 436th FS up: 1333 hrs., down: 1746 hrs. with no early returns.

The mission started out badly for the 434th FS, having had five of its P-38s return early. Four came back, all at the same time, arriving home at 1500 hrs. Capt. C.A.P. Duffié was escorted back by his whole flight, when he developed an engine problem. The squadron's leader also came back early with an engine problem. L/F was over Dunkerque, France at 1412 hrs./18,000 ft. for the 434th FS; over Ostend, Belgium at 1412 hrs./20,000 ft. for the 435th FS and over Nieuport, Belgium at 1409 hrs./17,000 ft. for the 436th FS. Heading in east, the squadrons reached their objectives and got to work. The 434th FS arrived at Mulhouse at 1500 hrs. and strafed southwest, following the rail and canal lines down to Belfort, France. The squadron netted four locomotives destroyed, plus assorted railroad cars, factories and barges damaged for their efforts there.

From Belfort, the squadron headed out, making L/O over Boulogne, France at 1645 hrs. The 435th FS went in to start at a point just south of Strasbourg, France. From there they strafed down along the railway and canal, to south of Colmar, France. Their strafing results were similar to those of the 434th, the squadron netting five locomotives, 25 goods cars, seven oil cars, a couple of factories and a power station damaged. They too, headed out, making L/O at Boulogne the same time, as did Newcross Squadron. Acting as top cover for Newcross and Lakeside Squadrons, Bison Squadron got off track near the target area and began strafing ten miles south of Strasbourg, heading down along a railroad that paralleled a canal. Starting at 1520 hours and winding up at 1532 hours, the squadron turned out of the area, north of Mulhouse and crossed out of the continent over Dunkerque at 1645 hrs. Bison Squadron claimed several locomotives, trucks and high-tension power lines destroyed, as well as another locomotive, some goods wagons, oil tankers and trucks damaged. The 436th FS had a two-plane relay covering the coast again. Radio transmissions became weak, so they had to penetrate inward from the coast in order to forward the messages.

A frame from First Lieutenant Harold (Bud) F. Grenning's gun camera film showing the locomotive he destroyed two miles west of Altkirch. *Courtesy of Harold F. Grenning.*

Observations made during the mission included noting the marshalling yard at Verdun, France was very active with three long trains standing in it. The runways at the airdrome immediately south of Douai were cratered as well as the dispersal area. One runway of the Cambri/Epinoy airdrome appeared to have white spots painted on it. The Abbeville/Drucat airdrome was camouflaged and in good shape. Two airdromes were sighted in woods near Yprés, France. Flak near the coast was heavy, moderate and inaccurate.

The difficulties of awarding credits for A/C claimed in Encounter Reports is well illustrated by this example. During the mission, all three squadrons, at different times, spotted the same B-24, situated in a large, open, grain field north of Mulhouse. An attempt to hide the brown-painted bomber had been made by covering the wings with straw and the tail section with netting. The plane was noted to have German crosses on it. Pilots from all three squadrons attacked the A/C, each firing upon it, observing flames resulting from their attacks and two of the three claiming it as destroyed. One pilot claimed only that he had damaged it.

4 August 1944

VIII FC FO 478

No. 114 Friday. Maj. Glover was the group's leader and he also led the 435th FS, which consisted of 16 P-38s. Capt. Duffié led the 434th FS, which consisted of 16 P-38s plus 2 relays.

Capt. Biscayart led the 436th FS, which consisted of 16 P-38s. Their assignment was a penetration to target and withdrawal escort for 2nd BD B-24s attacking their 8th AF Mission 514 primary target, a torpedo manufacturing plant at Kiel, Germany. 434th FS up: 1154 hrs., down: 1648 hrs. with three early returns. 435th FS up: 1158 hrs., down: 1645 hrs. with no early returns. 436th FS up: 1150 hrs., down: 1700 hrs. with one early return.

The mission started out on a sour note when Captain Elmer Hartman from the 436th FS struck a sign during take off. Damaged, the heavily loaded A/C sagged back down to the ground, caught fire on impact and ended up flipped over on its back. Repeated attempts to rescue Capt. Hartman were unsuccessful until the fire was brought under control. Finally recovered from the wreckage, he was pronounced dead at the scene. It was later learned he was killed instantly by the crash.

The Big Friends were met separately by each squadron at varying points and times along the course in over the North Sea, but basically across the cold water from the border between the Schleswig-Holstein area of Germany and Denmark. L/F was over Hooge Island, Germany for both the 434th and the 436th FSs, with the 434th crossing in at 1350 and the 435th in at 1347 hrs. The squadrons were spaced at 21-22,000 ft. respectively. The 435th FS made L/F over Langenhorn, Germany at 1357 hrs./22,000 ft. The mission was uneventful and the B-24s were escorted in, down, around and back out from the target. Immediate results were unobservable due to a heavy smoke screen covering the area, but later reconnaissance revealed the target to be well hit despite that bombers were reported to be in poor formation throughout the trip. L/O for the escorting squadrons was back up in the same vicinities as L/F, occurring between 1444 hrs./17,000 ft. for the 436th FS and 1510 hrs./20,000 ft. for the 435th FS. The 434th FS came out between the other two. The three squadrons broke away from the bombers over the North Sea near Cromer, England and headed home.

Observations made during the mission included sighting a number of vessels, including minesweepers along the eastern coast from south of Sønderborg, Denmark to in the harbor leading to Kiel. Two seaplanes, listed as possible dummies, were seen on Selenter Lake, ten miles east of Kiel and two airfields were noted to be in good condition along the route. Two probable jet contrails were seen trailing A/C traveling very fast and high. On the way out, one B-24 was observed to drop its bomb load on an airfield north of Husum, Germany. The results reported were excellent. Another B-24, with two of its engines on fire and props feathered, was seen heading towards Sweden at 1510 hrs. near L/O (probably a 492nd BG B-24 that went to Sweden). Finally, a large splash, explosion and later smoke was seen in the waters of the North Sea, about a third of the way home, after L/O. The cause was reported as unknown (probably a MIA 448th BG B-24). Flak was heavy, intense and inaccurate in the target area.

Lieutenant Walter M. Drake. *Courtesy of Clarence G. Haynes.*

Walter (Walt) M. Drake from the 434th FS remembers a mission like this one and later wrote about it:

> "Early in August I came back from a long escort run with two pilots from another unit. The 434th had performed its mission, but in the ensuing chaos over the target, I got separated from the squadron and joined these other two pilots as we made our way back to England. It was late afternoon, I was tired, and the sky was filled with dark storm clouds. We chatted with each other over the radio and kept a sharp look out for any break in the clouds in hope of identifying a landmark. We flew at 2,000 feet and watched our fuel gauges slowly edge down to empty. The clouds were thick, but broken. The clear space between the clouds was never more than a few hundred

yards. We were flying at 200 mph and just as we collectively decided to bail out and I began to release the canopy, I looked up at the last second and saw the dark image of a barrage balloon loom before me. I pulled the stick hard to the right and just missed the cable with my wing. I nearly choked on my heart, but I kept breathing and my two companions also avoided the danger. We now knew we were over London, but where? A few moments later one of the other pilots spied a small break in the clouds below us and we could see the countryside. He dived for the opening and I followed. We flew under the cloud cover and soon found ourselves over another P-38 base. [20th FG – Kings Cliffe] We each landed without mishap and as I touched down on the runway, I ran out of fuel and rolled to a dead stop. With each propeller silent and the engines still, I had a few moments alone before the ground crew arrived. I sat in the plane thankful to be alive and knowing I had nothing to do with it.

"The ground crew arrived and towed the plane off the runway. I spent the night at this base and reacquainted myself with Paul Denbo, [20th FG/79th FS] a friend who was stationed there. Paul and I trained together at Williams Field back in the states and it was good to see a familiar face. A few months later, I was saddened to learn he was killed in combat. [KIA – flak, 12 August.]

"The next day I flew back to Wattisham. The weather had improved some but there were still a lot of clouds. The flight time was less than thirty minutes and I expected this to be a simple ride. As I neared Wattisham, I saw familiar landmarks and I reduced my altitude to 500 feet and my airspeed to 175 mph. I saw the airfield from a distance and was comfortably setting up my approach when another P-38 broke out of the clouds directly in front of me. We were closing on each other at over 350 mph and with only a split second to react, I instinctively yanked the wheel hard to the right and miraculously we missed each other. I never knew who it was, but once again through God's grace, I survived another deadly situation."

5 August 1944

VIII FC FO 483

No. 115 Saturday. Lt. Col. Woods was the group's leader and he also led the 436th FS, which consisted of 17 P-38s plus one escort. Major Herren led the 434th FS, which consisted of 17 P-38s and Capt. Carter led the 435th FS, which consisted of 16 P-38s. Their assignment was a penetration to target and withdrawal escort for 3rd BD B-17s attacking their 8th AF Mission 519 primary target, the Krupp armament works at Magdeburg, Germany. 434th FS up: 0956 hrs., down: 1445 hrs. with two early returns. 435th FS up: 0950 hrs., down: 1455 hrs. with one early return. 436th FS up: 0947 hrs., down: 1500 hrs. with eight early returns.

The group's leader was forced to return home just after reaching the Frisian Islands, Germany. Lt. Col. Woods took half his squadron's strength back to Wattisham with him, leaving Maj. Herren with the lead and the remainder of his squadron. The group was joined by the P-51's of the 361st Fighter Group for this mission with the 361st taking the front of the formation and the 479th taking the rear. R/V with the B-17's was over the North Sea, with the group's three squadrons joining escort at differing times and places along the route. The bombers were reported to be in good formation, but ten to fifteen minutes late. The 434th FS and the 436th FS linked up at 1115 hrs./23-24,000 feet, while the 435th FS did so at 1135 hrs./24,000 ft. L/F was just south of Cuxhaven, Germany at 1135 hrs./25,26,000 ft. for the 434th FS and the remaining members of the 436th FS which had joined Newcross Squadron. L/F for the 435th FS was the same location, but at 1140 hrs./24,000 ft. Escorting the Big Friends inland, a lone Me 109 was observed to bounce the bombers from the rear at 1150 hours, northwest of Bremen, Germany. Two pilots from the 435th FS, Captain Raymond S. Carter and his wingman Second Lieutenant Norman R. Benoit, chased him off.

Capt. Carter gave this report:

> "As I drove into the fight, an Me 109 that was chasing a P-51, pulled around in front of me. I pulled in quickly and fired a very short burst, observing a few hits near the cockpit. The Me 109 fell into a spin and began smoking. The spin flattened out and the canopy or some part of the airplane fell away. The last time I saw the ship, it was in a flat spin on its back at about 15,000 feet. From the actions of the ship, I believe the pilot was hit and the airplane had no chance to recover."

Capt. Carter turned in a claim for the German A/C.

Five minutes later Capt. Carter attacked another Me 109 and downed this one also, giving this report:

Second Lieutenant Norman R. Benoit was no new comer to England, having been there during 1942 as an enlisted man. Then a Technical Sergeant, he is shown here standing to the far right in a photograph taken at Polebrook on 27 August 1942. The men pictured are posed in front of a C-47, which they had just flown. Also seen are radio operator Staff Sergeant Ted Lucas, pilot Captain E. F. Kiessig and the plane's navigator, Second Lieutenant Krieger. Technical Sergeant Benoit served as engineer onboard the plane. The occasion was the first awards ceremony for Americans in England. *Courtesy of Stephanie A. Benoit.*

"The second Me 109 pulled in front of me in a medium turn to the left at about 20,000 feet. I pulled in and fired a short burst at about 45 degrees off. I observed hits on the aircraft and white smoke pouring out. The Me 109 half-rolled and started down, doing rolls. I followed him down, pulling out of my dive twice. When I was sure my element leader was with me, I closed behind the Me 109 on the deck. I began firing at about 250 yards and closed to 25 feet. As I broke away, the pilot bailed out at about 1,000 ft. and the Me 109 crashed into an open field."

The pilot was seen to land and run away. Capt. Carter claimed this one also and was awarded a damaged and a destroyed for the two Me 109s.

Proceeding inward, two other pilots from the 435th FS, Captain George K. Sykes and his wingman, Second Lieutenant Carl W. Moore, chased another Me 109 down to the deck. Capt. Sykes wrote:

"I was Yellow Flight Leader and the squadron was flying flights in trail on the right of the bombers at 26,000 feet. We saw a gaggle of aircraft in what appeared to be a flight off to our right front and about 2,000 feet higher. As we turned to the right, a P-51 was coming right at my flight with an Me 109 about 300 yards behind it. I turned and got on the tail of the Me 109. He immediately broke off the attack on the P-51 and started a spiral descent. I followed him down with my flight behind me. He kept skidding from side to side during the dive and I was unable to keep my sight on him, although I did take several short bursts from about 1,000 yards. When we reached the deck, he went into a tight turn to the left. I dropped combat flaps and was able to turn inside him and get a few observed hits on his wings at about 30-degrees deflection and 300 yards. At that time, my wingman cut across in front of me and I had to cease firing. Then the Me 109 reversed his turn, which put me on his tail again. He began to smoke and fly almost straight. I fired from about 300 yards, closing to 100 yards. He crashed into some trees and hit the ground, skidding out into a plowed field, where he exploded. I claim one Me 109 destroyed."

After downing that one, they became involved in another fight on the deck when an Me 109 got on Lt. Moore's tail. Capt. Sykes got onto the 109's tail and around they all went, in a tight luftberry to the left, about a hundred feet off the ground. Smoke began coming from Lt. Moore's left engine and it appeared as though the engine was failing. His plane banked sharply to the left, then started to recover to the right, but mushed into the ground, hitting on its right wing and belly. It exploded on impact, about 30 miles due south of Hamburg, Germany. Lt. Moore was killed. This time the other side became the victor and the Me 109 was able to escape with only some damage to his A/C. Northeast of Stendal, Germany the group took a bounce from some 15 Me 109s, whose main target was apparently the 436th FSs Yellow Flight. The resulting fight saw two more Germans destroyed, giving the group a 4-0-2 record for the mission. Captain Clifford J. Moore from the 436th FS got one of the Me 109s. He stated:

Captain George K. Sykes, crew chief Technical Sergeant Harold J. Fox, assistant crew chief Sergeant Edwin R. Campbell and armorer Corporal Earl D. Ward. *From original 479th FG history.*

Arming one of the group's birds. *From original 479th FG history.*

Crew chief Technical Sergeant Stanley L. Steele's 436th FS P-38 is shown being readied for combat. *From original 479th FG history.*

"I was leading the seven ships remaining in our squadron, which was above and to the rear of the bombers. We sighted 16 plus Me 109s 3-5,000 feet above us. We were then at 27,000 feet. They began two or three passes at us, but broke back each time when we turned into them. Once, as I turned to get back to the bombers, at least one vic of three made a pass in formation and fired that way on my element leader who had not heard the warning to break. My number four man, Second Lieutenant Melvin S. Mickey, saw them, gave the warning and was seen to break into them and blow one up. By this time, I had turned back and saw an Me 109F or G going away from me at a light angle and long range. I closed on him slightly and fired, seeing puffs of smoke come from him. He began turning and skidding as evasive action, reversing his turn twice as he saw me turning inside him. He pulled up and as he began a split-ess, I hit his canopy several times. He then went into a vertical dive, smoking. As I spiraled down to about 15,000 feet, I saw his chute open. We then returned to the line of bombers." Lt. Mickey picked off the other Me 109 for the 436th, stating: "My element leader and I were bounced by three Me 109s. I called the break and broke left myself. Just after I broke, they all started firing. I kept my turn until I saw two of the Me 109s fall off. My action was all with combat flaps and full manifold pressure up to this time. The next thing I knew, there was an Me 109 in front of me which was racked up in a steep chandelle. I gave him four or five short bursts and he exploded from under the cockpit. I was closing fast at the end. The shooting was all large deflection, 60 degrees to 80 degrees, 400 to 200 yards."

Meanwhile, at 1200 hrs./25,000 feet, an unidentified E/A, thought to be a jet, made a pass at one of the B-17s in the front of the formation. Occurring just south of Hamburg, the E/A split-essed away when an attempt was made to intercept it. The B-17 that was the intended target, continued on with no apparent ill affects. Three Me 163s at 25,000 ft. were noted west of Lüneburg. This incident is one of many observations reporting enemy jet and rocket activity in the area between Uelzen and Stendal, Germany. There were another three sightings that told of these types of aircraft aloft as the B-17s and their escorts passed through. First, there were three Me 262s and an Me 163, reported at 32,000 ft. heading west. Then another two Me 163s and an Me 262 were seen. Finally, two more E/As, probably Me 163s, were observed at 30,000 feet, heading southeast. Recognizing that interception attempts were futile, the group continued escort through and out of the target. Bombing results were observable due to the CAVU weather and were excellent despite a smoke screen laid down by the Germans. Each of the three squadrons reported seeing B-17s exploding over the target area. There were no chutes from any of them. The return trip was nearly uneventful and the bombers were left at the Dutch coast in the vicinities of Alkmaar and Ijmuiden between 1315 hrs and 1401 hrs. Approaching the coast of England, a P-47 was seen to ditch in the waters about 40 miles east of Southwold. Air Sea Rescue was notified and one of the group's P-38s stood by until ASR arrived. It appeared as though the downed pilot could not get his dinghy inflated and his fate is unknown as the P-38 pilot had to leave as soon as ASR got to the location.

Observations made during the mission included 80 plus barges heading out to sea from the harbor formed by the Elbe Estuary at Cuxhaven, an escorted convoy of 20-30 freight barges anchored in the estuary near Neuhaus, Germany and numerous other water-borne transports seen along the waterway. Smoke screens were being used to cover the entrance to the Elbe River as well as the south end of the Kaiser Wilhelm Canal. Flak over Magdeburg was nil for the first box of B-17s, but then the Germans started shooting with determination and the last boxes were clobbered. Over Wesermünde, Germany it was heavy, moderate and inaccurate at 21,000 feet, but on the deck it was light, intense and accurate. Over Neunwald, Germany it was heavy, moderate and inaccurate.

6 August 1944

VIII FC FO 487

No. 116 Sunday. Major Herren was the group's leader and he also led the 434th FS, which consisted of 17 P-38s. Major Glover led the 435th FS, which consisted of 15 P-38s and Capt. Sullivan led the 436th FS, which consisted of 12 P-38s. Their assignment was a penetration to target and withdrawal escort for 2nd BD B-24s attacking their 8th AF Mission 524 primary target in Hamburg, Germany. While over the continent, they would be in the German homeland's airspace from landfall in, to land out. 434th FS up: 0920 hrs., down: 1410 hrs. with

A 436th FS P-38, armed and dangerous. *Courtesy of Kenneth D. Axt.*

two early returns. 435th FS up: 0915 hrs., down: 1420 hrs. with no early returns. 436th FS up: 0914 hrs., down: 1430 hrs. with no early returns.

The 434th FS recorded this day as: "...the usual lazy Sunday in the ETO, broken only by a rather boring visit to Hamburg in company with assorted Big Friends". The squadrons made R/V with the B-24s at varying points and times along the route to the target. Arriving at 1045 hrs./27,000 feet, the 436th FS was the first to take their place with the bomber stream, joining seven boxes over the North Sea at a point about 15 miles north of Germany's coast, above Wilhelmshaven. The 435th FS made R/V next, linking up with the proper bomber boxes over the North Sea waters, east of Heligoland Island at 1110 hrs./27,000 ft. The 434th FS contacted their five to six boxes of B-24s at a point west of the Elbe Estuary at 1115 hrs./27,000 ft. The bomber formation looked good heading in to landfall and a swing south. L/F for the squadrons began being made shortly afterwards, with the 436th FS entering near Tönning at 1105 hrs./29,000 ft. The 435th FS crossed in over Vollerwiek at 1112 hrs./27,000 ft. and the 434th FS followed, making L/F just a bit later and at a point in that vicinity. Continuing on in a northeasterly course and passing Friedrichstadt, the force then began a turn to the right that took them within eyesight of Kiel. The Germans were attempting to cover the last two places with smoke screens, but not having much success. Heading south now, the big and little friends continued on down to the target at Hamburg. The flak was murderous over the city. The 434th FS witnessed two B-24s hit and spinning down. Three chutes were seen to emerge from each one. The 435th FS saw three, possibly the two that the 434th saw, plus another, burning, then exploding over the target. Four chutes were seen from those. The 436th FS observed a B-24 explode over the target at 1155 hrs. Two chutes were seen. The clear weather permitted the bombing results to be observed and they were reported to be excellent. The hits were registered on the western part of the city causing tremendous fires reaching to 3,000 ft. and dense clouds of towering, thick, black smoke up to 10,000 ft. No enemy fighters appeared for the group's attention, but P-47s were observed in a dogfight with some Fw 190s west of Hamburg at 1200 hrs. Escorting the Big Friends out of the target area and on the route home, another bomber was lost near Altkloster. The plane crashed at 1205, probably as a result of damage sustained over the target. Heading to L/O, a lone B-24 that probably was not able to drop on the Hamburg target because of some problem bombed the Nordholz airdrome south of Cuxhaven. The target of opportunity suffered damage to its perimeter track. L/O for the group and their bombers was over Cuxhaven, between 1215 and 1245 hrs. Continuing on with their charges, the 434th and the 436th FSs took them down the North Sea, all the way to England, making L/F there at Cromer around 1350 to 1414 hrs. The 435th FS veered away from the B-24s over the sea and at a point about two thirds of the way home.

Observations made during the mission included miscellaneous shipping as well as three large freighters sighted near the Frisian Islands. A 15 ship convoy heading north in the bay by Wilhelmshaven. Two other convoys, one with 40 ships were also spotted in the North Sea. Twenty plus barges or transports were found in the water at Bremerhaven. Seen also, were one hundred plus jetties along both sides of the river Elbe, from Lauenburg to five miles southeast. A sub, an E boat and a tanker were located in the harbor at Den Helder, Holland. Also noted were construction activities at several airfields, including the east-west runways being lengthened at Lüneburg and Alterhausen. White streaks on the ground along those runways were also noted. (Possibly burn marks resulting from the hot exhaust of Me 163s taking off?) An airfield south east of Hamburg appeared to have eight A/C, possibly dummies, sitting around the perimeter. Flak along the coast from Bremerhaven to Cuxhaven was heavy, meager and accurate. At Cuxhaven it became intense. At Hamburg, it was heavy, intense and accurate.

7 August 1944

VIII FC FO 490

No. 117 Monday. Lt. Col. Woods was the group's leader and he also led the 436th FS, which consisted of 16 P-38s. Maj. Herren led the 434th FS, which consisted of 17 P-38s and Capt. Carter led the 435th FS, which consisted of 15 P-38s. Their assignment was a patrol and sweep in support of 3rd BD B-17s attacking their 8th AF Mission 527 target in France, where they spent all of their time. 434th FS up: 0922 hrs., down: 1350 hrs. with two early returns. 435th FS up: 0932 hrs., down: 1340 hrs. with no early returns. 436th FS up: 0914 hrs., down: 1351 hrs. with no early returns.

L/F for the group was over le Tréport at 1012 hrs./18-20,000 ft. Heading in, the group passed north of Paris and began patrolling an area bounded by Meaux to Melun on the west and twenty miles southeast of Vitry to Châlons on the east. The group flew around this uneventful area for a little over an hour, then began their sweep back, heading first west, then northeast, working their way up, off the coast. During the sweep, the 435th FS flew top cover while the other two squadrons had a field day destroying and damaging four locomotives, over 112 goods and coal wagons, 40 passenger/troop cars, switch houses, trucks, barges, factories, high-tension towers and a flak tower by the rail tracks near Meaux. Arriving at the coast, L/O was between Dieppe and le Tréport around 1255 hrs. for the 434th FS and the 436th FS. The 435th FS had split up and crossed out earlier near Le Havre and le Tréport at 1200 hrs. They must have been bored watching all the fun the other two squadrons were having below.

Observations made during the mission included the spectacle two B-17s lost to flak over Rouen. No chutes were seen. A serviceable air drome ten miles east of Dieppe was also noted. Flak at an airfield near Montmirat was heavy, intense, but inaccurate, while at Hanfleur, it was heavy, intense and accurate. At Rouen it was heavy intense and accurate, at Fère Champenoise, it was light, moderate and accurate and at Marigny, it was heavy, meager and inaccurate.

Two 436th FS enlisted men, Sergeant Charles K. Pruyne and Corporal Bart Massimino are seen clowning around with a few of the squadron's bombs. Cpl. Massimino appears about to blast his sergeant and himself to kingdom come. *Courtesy of Raymond Niekamp.*

8 August 1944

VIII FC FO 494

No. 118 Tuesday. Lt. Col. Riddle was the group's leader and he also led the 434th FS, which consisted of 16 P-38s. Maj. Glover led the 435th FS, which consisted of 17 P-38s and Capt. Sullivan led the 436th FS, which consisted of 17 P-38s. Their assignment was a fighter-bomber attack on rail and tactical targets in the Dijon, France area. 434th FS up: 1210 hrs., down: 1532 hrs. with one early return. 435th FS up: 1205 hrs., down: 1537 hrs. with three early returns. 436th FS up: 1200 hrs., down: 1540 hrs. with two early returns.

This was easily one of the best ground shows for the group to date. Two squadrons, the 434th and the 435th loaded up with 250-lb. and 500-lb. bombs. The 436th, tasked to provide top cover, carried drop tanks. L/F for the group was over le Tréport between 1250 and 1300 hrs./16-18,000 ft. Half an hour later, they arrived at the start point, northeast of Melun. The 436th FS broke into two sections and covered the other two squadrons. The 434th FS headed down the lower route from Melun to Argenteuil, following the railroad tracks. The 435th took the high route down, following the tracks from Melun to St. Parres. The total destroyed and damaged list includes three marshalling yards, a train loaded with heavy field guns, 18 locomotives, 98 freight cars, 18 oil cars, six box cars, sections of track, two railroad buildings, a railroad bridge, another small bridge, a viaduct, a dam, a factory, five staff cars and a number of assorted vehicles. A 434th pilot, Lieutenant John W. Hansen, did the neatest piece of work. He spotted a railroad tunnel entrance, lowered his flaps, headed for the opening and tossed his 500-lb. bomb cleanly inside. He did not stick around to assess the damage, but did report clouds of smoke coming from both ends of the tunnel. All of this havoc done to the German war machine came at a price, however. Captain John J. Courtney, Jr. from the 435th FS, going down after a truck during one of the many very low-level strafing passes the squadrons both made, struck a tree near Ravières, tearing off part of a wing. Pieces continued to come off as the P-38 struggled for altitude. Rolling over, the plane dove into the ground, exploding on impact and scattering wreckage all over the area. Fortunately, Lt. Courtney had bailed out, albeit at a low altitude of 300-400 ft. His chute opened about 150 ft. above the ground, barely slowing him down. He struck the ground hard and was not seen to move. Lt. Courtney had to be left behind because of flak in the area. Interestingly enough, he reappeared just 16 days later at Wattisham, dressed as a French peasant, complete with beret and bearing a bottle of vintage champagne. After a brief visit, rest and change of clothes, he was rushed off to London for the usual interrogation that followed the return of an evader from enemy territory.

Their attack completed, the squadrons headed northwest while reassembling and preparing to head home. East of Paris, they were directed to intercept and escort some bombers out.

Two boxes, 50-60 B-24s, were picked up southeast of there at 1345 hrs. Fifteen minutes later, a flight from the 436th FS went down to investigate unidentified aircraft below them. Lieutenants Hans J. Grasshoff and his wingman, Arlett G. Mosier, Jr., noted P-51s milling around as if in a fight. Three Me 109s went down on the 51s and when they split up, Lt. Grasshoff followed one into a cloud, firing as he chased him. Loosing the E/A momentarily, Lt. Grasshoff picked up the Me 109 on the other side of the cloud and began firing again. The three went in and out of clouds until all of Lt. Grasshoff's ammunition was consumed. Lt. Grasshoff continued to apply aggressive tactics in the hope that the enemy pilot would bail out, but that was not to be. The German escaped with some damage to his airplane. Returning to escort duty with the rest of the group, all continued on, until Dieppe, where the group broke away from the bombers at 1500 hrs. and made for home.

There were no observations recorded from the mission. Flak at Le Tourniquet was heavy, moderate and accurate. At Romilly airdrome, it was heavy, intense and accurate.

First Lieutenant William (Bill) H. Hehn by the P-38 his crew chief Technical Sergeant Milan J. Stanovich named Rumboogie. *Courtesy of Berkley E. Hollister.*

9 August 1944

VIII FC FO 496

No. 119 Wednesday. Lt. Col. Woods was the group's leader and he also led the 435th FS, which consisted of 17 P-38s. Maj. Herren led the 434th FS, which consisted of 16 P-38s and Capt. Biscayart led the 436th FS, which consisted of 17 P-38s. Their assignment was penetration to target and withdrawal escort for 2nd BD B-24s attacking their 8th AF Mission 533 primary target at Sindelfingen, Germany and their secondary target, the marshalling yards at Saarbrücken, Germany. 434th FS up: 0932 hrs., down: 1344 hrs. with no early returns. 435th FS up: 0930 hrs., down: 1332 hrs. with four early returns plus one escort. 436th FS up: 0920 hrs., down: 1335 hrs. with three early returns plus one escort.

The 8/10ths cloud cover played havoc with this mission, causing a diversion to the secondary target and making escort difficult due to the many cloud layers that the bombers kept disappearing into. L/F for the group was over Nieuport, Belgium at 1004 hrs./17-18,000 ft. Proceeding in and southeast, the group made an early R/V with the bombers over Trier, Germany. This was a piece of luck because the Big Friends were strung out and the group had to break into squadrons and go their separate ways in order to provide adequate cover. Continuing southeast, the force reached the primary target at Sindelfingen, just south of Stuttgart, Germany about 1100 hrs. Cloud cover prevented all the bombers from releasing their loads, but the results from those that did, appeared to be good. Gray smoke rising to 15,000 ft. was observed over the target. At 1120 hours, Yellow and Blue Flights from the 434th FS broke away from the formation during the swing around the target. Over Nürnberg, they sighted an airfield below. Having obtained permission from the group leader, they dove from 21,000 ft. Experiencing buffeting and the beginnings of compressibility, the P-38s reached speeds of between 550-600 IAS. Each pilot had some difficulty in pulling out of the dive, but oh, the speed was nice when they screamed across the field at 500+ IAS! The Germans on that field never knew what hit them. The time over the field was so short, that minimal quantities of ammunition were expended. First Lieutenant William H. Hehn only used 320 rounds of .50 cal. and 74 rounds of 20mm destroying/damaging three A/C and Second Lieutenant Tom D. Neely used only 140 rounds of .50 cal. and 22 rounds of 20mm on his He 111.

Making one east to west pass, the Lightnings did their damage and were gone in just moments. Pulling up from the attack and heading west, Major Frank J. Keller, Yellow Flight Leader, spotted another field a few miles west of the one they had just attacked. Diving from 5,000 feet, Yellow Flight made a pass on the airfield at Fürth. Flak there was intense so after the pass, the flight pulled up and left. The results of those attacks were:

At Nürnberg

2-0-0	He 111	1st Lt. William H. Hehn
0-0-1	Ju 52	1st Lt. William H. Hehn
1-0-0	Ju 88	1st Lt. George D. Hendrix
1-0-0	Fw 200K	Maj. Frank J. Keller
1-0-0	Fw 200K	2nd Lt. Harold E. Matthews
1-0-0	He 111	2nd Lt. Tom D. Neely

At Fürth

1-0-0	Do 217	Maj. Frank J. Keller
1-0-0	He 111	Shared by Maj. Keller and Lt. Neely

Unfortunately, at the second airfield, the two flights ran into intense, accurate, heavy and light flak, along with small arms fire. The AA fire followed them and approximately ten miles west of the Fürth airfield, the flights were bracketed while they were at 20,000 ft. Major Frank J. Keller received a direct hit on the left engine of his aircraft. The engine burst into flame and pieces started falling off. Flames enveloped the whole boom. He rode the plane down to about 13,000 feet, then bailed out just before the P-38 broke up. He opened his chute immediately. First Lieutenant William H. Hehn spiraled down and flew by him to see if he was alive. Maj. Keller waved vigorously to motion the Lieutenant away, so Lt. Hehn did not wait around to watch the Major land, as he was quite high and over a flak area. Maj. Keller was captured and became a prisoner of war.

The remainder of the squadron stayed with the B-24s, escorting them out of the primary target area and on up northwest, to their secondary target at Saarbrücken. The remaining, larger portion of the bombers unloaded on the marshalling yards there. Four chutes were reported as seen south of the target by the 436th FS. Heading out, the squadrons stayed as escorts, picking up more B-24s along the way. Like shepherds, the P-38s herded the stragglers back into the formations. Countless P-47s and P-51s were encountered along the way and these had to be avoided. South of Aachen, Germany, the remaining two flights from the 434th FS broke escort and went on out. L/O for the remaining 435th and 436th FSs was over Overflakee between 1230 and 1247 hrs. The squadrons then broke escort at mid-water and headed home.

Observations made during the mission included 30 to 40 twin-engine A/C spotted on the field at Nürnberg. Two unidentified towns near Sindelfingen had large fires burning in them. The Bierset airdrome at Liège, Belgium appeared to be camouflaged and the Dutch Islands as well as surrounding areas appeared to be 50% flooded. Flak over the targets was heavy, intense and accurate.

Second Lieutenant Tom D. Neely. *Courtesy of Frederick C. Hayner.*

Major Frank J. Keller. *Courtesy of Frederick C. Hayner.*

9 August 1944

VIII FC FO 497

No. 120 Wednesday. Capt. John A. Sullivan was the group's leader for this expedition. His force consisted of seven P-38s from the 434th FS and nine from the 436th FS. Their assignment was to escort three 482nd BG B-17s on their 8th AF Mission 535 into France for a flight test of the Micro H device. (A combination of beam radar and H2X, an airborne ground scanning radar used for blind bombing and navigation.) Time up: 1810 hrs., down: 2035-2100 hrs. R/V with the bombers was over Beachy Head, England at 1900-1912 hrs. L/F was over le Touquet at 1916 hrs./25,000 ft. The small force flew in, heading southeast to the target area near Amiens. Flak over Abbeville was heavy, intense, but inaccurate. Over Amiens, it was heavy, moderate and inaccurate. No enemy aircraft were sighted and the group returned, leaving the continent over le Trέport at 1950 hrs./25,000 ft. L/F over England was made, again over Beachy Head at 2025 hrs./ 20,000 ft.

Right: Lieutenant Colonel Kyle L. Riddle. *Courtesy of Frederick C. Hayner.*

Below: Lieutenant John W. Hedenberg by the P-38 he flew. *Courtesy of John W. Hedenberg.*

10 August 1944

VIII FC FO 498

No. 121 Thursday. Lt. Col. Riddle was the group's leader and he also led the 436th FS, which consisted of 16 P-38s. Capt. Jeffrey led the 434th FS, which consisted of 17 P-38s and Capt. Sykes led the 435th FS, which consisted of 16 P-38s. Their assignment was a fighter-strafing attack on rail transportation targets in southeastern France. 434th FS up: 0912 hrs., down: 1255 hrs. with one early return. 435th FS up: 0910 hrs., down: 1230 hrs. with one early return. 436th FS up: 0907 hrs., down: 1230 hrs. with no early returns.

In retrospect, Lt. Col. Kyle L. Riddle probably would have preferred to avoid this mission for reasons soon to be shown. The group's assignment was to attack rail traffic on the line that ran from Vesoul to Dijon and the line that ran from Arc, through Dijon, St. Florentin, Joigny and Melun to Paris. L/F in for the group was over Dieppe at 1002-1005 hrs./18-20,000 ft. Heading in and southeast, the squadrons, led by Col. Riddle, began drawing close to the target area, when at about 1030 hours, the 434th FS spotted rail activity in the vicinity of Oulchy le Château. The squadron called and asked permission to attack it. Permission was given and Newcross Squadron headed north, then southeast down along that rail line. Lt. Col. Riddle took the 436th FS along to provide top cover. The train that the 434th attacked was dispatched and at this point Lt. Col. Riddle decided to start another strafing run. He took his flight down from 6,000 ft. toward the marshalling yard at Meaux and began the run. Leading, he asked someone to follow him and strafe his drop tanks after he let them loose on the yard. On the deck and approaching his target, Lt. Col. Riddle and his wingman Second Lieutenant James E. Frolking started shooting at a large number of goods wagons in the yard. Defensive flak began coming up at the attackers and almost instantly after they dropped their tanks, Lt. Col. Riddle's left wing burst into flames and dipped dangerously, causing him to turn toward his wingman, Second Lt. Frolking. The Lieutenant pulled up to avoid being struck. Pilots from the 434th FS heard the Lt. Col. to say: "The SOB's hit me!" Then there was some heavy breathing heard. He straightened the plane somewhat and disappeared over a small hill. When his wingman called, Lt. Col. Riddle replied: "I'm okay." The 435th FS heard him to say: "I have to set this damn thing down, pull up on account of flak." Moments later, Lt. Frolking saw a crashed and burning airplane in a field about a mile or two northwest of the town. While all this was occurring, the 434th FS was continuing on down the rail line towards Épernay. The 435th FS continued to head down another of the lines that pointed towards Dijon.

Not one to be counted out without a fight, Lt. Col. Kyle L. Riddle become a successful evader and returned to his group a month later. He had felt the jarring of the flak explosion and immediately spotted the fire caused by the flak hit. Flames were pouring back from the gasoline fed fire near the leading edge of his plane's left wing and smoke quickly began entering the cockpit. Within seconds, the smoke obscured his vision. While trying to keep the damaged aircraft in the air, he began waving his free arm and hand in an attempt to clear some of it so that he could see to guide the plane. Enough cleared that he was able to see a tall tree directly ahead of him. Pulling back on the wheel, he was able to zoom up over the tree, but the rapid gain in altitude had bled off his airspeed and the P-38 began to mush down towards the ground. A grain field loomed straight ahead and Lt. Col. Riddle was forced to set his injured bird down there. He had landed near Boureches, about five or six miles northwest of Château-Thierry. Scrambling to get clear of the burning plane, Lt. Col. Riddle unbuckled his straps and got rid of his oxygen mask. In trying to rise up and climb out of the cockpit, he felt a tugging on his upper leg and realized that he had not undone one of his straps. Settling back down into his seat, he undid the remaining strap and then rapidly exited. After he jumped from blazing plane and hit the ground, he began running from the scene. He had in fact bellied the damaged aircraft in, gotten out and was off to the side of the burning fighter when Second Lieutenant Frolking passed nearby. Moments later he spotted several French farmers waving for him to lie down in the field. He did so and after a short period, he was guided from the area. Later he was moved much further away from the place of his downing. The resistance kept him hidden until the facial burns he had received could heal and the advancing Allied lines reached his place of hiding.

John W. Hedenberg was on that mission and recorded some details in his diary that are interesting to note:

> "Went on strafing run today. Lt. Col. Riddle led our squadron and the group. We were supposed to start at Vesoul, close to the Swiss border, and work our way back to just short of Paris. However, on the way, somebody called that he had seen a train and got permission to go down and get it – which he did. The Col. took the whole group down and decided to start strafing there. He called for someone to shoot up his belly tanks and set them on fire when he dropped them. I slid my element in behind him – I was leading the second element in his flight. He turned into a run toward a marshalling yard at Meaux and I do believe half the light flak in France was there. They clobbered him almost before he started shooting. His left wing caught fire and I think his left engine was shot out too, since he slued left at that moment. I instantly broke hard to the right in order to go around the town. I wasn't going to follow him across that mess of flak for anything; it would have been suicide. As I turned, I saw him just skim over a hill beyond the town and when I got over there, I saw the ship was smeared all over the landscape and was burning. He may have gotten out, but I doubt it. I took over the flight and we continued on up to Paris without seeing anything more to shoot up. Big city, Paris! From there, I brought the flight home."

At 1045 hours, about the same time as when Lt. Col. Riddle was having his troubles, First Lieutenant James E. Fleming, Jr. from the 434th FS, was hit by the heavy, intense and accurate flak coming from the area of Épernay. The squadron had followed the rail line down to there from Oulchy le Château. His P-38 received a direct hit at about 6,000 feet above the Épernay forest. The aircraft went out of control and dove into the woods, exploded and burned. There wasn't any chute seen, thus leaving little doubt that Lt. Fleming had been killed.

Continuing, the squadrons flew on, strafing until each plane's ammunition was either low or expended. Turning back then, they made their way back home. The 435th FS was able to see that they were over le Tréport and crossed out at about 1155 hours, but L/O was obscured mostly by cloud cover. The 436th FS crossed out approximately the same time and the 434th FS was later. The mission was successful and tallied a large quantity of destroyed and damaged rail stock, including: 13 locomotives, 103 goods wagons, two flat cars carrying tanks, eight gondola cars, two flak cars each bearing quad 40mm flak guns, seven passenger cars, ten flak towers, a switching tower and nine trucks. They also seriously disrupted a marshalling yard.

On the way back home, Lieutenants. George W. Gleason and John T. Tipps, flying as part of the 434th FS's Red Flight, spotted an isolated German motorcyclist with another occupant in a sidecar, traveling down a dirt road in France. Lt. Gleason asked his friend, Lt. Tipps, to provide cover for him and dove down behind the unfortunate cyclists. Lt. Gleason opened fire, giving the two Germans a short burst. That was all it took, the combined effects of four .50 cal. machine guns and a 20mm cannon were deadly. Lt. Gleason pulled back up into formation and the flight continued homeward. When Lt. Tipps asked Lt. Gleason why he did that, Gleason replied, "That might have been old Adolph down there! You can't tell when he might decide to go for a motorcycle ride."

Observations made during the mission included an Me 410 that the 434th went after near the Boulogne area, but could not catch. There was much activity in the forest around Épernay, including at least 20 trucks seen on a road through the wooded area. The marshalling yard at Meaux had at least 100 goods wagons located there. Flak over Dieppe was heavy, intense, but inaccurate. Over Boulogne and Villaroche, it was heavy, moderate and accurate. Flak was heavy, intense and accurate over Châlons-sur-Marne and the forest around Épernay. The area of Meaux put up both heavy and light, intense and accurate fire. At Leon, it was light, intense and accurate.

11 August 1944

VIII FC FO 504

No. 122 Friday. Maj. Herren was the group's leader and he also led the 434th FS, which consisted of 17 P-38s. Capt. Carter led the 435th FS, which consisted of 17 P-38s and Capt. Sullivan led the 436th FS, which consisted of 15 P-38s. Their assignment was an area patrol and bomber escort in support of 8th AF Mission 542 over the Brest Peninsula of France. 434th FS up: 1445 hrs., down: 1900 hrs. with one early return. 435th FS up: 1510 hrs., down: 1905 hrs. with one early return. 436th FS up: 1455 hrs., down: 1910 hrs. with three early returns.

The squadrons crossed out of southern England in the vicinity of Portland Bill, flew down the English Channel, passing over or near the island of Guernsey and making L/F over the peninsula at various times and places. The 434th FS arrived at the patrol area at 1638 hrs./18,000 ft. and began an uneventful circuit. The 435th FS passed in over St. Brieuc at 1650 hrs./19,000 ft. They then flew south, crossing the peninsula to the Vannes area, continued northwest along the coast to the southeast corner of the patrol area. From there, they continued circling the outer most portion of the Brest Peninsula for the remainder of the mission. L/F for the 436th FS was over Lannion at 1640 hrs./20,000 ft. They headed south to a point east of Lorient and began circling the peninsula to the west. They each patrolled for a little over an hour and then headed for home, with both the 435th and the 436th FSs leaving France behind at Batz Island, on the northern edge of the peninsula. They came back to Wattisham as they had left, crossing the southern coast of England and passing east of London. The patrol was uneventful with no enemy aircraft seen.

Observations made during the mission included a number of freighters and small boats seen throughout the flight. Large fires, flares, and black smoke were seen coming from Brest, where many hits from bombs were noted. There were also hits near the lighthouse located midway between Brest and St. Mathieu Point as well as at Roscanvel and Camaret, where bombs were seen exploding. The 434th FS watched, as bombers from the 1st BD attacked installations around the city of Brest. The bombs from the B-17s produced lots of smoke and dust. One large column of black smoke seemed to be coming from an oil dump that was hit northwest of the city. Flak in the patrol area was minor, with the 434th reporting that just one lone AA gun appeared to be firing "feebly and futilely" from Brest. The 435th recorded the flak there as heavy, moderate and inaccurate. The 436th FS said that flak was nil.

12 August 1944

VIII FC FO 506 A

No. 123 Saturday. Lt. Col. Woods was the group's leader and he also led the 434th FS, which consisted of 16 P-38s. Capt. Gates led the 435th FS, which consisted of nine P-38s. Their assignment was a fighter-bomber attack on tactical and railroad targets in France. 434th FS up: 0538 hrs., down: 0825 hrs. with one early return. 435th FS up: 0546 hrs., down: 0816 hrs. with no early returns.

The orders read: "ASSUMPTION OF COMMAND- Under the provisions of AR 600-20, the undersigned hereby assumes command of the 479th Fighter Group." Signed by Colonel Hubert Zemke and dated 12 August 1944, General Order Number 5 placed the familiar personality in command of the group. Having left the 56th Fighter Group at Boxted to take over the command of Lt. Col. Riddle, who recently "vacated the position," Col. Zemke was soon to make his presence known. From the sign that read: "KNOCK! I'M A BASTARD TOO! LET'S SEE YOU SALUTE!!" he had placed on his office door, to his leadership style, "The Big Z", as some of the men from the 435th FS called him, was there to make some changes and move the group in the direction that he felt it needed to go. It would be six days before Col. Zemke entered hostile airspace with the group. In the meantime, he became familiar with his new territory.

The group continued its series of attacks on the rail system in northwest France, carrying out four missions this day. Divided into A, B, C and D sections, the first target area struck was roughly bounded by Amiens to the west, Cambrai to the north, Guise and Épernay to the east and Compiègne to the south. The 435th FS provided top cover for the 434th FS. However, both squadrons carried five hundred pound General Purpose bombs for this mission. L/F was over point Haut Banc,

Left: The sign that Colonel Zemke had posted on his office door. These enlisted men found a use for it after it was discarded following the Colonel's loss. Pictured in the front row are Master Sergeant Jack E. Gowan, Master Sergeant Alvin R. Willhite and Technical Sergeant William M. Morgan. Behind them are Technical Sergeants Clifton M. Greene and Harold L. Greenlee. *Courtesy of William M. Morgan.* Right: Second Lieutenant George D. Hendrix by the P-38 he named Tarzana. *Courtesy of Clarence G. Haynes.*

south of Boulogne at 0631 hrs./16,000 ft. The 434th destroyed/damaged three locomotives, 40 goods wagons and 25 oil tank cars. Another train, apparently loaded with ammunition, was demolished in a huge explosion caused by one pilot. In addition, the squadron damaged three marshalling yards, destroyed/damaged a flak position, 18 trucks and two staff cars. They also damaged three factories and destroyed another, that when hit by four bombs, exploded in a green colored blast. The 435th bombed from their covering altitude, destroying a factory. L/O was about 0750 hrs.

Two experiences are notable from the mission: First, Second Lieutenant George D. Hendrix from the 434th FS, while flying near Compiègne, saw a plane flying on the deck. His brief Combat Report outlines what happened:

> "I went down and identified it as a Ju 88. I opened fire from astern at 400 yards, closing to 20 yards at an altitude of 25 to 100 feet. I saw strikes all over the plane and observed large pieces flying off the tail section and fuselage. Large holes appeared in the wing and both engines. The plane crashed into a power line and exploded. I believe both pilots and the gunner were trapped and killed by the crash."

First Lieutenant James M. Hollingsworth was with Lt. Hendrix at the time and confirmed the destruction. Now for the rest of the story: when Lt. Hendrix first sighted the unidentified aircraft, he thought it was a British Mosquito. Going down to check, Lt. Hendrix closed up and flew formation with the German A/C until he saw the unfamiliar cross and swastika painted on the plane. Then identifying it as a Ju 88, he dropped back into position and opened fire. Pieces and oil flew out of the enemy aircraft so thick and fast that Lt. Hendrix's windshield was covered over and he had to skid out to the side to find the 88's position, then slide back and fire some more. The plane's rear gunner fired a few bursts in the direction of Lt. Hendrix, but none hit. Lt. Hendrix finally overshot and Lt. Hollingsworth gave it a few squirts before Lt. Hendrix came back to give it the *coup de grâce*. Lt. Hendrix went back to Wattisham with a well-oiled machine. Certainly no squeaks were heard from that bird for a while. Well, maybe that is, because Lt. Hendrix flew the later mission that day, using the same P-38. This time he brought it back with about 70 flak holes. The plane's crew chief Staff Sergeant Henry J. Robitz was probably not very happy with Lt. Hendrix that day.

The second interesting experience from that mission concerns Second Lieutenant Harry E. Little, also from the 434th FS. It occurred during the first strafing run in the area of St. Quentin. Flying top cover above, both Captain William Gates and Lieutenant Stephen H. Zuchowski from the 435th FS, reported seeing a P-38 that appeared to go end over end in the air, down on the deck. Fearing trouble, they went down to investigate. Drawing alongside, they noted the pilot appeared to have recovered and was in fact, firing at something. They left the 434th FS plane and returned to their duty as protective cover. Again, here is the rest of the story: Lt. Little never came back home that day and was posted as "Missing". As luck would have it, he rang up the base the next day, asking for someone to please come and get him from some base in southern England. It seems as though Lt. Little hit a high-tension line during his strafing run, causing him to do two quick snap rolls from which he wound, right side up. As he straightened up, he saw a flak position firing at him so he gave it a good working over while flying on single engine. He then limped up to 1800 feet and started home. As he got over the channel, he began to get low on gas so he picked out a minesweeper, bailed out and parachuted down, landing in the water near the vessel. He returned to base with some wild tales about Navy hospitality.

Observations made during the mission were dealt with at the time. Light, intense and accurate flak was reported coming from a wooded area near where Lt. Little attacked an AA position.

12 August 1944

VIII FC FO 506 B

No. 124 Saturday. Capt. Sullivan was the group's leader and he also led the 436th FS, which consisted of 15 P-38s. Capt. Sykes led the 435th FS, which consisted of eight P-38s. This was the second fighter-bomber mission the group flew into northwest France for the day. Their assignment was to attack more rail and tactical targets. 435th FS up: 0754 hrs., down: 1016 hrs. with no early returns. 436th FS up: 0747 hrs., down: 1035 hrs. with one early return.

Carrying 500-lb. GP bombs again, the force made L/F over Berck at 0830 hrs./17-18,000 ft. Whereas the previous two squadrons had worked over the area about north-northwest of Paris earlier in the morning, this assembly went after that area just south of and farther northwest of the first strike area. Targets bombed and strafed extended to southeast of Paris and included Soissons, Crépy, Nanteuil, Lizy, Meaux and St. Mards. Destroyed and damaged totals were: a locomotive, 16 goods wagons, a viaduct, three bridges and a marshalling yard at St. Mards. Lieutenant John W. Hedenberg laid his two 500 pounders right between the rails of one stretch of track, putting it out of commission for a while. Howard G. Hightower used his two bombs on a bridge, scoring two direct hits and destroying it completely. L/O was over Dieppe at 0929 hrs./ 18,000 ft.

Observations made during the mission were dealt with at the time. Flak for the low flying planes was light, intense and accurate throughout their route.

12 August 1944

VIII FC FO 506 C

No. 125 Saturday. Maj. Herren was the group's leader and he also led the 434th FS, which consisted of 16 P-38s. Capt. Gates led the 435th FS, which consisted of nine P-38s. This was the third fighter-bomber attack of rail and tactical targets in northwest France for the day. 434th FS up: 1108 hrs., down: 1355 hrs. with one early return. 435th FS up: 1113 hrs., down: 1340 hrs. with two early returns.

The 435th FS provided top cover while the 434th FS bombed and strafed parts of the area that had been targeted previously during the day. Places hit this time included St. Quentin down to Roye, to Braine and to Meaux. L/F was over Dieppe at 1155 hrs./16-17,000 ft. In the target area, the squadrons began dropping their mixture of 250 and 500-lb. GP bombs as well as strafing targets of opportunity. The results included the following destroyed and or damaged: three marshalling yards, three locomotives, two ammunition cars, 45 goods wagons, 15 empty oil cars, a water tower, three flak towers, a tunnel, three trucks, an auto, four high-tension wire towers, 18 barges, two bridges and two factories. L/O was over le Tréport at 1251 hrs./16,000 ft.

On this mission George D. Hendrix was participating in an attack on a suspected ammunition factory/warehouse. As he told it later:

> " I made a run on a warehouse and just as I started to pull up, all hell broke loose. There was apparently a large cache of explosives in the building and it blew sky high. After I flew out of the debris, I had to shut down an engine because it was overheating. My plane's wings were full of holes, some the size of a fist. Metal was peeled back like a tin can. I became separated from the rest of the squadron, but luckily I didn't run into any German fighters. The flight back to Wattisham on one engine seemed like the longest mission of my combat tour. After I landed, my crew chief counted over 70 holes in the aircraft."

Observations made during the mission included sighting some factories believed to be steel mills. They were located between Béthune, Lille and Lens and appeared to be untouched by the bombings. A convoy of 15-20 trucks was seen on the highway from St. Quentin, heading toward Paris. (The pilots MUST have been out of ammunition!) Many barges in the rivers and canals of Guise, Somme and Aisne were also noted, particularly between Beauvais and Paris. Hidden under trees along the banks, they were believed to contain oil. Flak from St. Omer to Gravelines was heavy, intense and accurate. Light flak was prevalent around most target sites.

12 August 1944

VIII FC FO 506 D

No. 126 Saturday. Capt. Jules D. Biscayart was the group's leader and he also led the 436th FS, which consisted of 18 P-38s. Capt. Sykes led the 435th FS, which consisted of six P-38s. Their assignment was the fourth in a series of fighter-bomber attacks on the rail system and tactical targets in northwest France for the day. 435 FS up: 1350 hrs., down: 1616 hrs. with one early return. 436th FS up: 1330 hrs., down: 1625 hrs. with two early returns.

L/F was in the vicinity of Dieppe at 1425 hrs./18,000 ft. The squadrons, each loaded down with two 500-lb. GP bombs per plane, moved inward towards the target area. The 435th FS provided top cover again. Arriving at the assigned area, roughly bounded by Amiens, St. Quentin, Épernay and Paris, the pilots got to work. The shift's tally of destroyed and damaged targets included two barges, a locomotive, 42 goods wagons and oil cars, four passenger cars, four railroad bridges, a railroad intersection, a marshalling yard, a tunnel, two switch houses, five trucks and stretches of railroad track. L/O was over Point du Haut Banc at 1520 hrs./14,000 ft. for the 435th FS and over Le Crotoy at 1533 hrs./13,000 ft. for the 436th FS.

Observations made during the mission included two flak towers south of St. Quentin, 15 single-engine A/C on an airdrome at Piox, and another camouflaged airdrome with hangars and two runways forming a NW/SE-SW/NE "V", parallel to a woods four miles south of La Fère. Flak encountered in the area was generally light, meager and inaccurate. One lone gun was hidden in a haystack, the cover being moved away to expose the gun for firing.

A frame from First Lieutenant Harold (Bud) F. Grenning's gun camera film showing the train he attacked. He claimed 15 empty oil cars damaged. *Courtesy of Harold F. Grenning.*

13 August 1944

VIII FC FO 511 A

No. 127 Sunday. Maj. Glover was the group's leader and he also led the 435th FS, which consisted of 15 P-38s. Capt. Moore led the 436th FS, which consisted of eight P-38s. Their assignment was a fighter-bomber attack on tactical and rail targets in France. 435th FS up: 0510 hrs., down: 0705 hrs. with three early returns. 436th FS up: 0506 hrs., down: 0750 hrs. with one early return.

This was another day filled with activity as the group sent out four strikes during the course of the day, against targets of opportunity in the area above Paris. Today the roles were to be reversed with the 436th FS providing top cover for the other two squadrons during the day's missions. L/F was between Fécamp and Dieppe at 0600 hrs./18-19,000 ft. Entering the same target area as was covered the day before, the force again went after the transportation system carrying supplies to German troops. With 250-lb. bombs and by strafing, the P-38 pilots destroyed/damaged three locomotives, 20 goods wagons, a marshalling yard and sections of railroad track. The 436th FS was able to attack a locomotive and the first three cars of a train that was 25 cars long. Included in that length of cars were ten light flak guns, one to a car. That made attacking it a very dangerous business and as a consequence, the train escaped with only some damage. The squadron attacked another train, but again was driven off by return fire. The results of that attack were not observed due to the hasty retreat. L/O was for the 435th FS was east of le Tréport at 0643 hrs./22,000 ft. while it was south of Boulogne at 0645 hrs./13,000 ft. for the 436th FS.

Observations made during the mission included noting that Montdidier appeared to be the site of a lot of transport traffic. Several trains other than those attacked were seen. The runways at the Baumone-Sur-Ois Airfield, north of Paris had its lights on. Lights and blinker signals were going at the Abbeville airdrome. The 436th reported several unorthodox calls received from Colgate, the 65th FW Controller. The reception was louder than normal and the "calling out" signal was not given in the normal manner. Suspicion was aroused and it was felt that the calls had originated from German sources and that they were meant to be diversionary tactics. Most all flak encountered was light, intense, but inaccurate.

Crew chief Sergeant John Wendt, pilot Second Lieutenant Richard G. Simpson and assistant crew chief Corporal Mondell (Bill) G.Trimble. *Courtesy of Frederick C. Hayner.*

13 August 1944

VIII FC FO 511 B

No. 128 Sunday. Capt. Jeffrey was the group's leader and he also led the 434th FS, which consisted of 16 P-38s. Capt. Sullivan led the 436th FS, which consisted of eight P-38s. Their assignment was the day's second fighter-bomber attack on rail and tactical targets in northwest France. 434th FS up: 0700 hrs., down: 0918 hrs. with one early return. 436th FS up: 0657 hrs., down: 0930 hrs. with no early returns.

Returning to the area north of Paris, the two squadrons attacked with 250-lb. bombs and by strafing. With the 436th FS providing top cover, the yield this time was three locomotives, 11 goods wagons, two marshalling yards, a round house, a switch tower, seven stretches of track, six factories, six flak towers, two bridges, a highway overpass, and a truck. L/O was over Cayeux at 0827 hrs./13-15,000 ft.

Observations were prevented because of a ground haze in the area. Flak was light, intense and accurate to light, meager and inaccurate.

Along the route, Second Lieutenant Richard G. Simpson was hit by a lucky shot from some German infantryman taking pot shots at the planes from the ground. The flight had just crossed over a big bunch of trees when they came upon a lot of German soldiers, all dug in and waiting with rifles ready. The small caliber bullet hit his right engine and a piece continued on, entered his canopy and passed through the back of his helmet and scalp, grazing his skull. It almost knocked him out, blurring his vision momentarily. He hugged the ground and received no more hits. Out of range, he pulled up and had to shut down the engine that was hit because it was smoking. He came on home on one engine and through a lot of help from his squadron mates. Berkley E. Hollister recalls that the squadron had to keep Lt. Simpson headed towards Wattisham. It seemed as though the Lieutenant was dazed from the wound, because he kept trying to turn back into enemy territory. Upon his return, the plane's crew chief had a lot of blood to clean up from the cockpit as well as some repairs to the aircraft. Lt. Simpson suffered no serious injury however. After stitches and subsequent treatments by the squadron's doctor, he went back to work a short while later.

That was Lt. Simpson's second very close brush with death. His first occurred in the ZOI, Washington State, 9 November 1943. Lt. Simpson was flying the same kind of aircraft, a P-38:

> "I had been instructed to 'slow time' or in other words, break in and test an aircraft that just had its engines overhauled. I took the A/C up to 32,000 feet per my instructions, but by that time, had decided I didn't like the way the plane was handling. I banked left and pointed the nose down for a slight dive, intending to return to my base and land. Realizing that the plane was heading down faster then I wanted, I tried to bring the nose up, but the A/C would not respond. I tried pulling back on the control column, but no amount of force would ease the dive. By now the P-38 had entered a vertical dive and was picking up a considerable amount of speed. I tried cutting back the engines and I tried adjusting the trim tabs to gain some control. Nothing was working and the hurtling plane was vibrating and shaking so violently that I thought the wings would tear off at any second.
>
> "By now the Lockheed twin-engine fighter had entered what was known as compressibility back then, a situation where buffeting occurs, the A/C's control

surfaces loose their effectiveness, the plane becomes nose heavy and recovery from the dive becomes very difficult. During training, I had been taught that once a pilot was in that situation, there was no chance of survival. The plane could not be pulled out of the dive and the pilot could not bail out since the speed the A/C was traveling was 600+ mph. At that speed, it was thought that the pilot would be struck by the aircraft's empennage when he exited. With that in mind and recognizing that the ground was getting closer every moment, I decided my only chance lay with bailing out. Pulling the canopy release, I was sucked out as soon as the top of the cover was torn away. I did hit the empennage, but it was my parachute pack, which struck the rear part of the plane. The force of the blow knocked me unconscious and tore the chute pack open. When I came to, I was floating in space. My first thoughts were: 'Well, I guess that this must be how it feels to be dead.' Then I heard a fluttering sound and looked up above myself, seeing that my parachute was trailing my descent and had not opened. In fact the shroud lines were all tangled up. Disoriented, I reached for the ripcord, thinking that I needed to pull it and passed out momentarily, from pain. I believe that my shoulder must have been dislocated at the time.

"Coming to, I then looked up again and noticed that the chute had caught some air and opened partially, but also that there was a big tear in the canopy. One side of the parachute was higher than the other and the lower side's shroud lines were floating around. I also noted that I was about to hit the ground.

"I don't remember hitting the ground, but when I came to, I was face down. Getting up on my knees, I tried to unbuckle my chute, but could not use my right hand. Finally freeing myself of the harness and rigging, I stumbled up to higher ground in order to find any signs of civilization. I was in a rugged mountain region and there were none. There was nothing, save for a little something that I thought I saw off in the distance. Starting off, I began a slow decent down to what I saw. The temperature was in the thirties and my pant legs had been ripped off near the waist, but I really didn't notice the cold. I had walked very slowly for about a mile when I came upon a road. I began walking down it. Shortly thereafter, a pickup truck came rolling up and the driver recognizing the need for help, loaded me into the truck and took me to a cabin. I passed out again.

"When I came to again, my rescuers gave me some soup and informed me that they had arranged for my outfit to pick me up in an ambulance. What luck! Out of the many directions that I could have walked, I just happened to pick the route that would place me in the path of two hunters out in the wilderness. The hunters told me that they only came up there in the mountains to hunt once a year and that otherwise, there were very few people around. Back at base, the doctor examined me, but found no broken bones. I was black and blue all over from bruises. Even my eyes were bloody. The doctor said it was a wonder that my eyes weren't torn out of my head. My breastbone was so sore that I had to walk bent over and could hardly move my arms. My parachute was later located and reported as demolished.

"After I had recuperated, the army wanted to take me off flying status and retire me on 100% disability, but I would have nothing of that. I managed to convince the doctor of my firm desire to get back into the war effort and soon enough, found myself with the 479th Fighter Group."

Richard G. Simpson has always thanked, as he puts it, "The Man Upstairs", for sparing him those two times.

13 August 1944

VIII FC FO 511 C

No. 129 Sunday. Lt. Col. Woods was the group's leader and he also led the 435th FS, which consisted of 16 P-38s. Capt. Biscayart led the 436th FS, which consisted of eight P-38s. Their assignment was a continuation of the fighter-bomber attacks on the rail system and tactical targets in northwest France. 435th FS up: 1432 hrs., down: 1710 hrs. with one early return. 436th FS up: 1429 hrs., down: 1720 hrs. with one early return.

This mission was number three in the series of attacks for the day. L/F was north of Dieppe at 1512-1516 hrs./12-16,000 ft. The area attacked was northwest of Paris. Dive-bombing, the 435th using 500-lb. GP and the 436th using 250-lb. GP bombs and strafing, the two squadrons brought back news of more headaches for the Germans. They had destroyed/damaged two marshalling yards, two railroad bridges, some goods wagons, sections of track and a factory. L/O was over Valery at 1615 hrs./12,000 ft. for the 435th FS and over Cayeux at

1620 hrs./12,000 ft. for the 436th FS. There were no observations reported and flak was of the heavy type.

13 August 1944

VIII FC FO 511 D

No. 130 Sunday. Capt. Claire A.P. Duffié was the group's leader and he also led the 434th FS, which consisted of 15 P-38s. Capt. Sullivan led the 436th FS, which consisted of nine P-38s. Their assignment was number four for the day, in the series of attacks against rail and tactical targets in northwest France. 434th FS up: 1605 hrs., down: 1850 hrs. with two early returns. 436th FS up: 1559 hrs., down: 1855 hrs. with three early returns.

With both squadrons carrying 250-lb. GP bombs, L/F was over le Tréport at 1646 hrs./18,000 ft. for the 434th FS, and it was over Cayeux at 1648 hrs./19,000 ft. for the 436th FS. Arriving in the area of St. Quentin, the two squadrons started there and worked their way down south, bringing destruction and damage to the area. They went after two marshalling yards, ten railroad cars, six goods wagons, three factories and 15 barges. L/O was over Knokke, Belgium between 1815 and 1825 hrs./10-13,000 ft.

Observations made during the mission included some 100-150 barges loaded with coal, oil and gasoline seen between Tournai and Garde, on the Garde Canal, on the way out of Belgium. A well-camouflaged airdrome that appeared to be in good shape was spotted south of St. Quentin. Flak was light, meager and accurate at one spot and that was the only fire encountered.

14 August 1944

VIII FC FO 513

No. 131 Monday. Capt. Raymond S. Carter was the group's leader and he also led the 435th FS, which consisted of 13 P-38s. Capt. Turner led the 434th FS, which consisted of ten P-38s and Capt. Biscayart led the 436th FS, which consisted of 12 P-38s. Their assignment was another fighter-bomber attack in France against rail and tactical targets. 434th FS up: 0501 hrs., down: 0832 hrs. with one early return. 435th FS up: 0517 hrs., down: 0834 hrs. with five early returns. 436th FS up: 0500 hrs., down: 0835 hrs. with no early returns.

Take off for the 436th FS did not go well, with some confusion amongst the lineup for take off. As a consequence,

Second Lieutenant Arlett G. Mosier, Jr., with Tiger Lilly's crew, Staff Sergeant Ora Winn, Technical Sergeant Everett A. Sanborn and Sergeant John L. Dvorak. *Courtesy of Arlett G. Mosier, Jr.*

Second Lieutenant Thomas J. O'Holleran wound up taking off on the wing of another wingman, Second Lieutenant Arlett G. Mosier, Jr., instead of with his assigned element leader. After take off, the two, staying together, failed to locate their squadron so a course was set to take them across the channel with hopes of finding their mates. Approximately halfway across the water, they came upon another assembly of P-38s. Lt. Mosier proceeded to climb and to pull up to the left side of the P-38s in order to determine which squadron it was. At this point, Lt. O'Holleran broke away from his wing and pulled off to the right. That was the last Lt. Mosier saw of him, believing that he had joined another flight. Lt. Mosier recognized the squadron that he had pulled beside was not his and went on to later find and join his own. Lt. O'Holleran was not heard from again and went on the group's records as "Missing in Action". After the war was over, it was learned that Lt. O'Holleran had almost made it on his own to the target area, but was shot down by flak southeast of Laon, near Juvincourt. He had survived and become a POW for the rest of the war.

Carrying mostly 1000-lb. GP bombs with a few 250-lb. GPs mixed in, the three squadrons went after targets of opportunity, east of Paris, between Èpernay and Châlons. After the bombing and strafing, the total destroyed and damaged stood at four marshalling yards, a railroad station, a railway junction, three track sections, two locomotives, 70 goods wagons, five bridges, a canal lock, six trucks and a barrage balloon. Part of that action, but not shown in the totals of bombed and strafed, were two Fw 190s that Captain Robin Olds from the 434th FS claimed. He got mixed up with a couple of the Focke-Wulfs and knocked them both down. It wasn't part of the game plan, but it sure was nice. He recorded:

"I was flying Newcross Red Two. I became slightly separated from the rest of the flight on a dive-bombing run near Montmirail. I was alone on the deck, heading approximately 330 degrees, when I saw two unidentified aircraft, one to two miles away at one o'clock. They were in a turn to the right at about 300 feet off the ground. I cut across below them, pulled up behind them and positively identified them as Fw 190s. Then I opened fire on the trailing E/A from dead astern at about 400 yards, firing a five to eight second burst. I observed many strikes on the left wing and the left side of the fuselage so I changed my point of aim slightly to the right and put a concentrated burst into the fuselage. I observed big pieces flying off the German aircraft. Wisps of flame and heavy black smoke poured out from it. The E/A then went into an uncontrolled half roll, going down to the right. At this time we were both just above the trees at an altitude of not over 100 feet.

"The second E/A broke left in a violent evasive skid right on the deck and I followed so I did not see the first German hit the ground because my right wing blocked my view. I was turning inside the second German so I fired in short bursts at a range of approximately 350 to 200 yards, observing a few strikes. The E/A did a complete 360-degree turn and pulled out straight and level, still on the deck. I fired again, approximately a five-second burst, from dead astern and observed many strikes. Large pieces of the German ship flew off. He then zoomed up and I followed, continuing to fire, seeing still more strikes and pieces fly off. At the top of the zoom, the German pilot parachuted. His chute opened almost at once so I had to cock up a wing to keep from hitting him. I saw this second German ship hit the ground and explode." Second Lieutenant George W. Gleason was in the vicinity, at a higher altitude and after hearing Capt. Olds state on the radio that he had two Fws spotted and then that he had gotten one, saw the first Fw hit the ground and explode. Lt. Gleason saw the second hit shortly after. At the same time, he heard Capt. Olds transmit over the radio, " I have an announcement to make. I just shot down the other one, making two for the day."

L/O for the squadrons was at different points and times with the 434th FS crossing out at 0800 hrs./18,000 ft. over Cayeux, the 435th FS at 0755 hrs./18,000 ft. east of Ostend, Belgium and the 436th FS at 0759 hrs./18,000 ft. over Coxyde, Belgium.

Observations made during the mission included: A train made up of about 20 cars carrying tanks, trucks and flak guns was spotted in the area west of Châlons. Flak throughout the area was light, intense and accurate with a few locations firing heavy AA.

15 August 1944

VIII FC FO 516

No. 132 Tuesday. Maj. Glover was the group's leader and he also led the 435th FS, which consisted of 16 P-38s. Capt. Jeffrey led the 434th FS, which consisted of 16 P-38s and Capt. Sullivan led the 436th FS, which consisted of 15 P-38s. Their assignment was a penetration to target and withdrawal for 2nd BD B-24s attacking their 8th AF Mission 554 primary target, the airdrome at Plantlunne, Germany. 434th FS up: 1019 hrs., down: 1433 hrs. with one early return. 435th FS up: 1014 hrs., down: 1410 hrs. with two early returns. 436th FS up: 1021 hrs., down: 1400 hrs. with three early returns.

R/V with the bombers was made at different times and places by the squadrons. The 434th FS joined the B-24s at 1117 hrs./25,000 ft. over the North Sea. The 435th FS joined them at 1120 hrs./25,000 feet, also over the North Sea waters. The 436th FS met the bombers at 1122 hrs./25,000 ft. near the Dutch Terschelling Islands. Escorting the 20th and 95th CWs inland, L/F was north of Groningen, Holland between 1140 and 1200 hrs. Heading to the target airdrome, it was noted that proper escort was difficult to provide because the bomber formation was too spread out. However, after the strike, it was also noted that the bombing results were excellent. The hangars and barracks at the northwest end of the airdrome were burning with flames and black oil smoke reaching to 18,000 ft. Because of that, strafing after the attack was cancelled. Since the weather was CAVU, the airfields of Quackenbrück and Fürstenau in the nearby area were seen to be burning also. Returning the Big Friends home, the 434th FS broke away at about 1305 hrs. over Steenwijk, Holland to attack four plus E/A landing there. There were also nine plus A/C parked in line on the southeast end of the runway. Three E/A were shot down over the field and the parked A/C. were strafed. The results were as follows, with the first three listed being air combats:

1-0-0	Me 109	Capt. Arthur F. Jeffrey
1-0-0	Me 109	1st Lt. John W. Hansen
1-0-0	Me 109	1st Lt. Quentin S. Pavlock
2-0-1	Me 109	1st Lt. John W. Hansen
0-0-1	Trainer	1st Lt. John W. Hansen
1-0-2	Me 109	1st Lt. George D. Hendrix
1-0-0	Me 109	2nd Lt. Calvin J. Murphy

Some of the Combat Reports are reproduced here:

Captain Jeffrey:

"I was flying Newcross Leader with White Flight on a bomber escort when I heard 2nd Lt. George W. Gleason from Blue Flight call out three E/A landing at the Steenwijk airdrome. I made a 180-degree turn and went back over the field, circling to the left and losing altitude, descending from 20,000 feet down to 12,000 feet. As I circled, I could hear Blue Flight in a scrap. When I was just south of the field, I saw a dirty gray, single-engine A/C at 200-500 feet, flying east to west, right over the field at an estimated speed of 250 miles per hour. I made a 180-degree turn to head west and dive on him. Red Flight was to remain at 10,000 feet as top cover. The E/A made a 180-degree turn, heading back east and still at 200-500 feet. That put him right under me. By this time, I had positively identified the A/C as an Me 109 so I split-essed from 6,000 feet down on him. The E/A made a sharp turn to the left and since I was going so fast, I overshot. While I was trying to pull to the left after him, AA fire from the airdrome hit my left wing, knocking out the plane's pitot tube line. [A forward-projecting air intake tube placed on the exterior of the airplane, usually on the leading edge of a wing. The pitot-static system serves as the source of pressure used for operation of the A/C's flying instruments, *i.e.,* the airspeed indicator, vertical speed indicator and altimeter. The loss of these instruments meant that Captain Jeffrey was flying the airplane "by the seat of his pants" through skills built up from many hours of experience.] The E/A then turned back over the runway, as though to lead me back over the flak from the field. I made a 90-degree turn to the left and a 180-degree turn to the right to keep away from the field. As I rolled out, I observed Lt. William H. Rogers, Blue Four, attempting to make a pass on the Me 109, but his speed was also too great and he overshot. The Me 109 then headed back across the field from south to north and I made a 90-degree pass on him in a regular gunnery pattern. I opened fire at 60 degrees, range 350-450 yards and closed to 90 degrees, range 75-100 yards. I opened fire with one long five second burst and observed many strikes all over the E/A and saw many pieces fly off. During this time we were at an altitude of about 200 feet. The German pilot then zoomed up to about 300 feet, jettisoned his canopy and parachuted out. The A/C crashed into the ground almost beneath me and exploded."

Lieutenant Murphy, flying White Two, accounted for an Me 109 on the ground and Lieutenant Hendrix, following and flying White Three, destroyed another one and damaged two more, all on the ground. Lieutenant Hansen, flying Yellow Three:

"We were flying flights in trail, escorting some bombers when the call for bandits came through. We let down and Captain Hiram G. Turner, [he led the 434th FS in yesterday's last mission] Yellow Leader, called and told me to keep the flight at 10,000 feet while he went down to investigate some parachutes which were floating down near the field. He started down and then called for the rest of us to rejoin him, which we did at 5,000 feet, just east of the field. On command, we dropped our belly tanks, swung around west of the field and let down to start our strafing run. I went right down on the deck, three or four miles west of the field. Capt. Turner and Lieutenant James L. Wallace who was Yellow Two were about 200 feet ahead on my right and my wingman, Second Lieutenant John W. Morrow, Yellow Four, was pretty wide and on my left. Approximately two miles west of the field, I observed Yellow Leader break left and then roll out again. I didn't know what for until a moment later, when I observed an Me 109 coming at me almost head-on at zero altitude. Lt. Wallace turned and made a 90-degree deflection shot at the E/A, but I did not observe any strikes or smoke. Lt. Wallace then rolled out and continued his strafing run. I skidded left, to position myself for attack. The Me 109 broke right, as though to avoid my making a head-on pass and as he did, his right wing tip caught a tree causing him to cartwheel into the ground and explode.

"I continued my strafing run and at the west end of the airfield, I observed a multiple barrel AA gun with four gunners firing at Capt. Turner. His right engine caught fire, but he continued straight on down the field, still under control. I dropped my nose and opened fire on the gun position, observing strikes all over and around it. At this time, I was still on the deck and indicating approximately 410 miles per hour. I could see aircraft parked all along the southern edge of the runway so I opened fire on two Me 109s which were in line, firing from 500 yards to 100 yards and observing many strikes on the nearest one. As I closed, the nearest A/C burst into flames and the propeller came off the second one and flew up into the air. I raked a line of about 10-12 slate gray Me 109s that had red side markings as I pulled my nose up. Then, as I came to the east end of the field, I could get my nose down again so I fired a concentrated burst at an Me 109 parked just off the runway. The canopy flew off this A/C and I observed flames coming from the area around the wing roots. Right next to this last Me 109, I observed a fabric covered, low wing, single radial engine aircraft with the engine running. I gave it a squirt and saw the gear collapse and the aircraft fell to the ground. I continued across and away from the field, on the deck."

First Lieutenant Quentin S. Pavlock:

"I was flying Blue Three on a bomber escort mission when we went down to 10,000 feet in order to investigate some parachutes at an airfield. Lieutenant Gleason, Blue Two, broke right and called in two Me 109s attacking from four o'clock. The flight broke right as Lt. Gleason attacked one E/A which split-essed away, then Lieutenant Bailey A. Williams, Blue Leader, attacked the other. Lt. Williams pursued his lone Me 109 down to about 2,000 feet and got on its tail. My element was in close support behind and above him. When Lt. Williams did not open fire and moved out of attack position, I knew something was wrong so I took over the attack. [Lt. Williams tried to fire, but his guns failed to function.] I closed to approximately 300 yards at an altitude of 1,000 feet and fired a burst at 30 to 40-degrees deflection. I observed strikes on his right wing and gray smoke poured out. This gray smoke continued throughout the rest of the engagement. The German made a slight left turn and went down to the deck. I put on full power and closed, getting another deflection shot at a range of approximately 150 yards and again observed strikes on his right wing. Then the Me 109 pulled up to about 300 feet and did a vertical reverse, coming out in a right turn. Just as he reversed his turn, I fired a long burst from dead astern and observed pieces falling off his tail and heavy black smoke began pouring out. My windshield got covered with oil from the German aircraft so I had to skid out to the left a little. The E/A then made a 90-degree turn and straightened out. At close range, I gave it another long burst and the Me 109 dived straight into the ground and exploded. The pilot did not get out. There was another Me 109 on my right, but the oil was so thick on my windshield that I couldn't see so I disengaged and climbed back up to 8,000 feet."

Both, Captain Hiram G. Turner, Jr. and his wingman, First Lieutenant James L. Wallace were lost at that airfield during the course of the attack. As the leader of Yellow Flight, Capt. Turner took his flight down to strafe an enemy airfield. Starting out about five miles west of the field, the four P-38s accelerated towards it to gain speed for the attack. Spaced out about 100 yards apart and back from each other, Yellow Flight came into view of the field, flying 100 feet off the ground. As was already reported, a flak gun at the end of the field was firing at them and had hit Capt. Turner. The same gun probably also hit Lt. Wallace. Lt. Hansen fired at and silenced the gun, then continued his strafing run on the field. Reaching the east side of the field, he saw Lt. Wallace directly over him, with both engines on fire. Pieces were falling from the plane and shortly it rolled over to the right and exploded when it hit the ground near a canal. Lt. Hansen could see Lt. Wallace hanging partially out of the cockpit as it rolled over to his side. With his right engine on fire, Capt. Turner called to say that he was going to bail out so Lt. Hansen followed him in a southeasterly direction. The Captain bailed out from about 250 feet at 1320 hrs. Fire from the exploding airplane engulfed Capt. Turner as he landed beside the crashed P-38. He ran a few yards, dragging his smoldering parachute behind, then collapsed to the ground. He was still lying there when Lt. Hansen had to leave and was last seen being helped by some Dutch civilians. Capt. Turner was captured, hospitalized and made a POW.

L/O for the three squadrons was all over Holland with the 434th FS passing out in the vicinity of Egmond at about 1330 hrs. L/O for the 435th FS was over Zandvoort at 1310 hrs./ 23,000 ft. The squadron had broken from the bombers north of Meppel. L/O for the 436th FS was over Egmond at 1310 hrs./22,000 feet, but they did not leave the B-24s until mid-water over the North Sea. An oil slick was spotted by the 436th approximately 20 miles off the English coast near Lowestoft. It was thought to possibly be from a ditched A/C.

Observations made during the mission included an unidentified aircraft that was seen to crash south of Groningen. There were no chutes. Three P-51s were believed to have crashed north of Steenwijk airdrome at 1310 hrs. as seen by the 434th FS. The same squadron also noted that the west end of that airdrome appeared to be painted red and black. A large airfield was seen east of Meppel. It had long runways and what looked like an underground hangar. A convoy of 20 ships was observed heading east in the Zuider Zee. Flak near Groningen was heavy, moderate and inaccurate. At Steenwijk it was light, intense and accurate. In Germany, it was heavy, meager and inaccurate north of Lingen, heavy, intense and accurate at Borham as well as heavy, moderate and accurate at Emden.

John W. Hedenberg didn't make the mission this day, but there was plenty to keep him busy:

> "In the evening, I checked out in the AT-6 and made a few landings in preparation for flying the P-51 tomorrow. Our squadron Flight Surgeon, known affectionately as 'Doc' Cornelius, was a most likeable older man about forty. He fathered us benevolently and was heartsick whenever one of us was killed or became missing in action. He had to get in a certain number of hours of flight time as a passenger each month, it being required as a part of his job. He really disliked flying, however, and dreaded going up with those of us who couldn't resist teasing him with the acrobatics he dreaded and got airsick from. I offered him the opportunity to ride in the back seat of the squadron's AT-6 to get some of his time in, with the promise that I would play no tricks on him. He accepted gratefully, but blanched when he saw that the rear seat was equipped with a flexible-mount .30 cal. machine gun, saying he wouldn't have the slightest idea how to use it if necessary. I reassured him that the chances of that need actually occurring were essentially zero, and he found he actually enjoyed the ride when he knew he could safely relax and look around.
>
> "Later after the flight, we had a couple of drinks and spent several hours of straightforward 'What are you going to do after the war?' talk in the bar that evening. It developed that he was rather worried that he was losing ground with his skills while serving his Army time – in civilian life he was an obstetrician. Being a flight surgeon in a fighter squadron was giving him no opportunity at all to keep his hand in that, since scarcely any of us ever got pregnant!"

Sleepy Time Gal, the P-38 that First Lieutenant James L. Wallace regularly flew and was flying this date when he was lost. *Courtesy of Frederick C. Hayner.*

Elbow Dottie II and the great men who kept her flying. She went looking for a new pilot when Capt. Turner, the pilot who had named her, went down this date in another P-38. *Courtesy of Frederick C. Hayner.*

16 August 1944

VIII FC FO 518

No. 133 Wednesday. Lt. Col. Woods was the group's leader and he also led the 436th FS, which consisted of 17 P-38s. Newly promoted Lt. Col. Herren led the 434th FS, which consisted of 13 P-38s and Capt. Carter led the 435th FS, which consisted of 17 P-38s. Their assignment was a penetration to target and withdrawal escort for 65 3rd BD B-24s attacking their 8th AF Mission 556 primary target, the airfield south of Halberstadt, Germany. 434th FS up: 0903 hrs., down: 1340 hrs. with no early returns. 435th FS up: 0858 hrs., down: 1355 hrs. with three early returns. 436th FS up: 0851 hrs., down: 1345 hrs. with one early return.

This was an uneventful mission for the group. L/F was over Alkmaar, Holland at 0953 hrs./21,000 ft. for the 434th FS. The squadron also made R/V with their bombers at that time and place. L/F for the 435th FS was over Ijmuiden, Holland at 0954 hrs./22,000 ft. They had made R/V previously, east of the same place. L/F for the 436th FS was over Egmond, Holland at 0954 hrs./20,000 ft. where they also made R/V with a force of B-24s described as having vertical red stripes on their tails (possibly the 34th BG). The bombers were noted as being high, but the formation was good. They were escorted to, around and out from the target, which appeared to be well "clobbered". No enemy aircraft were sighted. On the way around the targeted airfield, three bombers were seen going down in flames over Magdeburg. L/O for the squadrons was 1248-1300 hours, at the same places as was L/F for them. They also broke from the bombers at these points except for the 436th FS, which continued on with escort until about mid-sea.

Observations made during the mission included noting two marshalling yards, one at Hameln and one at Bad Oeynhausen, Germany that had many trains with over 200 goods wagons sitting on their tracks. The letters N/W in 100-foot long lettering was observed on the ground approximately 18 miles northeast of Zwolle, Holland. Flak at Ijmuiden was heavy, moderate and inaccurate, while over the target area, it was heavy, meager and inaccurate. At Egmond it was also heavy, meager and inaccurate.

A part of the 436th FS medical team – Staff Sergeant Ralph E. Dewey is seated in the squadron's ambulance and Captain Frank J. Cornelius is standing beside it. *Courtesy of Travis M. Greenwood.*

17 August 1944

VIII FC FO 519

No. 134 Thursday. Capt. Jeffrey was the group's leader and he also led the 434th FS, which consisted of 15 P-38s. Capt. Sykes led the 435th FS, which consisted of 17 P-38s and Capt. Biscayart led the 436th FS, which consisted of 16 P-38s. Their assignment was a fighter-strafing mission against rail and tactical targets in France. 434th FS up: 0908 hrs., down: 1430 hrs. with no early returns. 435th FS up: 0914 hrs., down: 1430 hrs. with no early returns. 436th FS up: 0900 hrs., down: 1435 hrs. with two early returns.

L/F for the group was over Schouwen Island, Holland at 0950-1000 hrs./18,000 ft. Heading south down through Holland, then Belgium and on down into France, the group continued to Moulins, then made a left turn heading towards the assigned target area of Is-sur-Tille. Before they arrived in that area, they could see far enough ahead to recognize that the area to be strafed was covered by overcast so the group began an early run. As the 435th FS provided top cover, the other two squadrons went down on the deck. Starting around 1130 hours, three trains heading southwest were attacked on

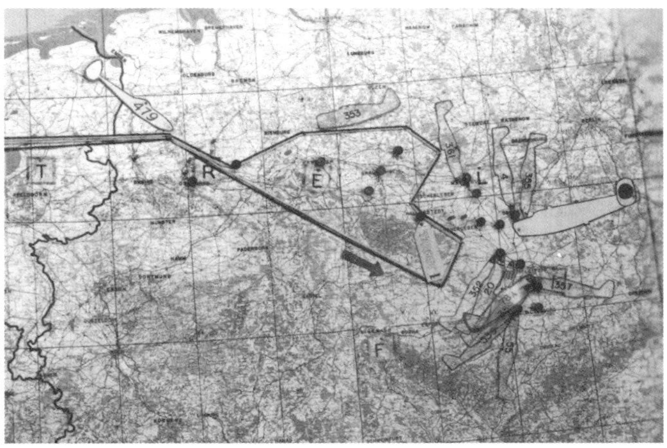

Right: A section of the mission map for this attack on the airfield. The routes in and out can be seen as well as silhouettes representing thirteen supporting fighter groups laid on. *Courtesy of Clarence G. Haynes.*

the line between Montceau and Le Creusot. Two of the trains were comprised of 10-20 cars each made up of goods wagons and flat cars carrying army trucks. One of the goods wagons exploded when it was hit. The other train was made up of 10-15 flat cars carrying armored vehicles. Numerous destroyed and damaged claims were turned in. After that work out, the group moved northeast towards Dijon as the overcast was lifting and the assigned target was being uncovered. At Is-sur-Tille, about 1200 hours, a marshalling yard with 300-400 goods wagons and oil cars was strafed. There were so many, that going after one or two was impossible. The two squadrons made three to four passes. From the vantage point that the 435th FS occupied above, the marshalling yard appeared to have been badly mauled. However, only a lot of damage was registered here, although there were some explosions. Members of the 434th FS commented during debriefing after the strike, that it would have been nice to have had some bombs! Heading out of the area at 1225 hours, the group headed northwest to exit the continent over Nieuport and Ostend, Belgium at 1330-1340 hrs.

There were no observations recorded from the mission. Flak over Ostend, Termonde and Dijon was heavy, intense and accurate. Over the railroad sites it was light, intense and accurate. Lieutenant John W. Hedenberg came back on one engine because his other engine had been hit by a 20mm shell and put out of commission. The hit also damaged his hydraulic system, making his landing gear inoperable and forcing him to belly the plane in back at Wattisham.

That brief note regarding John Hedenberg is better illuminated with his diary entry for this day:

> "August 17 – What a day! We started out on an ordinary strafing run to hit a marshalling yard just north of Dijon. Crossed in over the Dutch Islands, then went straight south to the target area. Overshot the area on account of the overcast and came down near Moulins on the Loire. Couldn't find the target and started working over the railroads around Le Creusot. Spencer, Frolking [Lieutenants Richard S. Spencer, Jr. and James E. Frolking] and I found three trains south of the town, and did we clobber them! I got one locomotive destroyed, one damaged and about 30 to 40 boxcars and flat cars damaged. The flat cars were loaded with camouflaged armored cars and we pretty well damaged them extensively. However, on the pass that I got the engine, I got a 20mm flak hit in my gun compartment (I was flying Andre Huycke's ship) and it knocked out my right engine. Feathered it up and started for home with Spencer escorting me. Then the other engine started acting up and I thought I'd had it. Couldn't gain altitude and after a while, started losing it. Chugged across half of France at 150 mph and at 3000 feet. Still don't know why I wasn't shot down; I was a sitting duck. Never expected to make it back and never would have had it not been for Spencer. I hardly ever saw the ground and never knew where I was. Just flew in the general direction of home. Spencer went upstairs and got me radio fixes – covered me all the way. Finally crossed out after what seemed like centuries. Told Spencer to go on home when we reached the English coast. Finally reached the field with a few minutes of gas left. When I started to put the landing gear down, I found out that the hydraulic system was shot out too. Didn't have enough gas or altitude to use the emergency hand pump, so I just bellied her in. Everyone else had gotten back long before and they were sweating me out. Had quite enough excitement for one day!"

John's comments added at a later date serve to give more insight to that experience:

> "This description of events, typical of the young man that I was, included very little of what the experience was like. In those days I thought such things were best ignored because they were only subjective and there≠fore unreal. Actually, I was quite surprised to discover, when that shell went off and the right engine nacelle promptly took on a remarkable resemblance to a colander oozing oil from every hole, that I was somehow calmly and deliberately doing all the right things. Since the oil was streaming back along the nacelle right toward the red-hot turbo-supercharger and beginning to smoke back there, I had to get the engine shut down at once before a fire started.
>
> "At the moment, I had only a few hundred feet of altitude, was still being shot at by ground fire, and had to do a lot of things all practically simultaneously in order to prevent fire and get the hell Out of there. So I did, at the same time marveling with an observing corner of my mind at the cool efficiency and speed with which all those things got done. I throttled back the damaged engine to the 'idle' position, set the fuel mixture control to 'idle cut-off', turned off the electrical switches and feathered the propeller to stop it rotating. (All of which let the turbo-supercharger wind down to a stop and cool.) At the same time, I started as steep a turn as I dared into the live left

engine, while re-trimming the rudder for easier control when I began to climb for altitude after getting a couple of miles away.

"I knew perfectly well that I was in real trouble. I had quite a few hundred miles to go before reaching any Allied-held territory, let alone getting back to home base. I called the squadron leader and told him I was heading for home, so he assigned Lieutenant Richard Spencer to go with me. As I started to climb, the left engine began to bang and sputter. Nothing I could do allowed me to draw enough power out of it to do more than get very slowly up to about 3000 feet. I could go no higher, but perhaps fortunately, there was a partial cover of cloud that I could duck into and out of from time to time to hide. After an hour or so, the engine's per≠formance deteriorated a bit more, and I began to lose altitude slowly. It looked now as though the left engine might fail at any time, in which case I would have to bail out and take my chances on evading capture.

"If that happened, I reasoned, I would almost certainly lose my cigarettes from the unfastenable knee-pocket of my flying suit when my parachute opened, and I wouldn't have anything to smoke for possibly a long time. So I did what seemed the only sensible thing to do, I started smoking them up one after an≠other while continuing to nurse the engine and keep the plane flying as long as possible, heading in the general direction of the nearest Allied territory in northwestern France. Crazy as that behavior seems from a distance, it probably was a very necessary psychological defense in coping with a most threatening situation.

"At any rate, for some never-discovered reason, as soon as I finally crossed out over the coast and headed for England the engine smoothed out and began to deliver all the power I wanted, as if there had never been anything wrong with it. I could again climb, and did, making better time from there back to home base. However, when I reached there and put the landing gear lever in the down position, all that I could see was the hydraulic pressure instantly drop to zero and stay there, while the landing-gear doors didn't even open. I began to cuss like a top sergeant. All I could think of was how annoyed my friend Andre Huycke would be to have his nearly brand-new plane that I was flying that day, reduced to an instant wreck, but there was no way out other than a belly-landing. When I called the tower to tell them what I was going to do, I could see all my fellow-pilots come pouring out of the Operations building to watch, while the crash-truck and ambulance went to the near end of the stretch of grass I was going to use. I felt I had better do a good job or would never hear the end of it.

"It actually turned out to be no big deal; the trucks and the Flight Surgeon's jeep pulled up alongside af≠ter the plane slid to a stop, even before I had time to jump off the wing after climbing out. I still have a good-sized chunk of that 20-mm shell; it was found just below the forward armor plate in front of the instrument panel. The shell had come in from dead ahead through all four nearly-empty .50 cal. ammo trays and the 20-mm ammo tray, finally exploding when it hit the armor plate about three feet in front of my stomach."

18 August 1944

VIII FC FO 522

No. 135 Friday. Col. Hubert Zemke was the group's leader and he also led the 435th FS, which consisted of 17 P-38s. Lt. Col. Herren led the 434th FS, which consisted of 17 P-38s and Capt. Moore led the 436th FS, which consisted of 16 P-38s. Their assignment was a penetration to target and withdrawal escort for 70 2nd BD B-24s attacking their 8th AF Mission 562 primary target, the Nancy-Essey airdrome in eastern France. 434th FS up: 1219 hrs., down: 1810 hrs. with no early returns. 435th FS up: 1218 hrs., down: 1806 hrs. with two early returns. 436th FS up: 1212 hrs., down: 1820 hrs. with no early returns.

This was one of the 479th Fighter Group's "Big Shows". It represented their best effort on the ground thus far in the group's history and was the greatest single source of victories for the men of the group since they became operational in May. The day's tally became a part of a Distinguished Unit Citation the 479th would receive, as well as the origin for a Commendation from 65th Fighter Wing Headquarters.

The commendation that went out to each man at AAF Station F-377, Wattisham, read:

> "1. I desire to commend all personnel on your station for your great victory against the German Luftwaffe in today's assault upon on of their airdromes in which you destroyed 43 aircraft and damaged 23 aircraft."

> "2. This is indeed a great blow struck at the enemy and could only have been accomplished through the cooperation of everyone of you."
>
> "3. It is this kind of cooperation and effort that is bringing victory for the Allies closer and closer, and I am confident that all of you will continue in this manner."

Dated 18 August 1944 and signed: Brigadier General Jesse Auton, Commander, 65th Fighter Wing.

The group crossed into France at Bayeux and made R/V with the B-24s all at about the same time and place, 1335 hrs./ 18,000 ft. Watching over their charges, all across France to the Nancy-Essey airdrome in eastern France, the three squadrons observed excellent results from the bombing. The ceiling and visibility was unlimited that day. Deciding to let down to get a closer look at the airdrome, Col. Zemke took both the 435th and the 434th FSs to a lower altitude and saw that the field was still a lucrative target. While the 436th continued on with the B-24s, taking them out of France, the other two squadrons began what would be their best ground attack against the German Air Force. In Col. Zemke's own words: "Group Leader and seven pilots of Lakeside started dive-strafing for two or three runs as soon as the dust cleared. That was followed by low level strafing by everyone when very little flak was found. Four to seven passes were made." When the strafing began, the airdrome had approximately 70 aircraft on it with only two having been hit by bombs. Due to conflicting claims, the total of claimed destroyed and damaged added to well over a hundred. After the matter had been settled through discussion, meetings, correspondence, etcetera, the victory credit board finally awarded 43 destroyed and 28 damaged with instructions for the group commander to distribute the claims fairly among those on the mission, taking into consideration: combat film, claims and strike photos. Col. Zemke, foregoing his own claims, gave what would have been his own awards, to others.

Some of the many Combat Reports listing claims have been chosen to represent the day's successes and they are as follows:

From the 435th Fighter Squadron:

First Lieutenant Verne E. Hooker: "I was leading Red Flight of Col. Zemke's section when he called in and said we were going to dive-strafe from north to south or approximately that direction. On my first pass, I slowly pulled my nose through the airfield, firing as I did so. My second pass, I did the same thing, only toward the end, I stopped on one twin-engine aircraft. I continued firing on it right on down. The bullets had not reached the ground yet when I started to pull out. On pulling out, I chandelled to the left and looked back. The aircraft at which I was firing upon was afire and I watched it explode. I claim this one as destroyed. On my third pass, I dove exactly the same way on another twin-engine aircraft. This time when I looked back, I observed it smoking and was about halfway around in this pattern when I saw it finally start to burn and explode. I claim this one as destroyed also. I then made a couple of other dive-strafing passes and not getting to see where my bullets hit, observed nothing. On my last pass, I came down on a twin-engine aircraft, firing all the way down to my tracers and even part of them. I saw some direct hits and I claim this one as damaged. I claim two He 111s destroyed and one Ju 88 damaged."

Second Lieutenant Theo J. Sowerby: "I was Red Flight Two and was the sixth plane to follow White Flight down. I made my first run north to south, parallel with the river on the west side of the airfield. I picked the first plane in the middle of the field, getting strikes on it. I moved to another near the south end of the field, getting strikes on it also. Just as I pulled up, it caught fire. I zig-zagged, pulled around to the east and started again. I got strikes on two planes on the next pass, but didn't see them catch fire. The next pass, I picked a plane just in front of a hangar, fired a long burst and saw strikes. Then it caught fire. It was on the east side of the field. I circled left to the north and as I was pulling up, I saw about three planes on a plateau. I circled and got a hit on a plane just outside of the trees. As I circled to the right, it caught fire. As I got in position, another P-38 picked out a plane on the same plateau. I followed him in and saw his strikes as I fired. Two planes caught fire. I went through the smoke on the field and saw about 14 S/E planes on the west side of the airdrome. I made a tight turn to the right and fired on one of the aircraft. When I pulled up, it started on fire. This was to the river side of the airfield. I ran out of ammunition on this pass so I climbed to about 5,000 feet and took pictures of the field below. It was covered by smoke from all the burning planes. I claim two He 111s, a Ju 88 and a Fw 190 destroyed plus an He 111, a Ju 88 and an Me 410 damaged."

Captain George K. Sykes: "I was leading Yellow Section. As we flew over the airdrome at Nancy, we saw approximately fifty aircraft dispersed in the open, all over the field. My section had acted as top cover for about four minutes when the group leader called us down to get in the strafing pattern. My flight made five dive-strafing passes across the field from northeast to southwest, individual airplanes in a string. I fired on two He 111s, seeing one explode and the other starting to burn as I pulled up off the field on my second pass. I claim two He 111s destroyed."

Second Lieutenant Charles F. Monsell, Jr.: "I was flying as Element Leader in Yellow Flight when we received instructions to come down and make our run. We came in on the airfield approximately east to west and on my first pass, the He 111 I was aiming at caught fire while I was still firing. Pulling up to the left, I made another pass, this time picking out another ship which gave out a red glow near the wing roots just as I finished firing. As I pulled up to the left again, I saw it burst into flames. On my next pass, I shot up some buildings on the airdrome while on my way going in, in order to neutralize possible small arms fire. I continued the run and this time I got good hits on another He 111 on the field. I did not see it burn until I had pulled up, but by then, I could not be sure whether it was from my fire or someone else's. On my next pass, I picked out an He 111 in between two other T/E ships that were burning and observed fire start, as I finished firing. On pulling up to the left, I could see all three ships burning fiercely. I made one more pass on two planes parked on a grass field just south of the main field. I got very good hits, but did not set either one on fire. Someone called in dummies, I supposed that they were and did not claim any destroyed or damaged. I have since found out that they were not dummy planes, but do not claim any damage to them as someone else may have already done so. I claim three He 111s destroyed and one He 111 damaged."

First Lieutenant Ray K. Friend: "I started my first run from east to west and was trying to shoot up everything on the south end of the field during that first pass. There were about six parked planes in a broken line there and as a result, I only damaged two or three. On my next pass, I came in the same way, concentrating on one plane and clobbered it good. Then I shot at a couple more on the way across. As I pulled up, I could see the plane burning that I had concentrated on. Again, I only damaged the others. On another pass, I hit another and stayed on it until it was really burning good. I made another pass, but there was too much smoke and I couldn't find a target to shoot at. Boy, what hunting! I claim two He 111s destroyed and three He 111s damaged."

Some leaders of the Nancy-Essey mission. Front row, left to right – Lieutenant Colonel James M. Herren Jr., Colonel Hubert Zemke, First Lieutenant George W. Gleason and Captain George K. Sykes. Back row, left to right – First Lieutenant Robert N. Pigg, First Lieutenant Howard C. Smith, Captain Robin Olds and First Lieutenant Thomas C. Olson. *Carroll C. Sprague Collection, courtesy of the East Essex Aviation Society.*

From the 434th Fighter Squadron:

Lieutenant Colonel James M. Herren: "I was leading Newcross Squadron [White Flight Leader or White One] on a bomber escort mission. The target was the airdrome and nearby installations at Nancy. After observing the bombing results from approximately 15,000 feet, I dropped down to 13,000 feet. Col. Zemke was leading Lakeside Squadron and called in an indeterminable amount of aircraft dispersed on the field. He made a dive-strafing pass with his White Section. Newcross Squadron furnished cover at 13,000 feet and after two or three passes, Col. Zemke called for a definite traffic pattern for strafing the drome. After seeing the large number of airplanes on the field, I called for permission to bring Newcross Squadron down. That being secured, we joined the pattern and made passes at the field."

"On my first pass, I couldn't get in position for a damaging attack, but on my second pass, I exploded an He 111 on the southwest part of the field. There were strikes only at first, but as I pulled over the plane, it burst into flames. Lt. Rogers, my wingman was in trail and saw it in flames. My next pass was ineffective, but on my fourth pass, I destroyed a Ju 52 on the south part of the field. There were so many airplanes burning on the field that it was dangerous to make any more passes so I called to Col. Zemke, who had climbed to give cover and suggested that we pull up for rendezvous. I claim one He 111 and one Ju 52 destroyed on the ground."

First Lieutenant Walter M. Drake: "I was flying Newcross White Three position in the squadron. We circled above the field while a few ships from Lakeside Squadron went down on the field to see how the flak was. Then our flight went down and made a pass from east to west on the field. On the first pass, I sprayed bullets into a couple of He 111s. We recovered to the left and made another pass, but this time at a lone Fw 190 southwest of the field, on the edge of a woods. My flight leader fired at it, but was short. I fired right after him and the ship caught fire. My flight leader's wingman observed my claim. We recovered again to the left and came in on the field from about southeast to northwest. I fired at a Ju 88 and observed it to burn. Its position was next to the hangars at the south end of the field. My wingman observed my claim. We continued on across the field and I shot up another Ju 88 at the extreme northwest end of the whole airdrome. This ship was not on the field itself. I recovered and looked back to see it beginning to smoke and burn. On our next pass, it was burned out so I claim it as destroyed because no one else claims shooting at it after I did. I claim one Fw 190 and two Ju 88s destroyed on the ground."

First Lieutenant Thomas C. Olson: "Our squadron was flying flights in trail and I was flying Newcross White Four in the lead flight. As we were circling the field above, a general traffic pattern from northeast to southwest, circling to the left was set up. When we went down, I made three passes from northeast to southwest, on the south edge of the field. On my first pass, I strafed four aircraft. The first was close to the hangar on the northeast edge of the field, two were close together near the center of the field and the fourth was to the extreme southwest edge of the field. These burst into flames. My next pass was slightly to the left of my first pass and I fired on three aircraft. The first was quite close to the hangars; this one caught fire and burned. The second and third ones were close to the second and third aircraft of my first pass. One of these caught fire. On my third pass, I strafed two aircraft. Although several hits were seen and the landing gear collapsed on one, they did not catch fire. On pulling out of this pass, I noticed aircraft on the edge of the woods northeast of the field. In one group, I noticed three Ju 88s and one He 111. I made two passes, concentrating mainly on one Ju 88 just outside the woods, noticing several hits and one landing gear collapse. On pulling out of my second pass here, I noticed another He 111 on the other side of the woods. I made one pass, noticing several direct hits and on pulling out to make another pass, it exploded. I then made one pass from north to south inflicting damage to one aircraft. I claim one Me 109, one Fw 190, two Me 410s, two He 111s and one Ju 88 destroyed on the ground." (You can bet he used all his ammunition!)

Captain Robin Olds: "I was Blue Flight Leader. After the bombers made their run, someone in Lakeside Squadron called out enemy planes on the field. My squadron circled left at about 10,000 feet, flights in trail. A Lakeside flight cut across in front of me while I was observing the field and upon looking up, I followed this flight instead of my squadron. [The whole flight followed the Lakeside flight.] We dive-strafed the field on the first pass, observing very little flak. On this first pass, I set an He 111 on fire. Circling left, we came back for another pass. By this time, there were several ships burning in the main portion of the field. All of my passes were from the northeast to the southwest and out across Nancy on recovery. The pattern continued left. My wingman [2nd Lt. Philip W. Manning] went in on this second pass. While positioning myself for a third pass, I noticed another box of bombers on a run. I called them in and all ships strafing drew off until the bombing had been completed. We then took up our strafing again. I picked out two ships, Ju 88s, parked close together in front of the hangars on the northeast side of the field. I made two passes at these two ships, and by the third pass they were both burning. I continued across the field and concentrated on another Ju 88 on the far side of the field. I made two more passes on this ship and ran out of ammunition. I pulled up and circled at 8,000 feet, trying to count the burning aircraft. I counted over 30 aircraft burning, but could not get the exact number due to smoke. We broke off from the field at approximately 1700 hours and headed home. One of the Ju 88s in the center of the field I share because another plane made a pass at the same plane. I claim one He 111, two Ju 88s and one Ju 88 shared."

Above: Frames of film taken from First Lieutenant Harold F. Grenning's gun camera film shot during his strafing passes on the Nancy-Essey mission. Since the loss back in mid-July of the original P-38J he regularly flew, Lt. Grenning had been flying a newer P-38L which had the gun camera mounted in the left bomb pylon instead of the nose. This eliminated much of the vibration that was present in the nose setup and resulted in clearer pictures. The first shows a Ju 88 that Lt. Grenning got hits on. Note the three strikes in the left wing root area. *Courtesy of Harold F. Grenning.*

Above right: Two He 111s that Lt. Grenning hit. Note the strike on the distant plane's wheel. *Courtesy of Harold F. Grenning*

Right: The first of two frames showing Lt. Grenning's pass on a He 111 parked near two hangars. Note the hits on the roof of the building in the foreground, the hangars and in the area of the He 111. Note also that Lt. Grenning's wingman has gotten ahead of him and has slid almost into the Lieutenant's line of fire. *Courtesy of Harold F. Grenning*

The second frame was taken a split second before Lt. Grenning passed over the two hangars and the first He 111 he was shooting at. He has now focused on a second He 111 a bit beyond the first. Note his wingman has moved into a position just above the Lieutenant's line of fire. *Courtesy of Harold F. Grenning*

One of the last frames of Lt. Grenning's 18 August 1944 gun camera film. It shows his last firing pass as his ammunition is nearly exhausted. His target, a He 111, is bracketed by his short burst, which empties the ammunition bins. *Courtesy of Harold F. Grenning*

Second Lieutenant Philip W. Manning was Blue Flight Two as noted in Capt. Olds' report. Following Lt. Manning, was Blue Flight Three, First Lieutenant Harold F. Grenning, Jr., Second Lieutenant Ronald L. Maley was Blue Flight Four. Following the flight on a strafing run, Lt. Maley ran out of ammunition so he switched to his gun camera only and was taking pictures of Lt. Manning on the pass. The two were good friends, having gone through flight training together and, in fact, their two army serial numbers were just two digits apart. Lt. Maley was Best Man at Lt. Manning's wedding just prior to shipment overseas. After the pass, Lt. Maley saw his friend pull up to about 200 feet and start a turn to the left. At that point, Lt. Maley saw what looked like a flash in Lt. Manning's cockpit. The stricken P-38 did a half roll at which point, Lt. Maley radioed his friend, urging him to roll the aircraft on over. It did no good because, apparently, Lt. Manning was hit and could not respond. The airplane, over on its back now, crashed into the town of Nancy at an intersection and slid into the corner of a red brick, two-story building. It exploded on impact.

First Lieutenant Harold F. Grenning, Jr.: "We started with Newcross Squadron, but became separated, joining with Lakeside Squadron, thinking they were Newcross Yellow Flight. After the second bombing attack, I made a pass from northeast to southwest and I fired at an He 111 next to a hangar and observed hits and saw it start burning. We recovered to the left and when I made a second pass, I came down the same way and in the same direction, firing at the ships on the south side of the field. I hit them, but they did not burst into flames. We made about three or four more passes that same way and I became separated from Newcross Blue Flight. I made the next pass alone and fired at a Ju 88 on the north side of the field, near some hangars. I fired a burst between two hangars and saw the Ju 88 start smoking. I recovered again to the left, looked back and saw the ship burning. I made another pass and then climbed up with the rest of the group as I had used all of my ammunition. I claim one He 111 and one Ju 88 destroyed as well as four Ju 88s damaged."

After the nearly thirty-minute attack, the group left, heading for the French coast. L/O was over Calais at 1745 hrs./9,000 ft. The 436th had crossed out over Bayeaux again, at 1731 hrs./18,000 ft. Observations made during the mission included construction activity at two airfields, one at Chambrey the other was unknown. There was a large amount of rail traffic at a standstill for five to ten miles around the Nancy area. Trucks on the road south of Nancy were heading towards the city. Flak at the Nancy-Essey airdrome was light, meager and inaccurate although two planes were hit. One was able to return home.

Among the congratulatory messages the group received after the mission, was a teletype from the 56th Fighter Group, Col. Zemke's old command. It read:

> "THE HUB WENT ON THE PROWL AGAIN,
> WHILE JERRY USED NO CARE.
> THE PLANES HE PARKED ON NANCY DROME,
> HE SOON FOUND WERE NOT THERE.
>
> 56TH FIGHTER GROUP"

A brief note from the diary of John W. Hedenberg for 19 August: "Checked out on the P-51. Damn fine ship – very light on the controls and easy to handle. Forgot to mention that yesterday tried out a new idea of Broadstone's [Lieutenant Chester W. Broadstone was in charge of the 436th FS armament section.] He rigged up clusters of 20 twenty-pound fragmentation bombs to be hung on our wing racks. When the cluster is dropped, it falls about 20 feet, then springs apart and the bombs spread out in a big dispersed pattern. Works pretty well."

24 August 1944

VIII FC FO 527

No. 136 Thursday. Maj. Glover was the group's leader and he also led the 435th FS, which consisted of 17 P-38s. Capt. Jeffrey led the 434th FS, which consisted of 14 P-38s and Capt. Sullivan led the 436th FS, which consisted of 17 P-38s. Their assignment was a penetration to target and withdrawal escort for 2nd BD B-24s attacking their 8th AF Mission 568 primary target at Brunswick, Germany. 434th FS up: 0837 hrs., down: 1348 hrs. with two early returns. 435th FS up: 0844 hrs., down: 1355 hrs. with three early returns. 436th FS up: 0830 hrs., down: 1400 hrs. with three early returns.

Rain, rain and more rain had kept most of the Eighth Air Force on the ground since the nineteenth, but finally that had changed. The weather over Germany was clear with ceiling and visibility unlimited for this mission. The 434th FS made

R/V with their bombers from the 448th BG, over the North Sea at 1007 hrs./20,000 feet, northwest of Heligoland Island, west of northern Germany. L/F for them was west of the Elbe River at 1023 hrs./20,000 ft. R/V and L/F for the 435th FS was just ahead of the bombers, near Cuxhaven, Germany at 1022 hrs. 12,000 ft. The squadron would continue to fly just ahead of the bombers for the mission. R/V for the 436th FS was a few minutes before their L/F which was between Cuxhaven and Wesermünde at 1022 hrs./24,000 ft. The B-24s were escorted to their target where it appeared to be well hit. For minutes on end, there were forty to fifty bombs exploding simultaneously in the target area. There were large fires and lots of black smoke seen rolling up to 10,000 ft. as a result of the attack. It was a fearful sight. One B-24 was seen to be hit over the target at 1135 hrs./ 23,000 ft. It exploded, but five to seven chutes were also seen. On withdrawal, another B-24 was seen hit west of Dümmer Lake, Germany at 1223 hrs./ 12,000 ft. The left engine started to burn and the plane dived to 7,000 feet, then exploded. Three chutes were seen to open while another, not opened and burning, went plunging downward. The B-24 was one of the 434th FSs charges from the 448th BG. On the way home, three planes were heard calling "Mayday". One stated he was crossing the Zuider Zee at Holland. The 436th FS reported on two B-24s, the first one marked: "...black tails with vertical silver [sic] stripes, C on wing, I on tails and EE on fuselage..." (389th BG, 565th BS). This aircraft was picked up at 1030 hrs./20,000 feet, ten miles north of Norderney, Germany and was escorted towards home. Despite the fact that the plane had one engine shut down and the prop feathered, early radio communications with the pilot indicated that he was all right. About an hour later, the B-24 made a 180-degree turn, giving it a heading of 80 degrees. Radio communications were lost at that point. Some of the squadron followed the bomber back for approximately 50 miles, at which point they were ten miles northwest of Vlieland, Holland. Low on gas, the P-38s had to turn away and head home. (This bomber was probably the 389th BG B-24 that landed in Sweden that day.) The other B-24 that the squadron reported, was identified as being marked with: "...horizontal silver stripe, I on wing, H on tail..." (448th BG?). This plane also had one engine shut down and the prop feathered when it was picked up 60 miles north of Norderney. The bomber was escorted back to England and taken to about ten miles east of Norwich, at which point the escorts broke away for Wattisham at 1220 hrs. Being at the lead of the force, the 435th made L/O near the Dutch island of Terschelling at 1225 hrs./12,000 ft. The 434th FS was out next, over Ijmuiden, Holland at 1248 hrs./15,000 ft. The remainder of the 436th FS broke escort approximately 50 miles northwest of Den Helder, Holland at 1300 hrs./12,000 ft. and L/O for them was near the same place as the 435th FS went out.

Observations made during the mission were sightings of mostly waterborne traffic. Five small boats, the size of "E Boats", were spotted in the bay at Heligoland. Another 15 were seen in the river south of the Weser estuary, at the German border. Just up the coast, there were nine large boats and another thirty of various sizes in the Elbe. The river near Hamburg, Germany had a whole fleet of various-sized boats on it. When the bombers approached both the boats and some cities, a very effective smoke screen was put up. Flak at those sites was a threat due to the presence of flak boats. Flak over the target area was heavy, very intense and accurate. It was heavy, intense and accurate over Bremerhaven, Hamburg and Dümmer Lake. At Westerschelling it was heavy, meager and accurate while at Heligoland, it was heavy, meager and inaccurate. The bombers were reported as receiving flak all along the route.

Two P-38s from the 436th FS flew an Air/Sea Rescue patrol this date also. Up: 1445 hrs., down: 1840 hrs. Taking off from Wattisham, the two flew over to Great Yarmouth and out, heading up into the North Sea. Reaching the northern point of their patrol, they turned south and headed down into the English Channel. Down to their southernmost point, they again turned north, completing a loop and eventually crossing in at Great Yarmouth and heading home.

25 August 1944

VIII FC FO 529

No. 137 Friday. Col. Zemke was the group's leader and he also led the 435th FS, which consisted of 18 P-38s. Capt. Duffié led the 434th FS, which consisted of 15 P-38s and Capt. Biscayart led the 436th FS, which consisted of 16 P-38s. Their assignment was a bomber escort for 2nd BD B-24s attacking their 8th AF mission 570 primary target, the aircraft industry at Wismar, Germany. 434th FS up: 0933 hrs., down: 1443 hrs. with one early return. 435th FS up: 0930 hrs., down: 1445 hrs. with no early returns. 436th FS up: 0923 hrs., down: 1440 hrs. with two early returns.

L/F for the group was over Holland, between north of Ijmuiden and north of Bergen at approximately 1025 hrs./16-

18,000 ft. Heading northeast into Germany, the squadrons pressed on, passing just north of Hannover. Continuing northeast, the 435th and 436th FSs reached the Lake Müritz area and turned north, passing the airfield at Rechlin. Winding around the east side of the lake and taking up a northwest heading, the 435th FS picked up their charges near Güstrow at 1212 hrs./22,000 ft. The 436th FS got to their assigned 2nd CW B-24s a bit later, over the north end of Schweriner Lake at 1220 hrs./20,000 ft. The 434th FS did not get that far. In the vicinity of Wittenberge, that squadron spotted 40 plus Me 109s. Pursuing them, the E/A were engaged between Plauer Lake and Rostock. The pilots of the 16 434th P-38s accounted for 7-0-1, and Captain Robin Olds became the squadron's first full-fledged ace:

2-0-0	Me 109	1st Lt. Berkley E. Hollister
0-0-1	Me 109	1st Lt. Walter M. Drake
2-0-0	Me 109	Capt. C.A.P. Duffié
3-0-0	Me 109	Capt. Robin Olds

First Lieutenant Berkley E. Hollister in claiming two Me 109s gave this narrative statement:

First Lieutenant Berkley E. Hollister by the second ship that he flew. *Courtesy of Berkley E. Hollister.*

"I was flying as Newcross Yellow Three on a bomber escort mission. Our squadron was flying a regular front formation on the left flank of the group formation. Just a few minutes before R/V time, my wingman, Lieutenant Walter A. Neumann, who was flying the number four position in the flight, called in bogies to our leader Captain Robin Olds, telling him that they were at 12 o'clock and on our level. The bogies were flying approximately 90 degrees to our course and heading north at about 360 degrees. We were flying at 19,000 to 20,000 feet at the time and turned left to chase the bogies. Newcross White and Red Flights followed us after them. Newcross Blue Flight had turned for home after having taken some flak hits on the way in. The other two squadrons from the group turned and tried to locate us, but never did. Our Yellow Flight was in hot pursuit of the bogies for about five minutes when Captain Olds went after the 109s on the extreme right. The E/A were now starting a fairly wide turn to the left and the two I was now after were also turning. They wound up being a little behind after the turn was completed. As they turned, I cut around the turn a little to get in closer to firing range. After turning 90-100 degrees, the two 109s I was chasing straightened out and flew almost straight, but in a slight dive at 350-375 miles per hour indicated at 18,000 feet. I closed in to about 250 yards and fired on the E/A to the left. I saw hits on the fuselage and center section as I fired from about five degrees deflection. Right after it was hit, white and black smoke came out and the ship almost half rolled, then went down. I passed over it fast and didn't ever see what happened to it after that. I then turned to the right to fire at the other 109 which was flying 150 feet to one side and almost line abreast to where the other had been. I was in close range by this time (100-150 yards) and fired on it from directly astern. I saw hits immediately and heavy, black smoke came from his engine. The airplane went into a violent skid, almost broadside, and was just beginning to roll over as I passed over the top of him.

"At that, Captain Olds said on the radio: 'Nice going Newcross ship that just shot one (or words to that effect). I'm below you now, come on down.' So I banked my ship and saw him about a 1,000 feet below me, chasing some 109s in a dive. I was indicating almost 400 mph by then and was having a difficult time losing altitude and clearing my tail at the same time. My wingman was too far behind me to keep in sight as the weather was very hazy and he had lost sight of me before I made my first bounce. While I was circling to let down, I heard Captain Olds call for some help down at 8,000 feet. He said one was on his tail and he was having trouble with his ship, having popped his side window out diving after the E/A. I circled at about 10,000 feet, looking for Captain Olds, but could not pick up his position. Then he called and said he got him, (his third one) but would really like some escort down there. Our flights were split up quite a bit by then, but I spotted Captain Olds plus another pilot circling the parachute of the last 109 he had gotten. When I got down to Captain Olds, two other P-38s, which later turned out to be Newcross White Leader, Captain Claire Duffié, and Lieutenant Walter Drake, were with him, having come to give help. These three ships and mine escorted Captain Olds home without any further activity. I claim two Me 109s destroyed in the air."

Lieutenant Walter A. Neumann, Lt. Hollister's wingman, followed the first Me 109 down and watched it crash, thus confirming the first of his claims.

Captain Robin Olds confirmed the second of Lt. Hollister's claims with this statement of support:

"I was Yellow Flight Leader and Lt. Hollister was my element leader, number three man. After my first pass at the E/A formation, I did a sharp 360 and ended up behind Lt. Hollister who was closing for his first pass. Just then the Jerries started a diving turn to the left, with small bunches of them falling into trail. As Lt. Hollister started around and down on one of these string formations, I called his attention to two 109s who were above and to the outside of the general flight path of the E/A formation. This position would have put them on Lt. Hollister's tail, had he continued his original bounce. He straightened out and then closed on the two E/A that I had called out to him. At this time, I was approximately 800 yards behind Lt. Hollister and slightly below. I saw him fire at both ships, obtaining many hits on one who broke away and many more on the other who skidded violently, apparently out of control. The pilot of this ship parachuted out. As I had turned down for a bounce myself, immediately after seeing the Jerry's chute, I did not observe what happened to the first ship that Lt. Hollister had hit. However, he seemed to get as many hits on the first ship as he did on the second. I confirm one Me 109 destroyed in the air by Lt. Hollister."

First Lieutenant Walter M. Drake damaged another Me 109 and gave this statement:

"I was flying Newcross Red Three position. Our flight followed White Flight as they dived down to engage 40 plus Me 109s. I had no wingman as he had aborted earlier. I got into a luftberry with some other 38s and 109s until the 109s finally all split-essed and went down. I broke very hard and got one Me 109's tail. I was still quite a ways from him, but I began firing short bursts at about 30-40 degrees deflection. As I was shooting, the 109 began smoking a little bit. I had to break off early though as three 109s were heading at me in a slight climb from the left. I did not get to observe what happened to the one I was shooting at after that. I claim one Me 109 damaged."

Captain Claire A.P. Duffié, the squadron's leader, gave this report of the day's encounters:

"At about 1120 hrs. in the vicinity of Wittenberge, Newcross Yellow Four called in bogies about ten miles directly in front of our squadron. Newcross Yellow Leader saw them at the same time and said they were heading north. He also said that there were about forty in number and flying in "V" formations of ten A/C apiece. I swung about 25 degrees left to cover the Newcross Yellow Flight, who had taken after them. When we reached Plauer Lake, we turned to a heading of about 355 degrees. At 1130 hours, Newcross Yellow Flight identified the bogies as Me 109s and attacked in the vicinity of Bützow. The E/A headed straight in the direction of the bay north of Lübeck and upon the second attack by Newcross Yellow Flight, they turned in a side-swiping, 180-degree turn to the left and started back at us. At this time, (1135 hrs.) I called Newcross Red and White Flights to drop tanks and told Newcross Red Flight to stay above at 20,000 feet. I immediately dropped my tanks, picked out what appeared to be the lead E/A and opened fire at about 1,000 yards. I fired all the way in on the head-on pass until forced to pull up and to the left in order to avoid a collision. As I pulled up, I noticed strikes and saw the right side of the

E/A flash. I was at 19,000 feet then. As the E/A formation passed underneath me, I made a 180-degree overhead pass on one of the last E/A in the formation. The E/A saw me, immediately split-essed and I followed. Very quickly, I reached compressibility. At about 10,000 feet, I passed the E/A, not being able to pull out or slow down. At about 8,000 feet, I trimmed the ship up, dropped combat flaps and pulled out in a climbing turn to the right with the E/A on my tail. I poured full RPM and throttle and kept a tight climbing turn. The E/A fired at me the whole time, but got no strikes. Finally the E/A stalled out of the turn, flipped over in a partial spin and recovered as I rolled over on his tail. He went straight for the deck over Rostock. Ground batteries of enemy flak consisting of all calibers, from light to heavy, opened up on both the E/A and me. The E/A then ruffed in a tight right climbing turn and chopped throttle. I pulled up underneath him and stalled out. He rolled to the left and I rolled to the right. I pulled around and made a head-on pass at him, then ruffed in to the left and caught the E/A with about a 75-degree deflection shot. I fired from 1,000 yards to about 400 yards, seeing strikes along his right wing and engine cowling. Immediately, the hatch flew off and the pilot bailed out. The E/A went straight in, crashing in an open field just east of Rostock. I turned on my camera and took shots of the burning E/A. Both light and heavy flack was becoming very intense so I left on the deck. The time then was 1220 hrs. I claim two Me 109s."

Three witnesses confirmed the two victories. First Lieutenant Quentin S. Pavlock, Newcross Red Leader and his wingman Lieutenant Calvin J. Murphy, saw part of the action and Lt. Pavlock confirmed that after Capt. Duffié's head-on attack of the first Me 109, the E/A had exploded. Captain Robin Olds and additionally, Second Lieutenant John H. Miller from Lakeside Squadron confirmed the second Me 109 as destroyed.

One of those witnesses, Captain Robin Olds, had his left side window blown out during a maneuver he had executed while keeping track of Capt. Duffié's second fight. The window's loss caused Capt. Olds to temporarily lose control of his P-38 and wind up recovering, down on the deck. (On the P-38, the two side windows, each of which rolled up like those of a car, had to be fully closed during flight, otherwise the airflow over the plane's empennage/tail section was disturbed and this in turn created a buffeting effect which made the plane unstable.) At this point, he saw the Me 109 that Capt. Duffié was pursuing, crash in a field. Escorted by First Lts. Walter M. Drake and Berkley E. Hollister and additionally Capt. C.A.P. Duffié, Capt. Olds took his disabled plane back home. That left his crew chief, Glen A. Wold, with the job of finding a replacement window.

Capt. Robin Olds was Newcross Yellow Leader and was busy at the same time as was Capt. Duffié:

"When the number four man in my flight, Lieutenant Walter A. Neumann called in the bogies at 12 o'clock and slightly low, our squadron had just begun a turn to the left. Our flight was positioned on the extreme left flank of the group. Upon picking up the bogies, I could see that there were 40 plus, traveling at about 45 degrees across our front. We immediately poured on power and fell in line astern, about ten miles behind. When we overtook the bogies, I was sure that they were Me 109s and dropped my belly tanks. By this time, my wingman and I were alone, numbers three and four having dropped back about half a mile. The squadron was another mile or more back and the rest of the group was so far behind that they had no opportunity to join the fight at all, having lost the bogies in the prevailing haze. I gave my course as 350 degrees, while closing. I picked the Jerry on the right flank of the top "V" and rode in, right on his tail. I fired at about 250 yards, seeing immediate hits. The E/A dove right and the pilot bailed out. I then broke left violently into the rest of the Jerry formation and continued this turn down for about 180 degrees and then violently up for the remainder of a 360-degree turn. This put me behind and above the E/A formation again. By this time, my number three man, Lieutenant Berkley E. Hollister had passed me so I covered his tail when he started a bounce. Our position was then slightly west of Rostock. The Jerries turned left, diving slightly. Lt. Hollister started around on a string of five, but I called his attention to two Me 109s above and to the outside of the general turn. Lt. Hollister broke up into these two. I saw his shooting and started down myself on the same five. As I started to shoot at the tail-end Charlie, he saw me and zoomed straight up into the sun. I passed below him and shot at the next Jerry in line, observing many hits and closing to about 50 yards. This one bailed out, too. Still in a shallow dive, I observed another P-38 and an Me 109 going round and round. It seemed that the 38 needed help so I started down. At about 4,000 feet, the Jerry, still way out of my range, turned under me and

> slightly to the right. He still had the P-38 on his tail. I rolled over on my back, following him and gave him an ineffective burst at long range. By this time I was traveling in excess of 500 mph. My left window blew out, scaring the hell out of me! I thought I had been hit by some of the ground fire I had observed in the vicinity. I regained control of the aircraft and pulled out above a wheat field. I tried to contact the flight to get myself recognized, but observed an Me 109 making a pass at me from about seven o'clock high. I broke left as well as my plane could and the dumb Jerry overshot. I straightened out and gave him a burst. He chandelled steeply to the left and I shot some more. He passed right over me and I slipped over in an Immelman. As I straightened out at the top. I saw the pilot bail out and followed his plane around to the left where it crashed in a field. I claim three Me 109s destroyed in the air."

First Lts. Berkley Hollister and Walter Drake confirmed Capt. Olds claims.

The bombing results were reported as excellent with the factory and railroad yard south of Wismar well hit. Escorting the B-24s back out, the force headed towards Kiel, then west, across the northernmost part Germany where the 435th FS made L/O south of Husum at 1255 hrs./21,000 ft. and then broke from the bombers out over the North Sea. The 436th crossed out north of Cuxhaven at 1300 hrs./20,000 ft. and broke from the Big Friends near the English coast, eight miles northeast of Lowestoft at 1405 hrs. The 434th FS never made R/V with the bombers and went back home on their own, making L/O at 1330 hrs.

Observations made during the mission included 20 plus unidentified aircraft seen on the ground at the airfield near Rechlin. A B-24 was seen to explode north of Bad Doberan. Seven planes were seen at an airfield near Tarnewitz. It was noted that Col. Zemke wanted to know about the flak at that airfield. Two unidentified aircraft were seen burning on the ground near Berkow. An airdrome north of Wismar had three Me 109s, two were on the runway and one was circling the field while another had been shot down by a P-51. A B-24 was sighted heading towards Sweden from the area of Kiel at 1230 hrs. Flak at Pellworm Island was heavy, intense, but inaccurate. At Bremen, Hanover and the airdrome north of Wismar, it was heavy, intense and accurate. At the Rechlin airfield, it was heavy, meager and inaccurate.

Some early artwork done of then Lieutenant Robin Olds. *Courtesy of George E. Falkner.*

25 August 1944

VIII FC FO 531

No. 138 Friday. Capt. Jeffrey led the 434th FS, which consisted of 12 P-38s. Capt. Gates led the 435th FS, which consisted of 16 P-38s and Capt. Moore led the 436th FS, which consisted of 16 P-38s. Their assignment was a penetration to target and withdrawal escort for multiple small formations of 2nd BD B-24s attacking their 8th AF Mission 572 chemical plant targets in Belgium. 434th FS up: 1630 hrs., down: 1921 hrs. with three early returns. 435th FS up: 1643 hrs., down: 1927 hrs. with four early returns. 436th FS up: 1636 hrs., down: 1952 hrs. with one early return.

L/F for both the 434th FS and the 435th FS was over Overflakkee Island, Holland at 1715 hrs./20,000 ft. The 436th FS also came in over Overflakkee Island, but at 1730 hrs./ 20,000 ft. The bombers were met at L/F and escorted south into Belgium where at Antwerp, the 93rd BG B-24s split up into small boxes of six, heading to their many assigned targets. The 434th FS's B-24s reached their target area at 1805 hrs. where the results were judged as good. Twelve bombers made direct hits, but six dropped short of the target. The 435th FS took part of their B-24s southeast to Liège to bomb an airfield there. Another section broke off, with six bombers going after a target at Termonde and eleven swinging back up to hit another at Antwerp itself. The six missed their target, but the eleven did better. The 436th FS went with their 18 B-24s to Alost. The results were also mixed, with one box getting excellent hits and the other poor. L/O was at 1850 hrs. over Overflakkee Island for the 435th FS and the 436th FS. All squadrons broke from the bombers at mid-water over the North Sea.

No observations from the mission were recorded. Flak over Overflakkee Island, Antwerp and Liège was heavy, intense, but inaccurate. Over Brussels it was heavy intense and accurate.

26 August 1944

VIII FC FO 532

No. 139 Saturday. Maj. Glover was the group's leader and he also led the 435th FS, which consisted of 16 P-38s. Capt. Jeffrey led the 434th FS, which consisted of 16 P-38s and Capt. Sullivan led the 436th FS, which consisted of 17 P-38s. Their assignment was a penetration to target and withdrawal escort for 73 2nd BD B-24s attacking their 8th AF Mission 576 primary target, the fuel dump at Dülman, Germany. 434th FS up: 1102 hrs., down: 1427 hrs. with no early returns. 435th FS up: 1104 hrs., down: 1440 hrs. with one early return. 436th FS up: 1054 hrs., down: 1449 hrs. with one early return.

The 434th FS made L/F north of Alkmaar, Holland at 1155 hrs./19,000 ft. They R/V'd with their B-24s northwest of Meppel, Holland at 1210 hrs./20,000 ft. The 435th FS made L/F over Ijmuiden, Holland at 1157 hrs./18,000 ft. and R/V with their B-24s north of Meppel at 1210 hrs./20,000 ft. The 436th FS made L/F also over Ijmuiden at 1144 hrs./18,000 ft. and R/V with their B-24s over Steenwijk, Holland at 1215 hrs./21,000 ft. The Big Friends were escorted through the target, which was reported as well-clobbered with dust, gray and black smoke rising up to 5,000 feet. Returning home, L/O for the 434th was over Texel Island, Holland where they also broke away from the bombers at 1335 hrs./17,000 ft. From there, the squadron went home. L/O for the 435th FS was also over Texel Island, where they separated from the bombers at 1318 hrs./18,000 ft. At 1323, Colgate [65th FW controller] called, telling the group leader to take his remaining force back to the area of Lemmer, Holland and look for stragglers. The 436th FS broke from their bombers west of Egmond and they joined the 435th in returning inland to search for strays. None were found so the two squadrons turned back and crossed out at scattered locations along the coast of Holland, around 1400 hrs.

Observations made during the mission included spotting shipping in the harbors and barges on the canals of Holland. Four jets were seen north of the target area, heading south. Flak over the target was heavy, intense, but inaccurate. Over the northern part of the Ruhr Valley, from Dortmund to Mors, flak was heavy and intense.

27 August 1944

VIII FC FO 535

No. 140 Sunday. Maj. Carter was the group's leader and he also led the 435th FS, which consisted of 17 P-38s. Capt. Duffié led the 434th FS, which consisted of 17 P-38s and Capt. Biscayart led the 436th FS, which consisted of 16 P-38s plus one P-38 relay. Their assignment was to be a penetration to target and withdrawal escort for 2nd BD B-24s attacking their 8th AF Mission 584 target at Oldenburg, Germany. Because of a large wall of Cumulonimbus clouds beginning over the Jütland Peninsula and extending northwest to southeast from 6,000 ft. up to 30,000 ft. covering the continent in the areas of L/F, the bomber force was recalled. 434th FS up: 1304 hrs., down: 1752 hrs. with two early returns. 435th FS up: 1304 hrs., down: 1830 hrs. with three early returns. 436th FS up: 1257 hrs., down: 1835 hrs. with one early return.

L/F for the 434th FS was over Alkmaar, Holland at 1357 hrs./17,000 ft. The squadron penetrated Germany and headed in east to the vicinity of Steinhuder Lake where they turned left and headed north to join the bombers heading home. In the vicinity of Heligoland, flak broke up the squadron formation. They reformed and made L/O over Norden at 1500 hrs./15,000 ft. Crossing down the North Sea, the 436th FS was seen circling a ditched bomber. The 435th FS made L/F and set a course into Germany to R/V with the B-24s, but northeast of Dümmer Lake, they took a 90-degree turn to the left and headed up north, passing between Oldenburg and Bremen. L/O was over Bremerhaven at 1510 hrs./20,000 ft. Heading home over the waters of the North Sea and the English Channel, the squadron was assigned to an air/sea patrol which they performed from 1610 hrs. to 1810 hrs. Nothing was seen. The 436th FS made L/F over Ijmuiden at 1400 hrs./20,000 ft. Lieutenant John W. Hedenberg from the 436th FS, flew radio relay up and down the Dutch coast. The Bison Gang got as far into Germany as did Lakeside Squadron when the recall was heard. Following a similar route north between Oldenburg and Bremen, they crossed out near Wilhelmshaven at 1500 hrs./ 19,000 ft. The squadron went down to 1,000 feet on the way home to look for dinghies. Two were found 100 miles northeast of Great Yarmouth at 1655 hrs. One P-38 circled the dinghies while another went up to altitude for a fix. The P-38s remained in the area until a rescue boat arrived at 1730 hrs.

Observations made during the mission included seeing 1st BD B-17s hit the waterfront and docks at Emden, Germany as a target of opportunity. Big fires were reported. A jet was seen at Leeuwarden, Holland at 1525 hrs. It was at 30,000 ft.

heading north. A convoy of six ships plus two escorts was sighted near Borkum Island. It appeared to be headed west to Emden. Another convoy was spotted at the mouth of the Ems River. Flak was heavy, intense and accurate over Bremen, Bremerhaven, Emden, Ijmuiden, Oldenburg, Wangerooge and Wilhelmshaven.

28 August 1944

VIII FC FO 538

No. 141 Monday. Capt. Jeffrey was the group's leader and he also led the 434th FS, which consisted of 17 P-38s. Capt. Sykes led the 435th FS, which consisted of 16 P-38s and Capt. Sullivan led the 436th FS, which consisted of 16 P-38s plus one P-38 relay. Their assignment in France was a fighter-bomber attack on rail and tactical targets in the area due east of Paris, near the German border. 434th FS up: 0647 hrs., down: 1129 hrs. with one early return. 435th FS up: 0710 hrs., down: 1125 hrs. with two early returns plus one escort back. 436th FS up: 0658 hrs., down: 1125 hrs. with three early returns.

L/F for both the 434th and 436th FSs was over Coxyde, Belgium between 0740 and 0745 hrs./14,000 ft. The 435th crossed in southwest of Dunkerque at 0738 hrs./15,000 ft. At 0810 hours, on the way southeast to the assigned target area, Capt. Arthur F. Jeffrey saw an aircraft taking off from the airdrome near Sedan. Leaving three of the four flights remaining above, he took White Flight down to investigate. At this point, the flight had to shed their bombs and drop tanks. While the flights provided cover, he closed on the plane. By then the German aircraft was about five miles north of the field and 300 feet above the ground. Capt. Jeffrey made a pass on what was identified as a Ju 52, firing two bursts, the first at 800 yards and the second at 350 yards. Both scored hits, the transport's right engine caught fire and about thirty seconds later the transport went into the ground. Reforming again and continuing on, the squadrons split up near the target to attack their respective areas. Each P-38 carried a 1,000-lb. bomb with a delay fuse and a drop tank. The 434th FS dive-bombed and strafed, following the rail line between Sarrebourg and Nancy. The 435th FS did the same along the line between Sarrebourg to south of Metz. The 436th FS followed a route similar to that of the 435th, but wound up heading southwest looking for more targets of opportunity. They found a fair-sized marshalling yard, six tracks wide almost immediately. They bombed that one, then ran across another one four tracks wide and bombed that one also. The 434th FS's route led them near

First Lieutenant Robert H. Hendrickson and the crew that maintained the ship that he flew. *Courtesy of Frederick C. Hayner.*

two airdromes, one at Sarrebourg and the other at Phalsbourg. Both were worked over, but the one at Sarrebourg yielded some claims for enemy aircraft destroyed and damaged:

0-0-1	U/I T/E	1st Lt. Robert H. Hendrickson
1-0-0	Do 217	1st Lt. James M. Hollingsworth
0-1-0	Fw 190	1st Lt. Thomas C. Olson
0-0-1	Me 109	1st Lt. Thomas C. Olson

Lieutenant Hendrickson's claim of one unidentified, twin-engine aircraft comes from a dive-bomb attack in which he hit both a hangar and an airplane with his 1000-lb. bomb The aircraft was probably hard to identify after the explosion.

Lieutenant Olson did some fancy shooting in his claims of one probable and one damaged. The Fw 190 was an air kill and should have been credited as destroyed, but there were no witnesses to the attack and no one saw the plane belly in and explode. The Me 109 that was strafed, was left in such a condition that Lt. Olson stated that: "...he did not believe the aircraft would ever fly again." Lt. Olson only expended 800 rounds of .50 cal. and 150 rounds of 20mm ammunition for the entire mission and that included other strafing.

The group's combined bombing/strafing attacks resulted in the following destroyed and damaged: three marshalling yards, a railroad station, five locomotives, 61 goods wagons and freight cars, ten flat cars, 12 oil tank cars, sections of track, a bridge, a flak gun emplacement and 12 trucks.

Heading out of the area and working themselves towards home, the 436th FS lost First Lieutenant William N. (Pop) Howard to intense, light flak. He was hit while the squadron was attacking targets in the vicinity of St. Mihiel. Bison Squadron had run across two trains a few miles apart and gotten both of them, but Lieutenant Howard got a little too eager. The Lieutenant was about 100 feet off the ground when he

First Lieutenant Thomas C. Olson is flanked by Lelah May's assistant crew chief, Corporal Alworth D. Larson and the ship's crew chief, Technical Sergeant Loy C. Slayton. *Courtesy of Frederick C. Hayner.*

was hit, just after making a lengthwise strafing pass. He had ignored a German truck convoy on a road running parallel to the train tracks. The gunners on the convoy shot his plane up. Hit in his right engine, the engine caught fire and in a moment his whole right tail boom was in flames. Lt. Howard turned to a heading of 240 degrees to take him in the direction of home and began a slow climb. As he flew on, engine burning, First Lieutenant Joseph R. Struby flew above him, doing esses back and forth and attempted to direct him away from any towns he might not have been able to see from his altitude. In radio contact with each other, the two continued on for 13 minutes. Lt. Howard's right engine and boom aft of the engine were still burning when, at approximately 1005 hours, when he called Lt. Struby to tell him he was going to have to bail out, the fire was just getting too hot. The two were at 2,000 feet and in the vicinity of St. Dizier when Lt. Howard left his P-38. His parting words were: "See you in a couple of weeks." His parachute opened close to the ground and for a moment, Lt. Struby thought his squadron mate might have been injured after he hit the earth. Lt. Howard got up though and dragging his chute behind him as he tried to free himself from the harness, headed for a woods at the edge of the field in which he had landed. As Lt. Struby circled above at 100 feet, he saw Lt. Howard disappear into the trees. It was a close call, for the Lieutenant's plane had crashed only 300 feet away from where he landed. It was noted at the time, that there was no other activity of any kind in the area and that it was felt that Lt. Howard stood a good chance of reaching friendly territory. (Lt. Howard was the kind of guy that could dive deeper, swim faster and come out drier than any other five men.) That proved to be an accurate prediction as Lieutenant Howard did in fact, successfully evade capture and returned to the group a short time later. He was picked up by a Maquis unit [French resistance fighters] almost as soon as he hit the ground just north of Dijon. He spent several weeks getting a close look at guerrilla warfare firsthand with the Maquis until he could be returned.

L/O for the 434th FS was over Cayeux at 1045 hrs./11,000 ft. L/O for the 435th FS was over St. Valery at 1045 hrs./10,000 ft. L/O for the 436th FS was scattered, extending from Cayeux to Ostend, Belgium at 1045 hrs./8,000 ft. The 435th left two of their pilots behind in France. Low on gas, the two landed at Ninth AF bases. One, Capt. William N. Gates, having crash-landed his plane, returned the next day from Meriere. Lt. Stephen H. Zuchowski ran out of gas and blew out a tire on landing. He came back three days later from Chartres. One other 435th pilot had the same problem, too. Lieutenant Charles F. Monsell was forced to land his P-38 on a road five miles northwest of Friston, England. He was reported to be all right, but the condition of his plane was unknown at the time.

Observations made by during the mission included rail and road traffic that the group was not able to deal with in the areas targeted. Shipping, including a large convoy was seen along the coast of France and Belgium. Flak was light, intense and accurate in the targeted area.

28 August 1944

VIII FC FO 539

No. 142 Monday. Major Carter was the group's leader and he also led the 435th FS, which consisted of 14 P-38s. Capt. Duffié led the 434th FS, which consisted of 16 P-38s and Capt. Biscayart led the 436th FS, which consisted of 16 P-38s. Their assignment was another fighter-bomber attack, but this time, in Belgium. This time they were carrying two 1,000-lb. GP bombs per plane and it was the second mission for the day. 434th FS up: 1708 hrs., down: 2006 hrs. with no early returns. 435th FS up: 1655 hrs., down: 1955 hrs. with no early returns. 436th FS up: 1654 hrs., down : 2000 hrs. with one early return.

L/F for the 434th FS and the 435th FS was over Walcheren Island, Holland, about 1742 hrs./13-15,000 ft. L/F for the 436th FS was over Vlissingen, Belgium at 1743 hrs./14,000 ft. Heading east to Eindhoven, Holland the squadrons turned south to reach their assigned target areas. The 434th FS provided top cover down to the St. Trond area at which point they dropped down to bomb the marshalling yards at Gossencourt and strafe the area. The results of the bombing were unobserved. The squadron reassembled over Gossencourt and headed out of Belgium, passing north of Brussels. They crossed out over Flushing, Holland at 1920 hrs./17,000 ft. The 435th FS began working over their assigned area, beginning south of Eindhoven at 1803 hours, heading southwest and breaking off at Hannut about 1850 hrs. Claims for the squadron were a marshalling yard, one railroad round house, two trains, 30 freight cars, one factory and an airfield, all damaged. They claimed six locomotives destroyed. L/O for them was also over Flensburg, at 1916 hrs. The 436th FS dive-bombed and strafed the area from Turnhout, Belgium to Roermond, Holland to St. Trond and over to Brussels. Arriving in the area at 1815 hours, they accounted for destroying and damaging a marshalling yards and round house at Beverlo, south of Turnhout and set some large fires at a factory near Roermond. L/O for the squadron was again over Vlissingen at 1855 hrs./18,000 ft.

Observations made during the mission include 30 unidentified enemy A/C on the airfield at St. Trond and three other airfields that appeared serviceable, one at Ursel, one north of St. Erremen and the other at Eeklo. Flak over Brussels was heavy, intense and accurate while at an airdrome ten miles northeast of Brussels, it was light, intense, but inaccurate. At St. Trond it, was light, intense and accurate.

29 August 1944

VIII FC FO 540

No. 143 Tuesday. Lt. Col. Woods was the group's leader and he also led the 436th FS, which consisted of 15 P-38s. Lt. Col. Herren led the 434th FS, which consisted of 17 P-38s and Capt. Sykes led the 435th FS, which consisted of 12 P-38s. Their assignment was a fighter-bomber attack on rail and tactical targets in the Saar area of southwestern Germany. 434th FS up: 0701 hrs., down: 1100 hrs. with no early returns. 435th FS up: 0707 hrs., down: 1103 hrs. with no early returns. 436th FS up: 0656 hrs., down: 1115 hrs. with no early returns.

L/F for the 434th FS was over Walcheren Island, Holland at 0750 hrs./10,000 ft. L/F for the 435th FS was over Schouwen Island, Holland at 0747 hrs./8,000 ft. L/F for the 436th FS was over Overflakkee, Holland at 0757 hrs./10,000 ft. The squadrons all ran into heavy overcast at Liège and were prevented from reaching their primary targets in Germany. They turned southwest, seeking targets of opportunity as they followed the Meuse River and the rail lines that run from Liège down southwest through Namur and Charleroi and over to Mons. The 434th FS used their 1,000-lb. GP bombs and the 436th FS used their 500-lb. GP bombs on a marshalling yard, a railroad roundhouse, numerous rail cars, sections of track and a tunnel which the Newcross pilots skip-bombed into oblivion. The Bison Squadron pilots had at first found an airfield before the rail targets, but flak at the field was so wicked and accurate that it's a wonder that there were no mid-air collisions in the mad scramble to get out of the area. The 435th

FS followed a different route, bombing and strafing from Dison, Belgium, down southwest to Revin, France. Their claims of destroyed and damaged include a triangular-shaped defensive strongpoint, a tunnel and sections of railroad track. Heading back home again, the 434th and the 436th FSs crossed out near Ostend at 1015 hrs./7,000 ft. The 435th FS went out east of Dunkerque at 1018 hrs.

Observations made during the mission included approximately 200 barges seen on the canal north of Valenciennes, France. That location was west of Mons and by then the squadrons had expended all their ammunition and ordnance. Heavy rail activity was noted in the marshalling yard at Tilburg. The group leader suggested that it was a good target for medium bombers. Several long trains were seen headed into Brussels. Flak at Liège was heavy, meager and inaccurate. At Ostend it was light, meager and inaccurate.

CHAPTER SEVEN

SEPTEMBER 1944

1 September 1944

VIII FC FO 543

No. 144 Friday. Lt. Col. Herren was the group's leader and he also led the 434th FS, which consisted of 17 P-38s. Lt. Col. Woods led the 435th FS, which consisted of 16 P-38s and Capt. Sullivan led the 436th FS, which consisted of 15 P-38s plus one relay A/C. Their assignment was a bomber escort to Saarbrücken, Germany in support of 8th AF Mission 595. 434th FS up: 0940 hrs., down: 1415 hrs. with one early return. 435th FS up: 0940hrs., down: 1355 hrs. with three early returns. 436th FS up: 0945 hrs., down: 1410 hrs. with five early returns.

L/F was made north of Ostend, Belgium between 1021 and 1030 hrs./16,000 and 17,000 ft. by all three squadrons. The 434th FS did not make R/V with the bombers because at 1050 hours, in the vicinity of Sedan, France, the squadron heard a call from Colgate telling fighter forces that the bombers had been recalled due to bad weather. The squadron continued in as far as Metz, France with a sweep that started at Namur, Belgium. Returning, they made L/O at Dunkerque, France at 1325 hrs./10,000 ft. No enemy aircraft were encountered in the air.

Observations made by the squadron during the sweep included heavy highway traffic headed east and marshalling yards full of cars, but with few locomotives present. It was noted the marshalling yards that had been attacked appeared to be partially repaired. Twenty trucks looking like U.S. 6x6s were seen heading northeast out of Namur. A truck convoy was seen heading south into Longuyon, France, while some trucks were noted as parked under trees. The marshalling yard at Longuyon showed heavy activity and some smoke was rising from what appeared to be burning oil tank cars. A group of oil tank cars were parked on a siding nearby, but there was no locomotive. West of there, near Jametz, France, a silver aircraft was seen on the ground in an open field. It appeared to be an allied plane that had bellied in. What were possibly balloons, were seen on the ground in an area north west of Metz. Fifteen to twenty S/E and T/E aircraft were observed at the Metz airdrome. Flak in the Mons, France area was meager, heavy and inaccurate.

The 435th FS drove in a little south of the tracked course, to a point northwest of Saarbrücken. A call to vector to Vinegrove 27 ("C" channel bomber call sign) was heard after it was found that the weather was bad. However, the originally assigned bombers to be escorted could not be found nor could be the newly-assigned Vinegrove force. L/O was north of Ostend at 1315 hrs./10,000 ft.

Observations made by the squadron during the mission included seeing fires and camouflage (simulated) bomb craters on an airfield south of Lille, France. An ammunition or stores dump of some sort was spotted in a woods west of Roulers, Belgium. There were oil tank cars seen in a marshalling yard at Valenciennes, France and the marshalling yard south of Longuyon was noted as full. The airfield south of Longuyon appeared to be shot up while the field south of Metz had 15 plus unidentified A/C. Heavy traffic in the form of transportation convoys heading north were seen in the Longuyon to Metz area.

The 436th FS made no R/V with the bombers before the Big Friends were recalled. The squadron penetrated as far as Saarbrücken before returning and making L/O near Ostend at 1315 hrs./1,000 ft.

Left to right – Lieutenant Colonel Sidney S. Woods, Deputy Group Commander; Lieutenant Colonel James M. Herren, Jr., 434th FS Commanding Officer; Lieutenant Colonel William F. Stenten, Group Executive Officer; Major Frank R. Silver, 434th FS Executive Officer; Captain Claire A.P. DuffiÈ, Flight Commander and Major William T. McElhinney, Group Flight Surgeon. The men are standing in front of the P-38 that Lt.Col. Herren regularly flew, L2-A. *Courtesy of Frederick C. Hayner.*

Observations made by the squadron during the mission include 50-60 barges along the canal from Ostend to Bruges, Belgium and three ships on the outer Enoke Harbor as well as several smaller craft in the inner harbor. Six to eight convoys were sighted in the area between Saarbrücken and Luxembourg. One was two miles long and consisted of 50 plus vehicles parked off the road. Another of twenty plus vehicles was heading northeast. Eighty plus vehicles traveling in groups of three in a convoy five miles long, were heading northeast at a good speed through Longuyon. These were all called in to the group leader. A very large railroad yard at Valenciennes was observed to be about one fourth full and did not appear to have been attacked in the past. There were ten to fifteen unidentified aircraft on the airfield at Metz. Flak over Lille-Roubaix was heavy, meager and accurate.

3 September 1944

VIII FC FO 548

No. 145 Sunday. Lt. Col. Herren was the group's leader and he also led the 434th FS, which consisted of 16 P-38s. Major Carter led the 435th FS, which consisted of 17 P-38s and Capt. Biscayart led the 436th FS, which consisted of 17 P-38s. Their assignment was a fighter-bomber attack against a tactical target on the Brest, France coast. This mission was in support of 8th AF Mission 601. 434th FS up: 1315 hrs., down: 1715 hrs. with no early returns. 435th FS up: 1320 hrs., down: 1710 hrs. with two early returns. 436th FS up: 1319 hrs., down: 1700 hrs. with one early return.

The group, after passing over Bournemouth, England on the way out and orbiting near the target area on the Brest Peninsula from 1510 hrs. until 1525 hours, was forced by weather to return to Wattisham. The group leader had reconnoitered the target while all other A/C were orbiting and determined that the 10/10ths cloud cover was too thick for bombing. All bombs were returned, much to the "enjoyment" of the armament people, except for two that were jettisoned over the channel. An explosion in the air at 3,000 feet, 12 miles north of London was observed at 1635 hrs.

Some of the 434th FS armorers posing on a bomb and dolly. *Courtesy of Loetta Taylor (Kennedy).*

5 September 1944

VIII FC FO 551

No. 146 Tuesday (First mission for the day). Lt. Col. Woods was the group's leader and he also led the 434th FS, which consisted of 17 P-38s. Capt. Sykes led the 435th FS, which consisted of 16 P-38s and Capt. Moore led the 436th FS, which consisted of 15 P-38s. Their first assignment of the day was a fighter rhubarb (strafing mission) in Germany that was laid on against rail and road traffic from Giessen to Hanau to Aschaffenburg to Würzburg and westward, as far as endurance would permit. 434th FS up: 0915 hrs., down: 1400 hrs. with five early returns. 435th FS up: 0930 hrs., down: 1405 hrs. with two early returns. 436th FS up: 0920 hrs., down: 1425 hrs. with two early returns.

435th FS armorers Corporal John P. Clodfelter and Corporal Stanley Kaufman are examining a .50 cal. machine gun as part of getting familiar with their new P-51s. *Courtesy of Carol Donaldson.*

This was the group's first strafing attack in Germany, the strafing attacks in France having been halted. The men were moving up on the rung, drawing closer in their part toward choking the life from the German war machine. L/F was made by the 434th and the 435th FSs near Blankenberghe, Belgium at 1000 hrs./14,000 ft. and 0958 hrs./14,000 ft. respectively, while the 436th FS made L/F over Ostend, Belgium at 1002 hrs./16,000 ft. The 434th FS arrived over Giessen at 1105 hrs./12,000 ft. and circled north of the town, spotting from there 20 plus aircraft on the ground at the grass airdrome of Ettingshausen, which was approximately six miles southeast of the town. The weather there was overcast with a base at 20,000 ft. and visibility unlimited underneath. Heading for the airdrome, no flak was seen, only two red flares that went up. Yellow and Blue Flights each made a dive-strafing pass to test for defenses, then two traffic patterns were set up from southeast to northwest, one right and one left. The entire squadron made a total of seven to ten passes, claiming 6-0-1 Ju 88s, 11-0-4 Do 217s and 8-0-0 Me 110s for a total of 25-0-5 twin-engine A/C. In addition to those planes, there were many gliders parked in small clearings in the woods to the south of the field. The group's leader, Lieutenant Colonel Sidney S.

Right: 436th FS armorers Corporal Paul E. Ellis and Corporal Melvin Bragman. *Carroll C. Sprague Collection, courtesy of the East Essex Aviation Society.*

Woods, filed a consolidated combat report after the attack. He stated:

> "I was flying with Newcross Squadron, leading the group on a strafing mission. We orbited the town of Giessen and nearby Ettingshausen Airdrome at 10,000 feet. One of the flights called in stating that many aircraft were parked on the airdrome's grounds. I circled the field and estimated that 30 plus aircraft were there, a few of which were later determined to be gliders or dummies. I sent Newcross Yellow Flight (six A/C) down to dive-strafe and held Lakeside and Bison Squadrons above, orbiting as top cover. After two passes by Newcross Yellow Flight, I took the other flights down to help complete the job, since there was no flak apparent.
>
> "We set up two separate traffic patterns: Yellow and Blue Flights strafed the south end of the field from east to west in a left-hand pattern while White and Red Flights strafed the north end of the field from east to west in a right-hand pattern. We made a total of eight to ten passes, then climbed and orbited the field at 8,000 feet. I counted nineteen planes burning, but smoke was so thick that it obscured sections of the field and prohibited a completely accurate count."

In order to facilitate the evaluation of claims, the above combat report was filed, noting that nineteen separate burning aircraft were definitely observed after the attack. The supported claims were as follows:

1-0-0	Ju 88	Lt. Col. Sidney S. Woods
1-0-0	Do 217	1st Lt. Robert H. Hendrickson
2-0-0	Do 217	1st Lt. James M. Hollingsworth
2-0-0	Ju 88	1st Lt. Berkley E. Hollister
1-0-0	Ju 88	2nd Lt. Harold F. Mathews
3-0-0	Me 110	2nd Lt. John N. Murr
1-0-0	Ju 88	2nd Lt. Thomas D. Neely
2-0-0	Me 110	2nd Lt. Thomas D. Neely
3-0-0	Do 217	1st Lt. Thomas C. Olson
1-0-0	Do 217	1st Lt. John T. Tipps
2-0-0	Do 217	1st Lt. Bailey A. Williams

After the attack, the squadron turned for home, making L/O at 1300 hrs./14,000 ft. Ten plus small boats were observed in the Rhine River. They were headed southeast towards Koblenz, Germany. Flak there was heavy, intense and accurate while over Bruges, Belgium, it was heavy, meager and inaccurate and over Liège, Belgium, it was heavy, intense and accurate.

A frame taken from First Lieutenant Berkley E. Hollister's gun camera film shot that day showing a Ju 88 that he was after. *Courtesy of Berkley E. Hollister.*

While the 435th FS and the 436th FS were circling and acting as top cover for the action below at Ettingshausen Airdrome, the 436th reported aircraft at nearby Mershausen Airdrome. First Lieutenant Andre E. Huycke narrates what happened then:

> "I was at 8,000 feet, orbiting to the left of the airdrome and flying element for the group leader, Lt. Col. Woods. Bison Squadron called in an airdrome at six o'clock to them. I advised Group Leader, reporting the airdrome. After asking for and receiving permission from both Group Leader and Bison Leader, I initiated a pass with my wingman, Captain Herbert H. Jordan, following. We made a dive-strafing run from 4,000 feet, traveling from east to west. On this pass, I hit one He 111 and saw it burst into flames. Observing no flak, I pulled back up to 4,000 feet and made a pattern to the left. The next two passes were spent trying to burn a remaining He 111. During the third pass, I saw several cannon hits on the nacelles and saw the Heinkel's entire cockpit blow up. On the fourth pass, I went after an airplane that I would identify as a Do 217, observing strikes on the fuselage and wings. After this pass, the group leader called us off. I claim two He 111s destroyed and one Do 217 as damaged."

When the 434th FS left for home, the remaining two squadrons continued on down the route to south of Giessen where the 435th FS took the opportunity to strafe rail traffic, putting in claims for two locomotives and ten goods cars destroyed as well as ten goods cars damaged. That squadron, in flying south from Giessen, to the Hanau area and back out, noted that the marshalling yard at Friedberg was loaded with freight cars, the Hoechst Oberau Airdrome had 20 plus unidentified A/C and the Langenselbold Airdrome had 50 to 60 A/C of all types. It was thought to be a depot of some sort because it had many large hangars and buildings. The 435th FS made L/O near Blankenberghe at 1333 hrs/10,000 ft. except for Lt. Stephen H. Zuchowski who had suffered an engine failure in the area of Hanau. He broke off from the force and escorted by two planes from Bison Flight, headed out from behind enemy lines, landing at Vitry-en-Artois airfield, 20 miles south of Lille, France. He returned the next day from that British C-47 base.

Continuing south, the 436th FS strafed the airdrome at Friedberg, just south of Bad Nauheim. They made five or six passes resulting in the following consolidated claims:

0-0-2	Fw 190	1st Lt. Edwin J. Fillipow
1-0-1	Fw 190	1st Lt. James E. Frolking
4-0-3	Fw 190	1st Lt. Hans J. Grasshoff
2-0-1	Fw 190	1st Lt. Vincent C. Hartnett
2-0-0	Fw 190	1st Lt. Edward C. Lewin
1-0-0	Fi 156	1st Lt. Edward C. Lewin
0-0-2	U/I biplane	1st Lt. Edward C. Lewin
0-0-2	Fw 190	Capt. Clifford J. Moore
1-0-0	U/I S/E	Capt. Clifford J. Moore
2-0-1	Fw 190	2nd Lt. Gerold M. Mulvany
2-0-1	Fw 190	2nd Lt. Zeymour Ogron
2-0-1	Fw 190	1st Lt. Victor Wolski

Most accounts of the strafing were similar to that of First Lieutenant Edward C. Lewin who gave this report:

> "I was number two man in the Bison White Flight. I followed Captain Clifford J. Moore, Jr. who was leading Bison Squadron, in the initial west to east dive-strafing attack. We dove on the field from 4,000 feet to ascertain flak concentration. Observing no flak, we made a left-hand pattern, coming in at deck level, west to east again. On the first run, I gave a short burst to a Fw 190 and saw it burst into flames almost immediately. We then changed our pattern to the right, still running west to east. On our first pass in this pattern, I observed two biplanes in a corner of the field. Heading that direction, I gave them a long burst and observed numerous strikes on both planes, but they did not burn. On the same pass, I gave another long burst to a Fw 190 that was to the far edge of the field. I saw strikes on this aircraft, but no fire. On the second pass in that pattern, I got a long burst in on a Fi 156 which was facing me at about a 45-degree angle. I observed strikes and saw the whole aft section of the plane, from wing on back, literally disintegrate, with blue-grayish smoke rising from the remains. As I passed across the field, I noted the whole plane had become engulfed in flames."

Left: A later photo of then Major Clifford J. Moore, Jr. *Courtesy of Clarence G. Haynes*. Right: Newly minted Second Lieutenants James E. Frolking and Edwin J. Fillipow pictured in California before shipment to the ETO. At the time the picture was taken, they were standing in front of Lt. Fillipow's home. *Courtesy of James E. Frolking.*

This action was seen and confirmed by Capt. Moore.

Two friends and roommates back at Wattisham had interesting experiences during this attack. First Lieutenants James E. Frolking and Edwin J. Fillipow were in Bison Blue Flight together and attacked similar targets. Lt. Frolking states:

> "I made my attack from west to east on the airdrome. On my first pass, I got strikes on one Fw 190, but it did not burn. Our flight made a right-hand gunnery pattern orbit and on my second pass, I got strikes on an Fw 190 that blew up and began burning right-directly in front of me!"

Lt. Fillipow:

> "I was flying Bison Blue Four. After the all-clear report, we came in and started our passes from west to east, making a right-hand traffic pattern. I observed numerous hits on two Fw 190s, but they would not burn.

I believe that one of these was definitely destroyed, because Blue Three and I hit it on three passes. On my fourth pass, I got a light-caliber bullet through my canopy that sprayed plexiglass all over the cockpit. The round also grazed my wrist so I pulled up from the pass. It was more than likely some foot soldier that took a pot shot at me. "

The 436th FS headed for home, having used most of their gas and ammunition. Capt. Herbert H. Jordan, flying on a single engine, was left at 1300 hrs./3,000 ft. approximately 30 miles south of Mézières, France. He landed at Meaux, France and returned to Wattisham later. Lt. Thomas H. Orrick, low on fuel, landed at the same airfield as did Lt. Zuchowski from the 435th FS. Lt. Orrick, getting fuel in just a short time was airborne again at 1500 hrs. L/O for the squadron was south of Walcheren Island at 1345 hrs./10,000 ft.

Observations during the mission were the same as those made by the other squadrons except the 436th also noted that three miles east of Ingelheim, Germany there was an airfield with five Ju 52s and ten to fifteen Me 110s and 210s parked on the eastern side of the field. The aircraft were marked with "RR+1".

5 September 1944

65th FW FO 110

No. 147 Tuesday (Second mission for the day). Capt. Duffié was the group's leader and he also led the 434th FS, which consisted of 10 P-38s. Maj. Carter led the 435th FS, which consisted of 13 P-38s and Capt. Sullivan led the 436th FS, which consisted of 11 P-38s. Their assignment was a late afternoon, return engagement to the morning's targets. There was more work to be done so this time the group's planes were loaded up with 500-lb. GP bombs (one bomb per plane, slung under the right wing, a drop tank under the left) for a fighter-bomber and strafing attack on the airdromes attacked previously that morning. 434th FS up: 1650 hrs., down: 2100 hrs. with no early returns. 435th FS up: 1657 hrs., down: 2125 hrs. with two early returns, one of which remained out as a relay. 436th FS up: 1644 hrs., down: 2115 hrs. with one early return.

L/F was made by both the 434th and 435th FSs near Blankenberghe, Belgium at 1730 hrs./12,000 ft. L/F for the 436th FS was south of Ostend, Belgium at 1725 hrs./13,000 ft. The 434th FS went back to the happy hunting grounds that they had visited during the morning. The weather in the area had remained unchanged with high overcast and visibility unlimited underneath. First Lieutenant James M. Hollingsworth filed this report of that action:

"I was Newcross Red Leader on a strafing mission in the Giessen, Germany area. Our squadron provided top cover while the other two squadrons dive-bombed and strafed various targets in the area. At the completion of their attack, I took Newcross Red Flight over to Ettingshausen Airdrome, where we had strafed earlier. We orbited the field at 8,000 feet and I observed eighteen burnt out wrecks plus one other aircraft which had not burned, but in fact, had been shot up so badly that it was completely destroyed. These nineteen destroyed aircraft were undoubtedly the result of our attack under VIII FG FO 551. In addition, I observed eight aircraft which were untouched. I called the observation in to the group leader and he ordered one of the other squadrons to strafe, but they could not find the field so he gave me permission to take Red Flight's four P-38s down. The other Newcross flights provided top cover while we went down in a southeast to northwest dive-strafing pass. We received light flak from the northeast section of the field so we made two strafing runs on the gun positions. Then we set up a traffic pattern on the undamaged aircraft and made four passes, southeast to northwest. We then changed our pattern and made two passes northeast to southwest to get some aircraft parked in the edge of the woods nearby. Following this, I took the flight up to 8,000 feet and as we reformed, I observed eight separate and distinct fires from burning aircraft on the field below."

Captain Claire A.P. Duffié supported that claim with this statement:

"I was leading the 479th Fighter Group on a dive-bombing and strafing mission in the Hanau, Germany area. At approximately 1850 hours, Newcross Red Flight called in operational enemy aircraft parked on Ettingshausen airfield. This is the same airfield they had strafed earlier in the day. I called Bison Squadron to attack and orbited the field at 8,000 feet. I counted eighteen airplanes that had been gutted by fire on the field. These obviously resulted from the first attack. Bison Squadron was unable to find the field so I gave Newcross Red Flight permission to strafe. I kept Newcross White Flight at 8,000 to 10,000 feet as top cover. Red Flight made a total of eight to ten passes on the field from various directions, then joined my flight above the field. As the group reformed, I counted eight fires and smoke from aircraft destroyed by Red Flight. Therefore, I confirm twenty-six of the twenty-seven aircraft claimed to be destroyed on Ettingshausen airfield, 5 September 1944. In addition, First Lt. James M. Hollingsworth, Newcross Red Leader, stated to me immediately after landing, that there was one other aircraft on the ground which they had not attacked on the second mission because it was shot up into wreckage. It had not burned."

The 434th FS's score card looked like this for the second mission:

1-0-0	Do 217	1st Lt. Robert H. Hendrickson
4-0-0	Me 410	1st Lt. James M. Hollingsworth
1-0-0	Me 410	2nd Lt. Calvin J. Murphy
1-0-0	Me 110	1st Lt. Thomas C. Olson
1-0-0	Do 217	1st Lt. Thomas C. Olson

Captain Claire A.P. Duffié. *Courtesy of Frederick C. Hayner.*

Below: Pilot Lieutenant John W. Morrow, crew chief Sergeant Maxcy O. Corder, Bolivar J. Dragass (the dog) and the remainder of Shoo Shoo Baby's crew. *Courtesy of Frederick C. Hayner.*

That made 27 aircraft destroyed by the Newcross squadron for the day. In addition to those, at another location, Second Lieutenant John W. Morrow was able to tally another enemy aircraft for the squadron's total. He gave this narrative: "I was flying Newcross Yellow Four on a strafing mission in the Giessen area. We observed two aircraft parked on a grass field south of the town and made a dive-strafing pass from northwest to southeast. I observed an Me 109 parked in an opening of a wooded section at the southeast end of the field, but just couldn't get my sights on it. The flight climbed back up and made another run, this time I got on the 109 and opened fire at about 400 yards. I observed many strikes along the wing roots and fuselage. The aircraft burst into flames just as I passed over it. I claim one Me 109 destroyed on the ground."

Capt. Duffié confirmed Lt. Morrow's claim:

> "I was leading the group on the above mission, flying with Newcross squadron. Newcross White Flight provided top cover for all of this strafing activity in the Giessen area. As I left the area, I observed flames and smoke from a burning aircraft in the vicinity of Grossenlinden, Germany. Newcross Yellow Flight had strafed this field. I confirm Second Lt. Morrow's claim of one Me 109 destroyed on the ground."

Newcross Squadron also put three locomotives out of action, south of Giessen before they made L/O over Blankenberghe, heading for home.

The 435th FS arrived at the Ettingshausen airdrome after the 434th FS was there and had stirred up a hornet's nest. Having been advised that the target was heavy with flak, the Lakeside P-38s moved on to look at the Gainhausen airdrome, but it had just been beaten up by a bunch of P-47 pilots, who left nothing, but dust, fires and smoke. They attacked two trains in the area and destroyed the locomotives along with damaging thirteen goods cars. The squadron continued on, following the railroad line down towards the vicinity of Frankfurt, Germany and winding up at the Langenselbold airdrome, where many aircraft had been reportedly seen during the morning's attacks. There was light flak and it was intense and accurate at the airdrome. The squadron's leader, Major Raymond S. Carter, was hit by that flak and was killed in the crash of his P-38. Maj. Carter's wingman, First Lieutenant Wilbert Muller, witnessed the event and documented the loss:

> "I was flying as Major Carter's wingman and I saw him go down to 500 feet above the deck to make a pass at one plane on the ground. When he pulled up, I noticed smoke coming from the pilot's nacelle and saw a flicker of flame. He then started a gradual climb and I saw flames inside the canopy. He leveled off at approximately 2,000 feet and then plunged straight downward. By this time, flames were pouring from the plane and it exploded on impact. I did not see a parachute leave the plane."

Second Lieutenant Nelson W. Butler was a witness also and he gave this report:

> "Our flight was circling the target airport at about 4,000 feet when Major Carter called and said that he was going to make a pass from south to north on one of the planes parked on the field. I watched him as he came in and fired on one of the planes. As he crossed over the edge of the field, I saw a flash on his plane and when he pulled up, there was a white spray of gasoline or coolant trailing from his plane. It then caught fire and flames spread very quickly over the airplane. He then rolled over and started to go in, but he recovered and rolled out again. He started down a second time and hit almost straight into the ground, exploding on impact. I did not see a parachute leave the plane."

The squadron left that hot spot and headed north to bomb and strafe the airdromes at Hochst Oberau, fifteen miles northeast of Frankfurt and at Friedberg, north of there. At Hochst Oberau A/D, First Lieutenant Verne E. Hooker attacked an He 111 on the ground and claimed one destroyed:

> "We approached Hochst Oberau airfield and made one or two circles, then the squadron leader called in two aircraft at the edge of the woods. He said they looked like real planes, not dummies so we dive-bombed these and scored near misses. The squadron leader then called in and said we would go down and make one pass, which we did. I fired approximately an eight-second burst into the closest aircraft, which looked like a He 111. All guns fired and the plane was riddled. I don't believe this plane can be repaired. After returning, however, some of the other pilots claim these planes may have been dummies. I request that my combat film be checked to confirm this."

Lakeside Squadron left both airdromes in a damaged state and headed home, making L/O east of Blankenberghe at 2050 hrs./ 10,000 ft.

Bison Squadron was assigned to dive-bomb gun positions around the airfield at Hanau in order to silence the flak. Three of the squadron's pilots successfully attacked defensive positions on the field, but they also succeeded in stirring up a hornet's nest. The flak became such a storm of tracers that it was decided the airfield was too hot to handle. They moved on to another airdrome just a short distance away. The flak there was not so bad, so the squadron set up a pattern and went to work.

In all, the 436th FS attacked three airdromes on this excursion and claimed these results:

At the Hanau A/D

2-0-0	Fw 190	2d Lt. Jesse V. Granger
2-0-1	Do 217	1st Lt. Travis M. Greenwood
0-0-1	Do 217	2nd Lt. Gerold M. Mulvany
0-0-2	Fw 190	Capt. Joseph H. Rosness
4-0-5	Do 217	Shared by Capt. John A. Sullivan, 1st. Lt. John W. Hedenberg and 2nd Lt. Melvin S. Mickey

At the Bad Nauheim A/D

0-0-1	He 111	Capt. John A Sullivan

At the Hochst Oberau A/D

0-0-1	Do 217	Capt. Joseph H. Rosness
0-0-2	Do 217	Capt. John A. Sullivan

Captain John A. Sullivan described his actions in this narration:

> "I was leading Bison Squadron. The weather in the area was good, with ceilings at 7,000 feet and visibility, five to six miles. I flew from east to west, along the north edge of the field at Hanau A/D and put my two flights into right echelons. When I got to the northwest edge of the field, I did a split-ess and started my dive-bomb run along the west edge of the field. There were a large number of airplanes parked along the field and in the woods. I dive-strafed and dropped my bomb in a group of nine airplanes. When I broke away from the field, I saw that all three of the bombs from my flight had been dropped into the group of nine airplanes.
>
> "From there, I took my squadron to Bad Nauheim Airdrome and made a dive-strafing pass from south to north along the east edge of the field. I picked out an He 111 and got numerous hits on it, but the aircraft would not burn. Flak was too heavy to make another pass here so I took my flights on to the Hochst Oberau Airdrome. I made one dive-strafing pass here from south to north along the east edge of the field, getting hits on two Do 217s, but they would not burn. I claim one Do 217 destroyed, four Do 217s damaged and one He 111 damaged."

Nose art on Piccadilly Rose, a 435th FS P-38. *Courtesy of Frederick C. Hayner.*

First Lieutenant John W. Hedenberg was in Capt. Sullivan's flight and reported this encounter:

> "I was flying Bison White Two, on Capt. Sullivan's wing. We flew from east to west along the north side of the field at Hanau A/D and successively peeled off and made our dive-bomb and strafing runs when we reached the northwest corner of the field. I released my bomb just as Capt. Sullivan pulled up. When I pulled up and looked back, I saw Lt. Mickey's bomb hit and explode amidst the smoke and dust caused by Capt. Sullivan's and my bomb, within the group of nine planes. Due to the intense flak, we did not press any further attack, but proceeded to Bad Nauheim Airdrome. I followed Capt. Sullivan on his

dive-strafing run there, but broke off before getting very low, due to the flak. When I pulled up, I lost Capt. Sullivan so I went with Lt. Mickey to Hochst Oberau Airdrome. There seemed to be no flak there so we made a couple of good passes. On my first pass, I got numerous hits on a small biplane, but it did not burn. On my second pass, I hit another biplane, which immediately burst into flames and blew up. I claim two Do 217s destroyed and one Do 217 damaged. I also claim one unidentified biplane destroyed and one damaged."

The third of the trio who dive-bombed together, Second Lieutenant Melvin S. Mickey had this to say:

"I was flying number three position in Bison White Flight. We were flying east to west, along the north edge of the field at Hanau A/D. Capt. Sullivan and Lt. Hedenberg peeled off, closely followed by myself. There were Do 217s and Ju 88s dispersed around three-fourths of the perimeter. At one point, near some trees, there were at least nine and probably twelve Do 217s bunched together. This was the point of our attack. There was very intense flak fire while I was in my dive and I was firing most of the way down. When I had pulled off the target, I observed that all three of our bombs had burst right in the middle of this large bunch of planes.

"From there, I went with my flight to Bad Nauheim A/D. Capt. Sullivan and Lt. Hedenberg peeled off on the only ship that I observed on the field, an He 111. I observed Capt. Sullivan firing at this aircraft, but I was too far away to see where he was hitting. As flak was too intense, Lt. Hedenberg and I turned away, losing Capt. Sullivan. Lt. Hedenberg and I then went to Hochst Oberau A/D. Here, I circled while Lt. Hedenberg made his first pass. I joined him on his second pass and observed his setting fire to one aircraft and I fired at a single-engine aircraft, but it did not burn. The smoke was heavy on this field. I claim one Do 217 destroyed and two Do 217s damaged."

First Lieutenant Travis M. Greenwood was leading Bison Red Flight and gave this statement:

"I followed White Flight from east to west along the north edge of Hanau Airdrome. I observed nine aircraft parked near the woods on the A/D. I relayed the command from Capt. Sullivan to echelon the flight to the right. I waited for White Flight to bomb and then followed with a wing over and dive-strafed the line of ships, releasing my bomb at about 3,000 feet. I believe the enemy aircraft to have been Do 217s. I pulled out and took evasive action. My flight reformed and soon after, I had to return home, escorting an abort. I observed two bombs to explode while following my flight's attack. My bomb destroyed two aircraft and damaged another; while the other bomb from my flight damaged or destroyed another. I claim two Do 217s destroyed and one damaged."

First Lieutenant Travis M. Greenwood. *Courtesy of Travis M. Greenwood.*

Bison Squadron made L/O between Overflakkee, Holland and Walcheren Island at 2020 hrs./10,000 ft.

Observations made during the mission included: P-47s were seen clobbering the Gainhausen A/D where there were 20 plus fires were noted. Barges in the river near Koblenz and heavy train traffic in the target area were also noted. Two of the trains were stopped because their locomotives were destroyed. Flak on the Rhine River near Koblenz was heavy, intense and accurate as it was over Koblenz itself. (John W. Hedenberg said on the way out of Germany, he made the mistake of flying over Koblenz and immediately regretted it.

He stated: "The gunners there were the sharpest I have ever seen anywhere, bar none! And they were shooting through solid cloud cover too! No matter what evasive action I would take, they were right on me. I don't like flak!!") The same was true of Wiesbaden and Hanau. At Friedberg, flak was heavy, meager and inaccurate, while at Langenselbold and Hochst Oberau, it was light, intense and accurate.

Second Lieutenant Calvin J. Murphy. *Courtesy of Berkley E. Hollister.*

6 September 1944

VIII FC FO 555

No. 148 Wednesday. Lt. Col. Herren was the group's leader and he also led the 434th FS, which consisted of 16 P-38s. Capt. Moore led the 435th FS, which consisted of 17 P-38s and Maj. Glover led the 436th FS, which consisted of 16 P-38s. Their assignment was a fighter rhubarb (strafing mission) to the Wiesbaden/Frankfurt area (the same general area that they had attacked the previous day) in Germany. 434th FS up: 1145 hrs., down: 1545 hrs. with no early returns. 435th FS up: 1150 hrs., down: 1555 hrs. with no early returns. 436th FS up: 1155 hrs., down: 1540 hrs. with one early return.

The 479th FG and four P-47 groups were the only large forces of Eighth Air Force planes in the skies this day. L/F was made near Blankenberghe, Belgium between 1220 and 1225 hrs./10,000 and 12,000 ft. by all three squadrons. Because the weather was bad, the group took a course directly to Koblenz, Germany, looking for good breaks in all the clouds. There were none. The group turned southeast, heading down the Rhein River towards Bingen, then onward southeast to as far as Darmstadt, Germany intending to head back up to the Hanau A/D again. The force had been stirring up German AA units all along the route and at 1320 hours, while the group was in the Darmstadt area, Second Lieutenant Calvin J. Murphy, flying Captain Arthur Jeffrey's P-38, "Boomerang", was hit by flak. When last seen, Lt. Murphy was in a steep dive, heading into the overcast. Second Lieutenants Walter A. Neuman and Richard G. Simpson gave this report of the loss:

> "Our squadron was flying southeast at 9,000 feet in the vicinity of Darmstadt at approximately 1315 hrs. We were forced to take evasive action by intense and accurate flak. Lt. Murphy, flying the White Two position, evidentially got a direct hit, for his plane was seen going down and on fire. He was observed going down in a 45-degree dive and later on failed to answer when called by his flight leader."

The 10/10ths undercast was just too much, preventing any strafing whatsoever so the group took a straight course out, making a somewhat scattered L/O between Blankenberghe and Dunkerque, France at 1435 to 1515 hrs./8,000 to 12,000 ft. After the war, Lieutenant Murphy's remains were recovered from a grave in the town near his crash site. He had gone down in the vicinity of Viernheim.

Observations made during the mission included: Heavy barge and road traffic northeast of Mullenback was seen as well as rail traffic along the Rhine River between Koblenz and Köln, Germany. Flak over Aachen was heavy, meager and accurate while south of Koblenz, it was light, intense and accurate along the Rhine River.

Back at Wattisham, Lieutenant McCarthy, a visiting pilot, was checking out in one of the 434th FS's P-38s and ran into a telegraph pole. The P-38 was completely demolished, but Lt. McCarthy escaped unhurt. Lucky fellow!

8 September 1944

VIII FC FO 557

No. 149 Friday. Col. Zemke was the group's leader and he also led the 436th FS, which consisted of 17 P-38s. Capt. Olds led the 434th FS, which consisted of 15 P-38s and Maj. Glover led the 435th FS, which consisted of 17 P-38s. Their assignment was a fighter rhubarb (strafing mission) of tactical targets in Germany, another try at the same area as the past few days. 434th FS up: 1255 hrs., down: 1630 hrs. with no early returns. 435th FS up: 1258 hrs., down: 1620 hrs. with four early returns. 436th FS up: 1250 hrs., down: 1645 hrs. with one early return.

The mission was unsuccessful due to weather. There was a huge front that extended from 2,500 to 29,000 feet in the target area. L/F was between Walcheren Island and Knokke, Belgium at 1330 to 1340 hrs./14,000 to 15,000 ft. The briefed course was abandoned and the squadrons flew into Germany to the area west of Koblenz, looking for a way through. From there they went north to the Bonn area, south to the Saarbrücken area and out. There was no getting through the cloud coverage. L/O was the same place as L/F, between 1545 and 1555 hrs./ 12,000 and 15,000 ft.

Observations made during the mission included: Barrage balloons were seen on the ground around a dam 15 miles south of Düren, Germany. Several trains were seen and one was strafed by Red Flight from the 436th FS. This yielded a damaged locomotive and seven oil cars and goods wagons. Between Louvain and Liège, Belgium, one pilot from the 436th FS saw what appeared to be hay on the ground. Spotted through a hole in the clouds, it was arranged in what he believed was an attempt to spell out about an eight-letter word. Further confirmation was impossible however. Flak over Köln was heavy, moderate and inaccurate while over Dilling, Germany it was light, meager and inaccurate.

This was the last mission flown with P-38s by the 435th FS. The squadron was released from combat for the next few days to make final check-ups and checkouts in the P-51s before beginning combat in the aircraft. The group had begun its transition over to the Mustang. On 9 September 1944, Second Lieutenant Everett P. Ford from the 435th FS failed to pull out of a dive while on a practice flight in the area of home base and was killed in the crash of his P-51. The tragedy of that hit home hard for T/5 Orie W. Cleous, who counted among his duties, part time barber and the job of ambulance driver. T/5 Cleous was friends with everyone and had just cut Lt. Ford's hair the previous day. This day however, he had to retrieve Lt. Ford's remains from the crash site and transport them to the mortuary.

10 September 1944

VIII FC FO 561

No. 150 Sunday. Lt. Col. Woods was the group's leader and he also led the 434th FS, which consisted of 16 P-38s. Maj. Sullivan led the 436th FS, which consisted of 17 P-38s. Their assignment was a fighter sweep, along with a bomber escort for 2nd BD B-24s attacking their 8th AF Mission 619 secondary targets, the marshalling yards at Ulm and Heilbronn, Germany. 434th FS up: 0855 hrs., down: 1440 hrs. with three early returns. 436th FS up: 0858 hrs., down: 1445 hrs. with three early returns plus one escort.

L/F was made near Coxyde, Belgium at 0938 hrs./16,000 ft. The group arrived in the target area and R/V'd with the assigned bombers at 1050 hrs. The Big Friends were escorted uneventfully through the targets and out. The weather there was clear, with scattered clouds at 5,000 ft. and this facilitated the search for airdromes during the escort and after the group broke away from their charges. The two squadrons looked around the areas of Ulm, Aalen, Stuttgart, Heilbronn, Mannheim and south of Frankfurt, Germany. There wasn't much that the group wanted to go after, but the 434th FS did find some targets at the Malmheim Airfield. At approximately 1100 hours, Second Lieutenant Ronald L. Maley claimed one He 111 as damaged in an attack on that field. His Combat Report states:

> "I was flying Newcross White Two on a bomber escort mission over the area of Malmheim Airfield in Germany. We were on a sweep ahead of the bombers in the area of Ulm. The bombers had come and gone when

A 434th FS P-38 (L2-E) taxiing to the take off runway on the way to forming up for a mission. *Courtesy of Arnold G. Helding.*

> we saw the airfield. There were three planes already burning on the field from a recent attack by some P-51s. There were still quite a few ships on the field so Highway [Lt. Col. Sidney S. Woods] called a dive-strafing pass to check for flak. I was on his wing and we started the pass from the east, heading west. At 1,000 yards, I opened fire on an He 111 and observed strikes on the right wing. I closed to 600 yards, firing a three-second burst. Flak was heavy so I pulled away and left."

Second Lieutenant Harold E. Mathews followed Lt. Maley down and he gave this report:

> "I was Newcross White Three. At about 1100 hours, we noticed numerous aircraft parked on the Malmheim Airfield. It also was under attack by some P-51s. We first did a 360-degree turn around the field and looked for another field in the area. Not finding one, we returned to the above-mentioned field just after the P-51s had left. I noticed three fires on the field. Newcross White Flight made a dive-strafe pass on the south side of the field, from 6,000 to 1,000 feet, to test for flak. We found intense, light flak and, in fact, Newcross White leader [Lt. Col. Woods] had his right engine hit by it. That was the only attempt made. During the pass, I saw Lt. Maley get hits on one plane and I scored hits on a plane to the right of that one. I claim one He 111 damaged on the ground."

L/O for the group was from Calais to Dunkerque, France at 1405 hrs./9,000 ft.

Observations made during the mission included seeing three aircraft burning at Boblingen A/D, southwest of Stuttgart, as well as another 25-30 twin-engine A/C that remained undamaged on the field there. There were many fires at various airdromes located between Stuttgart and Frankfurt. While there were eight to ten fires on the A/D at Odheim, north of Heilbronn, a like amount of planes remained undamaged. There were large fires and huge clouds of black smoke at Stuttgart and Frankfurt. Six plus Ju 88s were seen on an A/D east of Neustadt, southwest of Mannheim. There was a large explosion seen at Metz, France at 1035 hrs. Flak there was light, moderate and accurate. It was noted that the A/D at Boblingen had many 40mm guns.

From the diary of John W. Hedenberg:

> "Some days you just can't make a nickel! The mission was a bomber escort to south of the Frankfurt area. First Huycke [Andre Huycke] had me up for his plane instead of mine. I talked him out of that, only to have a bum prop governor show up during takeoff on the ship I did take. Succeeded in stopping before going off the runway. Went back to the line, got another ship and took off. Was only about five minutes behind, but couldn't catch the group even though chased them all the way to Brussels. Had to come back and call it an abort."

11 September 1944

VIII FC FO 563

No. 151 Monday. Col. Zemke was the group's leader and he also led the 436th FS, which consisted of 18 P-38s. Lt. Col. Herren led the 434th FS, which consisted of 15 P-38s. Their assignment was a bomber escort for 1st BD B-17s attacking their 8th AF Mission 623 primary target, the oil refineries at Merseburg, Germany. 434th FS up: 0930 hrs., down: 1440 hrs. with no early returns. 436th FS up: 0932 hrs., down: 1445 hrs. with six early returns.

L/F was made in the vicinity of Knokke, Belgium at 1020 hrs, 18,000 ft. Lieutenants Frederick M. Mead and Arlett (Art) G. Mosier, Jr. from the 436th FS flew an area in Holland between Ostend and Schouwen, acting as relays. R/V with the proper bombers was at 1120 hrs./27,000 ft. in the vicinity of Laacher Lake, about 12 miles northwest of Koblenz, Germany. The 434th FS stayed with the bombers, noting that the 4th FG was also present, their red-nosed P-51s joining in the escort. The 436th FS let down to look for attacking fighters, but none ever appeared. The B-17s were taken to within 20 miles of their objective. The squadron then moved to the rally point, waiting for the Big Friends to come off the target and begin heading home. They never reappeared. Some thought was given to the idea that the bombers had continued on to Russia as a "FRANTIC JOE" mission. There was such a mission that day, but the B-17 force that went on to Russia, was from the 3rd BD and had attacked a target in Chemnitz, Germany. That assembly, which was made up of two bomb groups, was escorted to their destination by the 20th FG. Whatever the case, the 434th FS picked up a box of 3rd BD B-17s and escorted them out and home, breaking away just before L/O at Gravelines, France. Earlier, Bison Red Flight had strafed a train north of Grafendorf, which is just east of Frankfurt, Germany. First Lieutenant Travis M. Greenwood got the locomotive. Col. Zemke's flight strafed a small convoy of five or six trucks northeast of Bad Kreuznach, Germany. That squadron made a scattered L/O. Col. Zemke's flight, plus Lts. Greenwood and Thomas E. Meyers, landed at Leon, France for gas, then continued on home. Lts. John W. Hedenberg, Vincent C. Hartnett and Gerold M. Mulvany also landed in France for gas. That trio had a difficult time at the English base where they landed. Per Lt. Hedenberg:

> "We landed at Amiens. The English there wouldn't give us gas, so we stole some out of a P-51 left on the field. We used a portable pump borrowed from the crew of a B-24 stranded there. Their plane had a couple of turbos out. It was too late to go on home then, so we decided to stay the night. We couldn't get any food out of the Limeys, so we hitched a ride into town. Got a meal at the Allied Canteen and stayed at the Hotel du Rhin – a small place. In the morning, ate again at the same place as before, caught a ride back to the field, took off and landed back at Wattisham about 3:30 this afternoon."

John Hedenberg, in writing later of this experience added this:

> "Here was another 'bare-bones' entry that lacked emotion or feeling for the situation at the time. That day so baldly described was full of an incredible variety of experiences. To begin with, the field at Amiens had only been liberated eight days previously. A squadron of RAF Typhoon fighters was operating out of it, under very difficult conditions. The runway was only just barely usable, having been heavily cratered with Allied bombs while still occupied by the Luftwaffe. The entire field was almost literally paved with bomb fragments; jagged pieces of bomb casing were lying everywhere only a couple of feet apart on the average (I picked up and brought back one, which I still have).
>
> "All of the gas for the RAF operations was being flown in on cargo planes of all descriptions. There was no control tower in operation and one end of the field was a park of assorted abandoned American aircraft that had landed there for various emergency reasons in the week since liberation. Naturally, with every drop of the RAF fuel being flown in, there was none to spare for non-combat use by us to get home. Some of the pilots and crews of those parked planes were still there, waiting for transportation back or for fuel to be flown to them, while others had bummed rides home in various ways. We exercised our ingenuity and borrowed the pump to steal gas from the tanks of a half-full P-51, whose pilot was nowhere to be found, but were then disconcerted to find that the RAF commander also would not feed us.
>
> "We asked which way the town lay along the road next to the field, went to that road, and stuck out our thumbs. There was a lot of military traffic, so it wasn't long before a truck full of friendly Canadian infantry troops picked us up. They let us off in the city, where we were evidently almost the first Americans seen since the fall of France in 1940. People everywhere would smile shyly and point, sometimes whispering to each other '*Americaine, Americaine*?'
>
> "With the aid of the very halting high-school French of the B-24's navigator, who had come into town with us along with the plane's tail-gunner, we found a canteen that had been set up for the Allied soldiers. There a frugal but tasty meal was to be had, though the town was still so newly liberated that the friendly people operating it would not accept any of the francs we had taken from our escape kits. They directed us to a nearby pension where we had no trouble getting rooms for the night – we were the only tenants. The entire staff consisted of a very old French lady who had very little to say, and a young red-haired woman who didn't seem to understand the little French we used among us. Eventually in the mutual incomprehension it became understood that the younger woman wasn't French, so she was asked where she was from. Her reply, repeated a number of times to penetrate our translator's lack of understanding, finally got through to me. It was something like '*Je suis Polonaise*?', so I burst out with, 'Hey, she says she's Polish!' At that point the tail-gunner told us he was second-generation Polish and could speak a little Polish but understood very little. With that, we could get a conversation of sorts going – we who knew neither language, could talk or ask questions in English, the tail-gunner would put them into Polish, the woman would answer in French, and the navigator would laboriously put what he got back into English. As might be imagined, it was a most amusing and unusual evening.
>
> "The next morning we took time enough to go look at the famous Amiens cathedral, but found it heavily barricaded with protective sandbags and not at its best. The nearby department store was just being opened, though with few customers. We took a quick look in there and I bought a scarf for my wife just to be able to say I

had something for her from France. Then we caught a ride back to the airfield, passing the quite large marshalling yard, which had very recently been bombed by our B-17s. We were all awed and sobered at the sight – the whole large area was one huge tumbled jumble of craters on top of craters, with twisted rails piled in utter confusion everywhere like jackstraws. There were no two rails end to end anywhere, and everything was as desolate and lifeless, as if it were a moonscape. Also, though the bombing accuracy had been in general excellent, there was a sprinkling of bomb craters just outside the yards, amongst surrounding shops and small homes. We became a bit more aware than usual of the human impact of the war, and didn't talk as much the rest of the way.

"Back at the field, we showed our friends from the B-24 crew how to crank up our inertia engine starters, (hand-wound flywheel type) since we had no electric starter carts here. Then I took the flight off as soon as we got a green light from the control van, only to find that Mulvany hit one of those newly filled bomb craters in the runway with his nose wheel and blew its tire. He had to abort his takeoff, pull off the runway, and await a rescue flight, which I told him by radio while circling the field, we would send as soon as we got home. He got back the next day.

"The final anticlimax to the whole crazy adventure was that I had to write a long report of justification for breaking open the escape kits for money, which wasn't supposed to be done unless there was need for actual evasion of capture. Since we were not at any time at risk of being taken prisoner, it wasn't easy to write a convincing letter. I was given to understand that unless I could convince higher headquarters, I would be subject to court martial. However, nothing further ever came of it, so my probably heartrending tale must have done the job. Interestingly, I remember the experience of the actual events vividly, all these years later, but haven't the vaguest recollection of what I said in that letter."

Lieutenants Zeymour Ogron and Henry P. (Porter) Plunk, also from Bison Squadron, made it across the channel, but landed at Manston.

The mission was uneventful and no notable observations were made or recorded. Flak over Koblenz, Germany was heavy, intense and accurate.

Second Lieutenant Gerold M. Mulvany's P-38, Jerry . *Courtesy of Sally Mulvany.*

12 September 1944

VIII FC FO 565

No. 152 Tuesday. Col. Zemke led the group's first joint P-38 and P-51 effort. Lt. Col. Riddle, having successfully evaded capture after he was shot down over France during the 10 August mission, returned to the group a few days ago and ready to saddle up again, led the 434th FS, which consisted of 18 P-38s. Col. Zemke also led the 435th FS, which, for the first time, consisted of the squadron's 20 newly acquired P-51s. Capt. Moore led the 436th FS, which consisted of 15 P-38s. Their assignment was a penetration to target and withdrawal escort for 2nd BD B-24s attacking an 8th AF Mission 626 target of opportunity at Hannover, Germany. 434th FS up: 0900 hrs., down: 1400 hrs. with three early returns. 435th FS up: 0855 hrs., down: 1353 hrs with two early returns. 436th FS up: 0905 hrs., down: 1415 hrs. with no early returns.

The squadrons were separated and made L/F over northeastern Germany, between Cuxhaven and the island of Föhr, about 1025 hrs. and between 24,000 to 27,000 ft. R/V was by squadron, each at a different point. The 435th FS, having made landfall at Cuxhaven, joined the bombers shortly after that, northeast of Bremerhaven, Germany. The 436th FS came in farther north at Föhr, and began escort ten miles south of Hamburg, Germany. They were on the tail end of the entire formation. All three squadrons stuck with the Big Friends through the target and back out. The target was obscured by smoke screens, but results were observable and reported to be good with most hits well concentrated. The bombers were taken back to the continental coast. On the return home, Blue Flight, from the 436th FS, shepherded one B-24 all the way from

Hannover to the emergency RAF airfield at Manston, England. L/O for the squadron was over Cape Gris-Nez, France at 1323 hrs./11,000 ft. L/O for the 435th FS was over Ostend, Belgium at 1325 hrs./14,000 ft. where they broke off with the bombers.

Observations made during the mission included spotting considerable barge traffic on the Rhine River between Koblenz and Mainz, Germany. Two unidentified twin-engine fighters were observed on an A/D southeast of Kassel, Germany. Another two unidentified twin-engine fighters were observed on an A/D at Giessen. A parachute was seen to open 15 miles southeast of Giessen at 1130 hrs. An unknown quantity of barrage balloons was noted floating in the vicinity of the A/D at Vogelsand, Germany. Flak northeast of Bremerhaven and south of Hamburg was heavy, moderate and inaccurate.

Colonel Hubert Zemke climbs into a P-51 to lead the group on a mission. *Courtesy of Frederick C. Hayner.*

13 September 1944

VIII FC FO 566

No. 153 Wednesday (First mission for the day). Maj. Jeffrey led the 434th FS, which consisted of 14 P-38s. Maj. Sullivan led the 436th FS, which consisted of 16 P-38s. Their assignment was a bomber escort for 2nd BD B-24s attacking their 8th AF Mission 628 primary target, the jet airfield east of (Schwäbisch) Hall, Germany. 434th FS up: 0900 hrs., down: 1345 hrs. with one early return. 436th FS up: 0900 hrs., down: 1345 hrs. with no early returns.

L/F was over and south of Ostend, Belgium between 0941 and 0944 hrs./17-18,000 ft. Driving southeast across Belgium, France and over Metz, the two squadrons crossed into Germany to R/V with their B-24s just north of Schaffhausen, Switzerland, in the areas of the Neckar River and Mühlheim, Germany. The 434th FS picked up four boxes of bombers at 1041 hrs./19,000 ft. and the 436th FS joining theirs at 1049 hrs./20,000 ft. The 436th FS noted that their bombers were well escorted by another fighter group's P-51s. The Big Friends were escorted through the target area, which at the time, was experiencing rain and a high overcast. However, generally good bombing results were observed and the 436th FS reported that the airfield was well-clobbered with many fires observed around the target area. Colgate reported bogies in the area and Newcross Squadron investigated these and swept north, but results were nil. Returning north of the target, the 436th FS picked up some B-24s that were identified as having black tails with silver stripes (white stripes?). One of the bombers with the letter "I" on its tail was escorted to Laon, France from Selestat, which is southwest of Strasburg, Germany. The bomber made a safe landing at Laon/Athies. The briefed return route was followed and the squadrons broke away from the bombers south of Ghent, Belgium. They made L/O between Ostend and Blankenberghe, Belgium.

Lieutenants John W. Hedenberg and Zeymour Ogron were the pilots who took the above mentioned B-24 to Laon, France. Per John's diary this date:

> "Bomber escort again this morning. Bombers hit an airfield a good distance east of Stuttgart. The Alps and Lake Constance were visible to the south – beautiful. Before reaching the target, a B-24 pulled out of formation. Ogron and I were detailed to escort him out. He was badly hit by flak. He told us on the radio that his number two engine was out, his flight instruments were shot out, there were several wounded aboard and he was losing his gas fast through a bad leak. We had to lead him to a safe field in a hurry. We took him to Laon, where his gas finally ran out just above the field at about 8,000 feet. We then saw trucks and men working on the runway, filling in old bomb craters. There was only one thing to do – scare them off by buzzing the hell out of them while the bomber was dead-sticking it down. We got them off just as the B-24 turned onto his final approach. He got it down okay. We stuck around long enough to see his wounded taken off and to see him wave to us, then we went on home."

John later wrote:

"Here too the account is rather skimpy. This plane was in deep trouble. While talking to whoever aboard the bomber was handling the radio, I had pulled up alongside in close formation, and could see that the windscreen was gone, that the pilot was slumped over in his seat bleeding from the head and unconscious and that the crew was frantically dumping overboard everything they could – guns, ammo belts, anything to lighten ship. It then developed that I was talking to the copilot. He was feeling awfully shaky, if the quiver in his voice was any indication, saying he didn't know whether he could set the plane down without power if the gas ran out. So we naturally wanted to do our best. By this time I had learned the area well, and could give him a course to steer right to Laon (the nearest friendly field). He told me the compass was shot out, so we dropped flaps and throttled back to his speed and flew right ahead of him as leaders (his navigator was one of the wounded).

"As soon as the field came in sight, I asked him if he saw it. When he said yes, I said we would go make sure he had a clear shot to go straight in. We put on the power and buzzed the field, only to find the runway being worked on. I told Ogron we would fly right straight at those workmen and hop over. If they didn't get off, I would fire a burst into the ground alongside, next time around. Fortunately for all, they did get the point and move. I would have fired too, which would have caused a ruckus all the way back to Washington! We continued circling the field at 50 to 100 feet altitude, watching our 'Big Friend' on final approach. He fired the red flare which signaled that there were wounded aboard, then touched down in a perfect landing while the ambulances and crash truck raced alongside. When slowed enough, he pulled off onto the grass.

"We continued circling and watching at about 100 ft. off the ground, while four or five wounded were taken off and the unhurt members of the crew waved and grinned up at us. We waggled our wings, straightened out and made one more low pass right over their heads and took off for home, feeling pretty good about having successfully done something worthwhile."

The only observations from the mission not already reported, were those from the 434th FS and unfortunately those are unreadable due to the poor quality of the preserved original copy. Flak over Nancy, France and Trier, Germany was heavy, moderate and inaccurate.

13 September 1944

VIII FC FO 567

No. 154 Wednesday (Second mission for the day). This was one of those super-secret, hush-hush jobs that showed up once in awhile. Maj. Glover led the 435th FS, which consisted of 15 P-51s on a bomber escort for 2nd BD B-24s attacking their 8th AF Mission 629 primary target, an oil refinery at Hemmingstedt, Germany and their secondary target, an ammunition dump at Kropp, Germany. This was an Azon (A secret experimental bomb that was directionally controllable to the left or right azimuth while in flight.) mission that employed only a dozen B-24s from the 753rd BS/458th BG, plus their escort. 435th FS up: 1440 hrs., down: 1920 hrs. with one early return.

The squadron left England from over Cromer, where they R/V'd with the bombers, at 1510 hrs./5,000 ft. The Big Friends were ten minutes late. Flying up over the North Sea, the 435th FS and "The Buck Rogers Boys", as the specially-trained bomber crews were nicknamed, made L/F northwest of Meldorf, in northern Germany at 1620 hrs. White section had gone in 35 minutes ahead of the small force to sweep the area. Yellow section remained with the bombers. Seven of the bombers attacked the primary target and the remaining five attacked the secondary target. They were in and out of the target areas quickly with no flak reported and no enemy aircraft. No results were reported except for resultant smoke and fires. L/F was again near Meldorf at 1745 hrs./17,000 ft. Lakeside Squadron broke from the bombers over the North Sea and all headed safely home.

Observations made during the mission noted only that there were no aircraft on the airfields at Rensburg, Jagel, Hussem or Lonnig, Germany.

Bad weather restricted Eighth AF operations from the 14th to the 17th of September, but the 479th FG flew training missions from morning to night so that the pilots could become familiar with their newly acquired P-51s.

14 September 1944

Thursday. It was only a training mission that was flown today, the men of the group were learning to work with their new P-51s. They were out to sharpen their skills and hopefully get a better chance at survival when combat occurred. Unfortunately, it did not work out that way for two men from the 435th FS. Lieutenants Ivan A. Ervin and Chester W. Granville were lost during the mission. Last heard from when Lt. Granville made radio contact with his flight leader, Lieutenant Robert N. Pigg, the two failed to return to Wattisham that afternoon. Their flight had entered dense overcast around 1500 hrs and had been flying through it for 15 to 20 minutes when the radio contact was made. At that time, they were on a heading of 150 degrees and at 9,000 ft. over England. An agreement had been made to maintain that course, but something went wrong. Estimates were made about where that radio contact and course heading would place Lt. Granville at least, the reckoning being along a line of 150 degrees from Carlingford, Eire. The Incident Report went out and a check began. An immediate reply came back stating that an unidentified aircraft was seen crashing on the coast of Ireland, at Carlingford. Checking further, it was found that the plane was completely destroyed and the pilot killed, however identification tags were found proving the pilot to have been Lt. Ervin. The whereabouts of Lt. Granville was not determined. It was felt that he had passed the area of Manchester, England and further checks were done as well as air and boat rescue searches of the area it was thought he might have gone down in, should he have crashed into the Irish Sea. The weather was bad, but the search continued for three days. The lack of concrete information concerning his disappearance allowed little to be done. Lt. Chester W. Granville was listed as MIA.

16 September 1944

VIII FC FO 573

No. 155 Saturday. Capt. George K. Sykes led the 435th FS, which consisted of 17 P-51s on a training mission. Up: 1420 hrs., down: 1654 hrs. with two early returns plus one escort.

L/F was north of Dunkerque, France at 1505 hrs./12,000 ft. From there, the squadron flew down the French coast to Le Havre and on over to Cherbourg where they made L/O at 1616 hrs./15,000 ft. Crossing the channel where the squadron observed a large amount of Allied shipping, they passed into far southern England over Selsey Bill at 1620 hrs./7,000 ft.

17 September 1944

VIII FC FO 576

No. 156 & 157 Sunday. The group was divided into two forces, A and B groups, both in support of 8th AF Mission 637, flak suppression for "D-Day", the airborne invasion of Holland. Maj. Jeffrey led A group, which was made up of the 434th FS and the 436th FS. He also led the 434th FS, which consisted of 18 P-38s. Capt. Biscayart led the 436th FS, which consisted of 18 P-38s. Capt. Sykes led B group, which consisted of 19 P-51s from the 435th FS. 434th FS up: 1127 hrs., down: 1450 hrs. with one early return. 436th FS up: 1132 hrs., down: 1440 hrs. with one early return. 435th FS up: 1135 hrs., down: 1530 hrs. with three early returns.

By early September 1944, Allied ground forces were fast approaching the Rhine River on a wide front. Field Marshal Sir Bernard Montgomery's forces were within 100 miles of Germany's Ruhr area, one of the two most vital industrial regions sustaining the Third Reich. General George S. Patton's army was within 100 miles of the Saar area, the other vital industrial region. The problem of logistics arose for the Allies at that point. Supplies moving to the advancing fronts, fuel and stores needed to sustain the advance, had become slowed down because the troops had advanced so fast. The ports in Normandy were too far away and the transportation means inadequate to keep the forward movement going for both forces. Montgomery went to the Supreme Allied Commander, General Dwight D. Eisenhower, with a plan to rush into Germany through the back door and seize the Ruhr. He proposed to drop three airborne divisions behind German lines in eastern Holland to capture five bridges on the main road linking the cities of Eindhoven and Arnhem. His plan then was to hold open a corridor until his ground troops could arrive and spearhead a dash into the German frontier. Unfortunately, the plan did not work and the operation, code-named MARKET GARDEN; MARKET, for the airborne side of the attack, GARDEN, for the infantry and armor that was to follow, became a disaster. The Germans successfully repulsed the attack and the bold operation ground to a halt in the Dutch city of Arnhem, its name becoming synonymous with the lost battle.

L/F for A group was north of Overflakee, Holland at 1215 hrs./8,000 ft. They arrived in their assigned area at 1230 hrs. and patrolled at 2,500 ft. Newcross Squadron remained in the area for about two hours, did some strafing and then headed toward L/O and home. Bison Squadron left early due to a misunderstanding. Bison leader's radio went out and when he attempted to signal this to his wingman, the wingman didn't understand. So when Capt. Biscayart broke away to head for home at 1330 hours, everyone followed him. L/O for the squadron was north of Ijmuiden, Holland at 1340 hrs./8,000 ft. Numerous C-47s towing gliders full of troops were seen by the squadrons and the 436th FS reported spotting three gliders down in the water six miles south of Orford Ness, England. Flak, beginning in the vicinity five miles southwest of Arnhem and continuing throughout the area was light, intense and accurate between 2,500 and 3,000 ft.

L/F for B group, consisting of Lakeside Squadron, was over Schouwen Island, Holland at 1213 hrs./10,000 ft. The squadron proceeded on, entering their assigned area where they patrolled from 1230 hrs. until 1435 hrs. Unfortunately, during the course of the squadron's time in the area, Lakeside's leader, Captain George K. Sykes, was hit by light flak in his aircraft's right belly tank. Luckily, the tank of gas did not explode. The Jerry round had only knocked off the rear of the tank, causing an immediate loss of the fuel. The A/C also sustained damage to its cooling system as shortly thereafter, white smoke began coming from the Mustang engine's exhaust. Down to about 200 feet, Capt. Sykes was faced with the necessity of having to belly his ship in. He reversed his course, jettisoned his canopy, bellied the plane in on a plowed field, got out and started running away from "Sugar Kayne", the newly acquired mount that he had named after his wife, Kay. Capt. Sykes set his plane down approximately eight miles east of Edge, Holland and was almost immediately surrounded by a number of people who appeared to be farmers. He appeared to talk with them for a few moments and then they all separated. At that point, Capt. Sykes ran for nearby woods. When some German troops began heading for the downed plane, the three remaining members of the flight drove them back with strafing runs. First Lt. Ray K. Friend, who was in the flight with Capt. Sykes, went down to destroy the bellied in A/C, but was forced to stop after he noted civilians around the plane. Capt. Sykes eventually became a successful evadee, returning October 24, 1944. L/O for B group was at 1435 hrs./10,000 ft. over the same place as entry.

Observations made during the mission included the sightings of 25 plus ships in convoy off the English coast as well as 300 plus C-47s, Albemarles and gliders on course from mid-water to the patrol area. Two of the transport A/C were hit by flak; one crashed while one was able to return. Also an oil tank farm was noted near Rotterdam, Holland. Flak in the areas of Arnhem, Doorn and along the Waal River was light, intense and accurate. Ground fire was very noticeable in the entire area.

18 September 1944

VIII FC FO 578

No. 158 Monday. Col. Zemke was the group's leader and he also led the 435th FS, which consisted of 16 P-51s. Capt. Olds led the 434th FS, which consisted of 16 P-38s and Lt. Col Woods led the 436th FS, which consisted of 16 P-38s. Their assignment was a bomber escort for 2BD B-24s and ground attack in support of 8th AF Mission 639, an aid to allied airborne forces in Holland. 434th FS up: 1432 hrs., down: 1930 hrs. with no early returns. 435th FS up: 1431 hrs., down: 1942 hrs. with no early returns. 436th FS up: 1430 hrs., down: 1920 hrs. with no early returns.

Upon reaching the R/V point, the force had to wait for the bombers, as they were 20 minutes late. L/F was then made by the force between 1540 hrs./8,000 ft. and 1550 hrs./6,000 ft. over Schouwen Island, Holland R/V with the B-24s was made at this time. The Big Friends were escorted to their drop zones where they unloaded their cargoes of supplies for the ground forces. The escorts swept a wide area as B-24s continued their mission, flying through an area as far north as the Arnhem, Holland area, by as far south as Malmédy, Belgium and on over to the Zuider Zee. The squadrons took time to attack a few trains while they were in the area, claiming a number of locomotives, goods wagons and flat cars. L/O was scattered for the squadrons with the 435th FS passing over Ostend, Belgium at 1815 hrs./8,000 ft. and because of an overcast, an unknown location around 1850 hrs./8,000 ft. for the other two squadrons.

Observations made during the mission included six glider fires seen north of Arnhem. The ground in the area of the landings and supply drops was littered with thousands of orange and blue parachutes as well as hundreds of abandoned gliders. Flak was reported to be light, intense and accurate in the area as well as from a flak train that was encountered.

20 September 1944

VIII FC FO 580

No. 159 Wednesday. Col. Zemke was the group's leader and he also led the 435th FS, which consisted of 8 P-51s. Lt. Col.

Herren led the 434th FS, which consisted of 16 P-38s and Lt. Col. Riddle led the 436th FS which consisted of 16 P-38s plus two additional P-38s which acted as relays. Their assignment was a fighter rhubarb in support of the allied airborne forces in Holland. 434th FS up: 1534 hrs., down: 1910 hrs. with no early returns. 435th FS up: 1540 hrs., down: 1900 hrs. with three early returns. 436th FS up: 1538 hrs., down: 1920 hrs. with one early return.

The mission was uneventful because 10/10ths cloud coverage up to 10,000 feet in the area made observation impossible. For the 434th FS, L/F was reached, the assigned area was patrolled, then it was back to L/O and home for more transition training for those not yet familiarized with the P-51. However, it was a slightly different story for the 435th FS. The squadron's small force was further whittled down when Lieutenant Theo J. Sowerby had to belly his A/C in just after take off, because of an engine failure. He landed near a farm building, one-half mile north of Bildesten. The plane burned and was a total loss, but Lt. Sowerby was able to walk away from it with only minor cuts and bruises. The two flights, White Flight, now down to three A/C and Red Flight, with four, continued on, making L/F 1640 hrs./18,000 ft. at Ijmuiden, Holland. They circled the area until 1720 hours, at which point White Flight broke away and returned to Wattisham, landing at 1800 hrs. Red Flight, flying at 17,000 feet, headed into the assigned area at Zwolle, Holland, then on southeast to as far as Wesel, Germany and back up again to Zwolle. Recalled by Tackline, (65th Fighter Wing) Red Flight returned home from south of Zwolle, citing flak at Valkenburg, Holland as heavy, inaccurate and moderate. The 436th FS made L/F over Egmond, Holland at 1552 hrs./16,000 ft. The squadron headed to Zwolle where they circled from 1643 to 1708 hrs./16,000 ft. They then turned south, splitting into two sections. One section went towards Wesel while the other headed west, then north. A course was set for home at 1800 hrs. by both, due to the cloud coverage. L/O was between Egmond and Haarlem, Holland at 1825 hrs./14,000 ft.

Previous to this date, because of fuel and ammunition shortages on the continent, an order had come down from Ninth AF HQ to send as many of the 370th FG's P-38s to Wattisham as possible. There they were to operate against enemy forces engaged in repelling the allied airborne invasion of Holland. The 370th FG was one of two P-38 groups from the Ninth AF helping to augment the Eighth AF in its efforts to support the invasion. The Ninth AF group came to AAF Station 377 (Wattisham) from their base at Roye-Amy (A-73) in northern France. Consisting of three squadrons, the 401st, 402nd and the 485th, the group brought about 51 P-38s to the home of "Riddles Raiders" and operated from there for a week. As had been the case for the 479th FG, the 370th FG's mission was flak suppression. Similarly, the 370th experienced the same circumstances as did the 479th when it came to doing that job. Both could see allied A/C receiving ground fire, but by the time they could arrive at the scene, the enemy gunners had fled or gone into hiding.

Private First Class Lester G. Kronberg and Sergeant Raymond Niekamp from the 436th FS, testing radios. *Courtesy of Raymond Niekamp.*

After their late afternoon arrival, it was to be three days before the 370th could take their ships into action against the enemy. Meanwhile, the men from the three 479th squadrons pulled extra duty on top of extra duty. They spent many long hours keeping the Ninth AF planes operational, attending to regular maintenance and problems like radio modifications as well as keeping their own group's P-38s up and flying, *plus* learning the mechanics of the new P-51s which were becoming operational with the 479th at the time. It was quite an undertaking. Humor did occasionally surface however. It was noted as a tongue-in-cheek entry in the 479th FG records, that the Ninth AF pilots were quite impressed with the setup at Wattisham. While Engineering was tearing their hair out in handfuls, trying to accomplish three things at once, the men from the 370th made themselves at home in the "luxury" of a permanent airfield, the former RAF station now on loan to the AAF. Sgt. Charles Falco, *maître de'* of the Officer's Mess, swore that he never saw one group of men eat as much as that bunch from the 370th did. Furthermore, it was reported that, believe it or not, the men from the 370th asked the attendants in the respective squadron snack bars for SPAM sandwiches between meals!

To add to the misery, the advancing allied forces had overrun the Pas de Calais area of France, thus eliminating the site that the Germans had been using to launch their V1 flying bombs toward England. However, the Jerries moved their equipment to the northern part of Holland, set up shop and began launching the infernal "Buzz Bombs" toward England again. The Germans also employed He 111s to carry the V1s from bases in their homeland to out over the North Sea where the robot bombs were launched from under the bomber's wings. Since London was a main target that put Wattisham on a direct line with the flight paths that the "Doodlebugs" took from where they were set off. Wattisham gained the name of "Doodlebug Alley" as many a night, time was spent in the base's bomb shelters as the gadgets putt-putted overhead. To cite an example, on the night of 23 September 1944, between the hours of 9:27 PM and 10:37 PM, a total of 21 Buzz Bombs passed over the coast of East Anglia. Many fell to the anti-aircraft gunners stationed along the coast, but some still got through. On another date, 4 November 1944, one of the Doodles that escaped being shot down, passed right over the field at a height of about a hundred feet. This one fell to the ground and exploded just southwest of the station. Putt-putting and passing overhead on all sides, it was felt that as long as they kept moving, no one would complain. Some did pass over to fall close enough so that the explosions shook buildings though. This was just enough to keep most men on the cautious side and the resultant loss of sleep from the several nightly passages had a telling effect. Sergeant Clarence (Clancy) M. Surges would take his flashlight, "Readers Digest" and a Cribbage Board along to the shelter. When his friend Sergeant Angus (Gus) W. Clark was there also, the two would play Cribbage to pass the time. However, some other hardened souls chose to forego the hiding in shelters after a while.

First Lieutenant William H. Rodgers and the crew that maintained the P-38 he flew. *Courtesy of Frederick C. Hayner.*

21 September 1944

VIII FC FO 581

No. 160 Thursday. Col. Zemke was the group's leader and he also led the 434th FS, which consisted of 20 A/C; a section of 8 P-38s, a section of 8 P-51s, one P-38 spare, one P-51 spare and two P-38 relays. This mission was the beginning of the 434th FS's operational transition to the Mustang. Major Glover led the 435th FS, which consisted of 9 P-51s and Lt. Col. Woods led the 436th FS, which consisted of 18 P-38s. Their assignment was a penetration to target and withdrawal escort for 3rd BD B-24s attacking their 8th AF Mission 644 primary target, the petroleum industry at Ludwigshafen/Opau, Germany. 434th FS up: 1228 hrs., down: 1800 hrs. with no early returns. 435th FS up: 1230 hrs., down: 1800 hrs. with three early returns. 436th FS up: 1232 hrs., down: 1755 hrs. with two early returns.

The weather was "unusually nasty" in the words of the group's historical records. The 479th FG took this mission over from the 55th FG whose pilots couldn't get airborne because of weather conditions at their field. The "Raiders" were given twenty minutes notice to brief and get ready for takeoff. At takeoff time, the ceilings in the area were at 800 to 1,000 feet with visibility down to a mile or less. During group form up, the two flights of P-51s from the 434th FS, White Flight and Red Flight, became separated from each other. Heading north to a hole that was supposed to exist in the clouds, none was found so the order was given to climb up through the overcast. Red Flight's Second Lieutenant Thomas A. Gavrys, tucked in close on his leader, Captain Robin Olds' left wing as the two began climbing through the dense clouds near the English coastal city of Lowestoft. He somehow became separated from Capt. Olds during the climb and disappeared. Capt. Olds, upon breaking through the clouds, saw immediately that Lt. Gavrys was missing and began circling, thinking that the Lieutenant had gone back down to try climbing through again. After three circuits, Capt. Olds set course towards the R/V, realizing that his wingman would never be able to catch up with him. Second Lt. Thomas A. Gavrys was never seen again and in all probability was lost in the North Sea. He is listed as MIA.

The exact area of L/F for the two 434th FS sections (White Section's P-51s were led by Col. Zemke and Yellow Section's P-38s were led by Capt. C.A.P. Duffié) was unknown. Bad weather which stretched from west of East Anglia, to across the North Sea and on over the continent make this determination impossible. Tops were reported to be at 13,000 feet. However, as the force followed the course that would bring it to the R/V point for the bombers, it was noted that by the time they had reached Aachen, cloud cover was down to 3/10ths, with cumulus tops only reaching 9,000 feet. Visibility was still restricted at the base of the clouds though. It was through all this that Col. Zemke's and Capt. Duffié's two sections made their way to R/V with the bombers. Yellow Section caught up with 2nd BD B-24s near Mannheim, Germany. The Big Friends were escorted through the target and back out again to Charleroi, Belgium, where the escorting fighters broke away from the bombers at 1450 hrs./20,000 ft. The force had been ordered to cease escort duty in order to provide top cover up at Arnhem. Arriving in that area, the ground could not be seen so the Little Friends orbited the Zuider Zee from 1450 until 1545 hrs./15,000 ft. White Section made R/V at 1325 hrs/20,000 ft. in the target area and wound up escorting some B-24s and B-17s out of the target area. Following the same directive to provide top cover at Arnhem as did Yellow Section, White headed for the Dutch city where they patrolled over the cloud covered location until around 1600 hrs. Finally, Col. Zemke was heard to say, "Oh, go home." By then the various flights had become so separated and the weather so bad, that planes wound up landing all over the continent and England. Col. Zemke took his White Flight, consisting of Lieutenants George D. Hendrix, Harold E. Mathews and the one of the spares, Lieutenant William H. Rodgers, to land at, of all places, Roye-Amy, the northern France home of Wattisham's visitors, the 370th FG!

The 435th FS, like the 434th, was scattered because of the weather and made separated L/Fs over Walcheren Island, Holland along a track north of the briefed course. As a whole squadron, they were not able to R/V with the assigned bombers, but three of the squadron's planes did pick up about 70 returning B-24s over the Moselle River. These were escorted out to within about 40 miles of the English coast, passing over the Ostend, Belgium area at 1330 hrs. From there, the three went home. They had heard the group had R/V'd with the bombers, then left on call from Colgate (65th Fighter Wing) to go to Arnhem. Two other pilots, Lieutenants Lewis E. Morris and Howard C. Smith, did not meet the group, but did meet the bombers and followed them out to Charleroi, Belgium. The two then headed to the Arnhem area where they looked for Highway (Col. Zemke). Failing to find anyone, the two returned to England, with Lt. Smith making Wattisham while Lt. Morris landed at Woodbridge. The squadron's leader, Major

A Ninth AF 474th FG/429th FS visitor to Wattisham stopped in for some repairs. *Courtesy of David L. Born.*

Glover, plus Lieutenants Ray K. Friend, William B. Gunn and Verne E. Hooker eventually landed at the St. Quentin airfield in France where they gassed up and continued on to Roye-Amy to join the other men from the 479th FG. They spent the night there, heading back the next day, save for one. Lt. Hooker had to remain another day due to a broken tail wheel.

The 436th FS was similarly thwarted by the weather. Having made L/F with the overcast below them, the four flights of P-38s succeeded in making a R/V with the correct Big Friends at 1400 hrs./23,000 feet, shortly after the bombers had completed their run on the target. In the mixed force of B-24s and B-17s, the Flying Fortresses were identified with the letter "L" inside a black square located on the Fort's tails (452nd BG). The bombers were escorted until the call from Colgate, vectoring the fighters to the Arnhem area, was received. Breaking away, the P-38s left their charges at 1450 hrs./22,000 ft. about 20 miles southeast of Brussels, Belgium. The squadron proceeded to patrol the Arnhem to Eindhoven, Holland area from 1530 hrs. until 1600 hrs./16,000 ft. From there they headed for L/O. Continuing poor weather back in England forced the squadron to seek air fields wherever they could, with Blue and Yellow Flights landing at Everett, Red Flight landing at Leiston and White Flight landing at Martlesham.

Few observations during the mission were made or recorded by the group due to the foul weather. However, it was reported that the bombing results must have been excellent because dense oil smoke was noted towering up to 15,000 feet. A burning B-17 was seen to go down near Neistadt, Germany at 1410 hrs./23,000 ft. No chutes were seen. Flak ten miles north of Kaiserslautern, Germany was heavy, intense and accurate while over Trier and Bergen, Germany it was heavy, moderate and inaccurate.

25 September 1944

VIII FC FO 586

No. 161 Monday. Lt. Col. Riddle was the group's leader and he also led the 435th FS, which consisted of 14 P-51s. Maj. Jeffrey led the 434th FS, which consisted of 17 P-38s and Maj. Biscayart led the 436th FS, which consisted of 18 P-38s. Their assignment was a bomber escort for 1st BD B-17s attacking their 8th AF Mission 647 primary targets in the Frankfurt, Germany industrial area. 434th FS up: 0839 hrs., down: 1328 hrs. with two early returns. 435th FS up: 0835 hrs., down: 1313 hrs. with one early return. 436th FS up: 0837 hrs., down: 1322 hrs. with one early return.

The group was joined in part by the 370th FG, the Ninth AF P-38 outfit that had been temporarily operating out of Wattisham for the past several days. This probably made quite a nice display, as there were 88 A/C; 74 P-38s and 14 P-51s that took to the air from the station that day. The 370th escorted

2nd BD B-24s to their 8th AF Mission 647 primary target, the marshalling yards at Koblenz, Germany. Both groups labeled this mission "a Milk Run" when they returned. The air temperature was cold though. It was minus 42 degrees Celsius (about minus 42 degrees Fahrenheit) at the 25,000 ft. altitude the men flew.

The 434th FS made L/F at 0910 hrs./10,000 ft. over Ostend, Belgium. The skies were undercast over the entire area. Passing Koblenz, on southeast to Mainz, and on to the Frankfurt area, the proper B-17s were picked up just north of there at 1030 hrs./25,000 ft. The Big Friends were escorted through the target and out. The results were not seen because of the cloud cover. The bombers were left shortly afterwards to investigate bogies called out by Colgate. Nothing was found and the squadron rejoined the B-17s and escorted them out at Ostend at 1206 hrs./14,000 ft. Circling back to check for stragglers, the squadron found none and headed out and home.

The 435th FS made L/F at 0900 hrs./9,000 ft. over Ostend. R/V with the bombers was at 1015 hrs./20,000 ft. over Hanau, Germany. The B-17s were escorted around the target area and out.

The 436th FS made L/F at 0905 hrs./18-19,000 ft. R/V with the proper bombers was 1020 hrs./20,000 ft. over Frankfurt. An area in Germany extending from Marburg, south to Darmstadt and east as far as Steinau, was patrolled from 1000 hrs. to 1040 hrs. The bombers dropped their loads through 9-10/10 overcast. No observations were possible. The squadron escorted stragglers from the target area to friendly territory. Both P-47s and P-51s were seen in the area when the group arrived. L/O was at 1245 hrs./10,000 ft. south of Boulogne, France.

Observations made during the mission included the sighting of a possible V2 rocket launched from the general area of Luxembourg at 1130 hrs. Pilots from the 435th FS reported seeing a twisting contrail going up at a steep angle and pointing towards England. The contrail went up so high that it dissipated in about two minutes. It was estimated that the contrail reached 40-50,000 ft. A freighter and a destroyer were spotted 3-400 yards off shore at Ostend. Flak over Frankfurt and Mainz was heavy, intense and accurate. It was heavy, heavy and inaccurate over Wiesbaden as it was over Koblenz.

26 September 1944

VIII FC FO 589

No. 162 Tuesday. Col. Zemke was the group's leader and he also led the 435th FS, which consisted of 12 P-51s. Lt. Col. Herren led the 434th FS, which consisted of 16 P-38s and Maj. Sullivan led the 436th FS, which consisted of 15 P-38s. Their assignment was a MEW fighter sweep in support of the Allied airborne invasion forces in Holland. 434th FS up: 1258 hrs., down: 1815 hrs. with one early return. 435th FS up: 1255 hrs., down: 1810 hrs. with no early returns. 436th FS up: 1300 hrs., down: 1805 hrs. with one early return and one escort return.

For this mission, the 479th FG was joined again by the 370th FG, which had been temporarily operating out of Wattisham. The Ninth AF P-38 group had been there for six days now and some bit of rivalry had developed between the two groups during the stay. Today, however, would definitely belong to the 479th Fighter Group. This was one of the big ones for the group, the stuff that records are made from and awards are given for. After yesterday's uneventful excursion over the continent, the weather had cleared and the Germans had taken to the air once more. The 370th FG, putting up 36 A/C, was to provide top cover for the 479th FG while the latter patrolled the assigned area. After assembly, the force crossed the North Sea and L/F was made at various points, with the 434th FS and the 435th FS crossing in over Schouwen Island, Holland between 1318 hrs. and 1320 hrs./10,000 ft. The 436th FS entered over Holland, a little further north, near Overflakkee at 1315 hrs./18,000 ft. The three squadrons from the 479th FG flew eastward over Holland, linking up over Zaltbommel. From there, Col. Zemke led his 12 P-51s from Lakeside squadron and kept them out front while the P-38s from Newcross and Bison Squadrons followed behind and above as top cover. The force broke off course in a southeastern direction to patrol the area of Roermond, Holland, and then north to the Zwolle, Holland area, back south to the Ruhr area and again north to Arnhem, Holland. They patrolled for an hour-and-a-half, making bounces on bogies only to find them turn out to be Allied aircraft. Finally they penetrated farther southeast into Germany. There, they were to step into a hornet's nest of Jerries. The weather continued to cooperate with 4/10ths bulging cumulus clouds floating at 4,000 to 8,000 feet above the ground. Sweeping eastward from Wesel over to Hamm and thence northwest, the group worked their way around toward Münster. Around 1600 hours while in the area of

Haltern, Col. Zemke spotted a small grass airfield that looked interesting. As the Colonel observed the field, he saw what appeared to be a plane flying directly over it. Calling Lakeside Squadron to go down with him to investigate, the dozen P-51s went over into a dive. As they got closer, more aircraft were seen and in fact they had spotted two gaggles of bogies flying at about 5,000 to 6,000 ft. The question was, were they friendly or hostile? As Lakeside Squadron drew nearer to the unknown A/C, they were identified as Me 109s and Fw 190s but by then the element of surprise lost. The bogies had become bandits, but they were alerted! Newcross Squadron joined that of Lakeside while Bison Squadron remained above as top cover. The group should have had the advantage of height, having arrived on the scene at 16,000 ft. and they should have had the element of surprise, but lost both when the bogies could not be identified quickly enough. It rapidly became a swirling battle and despite the lost advantages, the 479th FG emerged the unquestioned victor. Twenty-nine enemy aircraft were claimed as destroyed that day, with three pilots claiming triples. A further two were listed as probable and nine German fighters were reported as damaged. The group received a Distinguished Unit Citation for the day's action, its third for the ETO. The breakdown looked like this:

434th Fighter Squadron

1-0-0	Me 109	Capt. Claire A.P. Duffié
0-1-1	Fw 190	Capt. Claire A.P. Duffié
1-0-0	Me 109	1st Lt. Walter M. Drake
3-0-1	Me 109	1st Lt. George W. Gleason
1-0-0	Me 109	1st Lt. Harold F. Grenning, Jr.
1-0-1	Me 109	1st Lt. John W. Hansen
3-0-0	Me 109	Lt. Col. James M. Herren, Jr.
0-1-1	Fw 190	2nd Lt. Harry E. Little
1-0-0	Me 109	2nd Lt. Ronald L. Maley
1-0-1	Me 109	2nd Lt. Richard G. McChrystal
1-0-0	Me 109	2nd Lt. John W. Morrow
1-0-0	Me 109	2nd Lt. John N. Murr
2-0-0	Me 109	1st Lt. Quentin S. Pavlock
1-0-0	Fw 190	1st Lt. Quentin S. Pavlock

435th Fighter Squadron

2-0-0	Me 109	2nd Lt. Nelson W. Butler
1-0-0	Me 109	Capt. Richard R. Coursey
1-0-1	Me 109	1st Lt. Ray K. Friend
1-0-0	Me 109	1st Lt. Martin G. Gorian
0-0-2	Me 109	1st Lt. John P. McCann
1-0-0	Me 109	2nd Lt. Charles F. Monsell, Jr.
2-0-0	Me 109	1st Lt. William H. Pickering
2-0-1	Me 109	Col. Hubert Zemke

436th Fighter Squadron

1-0-0	Me 109	1st Lt. Hans J. Grasshoff
1-0-0	Me 109	2nd Lt. Gerold M. Mulvany

U. S. Fighters Down 28 Nazis, Lose One Plane in Big Air Duel

ALLIED SUPREME HEADQUARTERS, LONDON, Sept. 26 (UP).—American 8th Air Force fighters scored one of their most spectacular combat victories of the war today when a group of forty-three Mustangs and Lightnings tackled more than forty Nazi fighters near Haltern and in fifteen minutes shot down or damaged thirty-seven of the enemy planes with a loss of one American plane.

Led by Colonel Hubert Zemke, of Missoula, Mont., leading 8th Air Force ace, the Americans sent the German planes "falling like leaves," with twenty-eight definitely destroyed, one probably shot down and eight damaged.

Until today, the highest combat score by British-based American fighter pilots was twenty shot down with no loss to themselves. The greatest number of enemy planes destroyed by one American group in any one day has been thirty-two, with a loss of four. Today's victory may possibly have been the greatest on the basis of evenly matched forces, a rarely occurring situation.

The Germans were spotted at about 3,000 feet southwest of Munster, "looking as if they were assembling to go somewhere," when Zemke's outfit attacked. Zemke, who destroyed two Messerschmitt 109's and damaged a third, said: "We were getting ready to come home when I saw an ME-109 and took the boys down to investigate."

"Pretty soon we saw four 109's," he recounted. "Then some one shouted over the radio, 'Hell, I see ten.' In a few minutes there were more than forty, and every one was fighting." The battle swept the sky for more than a quarter of an hour.

"There were German chutes opening everywhere. I counted six open at once," said Lieutenant George Gleason, of Montrose, Col., who got three enemy planes. Lieutenant Colonel Jim Herren, of Ashland, Ala., and Lieutenant Quentin Pavolock, of Barnesboro, Pa., also got three each.

The pilots said that only a few of the Nazis showed any aggressive tactics. Most tried to get away.

The "Stars and Stripes" newspaper ran this article on the group's huge victory. *Carroll C. Sprague Collection, courtesy of the East Essex Aviation Society.*

8th Wins Greatest Dogfight, 37-1

By LEO S. DISHER

London, Sept. 26 (U.P.).—U. S. 8th Air Force fighters today scored one of their most spectacular victories of the war when a group of 43 P-51 Mustangs and P-38 Lightnings tackled more than 40 Nazi fighters near Haltern, and in 15 minutes shot down or damaged 37 of the enemy against a loss of but one plane.

Led by Col. Hubert Zemke of Missoula, Mont., leading 8th Air Force ace, the Americans waded in and sent the German planes "falling like leaves," with 28 definitely destroyed, one probably shot down and eight damaged.

Col. Hubert Zemke

NEWS AROUND THE CLOCK

from the Daily News is broadcast over WNEW at 1130 on the dial: Regular editions 24 times a day on the half hour. Wakeup editions weekdays from 6:45 to 8:15 on the hour and quarter hours. Extra editions on the hour, whenever news is urgent. Bulletins at once.

Until today, the highest combat score by British-based Yank fighter pilots was 20 shot down with no losses. The greatest number of planes destroyed by one U. S. group in any one day has been 32 against a loss of four. Today's victory, therefore, possibly may have been the greatest on the basis of evenly-matched forces—a rare situation.

The Germans were spotted at about 3,000 feet southwest of Muenster, "looking as if they were assembling to go somewhere," when Zemke's outfit pounced. Zemke, who himself destroyed two Messerschmitt 109s and damaged a third, said "We were getting ready to come home when I saw an ME-109 and took the boys down to investigate.

"Pretty soon we saw four 109s. Then someone shouted over the radio, 'Hell, I see 10.' In a few minutes there were over 40 and every one was fighting."

The battle swept the sky for more than a quarter of an hour, with the American guns firing until they were hot.

"There were German chutes opening everywhere. I counted six chutes open at once," said Lieut. George Gleason of Montrose, Colo., who got three planes.

Pilots said that only a few of the Nazis showed any aggressive tactics. Most tried to get away.

Another news article clipped and saved by Gerold M. Mulvany. *Courtesy of Sally Mulvany.*

Beginning with the 434th FS, what follows are some of the stories that tell of that action over Germany.

Lieutenant Colonel James M. Herren, Jr. was leading Newcross Squadron on the sweep and he wrote:

> "We were flying to the left and above Lakeside Squadron, which was being led by Col. Zemke. We were heading east when bogies were sighted on the deck, heading west. I followed Lakeside Squadron down and saw the group that they bounced, then sighted a larger gaggle ahead. Our rate of closure was very fast as we had dived from 16,000 feet. We hit the rear of the enemy formation. They were very slow to break from our attack, but finally did, turning to the right and up. I tagged on to two Me 109s and opened fire at close range from dead astern. I observed strikes all around the cockpit and then billowy black smoke poured out. The other 109 broke away and since I was out of position, I sent Lt. McChrystal, my wingman, to attack him. I pulled up and orbited to pick him up again, noticing the Me 109 that I had attacked, hit the ground and explode.
>
> "Before my wingman could rejoin, I sighted another Me 109 on the tail of a P-51. After two turns, I positioned myself behind the attacking 109, fired a long burst and observed strikes all over the E/A. Black smoke and flames began to pour out of the forward fuselage and wing roots as pieces of cowling flew off. The E/A then fell into an uncontrollable spin. Our altitude at this time was around 6,000 feet. I could not wait to see this German hit the ground since there was another one on my tail. I shook this one by climbing until he stalled out.
>
> "Then I saw another Me 109 attacking a P-38, so I moved in. The German had pulled up into a steep climb during his attack and was going very slow. After I got into position, I thought I had an easy target at close range, but before I could open fire, the pilot bailed out. He evidently saw me close in and figured that he had 'had it'. I didn't get a chance to take any pictures because I had to pull away sharply to keep from hitting the empty Me 109 which spun down. I didn't wait to see it hit the ground, I returned to the fight. I claim three Me 109s destroyed."

Lt. Col. Herren received credit for the three Me 109s he claimed, one of which was confirmed by his wingman Lieutenant Richard G. McChrystal. Lt. McChrystal also claimed and received credit for the Me 109 that he attacked during the course of performing his duties as Lt. Col. Herren's wingman. Lt. McChrystal stated:

> "I was flying Newcross White Two. The squadron was heading west at 16,000 feet when two gaggles of bogies, low and heading west, were called in. They were identified as enemy so White section dived on the rear of the lead gaggle, which was climbing to the right. We closed at an altitude of about 5,000 feet and Lt. Col. Herren, whose wing I was flying, attacked one of the two rear ships. As he did this, he told me to go after the other one. I closed to about 200 yards at the five o'clock position on that E/A, gave him one-half radii lead and opened fire. The German started into a steep turn to the right so I increased my lead to one-and one-half radii and observed strikes on the wing root and engine cowling. White smoke poured out, the German aircraft then leveled out and I observed the pilot take to his parachute.
>
> "I started climbing to the right and saw an Me 109 slightly above me, heading 90 degrees to the right of my course. I started after him and he turned into me. I opened fire, but didn't see any hits. After we passed, I made a sharp turn to the right and met him head-on again. This time I observed strikes on the fuselage of the E/A. We made two more head-on passes, but I didn't see any strikes from my firing. Then the German broke off and hit the deck. I climbed back up and joined the squadron. I claim one Me 109 destroyed and one Me 109 damaged."

First Lieutenant George W. Gleason picked up a triple also, giving this report of those encounters as well as one for the Me 109 that he damaged:

> "We were at 16,000 to 17,000 feet and I was flying Newcross White Three. When the enemy aircraft were sighted below and the order was given to go after them, I dropped my belly tanks and headed down from a three o'clock high position to one of six o'clock, right behind the end aircraft. I opened fire on the tail end Charlie, an Me 109, at about 400 yards. I observed strikes on his tail assembly and a big piece that looked like his rudder, flew off. I pulled on through, continuing to fire and getting strikes along his fuselage and wings. During this, the German was not aggressive and did not seem to take any evasive action. The E/A then went into a violent spiral,

out of control. I watched it crash into the ground. The pilot did not bail out.

"As I pulled up from that combat, I saw an Me 109 on a P-38's tail so I started after it to attack. When he saw me, he started a violent turn to the left. As we turned together, I closed from 60 to 30 degrees in about one-and-a-half turns, gave him one to one-and-a-quarter radii lead and opened fire. I observed strikes on his left wing and canopy. The canopy came off, the E/A rolled over on its back and the pilot bailed out. I did not see his parachute open however.

"While I was attacking this second Me 109, I could see another trying to position himself to get me, so I dumped combat flaps and turned into him. He climbed in a tight left spiral, but I gained on him. He then did a sloppy split-ess and went down to the deck. I followed and got in a short burst during the dive, observing a few strikes on his right wing. The German then chopped his throttle, dumped flaps and I overshot him, but quickly zoomed up to the right and to about 1,000 feet. He then did a wing over and started turning to the left again. I dived on him and we closed, meeting in a head-on pass. We each turned for another pass, but I rolled out of my turn a little before he did and opened fire again. This time, I saw strikes on his wings, fuselage and spinner. The E/A faltered momentarily, then rolled over, the pilot bailing out. I saw his parachute open.

"Then I saw a lone Me 109 stooging around by himself in front of me so I closed and fired a short burst from 30-degrees deflection with a one and one quarter radii lead. I observed a few strikes on his wing roots and fuselage, but I ran out of ammunition and could not finish the job. I claim three Me 109s destroyed and one Me 109 damaged."

Shortly after Lt. Gleason's last attack was aborted due to a lack of ammunition, he was attacked himself by an Me 109. This was seen by Second Lieutenant John W. Morrow who was flying Yellow Two, and came to the rescue during the churning melee:

"As I came out of a cloud, having lost my leader, Capt. C.A.P. Duffié in there, I saw an Me 109 on the tail of a P-38 about 2,000 feet below and three o'clock to me. I peeled off on him and he broke left and up. I gave him a two-and-a-half radii lead and opened fire at 300 yards, closing to 50 yards. I observed many strikes along both wings. I pulled up to the side to make another pass when I noticed that a big cloud of smoke was pouring out of the German. I started coming in again when he rolled to the left and the pilot bailed out. I watched the plane until it hit the ground and exploded. Then I joined up with P-38 'H' which the Me 109 had been attacking when I first engaged."

Lt. Gleason confirmed this claim.

First Lieutenant Quentin S. Pavlock got the group's third triple play for the day, claiming two Me 109s and a Fw 190 in the following Combat Report: He said:

"I was flying Newcross Red Leader when the bogies were called in. Newcross White and Red Flights dived from 16,000 feet, down onto the 20 plus unidentified aircraft flying at 7,000 feet. Lt. Col. Herren, White Flight Leader, identified them as E/A and we attacked the lead group. I led Red Flight in an attack against the last group of five, which were heading northeast. As I closed in from about 60-degrees astern, the lead E/A, a Fw 190, turned into me and we both fired in a 20-degree head-on pass at each other. I didn't observe any strikes on the E/A during my firing. I went into a tight right turn and came out slightly above the Fw 190. I gave him a short burst at 60-degrees deflection and observed a few strikes in his cockpit and engine. I closed from astern and fired another burst at ten-degrees deflection and observed hits on his tail. The E/A started smoking and went into a shallow dive. I overshot so I pulled into a tight left 360-degree turn and got onto his tail again at about 5,000 feet. The German aircraft was then on its back and in a moderate dive. I fired another short burst from dead astern, getting strikes on him. I then observed the German pilot bail out and the airplane dive into the ground and explode.

"Then I made a 45-degree left turn at an altitude of about 3,000 feet and observed an Me 109 heading west in a shallow dive. I stayed in the left turn and got on his tail. Firing three short bursts starting from ten-degrees deflection to dead astern, I observed many strikes on his tail and fuselage. He took no evasive action, but went into a shallow dive, pouring out black smoke and then began a very slow, shallow roll. I started to follow him, but I glanced in my rearview mirror and saw another Me 109, closing on my tail and firing at me from about 100 yards. I was at about 1,000 feet then so I shoved everything to the firewall and went into the tightest left turn I have ever made! The E/A followed me for about 50 degrees, then broke off and headed northeast in a steep climb. I completed my turn, got in behind him and fired two short bursts from 300 yards at 20-degrees deflection, as we began to climb to 8,000 feet. On the second burst, I observed many strikes on his right wing. The German flew through three small clouds without changing course and then went into a big one where I lost him for a moment. I picked him up again, almost 90 degrees off to my left and I noticed some bluish white smoke coming from his right wing. Just as I turned toward him, another single-engine aircraft came diving towards me, so I fired a quick burst from 200 yards, 40-degrees deflection at the plane that I had been chasing. I observed large pieces flying off his right wing and tail, then the pilot jumped out and his parachute opened. By this time I had identified the other single-engine aircraft diving on me as a Lakeside Squadron P-51. We orbited for a time at 8,000 feet, but no more E/A were around so I rejoined Newcross Leader and came home."

Second Lieutenant Walter A. Neumann was flying Newcross Red Four and confirms the Fw kill:

"When Red Flight attacked five E/A to the left of the main gaggle, the Fw 190 climbed and turned into Lt. Pavlock, Red Leader. They made a head-on pass at one another, firing until they went by each other. I didn't see any strikes on either ship. Red Leader pulled up into a climbing turn to the right and started another pass. Red Leader, Red Two and Three fired deflection shots at this same 190, but I didn't see any strikes. Then I made a 60-degree pass on the 190 without getting any hits. As I was coming around in my second 360-degree turn, I saw Red Leader on the Fw 190's tail and observed him getting strikes on the fuselage. The E/A rolled and I observed the pilot bail out at about 5,000 feet. I saw the German aircraft crash into the ground."

First Lieutenant Thomas C. Olson, flying Yellow Three with the squadron, confirmed the first Me 109:

"During the engagement, I observed an Me 109 with a P-38 on his tail so I fell in trail to give him cover while he attacked. I could see the letter 'K' on the P-38, which I subsequently identified as the aircraft flown by Lt. Pavlock. Lt. Pavlock fired from almost dead astern. I saw several strikes, and then Lt. Pavlock broke away. I saw the E/A start to smoke, then roll over into a split-ess position. The German pilot jumped out and I observed his parachute to open."

First Lieutenant William H. Pickering, flying the Lakeside P-51 described in the last section of Lt. Pavlock's Combat Report, confirms the second Me 109:

"I was flying a P-51 with the 435th Fighter Squadron during the above listed engagement and had been orbiting to the left for a few moments when I saw a red tail P-38 (Newcross Squadron) a thousand feet below me and in a luftberry with an Me 109. I started down to help, but had no sooner made up my mind to do so when I saw the P-38 'reef it in' and out toward the German and with a snap burst, get good direct strikes. I observed the German pilot bail out and his parachute open. Then the P-38 turned into me. From subsequent discussion of the fight, I am confident that the Newcross P-38 was flown by Lt. Pavlock."

A last account from the 434th FS serves to illustrate one of the many problems a pilot faced in situations such as the air battle being depicted. First Lieutenant John W. Hansen, flying Newcross Blue Three, tells of his encounter:

"Ours was the last flight to arrive at the battle and as we drove up, we saw ten Me 109s heading east, trailing smoke [normal exhaust emissions for that A/C, especially when under full power]. We set out in pursuit and caught them in about five minutes at approximately 10,000 feet. I opened fire out of range, but my gunsight bulb burned out so I closed in to approximately 200 yards and opened fire again from dead astern. The range was still too great without a sight so I drove up so close that I almost ran into him and held the trigger down. I fired at least half my ammunition and observed many hits on the fuselage and right wing. The canopy and big pieces flew off the enemy ship, which fell away to the left. As I went by, I observed the German pilot jump out and his parachute open almost immediately.

"I turned into a cloud to change gun sight bulbs. Just as I went into the cloud, I looked in my mirror and saw an Me 109 behind me. I changed bulbs and came out of the cloud again. My wingman started to join up with me, but he was jumped. I turned into the Me 109 on my wingman's tail and made a head-on pass at him, firing a short burst as I closed. I made two more head-on firing passes, but observed no strikes. The E/A then did a half roll and spun to the deck with me following. I closed from dead astern and opened fire at point blank range, observing four or five strikes along his left wing. Before I could finish him off, I ran out of ammunition. I pulled up and headed for home."

Lt. Hansen's wingman was Second Lieutenant John N. Murr, who drove what was actually two attacking Me 109s, off his leader. One E/A split-essed away, but the other pressed on the attack until Lt. Murr opened fire and closed on the German ship. Getting a good deflection shot from 100 yards away, he observed many strikes all over the plane. The Me 109 burst into flame, did a wing over and dove into the ground. The pilot did not escape. Lt. Murr went down to fly over the crash site and was hit in his right engine by ground fire. He had to shut it down, but could not feather the propeller. His left engine also began giving him trouble. Only able to climb to about 800-1,000 feet, Lt. Murr was quickly set upon by an Me 109. The German got on Lt. Murr's tail and he had to keep turning into the 109 and calling for help. This time Lt. Hansen came to Lt. Murr's rescue and chased the Me 109 away. Then Lts. Hansen and Murr headed for home. Over Holland, Lt. Murr recognized he was not going to make it to England that day and told Lt. Hansen he was going to try flying south into Belgium for as long as he could stay up. Lt. Hansen headed on to Wattisham and Lt. Murr started south. He flew on until his left engine finally quit and he was forced to belly in his ship on an open field. When he stopped sliding, a 1936 Chevrolet filled with about ten men came rolling up to him. They were with the Belgian underground and took him to a British airfield about ten miles away. He had landed just inside German lines. Three days later he was able to get a transport plane back home. When he arrived at Wattisham, all of the squadron's P-38s were gone. He needed to learn how to fly P-51s now. First Lieutenant Walter M. Drake had been assigned the duty of training the men to fly the Mustangs and found Lt. Murr was the only one he had not checked out in the new plane. That was taken care of quickly though and Lt. Murr was ready to rejoin the squadron in combat.

Several pilots reported seeing enemy aircraft on the tail of one or a number of P-38s. One such pilot seen being pursued by an Me 109 was Second Lieutenant Harry E. Little from the 434th FS. First Lieutenant Walter Drake told of noticing what he thought was a P-38 with an engine on fire at about 5,000 to 6,000 feet. He briefly observed the smoking fighter begin to spin down towards the ground, but had to turn his attention to other matters because as he stated: "We had been fighting with some 40 Me 109s for ten or fifteen minutes and I was pretty busy." Lt. Little became a guest at one of the German Stalag Luft "hotels" a short time later. His claims for the day were filed after the war ended and he had returned from captivity. He was the only casualty for the group that day.

The 435th FS accounted well for themselves during the day also, tallying three claims of doubles. Second Lieutenant Nelson W. Butler was one of those who brought two scalps home from the battle. (The Germans were caught up in the romance of Cowboy and Indian themes, having been intrigued with American Western movies prior to the war. Hence, German pilots sometimes referred to the American pilots and their aircraft as "Indians" using such statements as, "Here come the Indians" upon sighting American planes approaching.) Lt. Butler's report:

"I was flying number three position in Red Flight when about forty Me 109s were sighted. We dropped our wing tanks and made a bounce on them from the rear. My first pass was head-on with an Me 109. I fired a burst, but did not observe any hits. I turned to follow and got closer to him as he tried to climb away. I continued closing to about 100 yards and fired a good burst, which fairly got him. He broke into flames and finally, I saw him spin in.

"I saw another Me 109 flying along on top of about an 8/10ths overcast. I was about 2,000 feet above him so I went in to the rear and slightly to the left of him. As I started to close on him, he saw me and went into the overcast. I pulled up and over to the left and waited for him to reappear. He came out and I started after him again, but he saw me once more and went back into the clouds. I pulled up and waited for him again. We came to the edge of the overcast and he broke out again. I was close to him there so I got on his tail and tried a couple of shots, but he was using evasive action and I missed. He made a sharp turn to the left and went back into the overcast. I was very close to him then so I ducked under him and flew instruments with him for awhile. We broke out again, I raised up behind him and shot him down. When I hit him, he turned over and went straight in. I followed him down and took pictures when he crashed."

A second pilot to score twice from Lakeside Squadron was First Lieutenant William H. Pickering, the same Lt. Pickering who witnessed the outcome of 434th FS pilot Lt. Pavlock's third fight. Lt. Pickering was flying as Red Flight Leader and followed the original attack by Lakeside White Flight, Col. Zemke's flight. Lt. Pickering's words:

> "As we dove into the area of the fight, I saw two Me 109s at two o'clock low. I chased the wingman and got good hits, all in the center of his ship after he had turned left. The leader went right. The man I hit split-essed into a cloud and I followed, but turned out and dove underneath the same cloud. Just as I came under the cloud, the E/A popped out, too. I could see he was on fire and started to close on him again. He jettisoned his canopy and hit the silk. I started a turn to the left and saw two more Me 109s coming in under me. They evidently didn't even see me. I dropped down on the wingman's tail and got a good burst in at close range, but I overran him. As I went by his right wing, I saw fire coming from the engine and the pilot bail out."

The third pilot to knock down two for the day was Colonel Hubert Zemke, who got two Me 109s and damaged another. When the Germans broke right to evade the bounce, Col. Zemke picked out one of the Me 109s toward the center of a flight and gave it a burst from about 500 yards. The Me 109 pilot continued right, tightening his turn as Col. Zemke fired several more short bursts at him. There appeared to be no hits, but then Col. Zemke got in a 40-degree deflection shot and saw strikes on top of the German's wing surfaces and fuselage. The damage did not appear to be that much, however, the Me 109 pilot rolled over on his back and bailed out. Col. Zemke noted that he had forgotten range his gunsight during the fight.

Col. Zemke picked out another Me 109 and went after it. The German seeing the P-51 heading his way, flew into a cloud. The two played hide and seek until the German was finally able to give the Colonel the slip. After Col. Zemke lost sight of the Jerry, he was struck by the sight of a fighter in his rear-view mirror. He went into a series of violent evasive maneuvers to shake his pursuer, all without success. Every break, dive, climb and turn saw the fellow hanging on like glue. Finally Col. Zemke was able to see that the plane chasing him was a P-51. He had been trying to escape from his wingman, Lieutenant Billy C. Means.

No sooner had he recognized that he had been trying to escape from his wingman then he saw another Me 109 turning under him and fleeing toward the clouds to the south. Col. Zemke swung around and hit the German plane with several long-range bursts before the enemy aircraft entered the clouds.

A single Me 109 seen leaving a fight about a mile away came under the Colonel's scrutiny. Before he could get within range though, the German pilot appeared to have spotted him because the Me 109 began evasive maneuvers. Col. Zemke closed to 400 yards and fired a burst at 20-30 degrees deflection. His aim was good and after strikes appeared on the 109's fuselage, the plane's canopy flew off and the pilot bailed out. The aircraft dove down into a field and exploded. Col. Zemke took a picture of the crashing E/A with the K-25 camera mounted on the back of the headrest portion of the seat armor behind him.

First Lieutenant Ray K. Friend was number three in Yellow Flight and noted coming into the fight, "there were a bunch of 109s and P-38s going around." He continues:

> "I saw an Me 109 on the tail of a P-38 and firing at it so I broke into the German and started firing at about thirty degrees. The first burst hit the 109 in the left wing root. Observing strikes, I opened up with a second burst and saw the whole area around the cockpit blow up and start to burn. The canopy also had been knocked off. Evidently the pilot had been hit because he just sat there and made no attempt to get out, even though his whole cockpit and surrounding area was on fire. After a few seconds, the plane rolled over and plowed in from about 4,000 feet. The pilot of the P-38 that had this 109 on his tail was Lt. Neumann from the 434th FS. He will confirm this plane as destroyed."

Lt. Friend damaged another that perhaps should have been a kill for him:

> "I was climbing up off the deck and trying to find a wingman when I saw an Me 109 coming head-on, but slightly to the right of me. I broke into him and fired in the turn, but failed to hit him. As I came around on his tail, I closed too fast and fired one burst, which did hit the 109 and damage it. I pulled up to the right so that I could slice back in again, but five P-51s were all over him and shot him down."

Second Lieutenant Charles F. Monsell, Jr. almost had to chase his quarry into some woods before the Jerry gave up. Lt. Monsell:

"I was flying number four position in Red Flight when an Me 109 came right in front of and slightly below me. As my element leader did not see him, I immediately attacked him, firing a burst at an angle of about 45 degrees, but failed to get a hit. The enemy quickly started taking violent evasive action, skidding from side to side, then split-essing and rolling on the way down. I followed him and as he pulled out and climbed to the right, I got several hits near the wing roots and in the fuselage behind the pilot. The E/A then tried to turn with me to get on my tail, but didn't succeed. He then did another split-ess, almost going into some trees before he got it under control. He pulled up and bailed out at about 2,500 feet. The plane crashed, but did not burn that I could see; however, I didn't linger in the area to watch."

Lt. Pickering, who must have been all over the place, witnessed and confirmed this.

First Lieutenant Hans J. Grasshoff and Second Lieutenant Gerold M. Mulvany were the two victors for Bison Squadron, the 436th FS. While the squadron was flying top cover, two Me 109s dove through the squadron from somewhere above. They appeared headed for their friends below and did not seem to see the squadron. Diving after them, Lt. Grasshoff downed one of his "cousins" (He was kidded about his German name.) in an encounter with the Me 109s. He stated:

Crew chief Staff Sergeant Stanley L. Steele checking the gun switches on his P-38 to insure that it's ready for the next mission. *Courtesy of the 436th Fighter Squadron Association.*

"I was leading Bison Blue Flight south of Münster. At approximately 1600 hours, Lakeside and Newcross Squadrons bounced 30-40 Me 109s and Fw 190s flying at around 7,000 feet. Bison Squadron was at 18,000 feet, flying top cover. I took my flight down on a lone Me 109 that was flying about 2,000 feet above the fight. I didn't fire on this 109 because it was right on the tail of a P-38. I broke off and fired several bursts at long range. The 109 pulled away from the P-38. After several turns, I closed to approximately 100 yards, 30-degrees deflection and fired a long burst at him. There was an explosion and a gush of flames from just behind his cockpit. The Me 109s nose dropped and the plane went straight in."

Lt. Mulvany was in the flight that Lt. Grasshoff took down with him and wound up defending himself from another Me 109. He states:

"I was flying Bison Blue Two position. My flight leader made a diving pass at three Me 109s and we closed up fast. The Me 109 that my flight leader was following, split-essed. I was flying on the right side when a 109 made a pass, starting at one o'clock to me. I broke violently, head-on, into him and started firing. I out-turned him and he passed in front of me, pulled up and bailed out of his plane. I observed no good hits on the Me 109; he just straightened out his turn and bailed out."

Lt. Mulvany's gun camera film showed that the German pilot's chute spilled out of the Me 109's cockpit, apparently pulling the pilot half way out, but draped itself over the aircraft's rear fuselage and tail section. Lt. Mulvany's hits were in the cockpit area and on the parachute covered rear fuselage.

After the battle, which lasted for about fifteen or twenty minutes, broke up, the squadrons made their way back home, crossing out over Holland around 1710 hrs. Nothing much is recorded as to what was seen during the course of the mission. There was one note regarding some of the Me 109s attacked, as having had red and white candy-striped spinners. Flak over the Haltern area was light, intense and inaccurate while along the railroad between Münster and Rheine, it was light, intense and accurate.

27 September 1944

VIII FC FO 590

No. 163 Wednesday. Lt. Col. Riddle was the group's leader and he also led the 436th FS, which consisted of 17 P-38s. Capt. Olds led the 434th FS, which consisted of 8 P-38s, 8 P-51s and 2 P-38 relays while Maj. Glover led the 435th FS, which consisted of 13 P-51s. Their assignment was bomber escort for 2nd BD B-24s attacking their 8th AF Mission 650 primary target, the Henschel factory in Kassel, Germany. 434th FS up: 0730 hrs., down: 1300 hrs. with two P-51 early returns. 435th FS up: 0725 hrs., down: 1245 hrs. with two early returns. 436th FS up: 0736 hrs., down: 1310 hrs. with two early returns and one escort returned.

This was the last day that the 370th FG spent at Wattisham. When they took off from the station this time, they headed for their new Ninth AF home at Florennes-Juzaine (A-78) in southern Belgium.

The group suffered another loss forming up. Second Lieutenant William H. Rogers, from the 434th FS, disappeared in an area about forty miles east of the English coastal city of Lowestoft. He had called in stating that he was going to return and asked for a fix. This was about 0755 hrs. The weather in the area was 9/10ths with a stratus cloud deck at about 8,000 feet. Air-to-air visibility was reported as good, however. Lt. Rogers was never seen again.

L/F was in the vicinity of Egmond, Holland for all three squadrons who arrived over the area about 0815 hrs. and at 17,000 to 20,000 ft. R/V with the proper bombers was at 0930 hrs./23,000-25,000 feet, south of the target, Kassel. The group was up front escorting the Vinegrove 4-3 box of B-24s out of the target area when about 20 Me 109s slipped through to bounce the Big Friends in the last box, Vinegrove 4-2. The squadrons firewalled their throttles and strained every rivet in an attempt to get back in time to help, but by the time they arrived, the E/A had split-essed and dived down into the clouds. No contact was made, but other P-51s were seen tangling with the enemy. The last bomb group was seen to suffer the loss of 12 B-24s in less than three minutes between Hersfeld and Giessen, Germany, where the presence of Fw 190s was noted also. The 435th FS reported seeing a B-24 described as having black tails with a white stripe through them, tail letter "J" (445th BG) go down west of Stavalot, Germany. Seven chutes were seen to come out of the stricken bomber. The 436th FS reported on six B-24s, five of which exploded, the sixth, smoking and going down through the overcast. No chutes were seen from any of them. All totaled, from the dozen Big Friends noted as falling prey to the concentrated attack, only twenty chutes were seen. (On this day, the 445th BG suffered the worst loss for a single group in the history of the 8th AF. Setting out that morning, the Liberator group, a part of the 2nd Combat Wing, put up 37 B-24 bombers for the attack. By the end of the day, only nine had come back. Twenty-eight had been culled from the group by the determined efforts of up to 150 German Fw 190s and Me 109s. Having deviated 30 degrees from the main bomber stream at the Group I.P. and from the protection accorded by its protective firepower as well as that from escorting fighters, the 445th BG became wide-open to attack. Heavily armored Fw 190 *Sturmböcke* (The specially modified Fw 190s had thick armor plates added to the cockpit section, both sides and belly, of the aircraft. The purpose being to deflect the .50 cal. bullets shot at them when they attacked a bomber. Additionally, the plane's canopy had thick slabs of protective glass added to the area where the pilot sat. Consequently, visibility for the pilot was reduced and all the additional weight made the fighter heavy, which brought about a loss of maneuverability.) from the three *Sturmgruppen* formed by *Jagdgeschwader*'s 3, 4 and 300, accompanied by their escorting Me 109s, saw the opportunity, attacked and decimated the formation in the short period of a few minutes. Friendly fighters arrived shortly, but it was too late for most. German pilots reported that it was very unusual to see such a large formation of enemy bombers without fighter escort. Without the escorts, the bombers were virtually sitting ducks! One German pilot commented that while flying through the slaughter, his attention to the attack was hindered by having to watch out for the many fliers in parachutes as well as the small and large chunks of falling airplane debris.) The 479th FG broke away south of Koblenz, Germany and headed for L/O at Ostend, Belgium 1200 hrs. On the way back home, the group searched for Lt. Rogers, but no sign of him was found. Flak over the target was heavy, intense and accurate.

The exact date is unknown, but on a day similar to this one, an occurrence took place that illustrates the effort and the hardships that the ground crews went through in order to maintain and keep their aircraft flying. Eugene V. Venezia, then a Master Sergeant and Flight Chief with the 436th FS, told recently of an experience he had one morning:

> "When there was a lot of combat flying, mechanics often got little sleep. The P-38s needed a lot of work and most of this was tedious. Ground crews were often up at

three in the morning and out on their hardstands or the flight line until nearly midnight when things were busy. We had an assistant crew chief, a curly-headed fellow, pre-flighting a P-38 one morning for an early escort mission. He had the plane's engines going full out when it suddenly started to creep forward. The plane's brakes were locked on, but it was slowly sliding on the damp ground. The Lightning went across the hardstand and started chopping up a line shack made out of belly tank packing crates. There were a couple of guys inside and they took off like startled rabbits. Luckily, no one was hurt. The shack checked the P-38's forward motion, but the engines were still going full out. I ran over, climbed up onto the back of the wing and went to the cockpit. Looking through the canopy, I could see this guy's head pitched forward and I thought he was ill or dead. I released the hood, folded the top section back and when the cold air hit him, he suddenly sprang to life. With the canopy closed, he'd dropped off to sleep – it was warm in there, he was mighty fatigued and he'd been comfortable for a change."

28 September 1944

VIII FC FO 591

No. 164 Thursday. Col. Zemke was the group's leader and he also led the 435th FS, which consisted of 15 P-51s. Lt. Col. Herren led the 434th FS, which consisted of 8 P-38s, 7 P-51s and 2 P-38 relays. (Lt. Col. Herren led White Section's P-51s and Lt. Col. Riddle led Yellow Section's P-38s.) Major Biscayart led the 436th FS, which consisted of 15 P-38s. Their assignment was a bomber escort for 1st BD B-17s attacking their 8th AF Mission 652 primary and secondary targets in Magdeburg, Germany. 434th FS up: 0929 hrs., down: 1435 hrs. with one early return. 435th FS up: 0930 hrs., down: 1406 hrs. with three early returns, two escorts and one spare. 436th FS up: 0941 hrs., down: 1427 hrs. with four early returns plus two escorts.

This mission saw another strong attack by many of the same Fw 190 *Sturmböcke* that wrought such destruction to errant B-24s yesterday. This time, however, it was the B-17's turn to be on the receiving end. The 434th FS made L/F over the Dutch island of Texel at 1035 hrs./18,000 ft. The 435th FS made L/F just a bit south of that, but actually north of their course, over Den Helder at 1015 hrs./18,000 ft. The 436th FS,

Captain Claire A. P. DuffiÈ was forced to belly in his P-51 Give 'em Hell for H. L. near Martlesham Heath when his plane's engine failed. *Courtesy of Clarence M. Surges.*

following the briefed course, made L/F farther south still, over Ijmuiden, Holland at 1030 hrs./18,000 ft. Crossing into Germany and heading on to their R/V, bogies were called in at 1100 hours, near Minden. The group dropped their wing tanks, readied themselves for combat and bounced the bogies. The unidentified aircraft turned out to be P-51s that were painted a very dark olive drab with black and white diagonal stripes on their fuselages. They were very hard to identify. The group reformed and proceeded in to R/V with the proper bombers near Brunswick at 1110 hrs./29,000 ft. Eight boxes of B-17s were covered, especially the ones to the rear. At 1115 hours, the 434th FS sighted white-nosed P-51s that were engaged with 20 plus E/A. Weather in the area was 4-5/10ths with cumulus clouds from 2,000 to 7,000 feet and visibility unlimited. It was a good day for a scrap. The squadron went to investigate which resulted in a bounce on the enemy aircraft and a fight that ran from 30,000 feet to all the way down on the deck. The Germans dispersed in an area northeast of Goslar, 28 miles due west of Halberstadt. At this point, the 434th FS was forced to begin returning home due to a lack of gas.

Confirmed claims for the squadron were:

1-0-0	Fw 190	1st Lt. George W. Gleason
1-0-0	Me 109	1st Lt. George W. Gleason
1-0-0	Me 109	Lt. Col. James M. Herren, Jr.
0-0-1	Me 109	2nd Lt. Robert B. Kline
1-0-0	Fw 190	2nd Lt. Richard M. Lunstrum
0-0-1	Fw 190	2nd Lt. Eugene H. Wendt

Pilots flying P-51s made all of the above claims, except for that of Second Lieutenant Wendt, who was flying a P-38.

Lieutenant Colonel Herren, who led the attack, begins:

"I was leading the Newcross White Section of eight P-51s on the escort mission. Just after rendezvous with the bombers, we sighted an engagement at 28,000 feet, off to the right of the bomber track. I took the section over to investigate. It turned out to be about ten Me 109s and one or two flights of white-nosed P-51s. I joined in a luftberry and after two or three turns, I was in position on an Me 109. The German must have seen me because he started evasive action immediately. I chased him to the deck, where he started turning to the right. I was a little above him so I closed fast and got in a good burst from four o'clock, opening fire at 300 yards and closing to 150 yards. I observed many strikes in the cockpit and as he continued his turn, the strikes moved down to the tail, parts of which I saw fly off. I had to pull up to the left to keep from hitting him and as I did so, I saw the pilot bail out. I took pictures of the pilot in his chute."

Second Lt. Robert B. Kline was Lt. Col. Herren's wingman, flying Newcross White Two and confirms that claim. Lt. Kline also claimed an Me 109 as damaged when he shot it off Lt. Col. Herren's tail during the above engagement.

First Lieutenant George W. Gleason, flying as wingman to First Lieutenant Walter M. Drake in the other two positions of White Flight, got to take over from his element leader when Lt. Drake's guns jammed during an attack on an Me 109. Lt. Drake overshot the German and became the prey instead of the hunter. Lt. Gleason:

"I was flying White Four when we engaged in a fight with some Me 109s. White Three attacked an Me 109, but overshot and the German got on his tail. I turned into him, gave him one to one-and-one-half radii lead and opened fire. I observed many strikes on his tail and saw his rudder section come off. As I walked my aim up to his wing section, the Me 109 went into a violent, uncontrolled spin that continued until the E/A crashed into the ground. I did not see the pilot bail out."

Lt. Gleason continues:

"I saw a Fw 190 below me so I split-essed down on him and we wound up in a left-hand luftberry on the deck. I closed in on him to about 200 yards, gave him three-quarters to one radii lead and opened fire at 20 to 30-degrees deflection. I observed many hits on the left wing and fuselage. The German bellied his aircraft into an open field near a little village. The pilot got out and ran several yards, then fell flat on his stomach. At that point, the 190 exploded and began burning."

Second Lieutenant Richard M. Lunstrum confirmed Lt. Gleason's Fw 190 and got another himself:

"I was flying Newcross Red Three when the P-51s of the group became involved in a fight. Red Flight become separated from the rest of the group and wound up descending to 3,000 feet where we found several E/A circling an airport on which a few had already landed. A Fw 190 passed in front of our flight from the right as we were circling. Capt. C.A.P. Duffié, Red Leader, overshot so he told me to take him. I attacked the Fw in a turn to the right and gave him a short burst at 60-degrees deflection, but observed no hits. I closed and gave him another burst at five degrees, observing a few strikes. The German rolled into a left turn so I opened fire from dead astern, slightly high and observed strikes on his left wing. The E/A started a roll to the left again, the canopy came off and the pilot parachuted out. I saw the 190 crash straight into the ground."

Both Capt. Duffié and Second Lieutenant Donald W. Thorn, who was flying as a spare from the 435th FS and who became Lt. Lunstrum's wingman, confirmed the Fw's destruction.

Second Lieutenant Eugene H. Wendt, Yellow Two, wrapped up the day's scoring when the straggler from Yellow Section, Yellow Flight found two Fw 190s diving in front of him. He fired a short burst at one from about 1,000 yards and observed strikes along the fuselage. The Fw continued his dive for a thousand feet or so, then went into a spin. The E/A was still spinning when it went into some clouds at about 8,000 feet. There, Lt. Wendt lost sight of it so he could only claim a damaged for his effort.

The 435th FS left the bombers to check on what was reported as 100 plus Fw 190s and Me 109s in the Halberstadt area. They found a huge fight between the E/A, P-38s and P-51s going on, ranging from 28,000 feet to down on the deck and back up again. The lack of gas prevented the squadron from staying long and they also were forced to head for home.

The 436th FS, noting that the bombers were behind schedule, saw a gaggle consisting of 60 to 100 gray Fw 190s with yellow and blue-striped noses – two colored stripes about five inches wide, attack the B-17 bomber formation. The Fws were seen to spread out into line abreast formations, with ten to twelve aircraft to a formation, prior to attacking from six o'clock. The E/A came from 3,000 to 4,000 feet below the bomber level, moving up and aiming at the bellies of the B-17s. As the squadron moved in to intercept, no attempt was made to fire upon them by the Germans. Six to eight B-17s from the last box were shot down almost at once. Only one high side pass from the front quarter was made on the squadron before they waded into the Jerries. The squadron came away without a loss and tallied up a couple of triples as well as a double and a single:

2-0-0	Fw 190	Maj. Jules D. Biscayart
3-0-1	Fw 190	1st Lt. Donald A. Dunn
0-0-1	Fw 190	1st Lt. James E. Frolking
0-0-1	Fw 190	1st Lt. Howard G. Hightower
1-0-1	Fw 190	1st Lt. George Straub
3-0-1	Fw 190	1st Lt. Victor Wolski

Major Biscayart led the squadron and also was credited with two Fws:

> "I was leading Bison Squadron at 24,000 feet when at 1120 hours, I saw a gaggle of about sixty plus Fw 190s approaching the bombers from 22,000 feet, below the contrail level. We swung on down and in behind them. Several saw us and split-essed, but the main body continued driving on directly toward the bombers. I closed on one and put about a three-second burst directly into the cockpit area from about a 15-degree angle and 150 yards off. He peeled off slowly and spiraled down, winding up tighter and tighter, gathering speed and smoking profusely. He went vertically into the clouds that were topped at 4,000 feet. It is my belief that it was impossible for him to pull out at that altitude. I closed on the next man in the formation, with my flight alongside me. He split-essed and I attempted to follow him, but hit compressibility at around 450 IAS. I was able to level out at about 6,000 feet, saw another Fw 190 and gave chase. I closed on him and he bailed out before I fired. I passed right over the pilot in his chute."

Major Biscayart's wingman, First Lieutenant Jesse V. Granger, Bison White Two, confirmed the claims.

Major Biscayart, in a correspondence from 1995, described his feelings about that day:

"This encounter was one of the earliest uses of a completely new tactic being employed by the Germans against our bombers. Whereas previously, they made use of superior height and speed, attacking from the side or occasionally head-on in small sections or individually, they were now massing large numbers of fighters, some said up to 100, in a very close tight formation or gaggle for their attacks. Looking more like a flock of birds rather than a fighter formation, they came in level or slightly below the bombers at a slow closing speed and lined up dead astern. They pitted their massed firepower against that of the bombers from a deadly, no deflection firing position.

"On the 28th of September 1944, when we made rendezvous with the bombers, they were already under this kind of attack. The effect was devastating. The bombers were exploding and falling out of the sky. I had never seen so many aircraft going down in flames or pieces in so small of an area. There were some 20 to 30 parachutes, a few of which were on fire, floating down around us. The Germans were taking losses too. I saw one Fw 190, minus its engine and propeller, spinning down vertically. I was glad we were not on the bomber's radio frequency to hear the frantic calls they must have been making, calls we probably would never forget.

"I was leading our squadron's remaining nine P-38s. We were at 24,000 feet, behind and below the P-51s of the 434th squadron. The bombers were on our level and as we approached them, we could see the attack they were under. I called the enemy planes out to our group commander and we went after them. I got one and went after another, but lost him in a dive when I got into compressibility. This was the first time I had entered into this phenomenon. I lost control of the airplane and immediately forgot all about the FW that I was chasing. The dive had all of my attention. The airplane was shuddering, shaking and making lots of noise. In the case of the P-38, the plane stabilized in a slightly inverted dive and the elevator controls went completely slack, just as if you were on the ground, parked on a ramp. The aircraft's manufacturer, Lockheed, later came out with a modification consisting of a set of under-wing dive flaps that cured the situation, but that was after this happened and couldn't help me now. Fortunately, I had read a report about P-47s hitting compressibility and recovering when they got to denser air at about 10,000 feet. The report stressed that you shouldn't follow the notion to roll the aircraft's elevator trim back in order to raise the plane's nose as the wings had been pulled off of one P-47 that had the tab fully aft when it hit denser air, regained control and began recovery. When I got to a lower altitude, I was able to recover from the dive, pulling out at about 5-6,000 feet. I blacked out during the pullout and when my vision returned, there I was, right behind another Fw 190. I was traveling at a tremendous speed and must have scared the German pilot because in a split second, he bailed out. I never fired a shot. He must have seen me before I even saw him and figured himself for a goner. I nearly ran into him as I went sailing past. I put my gun camera switch in camera only position and made three runs on him, taking pictures only. His helmet had come off and I could see his blond hair. He threw up his hands and legs when I came at him, thinking that I was going to shoot him. That was not in my book though. Whether he was the one I had dove after, I don't know. I don't think so, the air was full of them."

Bison White Three, First Lieutenant Victor Wolski, the element leader and his wingman, First Lieutenant Donald A. Dunn, were the other two members of Maj. Biscayart's flight that attacked the formation of Fw 190s. They both got three each of the lumbering Fws. First, Lt. Wolski:

"As we came on down behind the enemy formation, a few saw us and went hell bent [sic]. The main group stayed and flew straight and level, taking no evasive action at all. I drove into the lowest flight and opened up on one, a bit too far away. I noticed hits on him and he split-essed away, damaged. I then closed to about 100 yards range on another one, throttled back and gave him the business. I saw many strikes at the wing roots and in the fuselage. Smoke began pouring out of the rear end of the fuselage, after which he slowly turned over and went straight down for at least 8,000 feet, still smoking furiously. I lost sight of him at that point because I had begun to concentrate on the next one. I closed in on him and gave him about a five-second burst, knocking his aileron off, after which, my wingman neatly polished him off. The Fw 190s were headed straight for a box of bombers when I opened up on my last one, observing hits and a couple of parts coming off him, when I ran out of ammunition. The 190 broke left and down. I pulled up to the left and saw the pilot bail out. I was going to take a picture of the pilot when a 190 came at me from a 90-degree angle. Having no ammunition, I pulled to a head-on attack and he didn't waste any time rolling over and going down. Two of my machine guns did not fire a shot due to faulty ammunition."

The P-38 that First Lieutenant Donald A. Dunn called his own. This had been a brand new bird when it arrived at Wattisham. *Courtesy of Steve Blake.*

These claims were substantiated by Lt. Dunn, as were his by Lt. Wolski.

Lt. Dunn, upon approaching the Fw 190 formation:

> "We closed on the rear and low outfit. My first bursts were out of range, but probably hitting, as we were dead astern of them and they split-essed each time I let go. As we closed in, I picked another and let go, well within range. I kept my plunger down until he fell apart and dropped down. That was number one. Seeing the A/C disintegrate, I then moved to another and let go again. This one started smoking when he went down and the plane was coming apart. That was number two. My next was hit by the number three man and turned right in front of my sights. I opened up and finished him off, watching the A/C disintegrate. That was number three. By this time I was on tracers and both of us had worked our way well into their formation. I opened up on the last one, knowing I was practically out of ammunition, but hoping. At the same time, I saw we had 190s on each side of us and we were too far up in the center of the formation. I had chopped throttle clear off to keep from overrunning, when all hell broke loose. Knowing I was well in their formation, I thought I was hit. Heading down, I pulled out, probably 5,000 feet below and went balls out for the first 38s I saw and came home with them. I had 27 rounds of ammunition left when I got home. My guns worked perfectly, happy day!"

First Lieutenants George Straub, James E. Frolking and Howard G. Hightower were numbers one, two and three in Red Flight and they all followed White Flight into the mass of Germans. Each of the three inflicted damage to the formation of armored Fw 190s, destroying one and tearing up three others. Still though, the enemy aircraft pressed on. This was to be another day for the *Sturmböcke* Fws of JGs 3, 4 and 300. Despite their losses yesterday, when 29 of the heavy, unwieldy planes were downed by American fighters and B-24 gunners, they were up again in force to attack the bombers. Weighted down by 400 pounds of armor to protect the *Sturm* pilot while he bore into the bomber formations for his kill, the Fws were no match for escorting American fighters. Sworn to bring down a bomber, even if it meant ramming, each Sturm pilot was determined and intent on his purpose. The massed attacks of the *Sturmgruppe* battle formations had proven to be effective and were very efficient against a single combat box of bombers,

Lieutenant George D. Hendrix had to belly land the P-51 he was flying this date when he had an engine failure southeast of Ipswich. *Courtesy of Clarence M. Surges.*

leaving destruction in their wake. Thus it was this date, when the battle formation of Fw 190s bore into the 1st BD B-17s belonging to the 303rd BG. Attacking from the rear and first opening fire on the tail section to knock out the rear gunner, the man who posed the greatest threat to the *Sturm* pilot, the Germans then proceeded to rake the hapless bomber with heavy fire. Eleven B-17s were lost by the group as a result of the persistent attacks. Ninety-nine men were missing in action.

There was to be one more Me 109 listed on Bison Squadrons tally sheet for the day, but Lieutenant Gerold M. Mulvany's thoughts for that claim were shattered when the 109 that he had lined up in his sights was blotted out by a P-38 that slid right in front of him just as he was squeezing off a burst. The P-38 pilot, almost adding injury to the offense, dropped his wing tanks as he passed in front of Lt. Mulvany. Lt. Mulvany thought he was going to hit one or both of the tanks for certain, but fortunately, both missed him. The Me 109 was lost process of trying to avoid the tanks and the other P-38. Upon returning to Wattisham, Lt. Mulvany reported probable damage to a friendly aircraft, sure he had hit the other P-38 with his fire, especially since his gun camera film showed a shining P-38 slide across in front of him. It was explained to him that the gun camera had an override that caused it to expose a few more frames of film after the pilot released his trigger and that the P-38 shown in his film in fact had not been hit.

L/O for the group was between Ijmuiden and Walcheren Island, Holland, from 1315 to 1320 hrs.

Observations made during the mission included seeing many planes at an A/D near Halberstadt. Several E/A that were encountered during the fight appeared to be new and silver in color. A rocket, heading almost straight up, but with a slight easterly slant, was sighted approximately ten miles southwest of Münster, a white smoke trail extending up to 35,000 ft. was seen at 1235 hrs. and a jet contrail was seen near Enschede, Holland. There were several distinct bursts noted in the

Right: Two unknown ground crew members flank Corporal Stanley Kellett as they stand beside Polly, a 436th FS P-38. *Courtesy of Stanley Kellett.*

Far right: The group's armorers serviced several aircraft and were not assigned to any one specific plane. Corporal Stanley Kellett is shown here with one of the P-38s he took care of. *Courtesy of the 436th Fighter Squadron Association.*

contrail. Flak over Texel was heavy, moderate and inaccurate. Twenty miles west of Oldenburg, Germany, along the Leda Canal, it was light, moderate and inaccurate. It was light, intense and accurate at Den Helder while over Hanover, it was heavy, intense and accurate.

30 September 1944

VIII FC FO 592

No. 165 Saturday. Col. Zemke was the group's leader and he also led the 435th FS, which consisted of 15 P-51s. Lt. Col Woods led the 434th FS, which, for the first time, was entirely made up of P-51s, 17, to be exact. Maj. Sullivan led the 436th FS, which consisted of 18 P-38s. Their assignment was a penetration to target and withdrawal for 2nd BD B-24s attacking their 8th AF Mission 655 primary target, the marshalling yards at Hamm, Germany. 434th FS up: 1148 hrs., down: 1655 hrs. with four early returns. 435th FS up: 1152 hrs., down: 1703 hrs. with one early return. 436th FS up: 1158 hrs., down: 1655 hrs. with two early returns.

Both the 434th FS and the 435th FS made an estimated L/F over Ostende, Belgium at 1226 hrs./20,000 ft. and over 10/10 cloud cover. The 436th FS made their L/F over Blankenberghe, Belgium at 1223 hrs./19,000 ft. per the briefed course. They picked up the bombers first, making R/V with the Big Friends 20 miles west of Antwerp, Belgium at 1245 hrs/ 19,000 ft. The 434th FS and the 435th FS joined the force later at 1315 hrs./24,000 ft. near the target. The proper bombers, identified by their black and silver [sic] tail markings, was escorted around the target, uneventfully. The B-24s maintained good formation and bombed through the overcast. No results were seen due to the cloud coverage. The 434th FS broke away from the bombers near Antwerp at 1435 hrs./24,000 ft. and headed northeast to sweep up east of Zwolle, Holland, then further on northeast, turning east of Steenwijk, Holland and heading to Münster, Germany, then back northwest to Lemmer, Holland and L/O at Ijmuiden, Holland at 1556 hrs./10,000 ft. The results of the squadron's stooging around were nil.

Observations made by the squadron during the mission included seeing a V2 contrail heading up to 30,000 feet, 15 miles from Brussels. Two unidentified A/C were seen to be knocked down 15 miles north of Wesel, Germany at 1310 hrs./ 24,000 ft. Three boats, one of which seemed to be unloading personnel, were spotted at Lemmer around 1537 hours. A huge explosion in a woods 15 miles west-northwest of Lemmer was sighted at 1540 hrs. Two large boats in the harbor at Ijmuiden were noted at 1556 hrs.

The 435th FS left the bombers over Eindhoven, Holland at 1435 hrs./18,000 ft. Heading north to the Arnhem, Holland area then southward and then back north to the Meppel, Holland area, that squadron looked for enemy aircraft, but they also found nothing. L/O was at Ijmuiden 1538 hrs./8,000 ft. for three of the squadron's flights, while it was farther south, between Schouwen and Walcheren Islands for the remaining flight, which crossed out at 1550 hrs./6,000 ft.

Observations made during the mission by the squadron included seeing two unidentified aircraft explode and go down in the area of Münster, one of which was believed to be a bomber. It was too far away to note any chutes.

Muz's Mighty Molecule usually flown by Lieutenant Richard S. Spencer, Jr., another of the P-38s that Corporal Kellett was responsible for. *Courtesy of the 436th Fighter Squadron Association.*

The 436th broke away over Antwerp at 1440 hrs./22,000 feet, turning north to sweep Holland from the northern end of the Zuider Zee, south east to Enschede, then south west to Nijmegen and over to L/O near Ijmuiden at 1600 hrs./9,000 ft. No results were to be had.

Observations made by the squadron during the mission included seeing an Me 262 heading south at 1530 hrs, north of Nijmegen and a large explosion such as a bomber crash or bombing near the north coast of the Zuider Zee at 1555 hrs. Flak over the target was heavy, intense and inaccurate.

During this month, the matter of drop tanks or auxiliary fuel tanks has figured into the mission accounts several times. It would be appropriate at this point, then, to add an account that relates to the use of them. The U.S.-made steel 165-gallon auxiliary gasoline tanks used by the P-38 Lightnings and later the British-made paper 108-gallon auxiliary gasoline tanks used by the P-51 Mustang, both came packed in wooden-framed, plywood crates. When the crates were broken down after the tank was removed, the framing material and the plywood provided adequate material from which to build serviceable huts near the dispersal points where the outlying squadrons were located. However, only so much material could be used in this manner before no more was needed and soon large hills of empty wooden crates began to accumulate. Most of these were burned in order to dispose of them. Corporal Stanley (Stan) Kellett, an armorer with the 436th FS, told of another use he found for the excess packing material. He said he previously had made friends with an English farmer whose fields bordered the 436th dispersal area. (Wattisham was/is located in a rural area made up totally of farms, some of which surround the airfield.) The farmer wanted some of the crating material that was being destroyed, but could not persuade the authorities to allow him to have any. The man was told the wood was government property and as such could not be handed out. Upon learning this, Corporal Kellett and a few of his friends made arrangements with the farmer to pass some of the boxes over the airfield's fence, under cover of darkness. The night the deed was to occur, the men arrived at the appointed place by the fence and began tossing the crates over. Stanley said that as soon as the crates hit the ground, they disappeared. They passed over maybe eight or ten that night. The next morning, they found a dozen fresh eggs by the fence. Boy, fresh eggs, Stan thought. What a wonderful surprise! As Stan put it, "Little did the farmer know that we would have given him a P-38 for those eggs."

One of the new P-51s that were arriving for the group, this one being assigned to the 434th FS. *Courtesy of Berkley E. Hollister.*

Stan also remembered that every once in a while one of the drop tank crates coming from the states would be packed with candy, cookies and other sweets in addition to the steel tank. The treats were put in there by the factory workers where the tanks were made. Those were always nice to find and much appreciated.

CHAPTER EIGHT

OCTOBER 1944

2 October 1944

VIII FC FO 594

No. 166 Monday. Colonel Zemke led the group, which consisted of 35 P-51s and 12 P-38s (17-434th, 18-435th & 12 P-38s-436th) on a 2nd BD B-24 escort and MEW controlled mission. Up: 1135 hrs., down: 1740 hrs. with three P-51 & two P-38 early returns.

The day started out badly when a P-51 belonging to the 434th FS failed to get airborne in time and ran into a small mound of dirt at the end of the runway. The plane flipped over on its back and First Lieutenant Quentin S. Pavlock was killed by the ensuing fiery crash. L/F was made by the group over Alkmaar, Holland at 1240 hrs./23,000 ft. Seeking their assigned Big Friends who, as it was discovered, were behind them, the group turned back to R/V with the B-24s, meeting them in mid-North Sea between 1250 & 1300 hrs./23,000 ft. The bomber formation was very poor with the Combat Wings not in their briefed order, A/C weaving and overrunning each other and some units as much as 20 miles apart. This made escort difficult. The 8th AF Mission 659 primary target, the marshalling yards at Hamm, Germany, were bombed at 1330 hrs./20,000 ft. with reported good results. At 1327 hours, a B-24 was seen to explode over Hamm. No chutes were observed. Flak over the target was heavy, intense and accurate at 24,000 ft. On return, one squadron descended to inspect airdromes, then swept south to the area bounded by Münster, Germany, the Zuider Zee and Arnhem, Holland. A second squadron swept the areas of Geldern, Lingen and Wulfen in Germany, as well as Apeldoorn and Urk in Holland. The third squadron having remained close to the bombers, broke off escort near Egmond, Holland at 1438 hrs./2,000 ft.

Observations made during the mission included heavy, intense and accurate flak, in both the Rheine, Germany and Walcheren Island, Holland areas. The airdrome southwest of Wesel, Germany put up light, intense, inaccurate flak. The other German airdromes that were surveyed were: Lippstadt, which had one unidentified A/C and a few unfilled bomb craters; Lippspringe, which had 25 plus, well camouflaged, probable single-engine A/C, Gütersloh, which had another 25 plus well dispersed, single-engine A/C and Plantlunne which had no A/C. The field at Steenwijk, Holland had one unidentified A/C. There was a lot of rail traffic in all directions between east of Dortmund and Ems, Germany. There was a possible Big Ben (V2 rocket) contrail heading west, seen 25 miles south of Münster, Germany. One Me 262 was seen in the Enschede, Holland area. It was chased, but could not be caught.

Milan John Stanovich, a crew chief with the 434th FS remembers this day vividly:

> "During the time we were maintaining the P-51 fighter A/C for combat operations at Wattisham, it was normal for all crew chiefs to informally gather along the take-off runway to watch 'his' aircraft get airborne. On October 2, 1944, our group was scheduled to escort B-24s to the marshalling yards at Hamm, Germany. After ensuring that my aircraft (not the subject A/C of this narrative) had successfully started and was taxiing out for take-off, some of the other crew chiefs and I headed for the runway to observe the 'launch'. Col. Hubert Zemke

was leading the group this day so he and his wingman, Second Lieutenant Clarence (Buck) G. Haynes took off first. Lt. Quentin S. Pavlock, who was leading the second element in the flight, and his wingman, were about 15-20 seconds behind Col. Zemke in taking off. As Lt. Pavlock approached the point where he should have normally become airborne, he failed to do so and it became obvious that he was not going to be able to get off the ground. As he ran off the end of the runway, he hit a pile of loose dirt or mud, flipped over and ended up on his back, engulfed in flames. I was closest to the point where the aircraft came to rest and I ran over to it. As a quickly-arriving fire truck dispensed foam on the burning plane, I called for someone to get the truck-mounted hoist so that the aircraft could be lifted, thus enabling us to attempt rescue of the pilot. Lt. Pavlock appeared to be still alive and actually was heard screaming for help. When the plane was finally lifted high enough to allow rescue of the pilot, I unbuckled Lt. Pavlock from the pilot's seat and he fell into my arms. With others helping, I laid him on a stretcher and placed him in an ambulance. Lt. Quentin S. Pavlock died while enroute to the base hospital."

A photo of the P-51 from which Technical Sergeant Milan J. (John) Stanovich rescued First Lieutenant Quentin S. Pavlock. The picture, taken shortly after the rescue, shows the airplane still coated with fire-fighting foam and suspended by the rescue truck. *Courtesy of Clarence M. Surges.*

This picture, taken at a later date, shows Second Lieutenant Robert F. Pfund in and crew chief Technical Sergeant Milan J. Stanovich on the wing of his P-51, Miss Georgia Carol/The Flying Dutchman. As always, the airplane belonged to the crew chief and T/Sgt. Stanovich was just letting Lt. Pfund fly it for a while. *Courtesy of Milan J. Stanovich.*

Crew chief Milan John Stanovich was later awarded the Bronze Star for his part in the rescue effort.

John W. Hedenberg started out on this mission, but lost a gas cap on take off and had to return for that reason. That gave him some free time for other things such as trying out the new P-51 he would be soon switching to. He wrote:

"Got my new P-51 today and test-hopped it. Very nice ship, in perfect condition. Has only one engine though! Fired in the guns offshore at the Wash. Seems funny as hell to have guns in the wings instead of the nose. Going to miss that cannon. Only six .50s in these. Since the combat tour length is still 270 hours, I guess I'll have to fly the damned thing in combat for several missions to finish up. George Straub finished today – first man in the group to do so. Not long for me though – I hope."

The pilots original to the group who had thus far survived combat, were beginning to finish their tours at this time and like the P-38s they had been flying, were being replaced by new blood.

Congratulations from all around go to First Lieutenant George Straub, the first Bison pilot to complete his tour. *Courtesy of Travis M. Greenwood.*

Some of the original P-38 pilots from the 434th FS are shown gathered around one of their birds in an early photo. *Courtesy of George D. Hendrix.*

The original pilots from the 436th FS are shown in their ready room. The picture was taken shortly after the group's arrival in England. *Courtesy of Travis M. Greenwood.*

3 October 1944

VIII FC FO 596

No. 167 Tuesday. Lt. Col. Riddle led the group, which consisted of 32 P-51s and 13 P-38s (16-434th, 16-435th and 13 P-38s-436th) on a penetration to target and withdrawal escort for 2nd BD B-24s attacking an 8th AF Mission 662 target of opportunity, the airfield at Speyer, Germany. Up: 0947 hrs., down: 1425 hrs. with one P-38 early return.

L/F was made by the group over Coxyde, Belgium at 1028 hrs./18,000 ft. R/V with the group's charges, the 2nd and 14th CW bombers, occurred at 1107 hrs./22,000 ft. in the Metz, France area. The B-24s were in good formation with the exception of several stragglers after leaving the target, but there appeared to be none in trouble. Flak over the target was heavy, meager and accurate. The 436th FS dive-strafed the airfield from 1,000 to 3,000 ft. at a 40-degree angle, getting many strikes on the field's hangars. The 434th FS broke away in the Arras, France area at 1315 hrs./23,000 ft. making L/O between Dunkerque, FRance and Ostend, Belgium at 1325 hrs./14,000 ft. The 435th FS broke away over St. Quentin, France at 1315 hrs./14,000 ft. making L/O over Coxyde, Belgium at 1325 hrs./ 14,000 ft. The 436th FS broke away over Guise, France at 1315 hrs./17,000 ft. making L/O over St. Inglevert at 1400 hrs./8,000 ft. The bombing results were mixed with a wooded area to the east along with all buildings on the east and west ends of the airfield clobbered. Three fires were sighted. A small town south of Speyer received some hits.

Observations made during the mission included 20 plus locomotives at the Saarbrücken, Germany marshalling yards as well as a climbing, 70-degree contrail over 30,000 ft. in the same vicinity. There was heavy, meager, inaccurate flak at 15-23,000 ft. coming from the yards.

434th FS armorer Corporal James E. Hamilton is shown standing beside one of the squadron's early P-38s. *Courtesy of Loetta Taylor (Kennedy).*

This was the group's last mission flown utilizing the P-38 Lightning. After this date, its entire fighting force would be made up of P-51s. The 479th Fighter Group TE, had flown the twin-engine, Lockheed-built aircraft since the group's first days in California. To some of the pilots, the newly transitioned to North American P-51 Mustang was a joy to fly and a needed shot-in-the arm for the group. To others accustomed to flying the outgoing "Cadillac of the Sky", the "Spam Can" was deserving of its name. Future replacement pilots would not know the difference.

The outgoing P-38s. Planes from all three squadrons can be seen parked and awaiting their disposition. *Courtesy of the 436th Fighter Squadron Association.*

Jules D. Biscayart, then a Major with the 436th FS, wrote later about the transition from P-38 to P-51:

> "During the transition to P-51s, we were given a couple of AT-6 Harvards [Texan] to fly and practice with, but we felt they were more difficult to fly than the 51s.
>
> "The P-51 was lighter, more maneuverable, had more range and had a better altitude capability. With it, our missions changed in length from four to six hours and operating altitudes increased from 24,000 feet, up to 35,000 feet. Along with this, we now had to sit on a hard, one-man dinghy instead of a more comfortable seat-type parachute. As a consequence, a masseur was assigned to each squadron to tend the sore muscles we had.
>
> "We had a few serious difficulties with the P-51 in the beginning. One such problem was that the aircraft's engine would sometimes quit during take-off. The culprit was spark plug fouling caused by the fuel we were using, a 100 octane gasoline which had been refined and blended with an additive which boosted its rating to 150 octane. [The use of a special 100/150 PN – Performance Number, octane rated gasoline, known by some as 'Purple Peril' or 'Purple Passion' because of its purple coloration, caused excessive maintenance and spark plug fouling. The 100/### numbering system arose from the fact that the octane rating scale only goes to 100, consequently, fuels with an octane rating higher than 100 are designated with a performance number expressed as an additional percentage of that scale's top. Therefore, 100/150 PN had a 50% higher rating than 100 octane.] In addition to replacing the spark plugs after every mission, we learned that we had to run the engine at high power for about a minute before take off, in order to clean the plugs. We also had to do this in the air about every 45 minutes or so if we were just cruising.
>
> "One other draw back to the P-51 was that we could see the flak exploding around us much better in it than we could in the P-38. This was because of the 51's blown plexiglass canopy and also because the location of the plane's wings, mid-wing for the P-38 verses low-wing for the P-51. Ignorance was bliss."

The exact date is unknown, but the incident to be described had to have occurred on or slightly before this date. Both William Hugill, then a Major and the Senior Flying Control Officer (ATC) attached to the 479th and William S. Culbertson,

One of the group's AT-6s taking off. *Courtesy of David L. Born.*

then a Corporal serving as a draftsman with the 436th FS, recently told about the flight of an inverted P-51 as it passed over Wattisham's field. William Hugill:

> "During the fall of 1944, the 479th was in the process of changing aircraft from the P-38 to the P-51. One afternoon while I was on duty in the control tower, I observed a P-51 approaching the airfield from the south and heading north, flying in an inverted position. The plane flew over and as expected, Colonel Kyle Riddle called on the phone and asked 'Who the hell was that!' He told me to have that pilot land and report to his office. The pilot was the above quoted Major Jules D. Biscayart, then one of the 436th FS's leaders. When he met with Col. Riddle, he explained that the P-51's T.O. (Technical Orders – written out, detailed A/C specifications.) stated that the P-51 could be flown in an inverted position for ten seconds before damage to the engine from lack of proper lubrication could occur. He said he just wanted to verify that data before he went out on a combat mission in the A/C."

Now for the rest of the story, William Culbertson added that Major Biscayart was fined $100 dollars and grounded for a week.

Lieutenant Henry P. (Porter) Plunk from the 436th FS also had an interesting experience transitioning from the P-38 to the P-51. He liked the P-38 and for him, the changeover was not all that welcome. He recalled that when flying the P-51, it seemed as though the pilot always had to keep one hand on the rudder trim wheel. The P-38 required less of that due to the counter rotation of its propellers. When fully laden with three full interior fuel tanks, two more exterior tanks, ammunition, armor, etc., the long-range fighter with its high torque Packard-Merlin engine was a tricky bird to fly. When Lt. Plunk made his first check out flight in the Mustang, he received a quick introduction to the plane's quirks. After

Major Jules D. Biscayart and the great crew that kept him flying. *Courtesy of Steve Blake.*

Crew chief Sergeant Herbert R. Green and First Lieutenant Henry P. Plunk by their P-51, Ambrosia. *Courtesy of James R. Helms.*

climbing to a safe altitude, he leveled off and flew straight for a while getting the feel of the aircraft. Then he pushed the stick into the right hand corner for a diving turn. Having using the same force he was used to applying when he was flying the Lightning, he received a rude awakening! He suddenly found himself going through five or six very fast snap rolls and felt like he was on some wild amusement park ride. Recovering, he flew straight and level for a long time before he tried any more maneuvers.

5 October 1944

VIII FC FO 598

No. 168 Thursday. Lt. Col. Riddle led the group, which consisted of 43 P-51s (16-434th, 15-435th & 12-436th) on a penetration to target and withdrawal escort for 2nd BD B-24s attacking their 8th AF Mission 665 primary target, the airdrome at Paderborn, Germany. Up: 0942 hrs., down: 1506 hrs. with eight early returns.

The group made L/F over Egmond, Holland at 1040 hrs./ 18-26,000 ft. R/V with the assigned yellow and black tailed B-24s was also made in that area at 1050 hrs./21-26,000 ft. The bombers were in good formation and they were escorted over the target, where the visual bombing was excellent. One chute was observed in the vicinity of the target. The 434th left the bombers at 1230 hrs. ten miles south of Steinhuder Lake, Germany to investigate a bogie that was later identified as an F-5 Lightning. The areas of Paderborn, Wesel and Krefeld in Germany as well as Arnhem and Zwolle in Holland were well covered by sweeps. The group broke from the bombers in the area of Zwolle. One squadron made L/O over Overflakkee, Holland at 1405 hrs./8,000 ft. while the other two squadrons made L/O over "The Hook" of Holland (Hoek van Holland, located south of The Hague) at 1425 hrs./12,000 ft. and 1445 hrs./8,000 feet, respectively.

Observations made during the mission included a 75-degree, upwards-traveling contrail at 1345 hrs./15,000 ft. believed coming from the woods halfway between Stavoren and Lemmer, Holland. An unidentified airdrome at Ahden, Germany 10 miles southwest of Paderborn was worked over by P-47s, leaving three fires. At 1230 hrs. six trains were seen to be moving between Hannover and Osnabruck, Germany. Twenty plus balloons were noted near Wesel, Germany as well as the same in the vicinity of Bramsche, Germany. Thirty plus silver balloons were at the canal junction north of Minden, Germany. An airdrome ten miles east-southeast of Lippstadt, on the west edge of the forest at Niederntudorf, Germany, was worked over by P-47s, who left eight or nine fires.

6 October 1944

VIII FC FO 599

No. 169 Friday. Col. Zemke led the group, which consisted of 51 P-51s (16-434th, 18-435th & 17-435th) on a penetration to target and withdrawal escort for 3rd BD B-17s attacking their 8th AF Mission 667 primary target in Berlin, Germany. Up: 0906 hrs., down: 1450 hrs. with four early returns.

L/F was made over Egmond, Holland 1000 hrs./16,000 ft. R/V with the assigned bombers was at 1100 hrs./23,000 ft. 20 miles southwest of Hamburg, Germany. The bombers were in good formation. Around noon, during the bomb run, the last five or six boxes of bombers were hit by 50-60 conventional and long-nosed Fw 190s as well as Me 109s a few miles west of Berlin, Germany. The E/A attacked from six o'clock high in waves of eight to ten, passing through the formations and continuing on down. The group's pilots turned into the E/A, attacking head-on while the accompanying 4th FG attacked from the rear. The Germans were very aggressive and made many attacks against the two fighter groups. After what appeared to be excellent bombing results, the Big Friends were escorted to Cuxhaven, Germany. by one squadron while the other two broke off in the Wesermünde, Germany area immediately after the combat. L/Os were north of Wesermünde at 1330 hrs./15,000 feet, Egmond, at 1355 hrs./9,000 feet, and Ijmuiden, Holland at 1400 hrs./11,000 ft. Two B-17s, apparently losing altitude, were picked up at 1000 feet, leaving Wesermünde. They were escorted to L/O. A shortage of gas prevented further help. No radio contact was able to be established with the bombers. The claims made were: in the 434th FS, 1-0-0 Fw 190 by Captain Robin Olds, 0-0-1 Fw 190 by First Lieutenant George D. Hendrix and in the 436th FS, 1-0-0 Me 109 by First Lieutenant Thomas E. Meyers.

Observations made during the mission included noting that the airdrome at Magdeburg, Germany contained forty single-engine and ten twin-engine A/C dispersed on the perimeter with a few in revetments in a woods. At 1030 hrs. from 20,000 feet, a tremendous explosion was seen in a forest just north of Bergen, Germany. There were 15 unidentified A/C at Rechlin airdrome and 15 twin-engine A/C on an airfield four miles west of Brandenburg, Germany. One P-51 was seen to spin in near Brandenburg, but the pilot was able to successfully bail out. Another opened chute was seen in the vicinity of Sulingen, northeast of Dümmer Lake at 1030 hrs. A B-17, just south of Brandenburg, was seen going southwest from Belzig and losing altitude. There was a convoy of 20 plus halftracks and tanks on the highway north of Ijmuiden spotted at 1050 hrs.

One of John W. Hedenberg's last entries in his combat diary concerns this mission, the first in his P-51:

"Longest mission yet and also the first for me in the P-51. It was an escort mission to Berlin – the first time we have hit Berlin in quite a while. Several industrial targets were hit on the western edge of the city and the boys did a damn good job. Just before the last box dropped their bombs, about 60 Jerry fighters hit them. Our group was a couple of thousand feet below at the time and we started up. It's a sickening feeling, watching bomber after bomber, go down in flames. Other fighter groups were there, giving the Germans hell, so they dove away, right through us. We saw them coming, dropped our tanks and turned after them. However, I fell off in a spin, not being used the 51 and trying to turn too tight. By the time I got straightened out a half a turn later, I couldn't see anything to shoot at. There was a hell of a melee of 51s circling around, which gradually got straightened out. During it, I saw a couple of tracers go past me from the rear. Naturally, I took evasive action and looked back, but nothing was there. Then all of a sudden, I was alone in the sky, with no idea where everybody had disappeared to, though I could hear them talking on the radio. While frantically searching about, first one, then another and another P-51 appeared and formed up on me as leader. So I then had a full flight, but we all had different tail markings and were from different groups – so did not have the same radio frequency crystals and could not talk to each other. On my own frequency, I heard a report that the bandits were tagging the rear of the bombers, away from the target. I called the group leader (who had been unsuccessfully trying to tell me where the group was) and told him I had a pickup flight of straggler P-51s and would escort the last bomber group to landfall out at Wesermünde. Having reached there, we would cover any crippled stragglers behind them. Group leader okayed that, wished me good luck and we were on our own. This was a very nerve-wracking thing to do with only four ships, but I felt it had to be done since I had spotted quite a few cripples limping out already. Fortunately, the bandits never did show, so after what seemed an interminable time, the last cripple was out over the North Sea and we headed for home, skirting the Frisian Islands along the way. Back at home, I found out later

The P-51 that John Hedenberg flew for the short time he remained at Wattisham before completion of his combat tour. Shown here parked on a hardstand after having been accidentally taxied off the perimeter track and into some mud. Note the mud splatters caked on that portion of the fuselage under the star and bar national insignia. Note also the short-lived black and white checkered rudder used for squadron identification. *Courtesy of John W. Hedenberg.*

that day that somebody had been shooting at me. Frank [Frank W. Watkins, the plane's crew chief] told me there were two bullet holes in my tail."

7 October 1944

VIII FC FO 600

No. 170 Saturday. Col. Zemke led the group, which consisted of 49 P-51s (17-434th, 16-435th & 16-436th) on a penetration to target and withdrawal escort for 3rd BD B-17s attacking their 8th AF Mission 669 target, the POL installations at Brux, Czechoslovakia. Up: 0915 hrs., down: 1528 hrs. with six early returns.

The spread-out squadrons made L/F over Alkmaar, Holland at 1015 hrs./16,500 feet, Bergen, Germany at 1022 hrs./15,000 ft. and Egmond, Germany at 1017 hrs./18,000 ft. Colgate reported the bombers were five minutes late at L/F. Having picked the B-17s up, the group followed the column until 1103 hours, at which point Colonel Zemke took half the group back six combat wings trying to find the proper bombers assigned for escort. The remainder of the group stayed with the front of the column. Past Nordhausen, Germany, as Col. Zemke was again moving up the column, a gaggle of 30-40 Me 109s was seen approaching from the north at a very fast speed. From what must have been 30,000 feet, they descended to attack the rear of the combat wing ahead. Closing speed was very slow. The enemy A/C attacked in mass from the rear

Another of the 436th FS aircraft sporting a checkered tail, 9B-O Ambrosia. *Courtesy of Steve Blake.*

First Lieutenant Norman R. Benoit with the crew that maintained the P-51 he called Victory Queen. *Courtesy of the Wings of Freedom Museum.*

Lieutenant Colonel James M. Herren, Jr. beside his P-51 L2-A Touché, one of the two planes that provided escort for the Big Friend. *Courtesy of Steve Blake.*

at six or seven o'clock and then split-essed to the left and down. The group saw some that tried to recover for another attack, but most of them hit the deck. After the attack, an orange-nosed P-51 belonging to one of the nearby escorting groups and described as chocolate colored with lightning markings along the fuselage, was noted as missing. The flak in the area was heavy, intense and inaccurate at 26,000 ft. The remainder of the group caught the correct bombers 50 miles short of the target and "went around the course" with them. Many parachutes were observed in the combat area as seven or eight Big Friends were seen to go down. One Me 109, chased by Major Arthur F. Jeffrey (434th FS) from 26,000 ft. down to 1,000 feet, was shot down by him. Col. Zemke spotted three more Me 109s that had made a firing pass on the bombers and were making an escape to the north. The Germans were several thousand feet below, so Col. Zemke and his wingman, Lieutenant Norman R. Benoit from the 435th FS, split-essed after them. Col. Zemke went after the leader who quickly turned into the attack rather than diving away. The German pilot tried to pull around onto Col. Zemke's tail and the aggressiveness of the maneuver surprised Col. Zemke. Having lost the advantage and not able to fire because of too much speed and deflection, the Colonel pulled into a near-vertical climb to cut his speed. At the top of his climb, Col. Zemke fell off on a wing and as he rolled over on his side to head back down, he saw Lt. Benoit. His wingman was making a pass on the German as he followed his leader. The Me 109 pilot turned into Lt. Benoit and he too went into a climb. As he headed back down, Col. Zemke made another pass at the German, but had no luck. Lt. Benoit followed, and when in position, tried to get on the Jerry's tail. The German turned in an attempt to reverse the attack and the two wound up in a luftbury. When Col. Zemke tried to cut the enemy aircraft out of the circle, the German dove down and away. Col. Zemke and Lt. Benoit went down after him and wound up in a 10,000 foot, 520 mph dive. At the moment that Col. Zemke was anticipating the German to begin pulling out of the dive, the Me 109's left wing folded back against its fuselage and the whole plane broke apart. It appeared that the pilot was killed in the break up of his aircraft for there was no parachute. Col. Zemke later stated that the German was very good and was the best that he had seen in some time. The Colonel and his wingman, Lt. Benoit shared the kill. (One source, John Foreman and S. E. Harvey, state in their book *The Messerschmitt Me 262 Combat Diary*, that when the Colonel and Lieutenant's combat films were processed, it was discovered that their opponent was actually an Me 262. The jet was later identified as being from *Kommando Nowotny*, one of a number such A/C up that day in defense of the Reich. However, this author has doubts that Col. Zemke and Lt. Benoit would confuse the two distinctly different aircraft and further more, there is no record of an amended claim.)

A B-17 with an "A" in square (94th BG) and the letter "Q" named "Clover Leaf" and with the name "Tommy" on a nacelle was escorted to south of Hanover, Germany where it crashed, diving to the ground from 8,000 ft. Four chutes were seen. Another B-17, this one from the 385th BG, was also in trouble. The plane and crew were returning from attacking their secondary target at Bielefeld, Germany. The flight crew was trying to keep the crippled A/C in the air after suffering a loss of power due to two runaway props on numbers one and four engines and the loss of number three turbo-supercharger. They were dropping at the rate of 1,500 ft./min. and were down to 110 mph in a bomber that didn't want to fly anymore. The crew jettisoned everything that wasn't tied, nailed or screwed down and was just able to maintain 10,000 ft. They had 150 miles to go before they were even out of Germany and they gradually found themselves alone in the sky. Flying that way for about 30 minutes and afraid to radio for help because they didn't want the Germans to find them, the crew got some unexpected company. Two P-51s from the 434th FS had drawn up beside the ailing Big Friend. L2-A Touché and L2-E My Jeanne had taken up escort.

They flew one off each wing, all the way to the Zuider Zee with the B-17. The P-51s had their gear down and some flaps in order to stay with the slow-flying aircraft. Low on fuel at this point, the fighters had to break off, but before they left, they radioed ahead to get some P-47 escorts that showed up to take over. The bomber made it safely back home. The group broke off from the bombers by squadrons, over the Zuider Zee at 1412 hrs./24,000 feet, over Zwolle, Holland at 1415 hrs./17,500 ft. and at mid-point over the North Sea, 1436 hrs./11,000 ft. The Zwolle area was searched for bandits without results, but a B-17 with a "Y" in square [sic] was escorted to a Ninth AF field east of Brussels, Belgium. L/O was over Bergen, Holland at 1430 hrs./9,000 ft. and Egmond at 1422 hrs./10,000 ft. for the two squadrons still over land. The claims were: from the 434th FS, 1-0-0 Me 109 by Major Arthur F. Jeffrey and from the 435th FS, 1-0-0 Me 109 (Me 262) shared by Col. Hubert Zemke and First Lt. Norman R. Benoit.

Observations made during the mission included heavy, intense and inaccurate flak in both the Chemnitz and Osnabrück, Germany areas, five trains heading north, south of Hannover and three more in the Hannover marshalling yards. There were six unidentified A/C on the Dessau, Germany airdrome, 20 single-engine A/C on an airdrome two miles east of Gotha, Germany, three single-engine A/C on an airdrome ten miles west of Bielefeld, Germany, and 50 plus twin-engine A/C on the Vechta Hesepe, Germany airdrome. Smoke and fires were seen coming from both Halle and Kassel, Germany at 1245 hrs. An area resembling a storage dump appeared to be well bombed along the railroad located five miles south of Chemnitz, Germany. There were dark rectangular objects floating at 28,000 ft. between Chemnitz and Brux. Twenty miles southwest of Chemnitz, five B-17s went down. Ten chutes were seen. Over the Leipzig, Germany area, the bombers split into small groups to bomb various targets. Four contrails believed to be from jets were seen in the target area, northeast of Leipzig. One jet, north of Leipzig hovered above the bombers during their attack. To this date, this was the longest mission, both in time and distance that the group had participated in.

First Lieutenants Victor (Vic) Wolski and James (Jim) E. Frolking became separated from the rest of their 436th FS mates during the chase of the Me 109s and started their return home alone. James Frolking later documented an experience that began during their return and has shared it with the author. Titled "Down in the Dutch Islands", it is reproduced in part here, through his kind permission. He picks up the story from the day's beginning:

> "The large map of Western Europe was uncovered during our pre-mission briefing on 7 October and we learned that our mission was to be a bomber escort to Brux, Czechoslovakia, a location southeast of Berlin, Germany. It would be the longest mission the group was to fly, both in time and distance. Our squadron was called Bison; we were the 'Bison Gang' and I was Bison 58, that being my radio call sign. The group had just completed conversion from P-38s to P-51s and our squadron was last to make the transition in aircraft. The day before, I had flown my brand new P-51 Mustang on a bomber escort mission to Berlin as wingman to our group commander, Col. Hubert 'Hub' Zemke. Having survived the six-hour mission on Col. Zemke's wing, I was feeling pretty good as a seasoned fighter pilot with 51 missions and about 200 combat hours of flying time under my belt.
>
> "For the Brux mission, we took off at 0915 hours. Lt. Wolski was the leader of our Bison Blue Flight and I was element leader to him. As we neared the target area, 30 to 40 Me 109s approached from below us. We immediately

gave chase after dropping our external wing tanks. The German fighters flew into the cloud cover below us and disappeared. During the chase, Lt. Wolski and I became separated from our respective wingmen and the rest of the squadron. We started our return to England alone. Because of the length of the mission and the jettisoning of our wing tanks, we decided to land and refuel at Antwerp, Belgium, rather than risk running out of gas over the North Sea. British forces had advanced into Belgium and the airfield at Antwerp was in their hands at this time. By the time we landed there, we had been in the air for over five hours. While our P-51s were being fueled, we checked into flight operations and received clearance to fly on to England. Ready to continue home, as I settled into the cockpit and strapped on my parachute, seat belt and shoulder harness, I noticed that I had not attached the hooks on my inflatable dinghy. I took care of that and after a wait, we were finally able to taxi to the end of the runway for our engine check. The direction of takeoff would be directly toward the city of Antwerp, which seemed very close to us as I looked ahead, down the runway. At approximately 1630, we started our takeoff roll and advanced full throttle. I was on Lt. Wolski's wing. No sooner had we become airborne and had our wheels retracted when my engine started to cough and sputter. My immediate thought was, 'Here I go, right into the buildings that loomed up ahead!' I reduced throttle and the sputtering stopped! OK! We began a climbing turn and took up a 310-degree heading towards Wattisham, England.

"We were flying abreast in a gradual climb with the Dutch Islands below us. At about 5,000 feet, I noticed light tracers right off Lt. Wolski's tail. I started taking evasive action as I called him on the R/T to warn that someone was shooting at us from the ground. He acknowledged, but kept flying straight ahead. Then I heard and felt a 'clunk' noise in the rear of my plane. I looked around and checked the instrument panel, discovering that my hydraulic pressure gauge was indicating zero. I would have to manually crank the wheels down to land. I'd had that experience several times while flying P-38s. We continued climbing, but within a minute or two, my right rudder pedal dropped from beneath my foot and the rudder pedal cable lay limp on the floor of the cockpit. As I held the left pedal steady, I began to wonder how I was going to land this airplane. Next, my control stick went limp!

Lieutenants James E. Frolking and John G. Glenn. *Courtesy of Herman C. Hoversten.*

The plane was trimmed for a slight climb, but I knew it would be only moments before the plane would be out of control. It was time to bail out.

"I radioed Lt. Wolski that I had been hit and was bailing out. I pulled the canopy release, unbuckled the seat belt and started to stand up. My oxygen mask hose and radio cord were still attached and restricting my attempt to free myself. Time was short, so I just took off my helmet and tossed it aside. Now, I could stand. From the seat, I dove out headfirst towards the right side of the aircraft, pulling the ripcord of my parachute when I had cleared the plane. Since I was wearing a back-pack type parachute, which opened faster than the seat-pack type, I neither felt the chute open nor the anticipated jerk we had been told to expect. I reached down to make sure the dinghy pack was with me, and it was!

"The plane went down into a spiral dive shortly after I left her and I watched as my brand new P-51 exploded on impact in the water below. Suddenly, it was quiet. Land was visible a few miles to the south. As I floated down, I felt secure, although the leg straps of my parachute harness were tight and uncomfortable. During training, we had been instructed that when landing in water, we should release the leg straps, fold our arms across our chest to prevent the harness from slipping free and when we were ten to twenty feet above the water, lift our arms and slide out of the chute into the water. The reasoning was that there was less chance of becoming tangled in the parachute's shroud lines away from it. I remembered though, how difficult it was to judge distance while descending towards the water.

"Abruptly, I splashed into the water. While fumbling around in the water, trying to release the chute strap, remove the harness and inflate my 'Mae West' life vest, I found that I could touch bottom with my feet! To my relief, the water was just chest deep. I unpacked my dinghy and inflated it with its CO_2 cartridge and climbed in, much relieved. I had landed on a sand bar and as I looked around, I could see a portion of the bar that was out of the water about 300 yards away. I paddled towards it.

"Meanwhile, Lt. Wolski, having watched the entire episode from above, circled the area, buzzed me and waggled his wings as I waved to him." Lt. Wolski notified Air Sea Rescue [ASR] that Lt. Frolking had gone down midway between the eastern ends of Schouwen and North Beveland Islands, then continued to circle him until 1900 hours when he was notified that planes were coming to relieve him. He then set course for home, only to find himself in difficulty a short while later. Lt. Wolski's own plane conked out at 1912 hours, possibly due to some AA fire encountered while patrolling over Lt. Frolking. The relief planes never arrived because at first, ASR determined that they were not needed and then later when it was decided that yes, relief was required, it was getting too dark. That left both Lt. Frolking and Lt. Wolski alone and in the water that night. Lt. Wolski was picked up by an ASR launch late afternoon the following day.

"The exposed sand bar was about 50x120 feet with nine bales of hay bunched together at its high point. Knowing that Lt. Wolski had radioed our position, I made the decision to stay on the sand bar in the hope that the British Air Sea Rescue Service would be looking for me. Fortunately, the weather was clear and mild; the water was calm and cool, but not cold. I was unsure of my location, only seeing land to the south, possibly two to four miles from the sand bar. My lightweight flight suit over a wool shirt and pants, plus my leather flight jacket and GI boots, suited me well. Luckily, my cigarettes were in my shirt pocket and had remained dry. The Zippo lighter, which had been in my pants pocket, lighted quickly after blowing on it a few times. We carried an escape kit in the leg pocket of our flight suit. The kit, which contained a map, compass, hard candy, razor and blades, Benzedrine tablets, sewing kit, language card and some French Francs, was sealed and dry, but to my dismay, I had no food or water.

"As the sun lowered and the tide advanced, I had to make a decision whether to stay put or make a dinghy trip to land. When the tide stopped rising, I decided to remain on the sand bar for the night, still hoping for ASR to appear. By this time my clothes and boots were practically dry and the sand bar was now 25x50 feet with the bales of hay still out of the water. It was a starry, moonless night and quite dark. I sat on the sand, leaning against a bale of hay, not wanting to fall asleep. I swallowed some Benzedrine tablets and smoked to stay awake. My thoughts turned to home. My mother would be grieving when she received that inevitable telegram from the War Department. I also wandered about my buddies back at the base and what Lt. Wolski had reported during his debriefing. At the time, I had no idea of his unfortunate episode in the North Sea. It was a lonely night and time passed slowly.

"During the night, a lighted ship approached, passing from west to east and I did something rather stupid. Could it be an ASR ship, I wondered? Hoping against hope, I shot off one of the flares included in the dinghy seat pack. I was standing next to the dinghy and didn't realize the flare had a kick to it when discharged. It popped out of my hand and landed in the center of the dinghy, burning a hole about 1/2 x 3 inches. The ship didn't respond.

"At daylight, the whole area was fogged in with visibility no more than 50 yards. With little wind and calm water, all was quiet. The fog lifted at around 1100 hours and it was another beautiful fall day. With the dinghy unusable, I put on my Mae West and waded into the water with my boots tied to the Mae West strap. The water was colder than I remembered from the day before and as it suddenly deepened, I remembered the sewing kit. Maybe my memory was awakened by the shock of the water and the distance of the land to the south. I retreated to repair the hole in the dinghy. The sewing job went well and when I was done, I inflated the dinghy with its fabric hand pump. I launched my boat at about 1300 hours. Although the dinghy had a sail, its two-piece horizontal board became my paddles. I was battling the current, which drew me laterally to my intended direction, but the company of a pair of porpoises made the journey interesting enough. The sewing repair held fast and didn't leak a drop.

"As I neared land at 1500 hours, I could see a dike along the shoreline. A solid wooden fence stood at the bottom of the 12 to 15 foot high dike. This short stretch of fence provided the perfect place to stash the dinghy and conceal it from someone walking above on the dike. I walked cautiously around the fence and slowly crawled to the top. I looked in both directions along the dike-top road and saw two men in civilian clothes, talking to one another about 150 yards to my left. I approached them in a friendly manner and it was obvious that they knew it was me who had parachuted from the downed plane. We walked a short distance to a small farmhouse, the only building in sight. It was the home of a young couple with an infant. The two men and the couple talked in Dutch and I soon found myself being escorted up a ladder to a second floor loft. The food and tea given me shortly thereafter was the first I'd had in about 36 hours. Reflecting on my good fortune, I fell asleep.

"The next day, October 9th, the same two men from the dike came to see me. We couldn't easily converse, but using the map, I learned that I was on the island of Noord (North) Beveland. I had wrongly assumed that I was on the Dutch mainland. Furthermore, the men said that the British forces were on the other side of the island, which I felt certain was not true. According to what I knew, the advancing allies were still in Belgium and had not yet crossed north into Holland. It became clear to me that these men wanted my stay in their area to be a short one. I could understand their reticence for I knew the consequences for them to be caught aiding me would be extreme. By means of the language card from my escape kit, I established that I would be moved on when it became dark. I thanked them as best as I could.

"At dark, one of the men led me down a road for about a half mile, advised me to continue walking on this road and bid me farewell. It was dark – no stars, no moon, no light. Finding my way was difficult. I passed some farmhouses and eventually an artillery battle began off in the distance. I learned later that the battle was on neighboring Walcheren Island and was a part of the Canadian Army's offensive. At some point, I came to a fork in the road and chose the left fork, being a left-hander. After walking a short distance, I came upon a barricade with a sign reading '*Verboten*'. Turning around, I headed for the right fork and eventually came upon a village. Having been advised in training, never to enter a town or village at night, I retraced my steps about a half-mile until I came upon a group of houses. Near one was a hay wagon. I crawled under it, covered myself with hay and went soundly asleep.

"Early daylight saw me awakened with a start and a sense that someone was nearby. It turned out to be a horse near the wagon. In a short while, he wandered off into the pasture and after making sure no one was in the area, I went to the nearest house. I knocked on the door and eventually was greeted by a young boy. I showed him the Dutch phrase on my language card that stated 'I am an American pilot'. He was obviously confused, for he turned around and left, leaving the door partially open. Shortly, the boy's father came to the door and I showed him the card. Looking me over, he immediately invited me into the house. I was taken upstairs to a room where I was made to understand I was to stay. Eventually food, drink, a towel and washcloth were brought to me and I ate and cleaned up. I felt better. "Later that morning, another man came into the room and handed me a sheet of paper typewritten in English, telling me that contact with the Dutch Underground had been made and that arrangements for my stay and eventual return to allied forces were being made. It detailed that the plan was to provide me with a set of civilian clothes and move me at dark to another location. They took the photos from my escape kit and made a print of my right index finger for a set of phony I.D. cards.

"Later that day, at dusk, a man arrived with a set of clothes for me. I changed, keeping only my GI boots and my dog tags, then off we rode into the night on bicycles. We eventually came to a farm in the village of Kats. We went to the back entrance of the house where I was motioned to wait by a tree. After a short wait, a young man came out of the house and greeted me in English. What a pleasant surprise! His name was Willem de Vor and he was a policeman, active with the Dutch Underground. He told me that I would be staying at this farm for the time being. It belonged to Izak and Marie van der Maas, who also had a five-year-old son, named Huib. We had arrived after Huib's bedtime as was intended. Marie served some tea and we became acquainted and the daily routine was explained. I was to remain in my bedroom until after dark and when young Huib was asleep, I was allowed downstairs to be with Izak and Marie, given my evening meal and permitted a trip to the bathroom. My room was accessed by a stair/ ladder and had a skylight, but no windows. There was also a storeroom there which had a hiding place concealed by a removable wall panel.

"Willem de Vor visited most evenings and since he spoke fluent English, we were able to converse, talking about the war, Holland, America and my flying experiences. Most of the evenings, the area was without electricity so candles provided our light. Occasionally, it was on and during those times, we listened to the BBC radio broadcasts for news of the war. Those times together were a comfort to me and served to relax me. During the day, tension would build in me because we were in enemy-held territory and in my windowless room, every noise from the outside brought dread. I was in good hands, however. Izak and Marie were prepared to help downed allied airmen and I wasn't the first to have received their hospitality. Settling into a routine, it was decided that I would remain there with them until the allies were close enough to be contacted and shortly afterwards, I was given a false photo I.D. card. I was now Nico van der Maas, a cousin of Izak and Marie. I was listed as a deaf and dumb baker living at the van der Maas farm.

"Marie van der Maas had scheduled some house cleaners to come some weeks before my arrival on the scene, this being a regular occurrence a few times a year. She did not want to disrupt the schedule as that could create some suspicion so I had to be moved to a neighboring village where Izak's father and mother lived. From the second floor room where I stayed, I could look out a window through the typical Dutch lace curtains and watch German soldiers walking along the road about 50 feet from the house. They were the first that I had seen. Five days later, I was returned to the farm.

"The days were long, the isolation being broken only by Marie bringing me my morning and noon meals and the books that she provided. I did exercises daily and moved about as much as I could in the room. I was grateful for the comfort and care, however. German troops were being pushed north and east by the advancing Canadian and British armies and a few times when little Huib was out of the house with his father, I was allowed downstairs, where I could look out from behind a lace-curtained window and watch the retreating German soldiers. Resting from their march, they would relax in the yard between the house and barns and fill their canteens with water from the well. Seeing all this activity, I figured it wouldn't be long before the Allies reached this island. Late one evening after dinner, while I was in the bathroom, which was off the small back entrance hallway, there was a knock on the back door. A signal word had been established that warned me to leave the bathroom immediately and head for my second floor room as quickly and as quietly as I could. I heard the knock, readied myself and waited. Willem, who was visiting at the time, and Izak went to the door, opened it and saw three German Army officers. Izak moved outside, closing the door behind him as Willem opened the bathroom door and gave me the signal. It didn't take me but seconds to get to my room. The Germans were not looking for anyone; they merely wanted a place to stay for the night. They were put in the spare bedroom on the first floor. It was directly below mine and I could hear their voices before they went to sleep and again in the morning before they left. I could not sleep the whole night and just laid motionless on my bed until Marie brought me breakfast and I knew that the Germans had left.

"A day or two after that, with no advance notice, I was taken to a nearby boat dock where two men rowed me across the causeway to the island of Zuid (South) Beveland. They directed me toward a small village nearby. It was there that I made contact with a Canadian army reconnaissance team, The Royal Canadian Dragoons. I was standing along the side of a road in this village when they drove up and stopped. As I introduced myself, the first comment by one of the Canadian troopers was 'We find you guys in the oddest places!' This all happened so fast that I didn't get the chance to say thank you or goodbye to Izak, Marie and Willem. I wanted to return to do so, but the Canadians wouldn't allow it because they had not liberated that island yet and there was the possibility of a few Germans lingering in the area.

"I spent the day with the Dragoons as they moved around the island, looking for German collaborators. We searched a small cabin cruiser belonging to a suspected collaborator and found some evidence in support of their suspicions. That evening I was driven by truck to Antwerp, Belgium where I was interrogated for three days by Canadian Intelligence and given a thorough physical exam. I was found to have contracted a case of Scabies during my stay on Noord Beveland and the treatment prescribed, was soaking for hours in a bathtub filled with some purple liquid. Fortunately, it washed off. The interrogating officer facilitated the sending of a cablegram to my mother to let her know that I was safe and uninjured. The last day I spent with them, I had to sign some documents, was issued a Canadian uniform without insignia and was given some money for a night out on the town. The next morning I was on my way back to London, England by C-47 transport. My squadron had been advised I was returning and my roommate and best army buddy, Edwin [Ed] J. Fillipow flew to London to meet me and to bring me a uniform to wear. Unfortunately, we missed connections and I returned to Wattisham as an unidentified Canadian soldier.

"Because I was classified as an 'Evadee,' my tour of duty in the European Theater of Operations was at an end, since there was a chance of my being captured should I ever be forced down again. In that event, I would have knowledge of those who had helped me and that would place them at risk. I left Wattisham and flew back to the States in a C-54 military transport Thanksgiving Day."

9 October 1944

VIII FC FO 603

No. 171 Monday. Lt. Col. Herren led the group, which consisted of 47 P-51s (16-434th, 17-435th & 14-436th) on a bomber escort for 2nd BD B-24s attacking their 8th AF Mission 670 secondary target, the marshalling yards at Koblenz, Germany. Up: 1300 hrs., down: 1730 hrs. with five early returns plus one escort.

R/V with the group's charge, the 20th CW, was made 15 miles south of Liege, belgium at 1410 hrs./21,000 ft. Split into two forces of 30 P-51s each, the group escorted the bombers on an uneventful mission that saw no enemy A/C. Flak was heavy to moderate, but inaccurate at 26,000 ft. in the target area. The group left the B-24s at 1605 hrs./24,000 ft. above an overcast sky. After L/O, the 436th FS patrolled the Walcheren Island, Holland area forty minutes in search of Lt. James E. Frolking who went down two days prior, on the seventh of October. No sightings were made. Two pilots from the 434th FS did not return with the group to Wattisham. Lieutenants Harold (Bud) F. Grenning and Douglas T. Holmes landed in the vicinity of Brussels, Belgium for unknown reasons.

Observations made during the mission included sighting a rocket trail extending from the Dutch Islands up to 30,000 ft.

Lieutenant Gerold M. Mulvany seated in the cockpit of a P-51. Note the piece of duct tape applied to the fuselage just below the forward part of the windscreen. That particular product has been around for longer than most of us think! *Courtesy of Sally Mulvany.*

12 October 1944

Eighth AF FO 1235A

No. 172 Thursday. Lt. Col. Riddle led the group, which consisted of 40 P-51s (14-434th, 14-435th & 12-436th) on a penetration to target and withdrawal escort for 2nd BD B-24s attacking their 8th AF Mission 674 secondary target, the marshalling yards at Osnabrück, Germany. Up: 0959 hrs., down: 1343 hrs. with three early returns.

R/V with the group's charge, the 14th CW, was made at 1100 hrs./18,000 ft. over the Zuider Zee. After making L/F, an Me 262 in the vicinity of Enschede, Holland made several passes at 25,000 ft. without firing. The 436th FS dropped their wing tanks and gave chase from 1120 to 1135 hours, pursuing the jet from Zwolle to Arnhem, Holland. They were not able to close on the enemy A/C, which disappeared east at a speed over 550 mph, IAS. It is possible that the purpose of the jet's tactics was to force the squadron to drop their tanks. The 434th FS and 435th FS continued to escort the proper bombers while the 436th FS escorted some unidentified B-24s through the target and back to the coast. No other enemy A/C was seen. The bombing was believed to be good. Flak over the target was heavy, meager and inaccurate, none-the-less, one bomber went down in that location. There were no chutes spotted. Upon returning, the area around Wattisham was experiencing some bad weather, forcing many of the group's A/C to divert to other fields. Seventeen landed at Martlesham Heath, six went to Rattlesden and one to Great Ashfield. Most had dinner where they landed and then returned home just before dark.

Gerold M. Mulvany a pilot assigned to the 436th FS usually had no difficulties in finding Wattisham. His method:

"I could always find our airfield in the soup. Some of the newer pilots said I must be able to smell the large burned out hangars on the base. I really came in on the deck and followed my time and distance points from the Wash, a prominent coastal feature a captured German pilot had said he used to find Wattisham when they came in on bomb runs. We met him when he was brought through our base."

14 October 1944

Eighth AF FO 1238A

No. 173 Saturday. Lt. Col. Riddle led the group, which consisted of 48 P-51s (17-434th, 18-435th & 13-436th) on a penetration to target and withdrawal escort for 2nd BD B-24s attacking their 8th AF Mission 676 primary target at Kaiserslautern, Germany. Up: 1052 hrs., down: 1515 hrs. with three early returns.

R/V with the group's charges, the 14th and the 96th CW bombers, was made in the vicinity of St. Vith, Belgium at 1215 hrs./22,000 ft. The heavies bombed through the cloud cover yielding unknown results. No enemy A/C were active in the area, but flak was heavy, meager and inaccurate at 21,000 ft. over the target. An unidentified bomber was reported as going to belly in about 17 miles east of Trier, Germany. L/O was over Ostend, belgium at 1415 hrs./2,000 ft.

Observations made during the mission included sighting a single contrail at 1310 hrs./30-35,000 feet, about 30 miles northeast of Antwerp, Belgium and an unidentified P-51 was seen to belly in south of Charleroi, Belgium at 1400 hrs.

15 October 1944

Eighth AF FO 1240A

No. 174 Sunday. Col. Zemke led the group, which consisted of 42 P-51s (16-434th, 17-435th & 9-436th) on a penetration to target and withdrawal escort for 2nd BD B-24s attacking their 8th AF Mission 678 target near Dusseldorf, Germany. Up: 0826 hrs., down: 1340 hrs. with three early returns.

R/V with the group's charges, the 2nd and 96th CWs, was made over the North Sea off Walcheren Island, Holland at 0900 hrs./15,000 ft. The bombers were strung out, but the group escorted them through the target where the bombing appeared excellent. The Big Friends were trying a new formation, utilizing spread out elements that seemed to confuse the flak gunners. Flak was heavy, moderate and very inaccurate at 24,000 ft over the target. At 1030 hours, one unidentified A/C on fire, spun in near St. Goar, Germany. It was too far to see if there were any chutes. After separating from the heavies in the area over Vielslam, Belgium at 1050 hrs./25,000 feet, a lone B-17 straggler, Vinegrove 2-7, was encountered. The pilot said he had two wounded on board and was going to land at Brussels, Belgium. The group then turned north to the Arnhem, Holland area, then east to Münster, Germany and on over to survey Gutersloh, Germany. Arriving over the Gutersloh airdrome at 1220 hrs./9,000 feet, it was noted to be filled with A/C, well dispersed in revetments and wooded areas. Nine mottled, twin-engine A/C, mostly He 111s and three unidentified, silver twin-engine A/C were reported there. The group did not strafe and the trip was uneventful. No enemy A/C were seen in the air, but a lot of unidentified highway convoy activity was observed heading east between Wesel and Münster. Heavy train activity was also seen traveling both ways between Gutersloh and Hamm. A rocket was noted climbing into the air near Trier, Germany.

17 October 1944

Eighth AF FO 1245A

No. 175 Tuesday. Lt. Col. Woods led the group, which consisted of 47 P-51s (17-434th, 18-435th & 12-436th) on a penetration to target and withdrawal escort for 2nd BD B-24s attacking their 8th AF Mission 681 target of opportunity, a marshalling yard in Cologne, Germany. The primary targets, chemical production facilities at Leverkusen, Germany were not attacked because of adverse weather conditions. Up: 0819 hrs., down: 1233 hrs. with one early return.

R/Vs with the bombers occurred over the North Sea and Knokke, Belgium while two of the squadrons made R/V with the group's charge, the 14th CW, east of Namur, Belgium and south of Aachen, Germany at 0923 hrs./20,000 ft. The mission was uneventful with the Big Friends bombing through the overcast. Results were not observed. Flak over the target was heavy, intense and accurate. The B-24s were escorted to the coast at Coxyde, Belgium where the group broke away at 1135 hrs./1000 ft.

Observations made during the mission included two rockets, one at 1000 hours, the other at 1010 hrs, seen to be climbing at a 60-degree angle from the Frankfurt, Germany

434th FS D Flight's Flight Chief, Master Sergeant James W. Smart and First Lieutenant Harold F. (Bud) Grenning, Jr. by Flat Top Jr. *Courtesy of James W. Smart.*

The original drawing of Flat Top that Chester Gould sent to Lt. Harold F. Grenning, Jr. *Courtesy of Harold F. Grenning.*

area and generally headed towards England. Another rocket was noted climbing at a similar angle from southwest of Koblenz, Germany. Two jet contrails were seen at 1000 hrs./ 35,000 ft. in the vicinity of St. Goar, Germany. Flak at Weisbaden, Germany was heavy, intense and accurate while flak five miles south of Düren, Germany was heavy, meager and inaccurate.

During 1998 Bud Grenning wrote:

> "By the time we got our brand new P-51s, I had picked the name Flat Top. I picked the name because of a combination of my 'hair style' and a Dick Tracy comic strip character called Flat Top. My buddy Bill Hehn [William H. Hehn] was called Stoneface after a Li'l Abner comic strip character. At the time, my parents knew Chester Gould, the creator of the Dick Tracy comic strip and happened to tell him about me, where I was and what I was doing. He sent me a note and a personal drawing of Flat Top. So when the guys were having nose art done on the P-51s, most of them were given the same name that their P-38s had worn, but with the addition of 'Jr.' Since I didn't care to name mine No Guts? Jr., I had chosen the name Flat Top and Sergeant Fred Hayner [Frederick C. Hayner] our squadron painter painted that on the plane's nose. Some time after I finished my tour, Dave Born [David L. Born] got Flat Top Jr. and renamed it Just Born."

18 October 1944

Eighth AF FO 1246A

No. 176 Wednesday. Lt. Col. Riddle led the group, which consisted of 47 P-51s (17-434th, 18-435th & 12 436th) on a penetration to target and withdrawal escort for 2nd BD B-24s attacking their 8th AF Mission 682 target in the Köln, Germany area. Up: 0947 hrs., down: 1355 hrs. with five early returns.

R/V with the mixed lot of bombers was ten miles west of Kiln, Germany at 1056hrs./24,000 ft. The bombers were late. They were escorted uneventfully through the target and back. Flak at the target was heavy, intense and accurate at 22,000 ft. No enemy A/C were seen. The group broke off escort in the vicinity of Brussels, Belgium. Due to the group's extensive flight time this escort, 13 pilots and their A/C were not able to return to Wattisham with the group because of fuel shortages.

From the 434th FS, Lieutenants Richard D. Creighton, Edward L. Hurtig and John T. Tipps landed at Brussels along with Lieutenants Ray K. Friend and Charles E. Monsell, Jr. from the 435th FS. Captain William Gates, Lieutenants William M. Barsky, Norman R. Benoit, Martin G. Gorian, David E. King, James H. Koerber, William F. Maier and William H. Pickering, all from the 435th FS, landed at either Brussels or St. Trond, Belgium.

Observations made during the mission included the sightings of one Big Ben contrail extending from 5,000 to 18,000 ft. at a 70-degree angle in the vicinity of Zuid Beveland, Holland, another Big Ben contrail two miles west of Bonn, Germany extending from 18-35,000 ft. at a 70-degree angle, another in the vicinity of Mannheim, Germany same altitudes and heading, and yet another in the vicinity of St. Vith, Belgium rising to 35,000 ft. and at a 70-degree angle. All rockets were heading west. Flak was heavy, moderate and accurate at 20-30,000 ft. along the Rhine River south of Koblenz, Germany and heavy, meager and inaccurate at 20,000 ft. west of Koblenz.

This was John W. Hedenberg's last combat mission. He wrote that it was a very ordinary run with lots of flak. After the group returned to Wattisham, he noted in his diary that: "Felt pretty good to set the old clunk down for the last time and realize I didn't have to stand for being shot at any more." John left for the ZOI on 13 November 1944.

Lieutenant George W. Gleason is seated in one of the Newcross Squadron P-51s. *Courtesy of George S. Gleason.*

Lieutenant Eugene E. (Elmo) Sears and his P-51 American Maid. Lt. Sears did his own artwork on the nose of the plane he flew. He also did the art on two other P-51s, Burn'n Bernie for his roommate Lieutenant Gail E. Jacobson and "Super Wabbit" for Lieutenant Richard D. Creighton. *From original 479th FG history.*

19 October 1944

Eighth AF FO 1249A

No. 177 Thursday. Col. Zemke led the group, which consisted of 45 P-51s (18-434th, 12-435th & 15-436th) on a penetration to target and withdrawal escort for 2nd BD B-24s attacking their 8th AF Mission 683 secondary target, the marshalling yards at Mainz, Germany. Up: 1050 hrs., down: 1647 hrs. with three early returns. R/V with the B-24s was above the overcast at 1201 hrs./21-26,000 ft.

The group drove [sic] down the column to the 4th CW, the bombers assigned to escorted. Some of the Big Friends were scattered while others were in good formation. The bombing results at Mainz were unobserved due to overcast. Flak, as seen at 27,000 ft. over the target, was heavy, intense, but inaccurate. At 1300 hours, one B-24 was seen going down from 15,000 ft. in the vicinity of the target. Six or seven chutes were noted. The group began a sweep east of the target, going about 25 miles, but the weather forced abandonment of that. Returning to the bombers at the Moselle River, north of Trier, the group accompanied them back until escort was broken over Ghent, Belgium. The group then went down under the cloud base, sweeping east, to north of Liège, Belgium and back to the coast, then heading down to Dunkerque and Calais, arriving in that vicinity at about 1620 to 1630 hrs. Allied gun emplacements one-half to one mile east of Calais fired on the fighters at that time. One A/C from the 434th FS, piloted by Lieutenant George W. Gleason, was hit about a mile southwest of Calais. Streaming oil and coolant at 1500 feet, he was instructed to bail out. Lt. Gleason asked if he was over friendly territory and was told he was. Lt. Gleason was understandably upset at this point and was heard to utter over the air: "Those son's of bitches..." just before his mike cord disconnected as he raised up to jump. He then left the A/C, but struck his ankle on the plane's tail as the doomed bird passed beneath his decelerating form. He opened his parachute and floated down, not realizing that he had suffered a broken ankle from the blow he received until he landed.

From there, while still under the cloud base, the group headed home. As they left the area, Lieutenant Eugene E. (Elmo) Sears, who was in the same flight as Lt. Gleason, watched that lonely parachute drift down as long as he could see it. Lt. Gleason was soon picked up and hospitalized by allied troops, first in Brussels, then in England. Back at Wattisham, the group's commander, Colonel Zemke, quickly made it known that he certainly appreciated the efficient manner in which their allies fired upon and shot down one of his returning fighters.

Three pilots, Lieutenants John T. (Tom) Tipps, Richard D. (Dick) Creighton and Edward L. Hurtig, took to the air and headed for home this day. They had landed the previous day at Brussels, Belgium because of flak damage to one of the aircraft, this having occurred during the group's mission to Köln, Germany. Lt. Tipps had led the flight, short one aircraft that had to abort early in the mission. The original intent was for the pilot of the damaged P-51 to leave his plane to be repaired and ride back to Wattisham on the lap of Lt. Tipps. After they had landed at Brussels, it was discovered that the damage was not serious enough to warrant leaving the plane behind. Lt. Tipps also discovered that he too, had some minor flak damage to his right wing, out towards the wing tip, in the vicinity of the aircraft's pitot tube. It seemed insignificant at the time. Taking off, they ran into some bad weather and while in a storm front, Lt. Tipps encountered a problem.

Tom Tipps, even now, remembers well what happened to him that day:

> "I had flown sixty missions prior to this one and had gained a lot of experience flying on instruments. We were climbing up through the clouds at 120 MPH and had reached around 20,000 feet. At that point, I noted that my airspeed was still showing 120 indicated, but my altimeter had begun going around and around and around! I was in a spin! It wasn't a head-down spin, but a stalled out, flat spin going around and around. I had no control over the aircraft, the stick and rudder pedals were ineffective. I was being badly knocked around inside the plane by the violent forces that controlled it. I knew after briefly trying to regain control, that I had no other choice, but to bail out, for there would be no reigning this beast in. I unloosened my seat belt and somehow got out. I really don't know how I did, but I was free of the ship and not hurt. I reached for my ripcord, but it wasn't there! (It had become tangled up in my shoulder straps.) I thought: 'Oh my God, I've lost my parachute!' I looked back and saw that it was still there so I reached back, found the cord and pulled it out by hand. The chute opened and I began to float downward.
>
> "It was a long flight down with nothing to do and nothing to see because of the clouds. Finally, I saw that I was coming down over a wooded area. I tried to control the decent by tugging on the risers, but to no avail. Boom! I hit a tree! My legs were separated and my left leg was twisted up, torn and broken so that it was only just barely hanging on. There I hung, all messed up, stuck up in a tree and to top it all off, it was snowing! I thought to myself: 'Damn! This is a hell of a note! The world's greatest fighter pilot is going to die in a damn tree!' It was kind of a lonesome feeling. I couldn't get down, I couldn't get up, I couldn't do anything. I thought that I was going to have to shoot myself, but I'd lost my .45 in the bail out. So I got into my escape kit and shot myself up with some morphine. I thought: 'Well I'll die happy, anyway.' I was feeling pretty good there for awhile, but all at once I heard a cowbell. There were three little 'ole cows coming through the woods with about a twelve-year-old girl herding them. I yelled down to her. I thought that

Crew chief Technical Sergeant Cullie D. Flynn and Lieutenant John T. Tipps by their P-51, The Wildcat. *Courtesy of Frederick C. Hayner.*

if I was in Germany, I'd rather get it over with than hang up there and freeze to death.

"They took off and in a little while she brought an old man about sixty to the tree where I was hanging. He was carrying a big old long barreled muzzle-loader rifle. Looking up at me, he called out; 'Bosch?' I replied: 'No, Americano!' He was a Belgian. They got a ladder and brought me down, putting me in a wheelbarrow. I'd been in that tree for two or three hours and I was hurting. Well, while I couldn't understand them and they couldn't understand me, once I was in that wheelbarrow, I said: 'Hell, Drive on!' They took me up to a house and pretty soon a Canadian Army truck came by. It had a steel bed on it and I was loaded on that. About that time, I passed out. I came to, about ten days later. I was in a hospital ward, incased within a big old body cast.

"Some days later, I happened to look up from my bed and saw my roommate from Wattisham, George Gleason, hobbling by on crutches. I flung a pitcher of water at him to get his attention. Lt. Gleason recognized me when he came over to see just who it was that just missed his head with that water pitcher. "Tipps, you SOB, I though you were dead!" said Lt. Gleason. Well, I told him I was pretty close, but still alive. The funny thing was that I thought he was dead after having been shot down over Calais. I enjoyed convalescing with George until I was shipped back to the states. When it was time for me to leave, I told him goodbye and he said that he would see me sometime in the USA. Unfortunately, we never saw each other again."

22 October 1944

Eighth AF FO 1254A

No. 178 Sunday. Lt. Col. Woods led the group, which consisted of 52 P-51s (17-434th, 18-435th & 17-436th) on a penetration to target and withdrawal escort for 2nd BD B-24s attacking their 8th AF Mission 685 primary target, the marshalling yards at Hamm, Germany. Up: 1120 hrs., down: 1550 hrs. with eight early returns.

R/V with the group's charge, the 2nd CW, occurred at 1320 hrs./25,000 ft. in the vicinity of Dümmer Lake, Germany.

First Lieutenant Price E. Henry is shown being congratulated by First Lieutenant Andre E. Huycke upon the completion of his combat tour. The two had both started at the same time in California with the 436th FS and should have finished up their combat hours about the same time. Lt. Huycke however, had chosen to extend his combat time and remained at Wattisham until December. *Courtesy of Herman C. Hoversten.*

The bombers were in good formation. Overcast weather prevented seeing the bombing or making any observations. Flak over the target as seen from 26,000 ft. was heavy, meager and inaccurate. There were no enemy A/C in the air and the mission was uneventful. Flak over Dümmer Lake was heavy, moderate and inaccurate while over Mersfeld, Germany, it was heavy, meager and inaccurate. The group separated from the bombers over the North Sea at 1525 hrs./15,000 ft.

25 October 1944

Eighth AF FO 1263A

No. 179 Wednesday. Col. Zemke led the group, which consisted of 51 P-51s (16-434th, 17-435th & 18-436th) on a

Right: Colonel Hubert Zemke beside his P-51, 9B-Z. He had recently shifted his presence from Lakeside Squadron to Bison Squadron. *Courtesy of Flamm D. Harper.*

patrol and escort of 1st BD B-17s attacking their 8th AF Mission 688 secondary target, oil refineries at Hamburg, Germany. Up: 1120 hrs., down: 1550 hrs. with nine early returns plus one escort.

The group patrolled Bremen to Lüneburg, Germany from 1235 to 1320 hrs. at 28-30,000 ft. No enemy A/C was seen. The B-17s bombed through overcast, so results were not observable. Flak over the target was heavy, intense and inaccurate. Flak over Neumünster, Germany was heavy, meager and inaccurate. The group did see two Big Ben contrails, one over the Ruhr area in Germany at 1205 hrs./ 16,000 ft. heading west and one over Wesermünde, Germany at 1420 hrs./45,000 ft. The mission was uneventful and the group separated from the bombers over the North Sea at 1430 hrs./28,000 ft.

30 October 1944

Eighth AF FO 1273A

No. 180 Monday. Col. Zemke led the group, which consisted of 62 P-51s (22-434th, 18-435th & 22-436th) on a penetration to target and withdrawal escort for 2nd BD B-24s attacking their 8th AF Mission 693 primary target, oil refineries at Hamburg, Germany. The group was divided into two sections; A section, led by Colonel Zemke and B section, led by Lieutenant Colonel Riddle. A section up: 1043 hrs., down: 1536 hrs. and B section up: 1112 hrs., down: 1600 hrs. with five early returns from the group.

The weather forecast for the mission called for visibility from air to ground over the target area to be ten to fifteen miles and air-to-air visibility to be unlimited. The forecast was wrong. When the group left Wattisham, the skies were clear there, but as they crossed the North Sea and headed towards land, they began to encounter a cloud build up. A section made L/F over the cloud shrouded continent and R/V'd with the 2nd CW bombers at 1210 hrs./25,000 feet, place unknown. All around were great, billowing stacks of cumulus clouds, rising three to four miles high from the ground. Escorting the Liberators became an effort of hide and seek. When the unwavering bombers entered the large banks of clouds, the accompanying fighters, for the sake of safety, would dodge around, above and below those clouds trying to meet the Big Friends on the other side. Pressing on and pulling contrails that turned to rime ice, A section continued the escort duty on a 70-degree heading. At 1310 hours, southeast of Hamburg,

Lieutenant Richard D. Creighton. *Courtesy of David L. Born.*

the bombers entered a huge, tall front that loomed up ahead. That presented Col. Zemke with the tough choice of going through it or loosing the bombers. Tightening the formation in order to maintain visual contact with each other, they plunged in at 24,000 ft. As soon as the section entered the murk, it became difficult for the pilots to see each other. The turbulence was violent and the fighters began to be bounced around. Any thoughts of finding the bombers quickly disappeared as the men fought the weather rather than the Germans. Col. Zemke quickly called for the section to turn around and head out of the front. He then banked left. At this point, the forces of nature took charge.

At 1315 hours, at a spot believed to be about 20 miles north of Celle, Germany, Col. Zemke and some of his force fought for their lives, in varying degrees, with a different enemy. Most were successful in their struggles, but some were not. The colonel and other men from the 434th FS: Lieutenant Colonel James M. Herren, Jr., the squadron's CO, as well as Lieutenants Harold M. Jenkins, Jr., Richard D. Creighton, Walter M. Drake, Douglas T. Holmes and Gail E. Jacobson, all battled the weather in their planes. Col. Zemke was tossed into a bad spin. Recovering from that, he found himself in a dive, still encased in the dark storm clouds. While gradually pulling out of the dive, the Col's P-51 disintegrated from the stresses and he was miraculously thrown free. Able to separate himself from the seat he was still attached to, Col. Hubert Zemke, on his last mission with the 479th FG before he was to give up his combat command and return stateside, opened his parachute and floated down to German soil. He was captured and become a POW the next day. His packed bags at Wattisham went waiting for his return.

Lt. Richard Creighton, Col. Zemke's wingman, followed the turn and found himself losing control of his A/C. He was in an uncontrollable spin, diving down from 24,000 ft. He tried to bail out of the seemingly doomed airplane, but his canopy would not open. With nothing else left to do, Lt. Creighton once again tried to get his Mustang out of the spin it was in. He had already lost 14,000 ft. Gradually, the A/C's nose came up as the airspeed was indicating 550 mph. Recovering at below 3,000 feet, he began a climb back to altitude. Lt. Creighton had pulled nine-and-a-half Gs.

Lt. Walter Drake, leader of the second element in Col. Zemke's flight, also tried to follow the turn. Walter (Walt) Drake, in recently documenting his experiences as a pilot with the 434th FS, told of his difficulties in the storm front that day:

> "The weather was extremely bad and my P-51 pitched and vibrated as we fought our way through the weather. I saw Col. Zemke flip over on his back and before I knew it, the same turbulence flipped me over too and began to spin and snap the plane downward. The gyros tumbled and were useless. I was hanging upside down from the seat belt and lost all sight of the rest of the flight as well as all orientation. I watched my wing tanks break loose and roll off the wings. In doing so, they hit my flaps and damaged them. I knew that I was in trouble. My airspeed was building and I began a furious struggle to regain control of the airplane. I felt my limbs grow numb as the plane fell faster and faster. The airspeed needle rose to 500 mph and I knew I was in an absolute vertical dive. I pulled back on my control stick and watched the airspeed slow to 100 mph. I figured I had gone from a steep dive to a climb, but I had no reference point and no horizon. I was completely disoriented. The air turbulence was horrific and bounced me around inside the cockpit like a pea in a jar. I tried to release the canopy several times to bail out, but I was unsuccessful. I needed both hands on the stick and I was still losing altitude quickly.

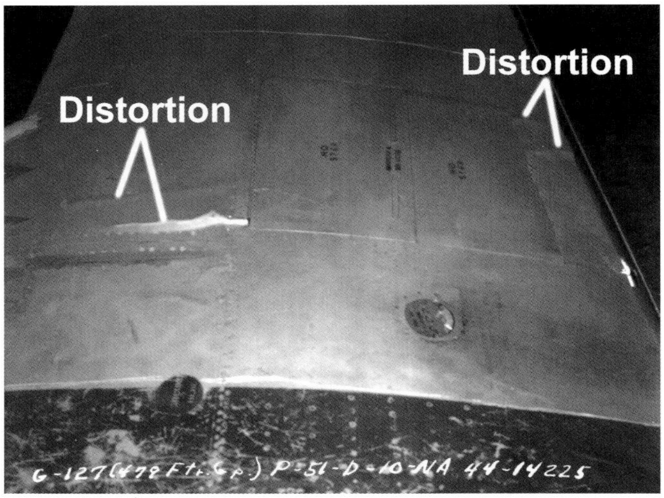

A photo showing one of the overstressed wings. Wrinkles can be seen formed in several places, both ahead and behind the gun bay doors. *Courtesy of the Wings of Freedom Museum.*

Lieutenant Walter M. Drake. *Courtesy of Berkley E. Hollister.*

> "The entire episode was very confusing and frightening, for each time, just when I thought I was getting control, my instruments would indicate otherwise. In the midst of this chaotic situation and with only moments before the plane would augur in, I remembered my training instructor teaching us to use the airspeed, needle ball, and altimeter gauges together to control the plane. I concentrated on flying by those three instruments and it

Margie, the P-51 that Lt. Walter Drake had named after his wife was not flown by him that day and thus escaped damage from the storm. However, the plane was lost due to an unknown cause 29 November 1944. *Courtesy of the 436th Fighter Squadron Association.*

worked. I broke through the cloud ceiling at 500 feet and still in a steep dive, but no longer twisting and turning out of control. I pulled out of the dive at tree-top level and regained attitude to the cloud ceiling. I was thankful to be alive. This was the last week of my combat tour and I had come within thirty seconds of crashing into the German countryside. I took a moment to look around for other members of the squadron, but no one was there. I used my magnetic compass and flew for England. I was mentally drained and ready to end this flight, but my thrills were not over.

"As I turned towards England, I tried to contact Wattisham and get a course heading to confirm my current heading. I tried several times to raise Wattisham while I continued to fly by my magnetic compass, but without success. The return flight was mostly over the North Sea and as I flew, I tried to radio the base. I had the engine running as slow as possible to conserve fuel and I kept a sharp look out for any planes, friend or foe. I was over the ocean when at last the radio came alive. The radio operator told me to change my course by sixty degrees! I was dumb founded. Change course by sixty degrees? Immediately I thought this was a ruse by the Germans to send me out into the North Sea where I would run out of fuel and perish. They were known to do that and by speaking in everyday English, you had no idea they were leading you astray. I flew for a moment longer and decided to trust the voice over the radio and change course. Once on my new heading I scanned the horizon looking for England's coast. After thirty minutes I crossed the English beaches near the Wash. The radio operator was for real and his directions saved my life.

Lieutenant Colonel James M. Herren, Jr. *Courtesy of Berkley E. Hollister.*

Left: Lieutenant Harold M. Jenkins. *Courtesy of David L. Born.* Right: Crew chief Sergeant John E. Wendt is shown by his P-51 that Lieutenant Richard M. Lunstrum, who is also shown, sometimes flew. At a point in time, the plane had been lettered Satan's Agent by Sergeant Frederick C. Hayner, the 434th FS resident painter/artist. Unfortunately, the paint was not dry before the aircraft had to be flown, hence some of the still wet lettering was streaked back from the wind force. It gave the nose art an appearance of "blurred speed". *From original 479th FG history.*

> "Back at Wattisham, the plane was scrapped. The wings were rippled and the rear stabilizers were bent up ward. The plane's accelerometer was pegged at nine Gs."

Walt gives all of the credit for his surviving the war to the Almighty God above, but he gives some credit to the G-Suit he was wearing that day.

Lt. Drake's wingman, Lt. Douglas Holmes, was number four in the flight. He suffered circumstances similar to those of Col. Zemke and disappeared completely at this time. Caught in the storm and torn by the forces of nature, Lt. Holmes bailed out of his damaged and uncontrollable A/C. Once on the ground, he was quickly captured and became another POW. Both he and the wreckage of his plane had come down near Offen, a small town about ten miles north of Celle. A few weeks later, he encountered his flight leader, Col. Zemke at the German *Dulag Luft* prisoner processing and distribution center at Wetzlar, north of Frankfurt, Germany.

Lt. Col. James Herren, leading the second flight, which was about a fifth of a mile behind and a few thousand feet above Col. Zemke's. On the course heading of 70 degrees and the weather around them worsening every minute, he tried staying with his leader as Col. Zemke first tried to climb away from the front, but then quickly leveled out and plunged in. Then came a call from Col. Zemke stating that he was making a 180-degree turn to the left. Lt. Col. Herren relayed the message and followed the turn. The clouds became so thick that Lt. Col. Herren and his flight lost sight of Col. Zemke. In an attempt to climb out of the clouds, Lt. Col. Herren led his flight upward. Second Lieutenant Gail E. Jacobson, who was flying Red Four in the flight, was indicating an air speed of 130 mph as the flight continued climbing. Finally Lt. Col. Herren was seen to level off or stall out, then enter a dive that appeared straight down to Lt. Jacobson. He was last seen going down from over 25,000 feet. His airplane apparently disintegrated on the way down as a German report indicated that from the wreckage, it appeared as though the plane had exploded. The body of Lt. Col. James Herren was found with the wreckage near Katensen, a small town about 15 miles north of Celle. His wingman, Lieutenant Harold M. Jenkins, who had followed the Lt. Col. in the climb, had been forced to level out with an IAS of 130 mph before reaching the 25,000 ft. altitude. He recovered and rejoined the section.

Red Flight Three, element leader Lieutenant Richard M. Lunstrum on observing Lt. Col. Herren's trouble, quickly lowered his seat and went on instruments. He made a very rough 180-degree turn out of the stuff and eventually joined Lt. Col. Riddle's section. His wingman, as noted above, was Lt. Gail Jacobson who also experienced the wild ride down in a violent spin similar to that of his flight leader. Fortunately, he was able to recover at a lower altitude and climb back up to rejoin the remainder of the section.

Ernest S. Lundstrom was the Group Weather Officer for the 479th FG and, as a consequence was popularly known as "Stormy". Then a Captain, his meteorological office and work area was on the first floor of the station's control tower. He was in charge of the station's detachment of weather specialists and observers. In addition to his many functions, he gave the

Left: A poignant photo of Lieutenant Colonel James M. Herren, Jr. pensively looking skyward. The date of the photograph is unknown, but the feeling of foreshadowing it projects is fitting to this date. *Courtesy of Berkley E. Hollister.* Right: First Lieutenant Donald A. Dunn is shown beside the P-51 that he named Ding Hoa II. *Courtesy of the 436th Fighter Squadron Association.*

weather briefings for the missions to be flown. In 1998, he recorded a few of his remembrances from his time with the group, one of which concerned a homemade 2 ft. by 2 ft. ouija board that was presented to him by Sergeant Charles C. Claybaugh during a mission briefing. The board had various weather conditions painted around it and an arrow in the center that could be spun to "forecast" the weather. Ernest said everyone got a real laugh out of that. Ernest said the board made light of the fact that predicting weather was a difficult task at the time. Many times the men were accurate in their predictions; but sometimes they were wrong because of various unknowns, one of which was what we now call the Jet Stream. In that case, the men were aware of high winds aloft, but did not have a working knowledge of the phenomena.

The "Met" officers received their data via teletype from Wing Headquarters and disseminated that information to Flying Control in the tower as well as used it to put their weather briefing together for any planned mission. Sometimes the information at hand was inadequate or perhaps the weather conditions were thought to be changing. Those times, a volunteer pilot would be called for and asked to fly the mission route to and from a target area in order to report on weather conditions along the route for more timely facts.

Above right: First Lieutenant Travis M. Greenwood, having just completed his 68th and final mission, is being congratulated by First Lieutenant John G. Glenn. *Courtesy of Travis M. Greenwood.*

Below: Lieutenant Arlett G. Mosier Jr., Major Edward F. Stoops Jr. and Major Edward R. Werner seem to have been enjoying themselves. *Courtesy of Arlett G. Mosier, Jr.*

Right: Lieutenant Victor Wolski and CWO Stephen H. Zuchowski have one of the local ladies cornered in front of a "Spirit" present at the affair. *Courtesy of Herman C. Hoversten.*

Left: Friends, food, spirits and fun. What more could be asked for? Lieutenants Thomas E. Meyers, Edwin J. Fillipow, Richard S. Spencer Jr. and Arlett G. Mosier Jr. were gathered together to enjoy a momentary reprieve from the war. *Courtesy of Arlett G. Mosier, Jr.* Right: First Lieutenant Walter M. Drake appears in a reflective mood in this photo. His required number of combat hours about finished; perhaps he was thinking about his having been blessed with survival so far while others had not been so fortunate. On the other hand, maybe he was just thinking about going home. *Courtesy of Berkley E. Hollister.*

Weather conditions predominately came out of the southwest and swept across the island toward the continent. Much of the time, those conditions were not favorable to a mission, but usually, the men pressed on. One of those difficult times was the mission of 30 October. Remembering that instance, Ernest said three days before that date, a large front had passed across England and headed for the continent. It was expected to continue on and provide good weather for several days after its passage. Consequently, the 30 October mission was laid on. Unfortunately, the front stalled over the continent and Col. Zemke and his pilots ran right into it.

A section rejoined the bombers at 1330 hrs./22,000 ft. in what was believed to be the Hamburg area. The bombers unloaded on the target, but the results were not observable because of the weather. Flak over the target was heavy, intense and accurate. The bombers were escorted to L/O over the Frisian Islands.

B section, led by Lt. Col. Riddle, made L/F at 1208 hrs./ 24,000 ft. and R/V with the proper Big Friends at 1240 hrs./ 26,000 ft. The location was unknown due to weather. Col. Riddle reported an uneventful trip, apart from the stinking weather, leaving the bombers at the English coast at 1425 hrs./ 13,000 ft.

During the month, a number of pilots completed their required combat hours and began returning to the ZOI. Lieutenants Donald A. Dunn and Travis M. Greenwood from the 436th FS were among those fortunate to have survived.

With the end of the month came the tradition of Halloween and of course, a party was laid on at Wattisham. These men from the 436th FS were typical of those participating.

CHAPTER NINE

THE SEVEN DOGS PUB

Mrs. Peter (Joane) Chevallier was a great friend to the men of the 479th Fighter Group. When the Red Cross opened its doors at Wattisham on 15 July 1943, Mrs. Chevallier began volunteering there through the Women's Volunteer Service and for the next two years, never missed a day. She had amassed a total of over 3,200 hours of service by the war's end. Her enterprising "Junk Shop" on the base earned over $8,000 worth of business from the men there, operating from May 1944 until August 1945. Profits from the shop were turned back into the Red Cross operation there and the men of Wattisham benefited through the organization's many services. Working most evenings at the Red Cross Aero Club, she always kept an invitation open for the men to drop in at her home anytime. There, hundreds of enlisted men from the station as well as other nearby bases became overnight and weekend guests at the 14th century Elizabethan manor named Nedging Hall.

Located at Nedging Tye, about a mile south of the Wattisham airfield, the estate's close proximity provided a nice bicycle ride to and from the airfield. The property featured about 70 acres of beautiful grounds and a lake, that boasted a punt, was near the large house. The GI's, in their typical humor, christened the house, naming it the Seven Dogs Pub because of Mrs. Chevallier's dogs. Ranging in size and breed from a three-year-old cocker spaniel to a fifteen-year-old Aberdeen Terrier named "Grandma", the seven dogs were at home with everyone. Capitalizing upon the nickname, Mrs. Chevallier often passed out to visiting servicemen, what looked like a pink and blue English Pound Note, but which in fact was a coupon that read: "Ration Coupon (Post War), for one good meal and a glass of beer at the Seven Dogs Pub (Good Deal!!). Joane Chevallier, Proprietress." The coupon was bordered with sketches of the seven dogs. Informality was the keynote to time spent there. The men nicknamed Mrs. Chevallier "Duchess" but she preferred to be known as "Chevy", "The Battleaxe" or "The Old Bag". Guests just dropped in, taking potluck and spending time relaxing from the war effort. They came away with memories of a day full of friendly talk, informal tasty meals, good music, hours of happy loafing and ideal surroundings.

Not everyone had to bicycle to the estate though. Staff Sergeant Clarence (Clancy) M. Surges, an NCO from the 434th FS's S-3 Operations section and his friend Staff Sergeant Angus (Gus) W. Clark, an NCO from the squadron's S-2 Intelligence section would occasionally get lucky. When that happened, the two regular visitors were able to hitch a car ride with Mrs. Chevallier as she returned home from the station's NCO club, the Rocker Club. On those fortuitous occasions, before they left, the men would sneak over to the mess hall and "liberate" cans of fruit and sardines to take along as gifts to the hostess. Clancy still remembers the three pairs of nylons that his wife Lila sent him to give to Mrs. Chevallier. Unobtainable in wartime England, Mrs. Chevallier was ecstatic over the hosiery when she received them.

There were rules of conduct that governed one's stay at the manor house (referred to as "The Dump" by Mrs. Chevallier). Arriving servicemen were requested to remove their uniform blouses and ties and get comfortable. When meal-time came most diners followed their hostess' example by taking their food from its place on the table and seating themselves comfortably on the floor or weather permitting, just outside in a corner of the manor's well-kept lawn. The grounds were kept neat through the courtesy of enlisted men, many of whom were regular visitors, spending their odd day off there helping with chores such as lawn care, gardening, window cleaning, exercising the horses and feeding the chickens. One of many thousands of British families who opened their homes to American GI's, Mrs. Chevallier's generosity was eagerly accepted, greatly appreciated and has long been remembered.

Mrs. Peter (Joane) Chevallier in front of one of the manor's fireplaces. *Carroll C. Sprague Collection, courtesy of the East Essex Aviation Society.*

Carroll C. Sprague; the seven dogs (eight actually!) – Baddle Dog, Snubby, Tipsy, Winkle, Shadow, Happy, Grandma and Rags; and Joane Chevallier. *Courtesy of Loetta Taylor (Kennedy).*

A left side view of the manor house. *Carroll C. Sprague Collection, courtesy of the East Essex Aviation Society.*

A view of the manor house taken in the back. *Carroll C. Sprague Collection, courtesy of the East Essex Aviation Society.*

A right side view of the manor house. *Carroll C. Sprague Collection, courtesy of the East Essex Aviation Society.*

An ARC worker, the seven dogs and Joane Chevalier at the back of the manor house. *Carroll C. Sprague Collection, courtesy of the East Essex Aviation Society.*

Another of the manor's many rooms. *Carroll C. Sprague Collection, courtesy of the East Essex Aviation Society.*

A view of the lake and grounds at Nedging Hall. *Carroll C. Sprague Collection, courtesy of the East Essex Aviation Society.*

Two friends standing near the lake bank at Nedging Hall. *Carroll C. Sprague Collection, courtesy of the East Essex Aviation Society.*

Walking along the lake bank. *Carroll C. Sprague Collection, courtesy of the East Essex Aviation Society.*

Flossie, the manor's cook. *Carroll C. Sprague Collection, courtesy of the East Essex Aviation Society.*

Making pastries in the manor's kitchen. *Carroll C. Sprague Collection, courtesy of the East Essex Aviation Society.*

Food preparation, and of course, the cleaning up of plates, glassware and utensils afterwards. *Carroll C. Sprague Collection, courtesy of the East Essex Aviation Society.*

Two friends engaging in a bit of tree climbing. *Carroll C. Sprague Collection, courtesy of the East Essex Aviation Society.*

The Nedging Tye grounds were well kept by those who spent time there as is illustrated by an ARC worker who is mowing some grass. *Carroll C. Sprague Collection, courtesy of the East Essex Aviation Society.*

Some visitors looking at Mrs. Chevallier's photo album. *Carroll C. Sprague Collection, courtesy of the East Essex Aviation Society.*

A few of the men enjoying time spent at the piano. *Carroll C. Sprague Collection, courtesy of the East Essex Aviation Society.*

A relaxing afternoon spent floating in a rubber life raft on the manor's lake. *Carroll C. Sprague Collection, courtesy of the East Essex Aviation Society.*

Naptime for both man and dog. *Carroll C. Sprague Collection, courtesy of the East Essex Aviation Society.*

CHAPTER TEN

NOVEMBER 1944

2 November 1944

Eighth AF FO 1281A

No. 181 Thursday. Lt. Col. Woods led the group, which consisted of 54 P-51s (19-434th, 18-435th & 17-436th) on a penetration to target and withdrawal escort for 3rd BD B-17s attacking their 8th AF Mission 698 primary target, the oil industry installations at Merseburg/Leuna, Germany. Up: 1002 hrs., down: 1530 hrs. with eight early returns plus three escorts.

The group made L/F and shortly thereafter R/V 1115 hrs./ 25,000 ft. in the vicinity of Steenwijk, Holland with their charges, two CWs of Fortresses. The B-17s were in good formation and the group, along with other P-51 groups, escorted them from above at 28-30,000 ft. The bombing results on the oil installations were unobserved because of cloud cover. Bomb release was at 1210 hrs./24-27,000 ft. During the attack, jet contrails were seen circling, just outside of the target area. Flak in the area was heavy, intense and accurate at 25,000 ft. Leaving the target, the group, while still escorting the Big Friends, observed enemy A/C. Two Me 109s were engaged at 1235 hrs./30,000 ft. in the vicinity of Zeitz, Germany. Lieutenant John C. Donnell from the 434th FS chased one Me 109 through the clouds and down to the deck, reporting that he had destroyed it. Missing after the action, Lt. Donnell called later, stating he was okay and had joined the bombers for the trip back home. However, he was forced to land on the continent before he could return to Wattisham. At 1240 hrs./ 30,000 ft. in the vicinity of Naumburg, Germany, one of the group's flights jumped three Me 109s, but lost them in the clouds when they were warned to break. In all, twelve Me 109s were sighted south of Merseburg. The group left the bombers at 1400 hrs./23,000 ft. above the Zuider Zee.

Observations made during the mission included spotting four sets of twin-jet contrails seen heading east from Nijmegen, Holland area at 1205 hrs./20,000 ft. At 1235 hours, two chutes were seen over the smoke screen at Zeitz. There were no bombers in the area. At 1310 hours, two B-17s were seen on fire and spiraling down, south of Merseburg. No chutes were observed. Flak was reported to be heavy, intense and accurate at 26,000 ft. in the Naumburg to Kölleda, Germany area; heavy, intense and accurate at 26,000 ft. in the Zeitz area and heavy, moderate and inaccurate at 25,000 ft. in the Bad Oeynhausen, Germany area. Fifteen to twenty white and gray puffs to 35,000 ft. were seen.

4 November 1944

Eighth AF FO 1286A

No. 182 Saturday. Lt. Col. Riddle led the group, which consisted of 52 P-51s (16-434th, 18-435th & 18-436th) on a penetration to target and withdrawal escort for 2nd BD B-24s attacking their 8th AF Mission 700 primary target, the oil industry installations at Hannover/Misburg, Germany. Up: 1000 hrs./ down: 1520 hrs. with two early returns.

R/V with the assigned bombers was made at 1131 hrs./ 29,000 ft. in the vicinity of Schiermonnikoog Island, Holland. The B-24s were escorted to the target. They were in good formation, but strung out. The results of the strike could not be observed due to the target being obscured by a smoke screen.

A 436th FS bird returns home after a mission. Note the checkered tail on this A/C that dates the photo as one taken of an early 436th FS Mustang. *Courtesy of Berkley E. Hollister.*

Assistant crew chief Sergeant Harper H. Nolan, Lieutenant Colonel Kyle L. Riddle and crew chief Technical Sergeant Harlan W. Leachman are standing beside the P-51 that Lt.Col. Riddle flew, J2-R. Note the K-25 camera mounted to the aircraft's headrest. *From original 479th FG history.*

Flak over the target was heavy, intense and inaccurate. Four bombers were seen to go down during the attack. No enemy A/C were noted to be nearby. There were no chutes observed. The Big Friends began heading towards their L/O at Egmond, Holland. At 1215 hrs./20,000 ft. in the vicinity of Oosterend, Holland an Me 262 making a pass on the bombers was repulsed by two relays from the group who turned into the jet. The jet broke away. The event was duplicated at 1230 hrs. Two other Me 262s were sighted between Dümmer Lake, Germany and Zwolle, Holland. These were engaged by another P-51 group at about 1240 hrs./25,000 ft. The jets outran the other P-51s, one breaking into the nearby 479th and allowing for a 90-degree deflection squirt, but no claim was made. At 1300 hrs./31,000 ft. in the vicinity of Muiden, Holland, three Me 262s in a vic formation appeared above the group. One bounced the rear of the first flight, shooting at them. They returned the attack, but the jet pulled away at 30,000 ft. even though the squadron leader was indicating 350 mph. The jet then made two head-on passes, one after another. No damage was caused, but the formation was broken up for 15 minutes. The jet then dove off into a cloud near Dümmer Lake. The other two Me 262s did not engage. The group broke away from the bombers at 1345 hrs./1,000 ft. over the North Sea.

The only observation made during the mission was the notation that the paint on some of the Me 262s seen, was a green with yellow markings on it. No Maltese [sic] crosses were visible. Flak in the areas of Terschelling, Holland as well as Borkum and Langeoog, Germany was heavy, intense and inaccurate. At 1131 hrs./29,000 ft. six boats about the size of ASR launches had formed a semicircle around the bay from Cuxhaven to Schillig, Germany. At 1330 hrs./14,000 feet, twenty silver tank cars on three or more tracks were seen in a marshalling yard across the bay north of Amsterdam, Holland. Two pilots from the 435th FS had to land at St. Trond, Belgium for an unknown reason.

5 November 1944

Eighth AF FO 1288A

No. 183 Sunday. Maj. Sullivan led the group, which consisted of 50 P-51s (16-434th, 16-435th & 18-436th) on an escort for 2nd BD B-24s attacking their secondary target, the marshalling yards at Karlsruhe, Germany and strafing transportation targets as per 8th AF Mission 702. Up: 0930 hrs., down: 1435 hrs. with two early returns. L/F was made at 1010 hrs./15,000 ft. north of Ostend, Belgium.

R/V with the proper B-24s was at 1042 hrs./23,000 ft. north of Bar-le-Duc, France. The heavies were very strung out. The escort went as scheduled, but the bombing results were unobserved due to overcast. Flak over the target at Karlsruhe was heavy, moderate and inaccurate. Returning, the group broke off escort 1315 hrs./18,000 ft. east of Rheims, France. Weather prevented the briefed strafing after the bombers were left so the group headed home, making L/O was 1322 hrs./5,000 ft. at Ostend, Belgium. Three straggling Big Friends were escorted to L/O where they indicated they were happy.

Right: Lieutenant Gordon L. Doolittle. *Courtesy of Edwin J. Fillipow.*

Far right: Lieutenant Thomas C. Olson. *Courtesy of Berkley E. Hollister.*

Observations made during the mission included two rockets heading west that were seen east of Luxembourg at 1032 hrs. and 1051 hrs. At 1050 hrs./40,000 feet, a rocket was seen over the Köln, Germany area, flying at a heading of 280 degrees. At 1150 hrs./40,000 feet, another rocket was seen on a similar heading over the Antwerp, Belgium area. An unidentified airdrome south of Saarbrücken, Germany was noted. The weather was 10/10ths with two decks; one at 3,000 ft. and the other at 10,000 ft. with openings in the Alts area.

Gordon L. Doolittle, in writing of his experiences with the 435th FS, recalled an incident that happened to him. He wrote:

> "About November 1944, the 479th was issued a UC-64 utility aircraft and I was told by the 435th Operations Officer to get checked out in it. When I looked into it, nobody at Group offered to check me out. I was told it had the same engine as an AT-6 and since I was current in that, I should be able to fly the '64. As I was sitting in it trying to feel comfortable before starting it, a corporal came up and asked if he could go along. Thinking he was the crew chief and thankful that he could help me through this self-training flight, I welcomed him aboard.
>
> "After starting and then take off, my first impression was that I was flying a truck that taxied, took off, climbed and cruised all at the same speed.
>
> "After getting a little feel for the plane, I decided to land and asked the corporal, who had not said a word yet, what the approach speed should be. He said: 'I don't know.' My questions about power, mixture, RPMs and landing speed all got the same answer. I then asked him if he was not the crew chief. He replied: 'No, I'm a parachute packer and just wanted an airplane ride.'
>
> "It wasn't humorous at the time, but is now."

6 November 1944

Eighth AF FO 1291A

No. 184 Monday. Lt. Col. Riddle led the group, which consisted of 51 P-51s (17-434th, 18-435th & 16-436th) on an escort for 2nd BD B-24s attacking their 8th AF Mission 704 primary target, the Mittelland Canal at Minden, Germany. (An important waterway that connected Berlin to the Ruhr.) Up: 0900 hrs., down: 1325 hrs. with one early return.

The group made L/F at 0947 hrs./18,000 ft. over Ijmuiden, Holland. R/V with the assigned bombers was at 1027 hrs./ 25,000 ft. north of Zwolle, Holland. The B-24s were in good formation. At 1040 hours, west of Bielefeld, Germany, three Me 262s in a vic formation at 30,000 ft. were sighted heading for the bombers. They were chased to the Lingen, Germany area and down to the deck. From there, the jets split up. One was chased to the Steinhuder Lake, Germany area where Lt. Colonel Sidney S. Woods managed to register some hits on it when he stood his bird on its tail and fired at the jet as it climbed away from him. The second turned south and was lost. The third was chased over Quackenbück, Germany where it escaped while the group was evading flak.

First Lieutenant Thomas C. Olson and Second Lieutenant Wendell H. Marlowe, both Newcross Squadron pilots, shared in the destruction of a Fw 190 they strafed at Hesepe Airdrome. They had been after the jets and came upon the parked A/C by accident. Lt. Olson gave this report of the action:

> "I was flying as Newcross Red Three [He was element leader and Lt. Marlowe was Red Four, his wingman.] on an escort mission to Minden, Germany. We were at 31,000 feet in the target area when jets were called in. We took up pursuit, but when I saw that I was not closing, I throttled back to save gasoline because I had not been able to draw

from my drop tanks on the way in. A few moments later the jets were reported going down, so I started losing altitude. At 10,000 feet I passed over a three- strip blacktop airfield, so I circled it. Then I saw two more fields of the same type close by and decided to patrol the three of them in case the jets tried to land there. My wingman, Lt. Marlowe and I patrolled at 7,000 feet between the layers of two to three tenths fair weather cumulus. During this patrol I saw only a few S/E and T/E aircraft dispersed about the fields. After circling one field and then going on to another, I saw that a Me 262 had sneaked in and landed there. We went after it, but the flak was too heavy to go in and get him. We then went back to an airfield which I later identified as Hesepe. I had previously spotted a Fw 190 there, parked in a revetment about 100 yards off the runway. There did not seem to be any flak, so I made a pass from southeast to northwest, firing a good burst and observing several strikes. I noted then that the Fw began to smoke a little. My wingman strafed the immediate area to button down any possible flak. We then pulled around and made another pass during which both of us fired on the Fw 190. This time it burst into flames. I claim one Fw 190 destroyed on the ground, shared with Lt. Wendell H. Marlowe."

The group continued escort of the bombers to their target and back to a point of break away at 1145 hrs./18,000 ft. over the Zuider Zee. Flak over the target was heavy, moderate and accurate as seen at 27,000 ft. Turning back in and down, the group sighted ground traffic and did some strafing, claiming 3-0-4 locomotives and damaging a passenger train east of Wesermünde, Germany. Heading north from there, they added 12-0-10 goods wagons, damaged a personnel carrier plus passengers and damaged a troop train in the vicinity of Soltau, Germany. The trains had light flak weapons mounted on them and gave the pilots some amount of grief. Finally, south of Meppel, Holland, they damaged a heavy truck and additionally, a 20-unit truck convoy that was armed with 20 and 40mm flak. The vehicles were heading north at the time. L/O was 1215 hrs./19,000 ft. at Alkmaar, Holland. At 1235 hrs./27,000 ft. near The Hague, Holland an Me 262 made a pass at the relays and was able to take a long burst at them. The jet then escaped in a cloud.

Charles H. (Henry) Darling, then a new Second Lieutenant who had recently joined the 436th FS, recalled this day quite well:

"It was my second or third mission. We were flying line abreast, far enough apart so that we could read the squadron letters on the other aircraft in the flight. Although it seemed to take a few missions before you really began to see a lot of things, I was catching on. Suddenly, someone called out bandits at six o'clock high. I looked but could not see them. Our flight leader called for us to drop our wing tanks and break left. I switched to my internal tanks, hit the switch to release my external tanks and broke left. Before I knew what had happened, I was in a high-speed stall and going into a spin. My left drop tank had not released.

"We had been told about spinning a P-51. The word was, do not do it, as recovery was very hard to accomplish. The warning was correct. I started the spin at about 25,000 feet. The prescribed recovery maneuver was the typical throttle back, stick to neutral position and opposite rudder to the spin. It didn't work. The spin continued and my efforts had no effect. I was getting a little panicky at this point. I neutralized the rudder and slammed it back to opposite of my rotation and held it there.

"I finally began to feel a change. The spinning had stopped, but by now I was passing through 8,000 feet and in a steep dive! Not wanting to go into another stall, I had to make my pull up as carefully as I could. When I finally leveled out and slowed down, I saw that I was only a 1,000 feet off the ground and somewhere in Germany. At that point, the hung-up tank finally released all by itself. I went to full throttle and began a spiraling climb back upstairs as fast as I could. After what seemed to be forever, I reached the altitude that I had left in actuality, not so long ago and began looking for some friendly aircraft. There was still a lot of chatter on the radio, but it appeared that the enemy was now gone. I caught sight of a flight of three aircraft making a wide turn to their left, so I cut into their turn and caught up with them. They were P-51s and I edged into the number four position. As luck would have it, it was my flight, the one that I had left a short while back. They seemed to not even know that I had been gone. I was very fortunate to have survived that one."

Observations made during the mission included four rocket contrails seen, one at 0945 hrs. south of Rotterdam, Holland heading west at 30,000 feet, one at 30,000 ft. in the vicinity of Rhein, Germany one at 1045 hrs. south of Dümmer Lake, Germany and one at 1123 hrs. in the Minden area. Two pilots, low on gas and heading home, sighted seven Fw 190s heading north at 1225 hrs./8,000 feet, ten miles east of Zwolle, Germany. At 1245 hours, an A/C believed to be a P-51 was seen diving straight down from 2,000 feet near Bohmte, just south of Dümmer Lake (Lt. Darling? See above.) Flak at Bohmte airdrome was heavy, moderate and accurate as seen at 17,000 ft. Flak at the marshalling yards south of Wesermünde was light, intense and accurate. The weather was CAVU.

Returning home to Wattisham, Lieutenant Marion W. Steele from the 436th FS ran out of gas and was forced to ditch in the North Sea. He was not seen to leave his plane.

Second Lieutenant Charles H. Darling shown in a P-40 during advanced training in Georgia during 1944. *Courtesy of Charles H. Darling.*

8 November 1944

Eighth AF FO 1296A

No. 185 Wednesday. Maj. Sullivan led the group, which consisted of 53 P-51s (16-434th, 20-435th & 17-436th) on an escort for 1st BD B-17s attacking their 8th AF Mission 705 primary target, the oil industry at Merseburg/Leuna, Germany. Up: 0910 hrs., down: 1433 hrs. with five early returns.

The group made L/F 0953 hrs./15,000 ft. between Bergen and Den Helder, Holland. R/V with the bombers was at 1035 hrs./26,000 ft. 15 miles north of Osnabrück, Germany. They were a half-hour late. The B-17s the group was assigned to escort were identified as having a triangle and red/yellow stripes on the A/C tail. (306th BG) These were found, but instead of being in the sixth CW position, they were in the first CW position and were already accompanied by a group of yellow-nosed P-51s. Therefore, the group cruised back along the bomber course, seeking the sixth box. Unable to locate it, they returned to the original bombers, rejoining them as they went to the target area. Flak over the target was heavy, very intense and accurate at 25,000 ft. One B-17 was seen making controlled circles and losing altitude over the target at 1115 hrs./14,000 ft. No chutes were observed. Jet contrails were seen at 30,000 ft. southeast of Leipzig, Germany. Weather was 10/10 overcast with tops at 10,000 ft. over the target. After the strike, the force turned back and headed towards Holland. At 1300 hrs./16,000 feet, an Me 262 made a weak pass at a lone B-17 east of Lingen, Germany. The jet was chased east to Dümmer Lake, but the enemy A/C pulled away from the pursuers. One burst was fired at the jet, but it was out of range. The Big Friends and their escorts arrived at a point 25 miles east of Zwolle, Holland at 1315 hrs./20,000 ft. While on that return trip, eight miles west of Minden, Germany in the Lübeck, Germany area, two members of a flight from the 435th FS had a mid-air collision. First Lieutenant Heinz W. Detlefsen was leading the flight when a right turn was called for. First Lieutenant Norman R. Benoit, who was flying number three in the flight, narrated the sequence of events as follows:

> "As the element started to cross over, First Lieutenant Thomas V. Smith, who was number four in the flight, crossed to my right [Lt. Benoit's] and in front of me. His position was close to the flight leader. Lt. Detlefsen then started a gradual right turn while Lt. Smith, apparently blinded by the sun which was at 90 degrees to his left, stopped his turn and assumed an almost level attitude beneath Lt. Detlefsen, who was also flying practically level. I then observed Lt. Smith gain altitude until he collided with Lt. Detlefsen, whose propeller cut the tail section off of Lt. Smith's plane at approximately the fuselage tank. Lt. Smith's plane immediately burst into flames and I broke sharply to the left and down, observing both planes spinning violently. Lt. Detlefsen's plane was trailing smoke and Lt. Smith's airplane ceased burning, but spun crazily with the canopy still on to about 2,000 feet, where I lost him. I followed Lt. Detlefsen down to the deck and called to him to get out, but received no reply. The airplane exploded on impact. The weather was 4/10ths cumulus clouds, with visibility 4,000 to 6,000 feet."

Lt. Detlefsen was killed as a result of the accident and Lt. Smith survived to become a POW. L/O was 1330 hrs./12,000 ft. at Ijmuiden, Holland. One flight from the 434th FS turned back towards Dümmer Lake to strafe. Results of that foray were a destroyed locomotive and four attached passenger cars damaged on a train found in the vicinity of Lembruch, Germany. A locomotive and five cars were damaged on another goods train that was found hidden in some trees at Quackenbück.

Observations made during the mission included heavy train activity that was spotted heading both ways between Dümmer Lake and Rotterdam, Holland. This was noted from 12,000 ft./1250-1315 hrs. At 1255 hrs./22,000 feet, three twin jet contrails were seen at 26,000 ft. just east of Dümmer Lake. When cut off, the jets disappeared into some patchy clouds. Both the jets at Leipzig and those at Dümmer Lake made no apparent move to attack, but rather ducked in and out of clouds. An Me 262 was seen northwest of Minden. At 1305 hours, a dinghy was seen in the water 15 miles west of Ijmuiden. Two P-47s, believed to be air-sea rescue planes, were circling the site. Between 1315 and 1330 hours, heavy marshalling yard activity at Rotterdam and Utrecht was noted from 8,000 ft. Flak over Naumburg, Germany was heavy, intense and accurate. Flak over Lembruck was light, moderate and accurate. Flak over Rotterdam was light-heavy, moderate and accurate. Heavy, moderate and accurate red puffs of flak were seen a mile offshore at The Hague, Holland. It was noted that the radio range seemed to be poor with the relay being unable to be read. Caboose Fifty (335th FS, 4th FG) asked Legacy, Manager and Colgate for a homing between 1245 and 1315 hrs. without apparent results.

Left: This is a picture of Lieutenant Thomas V. Smith taken by a base photographer for inclusion in his Escape and Evasion Kit. It was intended to be used in the fabrication of a false passport should he ever go down behind enemy lines. *Courtesy of James H. Koerber.* Right: Lieutenant Heinz W. Detlefsen is pictured near one of the hangars at Wattisham. *Courtesy of Edwin J. Fillipow.*

9 November 1944

Eighth AF FO 1299A

No. 186 Thursday. Maj. Glover led the group, which consisted of 49 P-51s (17-434th, 16-435th & 16-436th) on a penetration to target and withdrawal escort for 2nd BD B-24s attacking their 8th AF Mission 707 primary tactical targets, strong points on the ground at the front in the Metz, France area. Up: 0830 hrs., down: 1244 hrs. with three early returns plus one escort.

R/V with the assigned bombers was at 0945 hrs./23,000 ft. southeast of Rheims, France. The group escorted their charges through the target where the bombing was unobserved due to undercast. Flak over the target was heavy, meager and inaccurate, while flak in the Metz area was heavy, intense and accurate. The mission was uneventful and the group separated from the B-24s at 1055 hrs./9,000 ft. north of Calais, France.

Mission takeoff. *From original 479th FG history.*

Escorting B-24s from the 466th BG, 785th BS to target. *Courtesy of David L. Born.*

Observations made during the mission included contrails seen going northwest of France in the Saarbrücken, Germany area at 1050 hrs./12,000/35,000 ft. and at map area 4V0/3050, going west at 1130 hrs./30/35,000 ft. An explosion with flames and smoke going up 200 feet in the air was seen on the ground 15 miles northeast of Laon, France.

10 November 1944

Eighth AF FO 1301A

No. 187 Friday. Lt. Col. Riddle led the group, which consisted of 50 P-51s (17-434th, 15-435th & 18-436th) on an escort for 2nd BD B-24s attacking their 8th AF Mission 709 primary target, the airfield at Hanau, Germany. Up: 1032 hrs., down: 1538 hrs. with no early returns.

R/V with the assigned CWs was at 1146 hrs./25,000 ft. east of St. Vith, Belgium. Two of the combat wings were lagging far behind, with the 2nd CW in the last position instead of the fourth as was called for in the FO. The mission was uneventful and bombing was unobserved due to undercast. The group broke away from the bombers at 1415 hrs./22,000 ft. southeast of Brussels, Belgium. Weather prevented the group from strafing any targets.

Observations made during the mission included the sighting of a P-51 that was hit by flak over the Rhine River, 10 miles southwest of Nestatten, Germany. A chute was seen to open. A B-17, probably also hit by flak, broke in two over Wiesbaden, Germany. No chutes were reported from this one. Big Ben contrails were noted in the Bad Kreuznach, Germany area at 1145 hours, in the Frankfurt, Germany area at 1250 hrs. and heading towards the Zuider Zee, no location given, at 1430 hrs. Flak over Cochem, Germany was heavy, medium and accurate. Over St. Goar, Germany, it was heavy, intense and accurate while over Limburg, Germany, it was heavy, moderate and inaccurate.

11 November 1944

Eighth AF FO 1306A

No. 188 Saturday. Lt. Col. Woods led the group, which consisted of 22 P-51s (8-434th, 6-435th & 8-436th) on an escort for 1st BD B-17s attacking their 8th AF Mission 712 primary target, the oil refineries at Gelsenkirchen, Germany. Up: 1000 hrs., down: 1430 hrs. with no early returns.

After the group was airborne, their controller reassigned them to escort the second instead of their previously assigned third force. R/V with the bombers from the 41st CW was at 1115 hrs./25,000 ft. in the vicinity of Zwolle, Holland. The group watched over their B-17s with the yellow triangle tails (379th BG) through the target and back. While over the target, one Big Friend was seen to go down with no chutes appearing. The bombing was unobserved due to 6-8/10 overcast. Flak over the target was heavy, moderate and accurate. L/O for the bombers was at Bergen, Holland at 1240 hrs./22,000 ft. The group turned back in to sweep Antwerp, Belgium to Lingen, Germany to Groningen, Holland. They had an uneventful trip and made L/O was at 1355 hrs./10,000 ft. over the Dutch Islands.

Observations made during the mission included a possible Big Ben contrail that was seen to be inclining 80 degrees and extending up to 40,000 ft. in the Ruhr area. At 1230 hrs./20,000 ft. four relays were bounced by an Me 262 diving on then from 30,000 ft. As soon as the P-51s dropped their tanks and turned towards the jet, the enemy A/C scrammed. No shots were fired. Flak over Gladbeck, Germany was heavy, moderate and inaccurate while over Ijmuiden, Holland it was heavy, intense and accurate.

Lieutenants John N. Murr and Ronald L. Maley are seen standing next to Lt. Maley's Tommy Trojan, a P-51 he named for the university he attended – University of Southern California (USC Trojans). *Courtesy of Arnold G. Helding.*

18 November 1944

Eighth AF FO 1317A

No. 189 Saturday. Maj. Glover led the group, which consisted of 53 P-51s (18-434th, 18-435th & 17-436th) on a rhubarb to Freiham, Germany, in support of 8th AF Mission 716. Up: 1043 hrs., down: 1539 hrs. with two early returns.

L/F was made by squadrons between 1115-1130 hrs./5,000 feet, over Belgium between Ostend and Blankenberghe. A frontal condition with a 500 ft. maximum ceiling over Wattisham prevented the group from forming up over the base. The group was then briefed to form up at Brussels, Belgium but that was also prevented by the weather. Consequently, one

Below: Technical Sergeant William M. Morgan is seated on the wing of Little Wildfire, a P-51 named and flown by Lieutenant John N. Murr. *Courtesy of William M. Morgan.*

squadron swept east to the vicinity of the Rhine River and Wesel, Germany seeking targets of opportunity, but the prevalent weather hid them. The remainder of the group, vectored to similar targets, swept from Nijmegan, Holland to Luxembourg and then eastward. An A/C from the 435th FS, being flown by Lieutenant Wilbert Muller, was hit by flak at 16,000 ft. over Zevenaar, Holland, just southeast of Arnhem. Lt. Muller was able to glide to allied territory and bailed out in the vicinity of Grave, Holland. He was seen to get up and walk away from the landing. L/O was 1400-1445 hrs./10,000 ft. in the vicinity of Ostend. Lieutenants John N. Murr and Edward L. Hurtig, both from the 434th FS, landed at Brussels for unknown reasons.

The only observation made during the mission was the notation of hearing a radio message stating a yellow-nosed P-51 was seen burning in the woods in the vicinity of map coordinates 4VP 5150. Flak over Wesel was heavy, meager and inaccurate; over Zevenaar it was heavy, intense and accurate; over the Rhine River north of Venlo, it was heavy, meager and accurate. There was 10/10ths overcast at 3,000 ft. over the North Sea, 6-8/10ths overcast 4-5,000 ft. over Belgium plus over northern France and eastward, weather had closed the continent solidly.

A frame of gun camera film taken by Lieutenant Berkley E. Hollister showing some B-17s being escorted to their target. Lt. Hollister had acquired a "home made" movie camera from another Newcross Squadron pilot when that pilot rotated back to the US. The camera was made from a surplus aircraft gun camera and had a wooden handle with which it was held. Wired into the aircraft's electrical system by Staff Sergeant Thomas J. O'Grady, the plane's crew chief, the only time that it could be used was when Lt. Hollister was a flight leader. All other times he was too busy following his leader to utilize it. *Courtesy of Berkley E. Hollister.*

A frame taken from footage shot by First Lieutenant Berkley E. Hollister using his "home made" movie camera. It shows his flight in formation during a mission. *Courtesy of Berkley E. Hollister.*

20 November 1944

Eighth AF FO 1320A

No. 190 Monday. Maj. Biscayart led the group, which consisted of 53 P-51s (18-434th, 18-435th & 17-436th) on a ramrod to the oil storage facilities at Geislingen, Germany, in support of 8th AF Mission 718. Up: 1010 hrs., down: 1434 hrs. with five early returns.

Immediately after the group was airborne, Colgate contacted them and cancelled the original mission ordering instead, a sweep from Giessen, Germany to Wiesbaden, Germany and to strafe east of the Rhine River. L/F was made at 1100 hrs./10,000 ft. in the vicinity of Knokke, Belgium. The group swept to Köln, Germany area and on to the Dusseldorf, Germany area above the overcast, but the weather prevented any targets from being spotted. Flak in both areas was heavy, intense and accurate. Because of the 10/10ths cloud coverage over the continent and the layered undercast building up to a front east of the Rhine River area, the group was forced to withdraw. L/O was 1245 hrs./7,000 feet, again in the vicinity of Knokke.

The only observation made during the mission was a Big Ben contrail seen at 1145 hrs./20-40,000 ft south of Nijmegen, Holland. The group passed some bombers enroute out at 1130 hrs./20,000 ft. south of Eindhoven.

21 November 1944

Eighth AF FO 1323A

No. 191 Tuesday. Lt. Col. Riddle led the group, which consisted of 60 P-51s (19-434th, 21-435th & 20-436th) on a penetration to target and withdrawal escort for 3rd BD B-17s attacking their 8th AF Mission 720 target. Up; 0951 hrs., down: 1525 hrs. with two early returns.

Left: First Lieutenant Berkley E. Hollister beside his regular mount, the ship he named Pin Up Girl. The name was derived from the 1944 20th Century Fox movie *Pin Up Girl* that starred Actress Betty Grable. Lt. Hollister and Second Lieutenant John C. Donnell, Jr. had gone to London on a pass and had seen the movie there. At the time, Lt. Hollister was searching for a name for his new P-51 and the movie title clicked in his mind. The nose art was to include a Vargas Girl image also but time precluded that bit of work until later. *Courtesy of Berkley E. Hollister.* Right: Major Jules D. Biscayart, Lieutenant Joseph R. Struby, Corporal Stanley Kellett, Lieutenant Richard S. Spencer, Jr. and Lieutenant Edwin C. Lewin are seen standing beside Lt. Struby's Little Hemorrhoid. Of these men, only Cpl. Kellett remained at Wattisham by the end of December. The pilots had all completed their combat hours and returned to the ZOI. *Courtesy of Stanley Kellett.*

Just prior to joining the bombers, the group spotted an Me 262 near Zwolle, Holland, but were unable to engage it. R/V with three boxes of bombers was at 1055 hrs./25,000 ft. in the vicinity of Zwolle. They were closely escorted through the target and back out. On the way to the target, in the vicinity of Plantlunne airdrome in Germany, an Me 262 stooged around the formation trying to lure the escort away, but the group did not engage it. Four other Me 262s were seen at 6,000 ft. heading 160 degrees. The bomber formation was good. South of the target area, at 1215 hrs./16,000 feet, one B-17 spun out and disintegrated. Only one chute was seen to open. Neither enemy A/C nor flak was observed near this occurrence. Bombing was unobserved due to overcast conditions. On the way back out, one squadron picked up some B-24s near Bad Frankenhausen, Germany and escorted them out along the penetration course. Fifteen cars of a train were damaged by strafing near Quackenbrück, Germany. The group broke escort at 1423 hrs./ 10,000 ft. at Ostend, Belgium. Lieutenants Andre E. Huycke and T. E. Myers from the 436th FS had to land at Ghent, Belgium for an unknown reason.

Observations made during the mission included three Big Ben contrails seen north of Apeldoorn, Holland. One was seen at 1030 hrs./20-40,000 ft. and two were seen at 1150 hours, same altitude. Possibly, two more were seen at a 60-degree angle, ten miles northeast of Rotterdam, Holland at 1155 hrs./ 24,000 ft. A final Big Ben contrail was noted at 1200 hrs./ 24,000 ft. in the Gotha, Germany area. Flak over the Merseburg, Germany area and the Frankfurt, Germany area, was heavy, intense and inaccurate. Flak over the Quackenbrück area was light, intense and accurate. The weather over the target was 8-10/10ths overcast. There was frontal activity with cumulus to 31,000 ft. east of Leipzig. Arriving back at England, there were twenty bursts of AA from Clacton aimed at two P-51s heading 340 degrees at 8,000 ft. The bursts were ahead of the A/C.

25 November 1944

Eighth AF FO 1333A

No. 192 Saturday. Lt. Col Woods led the group, which consisted of 51 P-51s (16-434th, 18-345th & 17-436th) on a

A cartoon drawn by Captain Robin Olds that gives some illustration of the weather conditions this date. *Courtesy of George E. Falkner.*

MEW control and escort for 1st BD B-17s attacking their 8th AF Mission primary target, the oil industry at Merseburg/ Leuna, Germany. Up: 1004 hrs., down: 1535 hrs. with six early returns plus one escort.

In Germany, R/V with the assigned last five boxes of bombers was at 1130 hrs./25,000 ft. twenty-five miles northwest of Frankfurt. The Big Friends were escorted through the target and back to where the group broke away at 1345 hrs./20,000 ft. south of Bonn. The bombing results were not observed due to 10/10ths undercast cloud coverage. Flak over the target was heavy, intense and accurate. The group had a chance to do a bit of strafing and tallied up 5-0-0 locomotives (3-0-0 434th & 2-0-0 436th) and 1-0-4 goods wagons (1-0-0 434th & 0-0-4 436th). Some of these were shot up four miles northwest of Bad Nauheim, some two miles west of Giessen and others nearby those locations. Major Jules D. Biscayart from the 436th FS and Second Lieutenant Frederick L. Hart from the 435th FS, landed at A-83, a Ninth AF base on the continent for unknown reasons.

Observations made during the mission included spotting an Me 262 stooging around at 1130 hrs./35,000 ft. to the west of Düren, Germany. There was an unidentified A/C seen to explode at 1030 hrs./14,000 feet, 15 miles northeast of Ostend, Belgium. There were three V2 rocket contrails noted, all heading west. One was seen at 1050 hrs./30,000 ft. off the Dutch Islands of Holland, one at 1130 hrs./20,000 ft. over Walcheren Island, Holland and one at 1150 hrs./30,000 ft. northeast of Brussels, Belgium. Flak was reported as both light and heavy, moderate and accurate on the deck, north of Bad Nauheim, Germany. Along the Rhine River, south of Koblenz, Germany, the flak was heavy, intense and accurate.

Second Lieutenant David L. Born had this photograph taken of himself standing beside the Newcross Squadron P-51 that he flew his first combat mission in on this date. He had just returned when the picture was snapped. *Courtesy of David L. Born.*

First Lieutenant Berkley E. Hollister shot this photo through his P-51's gun sight using the "home made" movie camera previously described. While there only clouds "under the pipper", it gives some idea of what a pilot would have been looking at when sighting in on his target. *Courtesy of Berkley E. Hollister.*

Thanksgiving Day – the big meal at Wattisham. *Courtesy of the 436th Fighter Squadron Association.*

Bison Squadron members, armorer Corporal Carl E. Kelly, crew chief Staff Sergeant Gordon E. Evjan and First Lieutenant Edwin J. Fillipow by their P-51, Daisy Mae. *Courtesy of Edwin J. Fillipow.*

26 November 1944

Second BD FO 529B

No. 193 Sunday. Capt. Herbert R. Jordan led the group, which consisted of 49 P-51s (17-434th, 16-435th & 16-546th) on a penetration to target and withdrawal for 2nd BD B-24s attacking their 8th AF Mission 725 primary target, the rail viaduct at Bielefeld/Schildesche, Germany. Up: 1017 hrs., down: 1504 hrs. with eight early returns plus four escorts.

R/V with the bombers was at 1120 hrs./20,000 ft. over Zwolle, Holland. The CWs were not in the order given in the FO and were 22 minutes late. On the way to the target, the 434th FS was vectored to Rheine, Germany at 1125 hrs. in order to investigate bogeys, but were unable to locate any. They did, however, find some Spitfires and Typhoons at Münster, Germany while returning to the target area. The 435th FS was on the deck in the target area, but could not observe any hits on the rail viaduct. Weather did not affect the mission. A bomber exploded in the target area. No chutes were seen. The B-24s were returned to Holland, where the 436th FS, having escorted them the whole trip, broke away at 1315 hrs./ 20,000 feet, 15 miles north of Amsterdam, Holland. At 1300 hrs./1300 feet, a B-17, serial number 337955, with a green stripe and the letter "C" on the tail, was observed to be in trouble in the Zwolle area. (The 305th BG/365th BS B-17G was hit by flak over their target at Misburg, Germany. They ditched off the coast of Diepenveen, Holland where seven of the crew were captured and two evaded.) The 436th FS drove back toward the target area to look for stragglers. No other fighter escort was seen on withdrawal.

Meanwhile, the 435th FS, led by Lt. Col. Riddle, was back cruising around Rheine looking for enemy A/C on the fields in that vicinity. At 1300 hours, ten miles east of the city, a Fw 190 was seen to be flying west, down the nearby canal. The Fw was at approximately 3,000 ft. when it was spotted. Highway, (Lt. Col. Riddle) split-essed after it, but First Lieutenant Theo J. Sowerby, apparently having already seen the A/C, was quicker. Dropping his tanks, Lt. Sowerby began closing on the Fw which started twisting. When Lt. Sowerby opened fire with a 20-30-degree deflection shot, the Fw made a 360-degree turn to the left. The maneuver didn't separate Lt. Sowerby from the Fw's tail and he continued to get strikes on the enemy A/C. The Fw then dove towards the ground, but Lt. Sowerby registered more hits. The Fw pulled up and his pursuer began getting hits all over him. At that point, the Fw began to smoke, then burn and soon exploded, the wreckage crashing to the ground. Lt. Sowerby pulled around in a tight 360-degree turn and dove on the crash site, firing into it to take pictures. First Lieutenant Billy C. Means, who followed the action, confirmed the encounter. The airdromes at Achmer and Vorden, Germany were dive-strafed to test for flak. They were found to be too hot to handle. Flak at Vorden airdrome was heavy,

A Lakeside Squadron P-51 getting airborne for a mission – J2-N is just ready to break away from the runway. *Courtesy of Frederick C. Hayner.*

Two 435th FS birds as seen about to lift off runway 29.The pilots of J2-D My Buddy and his wingman in another P-51 have their fighters loaded down with fuel for a mission. *Courtesy of 435th Fighter Squadron.*

moderate and accurate from 3-8,000 ft. There were three light gun positions on the west side of the drome, just outside the perimeter. Flak at Achmer airdrome was light, intense and accurate at 3-8,000 ft.

Observations made during the mission included Big Bens seen at 1058, 1130, 1340 and 1350 hrs./20-40,000 feet, headed west from the Rotterdam, Holland area. Twenty plus partially camouflaged, single-engine A/C were seen at the Vorden airdrome where it was noted that extensions had been recently added. One single-engine A/C, as well as two unidentified A/C and some dummy A/C were seen at Achmer airdrome. Plantlunne airdrome had 20 plus single-engine A/C dispersed on the north side of the drome. Sixteen miles east of Rheine, there were decoy A/C dummies on a grass strip.

27 November 1944

Eighth AF FO 1343A

No. 194 Monday. Lt. Col. Riddle led the group, which consisted of 51 P-51s (16-434th, 18-435th & 17-436th) on a top cover/strafing mission, joining with the 56th FG as briefed, for their 8th AF Mission 727 target, an oil storage point in Germany. The purpose of this mission was to draw out and engage enemy A/C. In that, it was successful as 98 GAF A/C were destroyed. It was the only occasion that the bomber effort was subordinate to that of the fighters. Up: 1030 hrs., down: 1521 hrs. with four early returns.

L/F was made at 1130 hrs./18-20,000 ft. in the Egmond, Holland area. R/V with the 56th FG was at 1215 hrs./20,000 ft. in the area of Rütenbrock, Germany. The weather presented the force with only occasional holes in the cloud deck through which accurate orientation and pinpointing of positions was prevented. While heading towards the target, the two groups were vectored south by Nuthouse, their MEW controller. At 1240 hrs. they encountered numerous contrails at 30,000 ft. southwest of Dümmer Lake, Germany. The contrails were pursued, but no contact was made. Immediately afterward though, all thoughts of the target were cast aside when the combined force encountered a mixture of enemy A/C northeast of Dümmer Lake. The weather was clear with broken stratus clouds at 10,000 ft. in that area.

First Lieutenant Lewis P. Petterson from the 435th FS was leading the second flight when a gaggle of Fw 190s were spotted at 22,000 ft. Taken from Lt. Petterson's Encounter Report, he described the action as follows:

> "We turned to the left and jumped them from out of the sun. My first burst missed him and I shot a second burst at a 15-degree angle high. I saw hits on the wings

Right: First Lieutenant Hans J. Grasshoff is seated in the cockpit of a Bison Squadron P-51. *Courtesy of the 436th Fighter Squadron Association.*

and so I centered my aim on his canopy and wing roots. I continuing hitting him until smoke poured out, he lost his canopy and pieces were flying off the plane. He pulled up to the right and bailed out. I claim one Fw 190 destroyed." Captain Joseph J. Knofczynski, who was flying behind Lt. Petterson during the combat, confirmed the kill, noting that he saw the pilot bail out and that the pilot's chute was extended, but did not open."

Minutes later, Captain John W. Harrell Jr., also from the 435th FS, saw more Fws ten miles southeast of Dümmer Lake. The weather in this area was similar to that in which the previous encounter took place; there was good visibility with broken clouds at 5,000 ft. Capt. Harrell narrated in his Encounter Report:

"From 12,000 ft. I caught two Fw 190s on the deck. I dived to attack and damaged one of them. Closing to 50 yards, I was forced to take evasive action because of light flak coming from several barges. I claim one Fw 190 damaged." Second Lieutenant Fredrick L. Hart certified that he saw that action and that the Fw was damaged as claimed. The 436th FS flying back and more south of that, had a bit of action also. The weather where they were was 7-10/10ths cloud coverage.

First Lieutenant Hans J. Grasshoff was leading Red Flight of the Bison Squadron. They were at 22,000 ft. He reported: "At approximately 1215 hours, while in the Osnabrück [Ger.] area, two flights of Fw 190s, one of four and one of five, approached us at 25,000 ft. We climbed toward them head-on. The four ship flight split-essed and the five ship flight drove on. As we turned to give chase, they split-essed. I followed one and shot during the dive. I observed hits on my second burst and observed the pilot bail out at approximately 19,000 ft. I expended 220 rounds of .50 cal. ammunition. I claim one Fw 190 destroyed in the air." Second Lieutenant Stanley E. Derby was Lt. Grasshoff's wingman in this flight and was with him during the noted action. He confirms the kill stating that: "While cloud coverage limited vision of the entire action, I certify that a chute was observed at this approximate time and altitude."

The 56th FG had some business, too. Their 63rd FS accounted for three Me 109s. Unfortunately, the squadron lost one of their P-47s due to engine failure at the beginning of the foray.

First Lieutenant Thomas C. Olson with his Lelah May. *Courtesy of the Wings of Freedom Museum.*

Second Lieutenant Leo Czarnota, flying in Blue Two position with the 63rd FS made a circling descent to a lower altitude where he bailed out to become a POW. This was witnessed by the 479th and noted as one unidentified A/C that spun in and burned in the dogfight area at 1240 hrs. The force, scattered at this time by the action, began working its way back home. While on the way that direction, the 434th FS had a chance to do some strafing. First Lieutenant Thomas C. Olson damaged an Me 410 on the ground and later destroyed a locomotive. He gave this report for the Me 410 destroyed:

"I was flying as Newcross Squadron Blue Leader for the fighter escort mission. We were in the Dümmer Lake area when E/A were reported and later engaged. During this engagement, flights became separated and ours was no exception. A few miles north of the area, I spotted two airdromes and decided to look around them. At Vechta Airdrome I saw about ten plus Me 410s. I made a dive-strafing pass from 7,500 feet down to 3,000 feet, but drew no fire. I made another pass going down firing on a Me 410 and observed several strikes on the E/A. With this pass the field lit up with everything from .30 cal. to 40mm fire. I pulled away and claim one Me 410 as damaged."

Second Lieutenant John N. Morrow destroyed another locomotive. Both of the trains were located at Vechta, Germany, where one was headed south and the other was headed west. Second Lieutenant Wendell H. Marlowe damaged five goods wagons there also. L/O was 1345 hrs./10-21,000 ft. at Ijmuiden.

Observations made during the mission included three V2 rockets seen in Holland, one at 1200 hrs./21,000 ft. in the vicinity of Enschede, one at 1215 hrs./21,000 ft. coming from the vicinity of Apeldoorn and one at 1335 hrs./21,000 ft. southeast of Rotterdam. Enemy A/C were seen landing at the Hesepe, Germany airdrome. The runways appeared to be painted with orange stripes. Six plus A/C parked were on the southeast corner of Vorden, Germany airdrome and ten plus Me 410s were parked on the south side of the Vechta airdrome. At that airdrome there were light flak guns on the southeast and southwest corner as well as one of three located in a woods about one quarter of a mile south of the field. There were also 20 and 40mm guns on the west side of the field. Flak was light, moderate and inaccurate in the Osnabrück, Germany area at 1215 hrs./10,000 ft. to the deck. There was also an unidentified barrage of white puffs at 14,000 ft. in the same area. At 1230 hours, flak was heavy, meager and inaccurate over Oldenburg, Germany and at 1240 hours, it was light, moderate and inaccurate over Nienburg, Germany.

29 November 1944

Eighth AF FO 1348A

No. 195 & 196 Wednesday. The group was divided into two forces, A and B groups, both in support of 8th AF Mission 729. Lt. Col. Riddle led A group, which consisted of 32 P-51s (12-434th, 8-435th & 12-436th) on a penetration, sweep and withdrawal escort in support of 2nd BD B-24s. Up: 1012 hrs., down: 1533 hrs. with three early returns. Capt. Jordan led B group, which consisted of 28 P-51s (8-434th, 9-435th & 11-436th) on a penetration to target and withdrawal escort of 2nd BD B-24s. Up: 1059 hrs., down: 1600 hrs. with three early returns.

A group made L/F at 1055 hrs./16,000 ft. south of Ijmuiden, Holland. Lt. Col. Riddle led his group on a sweep through Germany at 22,000 feet, heading east to Einbeck, then north to Hanover, then back west to R/V at 1230 hrs./24,000 ft. south of Dümmer Lake with their assigned bombers, the 20th CW. The results of the bombing were unobserved due to undercast. L/O was 1440 hrs./10,000 ft. at Egmond, Holland. Flak at Hanover, Germany was heavy, moderate and accurate.

434th FS P-51, 44-14288 L2-I Margie, the mount named by Lieutenant Walter M. Drake, was bellied in this date. Lt. Drake had returned to the U.S. earlier in the month. *Courtesy of the Wings of Freedom Museum.*

B group made L/F and R/V'd with the proper bombers at 1225 hrs./23,000 ft. northeast of Zwolle, Holland. The B-24s were escorted through the target and back. Bombing results were unobserved due to 10/10 cloud cover. B group broke away from the bombers at 1330 hrs./12,000 feet, over the Zuider Zee. They then swept east to Dümmer Lake, looking for targets of opportunity to strafe. They found some, bagging 2-0-3 locomotives, 20-0-17 goods wagons, 0-0-6 troop cars and contents, 0-0-1 barge and 2-0-0 trucks. At a training camp located in a swamp in the Bourtanger Moor, just southwest of Meppen, Germany, the group saw twelve barracks and parade grounds with two towers. Also there were many straw-covered trenches filled with soldiers who were shooting with rifles at the P-51s. That was probably a bad idea for the Germans. The results were 0-0-1 trench of recruits and 0-0-3 barracks. L/O was 1455 hrs./10,000 ft. at Egmond.

Observations during the mission included noting that the Autobahn near the location of the training camp was graded, but then ended abruptly. A small road that led northeast to a clearing, joined it at that point. There was a small hangar, camouflaged brown and yellow in the clearing. No enemy A/C were seen there. Big Bens were seen headed west from southwest of Zwolle at 1050, 1100 and 1244 hrs.

30 November 1944

Eighth AF FO 1354A

No. 197 & 198 Thursday. The group was divided into two forces, A and B groups, both penetration to target and withdrawal escorts for 3rd BD B-17s attacking their 8th AF Mission 731 primary target, the oil industry at Merseburg/Leuna, Germany. Maj. Biscayart led A group which consisted

Left: Major Arthur F. Jeffrey onboard Boomerang Jr. *Courtesy of Frederick C. Hayner.* Top right: First Lieutenant Arnold G. Helding by Rumboogie Jr., a P-51 named by her crew chief, Technical Sergeant Milan John Stanovich. Lieutenant William H. Hehn was her pilot. He and Lt. Helding, had become part of the 434th FS back in the U.S. during January 1944. Since having come to Wattisham, the two shared a corner room at their BOQ with a third pilot, Lieutenant Harold F. Grenning, another pilot who had become a part of the 434th during that same January. Their time together as a part of Newcross Squadron forged a life-long friendship. *Courtesy of Arnold G. Helding.* Right: First Lieutenant William H. Hehn with his Rumboogie Jr. *Courtesy of Harold L. Stotts.*

of 32 P-51s (12-434th & 20-436th). Lt. Col. Woods was to have led A group, but he had to abort, thus placing Maj. Biscayart in command of the group. Up: 1020 hrs., down: 1610 hrs. Maj. Jeffrey led B group, which consisted of 29 P-51s (20-434th & 9-435th). Up: 1028 hrs., down: 1603 hrs. The combined groups had two early returns.

Both groups made R/V with the proper bombers at 1130 hrs./18,000 ft. northeast of Brussels, Belgium. The Big Friends were escorted to their target where they unloaded. Cloud cover was 10/10ths for most of the trip, however, in the Merseburg area, there were large holes, but still some haze was present. The results were observable and it was believed that most of the bombs hit in the target area. No enemy A/C were seen, but flak over the target was heavy, intense and accurate. Two B-17s were seen to explode at 1305 hrs./20,000 ft. over the target area. No chutes were noted. Two more B-17s were spotted gliding into some clouds at 1310 hrs./8,000 ft. in the Merseburg area. B group continued escort of the bombers, back to east of Brussels where they broke away at 1440 hrs./20,000 ft. A group remained in the target area to stooge around. They rejoined the bombers northeast of Frankfurt, Germany. A group broke away again, this time at 1430 hrs./20,000 ft. over the Rhine River. First Lieutenant Arnold G. Helding from the 434th FS, landed at St. Trond, Belgium. for an unknown reason. First Lieutenants Larry J. Cano and Howard C. Smith from the 435th FS, landed on the continent, both for unknown reasons.

Observations made during the mission included 20 plus barrage balloons spotted floating at 2,000 ft. over the dam north of Saalfeld, Germany and another 30 plus barrage balloons at 2-3,000 ft. south of Gotha, Germany. There were 25 plus unidentified A/C on the ground at Gotha. An airdrome two to three miles southeast of Gotha had two Do 217s and possibly some jet A/C. There were 15 plus unidentified A/C, possibly jets, at Weimar, Germany. Flak over the area crossed at the Rhine River was heavy, intense and accurate. In the Overflakkee Island, Holland area, it was light, meager and inaccurate while over Weimar, it was heavy intense and accurate. Captain John W. Harrell, Jr. who led the 435th FS in B group, made this observation:

"On returning from Mission FO No. 1354A, I was forced to take my section down from 27,000 ft. to approximately 16,000 ft. at a point about ten miles south of Koblenz by north of St. Goar and over the Rhein River. [Point located in Germany] We received moderate and inaccurate tracking flak at this point (at 16,000 ft.). The flak burst a dirty brown color with a smaller burst than 88mm fire and exploded in a round ball that did not dissipate after the explosion. The flak was received through the overcast. It is believed this could be 50mm flak described in a recent Teletype."

Lieutenant Chester W. Broadstone was in charge of the armorers for the 436th FS. He is shown here examining the breach of a .50 Cal. machine gun. *Carroll C. Sprague Collection, courtesy of the East Essex Aviation Society.*

436th FS armorers Corporal George W. Moyer and Staff Sergeant Daniel F. Pagano are examining a .50 cal. machine gun at one of the station's defensive positions. *Carroll C. Sprague Collection, courtesy of the East Essex Aviation Society.*

Newcross pilot Lieutenant Robert I. Bromschwig in his flight gear. *Courtesy of Robert I. Bromschwig.*

Right: Lieutenant Berkley E. Hollister took this photo of 434th FS Flight Surgeon, Captain Joseph F. (Doc) Schneider seated in Pin Up Girl. *Courtesy of Berkley E. Hollister.*

Technical Sergeant Earl L. Hicks and Master Sergeant Jack E. Gowan. *Courtesy of Clarence G. Haynes.*

Technical Sergeants Harold L. Greenlee and Victor R. Plassenthal. *Courtesy of Clarence G. Haynes.*

Chief Warrant Officer Earle L. Lewis a 434th FS engineering officer and Lieutenant John D. Foster, that squadron's supply officer, are by one of the squadron's new P-51s. *Courtesy of Marie H. Lewis.*

Lieutenant John D. Foster is standing by another of the 434th's new P-51s. *Courtesy of Marie H. Lewis.*

Staff Sergeant William M. Samples, Captain Philip D. Gossard and Sergeant Denver T. Susong by their 435th FS P-51 V for 'Val', a ship named for Capt. Gossard's wife. *Courtesy of Carol Donaldson.*

Lieutenant Berkley E. Hollister in and Technical Sergeant Thomas J. O'Grady on a 434th FS P-51. *Courtesy of Berkley E. Hollister.*

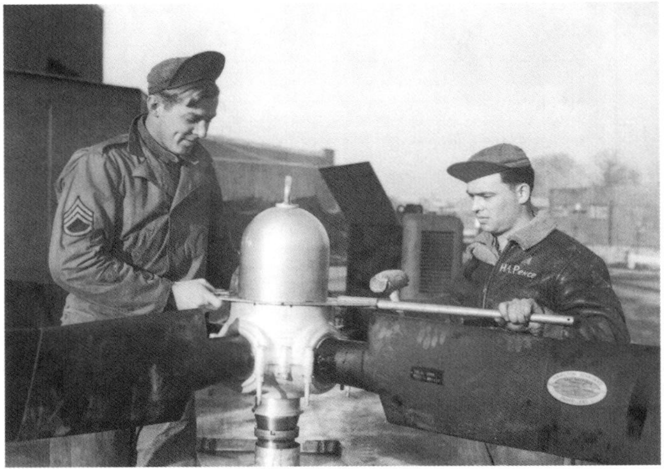

Staff Sergeant John J. Sipek and Sergeant H. A. Pence from the 436th FS are working on a Hamilton Hydromatic Propeller for one of their squadron's aircraft. Because of an urgent need in the 479th FG for men skilled in the maintenance of propellers, Sgt. Sipek was transferred from his beloved 56th Fighter Group to the prop shop at the 479th. He moaned about that until the day he died. There, I said it John. *Courtesy of John J. Sipek.*

Staff Sergeant Frederick C. Hayner has just put the finishing touches on some nose art he added to the other side of a 434th FS P-51 already named Pin Up Girl. Muriel was his wife and they were both from Troy, New York. *Courtesy of Frederick C. Hayner.*

Newcross pilot Lieutenant John W. Hansen finished his tour during this month. *Courtesy of Berkley E. Hollister.*

It wasn't always a combat mission or training that got a pilot into the air. Corporal Lucien Biernet, a photographer from the 436th FS and Lieutenant Norman R. Benoit, a pilot with the 435th FS are about to climb aboard one of the group's T-6s in order to take pictures of the group flying formations. *Carroll C. Sprague Collection, courtesy of the East Essex Aviation Society.*

CHAPTER ELEVEN

DECEMBER 1944

4 December 1944

Eighth AF FO 1370A

No. 199 & 200 Monday. Reaching its two hundredth mission, the group was divided into two forces, A and B groups, both penetration to target and withdrawal escorts for 2nd BD B-24s attacking an 8th AF Mission 736 target of opportunity, the marshalling yards at Koblenz, Germany. Capt. Jordan led A group, which consisted of 29 P-51s (8-434th & 21-435th). Up: 1046 hrs., down: 1603 hrs. Maj. Sullivan led B group, which consisted of 32 P-51s (12-434th & 20-436th). Up: 1051 hrs., down: 1610 hrs. There were no early returns.

A group made L/F at 1120 hrs./10,000 ft. at Knokke, Belgium. R/V with the 20th CW B-24s was at 1142 hrs./21,000 ft. northwest of Namur, Belgium. The bombers were in poor formation, all spread out. The group escorted the Big Friends as they went through their primary target area (the marshalling yards at Bebra, Germany) at 1252 hrs. No bombs were dropped. They wheeled around to the north and unloaded on the Koblenz target at 1320 hrs. The cloud cover was 10/10ths over the primary target with high-velocity winds aloft which were not forecast. Flak over the target was heavy, moderate and inaccurate. Upon returning, the group broke away from the bombers at 1440 hrs./24,000 ft. southeast of Liege, Belgium. L/O was at 1515 hrs./2,000 ft. south of Calais, France.

B group made L/F at 1121 hrs./19,000 ft. at Knokke also. They arrived at the R/V point at the proper time, but there were no heavies to be found there. Moving further inland toward the target area, the group encountered a single B-24 from the 20th CW, heading southwest at 1206 hrs./25,000 ft. near St. Goar, Germany. Continuing onward over Germany, they swept east to Frankfurt, northeast to Steinau, north to Giessen and southwest to St. Goar again. Heading back toward home from that point, high cross winds caused them to drift south to the area of Strasbourg, France. From there, the group then set a course of 270 degrees to try again to head home, but once more the winds caused them to drift southwest, eventually taking them near Orlèans, France. At this point, two flights landed at Orleans to refuel. Lieutenants Charles H. Darling, Albert R. DiPaola, Douglas L. Red and Richard S. Spencer Jr. from the 436th FS made up one of those flights. The other is unknown. L/F out for the rest was at 1500 hrs./deck-1,000 ft. at the Le Treport, France area.

Observations made during the mission included 75 plus barges seen at 1300 hrs. on the Moselle River southwest of Koblenz and a train with 20 plus cars seen at the same time, entering Koblenz from the southwest. Flak over the Rhine River, south of Koblenz, was heavy, intense and inaccurate.

5 December 1944

Eighth AF FO 1374A

No. 201 & 202 Tuesday. The group was divided into two forces, A and B groups, both penetration to target and withdrawal escorts for a force of B-17s attacking their 8th AF Mission 738 primary target, the marshalling yards at Berlin, Germany. Lt. Col. Riddle led A group, which consisted of 29 P-51s (12-434th & 17-435th). Up: 0829 hrs., down: 1355 hrs. Maj. Sullivan led B group, which consisted of 20 P-51s (8-434th & 12-436th). Up: 0825 hrs., down: 1356 hrs. The combined groups had a total of five early returns plus one escort.

A group made L/F at 0915 hrs./18,000 feet, north of Ijmuiden, Holland. R/V with proper bombers was at 0945 hrs./ 24,000 ft. in the vicinity of Dümmer Lake, Germany. B group made L/F at an unknown time and location due to the cloud cover that obscured the coastline. R/V with the proper bombers was at 0950 hrs./24,000 ft. ten miles south of Dümmer Lake. At approximately 1030 hours, as the group heading east to the target neared Stendal, Germany, Second Lieutenant Charles S. Kreger from the 436th FS reported he had a mid-air collision. At the time he was flying Bison Red Three and his wingman, Second Lieutenant Barrett B. Eskell was flying Red Four. According to Lt. Kreger, the following occurred:

> "I was to the right of my flight leader, First Lieutenant Thomas E. Myers, and flying at 27,000 feet. My flight leader made a 90-degree turn towards me and directly into the sun. I went down under him, started to turn and come up on the other side. While looking directly into the sun to see my flight leader, I felt a sharp jolt. I looked down and saw another airplane immediately under me. I stalled, recovered, looked to my right and saw my wingman, his left wing crumpled, going down. I stalled and recovered again. I noted that he seemed to be in a steep slip to the right. My aircraft was streaming gas at this point and as I did not know the extent of my own damage, I was not able to observe whether or not a chute emerged from the damaged aircraft. Both of my belly tanks had burst so I dropped them, called Snow White and came home."

First Lieutenant Norman R. Benoit and his wingman from the 435th FS reported seeing a chute at 1045 hrs. in the vicinity of the collision. Lt. Eskell survived the episode. He had bailed out, broken his leg and became a guest of the Germans for the duration.

The Big Friends were escorted through the target where flak was heavy, moderate and accurate. The time over the target was 1045 hrs./25,000 ft. Overcast prevented observation of the bombing results. One of the B-17s was seen spinning down. Five chutes from it were seen and then another bomber was seen, diving straight down in the target area at 1040 hrs. Two other chutes were seen in the target area at 1045 hrs. Still another B-17 was noted to be in trouble at 1050 hrs. Six chutes from it were seen, then it went into a downward spiral.

At about 1100 hours, ten minutes out of the target area, First Lieutenant Ronald L. Maley from the 434th FS called over the radio to say that he had been hit by ground fire and asked for an acknowledgement. He asked for acknowledgement several times, but all attempts to contact him failed. Apparently his receiver was not working. Lt. Maley had shot down a Fw 190 earlier this day, but now it was his turn to take some bad luck. With his engine about to quit, he tried to bail out of his plane, but he could not get his canopy open. It was jammed by flak that had hit it and torn some of it off. Lt. Maley was forced to belly land his P-51, "Tommy Trojan", named

A 436th FS P-51 landing at Wattisham. Note the external wing tanks are still in place, meaning that perhaps this bird could have been returning early or have been a spare that was not needed. *Courtesy of Arnold G. Helding.*

First Lieutenant Ronald L. Maley and his armorer Corporal Herbert Pastor. *From original 479th FG history.*

for his university, near Scharfenberg, Germany at 1125 hrs. He landed in a farm field and was captured by German soldiers before he could get out of his plane. He really did not have a chance at escaping because the area of trees to which he had planned to run after he got out of his ship was where the soldiers had come from. He was unhurt, but for him, the war was over. He has regretted every since that he never got to eat the Mars candy bar he had to leave on the plane's dash and that he never got to see his engine damage.

First Lieutenant Walter A. Neuman from the 434th FS was not so lucky. Last seen at 1100 hours, in the vicinity of a big air battle, he was reported by the Germans, in records found after the war, as killed in his crashed Mustang near Buchholz, Germany, 20 miles south of Berlin.

This was a big day for the 479th FG. Just after the strike, when the group and their charges had turned for home, Lieutenant Colonel Riddle spotted a group of 40 Fw 190s and 15-20 Me 109s near Neuruppin, Germany, slightly northwest of Berlin. They were carrying belly tanks and climbing on a westerly course about 1,000 ft. below. He immediately led the group down on them, initiating an air battle at 1045 hrs. that lasted twenty-five minutes and ranged from 22,000 feet, to all the way down on the deck. The official final score was 14-3-6 in the group's favor, but the cost was high.

The 434th FS tallied a score of 7-1-2 enemy aircraft claimed. Major Arthur (Art) F. Jeffrey had the biggest bag from that squadron. His claims were three Fw 190s destroyed and one Fw 190 damaged. He narrated the above action as follows. For Fw number one:

> "The clouds in the area were broken cumulus at 10,000 ft. and cirrostratus at 20,000 ft. I was leading Newcross Squadron's Section 'A' on an escort mission to the Berlin area. I was at about 26,000 feet in the vicinity of Neuruppin, which is ten miles northwest of Berlin. I sighted two formations of enemy A/C on a course of 330 degrees, [northwest] approximately 2,000 ft. below us, heading directly for the bomber formation. I gave the order to drop belly tanks and led White Section (9 P-51s) to attack in a diving left turn. I had started for the larger formation of about 40 plus Fw 190s, when my gunsight bulb went out. I dove right on through the smaller formation of approximately 15 Me 109s, which was slightly above and to the right rear of the big gaggle. The 109s split up every which way, with most of them hitting the deck. I finally got my gunsight back in operation and drove up to the rear of the 190 formation, closing on one to the left rear of the gaggle. I opened fire at 350 yards from dead astern, slightly high to low and closed to about 100 yards, observing strikes on the fuselage and belly tank. The belly tank exploded and then the whole A/C burst into flames and rolled over. I last observed him about 1,000 feet below me, spinning down out of control. During this attack, I could tell that all my guns were not firing and discovered later that two guns had frozen."

Fw number two:

> "I then moved over to the right, behind another Fw 190, and attacked from dead astern. Opening fire at about 250 yards, I closed to 50 yards, observing strikes all over his fuselage. The German started weaving slightly, but not violently. Finally I overshot and pulled up over him to the right, where I observed flames pouring out of his engine. The whole canopy and fuselage appeared to be blackened and seared. I repositioned for another pass, but then I saw the 190 go over in a spiral, belching flames and smoke, so I broke off to look for some more."

Fw number three:

> "Not immediately sighting any E/A at my level, I split-essed to around 4,000 feet, losing Lt. Jacobson, [Second Lieutenant Gail E. Jacobson] my wingman, while doing so. Almost at once, I picked up two Fw 190s stooging around rather aimlessly, evidently trying to find a hole in the undercast, the top of which was at approximately 3,000 feet. I drove up behind the rearmost one and in a fairly tight turn to the left, opened fire at about 200 yards, closing to less than 100 yards. While I was firing, I ran out of ammunition on the remaining right side guns so I had to skid to correct my fire coming from only the left side guns. I observed a number of strikes and flames began to pour out of the A/C. The 190 rolled over and spun, flaming into the undercast, out of control."

Fw number four:

> "I then tacked on to the remaining Fw 190 and opened fire from about 250 yards. However, after a very short burst during which I saw some strikes on his fuselage, I ran out of ammunition altogether. The Jerry immediately

started turning and weaving all over the sky in an attempt to shake me, but I stayed on his tail close enough to hit him with a club in hopes that I might scare him into bailing out as they usually do. Finally he ducked into a cloud, so I turned and lit out for the barn. I claim one Fw 190 damaged."

Maj. Jeffrey continues:

"I was driving along in a slight climb at about 5,000 feet, when I ran into another Fw 190 coming at me head-on. We each cocked up on a wing, glared at the other while waiting for a move, then went right on our respective ways. I for one, breathed a sigh of relief because I was all alone, out of ammunition and low on gas."

Maj. Jeffrey's wingman, Second Lt. Gail E Jacobson, in confirming what he saw of the attacks, narrates:

"I was flying Newcross White Flight Two, Section 'A' as Major A. F. Jeffrey's wingman, during part of his engagements. In the vicinity of Berlin, we sighted a formation of 40 Fw 190s a couple of thousand feet below us, with about 20 Me 109s slightly above and behind them. Maj. Jeffrey led White Section in a diving attack and drove right through the Me 109s, scattering them, and attacked one of the rear Fw 190s. I was on Maj. Jeffrey's right, doing a little shooting of my own, but covering him. I saw his German's belly tank explode, then the whole front end flamed up and the enemy A/C went tumbling down.

"Major Jeffrey then shifted over toward me and attacked another Fw 190 from dead astern. Again, I was attacking on my own hook while covering him. I saw the engine of his Jerry flame up and pieces fly off. Then the 190 rolled and went down, still on fire. While I was still firing at my E/A, Major Jeffrey split-essed off to the left and I followed, but lost him in the cloud and contrail level.

"I confirm the destruction of the first two Fw 190s claimed by Major Arthur F. Jeffrey."

Second Lieutenant Gail E. Jacobson, as he mentioned, had done some shooting, also. Claiming two destroyed, he continues:

"I was flying as Major Jeffrey's wingman when we attacked the Fw 190s from dead astern. He attached himself to one and I dived out to the right and positioned myself on another one. I opened fire from six o'clock, just slightly to the right side, at 200 yards, giving him about a two-second burst. I observed a few strikes on the left wing. The German didn't take any evasive action at all, and surprised me when he jettisoned his canopy almost at once. I cocked up on wing and watched him roll over to the right and bail out. I did not see his parachute open.

"I was still in formation with Major Jeffrey when I saw him move over toward me so I moved out to the right again and positioned myself for attack on an Fw 190 which had broken off from the enemy formation and was in a gentle left turn. I closed to 300 yards, opening fire from dead astern and just above his contrail. All my guns were not firing and I had to hold right rudder to keep the ball centered. I fired a two-second burst and didn't notice any strikes, but the Jerry popped his canopy at once and tumbled out the right side. The canopy almost hit me as it sailed past. I didn't wait to see if his chute opened, but followed Major Jeffrey, who had done a wing over to the left."

Major Arthur F. Jeffrey and his crew chief Technical Sergeant Nevoy C. Hummel by their P-51, Boomerang Jr. *Courtesy of the Wings of Freedom Museum.*

That took care of five destroyed and one damaged. First Lieutenant Richard G. McChrystal claimed another destroyed and one damaged. After sighting the 60 plus bandits, swinging around and making a diving bounce from the rear, he attacked the smaller bunch of Me 109s that Maj. Jeffrey and Lt. Jacobson zoomed through. Lt. McChrystal:

"I was flying Newcross White Three of Section 'A'. Two Me 109s broke right and dove through a cloud layer. I followed them and attacked one, firing from 45-degrees deflection at 300 yards to zero deflection and 50 yards range. I observed strikes on the E/A's right wing and gasoline came streaming out. He broke left in a dive. His prop wash flipped me right. I recovered and made another bounce on him from about 6,000 feet. I started firing at about 300 yards and closed to 50 yards. My fire was hitting him on the underside (he did not have a belly tank) and I saw a burst of flame. He half rolled and started going straight down, streaming smoke. He jettisoned his canopy as he went into the lower cloud deck.

"The second Me 109 was higher than I, so I started to climb towards him, commencing to fire 45-degree deflection shots from 300 yards, closing to zero degrees and minimal range. I observed strikes on the underside of his fuselage. He did a violent snap roll and went into a spin at 7,000 feet. I split-essed to follow him down. He went into the cloud layer and I followed him through. Below the layer, I found that he had recovered, but I lost him again when he ducked back into the clouds."

The score was now six destroyed and two damaged. First Lieutenant Harold (Smiley) E. Matthews, also from the 434th FS, claimed another. He stated:

"I was flying Newcross Yellow Flight Three, Section 'A', in a three-ship flight led by Capt. William H. Gates. After the group leader, Highway, [Lt. Col. Riddle] called in Bandits, our squadron dove to investigate, finding a gaggle of 40 plus Fw 190s. White and Red Flights made the bounce from the rear. The E/A broke into two bunches, one turning left and the other right. Newcross Yellow started after the right bunch, but these were bounced by another flight before we got to them. One Fw 190 broke, in a 180-degree turn from the formation. I called it, split-essed and started after him. I found I had but two guns on the right working and in the high-speed dive, I could not bring them to bear on him. We dove from 22,000 feet, through a number of cloud layers, attaining an indicated air speed of 475 mph by the time we hit 8,000 feet. We were diving at a 60-degree angle. At 5,000 feet, there was another cloud deck through which the 190 split-essed, taking a steeper angle of dive. I executed a sharp right diving turn and followed him through, easing up on the dive, as my ship was porpoising badly. We came out of this layer of clouds around 500 feet above the ground. My windshield had badly iced up after having dived through the cloud decks, but I could see that the Fw was apparently out of control due to the tremendous speed. He crashed straight in, causing smoke and debris to rise into the cloud deck."

Lt. Matthews expended 50 rounds of 50 cal. ammunition.

That made seven destroyed and two damaged. First Lieutenant Berkley (Berk or B.E.) E. Hollister, by claiming a probable, closed out the 434th FS's total, making it seven destroyed, one probable and two damaged. He continues the episode:

"I was flying Newcross Red Leader, Section 'A'. We were heading northwest when the E/A were sighted heading northwest, 2,000 feet below us. We let down as we turned and I followed White Flight into the attack. The main gaggle of Fw 190s held formation pretty well and made a turn to the right. I closed on a 190 at the left rear and opened fire at 250 yards, closing to 150 yards. As I got right in his contrails, I could not see very well, but I did observe a number of strike flashes and several pieces flew off the German plane and sailed past me. As I was overtaking him too fast, I put the stick forward and went under him, making a 360-degree turn. There were so many other P-51s attacking from other groups, that by the time I had completed the turn, I could not find him again, nor could I locate any unattached E/A, since most of them had split-essed into the clouds below."

Second Lieutenant Robert B. Kline, Newcross Red Two, supported Lt. Hollister's claim stating:

"I observed strikes all over the Fw that Lt. Hollister was firing at. Since we were closing too fast, we dived under and made a 360-degree turn, during which I lost sight of the E/A because of the clouds. Although I did not see the Fw 190 catch fire, from the number of strikes on it that I did see, I believe it improbable that it ever recovered at all."

Right: Captain William M. Gates. *Courtesy of Clarence G. Haynes.*

Fasr right: First Lieutenant Berkley E. Hollister. *Courtesy of Berkley E. Hollister.*

The group's CO and leader of A group, flying with the 435th FS, claimed that squadron's first victories. He successfully engaged and destroyed one Fw 190 and damaged another. That made the score 8-1-3.

Second Lieutenant Richard G. Candelaria from the 435th FS claimed two Fw 190s in that same engagement. His narrative of the action states:

> "I was flying Yellow Four position. We were heading 130 degrees at 30,000 feet when an enemy gaggle was sighted 4,000 feet below us, at eight o'clock and going away from us. The group leader called a bounce and I followed my leader into a sharp left turn. We closed on them as they started a gentle climbing turn to the right. My leader opened fire on one and got strikes on him. Two Fw 190s turned toward him and I opened fire on one at about 80-degrees deflection, but saw no strikes. The second one straightened and I closed on him and opened fire. I saw strikes in his cockpit and all over his fuselage. He went into a slow spiral to the right, trailing flames. I didn't see the pilot bail out, but a few seconds later the plane exploded. I pulled up toward my leader and watched his man bail out of the spinning aircraft. I followed my leader on another pass, but the E/A split-essed and went into the clouds.
>
> "We pulled up again and making another pass, my leader fired once more from very close range at another aircraft. I saw strikes on his fuselage and his canopy flew off. The E/A then pulled up sharply and fell away to the right. Two Fw 190s made a pass on us and I turned into them. They rolled over and started barrel rolling straight down. I followed, firing at them every time I got one in my sights. I saw no hits, but the canopy of the last plane came off and flew past me. A moment later I saw the pilot go out and go past my right wing, still in a half-sitting position. The plane went into a flat spin to the left. The other plane leveled off and caught up with four others. When they saw me closing in, all five peeled off to the right and dove into the cloud layer. I followed, but lost them in the clouds."

First Lieutenant Gordon L. Doolittle, the element leader and for whom Lt. Candelaria was wingman, confirmed those claims and that ran the total up to 10-1-3. Lt. Doolittle scored also, with two Fw 190s claimed as destroyed and one Fw 190 claimed as damaged. He said:

> "I was flying in Yellow Flight, number three position, when the E/A were sighted and the bounce was called. My wingman and I closed fast and I went clear into the center of the enemy formation. I fired a long shot at a Fw 190, 600 yards directly ahead of me. I fired a long burst and he rolled over, went into a spin and bailed out.
>
> "I pulled up to the left, above the formation and made another pass. I fired at one Fw 190, getting some hits on him. He split-essed and went into the clouds at 20,000 feet. I then pulled up behind another Fw 190 that was climbing. He was pulling heavy contrails and I drove up behind him, firing as I closed. I could not see strikes because of the contrail, but I closed to very close and saw his canopy fly past my plane. The Fw 190 then pulled up sharply and fell away to the right. I watched him in an uncontrolled spin, going into the clouds at 20,000 feet. I did not observe any parachute."

At a later date, Gordon Doolittle said that the sky seemed to be filled with fighters and that he had slid by one German plane close enough to see the pilot who was turning his plane to line up on him. That was the one that Lt. Candelaria picked off of him. Gordon also said that he remembered realizing on this mission that survival was critical if he planned to fly another day.

That made 12-1-4. Second Lieutenant Fredrick L. Hart, also from the 435th FS, bagged a Fw 190 that he claimed as destroyed:

> "I was flying in White Flight, in the number three position. Diving down on the melee, I closed fast and fired on a Fw 190 in the rear of the gaggle, seeing strikes on the underside of the engine. It started smoking and the pilot split-essed, heading straight down. I followed and when he leveled off in a cloud, I fired again, observing strikes on the fuselage. He dove again in a right turn, heading for the deck. I was right behind, firing and seeing pieces of the plane coming off. I overran him in a cloud as he was heading toward the ground from about 500 feet."

His wingman, Second Lieutenant George M. Salter, certified the claim to raise the sum to Thirteen-One-Four.

First Lieutenant Billy C. Means from the 435th FS claimed one Me 109 destroyed and brought back pictures to prove it:

> "I was flying Blue Flight Leader, on the right of the group leader. Being on the outside of the turn, I was late on the bounce. The gaggle had already broken and turned into me. I pulled up, picked an Me 109 passing under me and dove after him. He saw me, rolled over on his back, and then started a wide barrel roll going down. Following him, I closed to about 200 yards, then opened fire. I observed strikes all over the plane and parts came off. He steepened his roll until it was almost straight down. My controls stiffened until I could no longer roll with him. I pulled out straight ahead till I lost some speed, then turned after him again. He did about one more complete roll, then hit the ground and exploded. I took a pass at the wreckage to take pictures."

Number fourteen was dispatched.

Another pilot from the 435th FS, First Lieutenant Philip D. Gossard, joined the attack and claimed an Fw 190 destroyed. As the mixed gaggle of Fws and Me 109s began a slow, gentle right-hand turn, climbing to the right, Lt. Gossard, having dived down from over them, stated:

435th FS P-51, J2-O V for 'Val' – the fighter that Lieutenant Phillip D. Gossard had named and flew. *Courtesy of Steve Blake.*

> "I picked one on the outside of the turn, at the rear of the gaggle and closed to about 50 yards. I gave him a short burst and he blew up immediately."

Second Lieutenant Larry J. Cano confirmed the action and that became number fifteen.

The score was now fifteen destroyed, one probable and four damaged claimed, but then there were those from the 436th FS. First Lieutenant Thomas E. Myers damaged an Me 109 and shared the destruction of a Fw 190 with Second Lt. Peter C. Vassuer. Lt. Myers tells the story:

> "I had been leading Bison Red Flight, but after two aborts at the beginning of the mission, I sent my number two man to join White Flight and I joined Yellow Flight. When the box of bombers we were escorting were over the target, I called in a fight at nine o'clock to the bombers. After a minute or two, we went that way. I spotted a Fw 190 in a split-ess, so I peeled down and went after him. I started firing at 600 yards, closing to 100 yards and observed many hits on his wings and fuselage. He started burning fiercely and I overran him in the clouds, breaking out over the outskirts of Berlin at approximately 8,000 feet. I then pulled up through the overcast. My wingman lost me when I went into the clouds so I joined F/O Joseph [Flight Officer George Joseph] who took my wing and we stooged around. We found a B-17, 25 miles northwest of Berlin. Men were bailing out of it so we stayed with it until six of them were clear of the ship. The 17 then went into a tight spiral and was gone. We were at 14,000 feet when F/O Joseph called in bogies at three o'clock. We

went to investigate and one split-essed while another went under us. I went after the high one and called it in upon making positive identification that it was and Me 109. The 109 peeled off to the left and I followed, firing as best I could. The bandit went straight down, with me about 50 to 30 yards behind him. He was taking violent evasive action, but I got a few hits on him before he went through the overcast. F/O Joseph was on my wing all this time."

Second Lieutenant Vassuer continues the story:

"I was leading the element for Bison Yellow Flight and my wingman had aborted. Lt. Myers had broken up the remnants of his flight and joined us, so I flew wing for him. When he called out the bogies, we drove over in that general direction. Having identified them as bandits, Lt. Myers spotted one on the tail of a P-51. Lt. Myers peeled after him and I went on to cut them off. I was in a position of approximately four o'clock high on the Fw 190 when I fired. Missing, I reset my lead and observed hits on his wing. I gave him a pretty good squirt and he soon burst into flames and broke up. I went into the overcast and lost Lt. Myers so I joined up with another Little Friend. I claim one Fw 190 as destroyed, shared with Lt. Myers."

After that, Lt. Vassuer notes:

"I was getting low on fuel and could not locate my group so I started home on my own, joining at intervals with friendly aircraft. I escorted a B-17 with one engine dead as long as I could, then took a straight course home. In the vicinity of Osnabrück, Germany at about 1200 hours, I saw a bogie pop through the clouds below me and into the clear. I identified him as an Me 262. My altitude was 20,000 feet and I was up sun from him, so I peeled off at him, picking up speed from the dive. I was doing 450 mph and easily gaining on the jet, which evidently had very little power on. He started a turn, so I peeled off and started another turn to come inside of him. I sent a deflection burst at him and he flipped his belly at me and went into what seemed like a dive with the stick forward. I kept firing at him, seeing hits as I closed to about 350 yards. He rolled out and headed for a cloudbank at about 9,000 feet as I expended the last of my ammunition. I claim one Me 262 as damaged."

Numbers sixteen destroyed, one probable and six damaged as confirmed by F/O Joseph, First Lt. Myers and Second LT. Vassuer.

The big action was over now and the group was on the way home. A group broke escort at 1115 hrs./25,000 ft. ten miles northwest of Berlin while B group continued to escort the bombers back until they were southwest of Dümmer Lake. B group broke escort there at 1215 hrs./25,000 ft.

Before landfall out, A group had a chance to do a bit of strafing, picking up a couple of locomotives, a truck, a radio tower and some goods wagons as damaged and/or destroyed. First Lieutenant Norman R. Benoit from the 435th FS went down to strafe an airfield 30 miles west-southwest of Bremen, Germany. On his first pass at 5,000 feet over the field, Lt. Benoit saw something that looked like a plane that was camouflaged. Diving down and firing in that direction, but more toward some flak guns, he noticed that branches of some sort were covering what was definitely an aircraft. Becoming certain that it was an Me 262, he shifted his aim and began scoring many hits on the plane. Pulling up from his first pass, flak guns from north and west of the field, began a determined effort to hit him. Their rate of fire increased and Lt. Benoit observed intense and accurate light flak and tracer. The bursts were numerous, appearing all around him. He took violent evasive action, but the flak gunners evidentially tracked him with ease. They were putting up their defensive barrage wherever he went and the explosions were appearing closer, all around him. He stayed in the area for about ten minutes, attempting another pass, but the flak gunners continued to track him easily, even through six to eight-tenths overcast. Lt. Benoit left the area, claiming one Me 262 as "pretty well wrecked". The flak was too hot. This was certified by his wingman, Second Lieutenant David (Hot Shot Charlie) E. King, to make a grand total of sixteen enemy aircraft destroyed, one probable and seven damaged.

Major John A. Sullivan, the leader of B group called on the radio to state that his coolant had "popped" and that his engine was running rough. He joined the returning bombers to head home. The time was 1200 hrs. At approximately 1330 hours, he called Nuthouse (MEW Controller) saying he was leaving the bombers and could see L/O in the vicinity of Ijmuiden, Holland. He expected he would cross out in three minutes. Ten minutes later, at 1340 hours, Maj. Sullivan gave a Mayday call on "A" channel. This was heard by Captain Bailey A. Williams of the 434th FS. Capt. Williams called Maj. Sullivan and told him to switch to "B" channel, which he did. Capt. Williams then heard him call "Mayday, Mayday, Bison 30", twice. Capt. Williams waited for Air Sea Rescue to answer, but heard nothing from them. He then called them himself and asked if they had received the Mayday. ASR had not, so Capt. Williams told them to take a fix on his position as he wasn't too far from where Bison 30 should have been. A few minutes later, Maj. Sullivan gave another Mayday, but it was very distorted. At this point, Capt. Williams had to return to Wattisham because he was low on gas. Back home, nine P-51s were dispatched from the group to search for the missing Major, but the results were negative. Five ASR P-47s looked until dark, but found nothing. Major Jules D. Biscayart took another 17 P-51s from the 436th FS to look for an hour, but they also had no luck. Air Sea Rescue was to continue the search the following day, but the weather prevented that. All groups who were going out on missions were briefed to be on the lookout on their return trip. They were to let down and carry on the search. The results were nil. Major John A. Sullivan never came home.

L/O for A group was at 1230 hrs./3,000 ft. in the vicinity of Ijmuiden and for B group it was at 1315 hrs./17-18,000 ft. in the same location.

Captain Bailey A. Williams. *Courtesy of Berkley E. Hollister.*

Observations made during the mission included seeing a P-51 in a steep dive from 27,000 ft. to 20,000 ft. at 1000 hrs. It was trailing smoke and disappeared into the clouds near Nienburg, Germany. Flak in the Dümmer and Steinhuder Lakes was heavy, meager and accurate while over the Hook of Holland, (Hoek van Holland, located south of The Hague) it was light, meager and accurate.

A photograph taken from a sequence of movie film that Lieutenant Berkley E. Hollister shot using his hand held gun camera. The frame shows two 434th FS P-51s, L2-T- and L2-Z. In the foreground is "Hi-Baller", a Mustang named by Lieutenant Tom D. Neely. *Courtesy of Berkley E. Hollister.*

6 December 1944

Eighth AF FO 1383A

No. 203 & 204 Wednesday. The group was divided into two forces, A and B groups, both penetration to target and withdrawal escorts for 2nd BD B-24s attacking their 8th AF Mission 741 primary target, the marshalling yards at Bielefeld, Germany. Maj. Jeffrey led A group, which consisted of 31 P-51s (21-434th & 10-435th). Up: 1004 hrs., down: 1457 hrs. Maj. Biscayart led B group, which consisted of 22 P-51s (7-435th & 15-436th). Up: 1016 hrs., down: 1457 hrs. The combined groups had one early return.

R/V by both groups with the bombers was at 1030 hrs./15,000 ft. in the middle of the North Sea. The bombers were reported to be three minutes early, but were in fact ten minutes late. They were escorted uneventfully through the target area where the bombing was unobserved due to 6-9/10 overcast over the target. A group broke away from the bombers at 1215 hrs./22,000 ft. in the vicinity of Lingen, Germany and stooged around the Osnabrück, Germany area looking for targets of opportunity. They dive-strafed some barges on a canal west of Osnabrück, damaging three of six, plus canvas-covered barges. They also destroyed five locomotives, destroyed six goods cars and damaged another twelve, destroyed three trucks and two German GIs while they were at it.

B group broke away from the bombers at 1300 hrs./19,000 ft. in the Egmond, Holland area. They spent an hour searching fruitlessly for any sign of their missing CO, Major Sullivan.

Observations made during the mission included spotting V2 rocket contrails streaking 30,000 ft. into the sky seen at 1112 and 1215 hrs. in the Enschede, Holland area. Two airfields were investigated; one had a dummy A/C sitting on it and the other, located 20 miles west-southwest of Dümmer Lake, Germany, had three He 111s on it. First Lt. Norman R. Benoit, who strafed the field, damaged one of those. He concentrated on firing into one of two planes and a flak battery near the planes. The airfield put up light, meager and inaccurate flak from two towers located in a woods on the west side of the field. Flak in both the Egmond and Osnabrück areas was heavy, moderate and inaccurate. At Ijmuiden, Holland, and the shore of the Zuider Zee, near Zwolle, Holland, it was heavy, moderate and accurate. In the Hague area, it was heavy, meager and accurate.

Captain James M. Hollingsworth. *Courtesy of Thomas A. Hollingsworth.*

10 December 1944

Eighth AF FO 1404A

No. 205 & 206 Sunday. The group was divided into two forces, A and B groups, both penetration to target and withdrawal escorts for 2nd BD B-24s attacking their 8th AF Mission 745 primary target, the marshalling yards at Bingen, Germany. Maj. Jorden led A group, which consisted of 26 P-51s (20-435th & 8-436th). Up: 0909 hrs., down: 1300 hrs. Capt. James M. Hollingsworth led B group, which consisted of 27 P-51s (21-434th & 8-436th). Up: 0909 hrs., down: 1300 hrs. There were no early returns.

R/V by both groups with the 2nd CW B-24s was at 0955 hrs./22,000 ft. in the vicinity of Liège, Belgium. They were escorted through the target and out, uneventfully. The bombing results were unobserved due to overcast; there was a low deck of clouds extending from 9,000 ft. to 15,000 ft. in the target area. Flak over the target was heavy, meager and inaccurate. It was noted that over the target, there was a sequence of five light bursts, about 100 ft. apart, that ran in a vertical straight line through the undercast. The bursts appeared to be smaller than ordinary heavy flak (75 to 128mm) and round in shape (normal flak burst was upward and elongated, taller than wide).

A group broke escort at 1100 hrs./20,000 ft. to investigate bogies, but found nothing. B group broke escort at 1138 ft./ 20,000 ft. in the vicinity of Charleroi, Belgium. Two A/C from A group's 435th FS became separated from the rest of the group and did not return to Wattisham that day. They were both last seen together and apparently fine, headed west in the vicinity of Trier, Germany. First Lieutenants William D. Clarke and Robert (Marse) N. Pigg were both reported down safely on the continent, but only Lt. Pigg came home the next day. It seems that when he went down to land at an airfield that he spotted through a break in the clouds, Lt. Clarke pulled up and away. Later that day, Lt. Clarke was reported by telephone, as being safe at a RAF station. For several days, further inquiries as to his whereabouts brought forth no information. Finally, the news arrived that First Lt. William D. Clarke was reported as KIA near Dunkerque, France.

The mission take off was somewhat marred by an accident that occurred as two planes from the 436th FS were taxiing into position. Fog and ice had made both taxiing and take off precarious and this was well illustrated when Lieutenant Charles H. Darling in Ding Hoa over ran "My Best Bett IV" piloted by Lieutenant Charles S. Kreger. There were no serious injuries, but "My Best Bett IV" was scrapped. Landing at Wattisham after the mission, Second Lieutenant Wendell H. Marlowe cracked off the right wheel of his P-51 and battered the ship somewhat.

11 December 1944

Eighth AF FO 1408A

No. 207 & 208 Monday. The group was divided into two forces, A and B groups, both penetration to target and withdrawal escorts for 3rd BD B-17s attacking their 8th AF Mission 746 secondary target, the marshalling yards at Koblenz, Germany. Lt. Col. Riddle led A group, which consisted of 37 P-51s (17-434th & 20-436th). Up: 1008 hrs., down: 1435 hrs. with two non-effective. Capt. John W. Harrell led B group, which consisted of 23 P-51s (4-434th & 19-435th). Up: 1019 hrs., down: 1435 hrs. There was one early return.

R/V by A group with the third force of B-17s was at 1145 hrs./24,000 ft. in the vicinity of the target, Koblenz. The bombers were reported to be two minutes late, but were actually twelve minutes late. The formation was strung out, especially H box. The group stooged around the target area for a while, but Nuthouse, the group's controller, had no business for them. There were no enemy A/C in the nearby air. They eventually broke escort at 1300 hrs./25,000 ft. in the vicinity of St. Vith, Belgium.

R/V by B group with the proper bombers was at 1136 hrs./23,000 ft. in the vicinity of St. Vith. They escorted the Big Friends through the target and back to St. Vith, where they broke away from the B-17s at the same time that A group did. The bombing results were not observable due to undercast over the target. Flak around Koblenz and over the target was heavy, meager and inaccurate.

The observations made during the mission were only two Big Ben contrails seen within minutes of each other. One was seen at 25,000 ft. approximately 30 miles north of the target area and the other at 35,000 ft. approximately 35 miles east of Köln, Germany.

12 December 1944

Eighth AF FO 1412A

No. 209 & 210 Tuesday. The group was divided into two forces, A and B groups, both penetration to target and withdrawal escorts for 2nd BD B-24s attacking their 8th AF Mission 748 primary target, the marshalling yards at Aschaffenburg, Germany. For the third day in a row, the Eighth Air Force was pursuing a policy of striking the German rail system. This series of attacks was being relentlessly maintained to give the greatest immediate assistance to the allied armies in the west. All bomb divisions were engaged in a strong force on key rail centers heavily used in feeding badly needed replacements and material to the 1st German Army at the front. Maj. Jordan led A group, which consisted of 28 P-51s (20-435th & 8-436th). Up: 1019 hrs., down: 1530 hrs. with one non-effective. Capt. Hollingsworth led B group, which consisted of 28 P-51s (19-434th & 9-436th). Up: 1013 hrs., down: 1517 hrs. There was one early return.

R/V with the B-24s by A group was at 1130 hrs./27,000 ft. south of Liège, Belgium. The group escorted the bombers through the target and back out to south of Giessen, Germany. where they broke away from the Big Friends at 1300 hrs./ 27000 ft. The P-51s soon tied up with a force of 1st BD B-17s at 1310 hrs./27,000 ft. They were escorted further west to a point where they would cross the Rhine River. The Little Friends broke escort here at 1340 hrs./27,000 ft. While returning home, First Lieutenant Robert (Marse) N. Pigg reported that his engine had quit at 22,000 ft. While the actual cause of his engine failure is unknown, the possibility exists that it failed because of over-boosting. It is known that Lt. Pigg had the limit of his plane's engine boost control set higher than what was recommended. This gave him an extra amount of power when he went to full throttle, but it was hard on the engine. In fact, when he was cruising in formation for long periods and the call came through to clear engines – briefly go to full throttle in order to prevent spark plug fouling – the extra boost would push him ahead of everyone else in his flight. (For a further explanation of engine boost, see below, this date.) Gliding for a while, Lt. Pigg called again to say that he was down to 15,000 ft. and that he was going to bail out. Maj. Jordan advised him to bail out under the clouds below them. Apparently choosing not to heed the group leader's advice, Lt. Pigg jumped from his plane. After leaving his A/C and descending in his parachute, Lt. Pigg was reportedly struck by a B-26 while in the clouds. Found later on the ground, he died on the way to a hospital in Liège. First Lt. Robert N. Pigg was identified by his dog tags.

R/V with the B-24s by B group was at 1045 hrs./18,000 ft. in the vicinity of Ostend, Belgium but R/V with the proper bombers wasn't until 1130 hrs./22,000 ft. southwest of Koblenz, Germany. The formations were badly strung out and mixed up, making identification and escort difficult. The B-24s were taken through the target and back to Liège where escort was broken from the bombers at 1340 hrs./18,000 ft.

Observations made during the mission included a B-17 sighted going down ten miles northeast of Limburg, Germany. Seven men were seen to bail out of the stricken A/C, but only six chutes were noted. Two Big Ben contrails were watched as they trailed up and out at 1221 and 1233 hrs. south of the Ruhr area in Germany. Flak, eight miles south of Koblenz, was heavy, intense and accurate while at Wiesbaden, it was heavy, meager and inaccurate.

While the group was over the continent, back home at Wattisham, First Lieutenant Billy C. Means and Second Lieutenants Glen W. Hill, Robert H. Horman and Robert B. Hymans from the 435th FS were on a training mission. During that flight, Second Lt. Hymans became lost. The three Second Lieutenants had only arrived in England and been assigned to the squadron since the middle of last month. Here are the words of Lt. Means, describing the incident:

> "On the morning of December 12th, at approximately 1045 hours, we took off from our home field on a high altitude training mission. We had climbed to 21,000 feet when my engine began to surge, uncontrollably, from 40 to 60 inches Hg. [Manifold pressure or boost, as it is called, is the pressure under which the fuel mixture is supplied to the intake manifold, as measured in inches of mercury. The Packard built, Rolls-Royce Merlin, as was used in the P-51 Mustang, utilized an automatic boost feature which controlled the position of the carburetor throttles and ultimately the supercharger output. Therefore, no gas, no air, no go.] I tried several times to get by this point, but to no avail. Giving up on this, we chased some bombers south for a short while and then we began to simulate combat. At approximately 1130 hours, I pulled out of a shallow dive, on top of a cloud deck. Up to this time, Lt. Hymans had been right on my tail, but looking back, I could no longer see him. I immediately called him, but received no answer. Lt. Hymans was Lakeside Green Three, and at one time I thought I heard Colgate in contact with a Lakeside Green Three, giving him a steer of 200-plus degrees to a clear spot, but that was all that I could understand. We circled the spot where we had last seen Lt. Hymans for about five minutes, then took a 90-degree heading and held it for approximately ten minutes. After we had been on this course for two or three minutes, we received four or five bursts of flak off to our left. We then let down through a break in the clouds and saw that we were over water. We took a 290-degree heading and in about five minutes, made landfall in at Southend. We then turned north and flew up the coast to Ipswich Bay, then home, where we landed at 1230 hours."

Flying Control at Wattisham endeavored to contact Lt. Hymans on both "A" channel and "D" wing training channel, but met with no success on either. All three fighter wings were called for information as were RAF 11 and 12 Groups and The Royal Observer Corps. None had heard anything concerning the aircraft or pilot. Overdue action was started at 1533 hrs. Second Lieutenant Hymans was last seen northwest of the London area. [*Author's note*: during the summer of 1997, one of the pilots involved in this training flight and who happens to live near the author, told of the events surrounding Lt. Hyman's disappearance. Then a Second Lieutenant, Robert H. Horman tells of "rat racing" around the skies of England during this training mission. As he describes it, the formation of Mustangs were chasing each other around, simulating combat, when all of a sudden he looked around and could no longer find Lt. Hymans. They looked all over and called on the radio for him, but to no avail. He was gone, just disappeared! Ironically, later that summer it was unofficially announced that the remains of both Second Lt. Robert B. Hymans and the P-51 Mustang he had been flying were found in the mud flats about two miles east of Shoebury Ness near the mouth of the River Thames Estuary. Initial identification came from the serial numbers found on the aircraft's machine guns, guns that never had a chance to be fired at the enemy. Remains of Lt. Hymens were found amid the compacted aircraft wreckage, as was a piece of material that bore his name. It appeared that Lt. Hymens dove into the water from some height, but the reason will never be known.]

This cartoon drawn by Robin Olds, a member of the 434th FS, serves to illustrate the weather conditions that had been prevalent during this period. *Courtesy of George E. Falkner.*

18 December 1944

Eighth AF FO 1430A

No. 211 Monday. Lt. Col. Riddle led the group, which consisted of 57 P-51s (17-434th, 22-435th & 18-436th) on what was to have been a penetration to target and withdrawal escort for the first two combat wings of 2nd BD B-24s attacking their 8th AF Mission 754 target. A huge weather front over the continent changed that. Up: 1109 hrs., down: 1410 hrs. There were six early returns.

L/F was made at 1200 hrs./23,000 ft. in the vicinity of Ostend, Belgium. The group drove south at 1210 hrs. from west of Brussels, Belgium until 1240 hours, looking for a way around the front which extended up to 30,000 feet plus. Since L/F in, the undercast had been building to 10/10ths cloud coverage and increasing in height. At 1237 hrs, their controller, Nuthouse, advised the group that the Big Friends were at L/F. At 1300 hrs. Colgate advised the group that the Big Friends had been recalled and were returning home. The group made L/O at Walcheren Island, Holland at 1300 hrs./32,500 ft.

The only observation noted was an Me 262 seen headed east from south of Ghent, Belgium.

Second Lieutenant Dewey H. Hollis from the 434th FS, took off on a local flight and was not heard from again. He was found the next day, killed in his plane, which had crashed one mile south of Hundon. (located about 20 miles due east of Wattisham) Strange how those things happen.

On the bright side of things, Wattisham's Hangar One was the location of a formal awards ceremony. General Jesse Auton, commanding officer of the 65th Fighter Wing, presented an array of medals to the officers and enlisted men of the group. This was a sunny spot in an otherwise gray day.

23 December 1944

Eighth AF FO 1443A

No. 212 Saturday. Maj. Jeffrey led the group, which consisted of 64 P-51s (21-434th, 22-435th & 21-435th) on a MEW sweep. Up: 1244 hrs., down: 1717 hrs. There were four early returns.

This was another day of attacks on marshalling yards and rail centers by the heavies. However, the 479th was given a chance to do free-lance sweeps under MEW control which meant that anything the MEW controller, Nuthouse, could spot would be passed on as a target to the group. This was also an important day for the embattled American armies being hard pressed by the Germans in their offensive into the Ardennes area. Up until today, the snow, mists and ground fog that had shrouded the battle area and provided, for the most part, a protective barrier against allied air attacks for the attacking German armies, had been in the enemy's favor. Today that was to change. A frontal system had moved westward, clearing the covering clouds and foul weather from the skies. The sun came up and cast its bright rays on the snow-covered forests and hills of the battleground. It was a beautiful, clear morning and the allied air forces would be able to fly. Not only would air power begin crushing the enemy and forcing him back into his homeland, but also a great air battle was about to begin over the beleaguered Americans below. Lasting several weeks, the war in the air would drive the last big nail into the Luftwaffe's coffin. Germany's carefully built up and husbanded air force, reassembled over the last six months of

1944, was dealt a final deathblow. Granted, that until The Third Reich's surrender in May, there was still a German air force to be contended with, but it would not be seen in the strengths than had been present in the past and certainly not like what was to be seen during the final week of 1944 and the first weeks of 1945.

L/F by the group was made over Ostend, Belgium at 1400 hrs./15,000 ft. Nuthouse vectored the group several times, finally resulting in the 434th FS encountering enemy A/C activity in an area ten miles southeast of Bonn, Germany at 1500 hrs. and the 436th FS coming upon similar circumstances over Euskirchen airdrome, approximately ten miles northwest of Köln, Germany at 1450-1500 hrs. The 435th FS sped to an area south of Liège, Belgium to investigate bogies that later turned out to be Spitfires. They then went to Aachen Germany, stooging around the Aachen-Düren area without incident.

The enemy A/C encountered by the combined 434th and 436th squadrons were discovered on the deck, where snow aided in their recognition. They were heading generally west towards the battlefront. The majority were Fw 190s and Me 109s, but there were a few Me 410s, too. The 15 to 20 enemy A/C seemed to be in no visible formation, although pairs and three plane elements were seen. Some were carrying drop tanks. When the squadrons engaged them, almost all the German pilots seemed to lack any aggressiveness. The combat took place between 15,000 ft. and the ground, but most was on the deck. While there was still some haze and poor visibility present in this area, that did not slow the pilots from the 479th. The two squadrons racked up a total of 12 destroyed and one damaged against the loss of one 434th pilot. What follows is a rundown of the events:

Major Arthur F. Jeffrey, the group leader, was flying with the Newcross Squadron. Spotting the enemy A/C, Maj. Jeffrey called in the bounce and split-essed down on them. He takes it from here:

> "Due to the glare from the sun and the haze, I drove up close to positively identify them as Me 109s. I opened fire on the lead one from about 400 yards and closed to about 200 yards, this putting me alongside and a little ahead of the second aircraft. I observed strikes hitting the fuselage and then the enemy aircraft crashed into the ground. I pulled up and to the right to get on the tail of the other aircraft, which had peeled off to the right. He turned sharply to the left and I wound up dead astern of him and opened fire from about 300 yards. We passed over the edge of a clearing and he crashed into the trees at the opposite end. I then started climbing back up to rejoin the formation when I spotted another Me 109 heading east, about 4,000 feet above me. I chased him and had closed up to about 700 yards when I fired a short burst. I continued closing to 500 yards for another short burst and then finally to about 150-200 yards where I gave him a good squirt. The ship caught fire and I observed the pilot bail out before A/C crashed."

Maj. Jeffrey's claims of three Me 109s was confirmed by his wingman, Second Lieutenant Elbert N. Harris, who was flying Newcross White Two. Lt. Harris had this to add:

> "We peeled off from approximately 3,500 feet and made a stern attack. Maj. Jeffrey fired several bursts into the element leader and he nosed into the ground almost immediately. We then moved over and came directly astern of the second Me 109. As Maj. Jeffrey fired, I observed very many strikes, all up the fuselage. The enemy aircraft began smoking and turned to the left, crashing into a clump of trees, where it exploded. Neither pilot got out of their aircraft.
>
> "We then chandelled to the right and sighted another Me 109 above us and headed approximately north. Maj. Jeffrey immediately gave chase and after following the enemy aircraft for about a minute, he had closed to within range. He then fired one short burst, then another and finally a long one. The plane partially came apart and the pilot bailed out. I saw the chute open very close to the ground."

First Lieutenant George W. Gleason was leading Newcross Red Flight. He had recovered from the broken ankle he suffered as the result of having to bail out of his P-51 which had been shot down by friendly fire two months ago. As Maj. Jeffrey bounced the first two pairs of Me 109s, Lt. Gleason led his flight down on the second two pairs, these being identified as Fw 190s. He describes it the following way:

> "I drove right behind the first one and gave him about a five-second burst, observing strikes on the wings and cockpit. The ship caught fire and the German pilot pulled straight up and parachuted out.
>
> "The second one broke to the left, so after a couple of turns, I positioned myself for a good deflection shot at

thirty degrees. I put my pipper [the aiming point in the gunsight glass] on his cockpit and closed the diamonds in on him, giving him a good burst. Again, I saw strikes on the cockpit and wing roots as several large pieces of cowling flew off. The enemy aircraft burst into flames and the pilot bailed out.

"I climbed to about 6,000 feet, trying to locate another one and finally caught sight of a Fw 190 heading towards Bonn. I tagged on him and we got into a luftberry. I started closing in on him and got in one short burst, seeing strikes, but my guns jammed. I rechecked my switches and tried again, but they still would not work. Needing to get out of the situation, I started climbing in the luftberry to gain altitude in order to split-ess out and break off. In fact, I was almost flying formation with the German, hoping he would bail out, but he didn't, so I firewalled everything at about 8,000 feet and headed down for the deck. The Jerry tried to follow me, but I outran him."

Lt. Gleason was only able to expend about half of his ammunition, but claimed two Fw 190s as destroyed and another damaged.

Lt. Gleason's wingman, Second Lieutenant Ossie J. Huval, flying Newcross Red Two, confirmed the action. He added that the first Fw crashed and burned and that the pilot of the second Fw bailed out at about 700 ft. He also noted that Lt. Gleason's fire on the third Fw was striking the A/C's fuselage and wing roots. The aircraft was doomed had not Lt. Gleason's guns jammed. Lt. Huval got himself a locomotive while doing a little strafing later on.

Second Lieutenant Gail E. Jacobson was flying Newcross Yellow Three at the time and he does an excellent job of describing the situation:

"We had crossed the Rhine River, below Koblenz, Germany when our ground control station called in bogies thirty miles ahead, flying on a reciprocal course. About ten minutes later, Maj. Jeffrey, the group's leader went down to check the bogies and identified them as Me 109s. Yellow Flight stayed above to furnish top cover for White Flight. We circled to the left at 8,000 feet and I spotted a single bogie driving below us and in our direction. I called it in and got permission to bounce, so I peeled off to the right, doing a complete barrel roll. I dived from 8,000 to 1,000 feet, coming in from dead astern and identified him positively as a Fw 190. He must have seen me because he started to accelerate and black smoke poured out his exhausts. I was closing very fast, indicating around 420 mph, so I dropped ten degrees of flaps and closed my sight reticle to maximum range, waiting until he filled the ring. I tracked him in to about 200 yards range and pulled the trigger. My K-14 gunsight was in good working order because my strikes were evenly distributed over both his wings and canopy. The enemy aircraft started smoking immediately and broke sharply to the left, evidently sucking it in too tightly because the aircraft snapped and dove right into the ground, exploding on impact. I made two camera passes on the burning wreckage."

Staff Sergeant Bernard P. Dussling, Lieutenant Ossie J. Huval and Technical Sergeant Victor R. Plassenthal are shown here by Newcross ship Georgia Ann. *Courtesy of the Wings of Freedom Museum.*

Second Lieutenant Clifford W. Bowers, Lt. Jacobson's wingman and flying Yellow Four, confirmed the engagement. He states:

"Being number four man, I was looking up and around. Lt. Jacobson did a diving barrel roll to the right and it took me a few seconds to spot what he was after, but I soon saw the Fw 190, almost on the deck. We closed fast and I was off to the right and back a little as Lt. Jacobson open fire from dead astern. As soon as the smoke from Lt. Jacobson's guns appeared, I saw the API [Armor Piercing Incendiary ammunition] strikes all over the 190's cockpit and fuselage. The enemy aircraft then started a medium dive to the left and exploded in a patch of woods. I circled the spot, while Lt. Jacobson made two camera passes on the wreckage."

First Lieutenant Tom D. Neely, the leader of Newcross Purple Flight, claimed two Fw 190s for the day, but he never got back to Wattisham to celebrate the day's victories with the rest of the squadron. His squadron mates described his actions in Encounter Reports filed for him, because Lt. Neely was forced to spend the rest of the war on German soil as a POW after sending his second Fw 190 crashing down. First Lieutenant John N. Murr, who was flying number three in Purple Flight, gives part one of the story:

"When the bandits were called and Newcross Leader went down to investigate, we dropped our wing tanks and followed along. At 8,000 feet, I sighted a Fw 190 three o'clock to me and just a little below. I turned into him, but the German turned sharply to the left and started climbing. The E/A straightened out in front of Lt. Neely, who immediately closed from 400 yards down to 50 on him and opened fire from almost dead astern. I observed strikes all over the Fw 190 and then I saw flames lick out. The E/A rolled over and started straight down. The pilot was thrown clear of the plane and his parachute opened. I saw the plane crash. I claim one Fw 190 for First Lt. Tom D. Neely."

First Lieutenant Philip A. Brown, flying Purple Flight Four, confirmed the first kill by Lt. Neely. Second Lieutenant William H. (Hank) Daudistel, Lt. Neely's wingman, was flying Purple Flight Two and continues the narration:

"I was a little to one side during the kill described by Lt. Murr so I couldn't tell who was firing on the German since the rest of the Flight was closed up and the Fw 190 was right ahead. However, I did see the E/A catch fire and the pilot bail out."

Another flight leader, First Lieutenant Harold (Smiley) E. Mathews, Blue Flight One, saw the second Fw 190 that Lt. Neely destroyed:

"I saw Lt. Neely do a wing over and go down after a Fw 190 headed southeast. I had seen the German ship at the same time so I took Blue Flight down to 3,000 feet in order to give Purple better cover. I saw Lt. Neely attack and observed good strikes as he closed fast. The Fw 190 turned about 45-degrees left and drove right over the town of Westerburg, Ger. with Lt. Neely right on his tail at about 1,500 feet. The E/A rolled left and dived into a wooded area north of the town, exploding when it hit the ground. As Lt. Neely and his wingman, Lt. Daudistel, passed over the town, I saw a lot of 20mm stuff flying up at them from flak cars at a rail junction in the town. [Light, intense and accurate flak was reported coming from multiple barrel 20mm guns mounted on railroad cars, part of a train headed north, standing in the town.] Lt. Neely must have been hit somewhere in his coolant system because his ship started trailing white smoke. He was down to about 800 feet at this time. At that point, Lt. Neely called over the R/T, saying that he was bellying in. I saw him belly land in the snow, on an open field. Then I had to break left as the railway flak had opened up on my flight."

Lt. Daudistel followed his leader through out all this and confirms the second Fw 190 as destroyed. He also watched Lt. Neely crash-land on the open field, leaving only after the P-51 came to a stop and he saw that Lt. Neely was okay.

That was it for the 434th FS; 8-0-1 for the loss of one. While the 434th was doing battle with its foes ten miles southeast of Bonn, the 436th FS, south of the 434th's location and closer to Cologne, came upon a huge dogfight already in progress. Colonel David C. Schilling's 56th FG had been sent by a MEW controller to check out a large force of bogies. Striking pay dirt, the entire group had attacked a swarm of at least 90 enemy A/C orbiting over the airdrome. The 436th joined the battle already in progress overhead.

Captain Edwin C. Lewin was drawn into the fray when one of the squadron's flights was attacked. He was leading Bison Yellow Flight and picks up the events at the encounter:

"I observed a 'dogfight' at about 11 o'clock high, called it in to Bison White Leader and the whole squadron flew over to investigate. Upon arrival, we found a number of P-47, Me 109 and Fw 190 aircraft in such a tangle state-of-affairs that I found it impossible to get an idea of the number of friends or foe. We were flying five flights in trail at the time and Bison Purple Flight was at the rear of our squadron. Purple Two called for a break right and

Right: First Lieutenant Tom D. Neely. *Courtesy of Clarence G. Haynes.*

Far right: Another photo showing Lieutenant Neely standing on the wing root of a P-51 he later was forced to bail out of due to a structural failure. *Courtesy of Berkley E. Hollister.*

acting upon this, I broke right, dropping my tanks at the same time. I found the cause of the break to be an Me 109 which had come down on Purple Flight, apparently making a short pass at them while trying to evade a P-47 who was trailing him by approximately 800 yards. The Jerry started a straight shallow dive to the east when our squadron broke and entered the melee. The P-47 that had been trailing him was rapidly being outdistanced. I had about a 3,000 foot altitude advantage by this time and had no difficulty in closing rapidly. As a matter of fact, I closed too rapidly and overshot him when he broke into me. It took about two turns in an orbit to the right before I managed to get into a position about 500 yards behind him and open fire from approximately 25-degrees angle off. Using the gyro gunsight, I continued to fire and close on him to within 150 yards. Pieces flew from his plane and smoke began pouring out as I overshot him again. I kept the aircraft in sight, observed him to recover from a violent three-turn spin and followed him down as he bellied into a snow-covered field. He did a grand job of bellying in. While he was still sliding on the snow, I was getting ready to strafe him. Suddenly, as he came to the end of the field, the aircraft crashed into a stone fence there and exploded in a huge sheet of flame. I claim one Me 109 destroyed."

Second Lieutenant John K. Wilkins, Capt. Lewin's wingman, confirmed the action.

Captain Carl V. Ernst claimed another Me 109, stating:

"I was leading Bison Yellow Flight and was over an unidentified airdrome southeast of Ruhr [sic]. At 12-

Right: A later photograph showing by then, Captain Harold E. Mathews seated in a Mustang. *Courtesy of Clarence G. Haynes.*

Far right: Lieutenant William H. Daudistel. *Courtesy of Clarence G. Haynes.*

13,000 feet, I gave chase to a Fw 190 that passed in front of me and which was being chased by another P-51. My flight and I followed them down to about 1,000 feet, but overran them and lost both aircraft. We then broke off and climbed back in the general direction of the unidentified airdrome. Approaching it at about 5,000 feet, I observed an Me 109 on the tail of Lt. Thomas E. Myers. I came in for a 30-degree deflection shot and hit the enemy aircraft with a three to four second burst at very close range. The E/A began spurting coolant and then burst into flame. The pilot bailed out successfully at about 3,500 feet. I claim one Me 109 destroyed."

This was confirmed by Capt. Ernst's wingman, Second Lt. John R. Schuck.

Captain Joseph R. Struby took another of the 56th FG's quarry when he engaged and destroyed a Fw 190:

"I was leading Bison Purple Flight when we came upon a huge 'dogfight' in the air above us. There were P-47s, Me 109s and Fw 190s all in a heated, turning fight. I made a turn to the right, dropping tanks as I did and went after an Me 109. While I was giving chase to the enemy aircraft, my number two man called a break right. Glancing back, I saw another Me 109 coming in at five o'clock and firing at my number four man. My flight went into a violent right break. The 109 kept going and gained altitude. I continued to turn to the right and gave chase, but I had lost considerable speed in my break to the right. I opened fire at 600 to 700 yards, at the same time observing Capt. Lewin coming in high to my left and closing rapidly on the 109. I observed strikes and smoke, which were undoubtedly caused by Capt. Lewin scoring on the aircraft. I then turned south looking for other enemy aircraft and sighted two planes about half a mile away and slightly low, apparently engaged in a dogfight. As I approached, I identified one as a Fw 190 which then semi-split-essed and headed east, hitting the deck as he went. I gave chase with my flight, opening fire at about 400 yards and closing steadily. The 190 led me over a small town, just above the rooftops; then started a gradual pull up and turn to the right. He began taking violent evasive action at low speed, right off the deck, staying over and in the immediate vicinity of the small town. I had difficulty staying behind him and overshot him a number of times. I got in a good burst as he was in a turn to the right, observing strikes on the cockpit and wings. I overshot again and as I pulled up above him, he went into a violent snap to the right and crashed."

A later photograph of crew chief Staff Sergeant Roger F. Hofstra, Captain John R. Schuck and armorer Corporal Joe Diaz. *Courtesy of the 436th Fighter Squadron Association.*

Second Lieutenant Fred Zellman, wingman to Capt. Struby, confirmed the kill.

Captain Andre E. Huycke scored another victory for the squadron when he shot down a Fw 190. Flying as Bison White Three, he said:

"I was stooging around at 8,000 ft. with my wingman, Captain Hans J. Grasshoff. I spotted a P-47 on the deck, with an unidentified plane on his tail, shooting at him. I dropped tanks, rolled over and went down. While going down, I saw the P-47 split-ess and crash. Fortunately, the pilot bailed out. [He was one of three the 56th FG lost that day.] I pulled in on the aircraft I had now identified as a Fw 190. I took a shot at his tail and missed. I got a direct line astern shot while in a vertical bank and had to pull lead with my fixed sight because the gyro wouldn't catch up. At approximately 1200 feet, he fell off into a split-ess and didn't pull out. I pulled up and lost him for a second, but saw the fire and smoke from the crash below me."

Capt. Huycke's Fw was confirmed by Capt. Grasshoff.

Almost all of the scoring pilots from the 436th FS were from the original batch of fliers that had come over in May from Palmdale, California and each had also just received Captain's bars. Captains Lewin, Struby and Huycke, as well as Captain Grasshoff, who witnessed a kill, had each taken a tour extension and had over 300 combat hours apiece. This was their last hurrah, for their combat time with the squadron was at an end and they each would be heading home for some well-deserved rest.

L/O for the 435th FS was at 1600 hrs./12,000 ft. in the vicinity of Ostend and about the same for the combined 434th and 436th FS's except they made landfall out at Calais, France. On the way home, First Lieutenant Harold (Smiley) E. Mathews, Second Lieutenants David (Dave) L. Born and Clifford (Cliff) W. Bowers landed at Demain/Prouvy airfield in France for gas. Many years later, Cliff Bowers told the author why that happened:

"We were in our aircraft, with engines running, waiting at Wattisham to take off for the mission. We were all lined up and ready for the signal to go. Unfortunately, there was a halt called for some reason. It was getting warm in the cockpit so I took off my heavy flying gloves and laid them on top of the control stick. Well, one of the standard procedures for take off was to set the wing tank switches for emergency drop, just in case some emergency occurred during that time. The button that activated the drop was located on top of the control stick and you guessed it, the weight of the gloves pushed that button and my tanks released, falling on the taxiway. I was embarrassed, but I called to have the tanks rolled out of the way. I wanted to fly the mission because I wanted all the time that I could get and I didn't want to be left behind. I was one of the newer pilots to the group and wanted to gain experience. Besides, all my buddies were going! We eventually took off and got into a scrap over Germany, which used up extra fuel. On the way back home, we had to land in France for gas because I was running on empty. Smiley Mathews and Dave Born landed with me and we stayed overnight there. The base was crawling with women! That was the first time I'd ever seen anything like that. Smiley became our interpreter and by using his little French/English language guide, he tried to round up some food and a place to sleep. We felt a bit uneasy and out of place there, but we made do. Dave and I slept in the same bed, which sagged and dipped to the middle. We shared quarters back at Wattisham, but this was overdoing it. We were close there as roommates, now we were really close! In the morning, we got up, went to the planes and siphoned gas from both Smiley's and Dave's planes into mine. Then we headed home."

Captain Joseph R. Struby and his crew chief Technical Sergeant Walter J. Doyle with Little Hemorrhoid. *Courtesy of Stanley Kellett.*

Captain Hans J. Grasshoff by his P-51 Little Zippy. F/O Raymond E. King would be later lost in this aircraft when he was forced to ditch in the channel. *Courtesy of the 436th Fighter Squadron Association.*

A similar occurrence had happened to Lieutenant Gerold M. Mulvany of the 436th FS on another mission. He called his P-51 "Bottleneck" because he had dumped both wing tanks during run-up prior to taking off for the continent and as he claimed, stopped the war until the gasoline from the ruptured drop tanks could be washed away. The controller in the tower screamed "Get that damned bottleneck off the runway! Pilot report to the tower!" Mulvany said, "She was named."

Second Lt. William H. Daudistel, from the 434th FS, had to land at Framlingham, England due to weather. Lt. John H. Early had to land at airfield B-48 on the continent and F/O George Joseph had to land at A-58, also on the continent, both men from the 436th FS and both for unknown reasons.

Observations made during the mission included seeing eight to ten tanks in a woods believed to be east of Köln and many tank tracks in the snow covering the area east of Wuppertal, Germany. Flak over that area was seen to be put up in a large white barrage.

Lieutenant Clifford W. Bowers and crew chief Technical Sergeant Louis E. Kirby by Skunk Chaser's drop tanks. *Courtesy of David L. Born.*

First Lieutenant Gerold M. Mulvany by Bottleneck. *Courtesy of the 436th Fighter Squadron Association.*

24 December 1944

Eighth AF FO 1446A

No. 213 & 214 Sunday. The group was divided into two forces, A and B groups, both penetration to target and withdrawal escorts for 3rd BD B-17s attacking their 8th AF Mission 760 primary target, the airfield at Zellhausen, Germany. This assembly of 85 B-17s took part in leading the entire Eighth Air Force in what was part of the largest air strike operation of the war. The Christmas Eve Maximum Effort saw the 1st BD put up 542 A/C, the 2nd BD, 634 A/C and the 3rd BD, 858 A/C. The combined fighter groups put up 844 A/C in defense of the bomber force. While not all aircraft sent aloft were effectives, it still represented an unprecedented force that must have been a sight to behold. A high pressure area extending across Western Europe had brought clear skies again over the continent and allowed the Mighty Eighth to launch multiple strikes against German airfields and communication centers. Lt. Col. Riddle led A group, which consisted of 32 P-51s (20-435th & 12-436th). Up: 1054 hrs., down: 1620 hrs. Maj. Jeffrey led B group, which consisted of 29 P-51s (17-434th & 12-436th). Up: 1100 hrs., down: 1600 hrs. The combined groups had a total of six early returns.

A group made landfall at Belgium, then R/V'd with the Big Friends at 1200 hrs./25,000 ft. near Brussels. Proceeding inward towards the target, the group was notified of a number of bogie gaggles reported southeast of Liège, Belgium. They split up and went to investigate. Scattered elements were vectored to Frankfurt, Germany and Malmèdy, Belgium, a place gaining dark fame as the location of the December 17, 1944 slaughter/massacre of nearly a hundred American soldiers and Belgian civilians by German troops. Flying with one of those elements seeking the bogies, First Lieutenant Nelson W. Butler from the 435th FS witnessed the kind of killing so often seen taking place during the war in the air. At least in this instance, there was some retribution. Lt. Butler describes it:

"We were in the vicinity of Liège, Belgium and the weather was CAVU. I was flying number four position in White Flight when my element leader and I became separated from the rest of the squadron. We were flying along the bomber formation when I sighted three B-17s quite a ways ahead of us. I saw one of the B-17s explode and when I looked closely, I saw an enemy plane circling the remaining two. I called my element leader and started after what I had identified as a Fw 190. Before I could get to him, he had shot down the other two planes. [Lt. Butler reported the time of his attack to be at 1230 hrs. and located 20 miles southeast of Liège.] He was starting after another B-17 when I closed on him. I closed to about 100 yards and let go a couple of bursts. As I fired, I noticed numerous strikes in the fuselage of the 190 and several small pieces flew off. I was overtaking him pretty fast so I had to pull up to miss hitting him. As I pulled up, I saw his canopy fly off and the pilot bailed out. I claim one Fw 190 destroyed."

Second Lieutenant Ray K. Friend, from the same squadron, lends some confirmation to Lt. Butler's claim, stating:

"I was leading Yellow Flight and started after two bogies when I saw the front plane start to pour out smoke and at the same time, identified the rear plane as a P-51. I was only able to identify the lead plane as a single-engine and didn't know the type. In a minute or two, a parachute popped open so I pulled away to continue hunting. In talking with Lt. Butler, I feel that this was the same action he described in his Encounter Report, but I did not identify his plane for sure. This was in the same area as where Lt. Butler reported his claim."

Second Lieutenant Clark R Hoffman, also from the 435th FS, shared a Fw 190 with the group's leader, Lieutenant Colonel Riddle. They were in the same area as Lt.'s Butler and Friend. He tells of the downing:

"I was positioned on Lt. Col. Riddle's wing. As such, I assumed the responsibility of inter-communication with our particular boxes of bombers. I had trouble in contacting them and, therefore, had to resort to using "C" channel. We were on course and shortly after passing Liège, we made a 180-degree turn. It was standard rate and so I remained on "C" channel. Soon after this we made another 180-degree turn and started back on our original course. Within two or three minutes, I saw four aircraft approaching from our right, south-southwest to north-northeast and five or six thousand feet below our altitude. I switched to "A" channel just as Col. Riddle dropped his tanks and split-essed to go after them. I immediately dropped my tanks and advanced throttle to stay with him. I remained relatively alongside of him, but slightly closer that ordinary formation. The approaching aircraft dived slightly until they ascertained our identity. They then began an almost straight down dive. Our initial dive brought us almost straight down on them and I saw the crosses on their wings. The one that we chose to follow started to roll over. He was on his back and still diving at around 8,000 feet. We recovered at approximately 7,000 feet and pulled up high to our right. At that point, the enemy aircraft was still diving straight down. [It was seen to crash and burn after it failed to pull out of the dive.] I claim one Fw 190 destroyed, shared with Lt. Col. Riddle."

Parts of A group proceeded home by flights and part of the group stayed with the B-17s until 20 miles southeast of Giessen, Germany where they broke away for home at 1330 hrs./23,000 ft.

After crossing the coast and proceeding into Belgium, B group R/V'd with the bombers at 1200 hrs./17,000 ft. over Bruges, Belgium. At 1225 hours, their controller, Nuthouse, vectored them to an area ahead of their assigned bombers, up to the first box, which was under attack by approximately 40 enemy aircraft. The fight was over by the time they arrived. Thereafter, a general escort of the B-17s was maintained until 1445 hrs./25,000 ft. west of Stuttgart, Germany, where the group broke escort and headed home.

Observations made by the group during the mission included seeing chutes from the B-17s (reference Lt. N. W. Butler's encounter) shot down near Liège and also seeing another B-17 belly in' the same area. Two unidentified fighters were seen to collide in the vicinity of Köln, Germany at 1230 hrs./15,000 ft. (Fighter group losses for this mission included two P-51s, reported to have collided over enemy territory. One was from the 55th FG and the other from the 357th FG.) Balloons were seen over Koblenz, Germany and a smoke screen was seen along the docks at Weisbaden, Germany. Bombers going down, the result of enemy fighter attacks and flak, plus many chutes were noted between 1245-1300 hrs. along the Rhine River, below Koblenz. Three Me 262s seen at

1245 hrs./31,000 ft. southwest of Koblenz were chased, but could not be engaged. Flak in the Koblenz area was heavy, intense and accurate. At Worms, Germany, it was heavy and inaccurate. Twenty-five miles north of Hanau, Germany, it was heavy and accurate.

Lieutenant John H. Early, III, from the 436th FS, had to belly in between Knokke and Bruges. He reported he was okay after he came to a stop and returned to work a few days later. Captain Hans J. Grasshoff, along with Lieutenants Stanley E. Derby, Bernard R. Kleinman and George H. Witzel, all from the 436th FS, landed at Brussels for unknown reasons as did Captain William M. Gates , 435th FS, at St. Trond, Belgium.

Lieutenant John H. Early, III. Note the ever-present bicycle. *Courtesy of Charles H. Darling.*

25 December 1944

Eighth AF FO 1451A

No. 215 & 216 Monday. The group was divided into two forces, A and B groups, both penetration to target and withdrawal escorts for 2nd BD B-24s attacking their 8th AF Mission 761 primary target, a communication center at Prüm, Germany. Maj. Jeffrey led A group, which consisted of 27 P-51s (18-434th & 9-435th). Up: 0855 hrs., down: 1359 hrs. Capt. Moore led B group, which consisted of 26 P-51s (8-435th & 18-436th). Up: 0920 hrs., down: 1359 hrs. Christmas Day had dawned with excellent weather for the mission, but during takeoff, it suddenly grew very foggy and in a short space of time, Wattisham was completely closed in. The B group planes remaining on the ground continued, using instruments for their take off. One A/C skated off the runway, a victim of the fog and resultant icy conditions present. The combined groups had a total of four early returns.

This was another "Big Show" for the 479th Fighter Group. The group scored 15-credited enemy A/C kills in the air against the loss of four of their own.

A group made landfall in and then R/V'd with the lead box of B-24s at 1042 hrs./20,000 ft. near Ostend, Belgium. The Big Friends were ten minutes late for R/V. As they headed in with the bombers, at 1150 hours A group was vectored by Nuthouse, their controller, to bogies at 32,000 feet just northeast of the target area, south of Bonn, Germany. Arriving in the area southwest of Bonn, the force encountered two gaggles, one low and one high, totaling 50 plus enemy A/C. At that time, A group's Lakeside section was vectored south to the Eupen/Limburg area in Belgium where they intercepted 12 Me 109s and Fw 190s at 30,000 ft. As a consequence, air battles were fought in the skies covering territory ranging from southwest of Köln, Germany, to 20 miles southwest of Bonn and down to south of Aachen, Germany, all of which took place between 1200 and 1230 hrs. (All locations for claims from the 434th FS were given as 20 miles southwest of Bonn, while those from the 435th FS were as noted in the pilot's narratives.) The low gaggle of 20 plus Me 109s and a few Fw 190s were at 25,000 ft. and had come from the Ruhr area. They were on a course to intercept the bombers near the target. When A group attacked them, a high gaggle of 30 plus Fw 190s came in from the east at 28-32,000 ft. and bounced the already engaged group from out of the sun. (Beware of the Hun in the sun.) The Germans were extremely aggressive and fought in pairs or fours. They headed for the deck only when they were at a distinct disadvantage.

Major Arthur F. Jeffrey, from the 434th FS and leader of A group, gave this narrative of the beginning action:

> "The weather was clear with a slight ground haze and a few high cirrus clouds scattered about. I sighted twenty plus E/A coming in on us from the north, nine o'clock high to us, so I turned into them, calling for the group to drop tanks and attack. Due to my left tank failing to drop at first, I was a little slow in getting into the fight. When the tank finally did drop, I saw two Me 109s split-essing for the deck. I picked one and went after him. On

the way down, I observed the other Me 109 break into pieces after he had dived almost straight down from 10,000 feet. I had not fired on him, nor did I see any other Allied A/C attacking, so the E/A must have exceeded its stress limits in the dive. By this time, I was closing in on the other E/A. He must have seen me because he began to take evasive action. I closed in to about 400 yards from dead astern, high, and opened fire, observing strikes on the fuselage and wings. Smoke began to pour out and then I saw the canopy come off and the pilot bail out. I claim one Me 109 destroyed."

First Lieutenant George W. Gleason led the entire group in claims for the day, bagging three Fw 190s:

"I was leading Newcross Red Flight when I sighted the bandits we had been vectored to. They were in a luftberry, trying to gain altitude so I took my flight up in a tight, kinking spiral, with full power on. Just as we started working down on the luftberry, I saw another 20 plus Fw 190s coming in at us from about 32,000 feet and out of the sun. I called them in and broke into them, trying to climb above them, but I couldn't. I started turning with them. About the time that I would get lined up on one, there would be two or three lined up on my tail and I would have to break to get rid of them and start all over again. The E/A were all working in pairs or fours and were very aggressive. I finally cut one out and lined up on him after about two turns. I put the pipper on the cockpit, closed the diamonds and gave him a long burst. I saw his cockpit light up and observed strikes on his wings, engine cowling and forward fuselage. Parts of the ship began to fly off, including the canopy. I gave him another short burst and the 190 rolled over and went straight down in an inverted spin with flames licking out of the engine. The pilot never got out.

"Driving back into the fight, I saw a Fw 190 shooting up a P-51. I tried to get there, but could not do it in time to save the P-51. Finally I got on the German's tail and was positioning myself for the kill, but my sight was on the cowling of my plane since we were pulling as high as six-and-a-half Gs. When my speed died down to 300 miles per hour, I got everything lined up and gave him a long burst, observing strikes concentrated mainly on his left wing and cockpit. The E/A snapped through the air about four times with pieces beginning to fall off and smoke starting to pour out. Then I saw flames begin to lick out around the cowling and underneath part of his fuselage. The Fw 190 continued down in the uncontrolled spin and I followed him from 26,000 to 5,000 feet, where he was still spinning. I left him after that point because the pilot bailed out.

"I picked up another Fw 190 on the deck. He had two other P-51s after him, but the Jerry had the initial speed and broke towards the east. I broke to the right and down on him, finally catching him. I gave him a short burst at about 350 yards with the pipper elevated about one foot above his cockpit and observed a few strikes on his left wing. I closed right, lined up again, closed down my diamonds to about 100 yards and gave him another long burst. This time, I saw strikes on his canopy, tail and wing roots. Black smoke billowed out from his engine cowling. The E/A pulled straight up, the canopy came off and the pilot bailed out.

"I looked for more enemy planes, but could not find any so I pulled up to 12,000 feet and drove home by myself. I claim three Fw 190s destroyed."

First Lieutenant Phillip A. Brown, flying Newcross White Four from the 434th FS, continues the narrative:

"At 23,000 feet, southwest of Cologne, Germany, we picked up thirty plus E/A at ten o'clock high. We dropped tanks on order and broke into them. When the initial confusion straightened out, I was still flying number Four position, but I'm not sure what in what flight. We circled in a loose luftberry for several turns and then number Three, the plane that I was flying wing to in the flight, got on the tail of a Fw 190 and fired a short burst. I didn't see any strikes, but the E/A broke right and down, so I followed it. The E/A took violent evasive action, but I finally got in position, firing two long bursts at 15-degrees deflection. I didn't see any strikes, however. At 16,000 feet, I corrected my sighting and fired from about 200 yards. This time I saw many strikes on the left wing root and around the cockpit on the left side of the E/A. The Fw 190 immediately snapped into a violent spin and dived toward the ground. I watched it for a short time, noting that there was no apparent attempt to recover nor did the pilot bail out. Before I could see this E/A hit the ground, I spotted another Fw 190 at about 12,000 feet, just a little below me. I attacked and fired a short burst from above at

30 to 40-degrees deflection. Although I didn't see any strikes, the E/A went into a spin almost at once and dived straight into the ground, where it exploded. I claim two Fw 190s destroyed."

First Lieutenant Arnold G. Helding, flying 434th FS Newcross Blue One, was the leader of that flight and claimed two Fw 190s as destroyed:

"Our ground control station had called in a gaggle of bandits approaching our bombers from the left. We headed that way, climbing to their altitude. Just after we gained altitude, we caught sight of them, and they of us, for they immediately bounced us from the northeast. I was clearing my tail when I saw 20 plus Fw 190s coming down on us from the right at about 28,000 feet. My wingman and I, along with a P-51 from another group, turned into them. We got in a big luftberry and after a few turns, I positioned myself on the tail of a Fw 190. I had just gotten him centered and given him a short squirt, getting good strikes, when the E/A did a violent snap to the right. I tried to get in another burst, but he had snapped too far under me. I watched him going down for several thousand feet. He was still out of control, snapping violently as he went straight down.

"I then observed another P-51 from our squadron, off to one side and under attack. A Fw 190 was firing at him and after the P-51 went down, the German did a steep bank to the left to get away from me, since he must have seen me coming after him. I had more speed than he did however, so I got a little above him in the turn and cut down on him. The E/A then rolled to the right and I drove right in close and gave him a short burst, observing many hits on the canopy and cowling. His ship caught fire and just as the Fw 190 started to spin out of control, the pilot parachuted out."

First Lieutenant Richard D. Creighton, wingman to Lt. Helding and flying 434th FS Newcross Blue Two, confirmed the two Fws downed by his leader and got one himself:

"My flight leader broke into a gaggle of Fw 190s and shot down one E/A which snapped out of control and spun straight down. He then got on a second Fw 190, which winged over in a steep dive with both of us following. About that time, I checked behind us and was a little

Crew chief Staff Sergeant John B. Atteberry and First Lieutenant Arnold G. Helding are standing by the P-51 that Lt. Helding named Lil'Trouble! *Courtesy of Arnold G. Helding.*

excited to find a Fw 190 sitting on my tail, firing at me! I broke up to the left, trying to slice inside of him. At the end of the first turn, I was gaining on him. Then he started a shallow dive and pulled back up. I opened fire from about 300 yards with 30-degrees deflection and observed one or two strikes on the cockpit. The German split-essed and I followed him clear to the deck, where I got on his tail again. I opened fire, but forgot to range the K-14 and missed. I finally corrected and saw many good hits. He was right on the deck and after I hit him, he plowed smack into the ground, but bounced right back up. He started to pull up and bail out, but after he jettisoned his canopy, the ship went out of control and dived straight in from about 200 feet. I claim one Fw 190 destroyed."

First Lieutenant John N. Murr, from the 434th FS and flying Newcross Blue Three, was at 25,000 ft. when 25 plus Me 109s and Fw 190s were sighted at 12 o'clock:

"The lead flights made the bounce so I started climbing with my wingman and broke down into the dogfight. I picked out a Fw 190 and positioned myself on his tail. He was very aggressive and did not make any move to hit the deck, but instead, stayed and turned with me. After a few turns, I got in position and gave him a short burst, observing a few strikes. The E/A went into a gentle turn and the canopy came off. It looked to me as though the pilot was thrown out. I did not wait to see if his parachute opened, but instead, I climbed back into the fight.

"I got on the tail of an Me 109 pilot who was really sharp, because I had a job staying in position. I fired a short burst from dead astern and saw a few strikes, but I must have been caught in his prop wash because I found myself suddenly doing a half-loop and heading straight down. When I recovered, I had lost the Me 109, so I climbed back up to about 25,000 feet.

"I saw a number of E/A above me in a luftberry, so my wingman and I dropped to 20,000 feet and headed for the bombers. When we were almost there, I climbed back up to 29,000 feet to be above the bombers. Once there, I saw fourteen E/A below, at 25,000 feet and firing at the bombers. At first I thought they were P-51s because they were in four ship flights, but then I identified them positively. I checked for my wingman, but could not find him immediately, so I called the ground control station and my group leader to give them the word about the situation. I then dived down on the E/A. I came in on one Fw 190 from dead astern and opened fire from about 300 yards and closed to 50 yards. I saw hits all over the fuselage and wing roots. Flames began to lick out. I continued to fire in short bursts, getting strikes all the while. A big chunk came off his left wing, together with a piece of his cowling. I tried to pull up for another pass, but I had too much airspeed and overshot him. As I went by, I saw the Fw's whole left wing come off. At this point, the E/A had broken off their attack on the bombers, so I split-essed to the deck and headed home. I claim two Fw 190s destroyed and one Me 109 damaged."

Lt. Murr's wingman, Second Lieutenant Robert I. Bromschwig, flying Newcross Blue Four, had his own problems for part of the action:

"Just after the initial bounce, two E/A got on my tail and I had to take violent evasive action to lose them. I did not get back on Lt. Murr's wing until he started climbing back up to 29,000 feet. We bounced about 14 E/A which were firing at the bombers. Lt. Murr attacked a Fw 190 in a diving turn to the left and closed from dead astern. When he opened fire, I observed many strikes on the left wing. Then about a four foot section of that wing came off and the Fw 190 started straight down in a violent spin, trailing smoke. I confirm one Fw 190 destroyed by Lt. Murr."

First Lieutenant Gail E. Jacobson, also from the 434th FS and flying Newcross Yellow Three, went after a Fw 190:

Lieutenant Robert I. Bromschwig. *Courtesy of Robert I. Bromschwig.*

"Taking a vector from our controller, we ran into a gaggle of Me 109s with a gaggle of Fw 190s as their top cover. They were trying to gain altitude. Yellow leader took our flight up in a climbing left turn into the sun. We started our bounce from 27,000 feet. I singled out a Fw 190 in a circle to the left toward me and managed to cut across enough to get in a 90-degree deflection shot. I was using the K-14 gunsight and had the pipper right on him. I gave him one good burst and saw strikes right in his canopy and wing roots after which he rolled to the left and started straight down. Another P-51 from my squadron was following him at the time. As the German went down, he would roll to the right and then straighten out. After doing this three times, he went into a spin to the right at about 10,000 feet. I lost him then while checking for other E/A. When I last saw the Fw 190 I had hit, he was in an uncontrollable spin at about 10,000 feet. I did not observe any strikes by the other ship from my squadron as he tried to get on the Fw's tail. I claim one Fw 190 as probably destroyed."

Second Lieutenant Clifford W. Bowers, flying Lt. Jacobson's wing as Newcross Yellow Four, confirmed his claim of one Fw 190 probably destroyed, noting that Lt. Jacobson's 90-

degree deflection shot put four or five API bursts directly in the cockpit area, probably hitting the pilot.

First Lieutenant Eugene E. Sears from the 434th FS was flying as a spare for the Newcross squadron. Eventually being called upon to fill in as a part of Yellow Flight, he became involved in the action and gave this report afterwards:

> "Vectored to bandits, we dropped our tanks on orders, but mine would not let go until I salvoed them by hand and fired a short burst from my guns. By the time that I had done this, my element leader had dived away from me and I was unable to locate him in the general mix-up. I had dived down to about 22,000 feet in a left-hand spiral when an Me 109 passed in front of me, evidently intent on bouncing some P-51s below. I slid over and got a good close shot at about 20-degrees deflection. His tail wheel came down, so I moved my line of sight on up the fuselage, observing strikes all the way up to a point just back of the cockpit. Black smoke began to pour out and some stuff, evidently coolant, sprayed back and got all over my windscreen. The E/A then went into a vertical dive, streaming black smoke. I was unable to see if the pilot bailed out, due to the coolant on my windscreen, but I believe that he may have because I saw a pilot in a chute immediately afterwards and couldn't see any other A/C from which he might have come. Since I was alone and my vision was restricted, I broke out of the fight as some Fw 190s came down from above. I started climbing back up toward the bomber contrails until the wind cleaned the stuff off my windshield. After being unable to contact anyone else from our group, I came on home alone. I claim one Me 109 as destroyed."

First Lieutenant Harold M. Jenkins, flying 434th FS Newcross Yellow Three, knocked down a Fw, but almost became a casualty himself:

> "Soon after the vector to bandits, White Leader called in a gaggle of twenty plus E/A so I dropped tanks. White section engaged almost at once and was in a big luftberry when I came in high and singled out a Fw 190 on the outside of the circle. I closed to 250 yards and opened fire with about 15-degrees deflection. I saw a good concentration of strikes on his left wing root and in the cockpit; then flames began to stream back. The E/A did not seem to take any evasive action, but fell off to the left and started straight down, out of control. As I tightened up my turn to clear my tail, I saw the German pilot bail out and his parachute open.
>
> "As I started after another Fw 190, I felt vibration in my rudder pedals and on checking, found that I had taken a number of hits on the tail, so I broke off and headed towards home, making a forced landing at a forward base."

First Lieutenant Harold M. Jenkins. *Courtesy of Clarence G. Haynes.*

Lakeside's section, consisting of the 435th FS pilots assigned to A group, was vectored to the Eupen/Limburg area, south of Aachen where they intercepted 12 Me 109s and Fw 190s. Captain John W. Harrell, who was leading the Lakeside P-51s, had this to say:

> "I was leading the 435th Squadron [A group's section] on a bomber escort to Prüm, Germany. When the group was vectored to bandits by Nuthouse, I climbed with my section to give top cover. The remainder of the group engaged E/A at about 26,000 feet. Lt. Benoit [First Lieutenant Norman R. Benoit – see next report] and I attacked some twelve Me 109s at 30,000 feet. I became engaged with four Me 109s and fought to the deck. I scored numerous strikes on one of them, getting oil and coolant

from his ship all over my own. While chasing him, I lost my wingman and was forced to break my pursuit in order to defend myself against two other E/A. I am positive that the Me 109's engine was completely out of operation as I was overrunning him with everything completely chopped back. I did not see him bail out or crash because of the necessity to defend myself. I claim one Me 109 as probably destroyed."

First Lt. Norman R. Benoit, flying 435th FS Lakeside White Three, notes intercepting three gaggles of about 75 total Me 109s and Fw 190s southwest of Cologne:

"I saw about eight to twelve E/A Me 109s and Fw 190s above me and to my right. I put on the power and climbed into them. They started turning and firing at me. As I climbed into the gaggle, I started to shoot at an Me 109. Observing hits on him, I was forced to break off my attack due to the superior number of aircraft. I bored into another Me 109 and finally got him down to the deck level where he bailed out and his ship crashed. I claim one Me 109 destroyed and one Me 109 damaged."

Second Lt. Robert J. Baird, Lt. Benoit's wingman, confirmed the claims.

First Lieutenant Theo J. Sowerby, another member of the 435th FS section, gave this narrative:

"We were in a dog fight ahead of our box of bombers and I, along with two other P-51s, were following a Fw 190 near Bonn. The Fw 190 broke to the right, that being the side my wingman and I were following on. I fired, getting many strikes on the cockpit and at the wing roots. The Fw 190 went into a tighter turn to the right and then entered a tight spin. The pilot then bailed out. He seemed to be very limp in his chute. I think he had been hit. I claim one Fw 190 destroyed."

Second Lieutenant Donald W. Thorn, Lt. Sowerby's wingman, confirmed the kill:

"At approximately 1215 hours, while flying number two position on Lt. Sowerby's wing, we saw a Fw 190 off to our right. This was in the vicinity of Bonn, Germany. There were two P-51s on the tail of the Fw 190, but they broke off when the enemy plane went into a diving turn to the right. I called out the E/A to my flight leader, Lt. Sowerby, and he turned right onto the tail of the Fw 190. When he shot, I saw strikes on the wing roots and around the cockpit. The E/A went into a tight spin and the pilot bailed out. His chute opened, but the pilot hung very limp and I believe he had been hit while getting out of his plane. I confirm one Fw 190 as destroyed by Lt. Sowerby."

B group made landfall in and R/V'd with the 20th CW B-24s at 1030 hrs./16,000 ft. between Blankenberghe and Ostend, Belgium. They escorted the heavies bound for Prüm, around the target, at which point one section was vectored east of the target, but found nothing. Returning to continue escort, that section broke escort at Brussels, Belgium at 1215 hrs./24,000 ft. Meanwhile, the rest of B group continued west with the bombers.

At 1210 hours, fifteen miles southeast of Malmèdy, Belgium Captain Richard S. Spencer, Jr. ran across some Fw 190s:

"At 1205 hours, I was leading Bison Red Flight and had lost the rest of the squadron when I turned into some unidentified bogies. I had been flying over an unescorted box of B-24s at 23,000 feet when about five minutes later, I saw that another box, flying parallel to ours, was being attacked from astern by twelve to fifteen Fw 190s. I told Red Flight to drop tanks and we drove in on three of the E/A which were about 1,000 feet below us and pulling around for another pass on the bombers. I took a short deflection shot at a Fw 190 that was at a two o'clock position to me and then pulled around to on his tail. As I closed on him, I gave him another long burst from dead astern and saw many hits on the fuselage around the cockpit. The plane began to smoke. As I pulled directly behind the plane, the canopy flew off and the pilot bailed out. As I turned away, I saw a B-24 in a shallow dive at nine o'clock to me and about 1,000 feet below. There was a Fw 190 following him down and firing at him. I made a diving turn in his direction and he broke into me. I could not get my sight on him and we continued turning in a luftberry. We kept losing altitude and at about 10,000 feet, the 190 split-essed and I followed him. He pulled out, split-essed again and pulled out again. We were quite near the deck by then and we had picked up a lot of speed. The German saw that I was still behind him and split-essed again. He was too low to pull out, however, and he crashed just beside a small tower. My number two man was with me and we climbed back up and came out. I claim two Fw 190s as destroyed."

Second Lieutenant Albert R. DiPaola confirmed this action. The flight then rejoined the bombers and the remaining B group force flew on with the bombers to south of Ghent, Belgium, where they broke off escort at 1250 hrs./20,000 ft. From there, two flights returned to the target area for a sweep, but that was uneventful and they went home.

Observations made by the group during the mission included noting that the assigned bombers were ten minutes late for L/F in and 30 minutes late at the target. Two unidentified silver planes were seen spinning down at 1210 hrs./10,000 ft. ten miles north of Trier, Germany. The bombing results appeared to be excellent. One ammo train on or dump near the railroad ten miles south of St. Vith, Belgium received a direct hit. Flak over Prüm was heavy, intense and accurate. Two bombers went down on fire in the target area. No chutes were observed. One B-24 was seen shot down by a Fw 190, 16 miles southeast of Malmèdy. Six chutes were noted. A crashed B-17 was spotted on the ground.

The two forces had planes and pilots scattered all over the continent by the time this mission concluded. Most, like Lts. Philip A. Brown, John N. Murr and Harold M. Jenkins from the 434th, Lts. Norman R. Benoit, Ray K. Friend, Theo J. Sowerby and Donald W. Thorn from the 435th, had stopped for gas or repairs, but five did not. Three pilots from the 434th FS, Captain James M. Hollingsworth, First Lieutenants Edward L. Hurtig and Wendell H. Marlowe, along with Second Lieutenant Douglas L. Red from the 436th FS, never got home from Germany that day. Capt. Hollingsworth became a POW, while Lts. Hurtig, Marlowe and Red were killed in action, due to causes unknown. First Lieutenant Hurtig was found in the wreckage of his aircraft two days later by a German Signal-Corps Company. He had come down on the Nürburgring racecourse, which is located approximately at the intersection of lines drawn, southwest from Bonn and west from Koblenz. First Lieutenant Marlowe's body was found crushed and burned in the wreckage of his fighter which had come down about one mile southwest of Langenfeld. German Luftwaffe personnel recovered his body and buried him nearby. The two lieutenant's bodies were later disinterred and identified by U.S. Army Graves Registration Units working after the war. The whereabouts of Second Lieutenant Red was never determined. The three pilots from the 434th FS were a part of the A group

Second Lieutenant Douglas L. Red. *Courtesy of the 436th Fighter Squadron Association.*

that was involved in the air battle previously mentioned. The pilot from the 436th FS was with B group and was involved in their scrap with the Germans.

After the war ended, Captain Hollingsworth was able to tell his story and put in claims for one Me 109 destroyed (downgraded to a probable) and one Me 109 damaged when he returned from captivity. His Combat Report dated 13 June 1945 reads as follows:

"I was leading Newcross Yellow Section on an escort mission. At 27,000 feet while in the vicinity of Bonn, we encountered a gaggle of twenty plus Me 109s with about that many more Fw 190s in another gaggle. The Me 109s were a little above us and were making a 180 degree turn, so I took my section up in a climbing left turn into the sun. As we got into position, I tried an 800-yard shot at one of the last E/A in the formation, ranging with my K-14 sight. I fired a short burst, getting strikes, then closed up to point blank range and gave him a long burst. The Me 109 took most of my strikes on the fuselage and left wing, and then burst into flame with most of the fire coming from the left wing root and cowl. The E/A rolled over and went into a violent spin. I watched him snap around four or five times with no apparent attempt at recovery and then went after another Me 109. This second Jerry was in a turn to the left and I got several hits as he slowed down and rolled out of the turn. Just as I rolled out behind him, someone yelled out over the radio: 'There is one on your tail, Holly!' At that instant, .30 cal. slugs hit my canopy and a 20mm exploded in my right wing. Then came a crash that threw me forward in the cockpit and sent my P-51 into a very tight spin to the right. [His

> pursuer had struck him from behind, cutting off his tail.] After much struggling, I managed to get out and my parachute opened safely. As I floated down, I saw a dark colored parachute about a half-mile away which I assumed was the pilot of the Me 109 that I had shot down. I was taken prisoner about three minutes after I hit the ground. I claim one Me 109 destroyed and one Me 109 damaged."

Once Captain Hollingsworth was taken prisoner, his captors, two German soldiers, began walking him up a road. Both soldiers were walking behind him and one had his rifle pointed at Capt. Hollingsworth's back. As they proceeded up the road, hostile German civilians were heading down the road to intercept them. Capt. Hollingsworth knew that the German civilians would probably kill him if they got the chance. Recognizing he was in a bad situation, Capt. Hollingsworth quickly side-stepped the soldier who had the rifle to his back and by spinning him around, held him in front of the oncoming crowd. He held the German by his coat and kept him in front as he kept saying Geneva Convention, Geneva Convention – you can't kill me. To the soldier's credit, they refused to release Capt. Hollingsworth to the mob, which no doubt, intended him harm.

He went the route all captured Allied airmen traveled and eventually wound up in Stalag Luft 1 at Barth, Germany. He almost didn't make it to his destination though. His train was stopped at a station that was bombed and ran afoul of some more hostile civilians. Once again though, his luck held.

Clarence (Buck) G. Haynes, then a Lieutenant with the 434th FS, has good reason to remember this day vividly. The day is etched in his memory and will always carry a degree of sadness for him. In 1997, he wrote the following narrative about the day:

> "Although local flying weather was marginal on that Christmas morning, our group took off from Wattisham and set course for rendezvous with the bombers we had been assigned to protect. We were to meet them over Belgium and provide escort to the target. On that day, I was leading the second element of a four-ship flight led by Captain [James M.] Hollingsworth. Lieutenant Dave [David L.] Born was my wingman for the mission. About halfway across the North Sea, Dave and I both had to abort the mission because we both developed problems with our aircraft. Lieutenants Hurtig [Edward L.] and Marlowe, [Wendell H.] who were my two roommates back at Wattisham, were flying as spares, so they quickly moved in and took over our positions in the flight. Dave and I returned to England where the weather had deteriorated to the point that we could no longer land at our home base. We managed to make it into Framlingham, a B-17 bomber airfield. There we enjoyed a delicious Christmas dinner while our aircraft problems were being corrected. While standing in the chow line, I spotted an old friend from my hometown, Lon McCauley. He joined us and we three shared the turkey and dressing as well as swapped war stories. Each of us expressed mutual admiration for the role bomber and fighter crews were performing in the war.
>
> "Meanwhile, our group continued on the mission and the target was successfully attacked. Our section engaged a large force of German fighters in aerial combat and although we shot down 15 enemy fighters, four of our pilots did not return. Three of them were in the flight from which Dave and I had to leave when we aborted. Capt. Hollingsworth became a prisoner of war for the duration. Lts. Hurtig and Marlowe, my roommates and the men who had replaced Dave and I, were killed.
>
> "Life is full of 'What ifs?' and 'What might have beens?'. On that day, if Dave and I had not aborted, maybe our fates and lives would have been reversed and Lts. Hurtig and Marlowe might have experienced these 50-some years of family, home and friends which both Dave and I have been permitted to enjoy."

The last man home from the mission was Second Lieutenant James E. Bouchier from the 434th FS. He became separated from the rest of his squadron during the combat near Bonn. Finding friendly aircraft nearby, Lt. Bouchier joined two Mustangs from the 352nd FG. These were part of a flight vectored from the vicinity of Koblenz, Germany where they had emerged from a successful engagement with enemy planes, to Liège, Belgium. Major George E. Preddy and his wingman, Lieutenant James G. Cartee, were flying the two P-51s from the 352nd FG. Heading westerly towards their objective, the three-ship vee passed along at 1,500 ft. over the dense forests of the Ardennes, searching for the reported low flying Germans. In the vicinity of Düren, Germany, Maj. Preddy went down to 500 ft. to investigate something. Having spotted a Fw 190 flying at very low altitude, Maj. Preddy descended and gave chase at treetop level. He was followed by first, his wingman and then, lagging slightly behind him, Lt. Bouchier. Heading

Left: Lieutenant Clarence G. Haynes. *Courtesy of Clarence G. Haynes.* Middle: Captain James M. Hollingsworth as shown by a photograph the Germans took of him for his POW file. *Courtesy of Thomas A. Hollingsworth.* Right: Lieutenant James E. Bouchier. *Courtesy of Clarence G. Haynes.*

northwest, just west of the Roer River, between Düren and Jülich, Germany, Maj. Preddy started to break left in a climbing turn and began trailing coolant. He had been hit by friendly fire from an American quad .50 cal. AA gun mounted on a halftrack. The quadruple-mounted machine gun, emplaced along with a 40mm Borfors gun, was located in a heavily wooded area and was one of the units belonging to the 12th Anti-Aircraft Group, which had the assignment of protecting the area against German air attacks. The skies had been overcast for some time and aircraft were heard overhead, but only seen when they came in low to attack ground targets. The gun crews had recently been alerted that there were two Me 109s coming in, strafing ground targets. Surrounded by woods, the gunners had little time to identify and react to aircraft passing over them. The two 352nd FG P-51s, followed slightly behind by Lt. Bouchier, were momentarily mistaken for the Me 109s and fired upon. The gun crews immediately realized their error, but by then it was too late. All three planes were hit, with Maj. Preddy topping out his maneuver and diving straight into the ground. He was killed and America had lost her leading active ace. His wingman, Lt. Cartee, took a .50 cal. slug in his cockpit, but was able to fly through the fire to safety. Lt. Bouchier's aircraft, still at 500 feet, was hit in the radiator by a 40mm round. While his cockpit filled with smoke, he was able to climb to 1000 feet, jettison his canopy, undo his straps, roll the crippled A/C over and push out just like the book said to do. After his brief parachute descent to ground, Lt. Bouchier was picked up by American troops, his first inkling that he had been shot down by the good guys. He was taken to a field artillery command post at Langweiler and eventually returned to Wattisham to tell the tale. (An interesting note additional to Lt. Bouchier's story is that he saved the parachute canopy silk from his bail out and later, his bride used it as material for her wedding lingerie.)

As a final note added to this mission, the 435th FS's monthly history report recorded that the squadron was prepared on this mission to land at Rheims, France after the escort was completed if the weather was better there than at Wattisham. The intent being that the squadron remain there for several days and fly combat air support for the ground troops from that location. Supplies such as bedding, toilet articles and other necessary items were packed in the fighters – Lord knows where – before the mission. Though this is not noted anywhere else in the records, it is highly probable that the same applied to the other two squadrons. This process was repeated on three consecutive days.

26 December 1944

Eighth AF FO 1452A

No. 217 & 218 Tuesday. The group was divided into two forces, A and B groups, both in support of a MEW controlled escort for 2nd BD B-24s attacking their 8th AF Mission 762 primary target, a rail bridge at Sinzig, Germany. Lt. Col. Riddle led A group, which consisted of 20 P-51s (12-434th and 8-436th). Up: 0832 hrs., down: 1357 hrs. with no non-effective. Capt. Harrell led B group, which consisted of 26 P-51s (17-435th & 9-436th). Up: 0835 hrs., down: 1400 hrs. with one early return.

A group made L/F in at 1043 hrs./19,000 ft. near Ostend, Belgium. R/V with the 20th CW was at 1055 hrs./20,000 ft. north of Ghent, Belgium. The force provided escort on the

Christmas day services at Wattisham. *Courtesy of Kenneth D. Axt.*

Some of the English children who were invited to share Christmas with the men of the fighter group. *Courtesy of Loetta Taylor (Kennedy).*

first two boxes until another fighter group R/V'd at 1130 hrs. Sticking with the first box of B-24s, they continued escort until after the bomb run at 1155 hrs. The weather was CAVU, so results of the strike could be observed and they were noted to be good. Flak over the target was heavy, meager and inaccurate on the bombers at 22-25,000 ft. B group left the bombers at the rally point and swept areas south and west of Bonn. L/O for the group was at 1305 hrs./15,000 ft. in the vicinity of Knokke, Belgium.

B group made L/F in southwest of Knokke, Belgium at 1045 hrs./20,000 ft. R/V with their bombers was at 1200 hrs./20,000 ft. west of Brussels, Belgium. They stayed with the second box through the target and back to Belgium. The B-24s were spread out and in poor formation, making escort difficult. Their time over target was 1200 hrs. Bombing from 26,000 feet, the results were good to excellent. The group left the bombers at 1230 hrs./20,000 feet east of Ghent and made L/O at Ostend.

The group's controller, Nuthouse, called in bandits approaching the bombers from south of Liège, Belgium, but there was no contact.

Lieutenants Norman R. Benoit, Larry J. Cano, Norbert W. Rock and George M. Salter, Jr., all from the 435th FS, returned to Wattisham late because they were short on gas and had to stop on the continent to refuel.

27 December 1944

Eighth AF FO 1456A

No. 219 & 220 Wednesday. The group was divided into two forces, A and B groups, which both flew patrols in support of 3rd BD B-17s attacking their 8th AF Mission 764 primary target, the marshalling yards at Fulda, Germany. Lt. Col. Riddle led A group, which consisted of 24 P-51s (16-435th & 8-436th). Up: 1042 hrs., down: 1535 hrs. Maj. Jeffrey led B group, which consisted of 22 P-51s (14-434th & 8-436th). Up: 1055 hrs., down: 1542 hrs. The combined groups had a total of two early returns.

Take off for the whole group was delayed an hour due to fog and a heavy mist. Finally getting into the air, both forces made L/F at 1130 hrs./12,000 ft. over Ostend. At this point, A group was vectored to an area 20 miles south of Liège. From there, they were sent into Germany to the Giessen area and then on to Koblenz, where they patrolled in support of the 1BD heavies soon to be attacking there. R/V with the bombers was at 1215 hrs./24,000 ft. Following the B-17s through the marshalling yard target and around on out, the group continued to patrol along the course the bombers were taking home, looking for stragglers to help, but there were none. The target appeared to be well hit.

B group was vectored to escort bombers attacking in the Cologne, Germany area because other fighters had joined in escorting the groups assigned B-17s. The order was then changed to patrol from Cologne, down to Koblenz, over to Giessen and up to south of Kassel from 1230 to 1400 hrs. Flak over the Cologne area was heavy, meager and accurate at

17,000 ft. Along the route, they dive-strafed the Rhein/Main airfield at Frankfurt, Germany. There was light and heavy flak there and it was fully operational; therefore, the group didn't spend any time there. However, they noted 15-20 T/E and S/E aircraft scattered around in the open, mainly in dispersals southwest of the field. Noting heavy train activity heading west from Frankfurt, one was strafed by Major Jeffrey, just west of Eppstein, Germany. The attack destroyed the locomotive, but further activity was prevented by light, (both 20 and 40mm) intense and accurate flak coming from woods just south of the railroad track. The group looked for stragglers on the way back home.

Observations made during the mission included noting that the marshalling yard at Mendig, just west of Koblenz, was well hit and that there were barrage balloons in the Koblenz area.

Lieutenant John W. Morrow from the 434th FS was late by several days, returning home because he had to stop for gas on the continent.

28 December 1944

Eighth AF FO 1458A

No. 221 & 222 Thursday. The group was divided into two forces, A and B groups, both penetration to target and withdrawal escorts for 2nd BD B-24s attacking their 8th AF Mission 766 primary target near Kaiserslautern, Germany. Maj. Jeffrey led A group, which consisted of 22 P-51s (14-434th & 8-436th). Up: 1029 hrs., down: 1510 hrs. There were two non-effectives. Capt. Harrell led B group, which consisted of 26 P-51s (17-435th & 9-436th). Up: 1039 hrs., down: 1505 hrs. There were two early returns.

R/V by A group was at 1145 hrs./22,000 ft. and by B group, it was at 1150 hrs./22,000 feet south of Namur, Belgium. Both groups escorted their assigned bombers through the target and broke away back in Belgium. A group broke away at 1350 hrs./15,000 ft. in the vicinity of Ostend, while B group broke from their bombers at the same time, but east of Charleville and at 14,000 ft. The R/V and break away points are approximate due to the cloud coverage. The bombing results were unobserved due to 10/10 undercast over the continent; however, it was believed that some bombs fell in Kaiserslautern. That was possibly because the bomber formation was scattered, especially after the rally point. One B-24 was seen on fire over the target at 1245 hrs. It was descending from 23,000 ft. to approximately 15,000 ft. where it broke up. Seven chutes from it were seen, but of those, three were burning and one of the remaining men was on fire. Flak over the target was heavy, intense and accurate, appearing to be a barrage type that was quite accurate on the second box of bombers. Over Kaiserslautern proper, it was heavy, moderate and inaccurate.

Observations made during the mission included seeing a B-24 go down burning at 1235 over Zweibrücken, Germany. Four chutes were seen from it. Flak there was heavy, moderate and accurate. A P-51 was observed going down in a tight spiral at 1330 hrs. in the Metz, France area. The A/C pulled out of the spiral once, but went right back into it. A Big Ben contrail was seen north of the Ruhr at 1115 hrs./35,000 feet, headed west.

29 December 1944

Eighth AF FO 1463A

No. 223 & 224 Friday. The group was divided into two forces, A and B groups, both in support of 3rd BD B-17s attacking their 8th AF Mission 769 primary tactical targets. Lt. Col. Riddle led A group, which consisted of 25 P-51s (8-434th & 17-436th). Up: 1121 hrs., down: 1600 hrs. Capt. Phillip D. Gossard led B group, which consisted of 25 P-51s (8-434th & 17-435th). Up: 1126 hrs., down: 1550 hrs. The combined groups had one early return.

The group's assignment was amended after they were airborne. A group went on to R/V with 3rd BD B-17s Vinegrove 2-4, 2-5 and 2-6 at 1220 hrs./18,000 ft. southeast of Brussels, Belgium. A group swept ahead and on both sides of the bomber track. They were vectored to several bogies, but they all turned out to be friendlies. They patrolled from Bonn, Germany, southwest to Malmèdy, Belgium east to Trier and northeast to Koblenz until 1400 hrs when they were vectored to north of Neunkirchen, Germany, but there they found only one P-47. From there they patrolled south to Saarburg, Germany and finally over and out at Ostend, Belgium at 1500 hrs./17,000 ft.

B group made R/V with their bombers in the vicinity of Brussels at 1215 hrs./32,000 ft. The B-17s were escorted uneventfully through the target, which was well hit, and back, passing southeast of Liège, Belgium at 1330 hrs./23,000 ft.

Observations made during the mission included two Big Ben contrails heading west, one seen at 1210 hours, the other

Lieutenant George E. Witzel suffered a taxiing accident when he ran his 9B-E- into 9B-D being taxied by Lieutenant Stanley E. Derby. Fortunately, neither pilot was injured. *Courtesy of Charles H. Darling.*

at 1400 hours in the Hengelo, Holland area. At 1403 hours, a probable burning bomber was seen going down; no chutes were noted. An Me 109 was seen at 17,000 feet, two miles south of Sedan, France. When an attempt to engage it was made, it dodged into the haze and escaped. Flak north of Arlon, Belgium was heavy, meager and accurate at 22,000 ft.

There were three P-51s damaged at Wattisham during the course of this mission. One was declared Cat. A, the result of a locked tail wheel and two were Cat. E, having collided on the runway.

30 December 1944

Eighth AF FO 1467A
No. 225 Saturday. Maj. Jeffrey led the group, which consisted of 51 P-51s (16-434th, 18-435th & 17-436th) on MEW controlled mutual support for 8th AF Mission 770. Up: 1122 hrs., down: 1540 hrs. There were three early returns.

Take off was delayed for an hour due to bad weather, but the group got off and made L/F at 1145 hrs./16,000 ft. in the vicinity of Knokke, Belgium. From 1220 to 1400 hours, they patrolled Germany uneventfully, starting at Trier and going to Bad Kreuznach. Their controller, Nuthouse, had no business for them. At 1330 hours, the 434th FS picked up a box of B-17s, marked with black triangles on red tails, in the Trier area and escorted them to south of Brussels. They made L/O at 1515 hrs./10,000 ft. near Boulogne, France while the rest of the group made L/O at Dunkerque, France at 1430 hrs./16,000 ft. There were no observations made during the mission due to 10/10ths overcast.

31 December 1944

Eighth AF FO 1471A
No. 226 & 227 Sunday. The group was divided into two forces, A and B groups, both penetration to target and withdrawal escorts for 2nd BD B-24s attacking their 8th AF Mission 772 primary targets, rail bridges at Koblenz, Germany. Maj. Jeffrey led A group, which consisted of 27 P-51s (19-434th & 8-435th). Up: 0919 hrs., down: 1432 hrs. Capt. Richard S. Spencer led B group, which consisted of 25 P-51s (9-435th & 16-436th). Up: 0931 hrs., down: 1417 hrs. The combined groups had four early returns.

A group made L/F and then R/V'd with the 2nd CW B-24s at 1020 hrs./21,000 ft. south-southwest of Brussels. At 1041 hours, while near Bastogne, Belgium, they were vectored to the vicinity of Koblenz, Germany, but there were no E/A. They swept Trier to Bad Kreuznach, to Koblenz and to Köln, but had no success. At 1120 hours, their controller, Nuthouse, reported Vinegrove 2-4 being attacked, but the P-51s were unable to contact them either visually or via radio. By then, the bombers were in the target area and none were seen to be under attack. Escorting them out, the group broke away and made L/O at 1345 hrs./13,000 ft. near Calais.

B group made L/F and then R/V'd, the same as A group, and drove up the line (bomber stream) to R/V at 1100 hrs./ 20,000 feet, with Vinegrove 2-1, 30 miles northwest of Luxembourg. They escorted the bombers through the target and out to Ostend, Belgium, where they broke away at 1320 hrs./15,000 ft. It was noted that the second force formation was very poor, so strung out that it made proper escort impossible. One CW was ten miles behind and 15 miles south of the remainder of the force at R/V.

There were no observations made during the mission due to 8-10/10ths cloud cover over the target area; however, flak over Koblenz was heavy, moderate and inaccurate, while at Trier, it was heavy, meager and accurate. A high-pitched whine on the radio due to German jamming made communications with Nuthouse poor.

A group photo of the 434th Fighter Squadron posed in front of Satan's Agent. *Courtesy of The Wings of Freedom Museum.*

A group photo of the 435th Fighter Squadron posed in front of Colonel Kyle L. Riddle's P-51. *Courtesy of Ray K. Friend.*

A group photo of the 436th Fighter Squadron posed in front of a Bison Squadron P-51. *Courtesy of Arlett G. Mosier, Jr.*

Bison armorers Corporal Joseph C. Chism and Corporal James G. McCredie pose with a .50 cal. machine gun beside Major Clifford J. Moore, Jr.'s The Uninvited II. *Carroll C. Sprague Collection, courtesy of the East Essex Aviation Society.*

More of the Bison Gang – armorers Corporal John M. Hernandez and Private First Class James P. DiEujenio. *Carroll C. Sprague Collection, courtesy of the East Essex Aviation Society.*

434th FS – above: aircraft mechanics Master Sergeant James W. Smart and Corporal Carl O. Ayers below. *Courtesy of Clarence G. Haynes.*

434th FS – above: aircraft mechanics Technical Sergeant William A. Haas and Sergeant Maxcy O. Corder below. *Courtesy of Clarence G. Haynes.*

436th FS pilots – front: Captain Arlett G. Mosier, Jr., First Lieutenant Jay C. Malone, rear: Captain John R. Schuck, Major Clifford J. Moore Jr., Captain William C. Anderson and Lieutenant Douglas L. Red. *Courtesy of Arlett G. Mosier, Jr.*

436th FS pilot First Lieutenant Charles B. Elmgren is seen standing beside Dottie Mae. The lettering that can be seen is the original version. It was later redone. *Courtesy of Charles H. Darling.*

434th FS P-51 Teddie #4 is being readied by her crew chief. Teddie #4 was to become Lieutenant Clifford W. Bowers' Skunk Chaser in a short while. *Courtesy of Frederick C. Hayner.*

436th FS armorer Sergeant Alfred Bloom, Jr. beside Major Claire A. P. Duffié's Give 'em Hell for H. L. Jr. *Courtesy of Kenneth D. Axt.*

Below: A classic photograph of a fighter pilot, in this case it is First Lieutenant Berkley E. Hollister on the P-51 he named Pin Up Girl. Lt. Hollister completed his combat during this month and went home to stateside duty and his wife Edris. *Courtesy of Berkley E. Hollister.*

CHAPTER TWELVE

JANUARY 1945

1 January 1945

Eighth AF FO 1476A

No. 228 & 229 Monday. The group was divided into two forces, A and B groups, both penetration to target and withdrawal escorts for 1st AD (Air Division – Effective this date, the classification of Bomb Division was no longer used.) B-17s attacking their 8th AF Mission 774 primary target, the marshalling yards at Kassel, Germany. Lt. Col. Riddle led A group, which consisted of 25 P-51s (17-434th & 8-435th). Up: 1014 hrs., down: 1440 hrs. Capt. Edward C. Lewin led B group, which consisted of 25 P-51s (7-435th & 18-436th). Up: 1026 hrs., down: 1500 hrs. The combined groups had a total of five early returns.

Take off was delayed by 50 minutes due to fog, but the group finally became airborne. A group entered over the continent near Alkmaar, Holland at 1120 hrs./18,000 ft. and proceeded east into Germany. They were to R/V with the bombers near the target, but at 1215 hours, just north of Steinhuder Lake and in the vicinity of Nienburg, they encountered bogies. The unidentified aircraft were below the group so Lieutenant Colonel Riddle took White Section down after them, diving from 21,000 ft. Identifying the bogies as 12 Fw 190s, the section succeeded in isolating one before the rest dove into a cloud layer they had been flying above. Lt. Col. Riddle and Second Lieutenant Clifford W. Bowers chased the lone enemy aircraft to the deck, each firing at it during the chase. Many strikes were observed and the Focke-Wulf pilot finally bellied his plane in on a snow-covered farm field. As Lt. Bowers began the first of several strafing passes in attempts he made to set the downed fighter afire, the German pilot scrambled out of his cockpit and made a mad dash for the cover of a tree line that lead up to a farm house. He survived to fight another day. Back at Wattisham, Lt. Bowers' squadron mates gave him a rough time for allowing the German to get away. Their reasoning was that the escaped pilot would be back in the air again and would still pose a threat. Irregardless, the two Mustang pilots shared the credit for a destroyed.

During the course of the above-mentioned engagement, Yellow Section's leader, First Lieutenant Arnold G. Helding took his section down to about 9,000 ft. in order to provide top cover. They were orbiting to the left, just above a cloud deck when Yellow Three called in bogies at nine o'clock, level. The section turned and identified them as Fw 190s, traveling 180 degrees to the squadron's P-51s. An order was given to drop tanks and the section began turning into them. The Germans were not aggressive and by the time Yellow Section had completed about 90 degrees of their turn, the Focke-Wulfs began diving into the cloud deck. The section "fire-walled" everything and began closing in on the enemy aircraft fast, but all the Germans got into the clouds except for one who was lagging behind a bit. This enemy pilot leveled off on top of the clouds at about 8,000 ft. Second Lieutenant Robert I. Bromschwig was flying as Newcross Yellow Two, Lt. Helding's wingman in the section, when the enemy aircraft were spotted and chased. Lt. Bromschwig was in the right place and at the right time that moment because Lt. Helding had to hold his fire for fear of hitting his number three man, but Lt. Bromschwig had a clear field through which he could shoot. Opening fire at about 700 yards, Lt. Bromschwig allowed approximately a radii-and-a-half lead. He closed to about 300 yards, but saw no strikes. At that time he noted the Focke-

Wulf's tail suddenly snap up in a violent maneuver and the plane head into the clouds. As the enemy pilot performed this evasive tactic, both Lt.'s saw three large pieces fly off his airplane. They were certain that one of the pieces was the enemy fighter's canopy and suspected that the violent snap the pilot executed to escape had caused a structural failure of some sort and that the pilot had bailed out in the clouds. This could not be confirmed, however, so all that could be claimed was a probable for Lt. Bromschwig.

Reforming, A group proceeded south from the Steinhuder Lake area to Kassel, where they were to R/V with the bombers. None were seen. The decision was made to continue on in an effort to find the B-17s and the group continued around the target, looping in a south-southwesterly direction to the vicinity of Helmstadt, then northwest up to Koblenz. No luck was had. Their controller, Nuthouse, gave the group a vector, but shortly afterwards cancelled that. Unable to find the bombers, A group headed for home, making L/O over Calais, France at 1320 hrs./24,000 ft. It was believed that the predicted winds aloft were actually lighter and were from a more easterly direction than what was briefed, thus causing the group to be off an average of 60 miles for every 240 miles flown.

B group made R/V with the proper bombers in the area of Derben at 1240 hrs./26,000 ft. The Big Friends were escorted around Kassel and out of Germany to as far as Brussels, Belgium where escort was broken at 1355 hrs./20,000 ft. Their escort was uneventful.

Observations made during the mission included an oil slick spotted on the channel waters near Calais, twenty-seven

Lieutenant Clifford W. Bowers by his Skunk Chaser. *Courtesy of David L. Born.*

First Lieutenant Arnold G. Helding and his crew chief Staff Sergeant John B. Atteberry. *Courtesy of Arnold G. Helding.*

Lieutenant Robert I. Bromschwig in his Kraut Knocker. *Courtesy of David L. Born.*

unidentified aircraft seen at a serviceable airdrome near Quackenbrück, unidentified enemy aircraft spotted at the airfield near Zweschenahner Lake and there were barges on the Rhine River southwest of Frankfurt. Flak two miles north of Kassel was heavy, meager, but accurate. In the area of Derben, it was heavy, intense and accurate. From west of St. Goar to north of Trier, it was heavy, moderate and accurate. At Stolzenau, it was light, meager and inaccurate.

436th FS pilot Captain Joseph R. Struby was showing Technical Sergeant Walter J. Doyle and Sergeant Edward L. Akin, the crew of Little Hemorrhoid, how he got on the tail of an enemy aircraft. *Courtesy of Edward L. Akin.*

2 January 1945

Eighth AF FO 1479A

No. 230 & 231 Tuesday. The group was divided into two forces, A and B groups, both penetration to target and withdrawal escorts for 2nd AD B-24s attacking their 8th AF Mission 776 primary target, railroad bridges at Koblenz, Germany. Capt. Harrell led A group, which consisted of 26 P-51s (8-434th & 18-435th). Up: 0943 hrs., down: 1352 hrs. Capt. Joseph R. Struby led B group, which consisted of 25 P-51s (8-434th & 17-436th). Up: 0948 hrs., down: 1350 hrs. The combined groups had a total of two early returns.

A group R/V'd with the proper bombers 16 miles west of Bergen, Holland at 1042 hrs./20,000 ft. and began their escort duties. Along the route in and having passed into Germany, Nuthouse, their controller, vectored the group to the Dümmer Lake area to check out some bogies. Arriving there at 1110 hours, the unidentified aircraft were quickly found and determined to be eight P-51s. The group headed back south to rejoin the bombers, catching up with them at Gütersloh. No sooner had they arrived back with the Big Friends and resumed escort, when Nuthouse broke them away again to check on some more bogies. Vectored at 1145 hrs./24,000 ft. to a vicinity west of Siegen and then on to Giessen, the group ferreted out eight P-47s at 1200 hrs. Heading back to the B-24s, the group heard a call from Vinegrove 2-3 on the bomber channel. The caller indicated they were under attack, but when that was investigated, it was determined there was no attack. At Koblenz, the target was bombed through a cover of haze so no results could be observed. The escort was uneventful and the B-24s were returned, making L/O northeast of Ostend, Belgium at 1320 hrs./10,000 ft.

B group found their proper bombers at the same time and location, as did A group. Their escort was even more uneventful than was A group's. In taking the Big Friends into Germany, around the target at Neuwied, just north of Koblenz, and out again, the group soon found themselves at the break away point south of Brussels at 1300 hrs./20,000 ft. Crossing out over

Lieutenant Lawrence A. Keefe in his Lakeside Squadron P-51 J2-D Butch, over Germany. *Courtesy of James H. Koerber.*

Knokke, Belgium at 1330 hrs./17,000 feet, the force went home with no tales to tell.

Observations made during the mission included a small white balloon with a basket attached underneath that was seen in an area between Liège and Aachen. The rail traffic at Giessen had been bombed and it was noted that at least five locomotives were destroyed. The bombing attack at Frankfort appeared to be good. The target at Siegburg looked to be well clobbered and was marked by a huge cloud of white smoke coming from it. Flak in the vicinity of Koblenz was heavy, medium and accurate. In the battle area along the north end of Belgium, it was similar, but inaccurate. The same was true also along a track near Hachenburg.

The 436th FS suffered their first casualty of the year when Flight Officer George Joseph had his engine fail while flying over Merville, France. The weather was thick, with a cloud cover of 10/10ths. FO Joseph was low when the engine quit, but he managed to get to 1,500 ft. before he bailed out. In spite of following the correct book procedure for parachuting from the aircraft, the tail assembly struck his lower left leg, causing a compound fracture of both bones. He made a good landing on the seat of his pants, was found and cared for in a Royal Canadian Air Force hospital until he could be transferred back to England.

3 January 1945

Eighth AF FO 1485A

No. 232 & 233 Wednesday. The group was divided into two forces, A and B groups, both penetration to target and withdrawal escorts for 2nd AD B-24s attacking their 8th AF Mission 778 primary target, the marshalling yard at Landau, Germany. Lt. Col. Riddle led A group, which consisted of 26 P-51s (10-435th & 16-436th). Up: 0925 hrs., down: 1430 hrs. Capt. Gates led B group, which consisted of 23 P-51s (15-434th & 8-435th). Up: 0938 hrs., down: 1406 hrs. The combined groups had a total of two early returns.

The mission didn't start out well for First Lieutenant Jerome K. (Jerry) Nagel. Some fifteen minutes after becoming airborne, his engine cut out and quit. Lt. Nagel was forced to make an emergency landing at Ipswich, bellying the aircraft in. The P-51 was badly damaged and declared Category E, while the Lt. was just shaken up.

A group made L/O near Coxyde, Belgium at 1007 hrs./18,000 ft. and R/V'd with their proper bombers southwest of

Lelah Mae-the Slugger (first name on left side of nose, second name on right side of nose) after Lieutenant Jerome K. Nagel bellied her in at an RAF field near Ipswich. *Courtesy of George E. Falkner.*

Metz, France at 1054 hrs./24,000 ft. The B-24s were escorted to the target at Landau and back to an area 20 miles west of Metz, where they were broken away from at 1200 hrs./22,000 ft. After the group left the bombers, Nuthouse, their controller, vectored them first south, then north of Metz, in search of bogies. None were found and the group left the Metz area at 1225 hrs. and made L/O over Dunkerque, France at 1335 hrs./ 3,000 ft. Ten/tenths undercast was present for the entire mission.

B group found their bombers approximately in the area northwest of Nancy, France at 1049 hrs./23,000 hrs. They were escorted to and from the target and into Belgium where the group broke away in the vicinity of Brussels at 1303 hrs./ 12,000 ft. For both groups, the mission was uneventful.

The only observations noted as made during the mission were three Big Bens that were seen, one ten to twenty miles east of Amsterdam at 1010 hours, one near Charleville at 1015 hrs., and one near Trier at 1130 hrs.

There was no combat mission for 4 January 1945, inclement weather over the continent prevented the group from engaging

The train engine that Lieutenant Thurman E. Sands glanced off before he crashed. *Courtesy of George E. Falkner.*

in any activity over there. The squadrons did get in a bit of training time during the day, taking their planes up over England. Unfortunately, on one of those training missions, a 434th FS pilot lost his life. Second Lieutenant Thurman E. Sands was killed in a crash after he grazed a locomotive he was passing over near Stowmarket. At the time, he was on a low-level navigation flight in England.

5 January 1945

Eighth AF FO 1491A

No. 234 Friday. Capt. Harrell led the group, which consisted of 49 P-51s (17-434th, 15-435th & 17-436th) on a penetration to target and withdrawal escort for 2nd AD B-24s attacking their 8th AF Mission 781 primary target, a section of railroad at Pirmasens, Germany. Up: 1003 hrs., down: 1426 hrs. with a total of seven early returns.

The group made L/F in the Calais, France area at 1050 hrs./18,000 ft. and R/V'd with the proper bombers southwest of St. Quentin, France at 1105 hrs./21,000 ft. The B-24s were in good formation. The 436th FS took the first box, the 434th FS took the second box and the 435th FS freelanced on both as Capt. Herrell rode herd over his force as it headed into Germany. After the IP, (Initial Point) the first box of bombers failed to follow the briefed course, but the primary target, as well as the marshalling yards at St. Ingbert (a target of opportunity) were hit, both with good results. At St. Ingbert, the 435th FS lost the Big Friends because of the confusion. The squadron turned north to Kaiserslautern, then back to southwest of Saarebourg, but was unable to locate the bombers. Nuthouse, their controller, gave the B-24s position as west of Saarbourg, but they were not found. During the run into the target, White Flight from the 434th FS was vectored to Saarbrücken to investigate bogies, but nothing was found. After the group broke from the bombers at 1306 hrs./15,000 feet, they crossed out over Ostend, Belgium at 1335 hrs./15,000 ft.

Observations made during the mission included the noting of large fires in the area of St. Ingbert that had been previously struck by the bombers. An Me 262 was seen at 1230 hours, headed north in the Hengelo area. Flak in the target area of Pirmasens was heavy, meager and inaccurate while at St. Ingbert, it was heavy, meager, but accurate.

Two 436th FS P-51s became tangled when Lakeside pilot Lieutenant George P. Rossman in a war-weary P-51B over-ran Lieutenant Richard P. Thrall's plane. Fortunately, there were no injuries. *Courtesy of George E. Falkner.*

6 January 1945

Eighth AF FO 1496A

No. 235 & 236 Saturday. The group was divided into two forces, A and B groups, both penetration to target and withdrawal escorts for 2nd AD B-24s attacking their 8th AF Mission 783 primary target, a highway bridge over the Rhine River at Bonn, Germany. Maj. Jeffrey led A group, which consisted of 30 P-51s (22-434th & 8-436th). Up: 0931 hrs., down: 1440 hrs. Maj. Jordan led B group, which consisted of 26 P-51s (18-435th & 8-436th). Up: 0936 hrs., down: 1430 hrs. The combined groups had a total of three early returns.

Weather was again bad at Wattisham, barely permitting the group to get airborne. A group entered over the continent and made R/V with their force of B-24s at 1045 hrs./23,000 ft. southwest of Brussels, Belgium. It was noted that part of the bombers, Vinegrove 4-1, was not in formation at the time. Once in German airspace, the group provided a roving type of escort, sweeping the area from Trier, northeast to ten miles southeast of Koblenz. Their controller, Nuthouse, vectored them to bogies several times, but all turned out to be friendlies. They rejoined the bombers at 1220 hrs./23,000 feet, remaining as escort to L/O over Ostend, Belgium at 1311 hrs./13,000 ft.

Right: A Newcross Squadron P-51, L2-B, probably Beautiful Jan, is settling down for a landing. *Courtesy of David L. Born.*

Three Lakeside Squadron P-51s, J2- G, J and N, loaded down with belly tanks for the trip into Germany. Lieutenant James H. Koerber took the photograph with the K-25 aerial camera that was mounted to the back of his plane's seat armor. *Courtesy of James H. Koerber.*

B group had an uneventful escort through the target and out to the point of break away, southwest of Brussels at 1235 hrs./17,000 ft. Each of the bombing forces dropped through the overcast that covered the target area so the results were unobserved. Those clouds, which extended back over England, made for some difficult landings at Wattisham. The field was closed in about the time the groups were due back and about 1330 hours, aircraft were topping the trees, criss-crossing each other, just missing landing accidents, overshooting the field and going around. All of this occurring while B-17s and B-24s were passing overhead. The mess would have given future air traffic controllers nightmares. The pilots were all successful in landing safely, though a few diverted to other fields.

Observations made during the mission included the sighting of rockets at 1135, 1147 and 1155 hrs. coming from the Cologne area and heading west. Rockets heading west were also seen at 1110 and 1115 hrs. from the Utrecht area. An unidentified cherry red plane was seen on the ground in the vicinity of Bessaik [sic.] at 1025 hrs. An Me 163 was sighted 30-40,000 ft. northeast of Trier at 1200 hrs. Flak over Bonn was heavy, meager and accurate. It was heavy, meager and inaccurate at Mannheim and heavy, moderate and inaccurate at Koblenz.

7 January 1945

Eighth AF FO 1499A

No. 237 & 238 Sunday. The group was divided into two forces, A and B groups, both penetration to target and withdrawal escorts for 3rd AD B-17s attacking their 8th AF Mission 785 primary target, the marshalling yards at Cologne, Germany. Maj. Jordan led A group, which consisted of 24 P-51s (7-434th & 17-435th). Up: 0940 hrs., down: 1405 hrs. Capt. Duffié led B group, which consisted of 22 P-51s (7-434th & 15-436th). Up: 0946 hrs., down: 1420 hrs. There were no early returns.

A group made L/F south of Knokke, Belgium at 1019 hrs./15,000 ft. and R/V'd with the bombers north of Brussels at 1027 hrs./23,000 ft. Entering Germany, the B-17s were escorted to and from the target as far south as the Moselle River where they broke away at 1050 hrs./23,000 ft. Vectored by their controller, the group went north to Koblenz, then further north to Siegburg where they stooged around until 1120 hrs. Vectored back to the Moselle River area south of Koblenz, the group took up escort of another batch of bombers, H and K boxes of B-17s returning from their target, and took them on out to St. Vith, Belgium where they broke away at 1150 hrs./21,000 ft. They made L/O over Ostend, Belgium at 1300 hrs./15,000 ft.

B group crossed in with A group at Knokke and R/V'd with their assigned bombers. Escorting them towards the target, part of the group turned away when the force entered a front, but caught up later east of Siegburg. Cloud coverage was 10/

10ths through the target area. The remainder of the group continued escort through the target at Cologne and back out again. At Siegburg, the returning P-51s were then sent to stooge around in the area between Trier and Bingen. There was no activity and they rejoined the bombers 30 miles northwest of Trier. The portion of the group that had maintained continuous escort since R/V broke from the B-17s at Charleroi, Belgium at 1250 hrs./26,000 ft. The roaming Little Friends took the Big Friends to within 15 miles of Brussels where they broke away at 1300 hrs./20,000 ft.

Observations made during the mission included seeing two B-17s collide 15 miles north of Koblenz at 1120 hrs./ 26,000 ft. Another B-17 was seen to spin down in flames over the target at 1227 hrs./27,000 ft. No chutes were seen to come from any of the bombers. A Big Ben was observed heading west from the vicinity of Utrecht, Holland. Flak over Cologne was heavy, intense and accurate while over the Rhine River in the area of south of Bonn, it was heavy, meager and inaccurate. At Koblenz it was heavy, moderate and inaccurate.

The Ardennes Offensive was cause for an all out blood donor drive by the Army at this time. Type "O" the so called "Universal Donor" type was that which was urgently needed and the men of the 479th FG filled the station hospital as they sought to give blood during this time.

8 January 1945

Eighth AF FO 1503A

No. 239 Monday. Maj. Jeffrey led the group, which consisted of 35 P-51s (13-434th, 10-435th & 12-436th) on a fighter sweep in the Mannheim area of Germany in support of 8th AF

Corporal Stanley Kellett and Sergeant Richard F. Ryan in the remains of their line shack after it was knocked down because of the clean up efforts. *Courtesy of Stanley Kellett.*

Mission 787. Up: 0908 hrs., down: 1415 hrs. with a total of three early returns.

A deluge of snow whipped by a 30-40 mph wind impeded take off today, but the pilots pressed on. What began as an escort, changed to a fighter sweep once the group reached the Mannheim area. There was a solid undercast throughout the whole area except for there. L/F was over the vicinity of undercast Knokke, Germany at 1005 hrs./27,000 ft. From there, the Mannheim area was reached at 1050 hrs./27,000 ft. A few holes through the clouds, which had tops up to 27,000 feet, presented themselves at this point. The group patrolled from there in Germany to Frankfurt until 1140 hours, at which point they were vectored to escort some bombers. R/V with red-tailed B-17s was west of Wiesbaden at 1145 hrs./27,000 ft. Three of the bombers were straggling behind, unable to hold altitude. They went into the overcast in the vicinity of Trier at 1220 hrs. The rest of the bombers were taken as far as Sedan,

A P-38 visitor, stuck at Wattisham because of the snowfalls. *Courtesy of Harold L. Stotts.*

France where the group broke away at 1230 hrs./26,000 ft. L/O was in the vicinity of Calais, France at 1315 hrs./12,000 ft.

No observations were noted due to the cloud cover. Flak over Frankfurt and Mannheim was heavy, intense and accurate. Over Mainz and south of Koblenz, it was heavy, meager and inaccurate. At Wiesbaden it was heavy, intense and inaccurate.

Bad weather, poor visibility, continuing snowfall and icy runways were the cause for a number of days that passed without a mission flown. As the great flurries of snow fell with their accompanying gusts of wind, everyone jockeyed for a warm spot by a fireplace or stove as best they could. The arrival of a new C.O. at the 436th FS had brought some changes for that squadron as Captain Claire A.P. Duffié sought to make the squadron better and more efficient. One of those changes was a general cleaning up of the improvised shacks the ground personnel had built near the hardstands. Another was an establishment of a fuel policy that dictated who could burn coal, who could burn wood and who could burn gas or oil.

13 January 1945

Eighth AF FO 1513A

No. 240 Saturday. Capt. Duffié led the group, which consisted of 38 P-51s (11-434th, 13-435th & 13-436th) on an escort for 2nd AD B-24s attacking their 8th AF Mission 791 primary target, a bridge at Worms, Germany. Up: 1114 hrs., down: 1617 hrs. with one early return.

The snowfall had abated the previous day and that afternoon line personnel had been tasked with the job of snow removal in the hardstands and on the taxiways, perimeter and flying field. A fine mist began to fall and that aided the efforts to clear the snow accumulation, but it also kept the group grounded for another day.

This mission was different than other recent ones in a number of ways. First, it was a minimum effort show and secondly, the group was not split as it had been for a number of previous missions. Also, despite having left the doubtful weather at Wattisham late in the morning, and having flown through the same to and over the continent, by the time they arrived east of Brussels, Belgium, the clouds had cleared to a CAVU situation. R/V was near Mons, France at 1245 hrs./14,000 ft. Over the target at Worms, the group was able to observe the bombing which appeared to be good. Capt. Duffié reported that the bombs made a beautiful pattern and one of

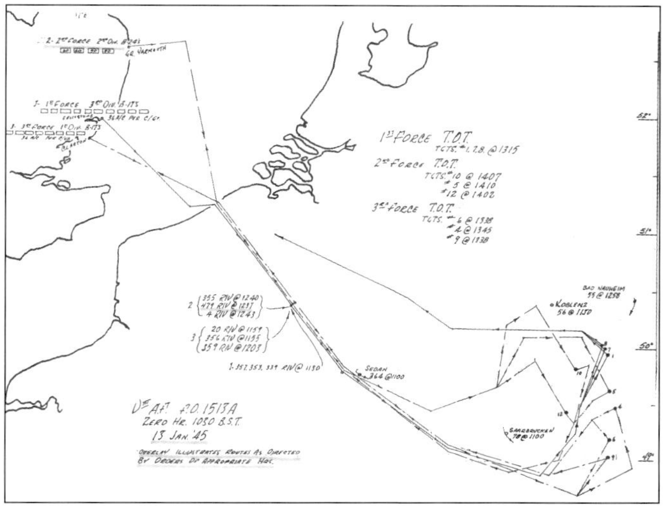

8AF escort mission map for this date. *Courtesy of the 436th Fighter Squadron Association.*

his pilots noted that he saw at least one direct hit and that both ends of the bridge were well clobbered.

Recalled by Colgate, the group broke from the bombers south of Worms and headed for home. They ran into what they generally agreed was the worst weather they had ever encountered during their time in the ETO. Wattisham was down to a 200-ft. ceiling with visibility next to nothing. Most made it home through the solid gray, but some did not and reported in from the various bases where they had landed. One pilot did not make landfall back at England that day. Flight Officer Raymond E. King from the 436th FS was flying escort to

Right: Captain Claire A.P. Duffié. *Courtesy of Berkley E. Hollister.*

Right: Flight Officer Raymond E. King. *Courtesy of Arlett G. Mosier, Jr.*

Far right: Lieutenant Fred Zellman and crew chief Technical Sergeant James H. Standiford. *Courtesy of the 436th Fighter Squadron Association.*

Lieutenant Fred Zellman, whose Mustang was having engine trouble. F/O King, in a P-51 named "Little Zippy" by her former pilot, was flying only his seventh combat mission since joining the group two months previously. Under the cloud base and at only two hundred feet, the two slowly crossed the North Sea. They were almost to the coast when the engine in F/O King's plane suddenly failed. He radioed for help and gave his position as 800 yards off the English coastline. His only chance at survival was to ditch the aircraft in the freezing cold water below for he had not sufficient altitude to continue further in a glide nor to bail out. F/O King had been a champion swimmer in high school back home, but his young, healthy body was no match for the inhospitable winter waters. Eight hundred yards wasn't much, but by the time the lifeboat from nearby Clacton reached him and pulled him from the water, life was ebbing away from the twenty-two year old pilot. He died later that day at the Clacton District Hospital from exposure and injuries received in the crash. "Little Zippy" sank to the bottom of the North Sea and became buried facing the shore, in the thick mud. In 1977, a fisherman discovered the remains of the plane and a local aviation museum sought steps to raise her. Time passed and finally during the summer of 1987, "Lille Zippy" was brought to the surface. The plane was reasonably intact and work began to stabilize the effects of being immersed in salt water for forty-two years. Those remains are now on display at the East Essex Aviation Society's Martello Tower Museum at Clacton.

Observations made during the mission included seeing a Big Ben heading west from the vicinity of Utrecht at 1150 hrs. and a B-24 that was burning on the ground, twelve miles northwest of Mannheim. Two Me 262s were seen, both apparently just observing the bombers and their escorts. One was spotted at 1240 hrs./35,000 ft. south of Mons, the other at 1400 hrs./30,000 ft. in the vicinity of Worms. South of Weisbaden, a huge ball of white smoke very suddenly appeared at 1330 hrs.

14 January 1944

Eighth AF FO 1515A

No. 241 & 242 Sunday. The group was divided into two forces, A and B groups, both penetration to target and withdrawal escorts for 2nd AD B-24s attacking their 8th AF Mission 792 primary target at Brunswick, Germany. Maj. Jeffrey led A group, which consisted of 26 P-51s (18-434th & 8-436th). Up: 1045 hrs., down: 1555 hrs. Lt. Nelson Butler led B group, which consisted of 22 P-51s (18-435th & 4-436th). Up: 1043 hrs., down: 1603 hrs. The combined groups had a total of two early returns. With fine weather again, (at least it was raining instead of snowing) the group took to the air.

A group headed up the North Sea and made R/V with their assigned B-24s off Terschelling Island, Holland at 1215 hrs./25,000 ft. They were escorted to the target area, which was hit at 1350 hrs. The bombing results looked good with several fires seen. Part of the group broke away at this point and the remainder stayed to continue escort until L/O ten miles north of Ijmuiden, Holland at 1450 hrs./21,000 ft.

B group made L/F and R/V north of the Elbe Estuary at Germany. The bombers were escorted through the target and back out again to L/O between Den Helder and Ijmuiden at 1455 hrs./20,000 ft.

Major Herbert H. Jordan and Lieutenant Larry J. Cano from the 435th FS became separated from B group in the Dümmer Lake region of Germany. They were coming out along the Ems Weser Canal when they turned south, having heard their controller, Nuthouse, give a vector for bogies. At 1430 hours, west of Wesel, Maj. Jordan spotted five planes, all looking like P-51s. Four were flying a good close formation and one was playing, just to the rear of them. Maj. Jordan decided to join them and go home. As the two 435th FS pilots crossed under the other five, Maj. Jordan noticed the fifth plane had crosses on it! He pulled up and tried a shot straight up, but stalled out. As he recovered, the enemy aircraft turned left. Pouring on the power, Maj. Jordan managed to turn inside the German and upon firing, got good hits on him. A fire started at the wing root. The enemy plane, identified as an Me 109, spun down out of control and its pilot bailed out close to the ground. The Me 109 crashed in a forest near Emmerich. Maj. Jordan reported later that he was certain that the other four P-51 pilots never knew the German was behind them, even after he spotted him. The Major received credit for one Me 109 destroyed.

Observations made during the mission included: near Baltrum Island, Germany, seeing a B-24 off in the distance being fired on by flak. The plane left its formation and turned in towards the continent. There were fires and smoke pots at the Elbe end of the Kaiser Wilhelm Canal. There were also smokescreens spotted at Ludwigslust, Hamburg, Wesermunde, Magdeburg, Bremen and Lübeck. Two large merchantmen ships were seen in the Elbe Estuary. Four Big Bens came from the Minden area. There was a wide clearing in the woods, about 25 miles long, southwest of Stendal. A train was shot up northeast of Dümmer Lake and a lot of train activity was seen in the Bremen and Hamburg areas. Flak in the Brunswick area was heavy, intense and accurate as it was in the areas of Hamburg and the Kaiser Wilhelm Canal near the Elbe. At Lingen it was light, intense and accurate.

15 January 1945

Eighth AF FO 1519A

No. 243 Monday. Lt. Col. Riddle led the group, which consisted of 51 P-51s (18-434th, 17-435th & 16-436th) on a MEW controlled fighter sweep into Germany. Up: 1024 hrs., down: 1215 hrs. with a total of three early returns. At L/F, Colgate advised the group that the 4th FG would not be joining them for the sweep. L/F was in the vicinity of Ostend at 1045 hrs./12,000 ft. The undercast was 10/10ths there and continued to remain that way all the way to the target area. Arriving in the target area at 1210 hrs./15,000 feet, the group swept, but was

Two 434th FS P-51s, L2-X and Z, can be seen taking off through some foul weather. *Courtesy of David L. Born.*

unable to strafe due to the cloud cover and fog, which extended to the deck. Lieutenant Colonel Riddle took his force west across the Rhine River and then home, making L/O over Ostend, Belgium at 1425 hrs./10,000 ft. No enemy aircraft were seen and their controller, Nuthouse, had no business for them. There was a total lack of enemy activity, both in the air and on the ground.

Observations made during the mission included seeing several Big Bens heading west from Frankfurt and Stuttgart. Two columns of smoke were noted coming from the area of Strasbourg. The Stuttgart target, as seen through a hole in the undercast, seemed well hit and smoking, the marshalling yard at Tübingen appeared well clobbered as well as the one at Reutlingen and there were smoke columns through the undercast in the vicinity of Günzburg. Flak was heavy, medium and accurate at Germersheim. It was heavy, intense and inaccurate at Stuttgart and heavy, moderate and inaccurate at Saarbrücken.

16 January 1945

Eighth AF FO 1521A

No. 244 Tuesday. Maj. Harrell led the group, which consisted of 48 P-51s (18-434th, 14-435th & 16-436th) on a penetration to target and withdrawal escort for 2nd AD B-24s attacking their 8th AF Mission 796 in Germany. Up: 0929 hrs., down: scattered. There were six early returns.

The weather frustrated efforts today, forcing recalls and cancellations, but the group made it off and L/F was at approximately 1030 hrs./23,000 ft. over the clouds. The squadrons R/V'd with their B-24s at 1050 hrs./23,000 ft. and later made contact with the 2nd ADs 96th CW in the area of Celle at 1115 hrs./23,000 ft. Holes in the undercast revealed good bombing results for the effort. The Big Friends were escorted as far back as Metz, France where the group broke away to find their way home. Again, this became a challenge because before they were able to get back, weather had forced the closing of Wattisham during the early afternoon. The weather was so bad there, that even the group's bicycles were not moving! Two pilots, who were not on the mission, had made test hops, leaving before the closing. They wound up landing at other bases and coming back minus their airplanes. In fact, no 479th FG aircraft returning from the mission came home that day. They were scattered around, most having landed on the continent (34 A/C) or if they had gotten that far, at

Staff Sergeant Clarence "Texas" O. Marlar, the crew chief for 436th FS P-51 Weezy, is seen perched on her wing root. Weezy was Flight Officer, later Second then First Lieutenant Thomas H. Thompson's nickname for his wife Louise. The promotion came as FO Thompson gained experience and because his CO, Major Claire A. P. Duffié was looking for flight leaders. Major Duffié felt his flight leaders should hold that rank rather than Flight Officer. *Courtesy of Thomas H. Thompson.*

other bases in England. Getting planes together for the next day's mission was nearly impossible and it was days before most returned.

Charles H. (Henry) Darling, a former Lieutenant who flew with the 436th FS recalled that mission. In writing about it during late 2001, he described the effort as full of hazards:

"We had just left the target and were escorting the bombers out when a message from our controller came over our radios. The controller informed us that a bad snowstorm was raging over England and instructed us to land where we could on the continent. My flight had separated from the rest of the squadron so we began looking for any open field that we could find. The first airfield that we spotted was in Belgium.

"As we circled the field to see if we should land, we saw that it was already pretty full of all kinds of aircraft that were parked along both sides of the runway as well as any other open space. What really helped us to decide the issue was what happened as we circled. A flight of B-24s was on approach and the bombers were about to begin landing. The first one landed and began breaking. When he got to the end of the runway, he could not clear it because parking traffic had backed up the exiting taxiway. The next B-24 was already touching down. As the heavy bomber rolled down the runway, its crew applied breaks and tried to stop, but ran out of room and crashed into the first. Meanwhile the third B-24 and subsequently the fourth touched down and the same thing happened. There was a four-bomber pile-up at the end of the runway. The other bombers waiting to land were able to go around and probable left to find another airfield. We left as quickly as we could and began looking for a safer landing site.

"Finally we found a place to land at Reims, France. No one had reached that airfield yet and we landed with no problems. We spent three days in Reims until we got word that it was okay to return to England. During that time we spent a lot of time sightseeing and sitting around, waiting.

"On the day we were to take off and return home, the weather was bad, completely overcast and cold. The weathermen assured us that the overcast was thin and that we would have no problems above 2-3,000 feet. We started our ships and got ourselves lined up for take off. I was flying the number two position. Our leader took off and after a few moments, I followed. No sooner was I airborne when the leader called reporting that he was taking on heavy ice and had not broken out yet. He stated that he was at 3,000 feet and was turning back. The two remaining planes in our flight aborted their take off leaving me trying to climb on instruments. I began taking on ice and the only thing that I could do, not knowing where my leader was ahead, was to keep on flying straight at the best climb I could maintain with the increasing weight of the ice. With the ice building up on my canopy, I worried about whether or not I could even see out when and if I ever got clear. Finally, after climbing slower and slower, I broke out into bright sunshine at about 10,000 feet. At that point, the ice began to melt.

"I was alone, but safe I thought, but was I? I took a heading for England and home. Suddenly the sky grew darker and I quickly realized that I was heading into another overcast of solid black clouds that seemed to be getting lower the further northwest I went. The upper overcast and the one below seemed to come together at a point I calculated to be near the coast of England. It looked as though I was in for another instrument let down and landing into the unknown. Just when the two cloud layers seemed to join, I saw a patch of clear sky where I could see all the way to the ground. I didn't waste any time diving down through the break. I came out below the overcast and had clear visibility all around me. I was able to return to Wattisham with no further problems."

Second Lieutenant Francis C. Schiess is about to board the truck that will take he and his fellow fighter pilots to their planes. *Courtesy of David L. Born.*

Two pilots from the 434th FS returned to England via Bremen and were successful in getting a little ground strafing accomplished. They bagged four locomotives destroyed and one damaged. They also damaged three passenger cars and a goods wagon.

There were no observations or flak reports recorded for the mission.

17 January 1945

Eighth AF FO 1525A

No. 245 Wednesday. Maj. Jordan led the group, which consisted of 21 P-51s (7-434th, 10-435th & 4-436th) on an area patrol in support of 3rd AD B-17s attacking their 8th AF Mission 798 primary target at Hamburg, Germany. Up: 0935 hrs., down: 1445 hrs. with four early returns.

Operating as what was squadron strength because of the many 479th FG planes grounded on the continent and at Martlesham Heath, L/F for those available was over Ijmuiden, Holland at 1024 hrs./15,000 ft. The group proceeded east into

Germany and through the vicinities of Dümmer and Steinhuder Lakes. They turned northward and continued on to the Hamburg area, where they arrived at 1200 hrs. They ran into 10/10ths-cloud coverage that extended from the Zuider Zee to Stendal during the trip. Beginning their patrol, it was noted that the force of B-17s arrived first at the target. They were followed by B-24s. At 1155 hours, an unidentified bomber was seen going down in flames. No chutes appeared. The bombing results were not observed, but there was white smoke coming from the target. The group circled the target area until 1230 hrs. and then flew northwest toward the mouth of the Elbe and then south toward Dümmer Lake again. They made L/O over Ijmuiden at 1355 hrs./9,000 ft.

Observations made during the mission included several Big Bens seen heading west in the Arnhem area. Flak over the target was heavy, intense and accurate. At Oldenburg it was light, meager and inaccurate, while that coming from the southeast corner of the Zuider Zee was light, moderate and accurate.

Only training missions were flown for the next three days because of bad weather and that was a good thing too as the availability of aircraft was poor. Most were still trapped where they had come down from the previous mission. A good 30-mph wind came up and raised havoc with the stockpiles of stacked paper belly tanks, scattering them about. It was also a problem with the tents and line shacks. Corporal Stephen J. Bardotz and Private First Class Louis D. Guernsey of the 436th FS had spent considerable time constructing a new shack and were enjoying the comforts of it when the winds came up. It only took a few brief moments for the wind to flatten it with ease. The men were once again out in the cold, especially since rumor had it that all stoves fueled with gas would henceforth be fueled with another form of combustible material. Everyone complained about the temperatures in the barracks and the line seemed to be the only place to keep warm. The rumor proved accurate as on the 20th, a fire inspector visited and warned that all fuel systems in shacks and offices would have to come out by the following morning. The following day, many were warming themselves from the heat produced by burning discarded wax-impregnated cardboard bomb rings. Good old Yankee ingenuity was at work again.

21 January 1945

Eighth AF FO 1539A

No. 246, 247 & 248 Thursday. The group was divided into three forces, A, B and C groups. A and B were penetration to target and withdrawal escorts of 2nd AD B-24s attacking their 8th AF Mission 803 primary target, the marshalling yard at Heilbronn, Germany. C group flew a photo reconnaissance escort into Germany. Capt. Duffié led A group, which consisted of 26 P-51s (9-434th & 17-436th). Up: 1003 hrs., down: 1530 hrs. Maj. Harrell led B group as a replacement for Maj. Jordan, who had been forced to return. The group consisted of 24 P-51s (8-434th & 16-435th). Up: 1010 hrs., down: 1555 hrs. First Lt. Gordon L. Doolittle led C group, which consisted of seven P-51s (2-434th, 3-435th & 2-436th). Up: 1330 hrs., down: 1740 hrs. The combined groups had a total of five early returns.

A and B groups were to R/V with their Big Friends at 1130 hrs./22,000 ft. about 20 miles north of Verdun, France, but they were unable to find the proper B-24s amongst those that they had been seeing. At 1145 hours, their controller, Nuthouse, advised them their assigned bombers were not able to get airborne and that they should stay with the bombers they had seen. A group tagged along, stooged around the target area watching the bombing through holes in the clouds and escorted some B-24s back to the vicinity of Metz, France where they broke away at 1415 hrs./15,000 ft. After crossing into Germany, B group departed escort to investigate some bogies for which they had been given a vector. The bogies turned out to be friendlies from the 4th FG, so the group spent some time strafing targets of opportunity before returning home. Two flights from the 435th FS strafed Leipheim airfield at Günzbourg, accounting for one Ju 52 and one Ju 88 destroyed by First Lieutenant Theo J. Sowerby, one Me 262 and one Ju 88 damaged by First Lieutenant Norman R. Benoit and one Ju 52 damaged by Second Lieutenant Edward H. Sims. Maj. Harrell made a single pass and strafed an unidentified airfield near Stuttgart, claiming one unidentified single-engine aircraft as damaged. The flak was too hot to stay around though. This claim was upgraded and confirmed to a destroyed by a pilot from the 4th FG who witnessed the attack. The remainder of the group tallied an electric locomotive and six steam locomotives as destroyed, plus six gondolas, three passenger cars, three goods wagons and two switch towers, all damaged at Stuttgart.

In the 25 February 2002 news column titled "Looking at Washington" written by Edward H. Sims (see above) for his "Editor's Copy", a syndicated news publication, former Lt. Sims gave further insight into the mission:

"Major John Harrell spotted a German airfield below. He called my flight leader, ordered him to dive down and make a pass over the field to see how much flak came up. Captain Theo Sowerby, the flight's leader, dropped his two wing tanks and dived. Having heard no order to stay up with the flight and knowing my primary obligation as his wingman was to stay with him, I also dropped my wing tanks and followed him down. (That immediately made our fuel supply critical for the return flight back home over the North Sea.)

"When Capt. Sowerby crossed over the German field, there was little flak, but my plane, The Uninvited had fallen far behind and when I crossed, the barrage of antiaircraft fire was heavy, in fact too heavy for more strafing. Both of us hit aircraft with our fire and left them burning.

"Capt. Sowerby and I were now forced to find an airfield in France on which to land and refuel. He found a B-26 medium bomber base and down we went. After we parked, I was astonished to see, jumping up on my wing with a cup of coffee, a cute 18-year old, with one of those smiles that has doomed so many males. So bomber bases had American Red Cross girls at their bases! We didn't.

"The weather was closing in and Capt. Sowerby had already informed me that we would probably have to wait until morning before flying back to England since refueling would take some time. Therefore, the question was, what was she doing that night? She had a date (understandably). Why not break it for a fighter pilot? She did. We toured Laon that night. The paddle-foot colonel (flyboys called the ground types that name) was gracious about the broken date. Capt. Sowerby had also plucked a knockout from the Red Cross girls and we were delighted.

"The next day the weather was still bad. The next day and the day that followed that one continued to be bad. Finally we returned to England. For the rest of the war, an excuse to land again at Laon was the goal, but it was never realized."

Hoarfrost as seen in the morning on a barracks building. *Courtesy of Kenneth D. Axt.*

Interestingly enough, after returning to the squadron, Lt. Sims found he was in trouble for having followed Capt. Sowerby down in the strafing dive. Apparently Maj. Harrell had intended for Capt. Sowerby to make the dive pass alone. As Lt. Sims reasoned however, the duty of a wingman was to follow and protect his leader.

Observations made during the mission included noting the airfield at Leipheim had six Me 262s, a six-engine Blohm & Voss [sic.], and three twin-engine aircraft parked on it. There

Right: The station weather vane located on top of the control tower. *Carroll C. Sprague Collection, courtesy of the East Essex Aviation Society.*

were no enemy aircraft on the snow-covered Goppingen airfield. There were approximately twelve burned out twin-engine plus four serviceable single-engine aircraft at the airfield attacked near Stuttgart. The airfields at Boblingen, Nelligen and Plieningen were heavily covered with snow, but the flak positions seemed to be freshly cleared. One box of B-24s bombed a small unidentified village eight to ten miles west of Heilbronn. The marshalling yard targeted at Stuttgart appeared to be well hit. Flak coming from a woods eight to ten miles northeast of Trier was heavy, moderate and accurate. At Esslingen, it was light, moderate and inaccurate.

No. 248 L/F for C group was north of Dunkerque, France at 1350 hrs./14,000 ft. The force headed into Germany and to the Freiberg area, arriving there at 1500 hrs./30,000 ft. The area to be photographed was covered by clouds reaching as high as 20,000 ft. which led to the mission being abandoned. L/O was near Hontleur, France at 1630 hrs. and on the deck.

That brief description does not begin to tell the whole story. Former First Lt. Gordon Doolittle as cited above, was the escort leader. In 1987 he wrote of his experiences during that mission. He stated:

> "One of my most memorable experiences involved escorting a P-38 photo reconnaissance aircraft [F-5] on a deep penetration mission into Germany. The recon plane was stripped and fast, while our six P-51 escorts carried oversize external fuel tanks, which made us heavy and slow during the flight in. As we got deeper into enemy territory, the recon pilot flew higher and faster so we had to use increasingly higher power settings to keep up. This resulted in using more fuel than we had planned to. Because of this, on the return phase, I became concerned about our ability to reach our home base. To compound this situation, the recon pilot descended to a very low altitude over western France, which precluded accurate visual navigation. As we reached landfall out near Dieppe, he followed a westward track that, by my compass, would take us below the entire south coast of England and out into the Atlantic Ocean. Upon advising the recon pilot of my concern, he (being senior to me) told me he was much more experienced than I was and that he knew exactly what he was doing. We stayed with him until he was safely out of German fighter range, broke off, landed at a base in southern England for fuel and then returned to Wattisham. I never found out if he returned safely or not."

Men in the radio shack at the 436th FS were staying close to their heater, made from a section cut from a steel belly tank. *Courtesy of Raymond Niekamp.*

There were no F-5s reported as missing that day so it appears as though the recce pilot made it home with his pictures.

There was another lull in combat operations, this one a week long, due to more foul weather. The group's records indicate that there was abundant fog so thick that it could have been cut with a knife. Even liberty runs were curtailed for the period. There was also more snow and cold to contend with, this having been the coldest recorded winter in 47 years. Per the group's records:

> "The word 'cold' does not adequately describe the weather so these must be added: freezing, unbearable, marrow-biting and spine-chilling. The ground is lying white with high drifts of snow; the trees have long strands of hoarfrost, snow and icicles hanging from them. All the while, people have moved closer to those beat-up, pot-bellied stoves scattered around the field, that is, if they are lucky enough to have maintained their right to possess a stove! [Some stoves and particularly oil-fired heaters were being removed on orders from authorities due to the various hazards they presented. See above.] With real wintertime here, it gives some of the northern boys a chance to revel in its coldness and remark about how it feels just like Michigan or Minnesota or Oregon. Meanwhile, the poor Californians and those people from the South, shiver in their boots! The hardier troops engaged in some fast and tricky snowball throwing and several times throughout the cold spell, the pilots and enlisted men took sides and slung themselves out. All there needs to be is a ski-jump and this place would be just like Lake Placid."

Four 434th FS CNS (Control Network Service) Corporals, John D. Chapin, Lewis J. (Jack) West, Henry A. Lamping and Aloysius G. Warth. *Courtesy of Lewis J. West.*

A raging snowball fight that broke out near the end of hangar one. *Courtesy of David L. Born.*

When it was possible, truck runs were made to area bomber bases to gather discarded bomb rings for fuel in the group's fireplaces and stoves. The wax-impregnated, compressed, wood-fiber shipping rings burned well and helped to make up for the scarce supply of coke that would have been normally burned. The weather also played a part in the men's health with a number of them becoming hospitalized and confined to quarters. It was also mentioned that the cooks were hardest hit and that there were no longer too many cooks to spoil the broth.

28 January 1945

Eighth AF FO 1563A

No. 249 Sunday. Colonel (recently promoted) Riddle led the group, which consisted of 38 P-51s (14-434th, 13-435th & 11-436th) on a penetration to target and withdrawal escort for 2nd AD B-24s attacking their 8th AF Mission 809 primary target at Dortmund, Germany. Up: 0959 hrs., down: 1415 hrs. with a total of three early returns.

Take off was delayed for twenty minutes because of a heavy snow shower, but the group did get off and made L/F over Den Helder, Holland at 1100 hrs./24,000 ft. R/V with Vinegrove 1-1, their assigned bombers, was at 1110 hrs./24,000 ft near Stavoren, Holland. At that point, one squadron was sent to cover Vinegrove 1-2 because their assigned escort was unable to take off. It was noted that the B-24s were strung out, making escort difficult. Arriving in the vicinity of Dortmund, the force found there was a large hole in the clouds that opened an area approximately 50 miles in diameter and was centered over the city. The Big Friends dropped their loads, hitting the south and west sides of Dortmund. Flak over the targets was heavy, intense and accurate, accounting for a number of losses to the bomber force. One B-24 was seen to explode over the target, another appeared to be spinning down at the same location and two (probably from the 392nd BG) were seen to collide and spin down. No one saw any chutes from the planes. Returning, a B-24 from Vinegrove 1-1 asked for an escort to Brussels. The pilot had a critically-wounded gunner onboard and wanted to land there in order to get help for his crewman. The request was cancelled shortly thereafter because the gunner had died. The pilot stayed with his group. L/O was over Den Helder at 1300 hrs./22,000 ft.

Observations made during the mission included the sighting of many parked goods wagons on the east/west tracks in the vicinity of Rheine. There were smoke pots putting out a smoke screen southeast of Hamm. The airfields at Münster, Osnabrück and Enschede were seen to have been cleared of snow and were ready for operations. A series of barracks and other miscellaneous buildings that appeared to be an army camp were spotted ten miles northeast of Lingen. In the areas of The Hague, the Ruhr and Amsterdam, V2 rockets were seen heading west. Flak over Münster was heavy, intense and accurate as it was from Dortmund to Altena.

29 January 1945

Eighth AF FO 1566A

No. 250 & 251 Monday. The group was divided into two forces, A and B groups, both penetration to target and withdrawal escorts for 2nd AD B-24s attacking their 8th AF Mission 811 primary target(s), marshalling yard(s) in central (Hamm and/ or Münster) Germany. Lt. Col. (recently promoted) Jeffrey led A group, which consisted of 26 P-51s (17-434th & 9-436th). Up: 1027 hrs., down: 1513 hrs. Maj. Jordan led B group, which consisted of 26 P-51s (17-435th & 9-436th). Up: 1034 hrs., down: 1502 hrs. with a total of three early returns.

A group R/V'd with their assigned B-24s at 1115 hrs./ 17,000 ft. over the North Sea and made L/F over the cloud-covered continental coast shortly afterwards. The bombers were escorted through the target area at 1255 hrs./23,000 ft. and out. The group then stooged around the Meppel, Holland area, keeping their Big Friends in sight at all times. They were easy to spot in the clear air above the undercast, which covered much of the area including the target. L/O was in the vicinity of Den Helder, Holland at 1355 hrs./13,000 ft.

B group R/V'd with their bombers 25 miles west of Ijmuiden, Holland at 1120 hrs./10,000 ft. They also were escorted through their target and back to Lingen, Germany where the Little Friends broke from them and headed homeward. The mission was uneventful for both groups except for a dummy convoy that was strafed east of Zweeloo, Holland.

Observations made during the mission included Big Bens seen in the areas of Zwolle, the Ruhr and Zuider Zee. A B-17 was seen bellied in southeast of Assen, Holland. Flak over Gutersloh, Osnabrück and the Bielefeld airfield was heavy, moderate and inaccurate.

The weather warmed during the last two days of January, but that brought mild flooding conditions to Wattisham, resulting in some buildings "invaded" by slush and water. No missions were flown during this period, but practice flights were being made.

434th FS pilot Lieutenant Eugene H. Wendt taking a break from a snowball fight. *Courtesy of Clarence G. Haynes.*

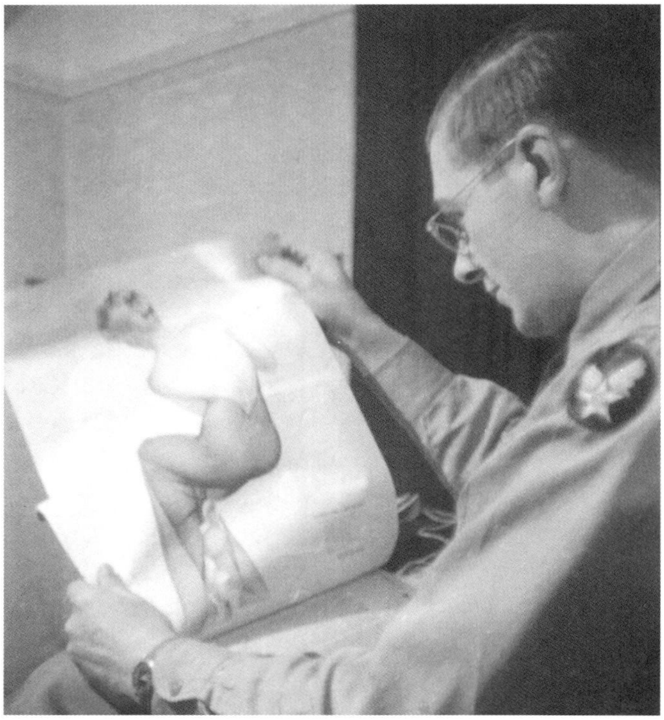

Captain Joseph F. (Doc) Schneider had turned his interests to thoughts of warmer pursuits. *Courtesy of Berkley E. Hollister.*

Left: First Lieutenant Chester W. Broadstone and about half of his 436th FS armorers. Lt. Broadstone is the man in the lower left corner. He is wearing an A-2 jacket and has a 436th FS patch on the coat. Corporal Stanley Kellett is the first man in the first row, just behind Lt. Broadstone's right shoulder. *Courtesy of Stanley Kellett.*

Left: 436th FS armorer Corporal William R. Bottenus, Jr. *Carroll C. Sprague Collection, courtesy of the East Essex Aviation Society.* Right: 435th FS armorer Corporal John D. McDufffie, Captain Ray K. Friend and Technical Sergeant Cleve G. Hewett with their charge, "Sweet El". *From original 479th FG history.*

Above: An enlisted men's party at their club. *Carroll C. Sprague Collection, courtesy of the East Essex Aviation Society.*

Above right: Lieutenant John W. Morrow, a pilot assigned to the 434th FS. *Courtesy of Arnold G. Helding.*

Right: Lieutenant John K. Wilkins, Jr. from the 436th FS was transferred to the Second Scouting Force during January. *Courtesy of the 436th Fighter Squadron Association.*

Above left: Lieutenant Ray L. Shewfelt from the 435th FS was also transferred to the Second Scouting Force during this month. *Courtesy of the 436th Fighter Squadron Association.*

Above center: Newcross Squadron pilot First Lieutenant Eugene E. (Elmo) Sears is shown standing between two belly tanks. The one in the left of the photo was made of steel, the other was made from paper. *© 2000 Elmo Sears, courtesy of Elmo Sears.*

Above right: Master Sergeant Alvin R. Willhite, one of the 434th FS's inspectors, is overseeing the work of another 434th FS crewmember. *Courtesy of Clarence G. Haynes.*

Right: Technical Sergeant Nevoy C. Hummel, a 434th FS crew chief, looks on as one of the squadron's sergeants performs maintenance on an engine. *Courtesy of Clarence G. Haynes.*

Below: First Lieutenant Berkley Hollister had gone home, leaving his Pin Up Girl to Lieutenant John C. Donnell, Jr. Lt. Donnell pestered Staff Sergeant Frederic C. Hayner to paint a Vargas Girl on the ship's nose. This photograph shows Pin Up Girl before the application. *Courtesy of Berkley E. Hollister.*

CHAPTER THIRTEEN

FEBRUARY 1945

1 February 1945

Eighth AF FO 1575A

No. 252 & 253 Thursday. The group was divided into two forces, A and B groups, both penetration to target and withdrawal escorts for 1st AD, 40th CW B-17s attacking their 8th AF Mission 814 primary target, the marshalling yards at Ludwigshafen, Germany. Maj. Duffié (recently promoted) led A group, which consisted of 26 P-51s (8-434th & 18-436th). Up: 1045 hrs., down: 1550 hrs. with four early returns. Capt. (recently promoted) Butler led B group, which consisted of 26 P-51s (8-434th & 18-435th). Up: 1055 hrs., down: 1625 hrs. with two early returns.

The weather over the North Sea was clear, but as the group drew closer to L/F, R/V and the target, a cloud cover appeared and became increasingly dense. From the North Sea to Brussels, it was 4-6/10ths. Passing through eastern Belgium after Brussels, they ran into a front and clouds that turned into 10/10ths.

A group made L/F over Ostend, Belgium at 1125 hrs./18-23,000 ft. and R/V with the proper bombers over Charleroi, Belgium at 1150 hrs./25,000 ft. The B-17s were taken into Germany where they unloaded on the target through undercast skies at 1230 hrs. The last box of bombers, identified as Vinegrove 1-5, bombed an unidentified target northeast of Karlsruhe. All results were unobserved due to the cloud coverage. The Big Friends were escorted out of Germany and one squadron broke from the force by Charleroi at 1430 hrs./13,000 ft. while the other broke near Mons, Belgium. at 1440 hrs./13,000 ft. L/O was over Calais, France at 1505 hrs./9,500 ft.

B group crossed in 15 miles west of Dunkerque, France at 1125 hrs./16,000 ft. R/V with their proper bombers was in the vicinity of Bastogne, Belgium at 1150 hrs./25,000 ft. The time over the target was 1230 hrs./26,000 ft. Bombing results were not observed because of the 10/10ths cloud coverage. Back out of Germany, break away occurred 20 miles northwest of Charleville, France at 1410 hrs./12,000 ft. and L/O was by Dunkerque at 1452 hrs./10,000 ft.

There were no observations noted as having been made during the mission, nor were there any flak reports.

3 February 1945

Eighth AF FO 1586A

No. 254, 255 & 256 Saturday. The group was divided into three forces, A, B and C groups. A and B were penetration to target and withdrawal escorts for 2nd AD B-24s attacking their 8th AF Mission 817 primary targets, synthetic oil plants and marshalling yards at Magdeburg, Germany. C group flew a photo-reconnaissance escort mission into Germany. Col. Riddle led A group, which consisted of 34 P-51s (12-434th & 22-435th). Up: 0936 hrs., down: 1440 hrs. with two early returns. Maj. Duffié led B group, which consisted of 30 P-51s (12-434th & 18-436th). Up: 0930 hrs., down: 1500 hrs. with one non-effective. First Lt. Charles B. Elmgren led C group, which consisted of 2 P-51s from the 436th FS. Up: 1110 hrs., down: 1625 hrs. with no early returns.

A group made L/F near Ijmuiden, Holland at 1022 hrs./17,000 ft. and R/V'd with their proper bombers in the vicinity of Zwolle, Holland at 1045 hrs./22,000 ft. The B-24s were six minutes late, but once joined by their Little Friends, the two made their way to the target and back. Bombing results were not seen due to the undercast. The group was able to see B-17s dropping their loads on Berlin, but those results also were not visible because of the clouds. For that city, the bomber stream with its attendant fighter escort was an estimated 300 miles long. The group broke away from their bombers south of Oldenburg, Germany at 1310 hrs./27,000 ft. There were no enemy aircraft spotted during the mission.

B group made L/F and R/V at the same times and places as did A group and escorted their bombers through the target and back to Terschelling Island, Holland where they broke from them at 1345 hrs./17,000 ft. Over Terschelling Island, a B-17 identified by a "C" in square on its tail (96th BG) was hit by flak causing its number three engine to fail and its number four engine to begin smoking. The bomber was lost sight of when it went down. A B-24 with an engine on fire was also seen in that vicinity. Again B-17s attacking Berlin were seen as well as those of two other bomber boxes that hit an unidentified target at Bremen on the way out. The pilots claimed the sky was filled with aircraft, including Russian.

Observations made during the mission included seeing three Big Bens south of Amsterdam and three south of Zwolle. A Big Ben site was seen on the way back at 1313 hrs. The V2 rocket there was just being launched. An Me 262 appeared to be paralleling the group south of Osnabrück at 1100 hrs./35,000 ft. and there were two unidentified contrails believed to be those of jets seen 20 miles east of Zwolle at 1355 hrs./23,000 ft. Flak over Berlin and Bremen was heavy, intense and accurate. Over Ijmuiden, it was heavy, meager and inaccurate, but over Terschelling Island it was heavy, moderate and accurate. Over Hanover, the Dümmer Lake area, Braunschweig and Magdeburg, it was heavy, intense and inaccurate.

Sergeant Theodore E. Cooper and Captain Nelson W. Butler. *From original 479th FG history.*

No. 256 C group made L/F near Ostend at 1150 hrs./12,000 ft. They were to go into the Frankfurt/Mannheim area, but instead provided escort as far as the vicinity of a front in the Bingen area, arriving there at 1355 hrs./12,000 ft. The PRU bird went in and came back out at 1425 hrs./12,000 ft. Escort was resumed, heading back until they were bounced from the rear by bogies. The escorts turned into the attackers and

A 359th FG, 368th FS P-51 bellied in at Wattisham this date. *Courtesy of the Wings of Freedom Museum.*

Left: First Lieutenant Norbert W. Rock. *Courtesy of Clarence G. Haynes.* Right: Little Chevy was the name that Lt. Rock placed on this P-51. He was not flying this aircraft when he plunged to his death and it became the mount of Lieutenant Edward H. Sims who eventually changed the name to The Uninvited. *Courtesy of Edward H. Sims.*

discovered them to be friendlies. Meanwhile, the PRU plane continued on. L/O was over Walcheren Island at 1530 hrs./ 8,000 ft.

On 5 February 1945, the 435th FS flew a dive-bombing training mission over the Wash, that section of water north of Wattisham and at the top of East Anglia. While in one of the training dives, the plane which First Lieutenant Norbert W. Rock was flying, started falling apart shortly before he could pull out of his dive. He crashed to his death in the Wash, approximately five miles out and northwest of King's Lynn.

6 February 1945

Eighth AF FO 1595A

No. 257 & 258 Tuesday. The group was divided into two forces, A and B groups, both penetration to target and withdrawal escorts for a 2nd AD CW of B-24s attacking their 8th AF Mission 821 primary target, the marshalling yards at Magdeburg, Germany. Col. Riddle led A group, which consisted of 39 P-51s (22-434th & 17-436th). Up: 0929 hrs., down: 1416 hrs. with three early returns. Maj. Jordan led B group, which consisted of 15 P-51s from the 435th FS. Up: 0932 hrs., down: 1402 hrs. with three early returns.

The weather was providing the usual cloud coverage, concealing the continent from Holland to Magdeburg. A group arrived at L/F in the vicinity of Ijmuiden, Holland at 1015 hrs./15,000 ft. and made R/V with their assigned B-24s west of Zwolle, Holland at 1025 hrs./20,000 ft. The Big Friends were escorted to the target and back until a point at which Nuthouse, their controller, instructed them to break away east of Hannover, Germany at 1220 hrs./21,000 ft. They were vectored to sweep back to Magdeburg, then down to the Leipzig area, but found nothing.

L/F for B group was at the same place and time as A group, but R/V for them was a bit farther east, joining their assigned bombers southwest of Meppel, Holland at 1040 hrs./20,000 ft. At 1100 hours, southwest of Meppel, Nuthouse instructed the group to also provide escort for the 20th CW so the group now had two combat wings to cover with only 12 A/C (three of the group were early returns). Fortunately, there were other fighter groups also providing escort. On the return trip from the target, Nuthouse instructed the group to break escort north of Brunswick, Germany at 1210 hrs./23,000 ft. They also engaged in a fighter sweep with no results.

Observations made during the mission included seeing a B-24 explode and fall in flames into the Zuider Zee just east of Hoorn at 1032 hrs./18,000 ft. No chutes were spotted. One of the bomb group formations, Vinegrove 3-3, was difficult to escort properly because they were spread ten miles wide by 30 miles deep. Flak over Alkmaar was heavy, meager and accurate. It was heavy, moderate and accurate at Hoorn and heavy, moderate and inaccurate east of Egmond. Over Ijmuiden, it was heavy, meager and inaccurate. At Magdeburg, flak was both light and heavy, moderate and inaccurate. It was light, meager and inaccurate at Steinhuder Lake.

8 February 1945

Eighth AF FO 1601A

No. 259 Thursday. Capt. Richard G. McCrystal led four P-51s from the 434th FS on a photo-reconnaissance escort to Berlin, Germany. Up: 1146 hrs., down: unknown because all A/C landed in France at airfield A-83, Denain/Prouvy. The generally poor weather prevented the group from participating in any combat mission, but the above listed PRU escort was able to be flown.

9 February 1945

Eighth AF FO 1605A

No. 260, 261 & 262 Friday. The group was divided into three forces, A, B and C groups. A and B were penetration to target and withdrawal escorts for a 2nd AD CW of B-24s attacking their 8th AF Mission 824 secondary target, the marshalling yards at Magdeburg, Germany again. C group flew a photo-reconnaissance escort mission to the Zwolle, Holland area. Capt. Clifford J. Moore led A group, which consisted of 38 P-51s (20-435th & 18-436th). Up: 0931 hrs., down: 1511 hrs. with six early returns. Newly promoted Maj. Robin Olds led B group, which consisted of 20 P-51s from the 434th FS. Up: 0941 hrs., down: 1506 hrs. with two early returns. Capt. McCrystal led C group, which consisted of four P-51s from the 434th FS. Up: 1145 hrs., down: 1445 hrs. on the continent at airfield B-58. There were no early returns from C group.

A group made L/F and R/V over the undercast near Den Helder, Holland at 1025 hrs./22,000 ft. and escorted the screening force through the target. After the bombers unloaded over Magdeburg at 1210 hours, the group stooged around the area for a few minutes. B group R/V'd with the proper bombers over an undercast covered Ijmuiden, Holland at 1026 hrs./ 26,000 ft. They also took their Big Friends through the target, but right after bombs away and during a wide turn to avoid flak, the group sighted a mixed formation of approximately 15 Fw 190s and Me 109s between Magdeburg and Dessau. The enemy aircraft came out of the cirrus clouds, heading east. B group turned left into the bandits and engaged them in an area bounded by approximately 30 miles southeast of Magdeburg to north of Dessau to southwest of Brandenburg. The Germans were very aggressive and A group joined in what became a twenty-minute battle that ranged from 26,000 ft. down to 6,000 ft. in the layered overcast skies. The totaled credits for the day were:

434th Fighter Squadron

1-0-0	Me 109	1st Lt. Richard D. Creighton
0-1-0	Fw 190	1st Lt. Richard D. Creighton
0-0-2	Me 109	1st Lt. John C. Donnell
1-0-0	Me 109	Capt. George W. Gleason
1-0-0	Fw 190	Capt. George W. Gleason
1-0-0	Me 109	Maj. Robin Olds
1-0-1	Me 109	1st Lt. Eugene H. Wendt

435th Fighter Squadron

1-0-0	Fw 190	Capt. Norman R. Benoit
1-0-0	Me 109	Capt. Gordon L. Doolittle
1-0-0	Fw 190	Maj. Herbert H. Jordan
1-0-0	Me 109	1st Lt. David E. King
1-0-1	Me 109	2nd Lt. John R. Rogers
0-1-0	Me 109	1st Lt. Frederick F. Shriner

Some illustrations follow to lend a feeling as to how the day's encounters went. Major Robin Olds gave this report concerning the Me 109 he destroyed:

"I was leading B group and when we arrived at the target, I took the group on a 180-degree turn to the right to avoid some flak. At this time I noticed contrails off to the southeast. Aircraft were apparently trying to use the concealment afforded by a long bank of cirrus clouds which was at approximately 26,000 feet and stretching in a southeast to northwest direction as far as the eye could see. I made positive identification and circled the squadron to the left, gaining position. The bogies were Me 109s and were at approximately 28,000 feet. They were flying their regular four-ship flight and were 2,000 feet higher than us. There were four ships in the closer formation and five or six more over to our left. The rest were sneaking along toward the north, just on the edge of the cirrus clouds. The last mentioned, were called in later and I warned my flights to keep an eye on them. I planned to get the first four with full squadron strength and then take out after the others. We were in good position to accomplish this. Completing a near 360 with the first four Krauts, we wound up right on their tails and had two flights in firing position. I opened fire on 'Tail-End Charlie' at about 250 yards and obtained strikes. The Jerry didn't leave formation, but went hog-wild using evasive measures. I closed to 100 yards and fired again. This time he was lit up from nose to tail on the left side and had the usual pieces fly off. He skidded out of formation. I radioed the rest of the squadron to continue on and that I was going to take care of this one. I circled and waited for a chance at another pass, though one would be unnecessary. Losing control completely, the pilot bailed out as the 109 went straight down, alternately half-rolling left and right. In bailing, the Jerry popped two panels in his chute and upon close inspection, looked quite unhappy about the whole affair. This action took place about five or six miles west of Dessau. I claim one Me 109 destroyed."

First Lieutenant Eugene H. Wendt was leading Newcross Red Flight:

"We had reached the target area and had swung to the southeast of it to avoid the flak when we noticed about eight contrails at approximately eleven o'clock high. I would say that they were at close to 30,000 feet. We were at about 20,000 feet when we started to climb up a bit to go after them. When we got to within a mile from them, they turned towards us and we saw that they were Me 109s. I was on the outside of the squadron and when we broke towards them, my flight was just a bit behind the other flights. We had been headed southeast when we started our turn and we had turned around to approximately a heading of north when we finally got to them. Four of the E/A were going left, across in front of me about a half a mile away and the other four were turning to the right, ahead of me and nearly the same distance or maybe a little more. As the four that were heading to the left in front of me were higher by at least a thousand feet or more and in a poor position for me to get at, I let these go and went after the four that were turning to the right. Also, the four above me already had a bunch of P-51s after them."

Lt. Wendt goes on:

"As I closed in on these other four, several P-51s went in and attacked them from the right. When they did this, two of the Me 109s turned to the left and the others kept to the right. I went after the tail-end 109 and managed to get on his tail just as he got on another P-51's tail that was chasing the other 109. I fired at him from a range of 300-400 yards and observed several hits on him. When I hit him, he broke to the right and dived into the overcast, which lay in layers from around 23,000 feet down. Although I could not see the ground, this overcast was very thin and flimsy, so I could see the sun through it and I could see him easily in it. In addition, I had closed to almost point blank range when we dove into the overcast. We chased around in the overcast, with me shooting at him every time I could get my sights lined up on him. I saw quite a few hits on him at different times and finally I must have really caught him square, as pieces flew off the plane and what looked like fire came back over my plane. I pulled to the right to avoid the pieces of his plane and cut my throttle to stay behind him. As I pulled aside, it looked as though his plane blew up, because pieces flew off all over it."

First Lieutenant Eugene H. Wendt by P-51 L2-R, Cactus Jack. *Eugene H. Wendt courtesy of Stephen Decker.*

Lt. Wendt continues:

"When I pulled aside then to avoid his plane parts, another Me 109 went by me on the left. Evidently he had been on my tail without me realizing it and when I had pulled aside and cut my throttle, he overran me. I immediately poured the coal to my ship and tried to overtake him. I did manage to get to within 300-400 yards of him and fired the rest of my ammunition at him. I saw several strikes on him, but ran out of ammunition before I could really close in on him. When this happened, I pulled back in a very tight turn to the left and went back the opposite way. I claim one Me 109 destroyed and one Me 109 damaged."

First Lieutenant Richard (Dick) D. Creighton was flying as an element leader in Newcross Yellow Flight:

"Just east of the target, at about 1211 hours, a group of five to eight contrails were reported at eleven o'clock high. My flight leader started climbing in a spiral to the left. I poured on the power to stay with him and then noticed what I thought to be two 109s positioning themselves on my tail. I pulled it in tight, stalled out and lost control momentarily. When I recovered, I could see no one on my tail and also had lost sight of my flight leader in the maze of ships. Then I noticed two lone contrails about 2,000 feet above me, at 28,000 feet. I started after them and they made a gradual turn into me and then started a shallow dive away, in front of me. One straightened his dive, flew into a cloud deck of high cirrus clouds, but the other continued turning in my direction. We passed each other, about 200 yards apart, in a head-on pass. I identified him as an Me 109. I pulled up in a steep wingover to the left in an attempt to get on his tail, but he had straightened out and was diving for the cirrus layers at about 25,000 feet. He got into it and I followed by continuing along his contrail, which was dense and persistent. We only went a short distance when I pulled out and saw him on a P-51's tail at about 26,000 feet. I closed to about 400 yards dead astern, fired a burst and blew up his external gas supply. I broke off then, as I had black soot on my windshield. I had picked that up as I flew through the explosion. I pulled up and saw him going down in a spiral, smoking badly. He appeared to have a little control though, as he managed to turn into some thin clouds. I followed, closing to about 400 yards again, fired and observed many hits. The clouds became quite thick and I lost him for about 30 seconds, but we broke out at about 23,000 feet. I saw him about 200 yards off to my left, definitely out of control. He jettisoned his canopy and I tried to get in position for another shot, but could not do so because of the 'violent evasive action' his loss of control was causing. Anyway, there was no need for another shot as he bailed out at about 20,000 feet."

Airplane mechanic Corporal Donald P. Busch is shown with "Super Wabbit", the plane that First Lieutenant Richard D. Creighton claimed as his own. The airplane really "belonged" to her crew chief and Lt. Creighton just got to borrow it once in a while. *Courtesy of Frederick C. Hayner.*

Lt. Creighton continues:

"I went down to about 9,000 feet on a bounce on what turned out to be some P-51s. I then saw four ships from Lakeside Squadron, which I tacked onto. We had started for home on a heading of 270 degrees and were at about 7,000 feet when, at 1300 hours in the Magdeburg area, I saw three Fw 190s in a tight vee. They passed directly beneath us, at about 5,000 feet. I called them in and started down on the bounce. Major Herbert Jordan, who was leading the Lakeside Flight, told me to take the left one while he took the middle one and his number two [second element] man took the right one. Being over eager, I got there first, closed to about 400 yards dead astern and started firing. I observed only a few hits before the German broke down and to the right into the other ships in his formation. I got a good shot at him from about 100-200 yards this time and saw many hits as well as observed pieces coming off his plane, just before he went into the clouds. I dived through after him. The clouds were only about 800 feet thick there at 6-5,000 feet. As soon as I broke out, I saw the other four ships in our formation right near me, but did not see any enemy aircraft. Shortly after, Major Jordan saw a Fw 190, closed on him and really clobbered him. We circled around looking for the others and observed two fires on the ground in the immediate vicinity. One was Major Jordan's and due to what had just happened, we felt sure the other was mine. We then came home. I claim one Me 109 and one Fw 190 destroyed."

First Lieutenant Billy C. Means from the 435th FS confirms Lt. Creighton's second claim with this statement:

"Lakeside White Flight was cruising at about 6-7,000 feet in the Magdeburg area when three Me 109s were called in to Major Jordan, my flight leader. Lt. Creighton from Newcross Squadron, who had joined us after being separated from his squadron, reported them. I immediately did a 180-degree turn and started after them. Lt. Creighton was a considerable distance ahead of me and opened fire before I was in range. I could see he was getting good strikes on the enemy aircraft, which I identified as a Fw 190, and it began trailing black smoke. As the 190s dove for the clouds, I picked one and gave it a three-second burst at extreme range just before he went into the undercast. I didn't see any strikes, however. Before I went into the clouds myself, I saw Lt. Creighton get more strikes on his Fw 190. Pieces, including the canopy, came off the E/A and flew back past me. We all went into and through the clouds. I broke out at about 3-4,000 feet and almost rammed an Me 109, which crossed directly in front of me. I turned onto his tail, but he lost me in the clouds. I went back down under the overcast and there I saw two planes burning on the ground and one parachute at about 2,000 feet. Then I saw another aircraft and started chasing him through the clouds, but finally recognized him as a P-51. I broke off and rejoined my flight above the overcast.

"At interrogation, it developed that my flight leader, Major Jordan, had also shot a plane down in the same engagement. Under the circumstances, I feel sure that the two planes, which I saw burning on the ground beneath the overcast, were the ones destroyed by Major Jordan and Lt. Creighton. I confirm Lt. Creighton's claim of one Fw 190 destroyed."

The Victory Credit Board gave Lt. Creighton credit for the Me 109, but downgraded the Fw 190 from a destroyed to a probable.

Major Herbert H. Jordan was in the mix-up reported above and gave the following Encounter Report:

"I was leading four ships, three from the 435th and one from the 434th, out of the Brandenburg area. We were west of Brandenburg, east of the Elbe River and over some clouds when Lt. Creighton of the 434th spotted three ships flying line abreast under us. We took out after them from 11,000 feet. Before we were in range, they broke to the right and went through the clouds [reported to be 10/10ths cumulus stratus at this time]. Lt. Creighton was the closest and called them in as Me 109s. Lt. Means was also ahead of me, but from my position, it looked as though we were all out of range. After the three E/A went through the clouds, we all went through after them. I picked up a Fw 190 at 4,000 feet. He was within range and one long burst was sufficient. A fire broke out at his left wing root. I didn't see his chute, but the other pilots said he hit the silk. I claim one Fw 190 destroyed."

Captain Gordon L. Doolittle was Lakeside's Red Flight Leader for the mission:

"We were flying on a heading of 300 degrees at 7,000 feet prior to the encounter. E/A were in the area and some of our flights were engaged. I saw two planes in close formation at eleven o'clock, slightly low. I checked my flight and finding all were present, banked sharply into the planes. I identified them as Me 109s at a range of about 800 yards. I closed to 300 yards and squeezed the trigger with no results. My gun switch was off. I ducked under the two planes as I called to my flight to get them and pulled up in a vertical climb. Looking back, I saw my number three man fire at one of the 109s and pass him up to chase the second one which had started after me. [This one was pressing his attack and was firing at Capt. Doolittle who saw a series of explosions ahead of him during the attack. Capt. Doolittle escaped by going into some clouds.] The Me 109 he first fired at went into a violent right turn, streaming coolant. He never recovered from the bank, did a two-turn spin and crashed. This plane was claimed as damaged by Lt. King, Red Three, as he did not see it crash. I believe this plane should be claimed as destroyed by Lt. King. The second Me 109 split-essed away from the three ships chasing him and went down to the deck. I saw him go down and dove after him, having the advantage of about 3,000 feet of altitude. I closed immediately, fired from 300 yards and continued closing to 150 feet. I was getting many strikes in the tail section and fuselage. The 109 rolled back at 300 feet and crashed into the edge of a forest. The pilot did not get out. I claim one Me 109 destroyed."

First Lieutenant David E. (Hot-Shot Charlie) King was the pilot who assisted Capt. Doolittle and who gave this report:

"I saw two ships flying close formation at eleven o'clock, slightly low. As I was very close to them, I identified them as Me 109s. I closed to about 300 yards. As I was about to fire, I saw my flight leader duck under the two ships, pull up in a vertical climb and one of the E/A pull up after him. I took a snap shot at the other one and observed strikes on his wing roots. He started a violent turn to the right and he was streaming coolant. (Capt. Doolittle observed that this Me 109 did not recover from his turn, but went down into a spin and crashed.) I ducked under this Me 109 and went after the one on Capt. Doolittle's tail. I chased this Me 109 until he split-essed away and Capt. Doolittle dove on him from above. He closed to about 50 yards, firing. The Me 109 rolled over and crashed into some woods. Since I had lost my wingman and Capt. Doolittle had lost his, I was trying to catch him when I saw another Me 109 at nine o'clock to me. When I started a turn into him, he split-essed. I split-essed after him and opened fire at about 3-400 yards. I didn't observe any strikes. The Me 109 pulled up into a vertical climb and I lost him in the clouds. I had previously claimed one Me 109 damaged, but because of Capt. Doolittle's observations, I claim the one damaged as destroyed."

Captain Norman R. Benoit and Captain Robert J. Baird are engaged in some fighter pilot talk. The two are on the wing of the P-51 that Capt. Benoit named Victory Queen. *Courtesy of Robert H. Horman.*

A period cartoon drawn by Major Robin Olds from the 434th FS. *479th FG records.*

Captain Norman R. Benoit gives this last illustration of the group's encounter:

"I was leading Lakeside Purple Flight in the vicinity of a fight and saw three high contrails. I called them out and a minute later, one of them came down through the squadron. I turned into him, identified him as a Fw 190 and shot him up. The pilot bailed out and the rest of the squadron witnessed the kill. Later I found an Me 109 flying in and out of the clouds and pursued him. I finally got him out into the open, closed on him and started firing at high deflection. The Me 109 pulled up, flying straight. Just as I was squared away on him again, Lt. Rogers, who was supposed to be flying my wing, dropped down on top of me, forcing me to break in order to avoid a collision. I had to watch Lt. Rogers shoot the Me 109 down. I had followed that Me 109 around and through the clouds for about ten minutes. The P-51 in Lt. Rogers' combat film is me! I claim one Fw 190 destroyed."

Norman R. (Benny) Benoit finished his tour with the 479th FG/435th FS on 14 February 1945. He had been with the squadron since early on and had started in their P-38s. He was a well-liked man who was praised as a natural pilot, a fighter pilot's, fighter pilot. He was young, strong and a tremendous flyer said squadron mate Ray Friend. Ray remembers one of Norman's tricks:

"...was to come in over the airstrip at Wattisham, going downwind – I'm not sure of the altitude, but he must have been at 1,000 to 2,000 feet. When he got to the end of the field, he would do a split-ess [an aerobatics maneuver whereby the aircraft, flying straight and level, is rolled over on its back and at the same time does a diving half-loop, thereby producing both a loss of altitude and a reversal of direction] and when he pulled out, his propeller would be clipping the field's grass. He would then do a peel-up and as we always said, never put his wheels down. He was putting them up because he was on his back." Ray continues, "I remember being in the squadron headquarters when Zemke was talking to Benoit about an Me 109 that tore off a wing trying to get away from the two of them [see 7 October 1944]. Colonel Zemke mentioned that he was one of the better German pilots that he had seen in a long time. After the Colonel had left, Benoit told us that all he (Norman) had been doing, was chasing the Me 109 back so Zemke could shoot at him. He wasn't about to shoot down the plane in front of a full colonel."

Norman Benoit was not an ace, only achieving two-and-one-half victories plus five damaged; but in his own right, he was a real hero. In his correspondence, Norman wrote of some of his experiences:

> "I tried to render both navigational aid and protection to the distressed and damaged strays leaving the target areas. Flak and enemy fighter actions forced those Big Friends 'crippled' by damage to fall back and lose the mutual protection afforded by their combat formations. Forced to struggle on their own, and usually carrying nine or ten crewmen, the strays were attacked unmercifully by the German fighter pilots and more often than not, shot down. My belief that saving these friends was a very important part of that protective assistance. Staying with them and often guiding them back to landfall at England saved many lives."

Norman continues:

> "There were many individual efforts that startled me at the time, but turned out well in the end. One such effort was when I picked up a B-17 bomber and the pilot said they would 'Bail' if I would nullify the ground small arms fire. So, I got right down to the trees, sprayed the area with gunfire and circled while ten chutes landed and the men waved okay to me. I reported the tail markings to intelligence and they were able to report the crew as missing, but alive! On another occasion, a badly shot up B-17 called me and said that if I would cover for them and navigate back to Woodbridge, they would unload. To my amazement, guns, ammunition, life rafts, bomb racks, boxes and even parachutes were thrown from the aircraft. Yes, they made it back! There were many other such incidents and at times in bad weather, I navigated back to England, bringing as many as 60 fighters from several groups with me. I was convinced many pilots did not know where they were going and needed someone to get them home efficiently. So, I would stay in an area, orbit to call them in and all manner of strays would show up and go back with me. I believe that I saved many fliers, which was more important to me than fighter-kill glory at the expense of lost American lives."

Norman R. Benoit flew 91 combat missions in Europe and was awarded the air medal with seven oak leaf clusters for his service with the 479th Fighter Group.

All of the losses were not on the German side, however. While at 12,000 feet, east of the target and circling left to cross over another flight, Second Lieutenant Carl B. Jarrell was engaged by a Fw 190 that dove on his flight from above. Lt. Jarrell split-essed to escape and in a battle similar to those described above, but with the roles reversed, had his aircraft put out of action by the enemy pilot. His flight leader, Capt. Norman R. Benoit, promptly shot down the Fw, but Lt. Jarrell's plane was badly hit. He tried to keep it going, but the P-51 caught fire and he was forced to bail out over the small town of Görzke, about 25 miles east of Burg. He drifted east, landing by a woods north of a road that headed to Belzig. His plane hit a building near the northeast corner of Görzke. His good friend Robert H. Horman, then also a Second Lieutenant, told me that he circled him as he parachuted down. (The two had been together since the beginning of flight school.) The former Second Lieutenant, who eventually became a Brigadier General in the Indiana Air National Guard, also told me the rest of the story: "When Lt. Jarrell hit the ground near a wooded area, he got up, waved, unbuckled his chute and was last seen running towards the woods."

Captured shortly afterwards, Lt. Jarrell became another POW interred at a German Stalag. For him "*...der war vas over*". Robert Horman continued:

> "After the war, Lt. Jarrell came back to Wattisham and told his buddies what happened after he ran into the woods. It seems that his airplane had crashed into a farmer's house and destroyed it. The area residents were all up in arms about that and the fact that Jarrell was a '*Terror Fleiger*'. They were after him with pitchforks and whatnot and having captured him, were set to do him harm. Fortunately, a Luftwaffe pilot arrived at the scene,

dragging his parachute behind. He was the pilot of the Fw 190 that had shot Lt. Jarrell down and was himself subsequently shot down. The German pilot had also been able to bail out and had landed in the vicinity of where Lt. Jarrell dropped down. He intervened and saved Lt. Jarrell from almost certain death at the hands of the hostile civilians."

What a piece of good fortune!

All of the battles over, the flights and squadrons made their way back home. A few with a little fight left in them, dropped down to strafe some ground targets. They destroyed and damaged seven trucks and a bus along the autobahn east of Burg. The Briest Airdrome southeast of Brandenburg would have made a good target as there were 50 plus single-engine aircraft observed parked around the field. Low on ammunition, gas and energy, the men passed it up. L/O was in the vicinity of Knokke, Belgium around 1400 hrs.

There were no observations recorded from the mission. Flak over Halberstadt and Magdeburg was heavy, intense and accurate.

No. 262 C group left England, passing over Orford Ness at 1200 hrs./5,000 ft. Climbing to 27,000 ft. and on instruments, the weather obscured their L/F over the continent. Cloud coverage was from about 5,000 ft. up to 27,000 ft. with an even denser layer of overcast clouds above that. The overcast was so bad that they lost sight of the PRU P-38 they were escorting. Dropping down, they finally broke through the clouds at 500 ft. in the area of Zwolle, Holland. The flak there was light, intense and accurate. Forced to abandon the mission, they landed at airfield B-58 on the continent, refueled and returned home later that day.

14 February 1945

Eighth AF FO 1622A

No. 263, 264 & 265 Wednesday. The group was divided into three forces, A, B and C groups. A and B were penetration to target and withdrawal escorts for 2nd AD, 14th CW B-24s attacking their 8th AF Mission 830 secondary target, the marshalling yards at Magdeburg, Germany again. C group flew a photo-reconnaissance escort mission to the Stettin, Poland area. This was a maximum effort by the group and 69 P-51s were fielded for the missions. Col. Riddle led A group, which consisted of 44 P-51s (24-434th & 20-435th). Up: 1048 hrs., down: 1625 hrs. with four early returns. Maj. Duffié led B group, which consisted of 20 P-51s from the 436th FS. Up: 1039 hrs., down: 1615 hrs. with no early returns. First Lieutenant Lawrence A. Keefe led C group, which consisted of five P-51s from the 435th FS. Up: 1126 hrs., down: 1625 hrs. with one early return.

Briefing in the pilot's room at the 435th FS. *Courtesy of Clarence G. Haynes.*

A group made L/F three miles south of Ijmuiden, Holland at 1126 hrs./14,000 ft. R/V with the proper bombers was 15 miles east of Meppel, Holland at 1148 hrs./20,000 ft. The 434th FS swept ahead of the force, responding to vectors from Nuthouse, their controller, after R/V. The 435th FS was vectored by Nuthouse to an area southeast of the R/V. They were looking for "Rats" (Me 262s), but found none to chase. They rejoined the heavies in the vicinity of Dümmer Lake in Germany, where the weather presented them with a mixture of 10/10ths overcast that clouded the skies from 14-25,000 ft. as well as a layer of low clouds with tops to 7,000 ft. They stayed with the bombers for the rest of the mission. The target at Magdeburg was reached at 1231 hrs./26,000 ft. and the Big Friends dropped their loads. The results were unobserved due to the weather there, which was again, a mixture of conditions: 6/10ths cirrus clouds to 26,000 ft. and 8-9/10ths cumulus clouds with tops 3-5,000 ft. The 435th FS took the B-24s on up north to the vicinity of Salzwedel and broke from them there at 1245 hrs./28,000 ft. They continued on and wound up doing some strafing in an area 30 miles northeast of Meppel. L/O for them was near Ijmuiden at 1459 hrs./12,000 ft.

Meanwhile, at about 1210 hours, the 434th FS was flying at 26,000 feet, southwest of Berlin. There they saw 15 Me

109s split into two gaggles of flights of four at 32,000 feet, five miles southwest of Berlin. Newcross Squadron climbed to meet them and attacked at around 1225 hrs. At the same time, another 20 Fw 190s were sighted farther below. Evidently the Me 109s were providing top cover for the Fws and both were heading southwest towards the Chemnitz area. The enemy Me 109 pilots were aggressive, although they dived for the deck. The Fw 190 flyers were even more aggressive. In the end, 434th FS gave old Adolph a headache for this Valentine's Day, costing him ten of his airplanes.

The claims were:

1-0-0	Me 109	1st Lt. David L. Born
1-0-0	Me 109	1st Lt. William H. Daudistel
1-0-0	Me 109	1st Lt. John T. Golden
1-0-1	Me 109	Lt. Col. Arthur F. Jeffrey
1-0-0	Me 109	Capt. Richard G. McChrystal
2-0-0	Me 109	Maj. Robin Olds
1-0-0	Fw 190	Maj. Robin Olds
0-0-2	Me 109	Capt. Donald J. Pierce
2-0-0	Me 109	1st Lt. Eugene H. Wendt

Lieutenant Colonel Arthur F. Jeffrey. *Courtesy of Clarence G. Haynes.*

Sorted by flights, the following Combat Reports represent the fight:

Lieutenant Colonel Arthur F Jeffrey: "I was leading Newcross Squadron [White Flight One] on an escort mission to Magdeburg. Between Magdeburg and Berlin, we encountered a small force of E/A at about 30,000 feet and on a heading of approximately 240 degrees. At first, I saw only three flights of E/A, two with three planes and one with four planes. We dropped tanks and turned into them, causing them to split up. One three-plane flight went north, one went west and the four-plane flight broke south. By this time they were identified definitely as Me 109s, so I took two of my flights and climbed in pursuit of the three E/A breaking west. Upon closing, I selected the 'Tail-End-Charlie' on the left of the formation and opened fire from about 400 yards, dead astern. I closed to 200 yards, observing a lot of strikes along the fuselage. Then the 109 broke to the left in a spin, flames licking out of his engine. Obviously not under control, the German plane spun down from about 30,000 feet, trailing smoke and flames. I saw several unidentified pieces fall off the plane before it disappeared in a cloud deck at around 6,000 feet."

Lt. Col. Jeffrey continued: "I then moved over to the right, behind the lead A/C and gave him one good burst, observing many strikes on his fuselage before he broke down and to the left. I followed, but in the ensuing chase, I could get in only two more short bursts before he went into the clouds. I claim one Me 109 destroyed and one Me 109 damaged."

Second Lieutenant Ossie Huval, who was White Two, Lt. Col. Jeffrey's wingman and First Lieutenant Eugene H. Wendt, who was flying as Red Leader, both confirmed the Lt. Col.'s claims. Lt. Col. Jeffrey only expended 206 rounds of .50 cal. API ammunition. That was good shooting!

Captain Donald J. Pierce: "I was flying Newcross White Three. We were southwest of Berlin at 28,000 feet when we contacted 12-16 Me 109s. They were at 32,000 feet and flying in a formation similar to ours. As we closed to attack, the enemy flights split up, so White Flight attacked three 109s heading southwest. We closed to about 250 yards and Lt. Col. Jeffrey, White Leader, attacked the E/A on the left, getting strikes on its belly tank, tail and wings. The other two ships broke, one to the left and one to the right. I started after the one that broke left, but the ranging cable in my K-14 sight broke and I was unable to use it. I closed in anyway, switched to fixed sight and opened fire at about 250 yards, while in a diving turn. I didn't actually see any strikes, but the 109s left gear fell down just before he went into a cloud. I lost him there."

Capt. Pierce went on: "I then started climbing back up to our fight level and at around 10, 000 feet, I saw a P-51 chasing an Me 109 just above a cloud deck. About the same time, another Me 109 closed in on the P-51. I started after the last one, which was somewhat on my level, closed on it and opened fire with a 60-70-degree deflection shot from 300 yards. I closed to 150 yards and observed a few strikes on the E/A's wing roots before he split-essed away into the clouds. I claim two Me 109s damaged."

Second Lieutenant Dalton F. Tommie, Newcross White Four, was Capt. Pierce's wingman and confirmed the two Me 109s damaged, adding that he saw hits on the fuselage of the first Me 109 and also saw its landing gear drop down.

First Lieutenant Eugene H. Wendt: "I was leading Newcross Red Flight when we encountered E/A at 30,000 feet southwest of Berlin. The squadron gave chase and just as we got within range and identified them as 12 Me 109s in three flights, they split up. White, Red and Yellow Flights dropped tanks and gave chase to three Me 109s heading west. After about five minutes, we closed to within range. White leader took the left E/A and White Two took the middle E/A. White Three and I took the right hand E/A. I opened fire at 300-400 yards from almost six o'clock and saw several flashes from strikes. The Jerry peeled off and kicked into a spin, losing a few thousand feet and then recovered. I followed him and was attempting to get back in firing position when three more Me 109s joined in from somewhere, so I called for help. We all got into a luftberry where I managed to pull through and line up on one of the 109s, giving him a short burst. I got strikes on his wings and fuselage. The 109 rolled over in a dive starting from 20,000 feet and I followed him down. At about 10,000 feet, I got in another burst from 400 yards or less and got a good concentration right on his fuselage and cockpit. The E/A continued to dive for a moment, then began a skid sideways and dove straight into the ground. I pulled out at about 1,000 feet and as I climbed back up, I saw smoke and fire from the crash.

Captain Donald J. Pierce. *Courtesy of the Wings of Freedom Museum.*

"On my climb back up and just as I had come out of some scattered clouds, I was bounced by the other three Me 109s. I got into a climbing luftberry to the left. Then I saw four P-51s off to my left, so I continued my turn to the left, then broke towards them. The Me 109s evidently didn't see the other P-51s until too late because they followed me and as we got close, we all set up in another luftberry to the left. I gained altitude in the turn, then knifed through and got a 30-degree deflection shot from 100 yards at one of the turning 109s. He reversed his turn which put me right on his tail, so I gave him a good burst at a range of about fifty yards, getting good strikes on his wings and fuselage. He straightened out and made a slight dive for the clouds. I got in another short burst from 100 yards after which the Jerry started a slight pull up. Then I caught him square, pouring in a good burst as I closed to point-blank range at ten-degrees deflection. I blew big pieces off his wings and most of his rudder and tail assembly. I flew right through the rubble that my fire knocked off the E/A. I then pulled up and as I did so, I saw the Me 109 spin into a cloud, trailing smoke and flame. Upon examining my plane after I returned to base, my crew chief found parts of this last Me 109 in my manifold scoop. I claim two Me 109s destroyed."

First Lieutenant David L. Born: "I was flying as Newcross Red Four when we encountered a small force of E/A at 30,000 ft. southwest of Berlin. My element leader closed to engage three Me 109s, but I had to leave him when one of the three pulled around on my tail. I broke to the left and ended up in position on one of the other 109s.

This sequence of five pictures are frames of gun camera film taken from the sequence shot by Lieutenant David L. Born of the German aircraft he claimed this date. His claim was for a Me 109, but upon close examination of the film in 2003, it has been suggested that his victim was in fact a Fw 190D. Frame one. *Courtesy of David L. Born.*

Frame two. Note the hits in the tail section. *Courtesy of David L. Born.*

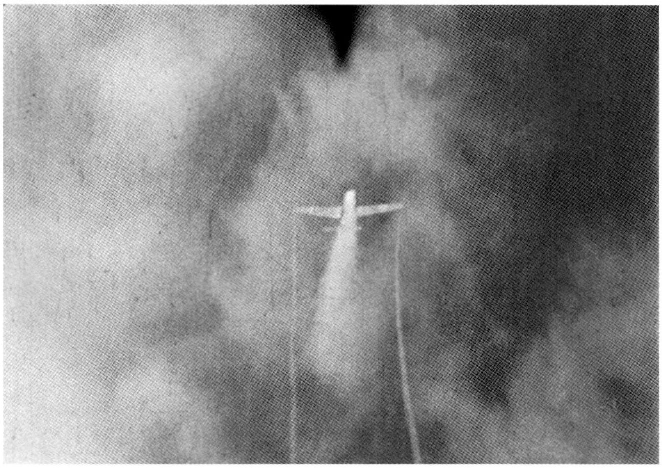

Frame three. Going down, smoking and pulling wing tip contrails. *Courtesy of David L. Born.*

Frame four. *Courtesy of David L. Born.*

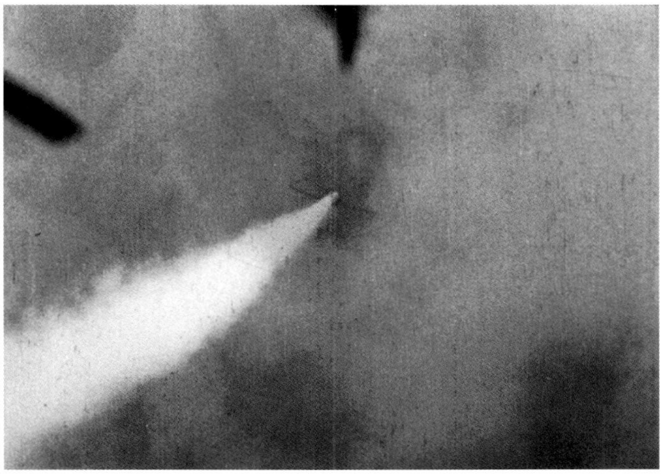

Frame five. The E/A is done for. *Courtesy of David L. Born.*

We went into a luftberry to the left and I managed to get three good bursts at the Jerry. I was using a K-14 gunsight and fired at about 20-30-degrees angle off, range 300-350 yards. During the first two bursts, I couldn't tell for sure if I was getting strikes or not, but I feel certain that I must have been because I had him ranged correctly and had the pipper right on him. On the last burst, I saw many strikes on the wing root and fuselage. We were in a turn to the left and when I next saw him, the 109 was smoking badly around the nose section. Then he broke to the right and dove for the clouds. I followed him into the clouds, which were fairly light. I couldn't see the 109 itself, but I could see the black smoke he was trailing and I fired a short burst in that general direction. Then a big piece of something, obviously off the 109, went sailing past me. I got a pretty good look at it and it seemed to be about eight feet long and one-and-a-half feet wide, with small ribs running across it. I assume it was a flap or an aileron. Fearing that I might run into more pieces and not knowing how high the base of the clouds was, I pulled up and joined with Lt. Dalton F. Tommie. When I last saw the Me 109, he was going down in a fairly steep dive at about 3,000 feet and I feel certain that he could not have recovered with the big piece off his plane. I claim one Me 109 destroyed."

Second Lieutenant Dalton F. Tommie, flying as White Four, confirmed Lt. Born's destroyed and added that he thought it appeared as though the Me 109's canopy had come off, but that the pilot was stuck part way out of his aircraft.

First Lieutenant John T. Golden: "I was flying Newcross Blue Four on an escort mission. At 1200 hours, we were at an altitude of 27,000 feet and more or less 20 miles southwest of Berlin when two enemy formations were sighted flying ahead of us. They were on a course of approximately 180 degrees and about 3,000 feet above us. The first enemy formation had 15 ships in flights of four plus one of three. The second enemy formation had maybe 25 planes. We turned into trail with the first formation, dropped our tanks and started to climb. As we closed with the E/A, they dropped their tanks and started to spread out. Our flights started to cross back and forth and I became separated from my flight. I drove on toward the E/A, on a parallel course with some other 51s. I closed to approximately 1,000 yards, in trail with three 109s. Two pulled up to the right and one did a wing over to the right.

First Lieutenant John T. Golden. *Courtesy of Frederick C. Hayner.*

I followed the one down, closed to 350 yards and opened fire at about a 20-degree angle off. I observed strikes all over the fuselage as I closed and overshot him. My airspeed at that time was nearly 400 MPH. When I overshot, I pulled up to the right and the 109 turned to the left. I turned back and came around to dead astern on him, slightly higher and at 350 MPH. I opened fire at about 350 yards again, observing strikes on his fuselage and cowling. As I closed, we went into broken clouds at 10,000 feet. I continued to follow him into the clouds and when we broke out into an open spot, I closed to 150 yards. As I brought my sight up to fire at him again, I saw his canopy fly off and he came out over the top of his ship. I did not see if his chute opened or not. As I pulled up, I could see flames coming from the E/A. I leveled off at 8,000 feet and finding myself alone, I climbed back up. I claim one Me 109 destroyed."

Maj. Robin Olds: "I was leading Newcross Green Flight. Our squadron was between Magdeburg and Berlin at an altitude of 27,000 feet and had started to make a 360-degree turn to the left when two bogies were called in at six o'clock low, passing from north to south. I glanced back and saw not two, but four bogies. As we made our turn, we lost altitude, going down to approximately 24,500 feet. In the meantime, these four bogies made a 360-degree left turn also, but they gained altitude during their turn. As we rolled out of the turn and headed about 90 degrees again, the four bogies were an estimated 3,000 feet above and behind our formation. I thought that they were enemy, but could not identify them positively. Then more bogies were called in at 12 o'clock high and passing 20 degrees across our front, towards us. We turned right and started climbing after them. At this time, they split into three small groups, one continuing southwest, one heading west and the other, north. The squadron split up to go after them. I was closest to the six bogies that went southwest. They were flying in one flight of four, as in a regular P-51 formation, with two 'Tail-End-Charlies' lagging behind. As we climbed, I identified them positively as Me 109s. Before I drew into range on the last two, the flight of four, well out in front, split-essed. The two bandits I was after continued at the same level. On reaching 30,000 feet, I closed to extreme range. One of the bandits dropped his belly tank and headed down. Lt. Golden, Newcross Blue Four, took out after him. Fearing that the other Me 109 would do the same, I ranged him carefully with my K-14 gunsight and allowed a small amount of deflection above to take care of the sizable 450-yard distance between us. I squeezed off a very short burst and got hits, much to my surprise! The Jerry started a slow break to the right. Taking my time, I ranged him again, still allowing a little for the distance. Another short burst produced more hits. Having closed in to a better range by this time, I put the pipper right on his cockpit, let up a trifle on the graticules and gave him another burst. He received more strikes this time, right where my pipper rested. Black smoke poured out of his engine cowling and he snapped into a spin, recovered drunkenly and then went into a violent, uncontrolled spin from which he didn't recover. I started to follow, but realized that he had had it and broke off.

Maj. Olds continued: 'Straightening up, I saw two more Me 109s ahead at 35,000 feet and 16 to 18 Fw 190s below them. All were heading southwest towards the B-17s attacking Chemnitz. I climbed again, figuring on bouncing the top cover first and then the main force. The same thing happened as before, one Jerry split-essed with Lt. Creighton hot after him and the other went straight. I fired at this one from slightly below and a dead astern range of 450 yards. As soon as I could see strikes, the 190 started right. Then with that beautiful K-14 sight, I got hits all over the right side of his fuselage. I obtained a few more hits as he rolled over into the inside of his turn, yawing and skidding. He must have been out of control, because this yawing and skidding continued for a bit; sometimes he was upside down; sometimes he was falling sideways, but then he went straight down.

He continued: "This last bounce left me in perfect position to hit the Fw 190s. Dropping my nose, I started down after them as they were making gentle left and right turns, in no apparent formation. I tacked onto the tail end man on the right side of the gaggle and closed into good range before firing. Just as I entered his contrail, I saw many strikes flashing and continued to fire for the next few seconds, placing my pipper midway between his wing tips, which were all that I could see. The 190 fell gently to the right and I realized too late that my closing speed was excessive. Even though I momentarily chopped my throttle, I glided on past him. I looked over and saw the German pilot slumped forward in his cockpit seat. His canopy was shattered and I went by slowly enough to note jagged holes in the left side of his fuselage.

"I blandly glided right on through the edge of the Jerry gaggle and out in front. As I had not the slightest intention to lead three Jerries anywhere, I did a half roll followed by a wing-low vertical 360 or loop. By the time I got three-fourths around in this maneuver, I looked through the top of my canopy and saw the 190s disappear into a thick cirrus formation that was between them and the bombers. I could still see my 190, because he was still in that steep diving turn to the right while the rest of his buddies turned left into the clouds. He disappeared momentarily, then reappeared underneath the cloud, going straight down. I watched him until he disappeared into a cumulus formation at 16,000 feet. He never could have recovered from a dive like that at that altitude, even if he had been intact.

"I circled, looking for the rest of the Fw 190s, but they had eluded me and I was all alone. I flew over to the last box of B-17s that hit Dresden and escorted a straggler halfway home. I claim two Me 109s and one Fw 190 destroyed."

First Lieutenant Gail E. Jacobson was Newcross Green Two, wingman for Maj. Olds, and gave these statements of conformation for the two Me 109s that Maj. Olds claimed: "Southwest of Berlin, we encountered 15 plus E/A at 30,000 feet, heading towards the B-17s bombing south of Berlin. The E/A split up as we positioned to attack and Green Flight ended up chasing six heading southwest. Just before we got in range, four of the six split-essed, leaving two, which we identified as Me 109s. They were still in a slight climb until one split-essed with a Newcross P-51 after him. At the same time, Major Olds started firing at the other 109, which was at extreme range. I observed strikes on its wings and cockpit section. At this time, I was four or five ship lengths behind and two or three to the right of Major Olds, where I remained during the rest of the encounter. The 109 was in a 15-degree right turn when Major Olds fired twice more, getting strikes on the E/A's canopy and wing roots. The 109 went into a spin and started to pour black smoke from the left wing root. He recovered momentarily and then fell off into an uncontrolled spin.

"Two more Me 109s were sighted ahead of us at 32,000 feet as well as 16-18 Fw 190s below them, all heading towards the bombers. The Jerries seemed to have a signal, because as before, one of the 109s split-essed when we started up after them. Major Olds lined up on the remaining one and I saw him get strikes on the ship's wing and canopy, lighting up the right side briefly. I was again on the right side and slightly behind Major Olds, since I had been trying to close in on his wing during a right turn. The 109 started a 15 to 20-degree turn to the right after the first burst and Major Olds fired again, getting hits on its wing. The Jerry then rolled to the inside of his turn, completely uncoordinated, went upside down and appeared to fall off on one wing. He ended up going straight down. These maneuvers were definitely out of control.

"After this bounce, we were at six o'clock high to the Fw 190s, so we dropped our noses and went down on them. The 190s dropped their tanks and went into a left turn, then cut back to the same heading. Major Olds closed on the E/A to the far right, so I slipped over to the left and tacked onto the middle one. Major Olds opened fire around 200 yards and dead astern of his 190. He got lots of good strikes all over the 190. I was within range of my own Jerry, so I opened fire, but hit prop wash and was thrown off. Major Olds' Fw 190 went off to the right and I didn't see him after that because I overshot and had to split-ess. I confirm Major Robin Olds' claim of two Me 109s destroyed and I also confirm that he scored many good strikes all over the Fw 190."

First Lieutenants Harold M. Jenkins, who was leading Newcross Blue Flight, and Robert I. Bromschwig, who was Newcross Blue Three, both gave confirmations for Maj. Olds' first Me 109.

Major Olds only fired 407 rounds of .50 cal. API ammunition during the whole of three successful encounters, which speaks well of his skill and experience. It also complements the functionality of the K-14 gunsight he was using. That little beauty was a gyroscopically actuated, lead-computing optical system which when properly used in circumstances of battle, assuming the pilot using it was the attacker, was called an "Ace-Maker". It computed the correct lead angle for target crossing speed at ranges from 200 to 800 yards. It contained two optical systems, one fixed, that projected a cross, surrounded by a 70-mil ring on a reflector glass. The other was the gyro system, which projected a circle of six diamonds that surrounded a central dot called the "pipper" on the reflector glass. The systems could be switched between or used simultaneously. The diameter of the diamonds could be changed by setting the span scale lever on the face of the sight or by rotating the throttle twist grip. This was called "ranging the diamonds". Once the target aircraft was engaged, properly framed and tracked for a minimum of one second, the sight computed the correct gunnery lead so that the pilot just had to keep what he wanted to hit "under the pipper". In actual usage, the sequence of operation was:

1. Identify the target and set the span adjustment lever to correspond with the span of the airplane.
2. Fly the airplane so that the target appears within the gyro reticle circle and rotate the throttle twist grip until the diameter of the gyro reticle corresponds to the target size.
3. Frame the target with the gyro reticle circle by rotating the twist grip as range changes. Track the target smoothly for one second and then fire.
4. Continue ranging and tracking while firing.

While all this was occurring, when firing, the pilot was releasing six streams of armor piercing incendiary ammunition at the rate of 550 rounds per minute, per gun. The rounds were constructed so that when they struck an object such as an aircraft's skin, they gave off a bright flash to indicate where they had struck.

First Lieutenant William H. (Hank) Daudistel was Newcross Green Four:

"We were at 25,000 feet, just east and south of the target when two gaggles of Me 109s were called in. White Flight went after one gaggle to the northwest and Green Flight gave chase to three Me 109s to the southwest. Newcross Green Leader, Major Robin Olds, attacked the 109s after climbing from 25,000 to 30,000 feet. He shot down one and the other split-essed for the deck. One Me 109 was left ahead of us, so Green Three, First Lieutenant Richard D. Creighton and I went after him. We had everything open, but I was losing ground. The 109 then split-essed with Green Three on his tail and me following along behind. Green Three hit compressibility, but the German didn't and got in position on his tail. Green Three recovered, started turning to the right and calling for someone to come and help him. I answered and made a pass from about 19,000 feet, opening fire at 700 yards, 90-degrees deflection and closed to 200 yards, 60-degrees deflection. I was going too fast and didn't get any strikes as far as I could see. I had a lot of speed, so I got in position for another pass from 16,000 feet. This time I opened fire at 700 yards, 90-degrees deflection and closed to 50 yards dead astern, getting good strikes all over the 109's canopy and wing roots. The E/A then reversed his turn to the left, began to trail white smoke and snapped over in a violent spin to the right, at about 14,000 feet. I rejoined Lt. Creighton and we began to wind back up to the main part of the fight. I watched the Me 109 as I climbed and when I last saw him, he was trailing great clouds of white smoke and was definitely in an uncontrolled spin as he went into a cloud deck at approximately 6,000 feet. I believe that the German pilot must have been killed on my second pass, because I saw a good concentration of strikes right in his cockpit and then the Me 109 spun down from 14,000 feet to 6,000 feet without any apparent attempt to recover or to bail out. I claim one Me 109 destroyed."

First Lieutenant Richard D. Creighton confirmed Lt. Daudistel's claim:

"After Green Leader made the initial attack, he told me to take the remaining Me 109, which was still at 31-32,000 feet, a few thousand feet above me. I firewalled everything and took out after him. I got on his tail at 32,000 feet and opened fire at about 700 yards, but the Jerry rolled over into a split-ess. I followed and got in a snap shot going straight down, but didn't get any hits. Then I hit compressibility and dived right on by the 109, without being able to make my controls take effect. In the meantime, the German positioned himself on my tail and when I recovered at 18-19,000 feet, he came in on me from about 2,000 yards, above and behind. I went a couple of turns with him and called for help. My wingman, First Lieutenant William H. Daudistel, answered and came in from 90 degrees, but didn't hit him. The E/A kept after me. Lt. Daudistel pulled into position and made another pass, firing from 90 degrees and closing to almost dead astern. This time I saw good hits in the cockpit and the E/A reversed his turn, started to roll off to the left going down, then snapped back to the right and into a spin. He was smoking badly and still spinning when I lost sight of him as he spun into the overcast at 5-6,000 feet. I am almost positive that the German pilot was dead, since he didn't bail out and certainly should have if he wanted to live. I confirm First Lieutenant Daudistel's claim of one Me 109 destroyed."

Captain Richard G. McChrystal heading for his aircraft. *Courtesy of David L. Born.*

Captain Richard G. McChrystal:

"I was leading Newcross Purple Flight on an escort of B-24s to Magdeburg. At 1200 hours, 26,000 feet and about 20 miles west of Berlin, I saw six E/A in two, three-ship flights, heading 180 degrees to us and about 3,000 feet above us. We pulled into a steep climbing turn. I saw two of the E/A shot down. We then came upon a gaggle of approximately 20 E/A, 2,000 feet above us. One Me 109 was trailing the formation by approximately one mile. I pulled into a steep chandelle to the left and fired a burst at 400 yards range and 20-degrees deflection. I saw many strikes around the underside of the cockpit and wing roots of the E/A. He went into a dive, trailing a lot of white smoke, popped his canopy and bailed out. I claim one Me 109 destroyed."

Second Lieutenant Hilton O. Thompson, flying as Newcross Purple Two, Capt. McChrystal's wingman, confirmed the captain's claim of one Me 109 destroyed, noting that he saw pieces flying off the E/A before the pilot jettisoned his canopy and bailed out.

As was many times the fact, the credit side of the balance sheet had a corresponding debit side. The cost that time was the loss of popular First Lieutenant John C. Donnell Jr., who was last seen by his fellow pilots late during the air battle. He had been flying as Newcross Red Three and was attacking three enemy planes while accompanied by his wingman, Second Lt. David L. Born. Lt. Born was forced to break off the attack when he was fired upon, himself. To Lt. Born's knowledge, there was only one Me 109 still in the area when he broke away. There were also two Newcross planes circling above. According to Lt. Born, about ten minutes later, Lt. Donnell was heard to radio, "I got one, Dick." (Referring to Lt. Richard G. Creighton, who heard him over his radio at 1240 hrs.) He was flying his own aircraft, a P-51 he had "inherited" from First Lieutenant Berkley E. (B.E.) Hollister, a fellow pilot who had returned home to the states. Lt. Hollister previously had the aircraft lettered with the name PIN UP GIRL by the squadron painter, Staff Sergeant Frederick C. Hayner.

When Lt. Donnell began flying the plane, he pestered S/Sgt. Hayner to paint a Vargas Girl on the nose; hence, the aircraft bore artwork representative of two pilots. Another special feature of the aircraft was that it carried the squadron's recently installed K-25 aerial camera, which was mounted on the backside of the pilot's rear armor, behind the headrest. Apparently hit by flak, Lt. Donnell crashed less than a mile north of Poetswchau, Dreiskau parish, which is about 12 miles southeast of Leipzig and 12 miles west of Grimma. He survived the crash and was taken to the Leipzig-Wahren hospital where he was admitted. Unconscious and suffering injuries to his chest and a lung, he died later that evening.

After the action, which lasted nearly thirty minutes, the 434th FS reassembled and tagged onto the last box of B-17s

First Lieutenant John C. Donnell beside Pin Up Girl. *Courtesy of Berkley E. Hollister.*

leaving the Chemnitz target area and escorted them to friendly territory. It was noted that a B-17 from the 379th BG, identified as having a yellow triangle with a black center and marked with the letter "K" on its tail, had a prop out west of Chemnitz. Having broken with the bombers, the squadron attacked some ground targets and destroyed/damaged 11 locomotives, three goods wagons and four passenger cars before coming home.

B group made L/F north of Ijmuiden at 1123 hrs./15,000 ft. R/V with the proper bombers was 20 miles northwest of Zwolle, Holland at 1145 hrs./20,000 ft. The group stayed with the bombers through the target and back, breaking away 20 miles northwest of Lingen, Germany at 1435 hrs./16,000 ft. They strafed the area of Almelo, 25 miles southeast of Zwolle, then headed out to L/O north of Ijmuiden at 1520 hrs./5,000 ft.

An observation made during the mission was that there was a lot of barge traffic on the canals in Holland. Flak over Magdeburg was heavy, intense and accurate while over Ijmuiden and Bremen, it was heavy, meager and inaccurate. Over Brunswick, it was heavy, intense and inaccurate and over Osnabrück, it was heavy, meager and inaccurate.

No. 265 C group made L/F over Den Helder, Holland at 1215 hrs./12,000 ft. They ran into the same weather that the groups previous to them had and found the area to be photographed at Stettin, Poland to be overcast. They turned back at 1420 hrs./18,000 ft. The photo recce bird took his pictures in the vicinity of Eindhoven, Holland instead. L/O

Staff Sergeant Frederick C. Hayner in his "office". *Courtesy of Frederick C. Hayner.*

Below: Three Lakeside P-51s J2-G, J and N in formation and on their way. *Courtesy of James H. Koerber.*

was south of Ijmuiden, Holland at 1535 hrs./12,000 ft. They escorted their charge as far as Ipswich, England and then broke away for home at 1619 hrs./2,000 ft.

Robert H. Horman remembers this or a very similar mission that he flew as an escort for a photo-reconnaissance plane. Then, just a Second Lieutenant new to the 479th FG and with only ten or so missions under his belt, he and the other remaining members of his flight were on their own for the escort. Their flight leader had been forced to turn back for home, having developed a rough engine while heading out over the North Sea. That left the new boys to carry on and in fact, one of them only had a few missions to his credit. They knew what they were supposed to do, but didn't know the details of the mission. They continued on, flying with the recce pilot and heading deep into Germany. Upon reaching the area of their target, which was located along the border between Germany and Poland and about 90 miles northeast of Berlin, the recce pilot dove down through the clouds to photograph his objective. The escorts were not expecting that and lost him. They went down to look for him, but could not see his plane anywhere. Giving up, they climbed back up and headed for home. They got almost back to the North Sea, when in the regular course of looking out for other aircraft, they glanced down and there he was! The Recce bird was just below them! The flight dropped down a little lower and followed him, all crossing the North Sea together. Arriving back at England, the PR plane disappeared again. They had thought he was going to go to Wattisham, but he apparently had landed somewhere for fuel. Back at home and a little bit later, in came the recce pilot, wanting to know where the men who flew as his escort were. The pilots thought: "Here it comes. We're in trouble now." Gathered together with the reconnaissance pilot, it turned out that he wanted to compliment them. As he put it: "Bloody good show! Every time I looked up, you fellows were right out there above me!" According to Horman, "We had lucked out."

15 February 1945

Eighth AF FO 1628A

No. 266 & 267 Thursday. The group was divided into two forces, A and B groups, both penetration to target and withdrawal escorts for 2nd AD, 20th CW B-24s attacking their 8th AF Mission 832 primary target, the oil industry at Magdeburg, Germany. Lt. Col. Jeffrey led A group, which consisted of 39 P-51s (21-434th & 18-436th). Up: 0930 hrs., down: 1505 hrs. with three early returns. Capt. Howard C. Smith led B group, which consisted of 22 P-51s from the 435th FS. Up: 0941 hrs., down: 1433 hrs. with no early returns. After becoming airborne, Colgate ordered the group to also escort the 96th CW B-24s as an additional responsibility. It was a beautiful day with beautiful flying weather over England and part of the continent.

A group R/V'd with the assigned B-24s north of Zwolle at 1045 hrs./23,000 ft. They had escorted the bombers to the vicinity of Dümmer Lake in Germany when their MEW controller, Nuthouse, vectored them after bogies. Nothing was found. Returning to the heavies, the group swept ahead as the force headed to Magdeburg. The bombers dropped their loads through 10/10ths cloud coverage so results were unobserved. The weather over the target had not cleared as it had in other areas. Returning, the group broke escort at 1200 hrs./26,000 ft. while in the area ten miles southeast of Ulzen, Germany to strafe railroad targets of opportunity. They destroyed and damaged five locomotives and five goods wagons. One of the goods wagons exploded with tremendous violence.

B group also R/V'd with the assigned Big Friends at the same time and place as did A group. They provided close escort through the target and back out to about 30 miles northwest of Meppel, Holland where they broke away at 1330 hrs./24,000 ft. For them, the entire escort was without incident.

Observations made during the mission included seeing many aircraft parked in a dispersal area south of a satellite flying field at the Fassburg airdrome. Large barges were seen heading upstream on the Elbe, southeast of Wittenberge. A Big Ben was observed at 0930 at the northeast polder in Hol. While over the target at Magdeburg, a red-orange sphere shot up vertically, bursting violently at 23,000 ft. Flak over the target was heavy, intense and inaccurate. Flak around the rail targets was light, meager and inaccurate. Flak at the airdrome was heavy, moderate and inaccurate.

19 February 1945

Eighth AF FO 1638A

No. 268 Monday. Maj. Duffié led the group, which consisted of 54 P-51s (18-434th, 18-435th & 18-436th) on a penetration to target and withdrawal escort for 2nd AD, 2nd CW B-24s attacking their 8th AF Mission 835 primary target, the marshalling yards at Siegen, Germany. Up: 1207 hrs., down: 1750 hrs. with a total of two early returns.

The group made R/V with the proper bombers 20 miles north of Terschelling Island, Holland at 1300 hrs./19,000 ft. They were escorted through the target, where the bombing results were unobserved, then back out again to an area 30 miles southwest of Koblenz, Germany where the group broke away at 1500 hrs./16,000 ft. After breaking away, the group stooged around and despite the poor visibility present for most of the mission, strafed some ground targets. Three trains southwest of Schweinfurt and two along the railroad between Fulda and Hanau were struck. From that action, the 435th FS turned in four steam locomotives and one electric locomotive destroyed as well as 24 goods wagons and eight passenger cars damaged. They also found a radio tower, which they strafed and damaged, about 15 miles northwest of Würzburg.

Observations made during the mission included the sighting of two Big Bens, one at 34,000 ft. coming from the Ruhr area and the other seen shortly after, about 40 miles west of Rheine. There was a small white balloon with a basket hanging beneath it, seen in the air at 25,000 feet, west of Koblenz. Rail traffic from Zweibrücken to Landau was noted as running eastward. A complaint was registered concerning "A" channel, the fighter channel, being cluttered with Becky, Ripsaw, Durham and 9th AF chatter. Flak was heavy, medium and inaccurate in the areas of landfall in; Dümmer Lake, Bielefeld and Bramsche. It was heavy, moderate and inaccurate over the target area and Lingen.

Due to poor weather at Debden, home to the 4th Fighter Group, a large number of their aircraft were forced to land at Wattisham along with the 479th FG's returning planes. They remained overnight and were sent out on the next day's mission from the station. This involved no small amount of confusion and hurrying to accomplish the extra work that arose; but all planes, both those of the 479th and those of the 4th FG, got off as scheduled. The weather improved during the day and the 4th FG made it back to their own base at the completion of the mission for 20 February.

First Lieutenant David L. Born, a Newcross pilot, is shown standing beside a P-47 that had been landed at Wattisham for an unknown reason. Lt. Born has his left hand bandaged, the result of having pushed his hand through a window in his BOQ room during some horseplay amongst a few of the pilots there. Captain Joseph F. (Doc) Schneider, the 434th FS flight surgeon was delighted to have a patient that he could practice his sewing skills on and took good care of Lt. Born. Unfortunately for Lt. Born, he was not going to be allowed to fly for a number of weeks until the injury healed. After a period of time, Lt. Born went to Doc Schneider and asked to be put back on flight status. Doc Schneider explained to Lt. Born that his stitched cut was not fully healed and after Lt. Born indicated he still wanted to go back to flying, Doc Schneider showed him the places where the wound had not yet closed and could be opened with just a slight tug. The wise doctor told Lt. Born that the same thing could happen while flying and as a result, Lt. Born could lose enough blood to pass out and crash. That was that then and Lt. Born did not fly. The good fortune of the accident is that Lt. Born found plenty of time to pursue his hobby of photography during his time off from flying. As a result, he accumulated many pictures he took of the squadron and this legacy will provided future generations with a wealth of images from his time there. Another interesting anecdote to this incident concerns Lt. Born's efforts to buy film for his picture-taking hobby. He recalls being sent to the Rolls-Royce engine school during his period of convalescence and while there, going into a near-by photo shop. When he asked the shop's proprietor about purchasing some bulk film, the man in turn asked Lt. Born how he came to receive his hand injury. Lt. Born told him how it happened and the proprietor promptly told him no, he didn't have any film. Wizened, Lt. Born went into another photo shop and asked about the availability of film. Once again, he was asked about the hand injury. This time Lt. Born gave the proprietor a story about being injured during an air battle, in order to garner a little sympathy. It worked and Lt. Born walked out of the store with his film. (Lt. Born loaded his own film, working in the dark of his closet back at the BOQ. He also built a photo enlarger from some scrap parts including old cans.) *Courtesy of David L. Born.*

20 February 1945

Eighth AF FO 1642A

No. 269 & 270 Tuesday. The group was divided into two forces, A and B groups, both penetration to target and withdrawal escorts for 2nd AD, 20th CW B-24s attacking their 8th AF Mission 836 primary target, the marshalling yards at Nürnberg, Germany. Maj. Jordan led A group, which consisted of 42 P-51s (21-434th & 21-435th). Up: 1014 hrs., down: 1556 hrs. with five early returns. Maj. Duffié led B group, which consisted of 20 P-51s from the 436th FS. Up: 1017 hrs., down: 1650 hrs. with no early returns.

The day started out poorly for the pilots of the 435th FS. The weather at Wattisham was cold and snowy and there was ice on the runways. These were bad conditions for taking off or landing, let alone flying in. On a snowy day, pilots sweated take off because the whole procedure was slowed down due to the extra caution that had to be exercised. That meant the Mustangs powerful Merlin engine had a greater chance of loading up and fouling its spark plugs as the planes in their long line up cautiously taxied to take off. Normally the fouling could be prevented by periodically revving up the engine to clear out the build up of carbon in the engine's cylinders. However, during slippery conditions such as these, the two main tires on which the plane rested and braked, many times could not prevent the plane from sliding forward when power was applied to the engine. Former Lieutenant Edward H. Sims recalled these circumstances in a February 2001 editorial article he wrote for his "Editor's Copy" newspaper:

> "My roommate, Lieutenant Frederick L. Hart wasn't able to keep his engine cleaned out. When he opened his throttle all the way to take off, black smoke shot out of the exhaust stacks on both sides of the engine nacelle. It was a terrible warning. If the smoke persisted, it meant the engine was not developing full power and wouldn't lift the heavily loaded fighter off the runway. We all watched in horror, hoping the smoke would clear up as he began his run down the strip.
>
> "When a Mustang was halfway down an icy runway, doing perhaps seventy miles an hour, should the pilot have wanted to stop, he no longer could have before the plane ran out of runway. I watched my roommate rocket down to the end of runway, swerve into the trees near there and crash. The mission had to be continued and we all took off through that foul weather. We found our box of bombers, but the weather was so bad that they were recalled. We continued on and picked up another box of bombers to protect, taking them to and from their target.
>
> "One of every ten Americans who died in World War Two, including all Army, Navy and Marine personnel, came from the 8th Air Force. The first question when we landed was did Fred Hart survive? Yes he did and lives today in Shawnee Mission, Kansas."

A group R/V'd with the bombers in the vicinity of Renaix, Belgium at 1110 hrs./24,000 feet, but a huge frontal line that topped out over 30,000 feet and extended from Brussels to the Vosges Mountains in France forced a recall of the bombers ten minutes later. At that point, they were still over Belgium. One flight, on instruments, escorted them back out. The remainder of the group was ordered to continue on and strafe ground targets of opportunity. Part of A group picked up Vinegrove 3-8, a batch of about 200 B-17s at 1125 hrs./25,000 ft. and escorted them as far as Donauwörth, Germany where they broke away at 1320 hrs./30,000 ft. First Lt. Richard D. Creighton from the 434th FS strafed a lumber train six miles west of Donauwörth, destroying the locomotive and damaging six goods wagons. Still looking for ground targets, they headed northeast as far as Cheb, Czechoslovakia and then turned south back into Germany to look. Maj. Robin Olds, who was leading the 434th FS, and his wingman, 1st Lt. Eugene E. Sears, found and strafed a train with a double locomotive that was headed south at Kirchenlaibach. Noticing activity eastward at Windischenlaibach airdrome, Maj. Olds took his squadron over to investigate. They found the 356th FG strafing there and having some success, with five aircraft already set afire. The 434th FS joined in and coordinated with the 356th FG in working the field over for about fifteen minutes, claiming 7-0-1 twin-engine and 1-0-1 single-engine aircraft destroyed/damaged. The fact that there was no flak allowed Newcross Squadron to press home attacks at minimum altitude. Making individual passes by elements, they searched out the well-dispersed and camouflaged enemy aircraft. There were 16 fires when they left. Continuing on, they made passes at Ottingen and Deiningen airfields, but were driven off by very intense, light flak. At Augsburg, they linked up again with the same group of B-17s they had previously escorted and took them as far as 20 miles east of Selestat where they broke away again, this time at 1430 hrs./30,000 ft. It was time to head home.

The ground strafing claims looked like this:

1-0-0	He 111	1st Lt. John T. Golden
2-0-0	Do 217	1st Lt. Robert B. Kline
0-0-1	Fw 190	1st Lts. John T. Golden & Robert B. Kline
1-0-0	He 111	1st Lts. John T. Golden & Robert B. Kline
1-0-0	Do 217	Maj. Robin Olds
1-0-0	Fw 190	Maj. Robin Olds
1-0-0	He 111	Capt. Donald J. Pierce & 1st Lt. Phillip A. Brown
0-0-1	U/I T/E	Capt. Donald J. Pierce & 1st Lt. Phillip A. Brown
1-0-0	Do 217	1st Lt. Eugene E. Sears

B group R/V'd with the B-24s at the same time as did A group, but south of Ghent, Belgium. The bombers were recalled and the group continued, eventually picking up two boxes of 94th CW B-17s near Selestat at 1220 hrs./27,000 ft. They were escorted through the target and back to the Black Forest area where they broke away at 1350 hrs./27,000 ft. The group stooged around in that area and found nothing of interest before setting course for home.

Observations made during the mission included seeing 35 plus enemy aircraft on the airfields at Cheb and Cheb/Oberschon. There were 50 plus unidentified single-engine aircraft on the northeast part of Ottingen airfield and another 20 unidentified single-engine as well as 10 unidentified twin-engine aircraft at Deiningen. The marshalling yard at Kirchenlaibach was filled with rail stock. There was a lot of train activity along the tracks northeast of Nürnberg. A twin-engine jet was seen to be flying parallel to the bomber track in the vicinity of Brussels at 1115 hrs./34,000 ft. Two V2s spotted between 1115 and 1135 hours were seen coming from the Rotterdam area. Flak over Nürnberg was heavy, intense and accurate. At Stuttgart, it was heavy, intense and inaccurate. In the Selestat area, it was heavy, meager and inaccurate. At the two airfields of Deiningen and Ottingen, it was light, intense and accurate.

First Lieutenant Robert B. Kline on the wing of the P-51 he named The Onley Genevieve. *Courtesy of Clarence G. Haynes.*

21 February 1945

Eighth AF FO 1647A

No. 271, 272 & 273 Wednesday. The group was divided into three forces, A, B and C groups. A and B groups were penetration to target and withdrawal escorts for 2nd AD, 2nd CW B-24s attacking their 8th AF Mission 839 primary target, the marshalling yards at Nürnberg, Germany. C group flew a photo reconnaissance escort mission. Col. Riddle led A group, which consisted of 38 P-51s (18-434th & 20-436th). Up: 0900 hrs., down: 1430 hrs. with one non-effective. Maj. Harrell led B group, which consisted of 17 P-51s from the 435th FS. Up: 0914 hrs., down: 1459 hrs. with one early return. First Lieutenant Harold M. Jenkins led C group, which consisted of four P-51s from the 434th FS. Up: 1253 hrs. down 1725 hrs. with no early returns.

Both A and B groups made L/F over Belgium in the vicinity of Ostend at 0950 hrs./12,500 ft. and were fired upon there by three lone B-24s, identified with black and white tail markings. R/V with the proper bombers was at 1015 hrs./22,000 ft. in the Brussels area. Escorting the Big Friends to Nürnberg proved difficult as they were strung out and also failed to follow the briefed course in the areas of Weisbaden and Frankfurt, thus receiving flak from both places. As the force approached the target, it appeared as though B-17s that were attacking the same location, forced the B-24s off their course near the target. That caused the B-24s to make a long turn before arriving over the marshalling yards and to be twenty minutes late. At that point the B-24s seemed to be flying by squadrons and were the last bombers over the target. The 10/10ths cloud coverage prevented observation of the bombing results.

A group broke from the bombers about five minutes after bombs away at 1200 hrs./28,000 ft. They stooged around north and northeast of Nürnberg, looking for ground targets. By the time they went home, they had accounted for the destruction and damaging of a railroad station, a switch house, nine locomotives, 29 goods wagons, 26 passenger cars, three oil cars, five flat cars, four trucks on flat cars, a caboose, two trucks, a tractor and trailer, a half track, two gas trucks and an unknown quantity of Germans. First Lieutenant Gail E. Jacobson, Red Flight Leader, and his wingman, Second Lieutenant Ossie J. Huval from the 434th FS, got a crack at Gotha airfield and made two passes, destroying an He 111 apiece. On the way home, a flight from the 436th FS landed at Charleroi in Belgium for gas and wound up going back into Germany to make a few passes at Nordhausen airfield. First Lieutenants Jay C. Malone, Fred Zellman and George H. Witzel each succeeded in damaging a Ju 188. The flight also strafed a train between Nordhausen and Eisleben, destroying the locomotive and three ammunition cars, which blew up and caused some damage to one of the planes. Debris, flames and smoke from the explosion went up to 5,000 ft.

B group stuck close to the heavies all the way around, flying south of the bomber course. They broke escort south of Saarbrücken at 1325 hrs./28,000 ft. L/O was over Dunkerque, France at 1415 hrs./10,000 ft.

Observations made during the mission included a lot of black smoke sighted at Cologne and an unknown quantity of Fw 190s at Nordhausen airfield. Flak was heavy, meager and accurate over the Rhine River south of Koblenz, Frankfurt, Weisbaden, Nürnberg and the Ruhr area. It was light, moderate and accurate at the Gotha and Nordhausen airfields.

No. 273 C group made L/F north of The Hague, Holland at 1340 hrs./22,000 ft. They took their P-38 recce birds into Germany and visited Lingen and the surrounding airfields, arriving there around 1410 hrs./22,000 ft. From there they went to Hannover where one P-38, Yardbush 1-5, turned back. He was escorted by two P-51s back to the Dutch Islands. The remainder of C group and their P-38, Yardbush 1-4, continued on to Magdeburg and that vicinity. Twenty-five miles southwest of Magdeburg, they were attacked by two Me 262s at 1540 hrs./22,000 ft. The jets caught them by surprise; their presence wasn't known until tracers from the first one went past them. He had slipped through the thin cirrus clouds, which shielded his approach, and made his attack on the P-51s. The escort pilots took violent evasive actions and the first Me 262 overshot and wound up with a P-51 on his tail. The jet was not able to turn as tightly as the Mustang, thereby enabling the escort to gain on the enemy aircraft by turning inside of him. Unfortunately, because of the hard turn, the escort pilot's gunsight became inoperative and he was unable to score any visible hits. The second jet quickly became a factor when he got on the P-51's tail. That forced the Newcross pilot to break off his attack and turn into the threat. The Me 262 passed with such speed that the Mustang was unable to get into position. Both jets escaped, disappearing in the distance and made no further attacks. During the fracas, the escorts lost the recce bird, but he soon called stating his intention to return home. They left the area at 1550 hrs./25,000 ft. and made L/O in the vicinity of Ostend, Belgium at 1700 hrs./15,000 ft.

22 February 1945

Eighth AF FO 1650A

No. 274 & 275 Thursday. The group was divided into two forces, A and B groups, both penetration to target and withdrawal escorts for 2nd AD, 2nd CW B-24s attacking their 8th AF Mission 841 primary target, the marshalling yards at Halberstadt, Germany. This attack was the opening phase of the 8th AF's Operation CLARION, an air offensive designed to disrupt German communications. By dividing the attacking force into smaller units of bombers with their accompanying fighter cover, a larger number of smaller targets were reached and assaulted. Often the bombers were at group strength and their fighter escort at squadron strength. An additional feature to this day's attack is found in that prior to reaching their targets, the bombers dropped to below 10,000 feet to achieve a high degree of accuracy and also to nullify some of the defensive anti-aircraft fire. After bombs away, the bombers returned to a higher altitude for the trip home. Maj. Duffié led A group from his lead position with the 436th FS. A group consisted of 40 P-51s (19-435th & 21-436th). Up: 0942 hrs., down: 1540 hrs. with four early returns. Capt. McChrystal led B group, which consisted of 24 P-51s from the 434th FS. Up: 1016 hrs., down: 1524 hrs. with no early returns.

A group made L/F in over Ijmuiden, Holland at 1110 hrs./ 17,000 ft. and R/V'd with their bombers ten miles southeast of Meppel, Holland at 1130 hrs./20,000 ft. B group made L/F north of Ijmuiden at 1110 hrs./17,000 ft. They R/V'd with their assigned bombers west of Dümmer Lake at 1136 hrs./19,000 ft. The B-24s had split into three formations for the bomb run, so in order to provide cover, the two groups had to split three ways, also. They continued southeast into Germany with the B-24s. At 1208 hrs./7,000 feet, while in the area of Meschede, the 436th FS was vectored to north of Kassel by their controller, Nuthouse. The results were nil, but time was taken to strafe a train in the area as well as another, ten miles east of Kassel. They rejoined their assigned bombers north of Eisenach. Shortly after rejoining, they departed again to look over the airfield at Kölleda. The defensive flak around the field was intense and drove the fighters off. There would be no strafing at this field today. Heading north to Nordhausen, the group observed what they described as "beautiful bombing" results on the marshalling yards there. The airfield at Nordhausen had few enemy aircraft on it, so the group didn't bother with them. Heading north again, the split force arrived at Halberstadt where the target was located. Once there, the 436th FS looked over the well-camouflaged airfield and found 15 plus twin-engine aircraft as well as a few Fw 190s. Flak was checked for by two dive strafing passes and when none was found active, Bison Squadron proceeded to have a field day from 1320 to 1355 hrs.

A left-hand strafing pattern running from southeast to northwest was set up, resulting in the following:

1-0-0	He 111	Capt. William C. Anderson
0-0-2	Ju 88	1st Lt. Charles H. Darling

1-0-1	Ju 88	Maj. C.A.P. Duffié
0-0-2	UI/TE	Maj. C.A.P. Duffié
1-0-0	Ju 88	1st Lt. Raymond E. Henry
0-0-1	He 111	1st Lt. Raymond E. Henry
0-0-1	He 111	2nd Lt. Ernest J. Hopcroft
0-0-1	Ju 88	1st Lt. Jay C. Malone
0-0-1	Ju 52	Maj. Clifford J. Moore
1-0-0	Ju 88	2nd Lt. Anthony J. Scordino
0-0-2	He 111	2nd Lt. Anthony J. Scordino
1-0-0	He 111	2nd Lt. Alfred J. Smigel
0-0-2	Ju 88	2nd Lt. Alfred J. Smigel

The strafing passes were in progress when planes from the 4th FG showed up and began making a pass 90 degrees to Bison Squadron. At that point, the planes of First Lieutenants Peter C. Vassuer and Albert R. DiPaola were hit and they both were forced to belly in. The group's leader for the mission, Major Claire A.P. Duffié first gave an abbreviated report of those two losses in the 479th FG's Mission Report, which went to the various 65th FW, 2nd AD, 8th AF and SHAEF headquarters. Describing what happened, he stated:

> "I was making my fourth pass on Halberstadt A/F and had started a fire. Out of the haze I saw four planes from the 4th Fighter Group headed for me, all firing. I pulled up to avoid being hit by their planes and bullets and carried on in the left-hand traffic. At this time Lt. Vassuer called on the R/T, saying that he had been hit. I called him and asked about the flak, but he replied that he had not, repeat, had not been hit by flak, making no further statement. He asked for support and I went along with him, seeing him belly in, throwing rods. At the same time, Lt. DiPaola called in stating that his engine was missing and felt he had been hit. He was on the same strafing run with me. It is believed that the 4th Fighter Group hit Lt. Vassuer's plane."

In a subsequent amendment to that report, Maj. Duffié recanted his accusation concerning the cause of Lt. Vassuer's loss. In doing so, he gave this withdrawal:

> "After careful investigation, the 479th Fighter Group wishes to retract the statement that their aircraft was shot down by the Fourth Group. It is not definitely known how the aircraft was lost. It is regrettable to us that this implication was made. (Signed) Major Claire A.P. Duffié."

That being the case, several points documented by records leave one to be curious about the unresolved cause(s) for the loss of both aircraft. Fact: Per the Mission Report, there was no flak active at the airfield during the strafing passes. Fact: The 4th Fighter Group was present and active on the Halberstadt Airfield at the time that Bison Squadron was there. The ground strafing claims for Halberstadt A/F submitted by members of that fighter group for 22 February 1945 verifies this. (Four pilots from the 336th FS/4th FG claimed a total of eighth E/A destroyed on Halberstadt A/F.) If friendly fire was not the cause and flak was not the cause, then just what did hit both 436th FS aircraft? The answer is unknown.

Maj. Duffié also gave this report as part of Lt. Vassuer's MACR:

> "I, Major Claire A.P. Duffié, was leading Bison White Flight on a fourth strafing pass from SE to NW on the west end of Halberstadt airfield about 1340 hrs. on 22 February 1945. As I was about to fire, I saw four aircraft, which I believe belonged to the 4th Fighter Group, coming in at 90 degrees to our pattern and firing their guns. I immediately pulled up, calling to the flight to watch out for these aircraft. Right at this time, Lieutenant Vassuer called that he'd been hit and asked for someone to come over and look at his aircraft. I saw him and went over. I saw that he was leaking coolant very rapidly. I called him and told him to take up a heading of about 295 degrees and I would cover him. Several minutes later, Lt. Vassuer called and said he had just thrown several rods and was getting out. I told him to belly it in on the field just in front of him. Prior to his touching down, I gave Lt. Vassuer instructions to head for a small woods about 150 to 200 yards north of the field he was headed for. He replied that he would. He bellied it in very nicely, called that he was all right and would see us later. I saw the hatch come open and he climbed out. He had bellied his plane in, setting it down at about 1345, between the two small villages of Hessen and Dedeleben. I left him and rejoined the squadron, which I had turned over to my Yellow Flight leader."

Lt. Vassuer was never seen again and is listed as MIA.

Lt. DiPaola also had problems during this time. Second Lts. Ernest J. Hopcroft and Carl W. Sherer gave statements concerning his whereabouts. Lt. Hopcroft:

Lieutenant Kenneth J. Hansen in his P-51 9B-D Jeannie. *Courtesy of Kenneth J. Hansen.*

"At about 1330 hours on the 22nd of February, when we were strafing this airdrome, [Halberstadt] I could hear Lt. Vassuer on the R/T saying that he was hit and would have to belly his plane in. Then I saw this plane, which I believed to be Lt. Vassuer. He was smoking and as I passed, I saw him jettison his canopy. He was at about 4,000 feet and south of the field. That is the last I saw of him. I don't know if he bailed out or bellied in. After the mission, I found out that Lt. Vassuer never got rid of his canopy till he was on the ground. Therefore, I believe the plane I saw was the one that Lt. DiPaola was flying because I am pretty sure it was a Bison aircraft."

Lt. Sherer:

"I last saw D (Lt. DiPaola) [Refers to the aircraft's squadron code, 9B-D]. Lt. DiPaola was flying Lt. Kenneth J. Hansen's P-51 named Jeannie instead of his regular mount, which he had named Jaybee Princess. As a side note, Al DiPaola and Ken Hansen, not having seen each other for nearly fifty years, met again at a squadron reunion only a few years ago. At that time, Al DiPaola took the opportunity to apologize to Hansen for having wrecked his airplane.] while circling the field at 7,000 feet as top cover for the strafing passes. After the flights were through making passes, he seemed to have come up from the pass and climbed up in back of me. I looked around and noticed it was him, so I just didn't pay any more attention to where he went. Later he was called in as missing from the formation."

Lt. DiPaola was forced to belly land the P-51 that he was flying, setting it down about two-and-a-half miles south of Quedlinberg and subsequently, became a prisoner of war. He kept a diary of his experiences that resulted from that mission and he has graciously allowed the author to reproduce it in whole as it appears:

"Diary of My P.O.W. Experience –
Albert R. DiPaola 0-720810"

436th Fighter Squadron, 479th Fighter Group,
8th Air Force, Wattisham, England.

"Escorted B-24s on a 10,000 ft. bombing mission to Halberstadt, flying Yellow 2 on Capt. Moore's wing. Bison

Squadron left bombers after target to strafe Halberstadt airfield. Made 3 passes, destroyed one Fw 190 in hangar on west side of field. Engine quit on deck after 3rd pass, pulled up to 100 feet, jettisoned canopy to bail out, called Duffié who advised me to try to start it. Good fields below so I tinkered with prop, throttle, mixture, primer and gas for a couple of minutes. No success. Belly-landed into wind, full flaps. No serious injuries – sprained ankle and back, cuts on arms and legs, gashed head. Lucky to get off so easily 'cause crash straps were off from when I started to bail out. Lost gloves, helmet and food kit in airplane (it was Ken Hansen's "Jeanne" – the "Jaybee Princess" was out for a power check) Left 'chute, forgot first aid kit, ran for nearby woods when two civilians headed towards plane. Dropped life jacket in field. Helmet, 'chute and life jacket had my name on them. Walked east in woods (small, thick pine trees) for 2 miles. Buried flying suit and boots, destroyed course card, walked a mile, saw German with rifle searching, so I hid under a bush until dusk. (2 boys passed within 10 feet once.) Walked southwest out of woods, through a small group of homes, exchanged greetings with several civilians and a German G.I. After a few miles of farms, came to Harz Forest and with aid of compass from escape kit, held to a generally southern heading on lumbermen's trails. Walked until 0600 with 10 min. break every hour. Took a couple of Benzedrine tablets to keep from falling asleep while resting. Spent Fri. 23rd in a clump of small trees. Couldn't sleep, kept saying the rosary (I found it in my hand when I got out of the ship and it stayed there. Lost the crucifix while pushing through the woods.) Tore up my A.G.O. card, scraped course off map, decided to try for Switzerland. Started walking at 1800, ankle very stiff. Came to a small town, (Stiege) saw road sign "*25 kl. nach Nordhausen*". Passed 4 officers (a la von Stroheim) who had some nasty things to say about my walking on the left side of the road. I meekly agreed with them and went on. Must have taken a wrong turn because Nordhausen not reached until 0800. Walked through several towns with "*Guten Morgen*" still a passport. By now both legs were in bad shape from limping, no food or sleep for 2 days (keep your seats folks, the ushers will pass out the hankies) so I decided to give myself up to the local priest. Passed numerous *soldaten* who had obviously never seen an American flying jacket, also a group of British POWs who were more observant, but who kept my secret! Received directions to church from an aged villager and arrived in time for Mass. After Mass, asked the pastor to hear me in the confessional. Told him who I was, asked for help, which he could not give, then told him I would give myself up. He took me to the rectory, got me some bread and coffee while he called the police. In a few minutes an officious police corporal arrived, searched me and dragged me off to the cooler in handcuffs. They took most everything, but missed my watch and compass in my watch pocket. Put in a cell with 7 others (Poles, Czechs and a Russian). I gave them encouraging news of the war (in a garbled mixture of English, French and German!) and ate or drank the Russian's soup. A member of the Wehrmacht took me to the local army post outside of town. There I was interrogated again and my watch was lifted. I was fed a piece of bread and a cup of coffee and given a wooden bed. Up at 0400 on Feb. 25th, left for "sweat box" at Oberursel (near Frankfurt). Supplied with half loaf of bread, 1/4 lb. "butter" and a decrepit 48-yr. old guard. Made good time during night as far as Kassel, having spent most of that day in an air raid shelter while "the boys massaged the town". Arrived Frankfurt about 0400 on the 26th. Waited in a storeroom with about 40 other POWs. Entrained at 0700 for Oberursel. Arrived, searched, (lost compass) quick interrogation, assigned cell 11B. Spent next 11 days there in solitary, slowly going mad. Had dysentery first 4 days. Meals were jelly sandwich and "tea" for breakfast, barley soup for lunch and butter sandwich and tea for supper. Saw Joe Evans in the hall, I was supposed to meet him in London on my next pass! Interrogated on 4th, 9th, and 11th days by a Lieutenant who had pics of my strafing runs. Name rank and serial number peeved him and he promised me a long stay until I "identified" myself by telling him everything I knew. However, the next day, Mar. 9th, everything except my money (3 pounds) was returned to me and about 150 of us left for the transient camp at Wetzlar. It was still dark when we marched down to the station at Oberursel and a small panic ensued when some crazy night-fighter pilot spotted a red light and decided to spray it. Fortunately, we had vacated that spot just 5 minutes before and nobody was hurt. In the morning we were about 8 miles from Wetzlar, just outside of a small town, when 8 bomb-laden P-47s passed over. Everyone piled out and took cover. The Thunderbolts circled and left, but we (and the guards!) decided to walk. The train continued on to the small town where it was promptly dive-bombed and strafed by a lone T-bolt.

"Reaching the Dulag Luft, we were issued clean clothes, allowed to take a shower (shaved for the first time in 17 days) barracked and fed. Went to Mass for the first time. Two meals a day of double Red Cross rations made all of us willing to stay for 3 or 4 weeks, but we were alerted for shipment tomorrow (Mon. Mar. 12th) Small library; read Willa Cather's "Death Comes to the Archbishop". Wrote home. Wetzlar (1/2 mile away) was bombed PFF with excellent results; optical works, small arms factory and railroad were hit heavily. Our departure was postponed.

"Left Wetzlar at 0600 with 1 G.I. blanket containing 4 rolls of "stationery", (on which the original of this hair-raising narrative was written) 1 bar of G.I. soap, a pack of cards, a pocket game, 1 brush, an extra shirt and socks. We walked back to the dive-bombed station, were issued 1 Red Cross parcel per man and put in boxcars (35 men and 4 guards in each – 1/4 of car for the guards). Two days and two nights were spent enroute to the Stalag Luft at Nürnberg. Crowded conditions made sleep impossible. German rations issued to us enroute were 1/7th loaf of bread per man and 1 can of meat (?) for 9 men. During an alert we were locked in the boxcars, which were left in the railroad yards in Gemunden while the guards took shelter. Luckily, the bombers went over to another target.

"Arrived Nürnberg (Stalag 3) Thurs. Mar. 8th. Terrific heat caused many of us to get sick while awaiting processing. Assigned to a "compound", we turned in our RC parcels (or what remained of them) to a communal mess. Meals at first were very poor, but they improved with the influx of more parcels. Two meals a day, not satisfying, but adequate to sustain life. Met Joe Evans again. He's working as a medical orderly in our compound. Jerry rations consist of 1/7th loaf of bread and 1 inch sq. of margarine per man, some dehydrated vegetables and a haunch of meat (probably horse!) for 1200 men. The RAF bombed the adjoining railroad, doing a good job, but scaring us under the bunks with the concussion of their blockbusters. News rumors are constantly circulated and occasionally substantiated by incoming prisoners. Hear that Bob Carr is two compounds away, trained with him in Texas.

"Sun. Mar. 18th. Heard Mass. Padre is an English priest shot down in the attempted airborne operation at Arnhem.

Sun. Mar. 25th. Latest "reports" say that Dortmund, Frankfurt and Mannheim have fallen and Yanks are advancing along Frankfurt-Nürnberg autobahn. If true, my prediction that the war will be over by April 30th may yet come true.

Sun. April 1st, Easter. Heard Mass and received communion. Prisoners evacuated from Sagan (east of Berlin) have been arriving all week. Our compound now numbers 2400 officers and enlisted men of all branches. With the approach of the American army we are alerted for a march, presumably south, to keep us "out of danger" per the Geneva Convention.

Weds. April 4th. Left Nürnberg 1300 for Moosburg. Column was dive-bombed as we passed through Feucht railroad yards. The lead ship of a 4-plane flight dropped two 500-lb. bombs; one scored a near miss on a bridge in the yard. The other landed in a ditch across the road about 35 yards away, killing 3 POWs and wounding 3. Slept in pine woods, fairly comfortable. Reached Neumarkt in afternoon. Waited all day for soup and bread. At 0200 we were told that there was no more soup, only 1/2 slice bread each. Started to rain so rather than sleep in it, we pushed on. My pack broke, ankle acted up, pace was fast. Tough day!

Fri. April 6th. Stopped for breakfast. Marched to Beilngries where we were billeted in a filthy barn. However, we met some French workers who took us (6 of us) to their quarters, a warm house, where we rolled our blankets out on the floor. They gave us some mashed potatoes and we left some cigarettes from the RC parcels we had been issued that day. (One parcel for 3 men and a piece of honey and 1 loaf of bread for 9 men.)

Sat. April 7th. Hoffman and I left after the main group and were picked up by a milk truck. I finally satisfied a 6-week longing! Caught up to the column, walked to Pondorf where we left the column again. Stayed in barn belonging to an old couple and their daughter. Scrounged a few eggs and a little bread.

Sun. April 8th. Stayed in Pondorf. No way to hear Mass. Supposed to leave tomorrow with a sick transport.

Mon. April 9th. Transport could take only 17 men.

Tues. April 10th. Left Pondorf on foot, baggage carried by cart. Walked 10 km. to a tiny village. Slept in barn, cooked in house.

Thurs. April 12th. Left village, but could not get transport or billets so returned to same barn for the night.

Fri. April 13th. Left in Luftwaffe truck. Past Pfeffenhausen, stayed overnight in barn in Holzhausen.

Sat. April 14th. Left on foot for Moosberg, 23 km. away. Walked 10 km. today, to Ubermunchen.

Sun. April 15th. Stayed in Ubermunchen. News is encouraging, but most of the large-scale activity seems to be taking place in northern "Goonland".

Mon. April 16th. Left Ubermunchen. Picked up by Red Cross truck, taken to within 5 km. of Moosberg. Dropped parcels to groups 3 and 4, heard that our group (1) was far back, so decided that we preferred the life of the open road to barbed wire and talked the truck driver into taking us back to Holzhausen. Groups 1 and 2 came into town tonight.

Tues. April 17th. Groups 1 and 2 left this morning, but Hoffman and I decided to stay with the "krankies" (sick group). Scheduled to leave this garden spot on Fri. We did, at 1030. Left at a slow walk (packs transported) arriving at Ubermunchen (yes, again!) at 1300.

Sun. April 22nd. Left "U" in the morning for a small town 6 km. away. Town filled with Wehrmacht, continued all the way to Moosberg, arriving at camp at 1730. Sacked in shower-dressing room.

Mon. April 23rd. Showered, rejoined group 1. Doing own cooking. 1 RC parcel daily for 6 men, plus frugal Jerry rations. Living conditions poor – 400 men to a barracks, slightly overcrowded! We may start walking again, and soon. Met 2 men from 479th, Capt. Calvin Butler and Lt. Thomas V. Smith (435th Sqdrn.).

Tues. April 24th. Not quite as much confusion today. News of the war is most cheering. Another march is now not probable.

Weds. April 25th. Armies 40 miles away on several fronts. Liberation likely within a week.

Fri. April 27th. German Red Cross says we will not be moved. Armies closer (24 miles from Munich). Col. Sidney Woods, (my old exec. off.) taken PW several days ago, just entered camp.

Sat. April 28th. P-51s have been around for several days – some obviously photo-recon.

Sun. April 29th. Allied PW guards have taken over the interior posts of the camp. 9th A.F. P-51s buzzed us and were fired on from outside. Fighting going on in immediate vicinity. One man was hit by a .30 cal. bullet (not serious). Tanks firing! Col. Jones says there is an armored and an infantry division 3 miles away. Tanks 300 yds. S.S. refused to declare Moosberg an open city, but the camp is open. Bridges being blown up. We are restricted to the barracks.

Still Sun. LIBERATED !!! 14th Tank Division, 47th Btn. (86th. Inf, 99th. Inf.)

"Allied flags over camp.

"Mon. April 30th. Generals and Red Cross girls in camp. War correspondent took a list of names to send home. I wrote 3 V-mails and gave them to the G.I.s to mail.

Tues. May 1st. Snowing lightly. Ate 1/4 loaf of G.I. white bread this evening; tasted like angel food cake! Patton was in this afternoon.

Thurs. May 3rd. 525 left today. 3000 were supposed to go, but weather held it up. Went into town to cook. Talked to a pastor; he had a beautiful chapel in the house.

Fri. May 4th. Nobody left today. Things seem to have come to a standstill and the weather isn't helping any. Snow (!) and rain. Wrote some V-mails. Got a 25-cent pen back for my Waterman. Nobody out Sat.

Sun. May 6th. Went to Mass this morning. Stood in line half an hour for 2 doughnuts. It was announced tonight that 19,000 would fly out tomorrow. Saw a movie in town today. "Tall in the Saddle" John Wayne.

Mon. May 7th. 19,500 men left today. We are scheduled to leave at 0530 for Ingolstadt Airfield. Tues. Left Moosberg at 0630. Arrived Ingolstadt 1000, found 3,000 waiting. Met a Sgt. who cooked a venison dinner. Looked over a jet, took its tachometer for a souvenir. A Stuka flew in to surrender. Mistaking its intentions (it carried bomb-like wing tanks) our AA opened up on it, getting strikes. It landed after going around once.

One C-47 landed today.

Weds. May 9th. Slept in non-com billets (a civilian house) in town. Ate a wonderful breakfast of pancakes! 50 planes in this morning. Left Ingolstadt 1735, arrived Reims 1935. Ate, showered, sacked.

Thurs. May 10th. Given clean clothes. Shots (6-hr. wait) Got on a list, moved to another camp on other side of Reims. (Tents). Slept.

Fri. May 11th. Up at 0400. Left Reims by C-47 at 0845. Landed Le Havre 1015. Truck to Camp Lucky Strike at St. Valery sur Coux. Showered. Assigned tents to await processing.

Sat. May 12th. Waiting.

Sun. May 13th. Heard Mass. Waiting.

Mon. May 14th. Waiting!

Tues. May 15th. Moved to "D" area for processing.

Weds. May 16th. Filled out a few intelligence forms. Issued one officer's uniform.

Thurs. May 17th. Physical exam.

Fri. May 18th. Partial pay: $80.70. Bought a hot-pilot hat!

Sat. May 19th. Waiting to ship out. Saw Crunk, Caselli, Joe Paragon (Queens College) Bob Carr and Haines. All were POWs.

Sun. May 20th. Truck to Le Havre. 15th Repl. Depot

Mon. May 21st. First professional haircut in 3 months. Went into LeHavre. Didn't seem like much of a town. Americans weren't very well liked 'cause the town had been clobbered by the Air Force.

Tues. May 22nd. Embarked in the evening on troopship S.S. Monticello. (former Italian liner "Conte Grande")

Weds. May 23rd. Arrived Southampton to pick up wounded.

Thurs. May 24th. Sailed 0800 in convoy. Docked in N.Y. Sun, June 3rd. (Staten Island). Train to Camp Kilmer.

Mon. June 4th. Train to Dix."

After working over the airfield at Halberstadt, the 436th FS was vectored to the Dümmer Lake area, but found nothing of interest. L/O for them was over The Hague, Holland at 1450 hrs./14,000 ft.

Lakeside Squadron, the 435th FS, was with their B-24s and flying east at 1150 hrs./16,000 ft. when just southwest of Berlin, they were attacked by 15 Me 262s. A bounce by four of the jets was directed at Red Flight as the squadron was making a shallow turn to the left from an easterly direction. It came from three o'clock, relative to their position and from the same altitude. The jets were described as flying the same type of combat formation as were the P-51s and the underslung engines of the Me 262s looked like the drop tanks on the American fighters. Red Flight broke into the jets, but they crossed in front of the flight and climbed up and away. A second flight of four Me 262s, appearing the same way, made a bounce from the rear at six o'clock high. Again, Red Flight turned into the German fighters and again, the enemy aircraft broke away, heading up and away. By this time, the first flight of Me 262s had come back, returning to attack from above and the rear. Red Flight broke into them once more with the same results; the Germans pulled away from the defenders. This continued on for three or four more breaks, with neither the Germans nor the Americans able to gain an advantage and get in close enough for a shot at the other. After each bounce, the attackers would climb straight ahead when confronted by the P-51s turning into them. They easily outdistanced us in pulling away. It was noticed that while turning, the fourth pilot in the German flight would fall behind and slightly above so that it would be necessary for the Mustangs to take him on first or he would slice in on their tails if they attacked the others. Both sides took advantage of the sun for their attacks.

White Flight from Lakeside Squadron encountered another four Me 262s in the same area. The jets came at them on a scissors-like pass from above, high and to the side with two ships on each side. The flight experienced cat and mouse activity similar to that of Red Flight, with the jets easily pulling up and away when confronted. The difference was that the jets used a defensive formation that gave them the advantage. Should White Flight be able to attack two of the enemy fighters, the remaining two Me 262s would be able to quickly return the attack. It left the P-51s open to a bounce.

The German pilots were experienced and aggressive. They flew excellent formation and never allowed themselves to be caught in a bad position. They were difficult to catch in a turn and if caught in such a position, would roll out and climb away, using their superior speed to an advantage. It was impossible to catch or climb with them. Apparently vectored to Lakeside Squadron, the jets attacked from the north and east from over the heart of Berlin. The dog fighting took place between 12,000 and 26,000 feet and was over by 1210 hrs. As was experienced, it was noted that a P-51 could not keep up with the Me 262 on the straight and level, nor could it climb with an Me 262, particularly if the jet had the initial altitude advantage. The jet's rate of roll was excellent, but its turning radius was poor. The P-51s could out turn the jets and, in fact, Red Flight out turned their attackers while still carrying their drop tanks. The attacking Me 262s were described as painted a light gray on their undersides and a dark green on their tops. Their job seemed to be to force the escorts to shed their drop tanks so the P-51s would have to leave because of a shortage of gas. This was a serious factor as the flights involved found that the expenditure of fuel was high because it was necessary to use full power at all times during the encounter. After the escorts had used up all but the minimum of gas required for the return trip and had left, the jets did not press any further attacks.

B group took their Big Friends through the target at Halberstadt where bombs away was at 1315 hrs./6-9,000 ft.

The B-24s were using the above-described, low-level technique for attacking their target. The weather over the target was clear and the visual bombing results appeared to be excellent. The group continued escort, returning to a point east of Zwolle, Holland where they broke away at 1425 hrs./14,000 ft. L/O was south of Ijmuiden at 1438 hrs./13,000 ft.

Observations made during the mission included eight balloons seen south of Minden, 12 seen at Hameln and 12 at Einbeck, all at 3,000 ft. The Langensalza airfield had 25 plus single, twin and multi-engine aircraft on it. The airfield at Mulhausen had ten to twelve unidentified aircraft parked on its west side. Flak along a railroad north of Giesa, southwest of Eisenach, was heavy, intense and accurate. From a train north of Kassel, it was light, intense and accurate. Over Ijmuiden, it was heavy, meager and inaccurate, while over Hersfeld, it was heavy, meager and accurate.

On this day, Second Lieutenant Cecil M. Peacock, a Newcross pilot, became engaged in the dangerous game of rat racing near Wattisham. When he attempted to better a record that Captain George W. Gleason had set for a rapid let down and fast landing, a maneuver some described as more of a controlled crash, Lt. Peacock in his P-51B suffered a high-speed stall from a thousand feet. He crashed and left the war-weary bird nothing but scattered wreckage. Lt. Peacock survived the incident, escaping with only minor burns although those who witnessed the fiery accident thought he had perished. However, seemingly raised from the dead, he appeared during the evening at the BOQ club. All swathed in bandages, Lt. Peacock drank his beer through a straw that night. *Courtesy of George E. Falkner.*

23 February 1945

Eighth AF FO 1654A

No. 276 & 277 Friday. The group was divided into two forces, A and B groups, both penetration to target and withdrawal escorts for 2nd AD B-24s attacking their 8th AF Mission 843 primary target, the marshalling yards at Fulda, Germany. This was the second day of Operation CLARION, but unlike the previous day, which was clear, this day the weather had provided a 10/10ths cloud cover. Maj. Jordan led A group, which consisted of 41 P-51s (23-434th & 18-435th). Up: 0852 hrs., down: 1505 hrs. with two early returns. Maj. Moore led B group, which consisted of 19 P-51s from the 436th FS. Up: 0925 hrs., down: 1503 hrs. with one early return.

A group R/V'd with the 2nd CW bombers east of Egmond, Holland at 1025 hrs./15,000 ft. and gave them close support until break away, east of Egmond at 1350 hrs./15,000 ft. It was noted that 28 bombers dropped their loads about 20 miles east-northeast of Fulda at 1211 hrs./20,000 feet, while the rest hit the target a few minutes later. A Mosquito was picked up 35 miles south of Steinhuder Lake at 1110 hrs./22,000 ft. and was also escorted through the target to the breakaway point near Egmond. (It was probably the division commander for the mission.) Newcross Squadron was the low squadron and was stooging ahead, looking for possible enemy aircraft. Turning at Heiningen, the squadron went to the vicinity of

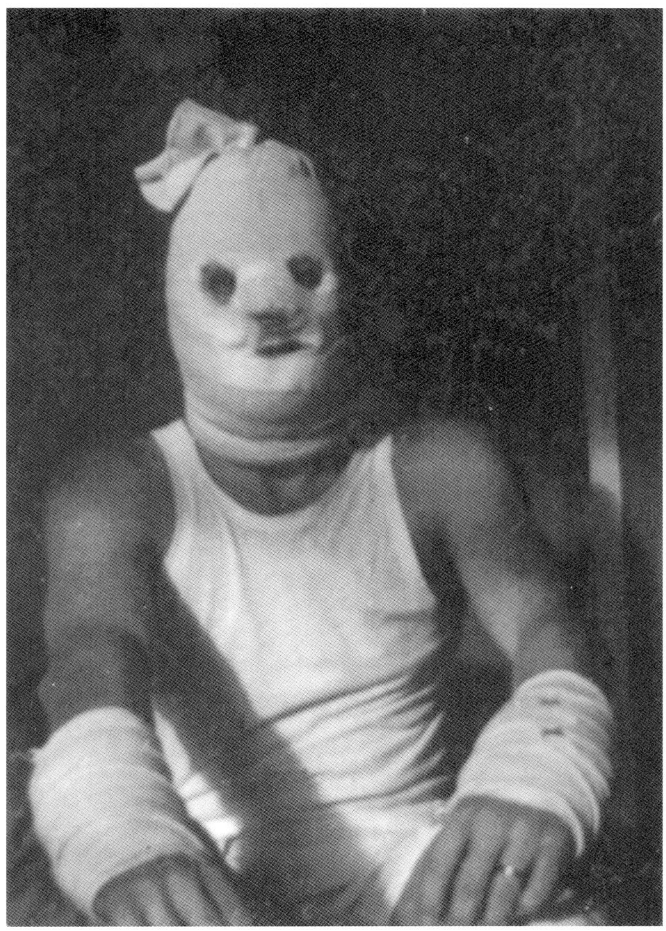

Right: Second Lieutenant Cecil M. Peacock in his "mummy dressings". The Lieutenant was back flying in a matter of weeks. *Courtesy of David L. Born.*

Halberstadt airfield, looking for available targets. There was an undercast extending to about 6,000 feet high and was probably 1,000 feet thick over this area. Green Flight found a hole southeast of Halberstadt, went down through it and while looking around, Green Flight Leader, Captain George W. Gleason, spotted a B-17 that had been bellied in. After close inspection, it was determined to be in good condition. Capt. Gleason and his wingman, First Lieutenant Clifford W. Bowers, each made a minimum altitude strafing pass on the bomber, setting it on fire and destroying it. This was done in accordance to a long-standing directive that required all intact Allied aircraft found to have come down in enemy held territory, to be destroyed in order to prevent enemy intelligence from gaining information useful to them from the aircraft. They both shared in the somewhat unusual credit. The two also came upon a German vehicle, which they dispatched. Clifford Bowers remembers this day well. In recently documenting it, he wrote:

> "I was flying as Captain George Gleason's wingman on the mission. Crossing the channel, we were just above the waves because of fog and it seemed as though my head was constantly popping in and out of the bottom of it. Once into Germany, we followed an autobahn looking for targets of opportunity. One that we came across was a German staff car, which Capt. Gleason promptly blew off the road. We were so low during the attack, that mud splashed all over our planes. As we were working our way back, I began running very short on fuel because wingmen use more gas than their leaders. The reason for that was wingmen always had to jockey their throttles back and forth in order to keep up with the leader. I radioed Capt. Gleason to advise him of this and we made a beeline for home. When I finally landed at Wattisham, my plane's engine quit as I was taxiing. I had to be towed back to my hardstand."

The remainder of the flight found other targets of opportunity to tackle. All in all, the Newcross pilots turned in as destroyed: one railroad station, two locomotives, two goods wagons, a tank car and a truck plus its semi-trailer. They also damaged the station control tower and two more goods wagons.

B group had an uneventful trip. They R/V'd with their Big Friends south of Meppen, Germany and took them through the target and back out to a point east of the Zuider Zee where they broke escort at 1332 hrs./15,000 ft.

The only observation listed for the mission was the 18 plus unidentified aircraft seen on the airfield at Quedlinburg. Flak over Magdeburg was noted as heavy, intense and accurate. It tracked the force for ten minutes. Upon return to friendly territory on the continent, 14 P-51s from the 434th FS stopped for gas before crossing the North Sea and heading home.

24 February 1945

Eighth AF FO 1658A

No. 278 Saturday. Maj. Harrell (recently promoted) led the group, which consisted of 46 P-51s (12-434th, 17-435th & 17-436th) on a penetration to target and withdrawal escort for 2nd AD, 2nd CW B-24s attacking their 8th AF Mission 845 primary target, the petroleum industry at Misburg, Germany. Up: 1050 hrs., down: 1605 hrs. with a total of three early returns.

The group made R/V with their B-24s between the Zuider Zee and Zwolle, Holland at 1140 hrs./20,000 ft. The Big Friends were escorted uneventfully through the target and back again to over the Zuider Zee where their escorts broke away at 1430 hrs./20,000 ft. Bombing results were unobserved because of 10/10ths cloud cover. After leaving the heavies, the group turned once again, towards inland, seeking targets of opportunity on the railroads and airdromes. The areas covered in both Holland and Germany included Zwolle, Polder, Borkum Island, Leewarden, Groningen, Dümmer Lake and Emden. Boats were strafed south and southwest of Borkum Island and another B-17 was found bellied in between Steenwijk and the Zuider Zee. It was spotted through a hole in the undercast and looked to be in good condition, sitting on a field of ice. Orders were orders, so First Lt. Eugene H. Wendt and Second Lt. Ossie J. Huval from the 434th FS dove on it from 10,000 ft. through the hole in the clouds. They opened fire at about 1,500 ft. and pulled out at around 500 ft. They then made a pass from south to north and caused the big bird to smoke. They repeated the pass and the bomber burst into flames. The two split the claim for one B-17 destroyed.

Observations made during the mission included seeing a B-24 (93rd BG) crash six miles southeast of Urk at 1435 hrs. No chutes were sighted. The airfield at Groningen was bombed out, but it was noted that the runways were under repair. The airfield at Steenwijk seemed to be in good condition, but no aircraft were seen there. An Me 262 was observed at R/V to be crossing the bomber track, but no attempt was made to hit the bombers. There was canal traffic on the Ems-Weser Canal south of Hesepe. Flak over Den Helder was light, intense and inaccurate, as it was, coming from a freighter south of Borkum Island. Flak over Bielefeld and Misburg was heavy, meager and inaccurate. It was heavy, intense and accurate over Hannover.

25 February 1945

Eighth AF FO 1662A

No. 279 & 280 Sunday. The group was divided into two forces, A and B groups, both penetration to target and withdrawal escorts for 2nd AD, 14th and 20th CW B-24s attacking their 8th AF Mission 847 primary target, the marshalling yards at Aschaffenburg, Germany. Maj. Olds led A group, which consisted of 33 P-51s (18-434th & 15-436th). Up: 0908 hrs., down: 1500 hrs. with two early returns. Maj. Harrell led B group, which consisted of 18 P-51s from the 435th FS. Up: 0917 hrs., down: 1515 hrs. with no early returns.

A group R/V'd with their B-24s over Nancy, France at 1048 hrs./25,000 ft. The bombers were ten minutes late and south of the briefed course. Passing into Germany, the group provided a roving escort to the target area at Aschaffenburg. Arriving there at 1210 hrs./22,000 feet, the heavies unloaded over the target five minutes later. The bombing results appeared to be excellent. The group broke away after the bombers had turned for home and swept the areas of Schweinfurt, Würzburg, (Schwäbisch) Hall and Frankfurt for targets of opportunity. They strafed some hangars at (Schwäbisch) Hall, damaging two and damaged two heavy lorries heading west between Dieburg and Darmstadt. A train that was heading north along the Main River was also strafed, resulting in the locomotive being destroyed as well as 13 goods wagons and six passenger cars damaged. One flight dive-strafed the airfield at Schweinfurt to test for flak, but the defenses were too rough so the airfield was passed up. Nuthouse reported rats (Me 262s) in the vicinity of Würzburg, but none were seen.

B group also R/V'd with the bombers over Nancy, a few minutes later that did A group. The group stuck with the heavies throughout the escort and watched the visual bombing attacks hit bridges, a factory and a marshalling yard. Results appeared to be excellent at all targets hit. B group broke from the bombers west of Metz, France at 1315 hrs./21,000 ft.

Observations made during the mission included 30 plus aircraft, mostly twin-engine, spotted at (Schwäbisch) Hall airfield. The airfield at Ansbach had 15-20 unidentified aircraft parked on it as did Schweinfurt. The Schweinfurt airfield also had some dummies. Nellingen had ten plus unidentified aircraft. A smoke screen was reported over Nancy. Eight balloons were seen over Heilbronn. A large explosion 20 miles south of Rotterdam was seen. It was thought to be a buzz bomb that was shot down. Flak at all of the airfields was light, intense and accurate.

Lieutenant Clark R. Hoffman had an engine failure and was forced to belly J2-B, Nobody's Baby in near Wattisham this date. *Courtesy of George E. Falkner.*

26 February 1945

Eighth AF FO 1665A

No. 281 & 282 Monday. The group was divided into two forces, A and B groups, both penetration to target and withdrawal escorts for 2nd AD, 20th CW B-24s and a screening force attacking their 8th AF Mission 849 primary target in northern Berlin, Germany. Maj. Duffié led A group, which consisted of 29 P-51s (15-435th & 14-436th). Up: 1025 hrs., down: 1627 hrs. with three early returns. First Lt. John N. Murr led B group, which consisted of 19 P-51s from the 434th FS. Up: 1032 hrs., down: 1635 hrs. with no early returns.

A group made L/F west of Ijmuiden, Holland at 1123 hrs./ 17,000 ft. and R/V'd with the proper bombers 15 miles west of Meppel, Holland at 1140 hrs./22,000 ft. Driving into Germany from there, they arrived over the target at 1239 hrs./ 25,000 ft. The weather had presented solid 10/10ths cloud coverage that extended from east of Zwolle, Holland to beyond Berlin, so observation of the bombing results was unknown. The group did some stooging around at various locations along the course, looking in at Salzwedel Lake, Luckenwalde, Fürstenburg and Landsberg without incident. The heavy overcast prevented any strafing, save for another B-17 that First Lts. Robert H. Horman and William M. Barsky spotted on an open field in Holland, near the southeast end of the Zuider Zee. They made three low-altitude strafing passes each on the bomber, putting lots of holes in it and eventually setting it on fire. They shared the credit, such that it was. Headed for home, the escorts and their Big Friends crossed out over Ijmuiden at 1535 hrs./12,000.

B group made L/F over Egmond, Holland at 1125 hrs./ 19,000 ft. and R/V'd with their proper bombers north of Lingen, Germany at 1140 hrs./23,000 ft. They provided close support to the target, where bombs away was at 1240 hrs./ 25,000 ft. through the overcast. Returning, the group broke from the bombers over Zwolle at 1520 hrs./18,000 ft. and made L/O south of Egmond at 1535 hrs./17,000 ft.

Both A and B groups provided escorts by elements for stragglers and early returning B-24s from their CW, specifically noting bombers from three different BGs. A B-24 from the 93rd BG, identified as having a vertical black stripe marked with the letter "M" on the A/C's tails and having a wheel hanging down, was escorted to Egmond. Another B-24 from the 446th BG, identified as having a horizontal black stripe marked with the letter "H" on the A/C's tails and named "Big Mitch" had two engines out. It was escorted to Amsterdam, Holland. A third B-24 from the 448th BG, identified as having a diagonal black stripe on the A/S's tails and named "YMI" had numbers two and four engines out and was escorted to the Dutch coast.

Observations made during the mission included sightings of a number of V2s; two from the Apeldoorn area, one from the Egmond area and one from the Rheine area. It was also noted that there was a lot of foot traffic heading north on the highway running from Kampen through Zwolle and up to Meppel. Flak over Berlin was of course, heavy and intense, but inaccurate.

27 February 1945

Eighth AF FO 1670A

No. 283 & 284 Tuesday. The group was divided into two forces, A and B groups, both penetration to target and withdrawal escorts for 2nd AD, 14th CW B-24s attacking their 8th AF Mission 851 primary target, the marshalling yards at Halle, Germany. Col. Riddle led A group, which consisted of 18 P-51s from the 435th FS. Up: 1025 hrs., down: 1640 hrs. with two early returns. Maj. Moore led B group, which consisted of 30 P-51s (16-434th & 14-436th). Up: 1030 hrs., down: 1630 hrs. with one early return.

A group crossed over the continent at an unknown place due to the 10/10ths cloud coverage that blanketed most of the area that their course was to take them. L/F was at approximately 1109 hrs./14,000 ft. R/V with their bombers was in the vicinity of Malmédy, Belgium. Because of the weather, the heavies and their escorts took a more direct route than the briefed southern course as they drove eastward into Germany. They arrived over the target at 1300 hrs./22,000 ft. and released through the clouds. The results were unknown. Heading west, A group broke from the bombers in the vicinity of Koblenz at 1450 hrs./24,000 ft. and made L/O northeast of Dunkerque, France at 1533 hrs./11,000 ft.

B group made L/F over the clouds at 1112 hrs./15,000 ft. Likewise, R/V with their B-24s was under the same conditions at 1146 hrs./26,000 ft. The Big Friends missed their primary target and went on to hit a target of opportunity at Bitterfeld, dropping their loads there at 1330 hrs./15,000 ft. Weather in the area was 7-8/10ths with a few breaks in the clouds. The 434th FS stooged ahead down into the Dresden area and back up again, rejoining the force at Torgau. Shortly there after, they headed south again down to Chemnitz and let down to strafe targets of opportunity. Along the railroad and the highway between Erfurt and Gotha, the squadron succeeded in destroying two locomotives and damaging another. They also damaged two goods wagons, two trucks and two carts. L/ F was at 1559 hrs./6,000 ft.

Two B-24s were escorted from the Greiz area. The one that was in the worst shape was a 392nd BG bird identified as having a horizontal black bar marked with the letter "V" on its silver tail. The bomber's number two engine had a feathered prop, number four engine was smoking and the bomb bay was shot away. No radio contact could be made with the ailing bomber. The other B-24 belonged to the 466th BG and was identified as having a white horizontal bar marked with the letter "C" and a bar on its red tail. This one had number three engine out, but said he was okay. They were escorted almost to the continental coast.

Observations made during the mission included a V2 rocket that was seen over the coast of England at 1045 hrs. and a B-24 that was seen hit by flak over Halle. The plane dropped in flames with no chutes spotted. Flak over Halle was heavy, moderate and accurate, as it was over Leipzig. Flak over Fulda was heavy, meager and accurate.

28 February 1945

Eighth AF FO 1675A

No. 285 & 286 Wednesday. The group was divided into two forces, A and B groups, both penetration to target and withdrawal escorts for a CW of 2nd AD B-24s attacking their 8th AF Mission 854 primary target, the railroad viaduct at Bielefeld, Germany. Capt. Gleason led A group, which consisted of 29 P-51s (13-434th & 16-436th). Up: 1214 hrs., down: 1755 hrs. with no early returns. Maj. Jordan led B group, which consisted of 13 P-51s from the 435th FS. Up: 1217 hrs., down: 1649 hrs. with no early returns.

Over eleven hundred heavies set out this day to attack German communications. They were supported by all fifteen fighter groups going along to defend against enemy fighters. The approach for the one long string of bombers was from over the Alsace in northeastern France. Heading in a northeasterly direction, once they got below the thickly populated Ruhr area, the various forces turned off for their individual targets.

A group R/V'd with their proper bombers in the vicinity of Brussels at 1316 hrs./22,000 ft. Because once again the weather provided nothing but overcast skies, all locations are approximate except for those involved with ground activity. Escort was maintained to and from the target, where the bombing results were unobserved. As an interesting note, there was no flak over the target. The 436th FS broke from escort early in order to look over potential targets of opportunity. They stooged around the areas of Warburg, down to Hersfeld, over to Eisenach, up to Nordhausen and back over to Northeim, like hogs hunting for truffles. The ground strafing claims they turned in consisted of a radar complex, three locomotives and a passenger car destroyed, as well as three more passenger cars, 18 goods wagons, a switch house and a water tender damaged. Most of the claims came from southeast of Kassel, on the rail line running north to south. The flak was thick, though, causing a lot of damage to the squadron's aircraft and more work for their sheet metal men to repair.

What they could not repair was the loss of Second Lieutenant Charles F. Schoen from the 436th FS. Lt. Schoen was flying in the number three position of Blue Flight. His flight, flying a line abreast formation, peeled off one by one and followed Yellow Flight down on strafing pass on a radar site located east-northeast of Kassel. He was last in line over the site, making a low altitude-strafing pass, as had the six others who preceded him. He was hit by what was believed to have been light flak or small arms fire coming from nearby woods. When the flights were rejoining, Lt. Earnest J. Hopcroft called, saying that Lt. Schoen was trailing black smoke. Lt. Schoen soon called to say he had lost his oil and would have to belly his plane in. Shortly thereafter, he called again, stating his concern for coming down in the middle of some town just over the hill. That was the last thing he said on the radio. The time was 1405 hrs. His squadron mates believed he went down near a small town west of Witzenhausen. They orbited the area several times looking for him, but could not locate him. He had crashed about half a mile north of a small village. He was taken to a nearby hospital, but died from his injuries several days later.

Lieutenant Ernest J. Hopcroft flying his 9B-G- Poontang II. *Courtesy of Kenneth J. Hansen.*

A group broke from the B-24s in the vicinity of the Zuider Zee at 1540 hrs./23,000 ft.

B group made L/F and then R/V'd with their bombers south of Bruges, Belgium at 1300 hrs./24,000 ft. The heavies were escorted through the target and out to a breakaway point north of Egmond, Holland at 1550 hrs./10,000 ft. For them, the escort was uneventful with no flak to contend with and the bombers in excellent formation. It was a "milk run".

The only observation recorded was that the B-17s appeared to be getting heavy flak over Kassel.

436th FS armorer Corporal William R. Bottenus, Jr. has uncrated one of the paper 108 U.S. gallon drop tanks and is carrying it to the flight line. *Carroll C. Sprague Collection, courtesy of the East Essex Aviation Society.*

Crew chief Staff Sergeant Clarence O. Marlar, Second Lieutenant Thomas (Tommy) H.Thompson and armorer Sergeant William M. Ferguson are gathered near Weezy, a Bison bird. Lt. Thompson wanted to make certain that his wife Louise saw the ship's name. *Courtesy of Thomas H. Thompson.*

436th FS armorers Private Frank W. Capers, Jr. and Private First Class Marshall F. White are getting a .50 cal. machine gun ready for one of the squadron's aircraft. *Carroll C. Sprague Collection, courtesy of the East Essex Aviation Society.*

435th FS pilot Lieutenant Floyd W. Salze with his Birmingham Kid. *Courtesy of Robert H. Horman.*

436th FS P-51 Little "Vic". *Courtesy of Kenneth D. Axt.*

435th FS P-51 J2-O. *Courtesy of James H. Koerber.*

434th FS P-51 L2-D Rabid Rebel – bellied in by Lieutenant John C. Donnell, Jr. after a mechanical failure. *Courtesy of the Wings of Freedom Museum.*

Some of the men who went out to pick up wrecked aircraft like Rabid Rebel, are shown by one of their recovery vehicles. *Courtesy of Clarence G. Haynes.*

An unknown Captain on the 435th FS flight line. *Courtesy of Robert H. Horman.*

Lieutenant Robert I. Bromschwig, a Newcross Squadron pilot, is pictured standing beside his Kraut Knocker. *Courtesy of David L. Born.*

CHAPTER FOURTEEN

MARCH 1945

1 March 1945

Eighth AF FO 1679A

No. 287 & 288 Thursday. The group was divided into two forces, A and B groups, both penetration to target and withdrawal escorts for 2nd AD, 96th CW B-24s attacking their 8th AF Mission 857 secondary target, a factory that manufactured jet A/C parts at Baumenheim, Germany. Maj. Moore led A group, which consisted of 32 P-51s (18-435th & 14-436th). Up: 1052 hrs., down: 1715 hrs. with one early return. Capt. Pierce led B group, which consisted of 15 P-51s from the 434th FS. Up: 1111 hrs., down: 1655 hrs. with three early returns. The weather at Wattisham hindered the group forming up and caused a delay in their R/V.

A group made L/F near Nieuport, Belgium at 1202 hrs./ 11,000 ft. Passing into Germany, R/V was in the vicinity of the target at 1330 hrs./25,000 ft. Cloud cover prevented observation of the bombing results. The 436th FS took the bombers back while the 435th FS stooged around the area south of Munich, shot up a train on the railroad at Murnau, then came home. The Bison Squadron escorts broke away over Nancy, France at 1530 hrs./15-18,000 ft. L/O for them was near Nieuport again at 1630 hrs./12,000 ft.

While the 435th FS was looking for targets of opportunity, the squadron lost Major Thomas F. Trabucco to an unknown cause. His squadron leader, Major Herbert H. Jordan gave the following statement concerning his loss:

> "South of Munich, we hit the deck through a hole in the clouds near Kochel Lake. This particular hole closed in while we strafed a train and looked for other targets. We all knew it was 10/10ths in the surrounding area, so when we finished, we climbed up on instruments to 8,000 feet and broke out on a course of 280 degrees. I circled and checked all flights. Everyone was up but Major Trabucco. I called him and he said he was below and would be up in a minute. I continued my orbit and called later. This time he said he was on top and would join us in a minute. Since we all broke out at the same spot, I assumed he was in the vicinity. We set a course of 280 degrees and I called him again with that information. I later checked and received no answer from Major Trabucco. I switched to other channels and listened for him, but never heard his call sign. All channels were busy, so I did not call him on anything but 'A' channel."

First Lieutenant Richard G. Candelaria was flying number two on Major Trabucco's wing and gave this statement concerning the Major's disappearance:

> "We went to the deck through a hole in the clouds around Kochel Lake. We strafed for several minutes and found the hole had closed in. We were behind the rest of the squadron as we made the last pass. We started up through the undercast, but half way through the clouds, we started back down for no apparent reason. We broke out below the clouds, did a 360-degree turn and started back up again. I had fallen slightly behind and a little off to the side. The clouds got very thick and I lost sight of Major Trabucco. I moved off to the side and climbed up by myself. I broke through and called him, telling him that I was on top, that I had found the flight and was with

the squadron leader. He answered and said he would soon join us. The squadron leader called him and Major Trabucco answered saying he was on top and would soon join us. He asked for our heading. We all presumed he was all right, but when the squadron leader called him again, he did not answer and failed to answer after that on all channels."

Approximately 45 minutes after he was thought to be missing, Major Trabucco was found dead in the wreckage of his P-51, about a quarter mile east of Haldenwang, which is about twelve miles southwest from Kaufbeuren.

B group made L/F at 1200 hrs./16,000 ft. over the overcast. They picked up their B-24s over the clouds in the vicinity of the Rhine River at 1330 hrs./18,000 ft. The Big Friends were escorted to the target at Baumenheim where they dropped their loads through the clouds. Under the direction of MEW control, they were escorted back over the Rhine River to where they were left in the Verdun area of France at 1526 hrs./20,000 ft. L/O was at 1625 hrs./9,000 ft.

There were no observations recorded due to the cloud cover, however, it was noted that the B-24s were early at R/V, early over the target and strung out, thus making escort difficult.

2 March 1945

Eighth AF FO 1683A

No. 289 & 290 Friday. The group was divided into two forces, A and B groups, both penetration to target and withdrawal escorts for two command Mosquitoes and 2nd AD, 14th CW B-24s attacking their 8th AF Mission 859 primary target, the POL industry at Magdeburg, Germany. Maj. Jordan led A group, which consisted of 35 P-51s (20-434th & 15-435th). Up: 0800 hrs., down: 1357 hrs. with one early return. Capt. Arlett G. Mosier, Jr. led B group, which consisted of 15 P-51s from the 436th FS. Up: 0830 hrs., down: 1340 hrs. with one early return.

A group entered continent over Holland and made R/V with their B-24s northeast of Zwolle at 0933 hrs./23,000 ft. While in Germany, part of the group swept ahead of the bombers, passing through the areas of Lingen, Hannover, Brunswick, Arendsee, Merseburg, Leipzig and Dresden. One flight, having R/V'd with the two command Mosquitoes in the area of Zwolle at 0935 hrs./23,000 ft. took them to the

This C-64 belonging to the Hitcham based 4th SAD wound up on its nose when a landing apparently went bad. *Courtesy of George E. Falkner.*

target area. While in the Magdeburg area, one of the flight's element leaders began to have engine trouble and had to break escort. He and his wingman left for home at 1040 hrs. Maj. Jordan immediately assigned another element as their replacements. The two replacing pilots continued escort of Mosquito VC 3-10 to the area of Steinhuder Lake. Contact was lost between them and the command A/C there at 1200 hrs. because, first, it became difficult to stay with the "Mossie" as it ducked in and out of bomber formations and, second, gunners in the bombers were shooting at the escorts. The second command Mosquito was taken through the target and out to east of Brussels, Belgium where escort was broken at 1255 hrs./22,000 ft. The remainder of A group took their charges through the target and back out again to east of Meppel, Holland where they broke away at 1230 hrs./22,000 ft.

Captain Arlett G. Mosier, Jr. with his My Best Bett. *Courtesy of Arlett G. Mosier, Jr.*

B group R/V'd with their bombers 12 miles southeast of Meppel at 0932 hrs./21,000 ft. The B-24s were taken through the target where they released their bombs at 1035 hrs./27,000 ft. Returning to Holland, the escorts broke from the Big Friends northeast of Zwolle at 1252 hrs./25,000 ft. For them, the escort was uneventful.

Observations made during the mission included the notation of a distinct lack of enemy fighter activity. The group's controller, Nuthouse, vectored some of A group's aircraft to the vicinity of Rheine to look for "Rats", but none of the jet fighters were found. At 1020 hours, a B-17 was seen to disintegrate after it was hit by flak over Merseburg. No chutes were seen. At 1030 hours, an unidentified A/C, probably a P-51, was seen going down in flames in the same vicinity. Again there was no chute seen. At 1200 hours, an unidentified bomber exploded 12 miles south of Dümmer Lake. The marshalling yards at Osnabrück, Hannover and Brunswick were all loaded with rail stock and there was heavy rail traffic between Hannover and Brunswick. Two V2 rockets were seen while over Holland, one near Meppel at 1220 hrs. and the other near Haarlem at 1200 hrs. Flak over the marshalling yards at Osnabrück and Hannover was heavy, meager and inaccurate. Over Brandenburg, it was the same. Flak in the vicinity of Dedelsdorf was heavy, intense and accurate.

L2-R Cactus Jack, a 434th FS P-51 that was damaged as it was being towed this date. The photograph is somewhat confusing because while the caption on the bottom of the photo indicates the date of the accident and the plane's serial number – 44-15086, from which it can be identified, there is a different serial number on the trim tab attached to the control surface of the plane's right horizontal stabilizer. (Many removable panels on the Mustang were stenciled with the last four or five digits of the plane's serial number.) That serial number, 44-63192, identifies the trim tab and possibly the elevator of which it is a part, as having come from a 436th FS P-51. A plausible solution to the mystery is that both in January and again in February, 44-63192 was involved in other accidents. It is reasonable to assume that the foreign part(s) was/were removed from 44-63192 during one of those times and replaced by new. The old salvageable part(s) then having been set aside for use when needed, found their way onto 44-15086. *Courtesy of George E. Falkner.*

9B-A "The Uninvited II", the aircraft that struck L2-R and knocked her tail and radio mast off. *Courtesy of George E. Falkner.*

3 March 1945

Eighth AF FO 1698A

No. 291 Saturday. Col. Riddle led the group, which consisted of 55 P-51s (23-434th, 16-435th & 16-436th) on an area patrol in support of 8th AF Mission 861 in Germany. Up: 0720 hrs., down: 1300 hrs. with a total of two early returns. There was potential and hope for Riddle's Raiders to have a great day this date. They had drawn a choice assignment, that of going in ahead of over a thousand bombers and their fighter escorts who were slated to attack oil targets in Central Germany. Their job was to catch enemy aircraft as they took off from their airfields. The previous day the Hun had come up in force in the same area and lost 63 planes to the Eighth's fighter groups. It looked like a set up for the Raiders and the pilots came away from their briefings wringing their hands in anticipation.

There was an 8/10ths overcast present with tops from 8-10,000 ft. covering the continent when the group made L/F in the vicinity of Ijmuiden, Holland at 0830 hrs./18,000 ft. Driving across Holland and into Germany, they reached their target

Second Lieutenant Elbert N. Harris and crew chief Technical Sergeant Earl L. Hicks. *Courtesy of the Wings of Freedom Museum.*

Armorer Corporal Theodore R. Butler, Jr., crew chief Sergeant John E. Wendt and First Lieutenant Richard G. Simpson with their P-51, Satan's Agent. *Courtesy of John E. Wendt.*

area at 1942 hrs. The weather had cleared a bit, becoming slightly hazy with scattered clouds 3-7,000 ft. Visibility was four to five miles. The group set up patrols in the area bounded by Magdeburg, northeast to Brandenburg, on to the western edge of Berlin, northwest to Neuruppin, west to Wittenberge and back down to Magdeburg. They cruised and fished for the enemy, but got nary a nibble. One flight was vectored to the area between Brunswick and Ulsen, but results were nil. West of Magdeburg, three jets believed to be Me 262s flying at 26,000 ft. were chased, but the jets pulled away without a fight. The day was a bust. The nearly 700 Eighth AF fighters aloft this date succeeded in bringing only one enemy aircraft down. Generally speaking, the Germans stayed on the ground. For the 479th FG, the day was a loss, both in terms of a lack of combat and also the loss of one of their own. Having left the patrol area at 1030 hours, Second Lieutenant Elbert N. (Neal) Harris, flying as an element leader in the 434th FS's Purple Flight, called twenty minutes later to report his engine was cutting out. His flight leader, First Lieutenant Richard G. Simpson, held the flight back and stayed with him as Lt. Harris tried first to keep the ailing engine going and shortly later when it quit, to get it restarted. Having no luck, Lt. Harris had turned east and was headed towards Russian lines in a glide down from 28,000 ft. All during this, Purple Flight circled above. Finally running out of altitude with which to continue his glide, Lt. Harris was forced to belly land his P-51 in a location about 15 miles east-southeast of Magdeburg by six miles northwest of Zerbst airfield. Lt. Simpson later reported that as the flight circled overhead, the last he saw of Lt. Harris was the Lieutenant walking slowly towards a wooded area. Lt. Simpson made three strafing passes and Second Lieutenant Harold L. Stotts made another on the P-51 named "Mary" on one side and "Georgia Ann" on the other. "Mary" was quite contrary and refused to burn. Lt. Harris was captured and became a POW for the short duration.

Taking the long way home on the way out, White Flight from the 435th FS bounced eight bogies north of Dümmer Lake. The bogies turned out to be Typhoons that were strafing a nearby airfield, but as the Lakeside flight pulled up off the bounce, First Lieutenant Richard G. Candelaria spotted an auxiliary airstrip five to six miles north of the lake. That one appeared to have about 15 enemy aircraft parked on it. Originally flying as Red Flight Leader, Lt. Candelaria had joined the flight that First Lieutenant Billy C. Means was leading after his own flight had lost him. In position to dive-strafe the secondary airfield, White Flight rolled over and went down after the parked targets. They had their way with some Me 109s, making four passes before the field's flak gunners awoke to the fact that they were being attacked and began to put up a lot of defensive fire. Lt. Means had just finished a pass when the first fire began coming up. He thought that the Germans were firing everything in the book at him – 40mm, 20mm and machine gun fire was all flying at him. Calling for the rest of the flight to break off and pull up, he felt the airfield was set up as a flak trap. Leaving it behind, Lts. Means, Candelaria and Second Lieutenant Charles E. Heathman tallied up 1-0-3 Me 109s and 3-0-0 dummy aircraft.

L/O for the group was north of Ijmuiden at 1145 hrs./ 10,000 feet, except for Purple Flight. Low on gas, they landed on the continent to refuel and then continued on home.

Crew chief Sergeant Stephan O. Coakley, Lieutenant Harold L. Stotts and armorer Corporal Raymond A. Martinez by their Yakima Chief. *Courtesy of Frederick C. Hayner.*

Observations made during the mission included the plumes of heavy smoke, black at the base and gray towards the top, that were seen reaching up to 15,000 ft. over Magdeburg. The bombing appeared to be excellent. There were numerous trains spotted within a 50-mile radius of Magdeburg. They all were standing still, but had their steam up. Flak over Magdeburg was heavy, moderate and inaccurate. South of there and over Braunschweig, it was heavy, intense and accurate. At Hannover it was heavy, meager and inaccurate while over Ijmuiden, it was heavy moderate and accurate.

4 March 1945

Eighth AF FO 1697A

No. 292 Sunday. Maj. Duffié led the group, which consisted of 40 P-51s (12-434th, 14-435th & 14-436th) on a penetration to target and withdrawal escort for 2nd AD, 96th CW B-24s attacking an 8th AF Mission 863 target of opportunity at Stuttgart, Germany. Up: 0813 hrs., down: 1258 hrs. with a total of one early return.

The group crossed over to the continent, making L/F over Belgium and made R/V in Germany with their B-24s 15 miles east of Selestat at 0945 hrs./31,000 ft. Heading towards the original target at Kitzingen, the bombers made a 360-degree turn east of the Rhine River, then turned towards Stuttgart where they bombed through the undercast. The results were unobserved because of a 10/10ths cloud cover that had been present since passing over Charleroi, Belgium. Heading out, escort was broken near Metz, France at 1130 hrs./21,000 ft. and L/O was from France.

Observations made during the mission included a V2 that was seen in the vicinity of The Hague at 0808 hrs. Radio reception and transmission with Nuthouse was excellent. The B-24s maintained an excellent formation, also. Flak over Stuttgart was heavy, intense and inaccurate. It was heavy, meager and inaccurate at both Heilbronn and Karlsruhe.

Three 434th FS P-51s (L2-G, L2-X and L2-J Satan's Agent) down for gas at an RAF TAF Typhoon base on the continent. That's Lieutenant Richard M. Lunstrum walking out to one of the birds. *Courtesy of Harold L. Stotts.*

5 March 1945

Eighth AF FO 1704A

No. 293 Monday. Maj. Moore led the group, which consisted of 50 P-51s (17-434th, 16-435th & 17-436th) on a penetration to target and withdrawal escort for two CWs of 2nd AD B-24s attacking their 8th AF Mission 865 primary target, the POL industry at Hamburg, Germany. Up: 0802 hrs., down: 1248 hrs. with a total of three early returns.

It was a clear, warm day with a cool prevailing wind breeze at Wattisham, but undercast clouds covered the continent beginning east of the Zuider Zee. While waiting for the Big Friends to arrive, a jet was spotted over Holland's Northeast Polder at 0845 hrs./21,000 ft. Lakeside Squadron gave chase, but the jet pulled away, heading north. R/V with the proper bombers was northeast of Terschelling Island, Holland at 0915 hrs./20,000 ft. The escorts were unable to locate the command Mosquito and they were unable to contact it via radio. It later turned out that the Mossie had to abort the monitoring mission. As the escorts and their charges passed north of Osnabrück after passing into Germany, Nuthouse vectored Newcross Squadron to bogies located 15 miles south of Dümmer Lake. The bogies were identified as Spitfires and the squadron returned to escort duty. Heading towards the target, contrails from a medium-sized gaggle flying at 30,000 ft. were seen paralleling the attacking force's course at 0940 hrs. They were flying to the south of the force and when investigated, they split-essed into the clouds. As the group drew closer to the target, Nuthouse had another vector at 1000 hrs./23,000 ft. Investigation found nothing. Over Hamburg, two jets were seen, chased and lost at 1015 hrs./23,000 ft. Bombing results were not observed due to undercast clouds hiding the target, but it was noted that the action of the clouds in that vicinity indicated large fires underneath. Turning back from Hamburg, two bogies were chased down to the ground, but lost in the rain at 1100 hrs. down on the deck. The group broke from the bombers east of the Zuider Zee at 1140 hrs./20,000 ft.

Lieutenant Robert H. Horman in his J2-A Lady Jean, ready to roll. *Courtesy of Robert H. Horman.*

The pilot of J2-L, Hell-Un is waiting in line for the flagman to give him the okay wave. *Courtesy of Robert H. Horman.*

Observations made during the mission included medium cargo vessels seen at 1155 hrs. along the coast, heading northeast from the Hook of Holland (Hoek van Holland, located south of The Hague.). Flak over Hamburg was heavy, moderate and inaccurate. It was the same over Wangerooge. Twenty miles north of Bremen, flak was heavy, medium and inaccurate.

B-24s from the 328th BS (squadron code GO) and the 409th BS (squadron code YM) are heading toward the target. Note the Mickey ship in the lead. *Courtesy of Harold L. Stotts.*

6 March 1945

Tuesday. Inclement weather scrubbed most of the Eighth AF activity for this day; but apparently, in anticipation of flying the scheduled mission, the 434th FS put up 16 P-51s led by First Lieutenant Eugene H. Wendt. Because of the bad weather, the squadron was diverted south from the briefed course. Entering France at Calais, they flew east to Lille, south to Le Havre, back north to Cape Gris-Nez and out. All aircraft returned safely.

The 328th BS presents a wide-open formation. *Courtesy of Harold L. Stotts.*

7 March 1945

Eighth AF FO 1715A

No. 294 & 295 Wednesday. The group was divided into two forces, A and B groups. A group was a penetration to target and withdrawal escort for 2nd AD, 14th and 20th CW B-24s attacking their 8th AF Mission 869 primary target, an old friend, the water viaduct at Bielefeld, Germany. B group flew a photo-reconnaissance escort for a 7th PG P-38 to and from the Åbenrå Fjord, a body of water between Åbenrå and Nordborg in southern Denmark. Col. Riddle led A group, which consisted of 38 P-51s (14-434th, 14-435th & 10-436th) Up: 0832 hrs., down: 1321 hrs. with no early returns. Capt. Mosier led B group, which consisted of four P-51s from the 436th FS. Up: 1405 hrs., down: 1755 hrs. with no early returns. A group was originally briefed for an area patrol along a route extending from Dümmer Lake to Rheine and Zwolle, but was diverted to the new mission by HQ via radio contact made during the course of the patrol.

The following photographs show 93rd BG (Ted's Traveling Circus) B-24s on a mission over Germany.

L/F for A group was approximately in the vicinity of Ijmuiden, Holland at 0926 hrs./18,000 ft. Clouds covered the continent at this point. Driving into Germany, the group was at 26,000 ft. and ten to fifteen miles north of Dümmer Lake

B-24s pulling those contrails that left a finger pointing right back at them. *Courtesy of Harold L. Stotts.*

German flak over the target. *Courtesy of Harold L. Stotts.*

Returning home over the North Sea. *Courtesy of Harold L. Stotts.*

when at 1000 hours, they received a course change to 220 degrees for a MEW controlled vector from Nuthouse to investigate bogies. Nuthouse lost the bogies five minutes later. Shortly after that, the group received a course change and orders to R/V with two combat wings of 2nd AD B-24s. R/V with the proper bombers, Vinegrove 1-3 and 1-4, was made 10-15 miles northwest of Dümmer Lake at 1025 hrs./27,000 ft. Over the target, bombs away occurred between 1050 and 1100 hours, with the bombers making bomb runs by individual groups from all directions. The results were unobserved due to 10/10ths cloud coverage with tops to 9,000 ft. over the target. The heavies were taken out of Germany and to the vicinity of Brussels, Belgium where the escorts broke away at 1215 hrs./ 23,000 ft. L/O was in the vicinity of Knokke, Belgium at 1220 hrs./10,000 ft.

Observations made during the mission included four V2s in flight that were seen while the group was passing through Holland. A smoke screen was noted at the airfield by Bad Oeynhausen. The Big Friends were happy, but noisy on "C" channel.

No. 295 B group R/V'd with the recce bird over Wattisham and escorted him over solid overcast to the vicinity of the target fjord. The weather gods were smiling at that moment and a hole over the fjord was found for the PRU P-38 to slip through and take its pictures. Flak at the target was heavy, meager and inaccurate. The work done, the five planes returned with the four escorts breaking away 30 miles north of Terschelling Island, Holland at 1715 hrs./17,000 ft. The mission was called uneventful.

9 March 1945

Eighth AF FO 1727A

No. 296 & 297 Friday. The group was divided into two forces, A and B groups, both penetration to target and withdrawal escorts for a screening force and a command Mosquito as well as 2nd AD, 20th and 96th CW B-24s attacking their 8th AF Mission 872 primary targets, the marshalling yards at Osnabrück and Rheine, Germany. Maj. Olds led A group, which consisted of 36 P-51s (16-434th & 16-435th). Up: 0815 hrs., down: 1314 hrs. with four early returns. Capt. Mosier led B group, which consisted of 15 P-51s from the 436th FS. Up: 0827 hrs., down: 1215 hrs. with no early returns.

A group made L/F north of Ijmuiden, Holland at 0923 hrs./17,000 ft. and once inside Germany, R/V'd with their proper bombers 40 miles southeast of Emden at 0945 hrs./ 24,000 ft. Reaching the target at Osnabrück, the heavies unloaded visually at 1000 hrs./24,000 ft. The bombing results seemed to be well concentrated on the target. On the way out, stragglers were picked up and given separate escorts. The group broke from the bombers near Urk, Holland at 1055 hrs./25,000 ft. Dropping down to 10,000 feet, they went back into Germany to sweep the areas along a route from Dümmer Lake, southeast to Bielefeld, northwest to Herford and back northwest to Dümmer Lake. There were 14 unidentified aircraft on one corner of the Hesepe airdrome. One of the 434th FS pilots dropped his belly tanks on them, but the results were unobserved. The sweep was uneventful and in returning home, L/O was over Ijmuiden at 1230 hrs./10,000 ft.

B group crossed in over Ijmuiden at 0922 hrs./20,000 ft. and R/V'd with their assigned bombers northwest of Meppel,

Holland at 0940 hrs/ 23,000 ft. The B-24s were taken over the target at Rheine, where bombs away was at 0955 hrs./23,000 ft. One B-24 was seen to receive what must have been a direct flak hit over the target. It exploded and went down. No chutes were seen because it was too far away. While over Holland and heading back, a B-24 straggler from the 467th BG, letter "P" on left wing and the number 286 on its nose, headed west at 1040 hrs./10,000 ft. This occurred while in the vicinity of the Zuider Zee. The bomber had no apparent trouble. Another 96th CW B-24 straggler, identified as having the letter "N" on its tail, had number three engine out and was leaking gas from its left wing. This Big Friend was escorted to Great Yarmouth, England where escort was broken at 1155 hrs./10,000 ft. L/O for the rest of the squadron was over Callantsoog, Holland at 1050 hrs./20,000 ft. Break away was mid-North Sea, 1053 hrs./23,000 ft.

Observations made during the mission included four V2s seen in The Hague area. The command Mosquito was heard on "C" channel, but could not be found. There were no aircraft visible at Diepholz, Vorden and Achmer airfields; however, at Bramsche, there were two He 111s and five unidentified aircraft on the field. Bad Oeynhausen had a very efficient smoke screen going. The marshalling yard at Bielefeld was loaded with rail stock and there was heavy traffic going both ways from it. The viaduct was STILL standing there! A B-24 was seen to explode over Münster at 0955 hrs. There was a smoke screen at Minden. Two ASR launches, a Catalina and a Wellington were seen searching the North Sea area between Ijmuiden and Southwold at 1155 hrs. There was a large oil slick south of the area. Flak 12 miles southeast of Enschede and over Rheine was heavy, meager and accurate. Over Osnabrück, it was heavy, moderate and inaccurate. At Münster, it was heavy, intense and accurate. In the Bramsche area, it was heavy, meager and inaccurate.

10 March 1945

Eighth AF FO 1731A

No. 298 & 299 Saturday. The group was divided into two forces, A and B groups, both penetration to target and withdrawal escorts for two CWs of B-24s from the 2nd AD attacking their 8th AF Mission 877 primary target, the rail viaduct at Arnsberg, Germany. Col. Riddle led A group, which consisted of 36 P-51s (18-435th & 18-436th). Up: 0952 hrs., down: 1400 hrs. with no early returns. Lt. Murr led B group, which consisted of 17 P-51s from the 434th FS. Up: 1000 hrs., down: 1410 hrs. with two early returns.

One flight of four 434th FS P-51s plus two more from another Newcross flight are pictured somewhere over the continent. *Courtesy of Clarence G. Haynes.*

The clouds were still present, providing undercast skies for the entire mission. A group made L/F over Belgium and R/V'd with their B-24s 25 miles south of Liège, Belgium at 1055 hrs./19,000 ft. Forty-five minutes later, the group had crossed into German air space and was about 20 miles north of Siegen, when Nuthouse called with a vector. They were sent to investigate some bogies, but no results were achieved that time. At the target, the bombing results were unobserved due to the cloud cover. Turning out, escort was broken 25 miles northwest of Trier at 1245 hrs./20,000 ft. During the course of the mission, Nuthouse advised Highway (the call sign for the group's leader, Col. Riddle) that Vinegrove was calling on "C" channel. Highway tried to reach both Vinegrove 1-5 and Vinegrove 1-6 for five minutes, but had no success. Nuthouse advised Highway once again that Vinegrove was calling. Col. Riddle continued trying to make contact and finally got through to the bombers. The message was of no importance.

B group also passed over Belgium and into Germany, making R/V with their assigned bombers southwest of Koblenz at 1100 hrs./22,000 ft. They took their heavies through the target where bombs away was at 1157 hrs./21,000 ft. The results were unobservable. Break away was at 1250 hrs./20,000 ft.

All geographical points of reference were problematical due to the undercast clouds. There were no observations and no flak reports recorded for the mission. It was an uneventful "Milk Run."

11 March 1945

Eighth AF FO 1738A

No. 300 Sunday. Maj. Jordan led the group on its 300th mission, which consisted of 48 P-51s (18-434th, 17-435th &

13-436th) on a penetration to target and withdrawal escort for 2nd AD, 20th CW B-24s attacking their 8th AF Mission 881 primary target, the Krupp Works at Kiel, Germany. Up: 1051 hrs., down: 1610 hrs. with a total of two early returns.

The long mission started out on a sour note when 30 minutes after takeoff, Lieutenant Lewis C. Smith from the 436th FS suffered an engine failure and was forced to bail out of his P-51. He landed in the cold inhospitable water below, about 20 miles east of Lowestoft, England. Despite the fact that rescue aircraft began to circle his position ten minutes later and that he was pulled from the water by ASR within a half hour of his parachuting down, Lt. Smith was found to have succumbed to the cold waters.

This was a long over-water trip for the group. Setting out and heading northeast over the North Sea, there were some breaks seen in the cloud cover below, but by and large, the frigid sea was hidden. They R/V'd with their proper B-24s about forty miles east of the southeastern tip of Denmark at 1232 hrs./26,000 ft. The group made L/F 35 miles southwest of Ribe, Denmark. at 1255 hrs./27,000 ft. Crossing down over Denmark and into Germany, the clouds became more dense and not much could be seen through the few holes in the 10/10ths cloud cover that laid over the land. The force arrived over Kiel at 1317 hrs. and released their loads through solid undercast, from 27,000 ft. It goes without saying that the results were unobserved. Heading back, L/O was three miles west of Meldorf at 1355 hrs./28,000 ft. One squadron broke off there and swept at 10,000 ft. from Meldorf up northwest to Sylt in the Frisian Islands, northeast to Vejle in southeast central Denmark and northwest to Ringkøbing near the western coast of central Denmark. They came home without incident, after having been in the air for almost seven-and-a-half hours. The remaining two squadrons broke from the bombers northwest of Terschelling Island at 1437 hrs./17,000 ft.

No observations were recorded from the mission. Flak over Flensburg and Kiel was heavy, moderate and inaccurate. Over Fockbek and Varde, it was heavy, meager and inaccurate. At Rendsburg and Eckernförde, it was heavy, moderate and accurate.

12 March 1945

Eighth AF FO 1742A

No. 301 Monday. Col. Riddle led the group, which consisted of 53 P-51s (18-434th, 18-435th & 17-436th) on a penetration to target and withdrawal escort for 2nd AD, lead CW B-24s attacking their 8th AF Mission 883 primary target, the marshalling yards at Swinemünde, Germany (Poland). Up: 0947 hrs., down: 1518 hrs. with a total of six early returns plus one escort.

L/F was south of Ijmuiden, Holland at 1047 hrs./15,500 ft. Having entered airspace over the German homeland, R/V with the proper bombers was in the vicinity of the target at 1212 hrs./27,000 ft. A 10/10ths overcast in the area prevented observation of the bombing results. One squadron stayed and stooged around the target area from 1206 to 1240 hrs. On the way back home, they were vectored to investigate bogies near Fehmarn Island, but no results were to be had. At 1225 hours, while in the vicinity of Rostock, a call was received from two bombers stating they were having trouble 25 miles east of Kiel. An attempt was made to investigate, but the Big Friends could

Colonel Kyle L. Riddle in his Bison Squadron J2-R is shown with his wingman in J2-S, ready for take off. *Courtesy of Robert H. Horman.*

not be located. The clouds had cleared while the force was over the Jütland Peninsula, but as they approached the Frisian Islands, it became hazy and closed to a 10/10ths situation again. L/O for the escorts that remained with the bombers was over Westerland at 1329 hrs./13,000 ft. They all could have waved at their former commanding officer, Colonel Hubert Zemke, as they passed near his current residence as a POW at Barth. Escort was broken 30 miles north of Borkum Island, Holland at 1355 hrs./15,000 ft.

Observations made during the mission mostly dealt with shipping and included: 1040 to 1111 hrs. – three V2s over Holland. 1130 hrs. – a large ship, single stack, in Elbe River, three miles west of Hamburg, direction of travel unknown. 1130 hrs. – two very low V2 contrails headed in the direction of Scotland, seen in the vicinity of Bergman Lake. 1300 hrs. – a ship believed to be a liner was seen headed southeast in the Fehmarn Channel. Two minesweepers and six smaller vessels were escorting it. 1305 hrs. – several large sailing vessels and one naval vessel, believed to be a destroyer, anchored in Kiel Fjord. 1310 hrs. – three large vessels anchored in the Flensburg Fjord. 1320 hrs. – twelve small ships headed northwest and a large ship escorted by three small vessels, all headed north, in the Kieler Bucht. Unk. time – ineffective smoke pots at the junction of the Elbe Estuary and the Kiel Canal. 1325 hrs. – one large vessel and three naval vessels anchored in the bay, north of Wilhelmshaven. 1410 hrs. – two V2s, one south of Groningen and one east of Ijmuiden, heading west. Flak ranged from heavy, meager and inaccurate to heavy, moderate and accurate at Stettin. It was heavy, intense and inaccurate at Swinemünde. At the bay east of Ueckermünde and at Neumünster, it was heavy, meager and inaccurate. Over the junction of the Elbe Estuary and the Kiel Canal, flak was heavy, meager and accurate.

One of two Bison P-51s that would not take to the air again. Having landed, 9B-C, was being taxied by First Lieutenant Frederick M. Mead when he was over run by Second Lieutenant Richard C. Palson, Jr. in 9B-A this date. The unfortunate Lt. Palson had run over another P-51 in the same Mustang just ten days prior. *Courtesy of George E. Falkner.*

13 March 1945

Tuesday. Weather forced a stand down of most Eighth AF operations, but Maj. Olds led 14 P-51s from the 434th FS on a training mission to the Maastricht, Holland area and back again. The 436th FS listed a fighter sweep flown to the area east of Paderborn, Germany as a mission in its records, but gave no details.

14 March 1945

Eighth AF FO 1752

No. 302 & 303 Wednesday. The group was divided into two forces, A and B groups, both penetration to target and withdrawal escorts for two CWs of B-24s from the 2nd AD attacking their 8th AF Mission 886 primary target, the marshalling yard at Gütersloh, Germany. Maj. Duffié led A group, which consisted of 31 P-51s (17-435th & 14-436th). Up: 1332 hrs., down: 1840 hrs. with three early returns. Capt.

Right: First Lieutenant Clarence G. Haynes and Captain John W. Morrow are standing near a low building that housed the 434th FS's ready room, briefing room, equipment storage, etc. *Courtesy of Clarence G. Haynes.*

Morrow led B group, which consisted of 18 P-51s from the 434th FS. Up: 1324 hrs., down: 1825 hrs. with no early returns.

A group entered over the continent and flew into Germany where they R/V'd with 20th CW B-24s 25 miles west-southwest of Bonn at 1435 hrs./24,000 ft. Continuing on, they additionally R/V'd with 14th CW B-24s near Giessen at 1506 hrs./26,000 ft. The bombers were not in the briefed sequence, but their formation was good. Escort was maintained through the target and out until the fighters broke away over St. Goar at 1615 hrs. After breakaway, Nuthouse vectored A group to south of Aschaffenburg, but they found nothing and left the area at 1643 hrs.

B group R/V'd with their B-24s east of Malmédy at 1429 hrs./23,000 ft. The bombers were escorted through the target and back towards home again as far as Koblenz, where at 1615 hrs./23,000 feet, the fighters were vectored to intercept some jets 50 miles to the southeast. No contact was made. At 1625 hours, a subsequent vector 20 miles east failed to produce any business either.

Observations made during the mission included the notation that the bombing results on the marshalling yard appeared to be excellent and well patterned. There were fires from oil dumps and a highway intersection was also seen to be hit. Ten miles north of Koblenz, an orange flashing explosion followed by black smoke and a parachute was sighted at 1605 hrs. P-47s were operating in the area. (It is probable that the explosion seen was that of one of the German Ar 234s destroyed near Koblenz that day by the 56th FG.) Flak north of Koblenz was heavy, meager and accurate. In the vicinity of St. Goar, it was heavy, meager and inaccurate.

15 March 1945

Eighth AF FO 1761A

No. 304 & 305 Thursday. The group was divided into two forces, A and B groups, both penetration to target and withdrawal escorts for two command Mosquitoes and 2nd AD, 2nd CW B-24s attacking their 8th AF Mission 889 primary target, an army headquarters at Zossen, Germany. Maj. Jordan led A group, which consisted of 28 P-51s (8-434th & 20-435th). Up: 1156 hrs., down: 1740 hrs. with no early returns. Maj. Duffié led B group, which consisted of 27 P-51s (12-434th & 15-436th) Up: 1211 hrs., down: 1736 hrs. with two early returns.

Newcross pilots Lieutenants Philip A. Brown and Hilton O. Thompson are sitting on board the fenders of a truck that was used to take the pilots to their waiting planes prior to a mission. Corporal Adolfo Ochoa is seated behind the vehicle's steering wheel. He was the squadron's regular driver for the pilots. *Courtesy of David L. Born.*

A group made L/F over Ijmuiden, Holland at 1244 hrs./ 16,000 ft. and R/V'd with the proper bombers 20 miles east of Meppel, Holland at 1302 hrs./20,000 ft. The heavies were escorted uneventfully through the target until breakaway near Medemblik, Holland at 1620 hrs./20,000 ft. L/O was by Alkmaar, Holland at 1630 hrs./18,000 ft.

B group made L/F over Ijmuiden, just behind A group, at 1254 hrs./17,000 ft. They R/V'd with their bombers over Coevordon, Holland at 1305 hrs./20,000 ft. and escorted them through the target where they dropped their loads at 1420 hrs./ 22,000 ft. with unobserved results. A flight from the group R/ V'd with the command Mosquitoes at 1405 hrs./21,000 ft. southwest of Brandenburg and took them through the target area ten minutes after bombs away. While escorting the Mossies, bogies were investigated, but they turned out to be P-51s. The flight picked up a Vinegrove 1-1 B-24, identified as having white on black markings, in the same area as the bogy P-51s were found. The Big Friend had its left outboard engine shut down and prop feathered. The damaged aircraft was escorted to Russian lines, crossing them at 1500 hrs./ 18,000 ft. At that point the bomber's pilot called saying he'd be back soon, he hoped. (The 445th BG crash-landed in liberated Poland.) Half a box withheld their bombs and dropped them 40 minutes later on a target of opportunity, a marshalling yard at Gardelegen, Germany. The results appeared to be excellent. The heavies and their escorts continued out to an area north of Bergen, Holland where they made L/O and separated at 1632 hrs./20,000 ft. Various vectors were given while the group and their charges were outward bound, but nothing was sighted.

Observations made during the mission included three twin-engine jets heading south, sighted at 1300 hrs. 15 miles north of Nijmegen. V2 contrails were seen headed west, one at 1332 hrs. from The Hague area and another at 1350 hrs. from over the Zwolle area. An unidentified bomber exploded over Jüterbog at 1455 hrs./20,000 ft. A B-17 was seen to be hit by flak and explode at 1500 hrs. No chutes were spotted. There was another report of an explosion seen in the air at the same time, ten miles south of Stendal. This may have been the same B-17. A battle damaged 20th CW B-24 with a smoking, shutdown engine, was escorted to the Zuider Zee. Twin-engine jets were seen at 1515 hrs. 15 miles south of Hannover and at 1550 hrs. southeast of the Zuider Zee. At the same time seven twin-engine aircraft were noticed on the ground at Ehra air drome. No aircraft were sighted at Rheine, Hesepe or Vorden airfields. Twenty to thirty barrage balloons were noted between Hannover and Steinhuder Lake. A large unidentified vessel was seen in the Weser River, about ten miles from its mouth, at 1530 hrs. Thirty miles east of Great Yarmouth, smoke was seen spiraling downward from 10,000 ft. to the water below at 1610 hrs. The smoke resembled a target marker. An aircraft similar to an OA-10 Catalina was observed coming out to that area, flying at 5,000 ft. (A 392nd BG B-24 ditched 30 miles northeast of Great Yarmouth. Six of its crewmembers were rescued.) Flak over Stendal was heavy, meager and accurate. Flak over Hannover was heavy, moderate and accurate. There was no flak present while the group was near Berlin or Bremerhaven.

435th FS pilot Captain Verne E. Hooker. *Courtesy of Verne E. Hooker.*

17 March 1945

Eighth AF FO 1774A

No. 306 & 307 Saturday. The group was divided into two forces, A and B groups for a MEW sweep and escort for 2nd AD, 14th CW B-24s attacking their 8th AF Mission 892 primary target, the marshalling yards at Münster, Germany. Maj. Olds led A group, which consisted of 29 P-51s (21-434th & 8-436th). Up: 1213 hrs., down: 1633 hrs. with one early return. Capt. Verne E. Hooker led B group, which consisted of 26 P-51s (20-435th & 6-436th) Up: 1223 hrs., down: 1635 hrs. with three early returns.

A group made L/F over Ostend, Belgium at 1242 hrs./12,000 ft. The continent was 9/10ths cloud covered. Passing into Germany, they arrived in the Kassel area at 1330 hrs. where Nuthouse began giving them MEW vectors. These included a patrol at 20,000 ft. to Brunswick at 1410 hours, to the Steinhuder Lake area at 1420 hrs. and over to the Dümmer Lake area at 1440 hrs. They found no business to conduct. Heading for home, L/O was over Ijmuiden, Holland at 1538 hrs./11,000 ft.

B group made a different L/F, having crossed in near Ijmuiden at 1314 hrs./23,000 ft. and connected with their assigned bombers northwest of Zwolle, Holland at 1320 hrs./25,000 ft. The B-24s were escorted without incident to the target at Münster where time over target and bombs away was 1346 hrs./25,000 ft. Escort was continued with the bombers being taken out to L/O and breakaway south of Ijmuiden at 1515 hrs./23,000 ft.

Due to the cloud cover, no observations were possible, although a number of V2s were seen over Holland. Flak was heavy, intense and inaccurate at Dunkirk. It was heavy, meager and inaccurate at Ijmuiden. It was the same between Münster and Gutersloh, although at Münster, it was heavy, intense and accurate.

18 March 1945

Eighth AF FO 1779A

No. 308 & 309 Sunday. The group was divided into two forces, A and B groups, both penetration to target and withdrawal escorts for a screening force and 2nd AD, 96th CW B-24s attacking their 8th AF Mission 894 primary target, an armored-vehicle manufacturing plant at Berlin, Germany. Maj. Duffié started out as A group's leader, but he was forced to abort and his position was taken over by First Lieutenant Walter B. (Becky) Steph. (This probably was a more than interesting mission for Lt. Steph because he always lowered the seat in his airplane when crossing the North Sea because he did not want to see the water. He could not swim!) A group consisted of 22 P-51s from the 436th FS. Up: 0948 hrs., down: 1526 hrs. with two early returns. Maj. Jordan led B group, which consisted of 27 P-51s from the 435th FS Up: 0948 hrs., down: 1521 hrs. with two early returns. The activities of the 434th FS are not recorded for this day.

A group crossed over Holland at Ijmuiden at 1029 hrs./ 18,000 ft. and R/V'd with their proper bombers over the northeast Polder there at 1041 hrs./20,000 ft. The heavies were escorted into Germany and onto Berlin, where they bombed with excellent results. After the attack, the B-24s dispersed into smaller units. This action broke up the squadron as one section then took up escort for 16 Big Friends while another covered 46. On the way out, five B-24s that had failed to release their loads, dropped their bombs through overcast on a target of opportunity that was thought to be Lüneburg. Breakaway was over the northeast Polder at 1425 hrs. and L/O was over Egmond at 1432 hrs./18,000 ft. The screening force was taken through the target where it was lost due to haze. The escorts for that then tacked onto the B-17 stream and came home.

B group made L/F at the same location as did A group. They came in at 1032 hrs./23,000 ft. and R/V'd with their assigned B-24s northwest of Lingen, Germany. Taking the bombers to their target, they reached Berlin, conducted their business and orbited the city heading out. Reaching Holland again, the escorts broke from the bombers over the northeast Polder at 1417 hrs./23,000 ft. and crossed out north of Ijmuiden at 1426 hrs./23,000 ft.

Observations made during the mission included a notation that the bombing was excellent on an unidentified marshalling yard in Berlin. One of the group's B-24 charges (467th BG) was seen on fire and going down over Berlin. There were no chutes spotted. There was a huge explosion seen south of

Mission return – 434th FS P-51s peeling off to land at Wattisham. *Courtesy of Clarence G. Haynes.*

Lichtenberg, near the Spree River. A P-51, described as having a blue spinner, red stacks, (probably a red panel under the exhaust stacks) a red rudder and no identifying squadron letters or numbers on it, joined two of the group's planes north of Magdeburg. (The aircraft probably was a bird that belonged to the 7th PG.) The plane stayed with them, flying wide, to Dümmer Lake. When the element leader's wingman crossed over his leader to the unidentified Mustang pilot's side of the formation, the stranger made a wide turn and departed. Eight to ten barrage balloons were floating southwest, over Nienburg. All the roads in the area north of Bremen were packed with horse drawn and motor vehicles headed southwest. The airfields at Wustermark and Schönewalde were crowded with a large number of aircraft. A B-17 identified as having a black triangle bordered with orange and the letter "E" on its tail was seen at 1340 hrs. heading from Zwolle to the Brussels area. The aircraft had number three engine shut down and the propeller feathered. It was observed dropping an unidentified article through its bomb bay over Zwolle. Flak over Berlin was heavy, intense and accurate. East of Salzwedel, over Wittenberge and over Lichtenberg, it was heavy, meager and inaccurate.

19 March 1945

Eighth AF FO 1785A

No. 310 & 311 Monday. The group was divided into two forces, A and B groups, both penetration to target and withdrawal escorts for 2nd AD, 96th CW B-24s attacking their 8th AF Mission 896 primary target, the airfield at Leipheim, Germany. Maj. Jordan led A group, which consisted of 33 P-51s (18-

435th & 15-436th). Up: 1225 hrs., down: 1834 hrs. with no early returns. Maj. Olds led B group, which consisted of 16 P-51s from the 434th FS. Up: 1226 hrs., down: 1831 hrs. with three early returns.

A group entered over the continent between Ostend and Coxyde, Belgium at 1300 hrs./15,000 ft. Driving in a southeasterly direction, R/V with the proper bombers was in Germany, 30 miles southeast of Strasbourg at 1408 hrs./21,000 ft. Time over target was at 1448 hrs./20,000 ft. with excellent bombing results. One squadron stayed with the Big Friends, taking them to 20 miles southeast of Aachen where the squadron broke from the bombers at 1620 hrs./17,000 ft. L/O for them was over Walcheren Island, Holland at 1700 hrs./ 7,000 ft. The other squadron broke escort in the area of Donauwörth, just northeast of the target airfield and stooged around, passing through the areas of Nürnberg, Bayreuth, Halberstadt and Hannover, finally making L/O over Ijmuiden at 1700 hrs./8,000 ft.

B group made L/F between Knokke and Ostend at 1308 hrs./14,000 ft. Over Germany, they R/V'd with the correct bombers east of Strasbourg at 1408 hrs./21,500 ft. The B-24s were taken to, through and from the target to Crailsheim where the squadron broke from the bombers and swept the areas of Giebelstadt airfield, Kitzingen, Würzburg, Volkmarsen, Paderborn and Münster. While in the Münster area, bogies were sighted at 1615 hrs./8,000 ft. The players were on the field and it looked to be a good day for a scrap. Even the weatherman had cooperated, providing skies that were excellent, except for haze, which caused contrails at 13-15,000 ft. The bogies were Fw 190D-9s from the First and Fourth *Gruppen* of JG 26, assigned a mission to provide airfield cover for Me 262 photo-reconnaissance aircraft based at Münster's Handorf airfield. Me 109s were also present from another *Gruppe*.

Major Robin Olds led Newcross Squadron in the attack on the patrolling 25 plus German aircraft. The 434th FS had the advantage in the bounce, having used the haze as cover in their approach on the enemy formation. Unfortunately, Yellow Flight became separated as the squadron closed on their adversaries. The remaining nine P-51s engaged the Focke-Wulf Doras, which having spotted the oncoming P-51s, went into a luftbury to the left, pulling contrails as they circled at 13,000 feet in the haze. Newcross Squadron joined in the luftbury, gaining altitude as the pilots waited for the Germans to break. The Dora pilots played coy, doing barrel rolls, shallow split-esses, et cetera and then pulled back up in an attempt to lure

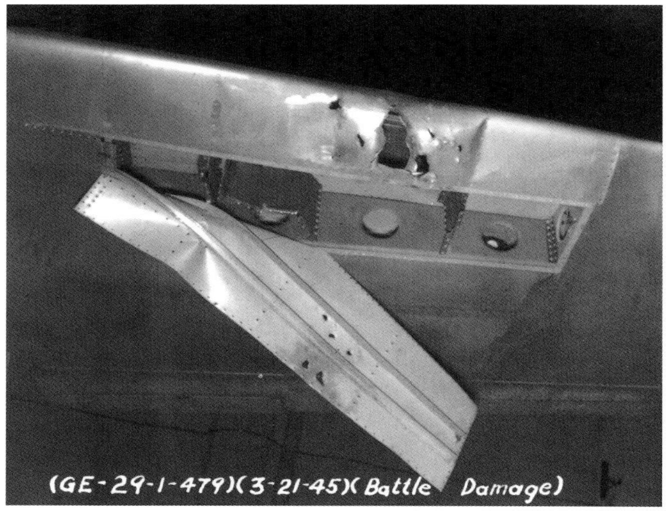

Battle damage (20mm) to the left wing's leading edge of a 434th FS P-51. Recently promoted to First Lieutenant, William H. (Hank) Daudistel received this hit during the above-described action while he was flying L2-Z, The Impatient Virgin. It occurred when Major Robin Olds told Lt. Daudistel to break because there was a FW after him. Just as he dipped his wing entering the break, a single round entered the wing from the top side and exploded, holing the wing and peeling back a lower sheet metal panel. The rolled back panel threw Lt. Daudistel into a spin from which he recovered and headed for home. Able to see only the entry hole from the slug while he was in the air, he could not understand why the aircraft was so difficult to fly. Upon landing, Lt. Daudistel was able to understand the problem. *Courtesy of the Wings of Freedom Museum.*

the Mustang pilots into following them down. Finally, as Maj. Olds reached the level of the enemy formation's leader, the bulk, but not all of the Fws, broke downward. At that point, elements of Newcross White, Red and Blue Flights took them on. Sort of patriotic, wouldn't one think? The German pilots were described as very competent and aggressive and they appeared to be flying very new, shiny aircraft. After a short eight minute dogfight, the Germans had lost two Fw 190D-9s and an Me 109. They were able to put a 20mm slug through the wing of one P-51, but the Newcross bird made it home okay.

First Lieutenant Richard G. Simpson confirmed the Fw 190D-9 that Maj. Olds claimed. Lt. Simpson:

> "I was leading Newcross Red Flight in the above engagement. Upon encountering the E/A, we climbed to about 13,000 feet and joined in their luftberry to the left. Red Flight was directly behind White Flight and as the luftberry got tighter, I saw an Me 109 roll over on his back, skid and then spin violently down. I did not see whether this 109 was under attack or not because of the haze and contrails, nor did I see any strikes. The German leader was getting uncomfortably close in the turn, so I

gave the word to break into them. Because of the contrails and haze, I continued the luftberry, not knowing whether the Jerries were on our tails or not. A few moments later, Major Olds, Newcross Leader, ordered us to get below the contrail level; so I split-essed, pulling out at about 8,000 feet. As I leveled off, I saw a Fw 190 with two P-51s on his tail. The 190 was smoking badly and then he rolled over and went down in a steep dive, losing pieces of cowling and other parts as they flew off his aircraft. I broke to the right with my flight in order to investigate two bogies, which turned out to be a P-51 attacking another Fw 190. The 190 pulled up sharply and I saw the P-51 firing and getting strikes all over the Jerry's fuselage. The 190 passed under my nose and after I completed my turn, I saw the E/A dive straight in and explode on impact.

"Because of the haze and thick contrails, it was impossible at the time to identify the pilots who had shot down the E/A described above; but at interrogation, it developed that Major Olds was the only one in the squadron who had attacked an Me 109. Additionally, the Me 109 that I saw was unquestionably out of control, spinning and skidding violently. The Fw 190, which I saw crash and explode, was the one claimed by Major Olds. I confirm Major Olds' claim of one Fw 190 destroyed."

First Lieutenants Gail E. Jacobson and Frank M. Taylor shared the other Fw. Lt. Jacobson:

"I was leading Newcross Blue Flight on a bomber escort mission to Leipheim A/D. Leaving the B-24s in the vicinity of Crailsheim, B group dropped to 10,000 feet and swept north. Between Paderborn and Bielefeld, bogies were called in at nine o'clock high, so we started climbing in that direction. In two or three minutes, I saw what looked like two flights of bogies in formation plus twelve more stringing along. At this time, I was directly

First Lieutenant Gail E. Jacobson, crew chief Corporal Elsworth Drais, Jr. and armorer Corporal Edward A. Tinker, Jr. by their L2-P Burn'n Bernie. *Courtesy of the Wings of Freedom Museum.*

Lieutenant Clarence L. Waters in L2-R, Setonia No. 3. *Courtesy of David L. Born.*

below Newcross leader. Upon identifying the bogies as Fw 190s, I tried to climb up behind them, but that put me directly behind their first flight, so I pulled out and drove in behind their second flight. I attacked the number two man on the far right of the enemy formation, opening fire at 600 yards from six o'clock, level, ranging with my K-14 sight. I saw a few strikes on his left wing and canopy. The German pilot was pretty clever in that he acted like he was hit and rolled over into a split-ess. I rolled to watch him and saw that he was pulling out, so I went after him again. The E/A pulled up in a steep chandelle to the left as I closed and opened fire from 200 yards at 50 degrees, but I didn't see any strikes. The 190 then rolled over again and repeated the same maneuver. This time he led me over the town of Münster where he pulled out and at 6,000 feet, I began to catch light flak. When the Jerry pulled up again, I closed in to 150 yards, ranged with my K-14 and got a few strikes on his left wing. The E/A did a complete barrel roll, pulled out in a turn to the left and then went down in a 50-degree dive. As I followed, I saw my wingman, Lt. Taylor, coming in from the left, so I pulled out and watched him fire. He got strikes on the German's tail. The 190 pulled up in a climbing left turn, did a half-roll and went down again. I moved over to attack again, but pulled up when I saw first his left wing, then his tail assembly and finally his canopy come off the plane. I did not see the pilot bail out. What was left of the 190 crashed and burned in a field, a little southeast of Münster."

Lt. Taylor:

"I was flying Newcross Blue Two, Lt. Jacobson's wing, in the above engagement. Lt. Jacobson led Blue Flight in an attack on the second flight of Fw 190s and fired on their number two man. The 190 split-essed and we followed. The German led Lt. Jacobson and me over the town of Münster where we started receiving light flak. The E/A then started climbing to the left and I saw Lt. Jacobson's fire getting strikes on the German's wings. The 190 went into a diving turn to the left and Lt. Jacobson fired again. Then, seeing that he was out of position, I moved over and fired a ten-degree deflection, one second burst at 600 yards, using a fixed sight. I didn't see any strikes. The 190 started climbing again and when he reached the top of his climb, he turned almost head-on to me. I dropped my nose and fired a short burst, closing from 500 yards, but again, I didn't see any strikes. The German pulled out and started to climb again and since Lt. Jacobson seemed to be out of position, I attacked at the top of the turn, ranging with my K-14. Closing from 400 to 150 yards, this time, I observed strikes on the Fw's wings, fuselage and tail – a large piece flew off of that. The E/A then went into a dive and the whole tail flew off. I then rejoined formation with Lt. Jacobson and did not observe the Fw 190 crash."

Second Lieutenant Clarence L. Waters and Flight Officer John S. Attwater both confirmed Maj. Olds' claim of an Me 109 destroyed. Lt. Waters:

"I was flying as Newcross Red Two in the engagement described above. We were in a luftberry to the left at about 12,000 feet, with Red Flight below and behind White Flight, when the Jerry leader knifed in on our tails. We broke to the left on an order from Red Leader and leveled out at 9,000 feet, successfully shaking the Jerry, who couldn't stay with us. As I leveled out, I saw an Me 109 crossing right in front of me. He was in a steep dive and trailing black smoke, which was pouring out of his engine section. Another P-51 from the squadron took a snap shot at the E/A as it went down, but didn't get any strikes that I could see. The P-51 broke off at approximately 4,000 feet. The Me 109 continued straight in, crashed into the ground and burned. I did not see any parachute.

"At interrogation, it was developed that Major Robin Olds was the only one who had attacked an Me 109. Since White Flight was above me at the time, I saw the Me 109 diving down, trailing smoke and since we were the only Allied fighters in the area, the Me 109, which I saw crash and burn, was undoubtedly the one claimed by Major Olds. I confirm Major Robin Olds' claim of one Me 109 destroyed."

F/O Attwater:

"I was flying Newcross White Four in Major Olds' flight. I became separated from my element leader in the contrails at 13,000 feet so I dived down out of them. Ahead of me and at 90 degrees to me, I saw two P-51s chasing an Me 109. The 109 was trailing black smoke and was in a slight dive when I first saw him. The Me 109 then did a half roll and dived straight down. The two P-51s broke off. As the E/A passed down in front of me, I took a shot or two at him, but I did not hit him. I pulled up around 3,000 feet to watch him hit, but my nose hid him from view.

"Major Olds was the only pilot in the flight who shot down an Me 109, so it must have been his that I saw go down. I confirm Major Olds' claim of one Me 109 destroyed."

After the battle, B Group regrouped and left the area at 1650 hrs./8,000 ft. L/O for them was in the vicinity of Overflakkee, Holland at 1730 hrs./7,000 ft.

Observations made during the mission included the note that the northern portion of the airfield at Leipheim and the southeast part of the field at Günzburg were both well clobbered. Following the bombing, there were numerous fires and explosions at the two locations. E/A were found parked at the following airdromes: Bayreuth/Bindlach – 12-14 A/C, Bayreuth/Laineck – 4-5 A/C, Kitzingen – 20-30 A/C, Kircheim – 26 single and twin-engine A/C, Halberstadt – 20-30 A/C, Schweinfurt – 12-15 A/C and at Fritzlar – 5 twin-engine A/C. At Giebelstadt – 12-15 Me 262s were parked and one conventional A/C was taxiing on the field, plus, for a distance of about five miles, there were revetments built off the highway between Giebelstadt and Würzburg. At Münster – 60-70 single and twin-engine A/C were on the field and in revetments. There were no A/C at Paderborn. At Volkmarsen, there were two formations of German troops parading in a barracks area. It was a good opportunity, but the field order read: "NO STRAFING!" North of the town of Paderborn, there was an area three to four miles square, that was covered with tank tracks and had many small shacks bearing red crosses. It was thought to be a tank testing area. The group's aircraft were pulling heavy, persistent contrails between 19-22,000 feet throughout the mission. Ten balloons were seen between Hannover and Steinhuder Lake. Flak between the Weser-Elbe Canal and the area 20 miles west of Hannover was light, intense and inaccurate. At Münster, it was heavy, moderate and accurate. There was light, intense and accurate flak present there, also.

20 March 1945

Eighth AF FO 1794A

No. 312, 313 & 314 Tuesday. The group was divided into three forces, A, B and C groups. A group flew a photo reconnaissance escort mission to Berlin, Germany and B group flew another photo reconnaissance escort mission to Leipzig, Germany. Both were in support of 8th AF Mission 898. C group, flying 8th AF Mission 899, was briefed to provide escort for a single 1st AD, 482nd BG B-17 going to Oberursel, near Frankfurt, Germany. Capt. Pierce led A group, which consisted of 16 P-51s from the 434th FS. Up: 1438 hrs., down: 2000 hrs. with no non-effectives. Capt. Hooker led B group, which consisted of 14 P-51s from the 435th FS. Up: 1459 hrs., down: 1500 hrs. with one non-effective. Captain William C. Anderson, a former member of the 4th FG, led C group, which consisted of 10 P-51s from the 436th FS. Up: 1453 hrs., down: 1940 hrs. with no non-effectives.

A group made L/F over Katwijk aan Zee, Holland at 1450 hrs./13,000 ft. They picked up their two P-38 PRU birds and escorted them into Germany and through the areas of Münster, Bielefeld and Dessau, to southeast of Berlin where White Section broke away to sweep back, passing north of Magdeburg on a route that took them south of Cologne and out. During the trip in towards Berlin, Ar 234s were seen twice, for a total of nine A/C spotted. The jets, in no apparent formation, were seen 15-20 miles south of Arnsberg. When an attempt was made to approach the enemy aircraft, they used their superior speed and fled. L/O for White Section was near Schouwen Island, Holland at 1910 hrs./9,000 ft. Meanwhile, Yellow Section kept escort and returned the photo recce planes to west of Münster, arriving in that area at 1730 hrs./23,000 ft. Then breaking away from the P-38s, the section swept southeast to Paderborn, then southwest through the Ruhr area to L/O by Knokke-Heist, Belgium at 1900 hrs./11,000 ft.

B group made L/F near Overflakkee, Holland at 1547 hrs./ 23,000 ft. They met their Spitfire PRU aircraft and accompanied it to Leipzig, Germany, arriving there at 1650 hrs./24,000 ft. From Leipzig, they went on to Erfurt, Germany, entering that area at 1715 hrs./24,000 ft. Following the briefed course, B group flew to a point about 30 miles west of Koblenz, where they broke from the Spit recce bird at 1812 hrs./22,000 ft. Heading for home, the group crossed out over Knokke, Belgium at 1845 hrs./10,500 ft.

Observations made during the missions included one jet that was seen on the ground at Halberstadt's airdrome and two more seen on the ground at Wittenberg's. There were 12-15 single-engine and two twin-engine aircraft on the field at Burg Airdrome, north of Magdeburg. Another 12-15 twin-engine A/C were parked in a wooded area to the southwest. The canal northwest of Burg was loaded with barge traffic. A chimney that was smoking heavily was observed at Merseburg. A small group of buildings seen in the vicinity of Grevenstein was exploding with a Fourth of July fireworks-like effect at 1720 hrs. Two fires were seen on the airfield at Paderborn. Flak was heavy, moderate and inaccurate at Burg. It was heavy, medium and accurate ten miles northwest of Dortmund. There were seven heavy, accurate bursts north of Dusseldorf. Almost home, one of the groups received heavy, moderate, but inaccurate flak over Lowestoft.

There were flames on the field at Wattisham when the highly volatile aviation gasoline from a refueling operation suddenly caught fire. The nearby men rushed to push the airplane being gassed away from the patch of burning ground. Fortunately, no one was injured, the plane was saved and the fire was quickly put out. *Courtesy of Clarence G. Haynes.*

Eighth AF FO 1797A

No. 314 C group was to escort a 482nd BG B-17 on a special mission. The 482nd was based at Alconbury and at this stage of the war, was engaged in training radar operators who flew in the radar equipped B-17s and B-24s used in sighting and bombing through overcast targets. The bomb group also flew its own radarscope sorties. This particular mission was the first operational test of Micro H Mk. II, the production version of the latest airborne ground-scanning device for blind bombing. The mission called for the use of a single B-17 to bomb the target. L/F for C group was over Walcheren, Holland at 1530 hrs./10,000 ft. The group had a SNAFU at the beginning of the mission. The late arrival of information for R/V with the B-17 prevented four escorts held in reserve for the mission from taking off. The balance of the squadron, having pressed on, was unable to find the bomber in the target area. They stooged around in the Frankfurt area from 1620 until 1745 hours, between 10-23,000 ft. Having had no luck, they turned towards Wattisham, making L/O over the Hook of Holland at 1835 hrs./10,000 ft. The B-17 completed its test mission and returned home, also.

Observations made during the mission included fifteen plus barrage balloons that were up over Rotterdam and another 30 plus floating over The Hague. Flak over Frankfurt was heavy, medium and inaccurate.

21 March 1945

Eighth AF FO 1801A

No. 315 Wednesday. Col. Riddle led the group, which consisted of 55 P-51s (18-434th, 20-435th & 17-436th) on a penetration to target and withdrawal escort for three different CWs of 3rd AD B-17s attacking their 8th AF Mission 901 primary targets, the airfields at Wittmundhafen and Marx, Germany. They were to also provide top cover for the 4th Fighter Group at Hesepe airdrome in Germany. Up: 0819 hrs., down: 1345 hrs. with no early returns.

The group R/V'd with the proper bombers over the North Sea, 20 miles north of Ameland Island in Holland's "Hook" at 0922 hrs./20,000 ft. Splitting up to cover the two attacking forces, they made L/F at 0935 hrs./20,000 ft. north of Groszes Lake and proceeded eastward into northern Germany, one force arriving over Marx airfield at 0941 hrs. and the other over Wittmundhaven airfield at 0950 hrs. for bombs away. Results of the attack at Marx A/F: a hardstand on the south side of the field, as well as the north, east/west runway were well clobbered. Results at Wittmundhafen A/F: The bombing results were excellent, especially in the hangar and barracks areas. Five minutes after the attacks, the escorts broke from the bombers in the vicinity of Winschoten and Zuidlaarder Lake, both in northern-most Holland. Heading back into Germany, the group, stacked up in layers ranging between 10-27,000 feet, arrived in the vicinity of Hesepe airfield at 1015 hrs. As they drew closer, they could see that the field, and especially the runways, appeared to be well hit by a recent bombing attack. When they approached the field, the 4th FG was already leaving and advised them to stay away because the flak there was terrific. Taking the advice as sound, the group made a left turn and followed the 4th to Achmer/Bramsche airfield, arriving there at 1025 hrs. They made one circuit of the area and saw numerous P-51s from the 353rd Fighter Group strafing and five or six fires on the ground towards the southeast and southwest corners. Recognizing the area was already receiving sufficient attention, the 479th left the two other groups to their business and headed east. Looking for targets of opportunity, they passed north of Steinhuder Lake and then drove northeast to Fassburg and Bremen, down to Quackenbrück, back southeast to Steinhuder Lake, south to Paderborn, west to Hamm and out. L/O was in the area of Schouwen Island, Holland at 1250 hrs./10,000 ft. Although the group received several vectors from Nuthouse, the bogies all turned out to be friendlies. Thus activity for pilots was nil.

Observations made during the mission included a grass airfield with many unidentified aircraft on it, seen eight miles northeast of Nienburg, between Rethem and Kerchboitven. There was what appeared to be either a military camp or a supply depot near the vicinity of Wietzendorf. There was a huge black funnel of smoke coming from a village on the north edge of Zuidlaarder Lake. Numerous oil fires were observed at Bremen, apparently the result of a RAF attack. There were two good-sized boats on the river just southwest of Delfzyl. Three Me 262s were seen, one in the Amsterdam area headed north, one in the Hengelo area headed northeast and one in the Ulzen area, headed east. Flak over Wilhelmshaven was heavy, meager and inaccurate. Over the airfield at Marx, it was heavy, meager and inaccurate. Along the coast south of Morderney, it was heavy, moderate and inaccurate.

21 March 1945

Eighth AF FO 1805

No. 316 Wednesday. First Lieutenant John T. Golden led a flight of four P-51s from the 434th FS to provide escort for a 482nd BG B-17 attacking its 8th AF Mission 903 special target at Oberursel, Germany. This was another test of the Micro H Mk. II airborne radar, blind bombing system. Up: 1518 hrs., down: 1930 hrs. with one early return.

The three P-51s reached the continent and made L/F over Ostend, Belgium at 1558 hrs./18,000 ft. They arrived at the assigned R/V point right on time, but no B-17 was to be found. Initial contact with Nuthouse indicated that the Big Friend was going to be a few minutes late, so the flight orbited the area waiting. Upon further contact with Nuthouse, it was learned that their bomber was orbiting Brussels. Off they went, but by the time they got there, the B-17 had set course for the target. The P-51s chased the bomber all the way to Oberursel, arriving in the target area before their charge. While waiting for the test plane, Nuthouse vectored the three escorts to investigate some bogies. During their absence, the big bird arrived over his target and dropped two tons of high explosives. His business finished there, the bomber pilot cleared the target area and headed back home. The three Mustang pilots never had a chance of seeing him. They also turned towards home and crossed out over Blankenberghe, Belgium at 1835 hrs./ 11,000 ft.

22 March 1945

Eighth AF FO 1810A

No. 317 & 318 Thursday. The group was divided into two forces, A and B groups, providing support both in the target area and during withdrawal for 15th AF bombers attacking their target, the largest remaining oil refineries at Ruhland, Germany. Maj. Duffié led A group, which consisted of 26 P-51s (7-434th & 19-436th). Up: 1008 hrs., down: 1615 hrs. with two early returns. Capt. Hooker led B group, which consisted of 30 P-51s (12-434th & 18-435th). Up: 1014 hrs., down: 1605 hrs. with no early returns.

This mission was the first time that the 8th AF had coordinated with the Italian based 15th AF by providing fighter support for an attack in Germany. The 8th AF fighter groups involved were the 4th, 339th and 479th. They belonged to the 2nd and 3rd ADs 65th and 66th Fws, respectively. It was a long-range escort and many a pilot had a sore backside by the time home base was reached at the conclusion of the eight-hour mission. The group's masseurs had their work cut out for them, straightening out all of the kinks the pilots developed during the flight.

A group made L/F ten miles north of Ijmuiden, Holland at 1100 hrs./22,000 ft. Driving in on an east-southeasterly course, the group arrived in the target area at 1225 hrs./27,000 ft. Because the 479th was split into two sections, they found themselves on opposite sides of Dresden as they patrolled the area. B-17s were seen in the area during the patrol, some marked with a three-foot checkered band around the fuselage center, some with yellow tails and others with orange tail corners. At 1230 hours, two of the group's P-51s had to leave the formation and return home. One had a problem with his oxygen system and the other acted as an escort for the ailing ship. First Lieutenant Charles H. Darling was flying in the position of the squadron's last spare. He had been shepherding several new replacement pilots, all of which were on their first mission. They had been assigned as spares and one by one, all except Lt. Darling had gone to take the places of other pilots who had aborted during the course of the long mission. When still another had to turn for home, this time because of a failing oxygen system, Lt. Darling volunteered to take him back since he himself was now alone. Flying as a two-plane element with Lt. Darling in the lead, the two Bison pilots began a descent and headed towards Wattisham. At about 20,000 feet, as the two passed near Torgau, they spotted a lone B-17 marked with a red rudder. The Big Friend appeared to be heading for its home in Italy. Lt. Darling attempted to contact the bomber to ask if help was needed, but that notion was quickly interrupted. He had just looked over his right shoulder and seen what at first he thought were two Mustangs that were joining them. The "friendlies" were approaching from four o'clock, level. The brief thought of company was fleeting, however when he saw the twinkling of their guns and realized the approaching aircraft were Me 262s! The two Bison pilots toggled off their wing tanks and began a rapid break to the left just as the two Me 262s made a pass at their P-51s. As they began their brake away, two more Me 262s were spotted coming at them from two o'clock, level. At this point, Lt. Darling had an additional problem to deal with. His left wing tank had failed to drop away. This had happened to the Lieutenant before and he had a quick remedy. Calling to his wingman and warning him to stay clear, he fired his guns during the tight turn and their vibration plus the G-force of the turn caused the tank to release.

The two elements of attacking German jets overshot the Mustangs, then dove on the lone B-17 flying almost directly below at 17,000 ft. The jets fired on the bomber, hitting the tail and starting a fire and starboard wing section. Two parachutes were seen to emerge from the bomber as the 436th FS P-51s dove to intercept the attackers. Lt. Darling was able to get close enough and he had the lead Me 262 in his sight, but could not fire because his wingman had gotten slightly ahead of him. Sitting on his lower right, the wingman would have been too close to the line of fire. Lt. Darling called to him, telling him to fall back as he wanted to fire, but the number two man replied that he was looking for the other jets and did not move out of the way. As Lt. Darling argued with himself about whether to fire or not, the Germans split up, with one element turning to the right and the other to the left. Despite the fact that the two Bison planes were at full throttle and in a dive, the Me 262s quickly outdistanced them and disappeared, not to be seen again.

Meanwhile, the group stooged around in the target area 28,500 ft. until 1245 hours, then escorted the lead box to Linz, Austria where they broke from them at 1335 hrs./25,000 ft. During that escort, at 1300 hrs./21,000 feet, two more Me 262s made a pass at another B-17 straggler. Coming in from below, the jets made a slightly high-to-low pass on the red-tailed Big Friend in the last box before the escorts could get into any kind of position to go after them. The jets flew a close formation and succeeded in getting some strikes on the bomber. As one section closed on the enemy aircraft, one jet broke left and headed back towards Dresden. The other broke right and disappeared. The B-17 kept going with no serious damage visible. A few minutes later and just south of that encounter, two Ar 234s went zipping along the entire length of the bomber formation, flying wide open. They disappeared and, fortunately, no damage was observed. While in the Frankfurt area, Nuthouse gave the several MEW steers, but no results turned up. L/O was over Walcheren Island, Holland at 1535 hrs./12,000 ft.

B group made L/F near Alkmaar, Holland at 1059 hrs./ 15,000 ft. Far into Germany, they R/V'd with their assigned B-17s, which were identified by a yellow-banded fuselage marked with an "A" on the band, in the area of Ruhland at 1221 hrs./25,000 ft. The bombers were in excellent six-to-twelve ship formations, but the boxes were strung out. The Big Friends bombed visually from 1230-1245 hrs./25-28,000 feet, their efforts resulting in a target that appeared to be well hit and that had dark smoke rising from it to 4,000 ft. One of the Big Friends was hit by flak and exploded over Ruhland. There were no chutes seen to be coming from it. Another target five to ten miles south of Ruhland was also bombed as well as the areas of Görlitz, Bautzen, Reichemberg and various other targets of opportunity struck along the way during withdrawal. During the attack to the south, one of the B-17s exploded and spun down in flames ten to twelve miles from Ruhland. The distance was too far to see if there were any parachutes. The escorts stayed with the bombers to the area of Passau, right on the Austrian border, from whence they broke away towards home at 1337 hrs./28,000 ft. L/O was over Walcheren Island at 1529 hrs./10,000 ft.

Mario V. Prevosti was a F/O pilot assigned to the 435th FS at this time. He flew on this mission and wrote of his experience during it:

> "I remember this maximum effort mission to a target in the general vicinity of Berlin. At the time, it seemed as though most of the German anti-aircraft guns were concentrated in this area. The guns created a huge black box of flak through which the bombers passed as they followed their course to the target. This box must have been a half-mile wide and deep by four to five miles long. How the bombers withstood this obstacle was not only incredible, but also a testament to the crew's courage and resolve. At that point, enemy fighter activity was also being concentrated so the proverbial 'All hell broke loose!' was an accurate statement.
>
> "We fighter pilots were trying to keep in formation with our flight leaders and at the same time swiveling our heads 360-degrees, looking for enemy aircraft. Our adrenaline was going at 100%. It only took a moment in this kind of situation for a pilot to become separated from his flight and squadron as we were all over the sky. That happened to me this time when suddenly I found myself with nobody around and deep in German territory. In our briefing, we were told the group was supposed to proceed south to a city called Chemnitz, near the Czech border. We were to pick up some planes from the 15th Air Force near there and escort them back towards home. They had come up from Italy to bomb near Chemnitz. I proceeded south and found a batch of 20-24 B-24 bombers flying fairly low and in a good formation. I positioned myself high and to the right which put the sun to my rear. That way, if there was any attack on the bombers, I would be in a good position to engage them.
>
> "The bombers flew at a much slower speed that my P-51 so I had to reduce my power to stay in position with them. I also leaned out my fuel mixture to conserve as much of it as I could. I learned this technique from Captain Robin Olds, [434th FS] who led several previous missions I took part in. As it happened, my lone escort of the 15th AF planes this day was uneventful. As I approached Munich, I left them to head home. I did not see another aircraft after that. Back home, on my approach flare out to land at Wattisham, my engine quit. I was out of gas! I made the landing and rolled to a stop. I had to call the tower to ask for someone to come out and tow me back to the squadron's hardstands. That was a long mission for me."

Observations made during the mission included the interesting notation that while the group was heading in and still over the Zuider Zee, an unidentified foreign language was heard on "A" channel. It was believed not to be German. A V2 was seen in the vicinity of Zutphen. There was a lot of smoke at both Celle and Hannover. The airfield at Wesendorf had three to five unidentified aircraft parked on it. Between Burg and Magdeburg, the Elbe Canal was loaded with traffic and there were fires along the canal, northwest of Magdeburg. One bomber was seen in the center of the airfield at Jüterbog. There were smudge pots at both Merseburg and Ruhland. While in the target area, it was noted that in addition to the three 8th AF P-51 groups, there was an unidentified 15th AF P-51 group present. There seemed to be a possible underground oil storage area to the west of Ruhland. That area was the most heavily defended by flak. It seemed like all the chimneys at Merseburg were smoking. The airfield at Biebelstadt had 15 plus single-engine aircraft parked on the southern portion of the field. There were also approximately six aircraft, believed to be Me

163s, parked on a road to the south of the east-west runway. Each of the Me 163s was surrounded by four light AA guns. Although the field appeared to have been heavily bombed, there were only three to four destroyed planes to be seen on it. Train traffic between Berlin and Magdeburg was heavy. The airfield at Ansbach had four twin-engine and ten single-engine aircraft parked on it. The field at Wertheim had 20 unidentified single-engine aircraft parked. A storage dump or an army camp was spotted at Köfering, about six miles southeast of Regensburg. While in the vicinity of Aschaffenburg, a large mushrooming cloud with a black base, similar in appearance to a thunderhead, was seen ballooning up to 20,000 feet north of the city. It was thought to be a violent explosion. Twelve to fifteen barrage balloons were seen at 2-3,000 ft. along the Rhine River below the Remagen bridgehead. Flak from Dresden to Ruhland and over Ruhland was heavy, intense and accurate. It was heavy, moderate and accurate over Torgau and heavy, meager and accurate at Halle.

23 March 1945

Eighth AF FO 1819A

No. 319 Friday. Capt. Hooker led the group, which consisted of 30 P-51s (10-434th, 10-435th & 10-436th) on a penetration to target and withdrawal escort for 2nd AD, 96th CW B-24s attacking their 8th AF Mission 908 primary target, the marshalling yards at Osnabrück, Germany. Up: 0905 hrs., down: 1440 hrs. with a total of one early return.

Having crossed into Holland in the vicinity of The Hague, the group R/V'd with their assigned B-24s eight miles northeast of Bergen at 1000 hrs./23,000 ft. The quick trip into Germany and to the target was uneventful, but successful, as the bombing results were called excellent. The attackers left the yards in ruin with large oil fires and columns of smoke rising in the clear sky. While returning, the escorts saw two B-24s from other CWs hit by flak and explode over Münster within minutes of each other. The first bomber went down at 1117 hrs. and the second was lost at 1122 hrs. No parachutes were seen to come from either one. A jet was seen in the Hamm area, but when the P-51s went after it, the enemy pilot poured on the coal and left them wanting. All they had for their efforts was the sight of a dissipating smoke trail from the jet disappearing in the distance. One of the 96th Combat Wing Big Friends had been hit by flak near the target. Identified as "6A" (467th BG, 789th BS), the bomber had its right inboard engine out. As the force headed home, escorts flew with the plane until east of the Zuider Zee where they broke from the Liberator at 1120 hrs./14,000 ft. The rest of the group broke from the heavies over the Zuider Zee at 1136 hrs./23,000 ft.

One flight was assigned the duty of escorting a command Mosquito. The Mossie, marked "N" was picked up 26 miles north of Meppel, Holland at 1000 hrs./24,000 ft. and escorted through the target and back out to break away near Meppel at 1150 hrs./21,000 ft. Communication with the command A/C was limited as the escorts were only able to raise it on "C" channel once. Nuthouse, their controller, also failed to raise the Mosquito.

After breakaway, the fighters turned back toward Germany and entered that country's airspace again to sweep the areas of Hamm, Kassel, Giessen and Frankfurt. In the vicinity of Giessen, they were vectored to bogies by Nuthouse, but the bogies turned out to be P-47s. With no activity to be had except for one jet, which was unreachable, the group left for home, making L/O over Walcheren Island, Holland at 1405 hrs./ 11,000 ft.

Observations made during the mission included a V2 that was seen between The Hague and Utrecht at 0936 hrs. The marshalling yards at Hamm and Rheine appeared to be well clobbered, as did the airfield at Achmer. The airfield at Nordhorn had ten plus single-engine A/C parked on it. A grass airfield was spotted east of Kassel, but there was no activity on it. Münster and Bremen were covered with smoke. Flak from a woods five miles west of Darmstadt, from a site twelve miles south of Dümmer Lake and from another site eight miles west of Osnabrück was heavy, moderate and accurate. It was heavy, intense and accurate over Osnabrück and Münster.

24 March 1945

Eighth AF FO 1828

No. 320, 321 & 322 Saturday. The group was divided into three forces, A, B and C groups, all in support of Operation VARSITY. Capt. Pierce led A group, which consisted of 27 P-51s (8-434th, 10-435th & 9-436th) on a withdrawal escort and area patrol in support of 3rd AD B-17s attacking their 8th AF Mission 911 primary targets, airfields in western and northwestern Germany. Up: 0700 hrs., down: 1235 hrs. with no early returns. Col. Riddle led B group, which consisted of 34 P-51s (9-434th, 12-435th & 13-436th) on an area patrol. Up: 1030 hrs., down: 1558 hrs. with no early returns. First

Lieutenant Robert J. Baird led C group, which consisted of eight P-51s (4-434th & 4-435th) on an escort for a 25th BG Mosquito flying a reconnaissance mission into Germany. Up: 0738 hrs., down: 1310 hrs with no early returns.

Operation VARSITY – the airborne assault across the Rhine River and into the German heartland by the British 6th and the U.S. 17th Airborne Divisions. Crossings had been made previously to this attack, i.e., the first Allied bridgehead via the Ludendorff Bridge and subsequently built pontoon bridges at Remagen allowed four U.S. divisions, including an armored division, to cross there. Further crossings had been made and troops were engaging the Germans east of the Rhine, but this was to be the great assault by land and air. Allied air forces had been concentrating their efforts for the past four days in an attempt to isolate the Ruhr area completely and to knock out German defenses in preparation for the operation. Airfields from which enemy aircraft might launch attacks were neutralized, as were marshalling yards through which reinforcements and supplies would be sent. Bridges and roads were also subjected to Allied ordnance delivered by strategic and tactical aircraft. General George S. Patton's forces crossed the Rhine at Oppenheim after a quick drive from their bridgehead at the Moselle. He had succeeded in getting some 5,000 men across the Rhine during the night of the 22/23rd with the loss of only eight men. Throughout the night of the 23/24th, British and U.S. artillery pounded German positions across the river in an attempt to soften the defenses as troops from both countries poured across the water. By dawn, the Allies had control of the eastern side of the Rhine between Wesel and Rees. Having learned their lessons the hard way at Arnhem, Allied planners sought first to have ground forces in place before the airborne troops were dropped. At 1000 hours, Operation VARSITY, that largest airborne invasion ever, commenced under the watchful eye of no less than that of Winston Churchill who was in a command post on the west side of the river. Escorted by almost 900 fighters, 2,029 U.S. Army gliders and their tow aircraft, plus 832 similar aircraft from the RAF, flew in an enormous two-and-a-half-hour long stream over the Rhine. Flak took its toll, but not a single GAF plane was able to get at the airborne operation. More than 40,000 paratroopers were dropped in the area around Hamminkeln and, in all, some 14,500 troops, 109 tons of ammunition, 645 vehicles, 113 artillery pieces, as well as numerous other quantities of equipment and supplies, were flown and landed across the river. The operation was a success and many German soldiers were taken prisoner.

A group made L/F north of Ijmuiden, Holland at 0748 hrs./18,000 ft. and arrived in the Bremen area at 0830 hrs./ 27,000 ft. after crossing into Germany. They patrolled the areas of Bremen, Steinhuder Lake and Dümmer Lake until 0940 hrs. when the last B-17s were leaving the target areas. Tacking onto a trailing formation of Big Friends, the Little Friends escorted the bombers as far as Meppen where they broke from the Forts at 1000 hrs./22,000 ft. and flew on to Area "C" where their next patrol assignment was located. Encompassing an area that contained a large network of roads, canal and railroad routes that all generally headed south towards the location of the invasion, the region posed a threat because of the possible routes available to the Germans for transporting reinforcements and supplies. Area "C" was located on the northeast/west Dutch/German border and was roughly bounded by Oosterwolde to Enschede in Holland and Haren to Uelsen in Germany. A group spread out, and flying from 12,000 ft. to down on the deck, they patrolled and strafed targets of opportunity in the territory. There was no heavy military-type traffic of any sort seen in the area, only trucks in two and threes, headed in every direction. The strafing attacks tallied 6-0-6 trucks, 1-0-5 autos and busses, 10-0-5 horses and wagons, 3-0-14 barges, 5-0-0 personnel, 0-0-3 small boats and a flak trap disguised as a house. By 1145 hours, they had reached the end of their assigned patrol time and the group headed out making L/O over Ijmuiden.

Observations made during the mission included thirty railroad cars with no engine seen in the Ommen marshalling yard. The airfields at Vechta, Cloppenburg and Quackenbrück were well hit and had numerous fires going. Ammo dumps were spotted just south of the perimeter track off the airfield at Havelta. There were numerous oil fires north of the airfield proper at Diepholz. Throughout area "C", but concentrated around Gramsbergen, Holland, there were barracks-like buildings arranged either in a square or a "U" shaped cluster. They each had a white flag flying from a pole in a central court and there appeared to be only women around. Flak 20 miles west of Lingen was light, intense and accurate. South of the tip of Vlieland, it was heavy, meager and inaccurate.

No. 321 B group made L/F north of Ijmuiden at 1113 hrs./ 12,000 ft. and arrived in area "C" (boundaries as described above) at 1136 hrs./11,000 ft. Stacked up in layers, the group patrolled and strafed by squadron, each heading down and back up in turn, until 1459 hrs. Results of the strafing were as follows: 5-0-1 staff and passenger cars, 3-0-4 trucks, 1-0-0 radio truck, 0-0-1 barrack, 0-0-20 camouflaged wagons, 1-0-

0 radar tower and adjacent installation, 0-0-9 personnel. During the time they were patrolling, Nuthouse gave them several vectors towards bogies, but all turned out to be friendlies. There was very little military activity of any sort. In fact, Col Riddle is quoted as having made the comment: "Not even kites were flying." L/O was through Holland.

Observations made during the mission included two camps and a stationary truck convoy seen near Gramsbergen. Twenty-five horse-drawn vehicles were leaving one of the camp's compounds. There were also 100-150 people, dressed in khaki uniforms, standing around outside a compound there and waving as the P-51s looked them over at 200 ft. The people made no effort to run or get under cover. At another location, what was described as a cluster of buildings surrounded by barbed wire and what was presumed to be a concentration camp, was investigated. It was noted that a person who was probably an inmate, stood in the yard and waved at the planes. Four buildings with red crosses painted on their tops were seen along some railroad tracks at another location. A radio station and a tower, both encircled by six more towers, was also spotted. Flak coming from a site near a barrack adjacent to a radar station was light, intense and accurate. Flak three miles north of Zwolle was heavy, but there were only eight or nine bursts. Flak at Almelo was light, intense and accurate. There was both heavy and light, intense and accurate flak at Hoogeveen.

No. 322 C group's eight P-51s joined the command recce Mosquito "Rollo" over Wattisham and escorted him from there through L/F over Knokke-Hiest, Belgium at 0813 hrs./11,000 ft. Crossing the Rhine above Koblenz in Germany, the escorts maintained top cover as the Mosquito investigated various areas while down on the deck. Heading north to Dümmer Lake and thence to Steinhuder Lake, then down along the Ems-Weser Canal, where "Rollo" made a dozen snappy orbits along the canal. In his wanderings, "Rollo" almost flew directly over Hannover and Bielefeld. The Mustangs were stalling out in their attempts to follow the recce bird. He was not making any points with his escorts. At approximately 1100 hours, "Rollo" told Nuthouse that he couldn't find what he was looking for and that his equipment wasn't working right anyway, so he was going home. The eight P-51s left "Rollo" ten miles southeast of Bonn at 1158 hrs./6,000 ft. when he said he was happy and that his Little Friends could go home. The timing was good as they were getting low on gas anyway. L/O was over Walcheren Island at 1230 hrs./11,000 ft.

Observations made during the wanderings of "Rollo" included four to five hundred goods wagons and three engines with their steam up spotted at Peine. The town of Hildesheim appeared to be on fire as seen at 1145 hrs. Thirty plus balloons were floating at 700 ft. near Giessen. Flak at Minden was light, meager and accurate with red tracers. At Limburg, it was heavy, moderate and inaccurate. At Brunswick, it was heavy, moderate and accurate. Over Hachenburg, it was heavy, meager and accurate.

24 March 1945

Eighth AF FO 1828A

No. 323 Saturday. In another series of missions for this date, Capt. Pierce led C group, which consisted of 29 P-51s (10-434th, 10-435th & 9-436th) on a MEW sweep from the Osnabrück area of Germany in support of Operation VARSITY. Up: 1529 hrs., down: 1935 hrs. with no early returns.

C group made L/F over Alkmaar, Holland at 1605 hrs./15,000 ft. and after crossing into Germany, arrived in the Osnabrück area at 1650 hours, 15,000 ft. Nuthouse took over control at this point and vectored the fighters to various locations including, Diepholz, Dümmer Lake, Kassel, Lippstadt, Fritzlar, back to Kassel, Paderborn, back to Lippstadt, on to Rheine and then out to L/O, which they made near Ijmuiden at 1840 hrs./13,000 ft. Everything that Nuthouse had to offer was identified as friendly. One bogie was chased from Osnabrück to Vechta, but was lost in the haze and smoke. The sweep was entirely uneventful.

Observations made during the mission included an oil fire spotted in the town of Rheine. The bombing results at Gutersloh appeared to be excellent. A grass airstrip northwest of Gutersloh was also clobbered and there was a fire there. The airfield at Vechta was still burning. Lippstadt's airfield was bare. There were no aircraft, no trucks, no nothing. Fritzlar's airfield showed no signs of activity, but looked serviceable. Most of western Germany seemed to be on fire and/or smoking. No trains or highway traffic were observed, nor was anything of a military nature spotted. Flak over Zwolle was heavy, intense and accurate.

No. 324 First Lt. Wendt led eight P-51s (4-434th & 4-435th) on an escort for a 25th BG Mosquito flying a reconnaissance mission into Germany. Up: 1510 hrs., down: 1845 hrs. with no early returns.

The escorts R/V'd with the Mossie over Wattisham at 1520 hrs./2,000 ft. and set course for Belgium. Making L/F over Knokke at 1615 hrs./12,000 feet, their charge took the escorts east past Antwerp, then turned to the southeast. Entering

Germany at Aachen, they continued on in the same direction, through the areas of the Remagen bridgehead and Limburg. Heading north, the nine planes flew to Siegen, then northeast toward the Kassel area. The Mosquito did a good bit of weaving, flying at 18,500 ft. with the P-51s tacked on slightly above at 19,000 ft. and 500-1,000 yards behind. About 1700 hours, Nuthouse called in bogies at one and two o'clock, headed west and others at three o'clock, heading east. The bogies heading west were identified as two flights of P-47s flying at 17,000 ft. Four of the eight P-47s made a 270-degree turn and flew in formation with the escorts and their charge. Two of the P-47s finally crossed under the Mustangs and the Mosquito, passing from left to right. The other two Thunderbolts stayed well out to the left and a little behind. The recce force tried contacting the P-47 pilots on "C" channel, but had no success. The Mossie pilot then turned into them to flash his colors as they came up. (25th BG Mosquitoes were frequently mistakenly identified as German Me 410s and attacked. As a consequence, the all-gray painted aircraft were distinctively marked, with their entire tail section, from the rearmost portion of the fuselage back, painted red as a means of identification.) Having completed a 360-degree turn to enable the intruding pilots to identify his aircraft, he then turned back on a northeasterly course. Noticing the maneuvers, Nuthouse contacted the force and asked what was happening, at which point the controller was informed as to what had occurred. Back on course, the Mosquito began to weave and then turned left. The two P-47s turned inside the Mustangs and closed down on the recce bird. One of the P-51 pilots radioed the Mossie pilot, telling him that the Thunderbolts were closing on him and he replied that he thought they were the 51s. First Lieutenant Eugene H. Wendt dropped his wing tanks and stated he was going down after the 47s. Meanwhile, the two P-47s got into position and began firing at the Mosquito. Its pilot yelled for his escorts to get them off his tail. Lt. Wendt called for the Mossie to break, but the airplane remained level and turning slightly to the left. The T-Bolts got hits on the recce A/C's tail and stopped both its engines, causing the left one to burst into flames. The Mosquito broke into three pieces and tumbled down. At 10,000 feet, one parachute appeared and opened safely. Lt. Wendt got into position on the P-47s numerous times, but each time the T-Bolt pilots rocked their wings violently, so he held off. After the Mossie had gone down, two other pilots from the escort group chased the P-47s all over the sky and stated that they were going to follow the intruding fighters to their base. The P-47s were described as having a yellow ring around their nose, yellow tails and bearing the markings 7UV and M70 (Ninth AF markings).

First Lieutenant Clarence G. Haynes in his L2-D Rabid Rebel over Hannover, Germany. *Courtesy of Clarence G. Haynes.*

Lieutenant William M. Barsky, who led the four 435th FS P-51s during the escort, gave this statement regarding the incident:

> "While on a course of 180 degrees, a flight of P-47s flew through us and the Mosquito we were escorting. The Mosquito made a slow turn to the left and a steep diving turn to the left, completing a 360-degree turn and pulled up. Two of the P-47s pulled up underneath us, in trail with the Mosquito and about 1,000-1,200 yards away from him. I advised the Mosquito pilot that two P-47s were on his tail and he acknowledged the call. The P-47s then closed on the Mosquito. As I nosed down to get on the P-47s and cut them off, the Mosquito pilot called and said he was hit and to clear his tail. A few seconds later, the Mosquito's left engine burst into flame, the aircraft broke in half and spun in. I closed on one of the P-47s and opened

The P-51 that First Lieutenant Eugene H. Wendt named and flew as much as possible. *Eugene H. Wendt courtesy of Stephen Decker.*

fire at 800 yards. I called my White Flight Leader [Lt. Wendt] to cover the Mosquito and told him I would take care of the P-47s. I closed on the P-47s and stopped shooting, as there was no continuation of aggression by the pilots. I pulled alongside the P-47s and spoke to one of the pilots on "D" channel, advising him that I would be going back to his base with him. I called Nuthouse and reported the P-47 markings and letters. I landed at the P-47 base and made a written report to Lt. Col. Slayden, the base C.O. [36th Fighter Group] The base is 20 miles west of Manager and is believed to be Le Culot [Belgium]. The remainder of the group flew to Siegen, Cologne and out to L/O over Walcheren Island at 1745 hrs./12,000 ft."

25 March 1945

Eighth AF FO 1835A

No. 325 & 326 Sunday. The group was divided into two forces, A and B groups, both penetration to target and withdrawal escorts for a CW of 2nd AD B-24s attacking their 8th AF Mission 913 primary target, the POL industry at Büchen, Germany. Capt. Anderson led A group, which consisted of 25 P-51s (9-434th & 16-436th). Up: 0723 hrs., down: 1234 hrs. with one early return. Maj. Jordan led B group, which consisted of 26 P-51s (8-434th & 18-435th). Up: 0729 hrs., down: 1231 hrs. with one early return.

A group made L/F in the vicinity of Den Helder, Holland at 0807 hours, layered between 19-21,000 ft. and B group made L/F near Bergen aan Zee, Holland at 0810 hours, stacked up between 23-30,000 ft. Colgate, their 65th FW controller, reported that the B-24s would be 35 minutes late so the P-51s orbited over their L/F areas, waiting for the heavies to appear. R/V was with the proper bombers at 0845 hrs./19-21,000 ft. over the coast of Holland. At this point, A group joined B group for the escort. During the R/V, five contrails were observed over the bomber stream at approximately 30,000 ft. They were to stay with the force, flying 15-20 miles ahead, apparently tracking the attacker's course. Maintaining those respective altitudes, the Big Friends were accompanied into Germany, where in the vicinity of Dümmer Lake, seven more unidentified aircraft pulling contrails joined the original five, coming in from the northwest. The dozen bogies stayed ahead and above the bombers and their escorts until 20 miles south of Büchen, where they were lost in other contrails. Arriving over the target, the B-24s dropped their ordnance at 1016 hrs. The results appeared to be excellent and resulted in heavy black smoke that changed to a dirty gray, covering the target area. At approximately 1020 hours, a call came from Vinegrove 2-1 in the bomber formation, reporting jets in the area. The caller also stated that some unidentified P-51s (possibly from the 352nd FG who were also in the area) had driven the jets down to the deck. However, one B-24 was seen at that time to be rapidly loosing altitude and apparently out of control. The eight Newcross Squadron aircraft from B group were up at 29,000 ft.

After the call, they swung to the north of the target and at approximately 1050 hours, saw two Me 262s attack the last box of bombers, about 20 miles southwest of Hamburg. Elements of *III./JG 7* had found the formation and were going after the Liberators. As the enemy aircraft attacked in line astern from five o'clock high, the 434th contingent dived into the attack in order to break it up. One B-24 flashed flame and then either it or another, peeled up in a steep climbing turn and three of the crew parachuted safely out. These were part of the four planes and crews lost to the swift German fighters by the 448th BG this day. One of the Me 262s went through the bomber formation with some unidentified P-51s after him. The other 262 pulled up to the right from about 21,000 ft. First Lieutenant Eugene H. Wendt, leading the Newcross section, attacked in a diving turn to the right from about 29,000 ft. Having the advantage of superior altitude from which he could dive and gain speed, Lt. Wendt caught up to the jet and opened fire from about 1,000 yards at 40-degrees head-on deflection. By the time he reached 25,000 feet, he had closed to only 50 yards. His continuous fire producing strikes all over the E/A, caused the Me 262 to break apart. It entered an uncontrollable spin to the right, crashed and burned. Two pilots from Lt. Wendt's Yellow Flight and another from Lakeside White Flight confirmed his victory, noting that many of the Lieutenant's strikes were in the cockpit area of his adversary and that they felt certain the German pilot was killed by the gunfire. German records also confirm these facts.

A few minutes later, Lakeside Squadron saw seven more Me 262s strung out in a line, making a pass at the bombers. The squadron went after them and five headed for the deck. Lieutenants Charles E. Heathman and Floyd W. Salze chased one of the remaining two to Hamburg where flak was put up between the E/A and the pursuers. Lt. Salze got some strikes on the aircraft, but it eventually got away. His report sheds some light on that action:

"We were flying behind and slightly above the box of bombers when I looked over to the right of the flight leader and saw about seven jets flying where another flight would be flying. I called them out to "Snow White" [the group's leader] and to my flight leader several times. Our original flight leader had gone home earlier [He would have been escorted by his wingman, number two in the flight.] so the number three man was leading the flight at the time. I was an odd man in the flight, so I flew as the second element leader. As the jet started in on the bombers from about five o'clock to them, I called them in as coming and I kept waiting for the flight leader to go after them. I later found that my radio was bad, so no one heard me. After the jets passed in front of me, I broke after them and fired at one. All but two went down in a dive at that point. Someone shot at one of the two and I followed the other one up and to the right. He went out about five miles and turned to the right again. Still on his tail, I fired a short burst at him, but he was out of range. As we got lower, I began to gain on him, but as we passed over Hamburg, I noticed that I was down to firing tracers and recognized that I didn't have much ammunition left. I observed some strikes around the fuselage and one wing, but then flak began coming up at me from the Hamburg area. I dodged the flak and lost the jet in the haze. Just before I lost him, he was giving out brown smoke from the plane's right engine and I assume he must have added power. I claim one Me 262 damaged."

German records indicate that Second Lt. Salze did in fact damage an Me 262 flown by *Oberfähnrich* Ullrich from *III./ JG 7*. The aircraft was reported as looking like a sieve, with more than thirty holes in it.

With all the action over, the escorts returned to duty and took the Big Friends out to L/O where A group broke away over Schiermonnikoog Island, Holland. and B group broke away 25 miles northwest of Groningen, Holland.

Observations made during the mission included the small ineffective smoke screens seen at Bad Oeynhausen and at Minden. Smoke pots were also present at Hannover and Magdeburg. At Hannover, there was a column of black smoke with a white boiling center raising to 19,000 ft. Osnabrück was suffering the same conditions, with black smoke/white center towering over the city. A jet airfield was spotted southeast of Lüneburg, in the vicinity of Hohenzethen. There were 20 jets parked there, all lined up in a straight row. Three Fw 190s were seen stooging around in the Büchen target area. Flak over Büchen was heavy, meager and inaccurate. It was heavy, moderate and inaccurate near Hamburg and over Hannover, it was heavy, intense and inaccurate.

26 March 1945

Eighth AF FO 1842A

No. 327 Monday. Col. Riddle led the group, which consisted of 39 P-51s (14-434th, 14-435th & 11-436th) on a penetration to target and withdrawal escort for a CW of 1st AD B-17s attacking their 8th AF Mission 915 primary POL target at Zeitz, Germany. Up: 1136 hrs., down: 1730 hrs. with a total of six early returns plus one escort.

L/F was over Ostend, Belgium at 1226 hrs./18,000 ft. and R/V was with their assigned bombers plus another box, Vinegrove 1-3, over Germany at 1358 hrs./18,500 ft. They were taken through the Zeitz area where the B-17s made two runs over the target. Although there was a front extending from England to Frankfurt, the skies were clear here, so bombing was visual and the bombing results appeared to be excellent. The escort was uneventful and the Big Friends were shepherded back as far as Fulda, where the fighters broke from the bombers at 1540 hrs./18,500 ft. L/O was in the vicinity of Knokke, Belgium at 1630 hrs.

Observations made during the mission included the sighting of a big oil fire southeast of Giessen and the notation that the airfield there also had a huge fire going on it. Giessen had eight large buildings marked with red crosses. The barracks and hangar areas at the airfield near Hanau were on fire. Five or six trains running east and west between Gotha and Erfurt were seen. A parachute was seen at 1307 hours, south of Aachen. This is about the same time that a radio transmission was heard concerning a B-17 crew bailing out. This was heard despite German jamming on the radios. There was no flak over the target at Zeitz. Flak over Limburg was heavy, meager and inaccurate as it was 20 miles northeast of Koblenz. Flak at Sieburg was light, meager and inaccurate.

Lieutenant Jesse F. Morris from the 436th FS had to bail out of his plane near Great Ashfield for reasons unknown. He was hospitalized with temporary amnesia.

30 March 1945

Eighth AF FO 1863A

No. 328 Friday. Maj. Olds led the group, which consisted of 55 P-51s (18-434th, 18-435th & 19-436th) on a penetration to target and withdrawal escort for two CWs of 2nd AD B-24s attacking their 8th AF Mission 918 primary target, the U-boat facilities at Wilhelmshaven, Germany. Up: 1215 hrs., down: 1855 hrs. with no early returns. The weather had held up most air operations for the past several days, but the offensive was on the roll once again even though there was a large front with 10/10ths cloud coverage extending from England's coast, up and over the North Sea and nearly to the continent.

L/F was over Den Helder, Holland at 1258 hrs./16,500 ft. and R/V with the proper bombers, Vinegrove 2-3 and 2-4, was north of Anjum, Holland at 1310 hrs./21,000 ft. The group provided close escort for the next ten minutes at which point their MEW controller informed them that the 355th FG would be replacing them as escorts for Vinegrove 2-4. They then moved up the stream and kept watchful eyes over Vinegrove 2-2 and 2-3 as the force approached the target. Wilhelmshaven came up fast with a time over target of 1336 hrs./26,000 ft. The group orbited the city at 27,000 ft. and picked up Vinegrove 2-3 and 2-4 as they came off the target, giving 2-2 over to the 56th FG. The Big Friends reported no enemy activity, but MEW control did have information on jets located between the target and Hamburg. The Little Friends did not leave to investigate. L/O was in the vicinity of Wilhelmshaven at 1348/26,000 ft. Three P-51s from the 436th FS, who had been tasked to escort a command Mosquito for the mission, followed the Mossie from the target, on over to Hamburg. The bombing was observed to be good there. The bombers were taken as far as 25 miles west of Terschelling Island where the fighters broke from their Big Friends at 1430 hrs./6,000 ft. After breakaway, one squadron, apparently looking for some sort of activity, swept back to Kassel and then on to Salzwedel, Brandenburg and finally homeward, all without incident.

Observations made during the mission included noting the bombing results were excellent, but there were possible hits in the city of Wilhelmshaven. One box of 12 B-24s trailing the second force orbited the target, but was not observed to release their bombs. False target markers were observed being fired into the air from the ground in an open area about ten miles south of Wilhelmshaven. The false markers were much like the real target markers, but the smoke plume fell straight downward without the curving, horizontal trajectory characteristic of markers released from moving aircraft. The false markers also appeared to be less dense and had a smaller flare than the genuine article. The false markers were first sighted just after the lead boxes of heavies passed over the deception area. There were a number of ship sightings reported, with 15 medium-sized vessels apparently evacuated from the dock area, seen dispersed in the bay by Wilhelmshaven, 11 medium-sized vessels anchored in the vicinity of Alte Mellum, 14 anchored south of Wangerooge and 10 anchored south of Schiermonnikoog. An ineffective smoke screen was being laid over the southern mouth of the Kaiser Wilhelm Canal (Nord-Ostsee Kanal). A single jet was seen parked on the perimeter of an airfield just north of Münster. The factories at Brunswick were in operation as smoke was seen coming from most of their chimneys. An OA-10 Catalina was spotted on the water 50 miles west of Texel Island at 1515 hrs. Neither of the aircraft's engines was running and a crewmember was shooting off green flares as three B-24s circled above. The situation and location were relayed to Colgate who gave the okay signal. Flak over Wilhelmshaven was heavy, intense and accurate. Over Heligoland, it was heavy, moderate and accurate. At Schiermonnikoog, flak was heavy, intense and inaccurate in the vicinity of Vinegrove 2-1. The rest of the force avoided it. Flak at Tönning was heavy, meager and accurate. Midway between Rheine and Osnabrück, heavy, meager, inaccurate flak was coming from a wood.

31 March 1945

Eighth AF FO 1874A

No. 329 & 330 Saturday. The group was divided into two forces, A and B groups, both penetration to target and withdrawal escorts for 2nd AD B-24s attacking their 8th AF Mission 920 secondary target, the marshalling yards at Brunswick (Braunschweig), Germany. Maj. Duffié led A group, which consisted of 32 P-51s (14-434th & 18-436th). Up: 0714 hrs., down: 1141 hrs. with no early returns. Maj. Jordan led B group, which consisted of 30 P-51s (8-434th & 22-435th). Up: 0726 hrs., down: 1152 hrs. with three early returns plus two escorts. The weather over the continent consisted of undercast clouds with tops 5-8,000 ft. from east of the Zuider Zee. Few breaks in the clouds were seen.

A group made L/F near Egmond, Holland at 0806 hrs./ 18,000 ft. R/V at 0818 hrs./20,000 ft. with the proper bombers was over Urk, on the western side of Holland's northeast polder. Escort for the heavies was provided to the target where time over target was 0906 hrs./24,000 ft. A layer of undercast obscured the bombing results. During the trip in to the target, two of the P-51s R/V'd with a command Mosquito flying above the bomber stream. The element of Little Friends provided close escort as the Mossie stooged all around above the formations. Just prior to arriving over the target, one flight took over the escort duty for five more Mosquitoes. These were flying as a screening force whose function was to dispense "chaff".

B group made L/F north of Ijmuiden, Holland at 0808 hrs./14,000 ft. They R/V'd with their B-24s over the Zuider Zee, in the Stavroen, Holland area at 0817 hrs./17,000 ft. Reaching the target area, bombs away was at 0912 hrs./22,000 ft. The undercast prevented the results from being seen.

Right over the target, four to six Me 262s, flying in elements, approached the B-24s from 12 o'clock and drove right down the bomber formation, turned and attacked from high and dead astern. The jets dived from 28,000 feet to below the bombers and then fired at them from below while in a climb. The jets did not rise above the bombers, but instead split-essed away to return and repeat the attacks. During the first attack, the lead box of the 2nd CW was hit and one of the bombers exploded. Two jets were also seen to attack a box of B-17s off to the right, but no results were noted. P-51s from both groups, along with fighters from the 361st FG and the 4th FG, immediately swarmed all over the enemy aircraft, causing them to split up. In breaking away, the jet aircraft ducked in and out of the cloud deck as they headed east. Before they got away, B-24 gunners managed to hit one of the jets in its right engine and thus slowed it down. Maj. Jordan chased that plane down to the deck where P-51s from the 355th FG came out of the clouds and clobbered the E/A at 1,000 ft. The jet crashed.

When the Me 262s were split up, two headed east were bounced by Newcross Red Flight in the vicinity of Braunschweig. An interesting coincidence occurred at this point. First Lieutenant Robert I. Bromschwig was flying as Newcross Red Three in the attacking flight. Lt. Bromschwig's family name was once Braunschweig, but was Americanized by the Lieutenant's grandfather on his father's side when he immigrated to the United States from Braunschweig, Germany. At the time, Lt. Bromschwig still had relatives living in the area he was flying above. The coincidence had no bearing, however, as the Lieutenant was successful in tacking on behind one of the swift German fighters for a few moments. He gave this report of the events:

A frame from the gun camera film First Lieutenant Robert I. Bromschwig exposed as he shot at the Me 262 he chased. A hit can be seen registering in the center of the jet's left engine pod. *Courtesy of Robert I. Bromschwig.*

"At 0910 hours, Me 262s were called in at 12 o'clock, high to the bombers flying at 21,000 feet. White and Red Flights were level with the bombers on the right side and the jets were reported on the left side, traveling 180 degrees to the bomber track. We started a 180-degree turn to the right and as I looked over my left shoulder, I saw a bomber explode, apparently hit by a jet. We had finished about 90 degrees of our turn when I first sighted the jet at 14,000 feet, off three o'clock to me. I reefed around to the left in a diving turn in order to head him off, as he was traveling parallel to the bomber stream at the time. I fell in line astern with him and framed the ship in my K-14 gunsight at 1,100 feet. I fired from 1,100 feet to about 2,400 feet, observing a few strikes right behind his canopy and a small puff of black smoke came from the aircraft's right nacelle. The 262 nosed down and rapidly pulled away from me in a 45-degree dive. I was indicating approximately 475 mph at the time I gave up the chase. I claim one Me 262 as damaged."

Second Lieutenant Clarence L. Waters was flying as Newcross Red Four, Lt. Bromschwig's wingman, and confirmed the damaged claim.

Shortly after Lt. Bromschwig's attack on an Me 262, First Lieutenant Robert J. Baird found another to go after north of Braunschweig. He wrote the following Encounter Report:

> "I was leading Lakeside Blue Flight and along with Yellow Flight, we were covering the bombers over the target. As we orbited, an Me 262 crossed beneath us at a lower altitude and at about 150 degrees to my direction

of flight. I rolled over and tried to close on him, using full power. I gave him a burst from 3-400 yards and noted strikes on his right wing root and on his fuselage. The E/A was gradually pulling away as I fired again, this time without results. With the jet out of range, I then returned to our bomber box in order to furnish further escort. I claim one Me 262 as damaged."

With the bombing attack completed and the fight over, the force was homeward bound. The fighters from A group broke from the Big Friends northeast of Alkmaar, Holland at 1045 hrs./24,000 ft. and L/O was north of Egmond at 1048 hrs./20,000 ft. L/O and breakaway for the escorts of the single Mosquito command ship was over Bergen at 1050 hrs./12,000 ft. L/O for the escorts of the chaff Mossies was over Vlieland, Holland at 1015 hrs./18,000 ft. The five Mosquitoes were accompanied as far home as Lowestoft, England, arriving in that area at 1050 hrs. B group broke away from the bombers over the Zuider Zee near Medemblik, Holland at 1047 hrs./12,000 ft. and made L/O over Bergen, Holland at 1050 hrs./6,500 ft.

Observations made during the mission included four Me 262s that were seen in the target area, but did not attack. One Me 262 had a white-tipped, red nose with a gray fuselage and wings. Some of the jets looked blue-black with yellow markings. It was believed that the 361st FG destroyed one Me 262. One bomber from the third box of B-24s exploded over the target. No chutes were seen. During the trip back home, one unidentified aircraft exploded southeast of Alkmaar and crashed to the ground. An oil slick was spotted in about the middle of the North Sea when the groups were crossing from England to the continent. Flak over Brunswick/Braunschweig was heavy, meager and accurate. Three miles north of the target, it was heavy, meager and inaccurate.

436th FS armorers Private First Class Thomas W. Richards and Staff Sergeant Carl F. Withrow. *Carroll C. Sprague Collection, courtesy of the East Essex Aviation Society.*

436th FS armorers, the first of which is unknown and Corporal Thomas E. O'Malley are posed by Major Clifford J. Moore's P-51 The Uninvited. *Carroll C. Sprague Collection, courtesy of the East Essex Aviation Society.*

Lieutenant Clifford W. Bowers is pictured flying his Skunk Chaser near a British B-25. *Courtesy of David L. Born.*

Right: 435th FS crew chief Technical Sergeant Charlton N. Harmon is beside his Lady Jean, a P-51 named by Lieutenant Robert H. Horman. *Courtesy of Robert H. Horman.*

Captain Thomas R. Brown was the Protestant Chaplain for the group and he is shown here, busy as usual. *Courtesy of Clarence G. Haynes.*

Crew chief Staff Sergeant Thomas J. O'Grady and Captain Donald J. Pierce are standing beside their P-51 Setonia No. 3. The aircraft was the third of three presentation aircraft purchased through the efforts of the students at Seton Hall Preparatory School (then located in South Orange and now West Orange, New Jersey) in a War Loan Drive. The first Setonia went to the 12th Tactical Reconnaissance Squadron in England and the second went to the 2nd Air Commandos in India. The students placed a letter in the cockpit of each of the aircraft requesting that the Setonia name be painted on the plane's nose so that the name of the school would always be held aloft. Further, the letter explained how the students were able to purchase the aircraft and noted that the pilots would always be in their prayers. *Courtesy of Berkley E. Hollister.*

The pilot and crew of L2-Y, Just Born, a Newcross bird. First Lieutenant David L. Born, the man who named the plane, is seen crouching top center. He is surrounded by, from left to right, assistant crew chief Corporal Guy M. Purdy, crew chief Technical Sergeant John E. Gilchrist and armorer Corporal James B. Dillon. *Courtesy of David L. Born.*

Right: Some of the guys who maintained the Bison aircraft are seen here with one of their charges. *Carroll C. Sprague Collection, courtesy of the East Essex Aviation Society.*

Lieutenant Dalton F. Tommie flying L2-O, Boomerang "Jr." *Courtesy of David L. Born.*

The P-51 that Lieutenant Eugene E. Sears painted the name American Maid on is being fueled for another mission. *Courtesy of David L. Born.*

Some of the 434th FS armorers gathered for this picture of another 434th Mustang, L2-T, being readied for bore sighting. *Courtesy of Loetta Taylor (Kennedy).*

Lieutenant Thomas (Tommy) H. Thompson and crew chief Technical Sergeant Clarence O. Marlar by their 436th FS plane, Weezy. *Courtesy of Thomas H. Thompson.*

Left: Darlin Fran was the 435th FS airplane the Lieutenant Glen W. Hill named and flew during his time at Wattisham. *Courtesy of Robert H. Horman.*

Scat VI, one of Major Robin Olds' 434th FS aircraft. *Courtesy of David L. Born.*

Below: Rosita, a 436th FS P-51. It is possible that this is the aircraft that Lieutenant Raymond E. Henry named King's Queen, but that is only speculation. *Courtesy of James R. Helms.*

435th FS armorers Staff Sergeant Ralph N. Piepenburg and Corporal Clayton J. Lanning. *Courtesy of Clarence G. Haynes.*

434th FS airplane mechanics – Corporal Regis P. Marhefky and Technical Sergeant Henry J. Robitz were the men who kept The Rabid Rebel well-tuned. *Courtesy of Clarence G. Haynes.*

CHAPTER FIFTEEN

APRIL 1945

2 April 1945

Eighth AF FO 1882A

No. 331 & 332 Monday. The group was divided into two forces, A and B groups, both penetration to target and withdrawal escorts for 2nd AD, 96th CW B-24s attacking their 8th AF Mission 922 primary targets, airfields at Ringkøbing and Tirstrup, Denmark. Maj. Jordan led A group, which consisted of 17 P-51s from the 435th FS. Up: 1412 hrs., down: 1838 hrs. with one early return. Maj. Olds led B group, which consisted of 33 P-51s (17-434th & 16-436th). Up: 1414 hrs., down: 1830 hrs. with two early returns.

The climate over East Anglia had taken a turn for the better and would remain so until mid-month. It seemed as though spring had had finally arrived and the men of the 479th Fighter Group were enjoying the finest weather they had experienced in some time. It was like that of Los Angeles, Hollywood and Santa Monica, California all rolled into one. The flying conditions were the best imaginable and all who could spare themselves from jobs, fled for the baseball diamonds, the volley-ball courts or wherever, just to let "Old Sol" bake their sun-starved bodies. This was in sharp contrast to what the pilots were to experience during this and later missions.

A group R/V'd with their assigned B-24s over the North Sea at a point approximately 50-60 miles northeast of Great Yarmouth, England at 1503 hrs./16,500 ft. B group R/V'd with their bombers at 1515 hrs./17,000 ft. and about another 110 miles farther northeast of A group's R/V point. The heavies were in poor formation with the boxes mixed up and not in the briefed order. Referencing the A/C tail markings, it was noted the boxes ran in the order of black on silver, black on white, white on red and yellow on black. As the lead groups approached the Jütland Peninsula, they began encountering a bad front with cloud tops up to 27,000 ft. that was present over the coast and inland. Due to the weather conditions, the mission was recalled. A and B groups began returning just after L/F in the vicinity of the Ringkøbing Fjord at 1605-1610 hrs./24-26,000 ft. The escorts broke away from the bombers over the North Sea near where they had first R/V'd with them. Breakaway was at 1745-1750 hrs./11-12,000 ft.

Returning to Wattisham, the 436th FS lost an aircraft when its pilot First Lieutenant Carl W. Sherer had an engine failure and had to bail out of his ship west of Ipswich. The plane dove into an open field and the Lieutenant landed nearby, shaken, but unhurt. For his successful egress, Lieutenant Sherer was awarded membership in the Caterpillar Club.

Observations made during the mission included many small boats seen milling around in the Zuider Zee just south of the causeway. There were four medium-sized merchantmen ships south of Borkum Island. No flak was reported.

4 April 1945

2nd AD Order Unk.

No. 333 Wednesday. First Lieutenant Clark R. Hoffman led four P-51s (2-434th & 2-435th) on an Air-Sea Rescue mission to the vicinity of Holland. Up: 0550 hrs., down: 1110 hrs. with no early returns.

The four P-51s R/V'd with an RAF Warwick over the vicinity of Beccles, England at 0615 hrs./2,000 ft. The five headed east across the water, arriving off the coast of Holland where they searched the area north of Borkum Island from 0730 to 0945 hrs. At 0755 hours, they spotted a smoke signal from the six survivors of an OA-10 Catalina that had been unable to take off after rescuing some ditched bomber crewmen on 30 March 1945. (See observations made from 30 March 1945.) A second smoke signal was observed at 0810 hrs. Twenty minutes later, the Mustangs and the Warwick were contacted by radio and informed that a patrol boat had picked the six men up. The five pilots of the search party never saw the boat, but believing all went well, split up and left the area of Ameland Island for the return trip home at 0945 hrs./2,000 ft. On the way home, at 1000 hours, they heard a report on "D" channel concerning a mid-air collision. (Probably 385th BG B-17s that had a mid-air over the sea.) A chute was also reported as one of the planes involved disappeared into the clouds.

4 April 1945

Eighth AF FO 1896A

No. 334 & 335 Wednesday. The group was divided into two forces, A and B groups, both penetration to target and withdrawal escorts for 2nd AD B-24s attacking their 8th AF Mission 926 primary target, an airfield at Kaltenkirchen, Germany. Maj. Olds led A group, which consisted of 22 P-51s from the 434th FS. Up: 0730 hrs., down: 1300 hrs. with no early returns. Capt. Anderson led B group, which consisted of 42 P-51s (20-435th & 22-436th). Up: 0735 hrs., down: 1250 hrs. with one early return.

A group R/V'd with the proper bombers north of Juist Island, Germany at 0904 hrs./23,000 ft. Staying out over the North Sea, the bombers and their escorts continued to fly northeast and did not make L/F over Germany until they entered west of Heide at 0917 hrs./23,000 ft. After turning and heading southeast, Kaltenkirchen was reached where the time over target was 0936 hrs./23,000 ft. The target area was covered by a low layer of 10/10ths clouds that had tops at 3-4,000 ft. so bombing results were not seen. Avoiding the Hamburg area while homeward bound, the group saw a single Me 262 bounce some B-17s at 0950 hrs./22,000 ft. in the Lübeck area. The jet made a level attack from the rear, followed that up with a 360-degree oblong turn and passed through the bombers once more as he continued eastward. The Jerry was successful and brought one of the B-17s down. No parachutes were seen to emerge from the stricken bomber. At the beginning of the initial attack, the jet was being chased by some P-47s, but the German pilot broke from them to make the first attack. His speed was too great for the P-51s from Newcross Squadron

The remains of the P-51 that Lieutenant Carl W. Sherer was forced to bail out of this day. *Courtesy of George E. Falkner.*

Lieutenant Clarence G. Haynes in his Newcross Squadron L2-D. *Courtesy of Clarence G. Haynes.*

Another good shot of Lieutenant Haynes. *Courtesy of the Wings of Freedom Museum.*

to be able to cut him off. They fired at the E/A, but the distance was beyond their effective range. He got away. Continuing on in a generally southwestern course, the force passed south of Dümmer Lake at which point the escorts broke away to sweep back north to the Bremen area. Breakaway was at 1030 hrs./ 23,000 ft. and the sweep was fruitless. L/O was over Ijmuiden, Holland at 1154 hrs./12,000 ft.

B group made L/F and R/V'd with their bombers in the Heide, Germany area at 0915 hrs./20-21,000 ft. Arriving in the target area, smoke markers were seen, but no bombs were spotted falling. Time over target was 0932 hrs. On the way out, south to L/O, a lone Me 262 attempted to bounce the group's rear box of B-24s in the Lüneburg area at 0955 hrs. When Bison Squadron turned into the jet for a head-on pass, the E/A dove for the deck and Second Lieutenant Alton (Al) A. Massey went after him. Lt. Massey gave the following report of his efforts to bring the jet down:

> "Bison Squadron was giving our bombers close escort when I saw a jet attacking the rear bombers just after leaving the target at Kaltenkirchen. I called him in to my flight leader, but got no response. I did the same again and my flight leader acknowledged my call. Upon hearing his response, I peeled off to the left as the jet passed below me. I was at 27,000 feet and began a steep dive after him. I got into compressibility twice, but kept control of my plane as I closed to approximately 1,300 yards. I didn't seem to be getting any closer, so I gave him a short burst and saw a flash just behind the E/A's canopy. At this time, I was still about 1,300 yards away from him. The E/A gained distance on me and then disappeared after having gone through a hole in a cloud. I claim one Me 262 damaged."

Shortly after Lt. Massey's unsuccessful attack, Second Lieutenant Edward H. Sims from Lakeside Squadron pursued another Me 262, eight miles west of Lüneburg. Lt. Sims, who later became a well-known writer of aviation history, wrote the following Encounter Report concerning the events of his combat with the German jet aircraft:

> "I was flying White Two position, covering the bombers on the left side of the formation. One lone Me 262 started a pass from six o'clock and a little high, on the last box of B-24s. White Flight swung right and turned back to meet the jet. Closing on him, I opened fire on the Me 262 from about 45-degrees, head-on. As I passed fairly close by him, I observed a strike on his fuselage, just behind the cockpit. The film from my gun camera would not have recorded it as I had stopped firing by that time. I turned as tightly as possible to the left, rolled out, put my pipper directly on the E/A and fired four or five good bursts before he got out of range. I should have gotten 50-100 hits, but at that distance and without tracers, it is extremely difficult to give an accurate tally. The Me 262 pulled steadily away, dove and turned slightly left, heading for the clouds into which he went without further variation. I lost him completely in those clouds. I claim one Me 262 damaged."

B group continued escort until they broke away in the Tilburg area of Holland at 1125 hrs./15,000 ft. L/O for them was over Walcheren Island at 1143 hrs./4,000 ft.

Observations made during the mission included a notation that the bomber formation was poor. The Big Friends lost a B-24 described as having black on white tail markings (2nd Combat Wing) north of Kaltenkirchen. The bomber was seen to explode and, unfortunately, no chutes were spotted coming from it. The Liberator was possibly a victim of a rocket attack made by one of the intercepting Me 262s. The airfield at Bremen was in use, with the east-west runway active. Five plus unidentified twin-engine aircraft were also parked there. The roads north of Bremen were lined with parked army vehicles. Flak over Itzehoe, Bremen and west of Heide was heavy, meager and inaccurate. Flak over Hamburg was heavy, intense and inaccurate.

Crew chief Staff Sergeant Harold E. Virgin, Jr., Lieutenant Alton A. Massey and assistant crew chief Edward L. Akin by their P-51. *Courtesy of Edward Akin.*

5 April 1945

Eighth AF FO 1903A

No. 336 Thursday. Maj. Duffié led the group, which consisted of 52 P-51s (17-434th, 18-435th & 17-436th) on a penetration to target and withdrawal escort for 2nd AD B-24s attacking their 8th AF Mission 928 primary target, the marshalling yards at Plauen, Germany. Up: 0831 hrs., down: 1410 hrs. with a total of nine early returns.

The group history cites the weather present on this mission as "Rawthur (long 'a') nahsty, (another long 'a') what with fronts and 10/10ths cloud cover." L/F for the group was over an undercast continent, location unknown, at 0957 hrs./28,000 ft. R/V with the proper bombers was five miles north of Domazlice, Czechoslovakia at 1110 hrs./19,000 ft. While enroute to the target, Me 262s hit the bomber formation, which was strung out and in a very poor state of assembly, conditions inviting for such an attack. The 434th and 435th FSs were flying slightly higher than the B-24 formation with one on the left and one on the right. The 436th FS was providing top cover at about 26,000 ft. Upon sighting the jets, Bison Squadron went down after them. Bison Leader and his wingman, Second Lieutenant Alton (Al) A. Massey led the counterattack, with Bison Leader dropping his external fuel tanks when he began the dive. As Lt. Massey was in the process of trying to stay on his leader's wing and release his tanks also, his leader suddenly pulled up in a four to five G climbing, left bank. Lt. Massey had been reaching for both his tank release and gun switch at that moment and the pull of the high G climb caused him to struggle for the switches. He released the tanks, but due to the high G maneuver, Lt. Massey thought only one tank dropped when he toggled them both off. His aircraft went onto an immediate two-and-a-half turn snap roll. Recovering from the unexpected roll, Lt. Massey's suspicions were confirmed when the other drop tank came off and flew over his canopy. Looking in the direction of his leader, Lt. Massey began heading toward him, radioing that he was not with him at the moment. He received no answer and just as he was about to call again, he felt a strong tap on his right shoulder. Instinctively turning his head to look in the direction of the tap, he saw tracers flying over his canopy and an Me 262 coming up from behind him. He automatically broke left in a tight turn and within a few seconds or less, the jet appeared in his windshield, straight ahead. It was in an almost stall position and so close, he could see the pilot looking at him. He let up on his turn and pulled the gun trigger. Nothing happened. In the turmoil, he had not lifted the gun switch safety and turned on his guns. The opportunity was lost. For one fleeting moment, the grand chance was there. But, was it? Had Lt. Massey fired at point blank range, the jet no doubt would have exploded or come apart directly in front of him and his flight path. It would have been a double kill, with the Lieutenant getting the jet and the jet taking him down, also. To this day, Al Massey claims emphatically that it was an angel who tapped him on the shoulder and saved his life during those few seconds of combat. He is certain an angel both warned him and distracted him from arming his guns when he saw the German jet and he has religiously believed in their existence since that April date.

A nice view of 434th FS L2-H Hot Toddy, taken right after one of the rains that fell so often during that time of year. *Courtesy of David L. Born.*

Another view of the same plane. This airplane had a lengthy service record; having been one of the original P-51s assigned to Newcross Squadron. Flown primarily by Lieutenant George W. Gleason (except during his convalescence because of a broken ankle) the ship was to be lost later this month when another pilot, First Lieutenant Frank M. Taylor who was flying it at the time, was hit by enemy fire during a strafing run. A nice story that involves this particular plane and her regular pilot, Lt. Gleason, took place back during the month of October. It seems that during that time and on the eve of his first mission, Second Lieutenant Clifford W. Bowers, one of the new pilots, approached First Lieutenant George W. Gleason in the BOQ Club asking the experienced veteran for some advice on flying combat. Lt. Gleason reportedly refused the request, telling Lt. Bowers: "Why should I waste my time with you! You're probably going to be dead tomorrow. Taken aback, Lt. Bowers retreated and left Lt. Gleason alone. The story does not end here however. Lt. Gleason later made arrangements for Lt. Bowers to be assigned Hot Toddy and spoke with his crew chief asking him to make certain the bird was perfect working order and to do his best to help the new pilot feel comfortable for the mission. *Courtesy of David L. Born.*

Lt. Massey rejoined his flight and with the attack over, the group continued heading northwest to Plauen with the Big Friends. The time over target was 1135 hrs./19,000 ft. and the results were unobservable due to the cloud conditions. Heading out towards home, Lakeside's commanding officer, Major Herbert H. Jordan, was hit by light flak while flying over Siegburg, southeast of Cologne, Germany. The flight encountered the moderate, accurate flak at 2,500 ft. During evasive action, Maj. Jordan's P-51 was hit and his hydraulic system was damaged. After herding the crippled plane along for awhile, he was forced to crash-land, accomplishing a one-wheel landing on a strip 16 miles southeast of Aachen, Germany. Maj. Jordan's landing brought light damage to the plane and none to himself. The irony of the situation was that this was his last mission; his tour would be complete with his return. That was delayed by a day, however, since he spent the night on the continent. The next day he returned to Wattisham.

The escorts broke from the bombers over the Fulda, Germany area at 1210 hrs./16,000 ft. L/O was over Knokke, Belgium at 1330 hrs./8-9,000 ft.

Observations made during the mission included another note that cited the escort as having been made difficult due to poor bomber formations. The note went on to add that the bombers were strung out in little bunches of six. One group of bombers identified as Vinegrove 1-4, called for two groups of Little Friends to come help them, but the bombers could not be located, even after two searches. Another single B-24 kept calling for help, but he was under the bomber stream and in direct sight of the escorting fighters at all times. "A" channel was filled with too much chatter during most of the flight in to the target. Black smoke rising up to 11,000 ft. was spotted in the area of Bayreuth. Flak over Siegburg was light, moderate and accurate.

6 April 1945

Eighth AF FO 1909A

No. 337 Friday. Capt. Hooker led the group, which consisted of 42 P-51s (14-434th, 14-435th & 14-436th) on a penetration to target and withdrawal escort for 2nd AD B-24s attacking their 8th AF Mission 930 primary target, an oil depot at Stassfurt/Leopoldshall, Germany. Up: 0719 hrs., down: 1250 hrs. with a total of four early returns.

L/F was over Ostend, Belg. at 0759 hrs./16,000 ft. After passing into Germany, R/V with their proper bombers was made by two of the group's squadrons in the Marburg area at 0900 hrs./23,000 ft. One squadron lost their bombers during R/V, because of the clouds. They wound up escorting some B-17s from the R/V area to south of Magdeburg where they broke from them and drove farther south to the target area looking for the B-24s. Failing to find them, the squadron headed home. The proper Big Friends and their escorts arrived in the target area at 0950 hrs./24,000 ft. where an unidentified target, not the primary, was struck with unknown results. Turning towards home, the force swung around Leipzig and headed west. The remaining escorts broke from the B-24s ten miles north of Koblenz at 1107 hrs./23,000 ft. L/O was over Walcheren Island at 1200 hrs./15,000 ft.

Lakeside Squadron P-51s J2-O, J2-P, J2-V and J2-S are seen flying above some heavy cloud cover during an escort mission. *Courtesy of Robert H. Horman.*

No observations were recorded from the uneventful mission due to the heavy cloud cover. Flak over Magdeburg and Leipzig was heavy, intense and accurate.

Verne E. Hooker, who led the group on this mission, recently wrote of his experience during the flight. He stated:

> "Weather played a prominent part in flying during the war. On this mission we rendezvoused above the clouds and never saw ground until we returned. As group leader that day, I had to get our planes to the proper bombers, take them to their target and return, essentially all on instruments. As we returned to Wattisham, we learned the ceiling there was only one to two hundred feet. It had been a long mission and some of the guys began telling me they were low on gas and would have to set down soon. Still on instruments, we began our descent through the clouds and popped through the ceiling right over our base. One of the pilots exclaimed 'We're here!' and they began peeling off to get on the ground as soon as

possible. It was a moment to remember – hitting the base that well on instruments."

7 April 1945

Eighth AF FO 1914A

No. 338 & 339 Saturday. The group was divided into two forces, A and B groups, both penetration to target and withdrawal escorts for 2nd AD B-24s attacking their 8th AF Mission 931 primary target, the munitions works at Düneburg, Germany. Maj. Olds led A group, which consisted of 30 P-51s (22-434th & 8-435th). Up: 1017 hrs., down: 1535 hrs. with no early returns. Maj. Duffié led B group, which consisted of 29 P-51s (8-435th & 21-436th). Up: 1047 hrs., down: 1510 hrs. with five early returns plus three escorts.

A group made L/F over an undercast covered Holland in the vicinity of Ijmuiden at 1121 hrs./18,000 ft. R/V with their B-24s was northwest of there, over Bergumer Lake, Holland at 1140 hrs./22,000 ft. The Big Friends were 17 minutes late for the rendezvous, forcing A group to orbit the area as they waited. The 355th FG was also present and waiting to join in the escort. Once the proper bombers were identified, the escorts moved to their positions as the force flew over Holland and headed into Germany where the skies were 7-9/10ths undercast with tops to 8,000 ft. In addition, a light haze layer was present at 28,000 ft. Heading east and having passed Bremen on a heading of 70 degrees, the B-24s were bounced by 12 Me 262s in an area 20 miles west of Soltau, at 1225 hrs./20-22,000 ft. A group, flying at 31,000 ft. and to the left of their bombers, had first spotted the jets about five minutes earlier. The enemy aircraft were flying at 33,000 ft. and paralleling the formation's course. As the Germans turned towards the Liberators and began a nine o'clock pass by elements on the heavies, Newcross Squadron dropped their wing tanks and engaged the jets. As the E/A went through the formation in twos, the defending fighters chased them. The jets turned and attempted to make another attack from six o'clock. The squadron tried to help ward off the attack as the area filled with both B-24s and B-17s going to their targets, the German jets after them and all of the fighter escorts trying to protect the bombers. It was inevitable that nervous gunners onboard the heavies would shoot first and ask questions later. Evidence of this was born by several of the group's returning P-51s, which had been hit by fire from both bomber types. In the end, it was believed that only one Me 262 succeeded in getting at the bombers, but

This photo taken during the summer of 1945 shows crew chief Staff Sergeant Victor C. Potts, Captain Verne E. Hooker and assistant crew chief Sergeant John D. Alexis by a Bison P-51. Close examination of the photograph reveals two points, the first of which is Colonel Kyle L. Riddle's P-51 J2-R in the background. The second is that the P-51 immediately behind the three men has mounting pylons for rockets on its wings. *Courtesy of Verne E. Hooker.*

that attack was successful in downing a B-24. A group's leader, as well as leader of the entire fighter group; Maj. Robin Olds caught a piece of one 262, but his adversary escaped with only a damaged ship and his luck still intact. Lieutenant Hilton O. Thompson from the 434th FS shot another down as it tried to cut back in. The rest dove away, heading down to 8,000 ft. in an attempt to evade the defending fighters. Maj. Olds and Lt. Thompson described the action in their Combat Reports, reproduced here to add insight. Others are included in part, to give further information for the purpose of illustrating the encounter.

Maj. Olds:

"I was leading the group [the 479th FG] on this escort mission to Düneburg. By an agreement made over the radio with the 355th Fighter Group, who was also escorting the first box of B-24s, I positioned my group on the north side of the box. The 355th Group took the south side.

"At about 1220 hours, we were at 27,000 feet, nine o'clock high to the bombers. Our position was approximately midway between Bremen and Dümmer Lake. I noticed contrails popping up over a cirrus bank nine o'clock to us. This cirrus layer ran from east to west. Someone in the squadron called the contrails in about a minute later. I left two squadrons very close to the bombers [Lakeside and Bison] and with Newcross Squadron only, I eased over towards the bogies to investigate them. The

First Lieutenant Robert I. Bromschwig by his Kraut Knocker. *Courtesy of Robert I. Bromschwig.*

contrails cut off and a few seconds later, I saw 12 Me 262s diving on the bombers. The jets were flying good formation, being in three flights of four each, line abreast in flights, flights in trail. At this moment, Nuthouse called in bogies approaching our bomber force from the southwest. The jets were approaching the bombers from nine o'clock high. I split-essed on top of them, stalled, shuttered and fired. It was a snap shot that achieved no hits. At the end of the split-ess, I found myself directly behind the jet jobs and heading for the bombers with them. I ranged and fired on the Me 262 playing tail-end Charlie, but was far out of range. I did see one large puff of black smoke emitted from the jet while I was firing, but cannot say whether or not I had gotten a strike on him. This particular jet went right between two boxes without firing a shot. He then started to turn to the right, presumably for another pass. He must have seen the two flights of us that were behind him, for he straightened out and left us far behind. He seemed to be heading for the B-17 stream to our south. I claim one Me 262 damaged."

Maj. Olds' wingman, Second Lieutenant Roy M. Rossel, Jr., gave confirmation to that claim.

Lt. Thompson:

"I was flying in the position of Newcross Purple Three on the escort mission to Düneburg. Our squadron was positioned on the left-hand side and high to the leading box of bombers. My flight was on the extreme left, or north side of our squadron. West of Düneburg, just prior to the target, we sighted at least six Me 262s coming in at nine o'clock and headed toward the bombers. They were flying in elements of twos, with the first element leading the other two elements who were flying almost line abreast. We turned with them, but by the time I had my sights on one, he was out of range due to his extreme high speed.

"While flying at about 26,000 feet in the direction of the bombers and in hopes of finding some more E/A, I discovered that I was separated from my squadron, lost, without even a wingman. While hunting for some other members of the squadron, I sighted an Me 262, possibly 2,000 feet above me and in a gentle climbing turn to the left. I began climbing up to him and closing by cutting inside of his turn. After having chased him to 31,000 feet, I had closed to within about 800 yards. Upon firing two short bursts, I saw a few strikes on the left wing of the Me 262 and at the same time, he increased his turn to the left. He finally rolled over and went straight down. I fired several more bursts during this time and saw many hits on and around the cockpit. After following him down about 5,000 feet, I saw large pieces fly from his aircraft. At that point, I pulled out of my dive since my speed was becoming very high. I did not see the Me 262 again. Shortly before I fired my first two bursts at the jet, I noticed three or four other Newcross ships off to my left and below me. They apparently were chasing the same Me 262. I claim one Me 262 destroyed."

Lt. Thompson's claim was supported by First Lieutenant Robert I. Bromschwig, who filed this confirmation report:

"I was flying as Newcross Spare during the above engagement. My wingman and I were flying with two Lakeside ships about 2,000 feet above and on the left side of the bomber stream. I saw an Me 262 make a diving pass from six o'clock high, on the lead box. He fired, then pulled up in a forty-five-degree climb and started a turn to the left. I immediately started a turn to the left and climbed to intercept him. After turning about 180 degrees, I saw Lt. Thompson was slightly higher than I and was also turning inside of the Me 262 to cut him off. At about 31,000 feet, Lt. Thompson had closed in to about 800 yards behind the jet. I saw him fire two bursts and get many hits on the 262. The Me 262 rolled slowly to the left and Lt. Thompson fired all the way around until he was going straight down. All this time he was scoring many hits around the cockpit. I saw a few large pieces fly off the jet as it went down. I watched the Me 262 go down and saw the pilot bail out and his chute open at about 15,000 feet. The plane went straight into the ground and exploded. I confirm one Me 262 destroyed by Second Lt. Hilton O. Thompson."

First Lieutenant Gail E. Jacobson:

"I was flying Newcross Yellow Leader. Our group was assigned to escort the lead box of B-24s. At 1220 hours, contrails were called in at nine o'clock high and approximately 30,000 feet. There appeared to be four and they were flying parallel to the bombers. As they turned and came in from nine o'clock, I turned to meet them and as we closed, I identified them as Me 262s. The four Me 262s dived under us and headed for the bombers. I lined up with the two tail-end Charlies and then tried to drop my wing tanks, but my right tank hung up and would not release. We gave chase and the two jets crossed the bomber stream at 90 degrees, pulled up into a chandelle to the left and tried to come in from six o'clock high. I cut the two jets off in their left-hand turn and was closing on them when the lead jet disregarded the bombers and dived away from us, heading towards Bremen. I couldn't close because of my right drop tank, but we chased them down to 15,000 feet, still in the direction of Bremen. All along the way, I was trying to release my tank. I finally lost it, but then we lost the jets a bit later. I last saw them at 12,000 feet, heading north past Bremen."

First Lieutenant Jerome K. Nagel:

"I was flying Newcross Yellow Three on a bomber escort to the Düneburg ammunition dump, southeast of Hamburg. About eight Me 262 jets were called in as coming from the north on the bombers. They passed under us, so my wingman, Second Lt. George H. Looney, and I dropped our wing tanks and started to chase them. The jets pulled up, over and back around for a pass on the bombers from five o'clock, high above. I followed them through, firing several bursts, but the range was too great and I didn't observe any strikes. We chased the jets north for about five minutes, but could not close as they were diving slightly. As they were leading us over Hamburg, I broke off the chase and turned back to the bombers because I heard that they were being attacked by Me 109s."

At 1230 hours, a MEW report of bogies flying south of the course the B-24s were on was received from Nuthouse. By this time, A group was split up from their pursuit of the Me 262s, so individual flights climbed to intercept the unidentified aircraft. Ten minutes later, ten plus Fw 190s and Me 109s were encountered in the vicinity of Ulzen. The E/A were carrying belly tanks and appeared to be forming up from the Ulzen-Salzwedel area. The bandits were engaged and combat ranged from 33,000 ft. to down on the deck. A group's leader, Major Robin Olds, knocked down an Me 109 that had just destroyed a B-24, while three more were accounted for by other members of Newcross Squadron.

The 434th FS claims for the encounter were:

1-0-0	Me 109	1st Lt. Gail E. Jacobson
1-0-0	Me 109	2nd Lt. Robert L. Munson
1-0-0	Me 109	1st Lt. Jerome K. Nagel
1-0-0	Me 109	Maj. Robin Olds

After Maj. Olds had the above-described brush with an Me 262, he ran into the pack of German fighters from which the previous claims came to be filed. Maj. Olds (After the combat with the Me 262):

"I turned around and headed back for our bombers which were not far distant. As I passed the second box in the force, I saw an Me 109 going in on the bombers. I tacked onto him and followed him right through the box. I couldn't fire until he passed through the box for fear of hitting a bomber myself. The Me 109 fired at one bomber from eight o'clock high, while in a steep dive. He clobbered the bomber. Being in range, I cut loose at him then and immediately got strikes. He rolled into a dive and I followed, getting a few more strikes. The pilot bailed and his airplane went straight into the ground. I lost a wheel-fairing door during my dive after the Me 109 and from there on out, the airplane would not fly properly. The rate of climb and airspeed were poor. I got the Me 109 at approximately 1240 hours, 11,000 feet, just as the bombers turned into their I. P.

"Afterwards, I tried to climb up to some Me 109s several thousand feet above me, but couldn't do any good with my damaged plane. I circled there to watch and wait for more P-51s to show up. I claim one Me 109 destroyed."

Second Lieutenant Roy M. Rossel, Jr. confirmed Maj. Olds' Victory.

First Lt. Gail E. Jacobson continued his preceding Combat Report, the first part of which described his encounter with an Me 262, in this manner:

"My wingman, Second Lieutenant Robert L. Munson and I then climbed back up to the bombers, meeting them in the vicinity of Soltau. There I sighted high contrails, coming from three o'clock and headed for them. As we closed, I could see there were six to ten mixed 109s and 190s. The 190s were leading and the 109s were five hundred feet higher, around 32,500 feet. I called Highway, [479th FG leader, Maj. Olds] telling him that there were 109s and 190s in the area. I kept climbing, trying to reach their altitude, but met them first at 1240 hours, 32,000 feet. I picked what I thought was the last one and made a right turn to come in from six o'clock, low. I was just within range when my wingman called and said there was a 109 on his tail and that he was breaking right. I broke right while my wingman, Newcross Yellow Two, Lt. Munson, did a 360-degree turn, coming up from six o'clock low, in a 40-degree bank. He fired about a three second burst, getting hits in the 109s canopy and wing roots, blowing his coolant and setting him on fire. The 109 went into a vertical dive and the pilot bailed out. I then turned around to the right and spotted a 109, who didn't look very friendly, setting behind me. I did one turn to the right and he lost interest. I then started off south and saw another 109 much closer. This one started to get sassy. I did a 360-degree turn, closing on him to about 200 yards from six o'clock, low. Using my K-14, I ranged him carefully and fired a two or three second burst. I observed strikes in his engine section and wing roots. His coolant was also hit and he started burning on the left side, at the wing root. The 109 started down in a dive; the pilot jettisoned his canopy and bailed out. I didn't see his chute open, but his plane crashed south of Celle. I claim one Me 109 destroyed."

Lieutenant Jerome K. Nagel. *Courtesy of David L. Born.*

Second Lt. Robert L. Munson confirmed Lt. Jacobson's claim and submitted his own claim for an Me 109 destroyed. Lt. Munson:

"I was flying Newcross Yellow Two in A group escorting 2nd Air Division B-24s to Düneburg. I was flying as wingman to First Lt. Gail E. Jacobson. After chasing two Me 262s down to 15,000 feet and almost to Bremen, we turned back towards the bombers and climbed up to 32,000 feet, reaching the rear of the bomber stream in the vicinity of Soltau. At 1240 hours, we saw two Me 109s at 30,000 feet and coming in at the bombers from three o'clock. Lt. Jacobson made a pass on these from seven o'clock. At this time, an Me 109 came at me from six o'clock and we broke sharply right. I completed a 360-degree turn and came in on the 109 from four or five o'clock. I began firing at him from about 1,500 feet, using my K-14 sight, and continued firing on around the turn, until I was almost right in line with him and about 500 feet away. I observed several hits around the cockpit and

> right wing before a flame and black smoke gushed out of the wing root and cockpit area. The plane went into a spin and the pilot bailed out. I watched it go into the undercast at 4,000 feet, still burning. I claim one Me 109 destroyed."

Lt. Jacobson confirmed Lt. Munson's claim for the Me 109 destroyed.

First Lt. Jerome (Jerry) K. Nagel completes the narrative with the second part of his Combat Report:

> "We stooged around just below some B-17s for about fifteen minutes looking for E/A, but saw none. Finally, I took up a heading of 300 degrees to intercept our assigned box of bombers. While in the vicinity of Soltau, I observed a lone plane heading east, down on the deck. We were at about 11,000 feet when I began my dive down after him. I lost him temporarily behind a cloud puff. When we had passed under the cloud, I saw him again at three o'clock to me and recognized him as an Me 109. He was in a turn to the right. I pulled around steeply to the right and within 180 degrees, was hot on his tail. I was just lining up my sight on him when I saw him level out and jettison his canopy. I opened fire anyway, saw the pilot pop out and the ship roll over. Turning, I saw his chute, but as two other planes had appeared, my attention was drawn to them until I identified them as P-51s. I did not see the Me 109 go in. The fight took place at approximately 1300 hours and at 1,500 feet. My wingman and I were both fairly low on gas by then, so we headed on out. I claim one Me 109 destroyed."

Newcross Blue Two, Lt. Nagel's wingman, Second Lt. George H. Looney, confirmed Lt. Nagel's claim of one Me 109 destroyed.

After having chased the Me 262s at full power, the fight with the 109s and Fws had to be broken off short in order that fuel would remain sufficient for the group to return home. The previous full power chase and the gas consuming air battle that was being fought had depleted the supply in the Little Friend's tanks. Leaving what could have been a greater tally behind, the planes of Newcross Squadron were forced to turn towards Wattisham. Continued withdrawal support for the bombers was also out of the question, despite a request from Nuthouse to do so. L/O was at an unspecified location over the Dutch coast at 1405 hrs./14,000 ft. The Lakeside Squadron contingent of A group continued on with their escort of the bombers and returned later.

B group made L/F over the Dutch coast in the vicinity of Den Helder at 1128 hrs./21,000 ft. R/V with the proper bombers was two minutes later at the same altitude, 15 miles east of there. Once across Holland and over Germany, the force ran afoul of enemy fighters northeast of Nienburg at 1225 hrs. Two Me 262s came in from the seven o'clock position, underneath the tail end formation of B-24s. Two of B group's Lakeside Squadron P-51s went after the jets, one of which Captain Verne E. Hooker destroyed with a long shot. The other jet escaped, only to be replaced moments later with a second pair making a similar pass at the bombers. During this time, an unidentified single-engine aircraft made a bounce on the rear B-24s, diving from above and climbing straight up again. Within minutes of those attacks, two more Me 262s, using the same tactics as the other pairs of jets had, made a pass on the Big Friends, heading up the bomber stream and towards the lead box. First Lieutenant Richard G. Candelaria shot one of these down approximately 20 miles northwest of Nienburg.

By 1232 hours, the Me 262s had left and were replaced by Me 109s after the bombers. About fifteen miles north of Celle, in an area five miles west of Fassburg, ten plus Me 109s made bounces on the bombers from all directions and altitudes. The enemy aircraft were definitely aggressive and determined to get at the heavies. One E/A cut his throttle while attacking and also made a pass on his back! The Germans did not use their "Company Front" formation and it appeared as though the leader did all the firing. Again Capt. Hooker and Lt. Candelaria were in the thick of it and did the scoring.

The 435th FS claims for the encounters were:

1-0-0	Me 262	1st Lt. Richard G. Candelaria
4-0-0	Me 109	1st Lt. Richard G. Candelaria
1-0-0	Me 262	Capt. Verne E. Hooker
1-0-0	Me 109	Capt. Verne E. Hooker

First Lieutenant Richard G. Candelaria:

> "I was flying Lakeside Blue Three in a three ship flight and due to bad weather during forming up and a mix up on my part, I made R/V with the bombers by myself. I went to my appointed place, which was at the rear of the lead box of the first force. I stayed around at the bomber altitude, alongside their low squadron. At 1220 hours, I heard the group leader, Major Olds, give his squadron (434th) the order to drop their wing tanks. I looked around, but could see nothing so I hung onto mine. Approximately five minutes later, the bombers started

shooting flares, signaling enemy fighters. Then I saw two Me 262s at seven o'clock and slightly low, coming up along the bomber stream. I went at the leader head-on, trying to make him break, but he avoided my pass by diving. However, he did not alter his course and that made it very difficult for me to hit him. I tried to drop my tanks on him, but missed completely. I did a half-roll and lined up on his tail as he opened fire on the bombers. I opened fire on him and observed hits on both sides of his cockpit and large puffs of smoke emanating from his fuselage and wings. In the meantime, the pilot of the second jet had positioned himself on my tail and opened fire at me. I saw white and red shells like golf balls, going past me. Looking up in my rear-view mirror, I could see him firing away at me. A moment later, he hit me in the right wing. At this time, the first jet broke away to the left in a lazy half-roll and went straight down, trailing smoke. I broke hard into the jet behind me, but he went off in a shallow dive towards his buddy. He was going much too fast for me to ever hope to catch. I had a good look at the jets and would describe them as being painted a mottled brown with yellow polka dots [sic] the entire length of the fuselage and wings.

"I went back to the bombers and once there, saw ten to fifteen Me 109s coming in from different directions of the clock. They were on the same level as the bombers. I screamed them out over the radio, then tried to get on the leader of the 109s. I did my best to keep him from getting to the bombers, but he made a fool out of me by completely out-maneuvering me, making pass after pass on them and finally knocking one down. Each leader had four wingmen who did not fire at the bombers or attempt to bother me. Their job seemed to be to stick with the leader. The leader I had picked to attack was a superb acrobatic pilot; making passes on the bombers in an inverted position and even firing while he was rolling. He continued to easily elude me in spite of my best efforts, but finally I succeeded and got on him. I fired, hit him and he broke away from the bombers with the whole gaggle in tow behind him. He went barrel rolling down and when I hit him again, he started trailing smoke and coolant behind. It was then at that point his buddies tried to clobber me. They began making passes at me, but they were evidentially green pilots because none of them managed to hit me. I saw the pilot's chute from the 109 I had first attacked open at 2,000 feet and saw that the plane had crashed in a wood.

"A second leader then made a pass at me and overshot. As he passed in front of me, I gave him a squirt and hit him. I tried to get back on him, but this time I overshot because he had cut his throttle. I was just sitting alongside him when he up and bailed out.

"By this time, the rest of the Jerries were giving me a hard time and having gotten into a Luffberry, I out-turned them, got behind and fired a short burst. Although I observed no strikes, one of them leveled off and bailed out. Another one that had been behind me failed to out-turn me on the second turn and snapped suddenly, going into a spin that resulted in his crashing and exploding on the ground. The pilot never got out of the aircraft.

"Just at this time, Lieutenant William M. Barsky, along with six other P-51s, arrived on the scene. They witnessed the last actions and saw the 109s hit the ground and burn. I then went around and took pictures of the fires and the parachutes. Before Lt. Barsky and the other planes arrived, an unidentified P-51 came down to help me, but he was shot down by the 109s. I circled his chute while he waved at me and I continued to circle him until he landed and walked away to a woods. His plane crashed and burned. I'm certain that had it not been for the intervention of the unknown pilot, along with the timely arrival of Lt. Barsky and the others, I would have likely 'had it'.

"The above events might not have happened in the exact sequence that I have put them down as everything happened so quickly, I am not absolutely positive of their order. Lieutenants Barsky, King, Heathman, Williams and Salze, along with the remainder of the flight, witnessed most of this action and counted the fires and chutes.

"The following is my opinion of the tactics used by the enemy fighters during this encounter: The Me 262s were used to lure the escorting fighters away, while the Me 109s made the determined attacks. The leader of each group was definitely an experienced and "hot" pilot, while their wingmen were not aggressive and seemed to get in each other's way. I suggest that the bomber gunners open up at maximum range and stay alert. I also swear by the K-14 gunsight. I claim one Me 262 destroyed as witnessed by Lt. Floyd W. Salze and four Me 109s positively destroyed."

First Lieutenant Richard G. Candelaria never got a chance to sign the above Combat Report. The original report was written in longhand by Lt. Candelaria and subsequently sent for typing. By the time the report was fully prepared and ready for his approval signature some days later, the tables had been turned on him. Lt. Candelaria had been hit by flak and forced to bail out over enemy territory. He became a POW for the short duration of the war.

The following are confirmations for Lt. Candelaria's claims:

First Lieutenant Richard G. Candelaria. *Carroll C. Sprague Collection, courtesy of the East Essex Aviation Society.*

> First Lieutenant William M. Barsky: "I broke out of the clouds at 3,000 feet and saw Lt. Candelaria fire on an Me 109 which was in a turn to the right. I observed strikes on the 109. Lt. Candelaria immediately opened fire on a second Me 109. Both planes hit the ground almost instantaneously within 100 yards of each other. A third 109 was hit and exploded in the immediate vicinity of the first two. I confirm three of Lt. Candelaria's claims of four Me 109s destroyed."
>
> First Lieutenant Charles E. Heathman: "We were escorting bombers near Lüneburg when Me 262s hit the bombers. Then we heard Lt. Candelaria calling for help because he had some Me 109s cornered down around 4,000 feet. As we broke out below the clouds, I saw four fires, all within five miles of each other. I confirm Lt. Candelaria's claim of four Me 109s destroyed."
>
> First Lieutenant David E. King: "I broke out of the clouds at about 3,000 feet and saw Lt. Candelaria circling the wreckage of three fighter aircraft. I made one circle and saw one of the wrecks explode. I then joined Lt. Candelaria and flew his wing for the remainder of the mission. I confirm three of the four Me 109s that Lt. Candelaria claimed."
>
> Second Lieutenant Floyd W. Salze: "We were flying at about 19,000 feet when two jets made a pass at the bombers. Lt. Candelaria broke after the leader and fired at him while at the same time, the second jet was firing at Lt. Candelaria. The first jet did a left wing over and, trailing heavy smoke, went straight down from 17,000 feet and into the clouds, which were below, at 2500 to 3000 feet. The jet was still going straight down when he entered the clouds. The German's wingman did not follow him on through the clouds. I confirm Lt. Candelaria's claim of one Me 262 destroyed."
>
> Capt. Verne E. Hooker: "I was leading Lakeside Squadron, covering the tail end of the bombers when I saw two Me 262s coming in from seven o'clock, slightly low, to make a pass on the bombers. I turned in to them and took a long shot at the leader, observing some hits on the aircraft's left wing. He pulled off to the left and away from the bombers. When he did this, I saw two other Me 262s coming in for another seven o'clock pass at the bombers. I left the other jets in an attempt to drive the second pair away from their intended attack. I didn't see anymore of the first jet that I had fired upon. Lieutenant William M. Barsky, who was one of my flight leaders, said this jet pulled over to the left and the pilot bailed out. He also saw the Me 262 hit the ground.
>
> "Then I spotted another jet at nine o'clock, flying along the left side of the bombers. He appeared to be trying to decide whether or not to make a pass. I had just gotten between him and the bombers when the 109s hit the front end of the box we were protecting. I spotted a 109 making a pass at the bombers from seven o'clock and slightly low. I closed in on him and began firing from 100 yards. I continued firing and closing until I was within 50 feet of him. I saw strikes hit all over the 109 and smoke started coming out of the aircraft. I broke to the right and as I passed the 109, he pulled off to the left where the plane caught fire and the pilot bailed out. My wingman, Lieutenant Sylvan R. Routh, also observed the 109 catch fire and the pilot bail out. I claim one Me 262 and one Me 109 destroyed."

Recently, Verne Hooker gave further insight into the Me 109 attack described above. He said:

> "I had spotted a Me 109 that had gotten through our fighters and was in formation just behind the bombers and shooting at them. I thought surely the B-24 gunners would get him, but for whatever reason, they didn't. Although we had been cautioned not to venture too close to the bombers during actual combat because they could mistake us for Germans and accidentally shoot at us as well, something had to be done about that attacking Me 109. I took my wingman and went in after the 109 and got him out of there. The German was last seen going down and the pilot was reported as having bailed out. Sometimes you just have to do what you have to do and hope for a little luck."

First Lieutenant William M. Barsky confirmed Capt. Hooker's claim of one Me 262 destroyed, stating:

> "I saw White Leader Capt. Hooker pull in a climbing turn to the left behind an Me 262. He fired and I saw intense strikes on the left wing and fuselage of the 262. The jet peeled off to the left and went straight down from 26,000 feet. Captain Hooker broke away to the right and I followed the 262 down. At about 10,000 feet, the pilot bailed out. The 262 hit the ground and exploded. I watched the pilot in his chute until he almost hit the ground, then I pulled up and rejoined the bombers."

First Lieutenant Charles E. Heathman also confirmed Capt. Hooker's Me 262 claim, citing the smoke coming from the stricken jet.

Second Lieutenant Sylvan R. Routh confirmed Capt. Hooker's destruction of the Me 109:

> "I was flying wing to Captain Hooker, in the position of Lakeside White Two, when 109s made a pass from about seven o'clock and a little low. A 109 began firing at the B-24s and Captain Hooker got behind him and really clobbered the 109 with his first bursts. The Me 109 caught fire immediately and the pilot bailed out right after the fire started."

On this date, the insanity of war reached a high point for the German Luftwaffe when a specially formed unit known as *Sonderkommando Elbe* flew its only operation of the war. The proposed objective of the all-volunteer unit was to bring down heavy bombers by, if no other means, ramming them. Previously, about a hundred and fifty very young, not more than boys with minimal flight training, attended a ten-day course in the tactics they were to apply. During the classes, the pilots were instructed to make a diving attack, firing on a bomber. If the attack failed to score hits adequate to begin sending the victim down, the pilots were to ram the *Viermot*, preferably striking the bomber's midsection with the fighter's wing. It was hoped that this method would enable the attacker to survive the crash and give him a chance to bail out. The curriculum also included heavy doses of Nazi indoctrination designed to put the volunteers into the right frame of mind in order to carry out their task. The unit became ready and over a hundred pilots flying their Me 109s, plus a dozen Me 262s assigned to provide them cover, went after the bomber formations. Urged on by radio communications that included slogans like "*Deutschland über Alles*" and patriotic music, the *Ramstaffel* pilots attacked. Members of B group, and those who remained from A group, both reported seeing instances or evidence of ramming: At 1235 hours, ten miles west of Lüneburg, an Me 109 was seen to ram a B-24, which in turn, struck another B-24 as it went down. Pilots from the group who witnessed the attack did not note any chutes coming from either of the stricken airplanes. Similar observations by others at the same location, did however, describe seven or eight crewmembers exiting from the two burning bombers as they plunged downward.

Seven miles south of Lübeck, a B-17 was spotted spinning down, the reason unknown. Two parachutes came out of the plane. Five miles north of Lüneburg, a B-17 with its right elevator missing was seen to be spinning down from 19,000 ft. at 1305 hrs. Five chutes were watched as they emerged from the damaged bomber. Another of the crew appeared to be caught on the plane as he was seen hanging from his chute which seemed to be caught on something near the ship's nose. A 467th BG B-24, identified as having a white on red tail and marked with the numbers 931, had its right stabilizer severely damaged. This aircraft was closely escorted on a course of 254 degrees from the target area to east of Dümmer Lake where the plane was left on its own at 1325 hrs./15,000 ft. No radio contact could be made, but the bomber appeared to be flying well enough on its own. In all, it is thought that eight heavies were brought down by *Sonderkommando Elbe*. The rammers paid a heavy price though, as the majority of the nearly sixty German fighters brought down in battle were from that unit.

Finally, despite the opposition, the target was reached and bombs were released to fall away. The time over target was

1258 hrs./18,000 ft. Results of the strike were observable and they were reported to be excellent. Debris-laden smoke raising to 15,000 ft. stood in testament to that fact. The trip out and back home was uneventful with L/O occurring over the Elbe Estuary at 1350 hrs./20,000 ft. B group remained with the bombers until the force reached a location 40 miles northwest of Vlieland Island, off the coast of Holland. There they broke from the heavies at 1430 hrs./22,000 ft and made for AAF Station F-377.

Observations made during the mission included: Twenty miles northeast of Nienburg, a B-24, identified as having a black tail, was hit by a jet, but seemed only to suffer damage. The A/C did not go down, but instead, broke formation, did a 180-degree turn and calling for escorts, headed for home. An Me 262 dropped four star flares over Ulzen at 1230 hrs. Fifteen miles east of Hamburg, a P-51, identified as having a blue tail, collided with a B-24 while chasing an unidentified enemy aircraft. The E/A had bounced the Liberator and set its wing on fire. Trading tit for tat, one of the B-24s clobbered two Me 109s ten miles west of Lüneburg. Ten miles west of Fassburg, a tail gunner in another of the bombers nailed a unidentified fighter. There was a large explosion in the air at 1310 hrs/17,000 feet, ten miles northwest of Steinhuder Lake. B-17s were in the area at the time. Two miles south of Ratzeburg, an unidentified fighter exploded at 1340 hrs. Red-nosed P-51s (4th FG) were operating in the area. Nine transport ships being escorted by 12 destroyers were seen in the Elbe Estuary. They appeared to be headed towards Hamburg. There seemed to be quite a lot of shipping activity in Lübeck Bay. There were 15 unidentified single-engine aircraft and three Me 262s parked in revetments at an airfield near Bad Kleinen, just north of Schwerin Lake. An airfield near Lüneburg had another eight unidentified, silver-colored twin-engine and 15 unidentified single-engine aircraft parked on it. Twelve to sixteen Me 262s were parked on the airfield at Reinsehlen. Buildings on the west side of the field had red crosses painted on their roofs. Thirty-five unidentified single and twin-engine aircraft were seen well dispersed in a wooded area near the airfield at Wenzendorf. There were also eight dummy A/C placed on the south side of the field. The city of Wilhelmshaven was putting up a smoke screen. The marshalling yard at Lüneburg was loaded with goods wagons. Flak over Blauort Island was heavy, meager and accurate while at Elmshorn and an area just north of Soltau, it was heavy, meager and inaccurate.

Jack M. Clark was a Warrant Officer in the armament section of the 479th FG while it was stationed at Wattisham. He served with the group and the 435th FS from 21 October 1943 until October 1945 when he was shipped out prior to its returning to the U.S. In 1987 he wrote a brief essay in which he recalled the section's achievements and some humorous stories that happened during his time with the group and squadron. One of those concerned the crack outfit he worked with and party held just prior to a mission. He wrote:

> "I got along well with the men in the 435th's armament section and considered them the best darned armorers around. I had come up through the ranks and was a Chief Warrant Officer during most of my tenure with the squadron. The men seemed to like the fact that they could call me Mister. [The proper form of address for a warrant officer. During my time of service in the army, I must confess that I thought well of the term and enjoyed working with W.O.'s also. They were stuck in the middle of the command structure, neither enlisted men nor officers either.] They knew that I had been at all of their rank levels before and understood their problems and desires. As a team we helped make the P-51 Mustang an outstanding gun platform by analyzing each malfunction and doing things which had not been done before. For example, we did not oil the guns after cleaning them. We added a second heater to the guns, which prevented them from freezing up at high altitudes. That was one of the major causes of gun malfunctions for us. We realigned and secured the ammunition feed chutes to reduce drag as the belted .50 cal. ammunition fed into the guns during firing. We designed a gun spread harmonization pattern that gave the pilots greater odds for a kill once they had an enemy plane in their sights. We installed the K-14 gyroscopic lead-compensating gun sights at our squadron level, which prevented long installation delays at our depot. Through their ingenuity, ability and desire, the armament section attained the best record in the 8th Air Force, firing an average of over 8,000 rounds per malfunction.
>
> "With these achievements in mind, I felt obligated to the men to do something special for them other than the normal promotion and decorations. Yes, those came, but what I had in mind was a celebration party and so one was organized. Kegs of English beer were ordered along with food fit for a king. All of this was delivered to our armament shop for the big bash. It didn't take long to determine that there would be many 'chug-a-lugs' that

evening and that I would become the center of attention. I made one provision though. That was the men were to drink a pint to each of my half-pints. What I didn't realize was as each of them finished his pint, he would slip outside, stick his finger down his throat and throw up the beer. Then he would return for another. Needless to say I soon lost, much to the pleasure of all.

"The next morning I knew that I would have to be at the flight line bright and early in order to set an example. When I got there, the place was quiet except for some singing coming from the aircraft parking area. I walked to that area only to find gun bay doors up on the planes and all the men were getting their .50 cal. machine guns ready for the day's mission. Oh, yes, there was one difference; there were partially filled pints of 'good old English mild and bitters' on each wing. As I remember, the days mission was one of the better."

Warrant Officer Jack M. Clark (front center in the dark uniform) with his armorers for that party. Master Sergeant Arthur H. Wilcox, his right-hand man is to his immediate right. *Courtesy of Albert M. Myers.*

8 April 1945

Eighth AF FO 1918A

No. 340 & 341 Sunday. The group was divided into two forces, A and B groups, both penetration to target and withdrawal escorts for a CW of 2nd AD B-24s attacking their 8th AF Mission 932 primary target, the airfield at Fürth, Germany. Maj. Duffié led A group, which consisted of 30 P-51s (10-434th & 20-436th). Up: 0911 hrs., down: 1435 hrs. with no early returns. First Lieutenant Theo J. Sowerby led B group, which consisted of 30 P-51s (10-434th & 20-435th). Up: 0919 hrs., down: 1437 hrs. with no early returns.

A group made L/F over Walcheren Island, Holland at 1000 hrs./17,000 ft. Once beyond the German border, R/V with the proper bombers was 40 miles west of Koblenz at 1043 hrs./ 23,000 ft. The B-24s were escorted through the target, where bombs away was at 1207 hrs./23,000 ft. Results were excellent and appeared to be centered on buildings and the northwest corner of the field. The Big Friends were taken back out to the breakaway point which was the same location as was R/V.

B group made L/F over the same area as did A group and about a minute later at 16,000 ft. R/V with their assigned bombers was ten miles southeast of Aachen, Germany at 1046 hrs./24,000 ft. The B-24s were escorted through the target and back out again to southeast of Bonn where the escorts broke from the bombers at 1305 hrs./13,500 ft. Bombing results were excellent, but the first box dropped their loads on an open field near an already beat up airfield. L/O was over Walcheren Island at 1331 hrs./12,000 ft.

Observations made during the mission included bogies that were called in at 1145 hours, ten miles south of Crailsheim. They turned out to be friendlies. The bombers were pretty well spread out and Vinegrove 3-3 and 3-4 reported being hit at 1200-1205 hrs. Vinegrove 2-10 reported enemy aircraft taking off below it. At 1240 hrs./17,000 ft. and eight miles west of Weisbaden, a B-24 identified as having a vertical black stripe on a white tail (44th BG) fired a burst at the number four P-51 in Purple Flight. This occurred after the same P-51s had provided the bombers close escort for almost two hours! The airfield at Illesheim had 15 plus unidentified twin-engine aircraft parked on it. Black smoke was seen coming from a factory at Nürnberg. Radio communications were difficult due to so much traffic and German jamming. Flak over Nürnberg was heavy, intense and inaccurate. It was heavy, moderate and accurate over Karlstadt.

9 April 1945

Eighth AF FO 1929A

No. 342 Monday. Capt. Hooker led the group, which consisted of 54 P-51s (18-434th, 18-435th & 18-436th) on a penetration to target and withdrawal escort for the fourth force, first CW of 2nd AD B-24s attacking their 8th AF Mission 935 primary target, the airfield at Landsberg, Germany. Up: 1432 hrs., down: 1940 hrs. with no early returns.

For the first time in the past two weeks, the wind was not blowing at Wattisham. However, a ground hugging fog that shrouded the landscape, settled in to take its place there. By mid-morning it had lifted enough to think about allowing the day's mission to proceed, but still the scheduled take off time was delayed about an hour.

Beginning with this mission, the 8th AF went after those airfields on which Me 262 jets were based. L/F was over Ostend, Belgium at 1523 hrs./16,000 ft. Heading southeast and crossing into Germany, the P-51s R/V'd with their assigned B-24s 15 miles northeast of Freiberg at 1630 hrs./25,000 ft. From there the force continued on east toward the target, the Big Friends making it difficult along the way for their escorts to cover them properly because their formation was scattered, with bombers trailing behind. The situation could have been favorable for an attack by enemy fighters and in fact, two possible jet contrails were sighted west of Lake Constance (Bodensee) at 1711 hours, but nothing came of it. On the way in, it was noted that there were two huge oil fires; the first was about 24 miles northwest of Kempten and the other was about ten miles north of the target area. Just prior to entering the target area, one of the B-24s was hit in an engine by flak. The plane dropped back, but seemed okay. Landsberg was reached at 1730 hrs. and the heavies released their bombs to fall upon the airfield there from 22,000 ft. The weather was good so results of the strike could be observed. Unfortunately, those results appeared to be poor except for hits on the runways, which were well clobbered. The observers in the two command Mosquitoes present in the area were probably not happy. Turning out to head home, another large oil fire was seen 15 miles west of Ingolstadt. Escort continued back west until 1820 hours, at which point the fighters left the bombers for L/O over Knokke, Belgium at 1903 hrs./11,000 ft.

The only observation made during the mission was an ineffective smoke screen that was seen along the Paar River, between Ingolstadt and Augsburg. Flak over Landsberg was heavy, meager and accurate.

10 April 1945

Eighth AF FO 1936A

No. 343 & 344 Tuesday. The group was divided into two forces, A and B groups, both penetration to target and withdrawal escorts for 2nd AD B-24s attacking their 8th AF Mission 938 primary target, the airfield at Parchim, Germany. Col. Riddle

Lieutenant Wallace A. Rudat on his Little Joan. *Courtesy of Mario V. Prevosti.*

led A group, which consisted of 38 P-51s (21-434th & 17-436th). Up: 1209 hrs., down: 1727 hrs. with no early returns. Capt. Hooker was to lead B group, but had a mechanical failure a few minutes after take off and had to abort the mission. That put First Lieutenant William M. Barsky in position to lead the group, which consisted of 21 P-51s from the 435th FS. Up: 1216 hrs., down: 1712 hrs. with one early return.

After a trip up northeast over the North Sea, A group made L/F southwest of Husum in the Schleswig Holstein area of Germany at 1355 hrs./20,000 ft. Driving eastward, R/V with the proper bombers was 25 miles southwest of Kiel at 1424 hrs./22,000 ft. Time over target was 1454 hrs./23,000 ft. The bombing results classified as good, were observable through the hazy, 5/10ths cloud coverage. Returning on a southwest course, the group broke from the bombers in the area of Steinhuder Lake at 1600 hrs./23,000 ft. L/O was over Walcheren Island, Holland at 1640 hrs./9,000 ft.

B group also flew up the North Sea and made L/F to the north of Husum at 1352 hrs./24,000 ft. The group picked up their assigned B-24s 25 southeast of Husum at 1423 hrs./24,000 ft. Heading east by southeast, their time over target was also 1454 hours, but at 24,000 ft. B group followed the same route as A group took back towards home and broke from their bombers 15 miles north of Münster at 1600 hrs./18,000 ft. L/O was north of Ijmuiden, Holland at 1626 hrs./11,000 ft.

Observations made during the mission included, after making L/F at Husum, a bogie was sighted heading north, but the aircraft could not be identified. A smoke screen was put up to shield the area of Kiel, but it was ineffective. Enroute to the target, one of the B-24s left the formation in the vicinity of Neumünster, turned back and appeared to be heading for Denmark. Fifteen to thirty naval vessels were seen in the harbor

Captain Richard M. Lunstrum. *Courtesy of David L. Born.*

Captain Arlett G. Mosier, Jr. *Courtesy of Arlett G. Mosier, Jr.*

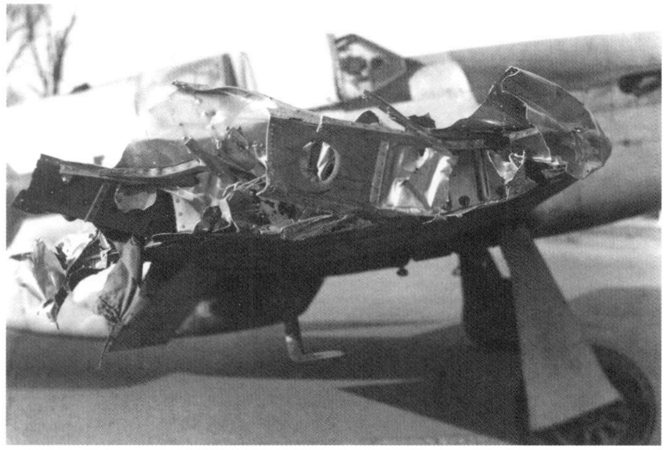

L2-3, a 434th FS war-weary aircraft that was damaged in a taxiing accident on this date. *Courtesy of George E. Falkner.*

northeast of Lübeck. There was also a great amount of traffic seen in the marshalling yard there. Fifteen miles east of Lüneburg, what was possibly a bomber, was seen explode. Twenty miles south of Ulzen, a B-24 exploded, but it was too far away to see if there were any parachutes that came from it. Twenty-five miles northwest of Magdeburg, a yellow-tailed B-17 was seen blow up while another spiraled downward before doing the same. (Probably both A/C were from the 486th or the 487th BGs, which between the two, lost a total of six B-17s during the mission.) This time, five chutes were spotted. Smoke and flames could be seen in the vicinity of Deventer, Holland. Flak over Ludwigslust was heavy, moderate and inaccurate. It was heavy, meager and accurate over Rhenen and in the Emmerich area. Southwest of Osnabrück, it was heavy, meager and inaccurate. Over Wittenburg, flak was heavy, moderate and accurate.

Previous to this date, Captains Richard (Swede) M. Lunstrum from the 434th FS and Arlett (Art) G. Mosier, Jr. from the 436th FS had been assigned the duty of picking up a pair of P-51s from the 8th AF's Warton Base Air Depot (BAD 2). Their assignment was to deliver them to Stockholm, Sweden. The then classified flight was part of a U.S. State Department aircraft sale to Sweden. The two pilots had left Wattisham for the air depot, which was located near Blackpool on the western coast of England. From BAD 2 they flew two P-51s eastward across England to Metfield, an AAF station near the eastern coast and south west of Lowestoft. The former home of the 491st BG, a 2nd AD group, was now occupied by the European Division of Air Transport (USSTAF) whose main function there was to provide a link with Sweden for the purpose of secretly ferrying personnel and transporting special materials out of that country. The two 479th FG pilots departed Metfield on this date and flew to Stockholm where they dropped off the two birds. (As a matter of interest, the aircraft flown by Capt. Mosier, serial no. 44-72105, became the longest serving Mustang in the Swedish Air Force.) Capt. Lunstrum, who was of Swedish descent, received an extra warm welcome upon their arrival. After a short stay, the two were returned to England and the shooting war.

11 April 1945

Eighth AF FO 1944A

No. 345 & 346 Wednesday. The group was divided into two forces, A and B groups, both penetration to target and withdrawal escorts for 2nd AD B-24s attacking their 8th AF Mission 941 primary targets in Germany, an ordnance depot at Regensburg and the marshalling yard at Amberg. Maj. Duffié led A group, which consisted of 18 P-51s from the 436th FS. Up: 1027 hrs., down: 1640 hrs. with one early return. Maj. Olds led B group, which consisted of 45 P-51s (23-434th & 22-435th). Up: 1038 hrs., down: 1632 hrs. with three early returns.

This mission fell into the category titled "Milk Runs". The trip was totally uneventful and, in fact, the entire force returned safe and sound. The weatherman even outdid himself, providing better than forecast skies for the mission. A group made L/F in the vicinity of Knokke, Belgium at 1115 hrs./ 17,000 ft. After passing over Belgium and crossing into the airspace over Germany, they R/V'd with their assigned B-24s near Bingen at 1218 hrs./15,000 ft. Having provided escort for the heavies to their target area at Regensburg, they broke from them at 1325 hrs./25,000 ft. Under orders not to strafe, they went hunting for other trouble. Stooging south to Landshut, then back up to Regensburg and finally along the exit course the Big Friends were taking out, the group looked for adversaries. Finding nothing, the group rejoined the bombers 15 miles southwest of Koblenz, staying with them until near Aachen where they broke escort at 1500 hrs./8,500 ft. L/O was by Westkapelle, Belgium at 1551 hrs./8,000 ft.

B group made L/F at Knokke slightly higher and a few minutes later than A group. They R/V'd with their proper Big Friends in the Wiesbaden area at 1218 hrs./22,000 ft. Escort was to and from the target area at Amberg, which is 30-35 miles north-northwest of Regensburg. Escort was broken near Würzburg at 1415 hrs./17,000 ft. and L/O was by Overflakkee, Holland at 1546 hrs./5,000 ft.

Observations made during the mission included: At R/V, the B-24s were spread all over the sky. The bombing results at Regensburg were good while those at Amberg appeared to be poor. There were many fires spotted in the Ruhr area as the group passed over that locale. Red crosses were seen on the ground, 13 miles east of Würzburg. Six single-engine and four twin-engine A/C were parked in revetments at Straubing's airfield. There were 50 plus single-engine aircraft parked on the southeast side, at the base of a hill, at the Landshut/Lutzenjof Airfield. The marshalling yard at Landshut was well clobbered. Another ten single-engine aircraft were setting around the hangars on the west side of the airfield at Obrtraubling. Ten trains in the marshalling yard at Regensburg looked to be stationary. There was a hospital train consisting of ten cars seen at Neumünster. An airfield near Schierling had many camouflaged emplacements and roads. There were also 50 plus buildings located there. Flak over Regensburg was heavy, meager and inaccurate.

First Lieutenant William H. (Hank) Daudistel from the 434th FS shows off his full set of flight gear. *David L. Born.*

13 April 1945

2nd AD FO 686A

No. 347 Friday. Capt. Hooker led the group, which consisted of 48 P-51s (21-434th, 13-435th & 14-436th) on a penetration to target and withdrawal escort for a CW of 1st AD B-17s attacking their 8th AF Mission 945 secondary target, a marshalling yard at Neumünster, Germany. They also strafed targets of opportunity. Up: 1355 hrs., down: 1930 hrs. with a total of two early returns.

The ban on strafing had been lifted and the boys went out looking for some business. The wrecking crew was about to strike. There was just one problem that day; it was a "Friday the Thirteenth".

L/F and R/V both occurred over the same place, Westerhever in the Schleswig-Holstein area of northern Germany at 1516 hrs./21,000 ft. The Big Friends were not able to make the primary target, the airfield at Hagenow, so the secondary was bombed through haze and smoke at 1535

J2-O, a 435th FS P-51 takes to the air for a mission. *Courtesy of Albert M. Myers.*

hrs./22,000 ft. For the most part, actual observation of the results was not possible due to the cloud coverage noted previously; however, the results were believed to be good. Dropping nearly straight south, the escorts broke from the B-17s 15 miles northwest of Brunswick at 1615 hrs./22,000 ft. Heading back up north, the squadrons attacked airfields located at Salzwedel, Lübeck-Blankensee, Tarnewitz, Kaltenkirchen and the Ratzeburger Lake area. When all was finished, the claims stood at 47-0-33 destroyed and damaged on the ground as well as 5-0-0 locomotives rendered up as scrap in the Gadebusch area, east of Ratzeburger Lake. Final confirmation of the claims resulted in awards of 37-0-28, plus those shared. The group lost three of its own and almost another as a result of the strafing runs. The claims were broken down thusly:

434th FS

1-0-0	Ar 234	Maj. Robin Olds	Lübeck-Blankensee
1-0-0	Ar 234	2nd Lt. Roy M. Rossel	Lübeck-Blankensee
0-0-1	Me 410	Maj. Robin Olds	Tarnewitz
1-0-0	Fw 190	1st Lt. Lauri A. Hendrickson	Kaltenkirchen
0-0-1	Ju 88	Capt. Donald J. Pierce	Kaltenkirchen
1-0-0	Ju 88	1st Lt. Jerome K. Nagel	Kaltenkirchen
4-0-12	UI/SE	Shared*	Ratzeburger Lake

* Unidentified single-engine floatplanes described as looking like Fw 190s on floats (possibly Ar 196s) shared equally between 1st Lieutenants Clifford W. Bowers, Phillip A. Brown, Richard D. Creighton, John T. Golden, Ossie J. Huval, Robert B. Kline, Richard G. Simpson and Frank W. Taylor.

435th FS

1-0-2	Ju 88	Capt. Verne E. Hooker	Tarnewitz
1-0-4	Ju 88	Capt. Theo J. Sowerby	Tarnewitz
1-0-2	Ju 88	1st. Lt. William B. Rourke	Tarnewitz

436th FS

1-0-0	Fw 190	2nd Lt. John M. Archibald	Salzwedel
0-0-1	Me 110	2nd Lt. John M. Archibald	Salzwedel
2-0-0	Fw 190	1st Lt. Charles H. Darling	Salzwedel
0-0-1	Me 110	1st Lt. Charles H. Darling	Salzwedel
0-0-1	UI/TE	1st Lt. Charles H. Darling	Salzwedel
1-0-0	Fw 190	1st Lt. John R. Early III	Salzwedel
1-0-0	Me 110	1st Lt. John R. Early III	Salzwedel

0-0-1	Me 410	1st Lt. John R. Early III	Salzwedel
3-0-0	Fw 190	1st Lt. Kenneth J. Hansen	Salzwedel
1-0-0	Me 110	1st Lt. Kenneth J. Hansen	Salzwedel
1-0-0	Me 109	1st Lt. Ernest J. Hopcroft	Salzwedel
2-0-0	Me 410	1st Lt. Ernest J. Hopcroft	Salzwedel
1-0-0	Fw 190	1st Lt. Bernard R. Kleinman	Salzwedel
1-0-0	Me 110	1st Lt. Bernard R. Kleinman	Salzwedel
2-0-0	Fw 190	2nd Lt. Sylvester F. Long	Salzwedel
2-0-2	Fw 190	Capt. Jay C. Malone	Salzwedel
1-0-0	Me 110	Capt. Jay C. Malone	Salzwedel
0-0-1	Me 410	Capt. Jay C. Malone	Salzwedel
0-0-1	Fw 190	2nd Lt. Richard C. J. Palson	Salzwedel
2-0-1	He 111	2nd Lt. Richard C. J. Palson	Salzwedel
1-0-0	Fw 190	2nd Lt. Charles H. Philbrick	Salzwedel
1-0-3	Me 109	2nd Lt. Charles H. Philbrick	Salzwedel
0-0-1	UI/TE	2nd Lt. Charles H. Philbrick	Salzwedel
0-0-1	Me 109	Capt. Presson S. Shane	Salzwedel
1-0-0	Me 410	Capt. Presson S. Shane	Salzwedel
1-0-0	UI/TE	Capt. Presson S. Shane	Salzwedel
1-0-0	Fw 190	1st Lt. Walter B. Steph	Salzwedel
0-0-1	Me 109	1st Lt. Walter B. Steph	Salzwedel
2-0-1	Fw 190	1st Lt. George H. Witzel	Salzwedel
0-0-1	Me 110	1st Lt. George H. Witzel	Salzwedel
1-0-1	Me 109	1st Lt. Fred Zellman	Salzwedel
1-0-0	Me 410	1st Lt. Fred Zellman	Salzwedel

Documentation of the strafing was done by squadron leader or flight leader. Starting with Newcross Squadron, the events are laid out by Major Robin Olds:

> "I was leading Newcross Squadron on an escort to Neumünster, Field Order No. 1964A. I took the squadron down on Lübeck-Blankensee airdrome shortly after target time, approximately 1550 hrs. The weather there was CAVU. I had the flights circle while White Two, my wingman, Second Lieutenant Roy M. Rossel, Jr., and I went down on a dive-strafe to test for flak. We managed to pot two Ar 234s on the pass. They were situated on a hardstand off the northeast end of the runway. I broke left on recovery and went directly over a flak position on the northeast side of a lake, which was located on the southeast side of the field. I called this in to the rest of the squadron and told them to eliminate the position. They hesitated due to a misunderstanding and since I had attained position again, I told them to follow me down this time. I made a pass at the guns. One flight followed me. By then, other guns began opening up. We had too few airplanes to knock out all the flak, so I told the boys to leave. Two fires were left on the field, both verified by the flights circling above.
>
> "I then went to Tarnewitz and pulled a dive-strafe by myself. I managed to damage an Me 410 on this pass, but the flak here was both intense and accurate. In fact, they knocked off one of my flaps and punched a couple of holes in my wing. I told the boys to leave that field alone and headed home myself. The time was approximately 1615 hrs. and the weather still CAVU. I claim one Ar 234 destroyed and one Me 410 damaged for myself and confirm Lt. Rossel's Ar 234 destroyed claim."

A number of years later, then Brigadier General Olds, Ret., told of his difficulties in bringing his wounded bird home:

> "I was hit by flak as I was pulling out of a dive-strafing pass on an airfield called Tarnewitz, located in Germany, up on the Baltic. Five P-51s made a pass on the airdrome that April day. I was the only one to return home. It was

Friday the Thirteenth! The trip home to England was long and lonely. When I tested the stall characteristics of my wounded bird over our home airfield, I found it quit flying at a little over 175 mph indicated and rolled violently into the dead wing. What to do? Bailout seemed the logical response, but here's where sentiment got in the way of reason. That airplane had taken me through a lot and I was damned if I was going to give up on her. We had a long stretch of flying field running northeast to southwest and I thought I'd put her down on the grass next to the PSP. At least the grass was smoother than the steel matting and I'd have a better chance of keeping contact with Mother Earth as I bled off speed. So with no flaps and no right aileron control, (see the severed cable dangling on the far right of the picture?) I lined up way out and dragged her in at 180. I didn't put her down; I had to force her down and keep those wheels in contact with the grass. Sure enough, the right wing quit flying at about 176 mph and the left wing was still happily full of lift. With only one aileron, it turned out to be a wild ride. Fortunately for me, the rudder and good left aileron sufficed to keep me upright, though why the bird and I survived the careening, bouncing and juttering ride down the length of the field, I guess I'll never know. My crew chief, T/Sgt. Glen A. Wold and some of the hangar crew put a new wing on my SCAT VI that night and I test hopped the bird the next day. Unfortunately, the plane was soon declared War-Weary."

Kermit Brickson, then a clerk typist in the Operations Section of the 434th FS, tells another side of that story:

"It was Friday the Thirteenth, an unlucky day if you believe in those sort of things. I can remember telling Major Olds to be careful and wishing him good luck as he left our office for the mission he was about to go out on. Later in the day, when he wasn't back yet, I became concerned, as we knew that there had been a lot of action where they went. Finally, we heard him talking on the radio to the control tower, as he made his approach. (We could listen to the radio in the nearby S-2 Intelligence Section.) Robin told the tower he was coming straight in for a landing, as his plane was pretty badly shot up. As he made the approach, he was singing 'The Hard Way, The Hard Way'. After he had landed, he taxied his plane up to the main repair hangar, which was just next to our office. I ran out to take a look at it and could not believe that he had made it back in that wreck. When I saw him, I reminded him of what I had told him before the mission. His answer, 'I made it back, didn't I?' Yes, he certainly had."

This photo shows flak damage to the P-51 (44-11746, L2-W SCAT VI) Major Robin Olds was flying 13 April 1945. The plane was hit by flak over Tarnewitz A/D that date. Notice the missing wing flap and dangling control wires. *Courtesy of the Wings of Freedom Museum.*

Captain Donald J. Pierce:

"I was leading Newcross Red Flight on an escort mission to Neumünster. Shortly before reaching the target area, Newcross Leader, Major Olds, directed me to check Kaltenkirchen Airdrome. I took my flight down and found two flights of P-51s, believed to be from the 364th Fighter Group, circling the field. We circled above and watched

Lieutenant Lauri A. Hendrickson is standing on the wing of a P-51 named Miss Georgia Carol. The plane's crew chief, Technical Sergeant, Milan J. (John) Stanovich had that name applied in honor of his daughter. Lieutenant Hendrickson was nicknamed "The Flying Dutchman" and later had that name applied to the plane's canopy rails. *Courtesy of Frederick C. Hayner.*

them make a pass across the field, leaving behind one A/C burning. As they pulled away, I positioned my flight to make a dive-strafing pass from out of the sun. Jerry was alert by this time and we received both heavy and intense light flak, which was altogether. It discouraged us from pushing our attack. On the one pass made, we concentrated our fire on two Ju 88s and one Fw 190. The Fw 190 and one of the Ju 88s burst into flames. Although I saw repeated strikes from my own fire on the other Ju 88, it did not burn. Immediately thereafter, we left the area to report back to the group. I claim one Ju 88 damaged and confirm the Ju 88 destroyed by Lt. Nagel and the Fw 190 destroyed by Lt. Hendrickson."

The approximate time of the attack was 1550 hrs. and the weather there was CAVU with just a slight haze.

First Lieutenant Robert B. Kline:

"On Friday, April 13th, I was leading Newcross Blue Flight and we were on a bomber escort mission to Neumünster. We gave close support to the target area and as there were no bandits in the vicinity, we dropped down to look for targets of opportunity. At Ratzeburger Lake, we found nineteen (19) single-engine aircraft on floats, parked along the southeastern shore of the lake. We dropped our wing tanks and I took my wingman down for a pass to test for flak. Finding practically none, I set the flight up on a strafing pattern that ran northwest to southeast. At that point, Newcross Purple Flight joined us. Two passes were made in the NW to SE direction and then we changed direction to a south to north pattern. On the first pass in the new direction, we met the 4th Fighter Group coming in, head-on, and ruining the hell out of our strafing pattern. We got them on "C" channel and told them to join our pattern, which they did. When we got the pattern set up and the directions fully organized, we made approximately fifty (50) collective passes on the base. I pulled up after one pass as there was too much confusion and, also, I wanted to circle above and observe the results of the firing passes. After about ten minutes, The 4th Fighter Group pulled out, claiming three damaged. Then I called up Blue Flight and we pulled out ourselves, leaving Purple Flight to continue strafing. Purple Three and Four were the last to leave. About 45 minutes later, I flew back over the same area at about 50 feet and there was not a single floatplane there that had not been well clobbered. One was still burning and two others were smoking.

"As every man in the two flights made repeated passes from varying approaches and angles, it is impossible to credit any particular individual with a definite claim. Although every A/C parked in the area was repeatedly strafed, unfortunately only four were observed to burn. In view of this, I claim four (4) unidentified single-engine floatplanes destroyed and twelve damaged, to be shared between the members of Newcross Blue and Purple Flights who participated in the strafing runs, those members being First Lieutenants Bowers, Brown, Creighton, Golden, Huval, Kline, Simpson and Taylor. In addition to those claims, I also confirm three (3) damaged claims for the 4th Fighter Group."

The time of the attack was 1625 to 1645 hrs. and the weather was reported to be CAVU.

Lakeside Squadron, Captain Theo J. Sowerby:

"After our bombers hit their secondary target, we circled an airfield which some Newcross planes were strafing. [Probably Kaltenkirchen, see above.] After circling for approximately ten minutes, we decided there was too much flak so we set course for Tarnewitz, our originally assigned airfield, which we were going to strafe. We orbited that field, observing many planes of all types below. I led Lakeside White Flight on a dive-strafing pass at 1630 hours and I shot up one plane, which I believed to be a Ju 88, right inside a hangar. Lakeside Yellow Flight was reporting lots of flak at this field, but after I pulled up, White Three, First Lieutenant Richard G. Candelaria, asked to make one more pass, as he had picked something to fire upon. I okayed his request and he started a shallow dive on a course of 30 degrees, heading in toward the airfield from the nearby bay. He picked up a lot of flak and soon called on the radio, reporting that he had been hit and had no oil pressure. He asked for the best steer for friendly territory. [Theo Sowerby had the reputation of having a good sense of direction and often times would wind up bringing other units that had lost their way, back to England. His previous experience as a surveyor came in handy and it was known in the squadron that Sowerby could get them home.] I told him to fly a course of 200 degrees, which he did for about five minutes. He then called and said his ship was pretty hot and guessed he would have to bail out. This was right near the town of

Wittenburg. He bailed out okay and on reaching the ground, ran into some nearby woods. There was neither traffic nor people to be seen near him. His plane crashed and exploded in the woods, some ways to the north of where he landed in his chute. I think Lt. Candelaria had a good chance of escaping." [That was not to be, as Lieutenant Candelaria wound up becoming a POW.]

"We set a course of 240 degrees and passed over a grass auxiliary field near Lüneburg. [Located approximately near Darchau, 20 miles east of Lüneburg.] There were about 15 Ju 88s parked on it. Three of us from White Flight, Capt. Hooker, Lt. Rourke and myself went down on this field at about 1700 hours and after about six passes, we got three of the Ju 88s burning. The other planes we attacked would not burn, although we shot them up quite badly. Evidently, they had no gasoline or oil in them. I definitely saw three planes burning on the airfield when we left. I believe Capt. Hooker, Lt. Rourke and I each started one of these planes burning. I claim one Ju 88 destroyed and three Ju 88s damaged on this field as well as one Ju 88 damaged on the Tarnewitz airfield. Captain Hooker claims one Ju 88 destroyed here and two Ju 88s damaged on the unidentified airfield and Lt. Rourke claims one Ju 88 destroyed here and two Ju 88s damaged on the unidentified airfield."

Lieutenant Theo J. Sowerby. *Courtesy of Oranne (Sowerby) Hilgerman.*

Bison Squadron's Captain Jay C. Malone:

"I was leading the squadron on a bomber escort mission to Hagenow airfield as per 8th AF FO 1964A. We were briefed to be close support for the heavies from R/V through the target and back over friendly territory. Bison Squadron followed the briefed procedure and after calling Nuthouse to inform him that we were leaving the heavies, we did so west of Celle. We were over a 5-8/10ths undercast at the time, so closer geographical location was impossible. We then turned back toward our strafing area. I found a large hole in the undercast at about 8,000 feet and took the squadron through it. The cloud base ranged from 3,500 to 6,000 feet with the coverage consisting of fair weather cumulus. Beneath the undercast, there was a haze that limited visibility to about five to eight miles. We discovered an airfield, which I first believed to be Ludwigslust, but wasn't certain because we didn't know our exact position. Later, upon returning to base, I determined that we had been at Salzwedel.

"The field was covered with aircraft and despite the low ceiling, I decided to check it for flak. I put on full boost at about 3800 feet, did a wingover and headed at a Fw 190 parked on the end of a runway. I hit the Fw on this pass and to my surprise, there was no flak. After checking with the remainder of my squadron, who had stayed above, I found they had observed no flak either. Still not believing my eyes, I decided to test the airfield again. I made a pass at the same Fw 190, which was on the opposite end of the field from the building area I was above. Heading towards it, I observed strikes all over the Fw 190, but it still didn't burn. Again, I observed no flak and the remainder of the squadron reported no flak. Still distrustful, I made one more pass at the Fw 190 and this time it burned. As no one in the squadron observed any flak, I called the remainder of White Flight plus Red Flight down and we set up a strafing pattern that ran from north to south. We made about three more passes and as there was absolutely no flak, I radioed instructions to reduce power to 35 inches manifold pressure at 2400 RPM and

Crew chief Technical Sergeant Stanley L. Steele, First Lieutenant Charles H. Darling and an unknown armorer by their 436th FS P-51, Dottie Mae. *Courtesy of Charles H. Darling.*

Master Sergeant Ray L. Robertson, Staff Sergeant Kenneth G. Shoemaker, Lieutenant Walter B. (Becky) Steph and Corporal Joseph G. McCredie by their Bison Squadron ship. *Courtesy of Thomas H. Thompson.*

told everyone to use ten degrees of flaps. White and Red Flights made about five more passes at the field and I counted fifteen plus fires going after they finished. At this time, Yellow Flight and the two spares, which were left as top cover, called stating that there were many more planes in a wooded area northeast of the field we were currently strafing. This was a rather nasty break as the wind was from 280 degrees and the smoke from burning planes partially obscured the Me 110s, Me 410s and single-engine aircraft setting in that woods. The planes were very well camouflaged, being parked in amongst the trees along the edge of the woods and covered with nets over them and pine boughs strewn along over their wings. I reversed the traffic pattern and we started working on the concealed aircraft. I called White and Red Flights, telling them to stop shooting when they got down to tracers. [Their P-51s were armed with six .50 cal. machine guns, with each weapon having a linked belt supply of 270 rounds of ammunition for a total of 1620 rounds. All of the ammunition in each of the six belts was .50 cal. API (Armor Piercing Incendiary) except for the last rounds in each belt. Those last rounds were tracer bullets and they were loaded in the belts as an indication to the pilot that he was down to the last of his ammunition. This signal could work to a pilot's disadvantage, though, as an enemy pilot being pursued and aware of the loading method, upon seeing tracers, could recognize that his adversary was out of ammunition in a fight and thus gain the advantage.] A few minutes after this, I called, telling White and Red Flights to go up as top cover and for Yellow Flight plus the spares to come down and go to work. I stayed down to direct Yellow Flight and to try and count the fires. Salzwedel was evidently some kind of a repair depot. I make this statement due to the many different kinds of aircraft observed there. Some of these aircraft were apparently not serviced with gas because I personally saw three different aircraft start smoldering before they finally began to burn. Likewise, during interrogation, some of the pilots only claimed aircraft as damaged; but with no further strafing of the claimed aircraft having occurred, other pilots reported the same planes as burning when they saw them. We arrived at Salzwedel about 1635 hours and we strafed there until 1735 hours. When I told the squadron to pull up, I stayed down and attempted to count the fires. I definitely counted 26 separate fires. I have no doubts that there were more, but smoke from the many fires was covering them. I firmly believe our claims on this occasion are very conservative. My only regret is that we had no K-25 camera ship in the squadron to substantiate our claims because many of the claims of A/C destroyed will not show on gun camera film due to the fact that the aircraft did not burn during the firing pass.

"I would estimate the number of aircraft on and around this field at sixty plus.

"As Squadron Leader, I am satisfied that the claims made are true and valid and as supporting evidence, the signatures of the other flight leaders are affixed."

The squadrons made their scattered ways home by squadrons and flights. The 434th FS lost two pilots, First Lieutenants Robert B. Kline and Ossie J. Huval, both of which were lost on the route home after they and First Lieutenant Richard D. Creighton took time out to shoot up some locomotives after leaving the Ratzeburger Lake area. The three-ship formation continued on after strafing the trains, but was hit by light flak at 2,000 ft. on the outskirts of Bremen. The two lieutenants were able to continue on a short distance towards friendly territory before having to abandon their damaged aircraft. Lt. Kline bellied his P-51 in at 1630 hours, seven or eight miles behind enemy lines, southeast of Bremen. He came back to Wattisham three days later, telling of having landed, taken a German farmer hostage using his .45 Colt Semi-Automatic sidearm and making the farmer's son direct him to the British, who were near the place he bellied in. It seems as though he landed in the center of a pocket of resistance just outside of Bremen. Lt. Huval, a member of Lt. Kline's Flight, wasn't so lucky when, having been able to continue on a while longer then Lt. Kline, he was finally forced to bail out of his plane. Upon landing, he was captured and became a POW for a few weeks.

Observations made during the mission included one squadron's report of seeing 45 plus large boats, several submarines and one carrier [sic] in Lübeck Bay near Seebad Neustadt. The ships were clustered together, but there was no apparent activity such as smoke from their stacks. The carrier lay farther out in the bay. Another squadron reported eight large and twelve small vessels, all looking like merchantmen, in the same bay. Some of the merchant vessels seemed to have steam up. Also spotted, were six E-Boats heading south. Flak over Kaltenkirchen, Lübeck/Blankensee and Tarnewitz airfields was light, intense and accurate by rapid firing guns. Over the Bremen area, it was the same, while at Hamburg and Heligoland, it was heavy, meager and inaccurate. Over Neumünster, flak was heavy, moderate and accurate.

First Lieutenants Harold M. Jenkins from the 434th FS and Paul J. Shonborn from the 436th FS both missed this days action as they were in the air elsewhere, delivering another two P-51s sold to Sweden.

16 April 1945

Eighth AF FO 1997A

No. 348 Monday. Col. Riddle led the group, which consisted of 70 P-51s (23-434th, 22-435th & 25-436th) on area support for 2nd AD B-24s attacking their 8th AF Mission 954 secondary target, the marshalling yards at Landshut, Germany as well as strafing attacks on German and German-held airfields. Up: 1246 hrs., down: 2012 hrs. with a total of just two early returns.

This day was a "Grand Slam" home run hit for the Mighty Eighth fighter pilots. Almost everything was in their favor.

Lieutenant Richard D. Creighton. *Courtesy of Berkley E. Hollister.*

Lieutenant Ossie J. Huval. *Courtesy of Clarence G. Haynes.*

The brass had given them the go ahead to strafe. The weather was perfect, CAVU in fact; they were able to see for miles. Escort of the heavies had not used up all of their gas, for the Luftwaffe had none of their own and thusly were not able to get off the ground. These reasons plus others added up to what the English called "A jolly good show"! Final tallies for the day's actions showed the Eighth's scorecard at 724-0-373. The 66th Fighter Wing claimed the most because they were lucky; their bomber's original missions were scrubbed in favor of coastal attacks along the French Atlantic seaboard. Their targets were German strongholds in Bordeaux, where there were no longer enemy fighters to defend against, thus freeing up the wing's fighters for other purposes. This then allowed the wing to enter into the strafing area, way ahead of anyone else. All three wings did well though, all of them hitting the same general area bounded by Munich and Karlsbad, Germany; Prague, Czechoslovakia and Linz, Austria. Col. Riddle took off with 70 P-51s. It was supposed to be a reduced effort mission, but somehow, what was supposed to be a training flight which took off right after the planes that were operational for the mission, tagged onto the rest of the group and went along. Mysteriously, the extra pilots just happened to have maps of the strafing area and their planes just happened to have full wing tanks. Strange how those things happened.

The heavies were given the area support prescribed in the field order, although the B-24 jockeys went after their secondary rather than their primary target at Rosenheim because they could see it better. After the bombers hit the town, the group broke support and the squadrons went their separate ways to attack airfields. It was one of those days when the pilots saw so many aircraft parked on the ground that they couldn't resist going down despite the strong defenses. That cost the group in men, but they were paid for in part by a 52-0-11 loss to the Germans.

L/F was in the vicinity of Ostend, Belgium at 1318 hrs./15,000 ft. The group crossed into Germany and picked up the bomber track in the vicinity of Mannheim at 1415 hrs./22,000 ft. Nuthouse reported they were five minutes ahead of the Big Friends so the fighters continued on, sweeping towards Landshut where they arrived at 1520 hrs./20,000 ft. Ten minutes later, the B-24s came upon the scene and bombed their secondary target, the marshalling yards. The results were reported to be excellent. As the group patrolled there, Nuthouse gave them a vector to bogies in the vicinity of Munich. The investigating fighters never found the unidentified aircraft and returned to the group. After the bombers were safely away from the target area, the squadrons split up. The 434th and 435th FSs headed eastward into Austria, where Newcross Squadron ran up 17-0-8 at Reichersburg, 1-0-0 at Kircham and 2-0-0 at Eferding, while Lakeside Squadron got 1-0-3 at Pocking in Germany, then crossed the border into Austria and tested Wels, Traun, Linz and Eferding. The squadron found the flak too intense at all of those to risk an attack. 436th FS went down and strafed the airfields at Landshut and nearby Ergolding, between 1535 and 1635 hrs. Bison Squadron claimed 25-0-0 at Landshut and 6-0-0 at Ergolding. The final score stood at:

434th FS

3-0-0	U/I E/A	1st Lt. John T. Golden	Reichersburg
2-0-1	Fw 190	1st Lt. Gail E. Jacobson	Reichersburg
0-0-1	Ju 88	1st Lt. Gail E. Jacobson	Reichersburg
2-0-1	Fw 190	2nd Lt. Robert L. Munson	Reichersburg
1-0-0	He 177	Maj. Robin Olds	Reichersburg
2-0-0	Ju 87	Maj. Robin Olds	Reichersburg
1-0-0	Me 109	Maj. Robin Olds	Reichersburg
1-0-0	Me 110	Maj. Robin Olds	Reichersburg
1-0-0	Fw 190	Capt. Donald J. Pierce	Reichersburg
1-0-0	Ju 88	Capt. Donald J. Pierce	Reichersburg
1-0-2	Me 109	Capt. Donald J. Pierce	Reichersburg
1-0-0	Fw 190	2nd Lt. John A. Plazibat	Reichersburg
1-0-1	Ju 88	1st Lt. Harold L. Stotts	Reichersburg
0-0-1	Fw 190	1st Lt. Dalton F. Tommie	Reichersburg
0-0-1	Me 109	1st Lt. Dalton F. Tommie	Reichersburg
1-0-0	Me 109	Capt. Donald J. Pierce	Kircham

1-0-0	U/I T/E	1st Lt. Philip A. Brown	Eferding
1-0-0	U/I S/E	1st Lt. Donald H. Stott	Eferding
435th FS			
0-0-2	U/I E/A	1st Lt. Russell B. Frost	Pocking
0-0-1	Me 109	Capt. Verne E. Hooker	Pocking
1-0-0	U/I E/A	Capt. Verne E. Hooker	Pocking
*436th FS**			
1-0-0	He 111	1st Lt. Charles H. Darling	Landshut/Ergolding
4-0-0	Fw 190	Maj. Claire A. P. Duffié	Landshut/Ergolding
4-0-0	Fw 190	1st Lt. Charles B. Elmgren	Landshut/Ergolding
1-0-0	He 111	Capt. Carl V. Ernst	Landshut/Ergolding
3-0-0	Fw 190	1st Lt. Raymond E. Henry	Landshut/Ergolding
1-0-0	He 111	1st Lt. Ernest J. Hopcroft	Landshut/Ergolding
1-0-0	Fw 190	Capt. Jay C. Malone	Landshut/Ergolding
2-0-0	Fw 190	1st Lt. Grover G. McLaurin, Jr.	Landshut/Ergolding
2-0-0	Fw 190	2nd Lt. Richard C. J. Palson	Landshut/Ergolding
1-0-0	Me 109	2nd Lt. Charles H. Philbrick II	Landshut/Ergolding
1-0-0	Fw 190	2nd Lt. Walter N. Rawley, Jr.	Landshut/Ergolding
2-0-0	Fw 190	Capt. Presson F. Shane	Landshut/Ergolding
2-0-0	Fw 190	1st Lt. Alfred J. Smigel	Landshut/Ergolding
1-0-0	Me 109	1st Lt. Alfred J. Smigel	Landshut/Ergolding
1-0-0	Me 109	1st Lt. Walter B. Steph	Landshut/Ergolding
1-0-0	He 111	1st Lt. Thomas H. Thompson	Landshut/Ergolding
3-0-0	Fw 190	1st Lt. George H. Witzel	Landshut/Ergolding

* The claims totaled 25-0-0 at Landshut and 6-0-0 at Ergolding, but no separation or identification of location for individual claims was made in the records.

Beginning with the 434th, each squadron submitted combat accounts of the strafing attacks and they are reproduced below.

Colonel Kyle L. Riddle for Newcross Squadron:

"I was leading the group, flying with Newcross Squadron on a free-lance patrol along the bomber track and in the target area. The bombers hit their secondary target, the Landshut marshalling yard and after their withdrawal, the group split up into squadrons to strafe airdromes in the briefed area. Bison Squadron attacked Landshut A/D as briefed while I took Newcross and Lakeside Squadrons over to Wels A/D. Enroute at about 10,000 feet, we passed over Kircham, Pocking and Reichersburg where I could see other P-51 fighter groups strafing. I saw 30-40 fires from burning A/C on Reichersburg, but Newcross Yellow Leader reported many more E/A dispersed in the woods to the south. I gave Yellow Section permission to strafe, which they did at minimum altitude. I took Newcross White Section in on the deck to attack E/A parked in the woods on the southeast corner of the field. I made three or four passes, but my gunsight was out and my fire ineffective, so I withdrew from the pattern to serve as top cover and to spot flak. One 20mm gun finally opened up, but I was unable to locate its position, possibly due to the smoke from so many fires.

"The strafing pattern set up was somewhat confused due to the number of fires burning in the dispersal area and on the field. Likewise, the blanket of smoke covering the field made it impossible for me to observe or to confirm the exact amount of destruction. The E/A being worked over by White Section on the southeast side of the field were finally given up on, as they would not burn. There were a few others that were observed parked in the center of the field, which were not burning when we first arrived, but they were burning when we left. I believe that this group destroyed these planes, together with many other claimed A/C destroyed on individual passes. Several of the men strafed Kircham A/D as they pulled up from a pass on Reichersburg. After approximately 25 minutes, the smoke got so bad that I called the group to pull up.

"We drove to Wels A/D at 6,000 feet, but the flak was intense there and also at the auxiliary field to the northeast, [Traun] so we did not attack. Approaching Eferding A/D from the south, I took Newcross White Flight, plus an element from Red Flight, down on a dive-strafing attack from 6,000 feet, pulling out at 2,000 feet. Three E/A were on fire when we pulled away, but the flak was too heavy to continue the attack. I reformed the group and we drove out at 6,000 feet, pausing again at Reichersburg while a few individual passes were made at isolated undestroyed aircraft.

"In spite of the confusion at Reichersburg A/D, every effort was made to coordinate our attack with the group already there. The thick smoke and the individual passes made at isolated and dispersed A/C made the confirmation of separate claims impossible. Four pilots were lost on the attack and several others crash-landed in friendly territory on the continent, making the documentation of a coherent story of the attack impossible. I am, however, confirming two; First Lieutenant John T. Golden called on the radio stating that he had destroyed three aircraft, one of which was confirmed by First Lieutenant Dalton F. Tommie. First Lieutenant Donald H. Stott was in one of the flights which strafed Eferding A/D with us and it is believed that he destroyed one of the two E/A seen burning on that field after we left."

First Lieutenant Dalton F. Tommie:

"I was flying 1st Lt. John T. Golden's wing in the above engagement and confirm his destruction of one unidentified enemy aircraft. I became separated from him and did not see the other two he claimed destroyed over the radio before bellying in."

Major Robin Olds:

"I was leading Newcross Yellow Section in the above engagement. As we approached Eferding A/D, I counted four fires from burning A/C. After Colonel Riddle and White Flight pulled up from their dive- strafing pass, I

L2-W, Scat VII, the plane that Major Robin Olds flew at this time and L2-D, Rabid Rebel, a ship flown by First Lieutenant Clarence G. Haynes, are seen in formation. *Courtesy of David L. Born.*

counted a total of six separate burning planes; the two new ones were undoubtedly the result of their attack. Since one of these is claimed by Second Lieutenant John A. Plazibat, the other must have been destroyed by First Lieutenant Donald H. Stott, who failed to return from the mission for reasons unknown."

The men who were lost during the airfield attacks were all from Newcross Squadron. They were First Lieutenant John T. Golden, Second Lieutenant Harold F. Krauss, Jr., First Lieutenant Donald H. Stott and First Lieutenant Frank M. Taylor. Lieutenant Golden was hit by light flak or small arms fire during the squadron's second attack on Reichersburg. First Lieutenant Philip A. Brown was flying as Newcross Yellow Three during the mission and later detailed what happened:

"After starting home, we passed a field that had been worked over a bit earlier and several of us went down on it. After making two passes at the field, I heard Newcross Red Three, who was Lt. Golden, say he had been hit and was losing coolant. He took up a course of 310 degrees and I joined him. I went up to 17,000 feet in an endeavor to contact Nuthouse in order to get a steer for Red Three,

Second Lieutenant Harold F. Krauss, Jr. *Courtesy of David L. Born.*

but had no luck contacting them. I could go no higher as I was out of oxygen. I went down, joined Lt. Golden again and stayed with him until he had to belly in about ten miles west of Regensburg. He got out of the plane all right and I last saw him with half a dozen German farmers who had been plowing nearby. Their actions appeared more friendly than hostile as they waved when I buzzed them."

Lt. Golden became a POW.

Lieutenant Brown also told what happened to Second Lt. Taylor:

"I had become separated from my squadron and while trying to find them, it became evident from radio transmissions that they were attacking an airdrome [Reichersburg]. I heard Newcross Yellow Two [Lt. Taylor] say that his coolant had been hit and that he was heading due east [toward Russian lines]. Within a few minutes, he said he was bailing out and that was the last I heard from him."

Lt. Taylor bailed out 20-30 miles west of Linz, was captured and he, too, became a POW.

Lieutenants Krauss and Stott were last seen during strafing passes at the Reichersburg airfield. Lt. Krauss had been hit and tried to head homeward but could not make it. He died of wounds in Allied-held territory. Lt. Stott was also probably hit there but his actual cause of death is unknown. His body was recovered in late June 1945. He had been buried in a cemetery at Weilbach, Austria. Found in "Shoo Shoo Baby", the plane he had been flying, he had gone down approximately two miles east of Weilbach, near the town of Vilshofen. The plane was found nearly intact.

Lieutenants James E. Boucher and Francis C. Schiess had to land on the continent and returned to Wattisham later.

Lakeside Squadron's Captain Verne E. Hooker and his wingman, First Lieutenant Russell B. Frost, joined the 434th FS pilots in their attack on an airfield along the Inn River at a location due south of Pocking. They spotted a couple of parked aircraft on the field that were not touched yet. The two made four or five passes on one of the planes before it started smoking and finally caught fire. On one of the passes, Capt. Hooker spotted another E/A that had been well camouflaged. It was off to the left of the one he was attacking so he made one pass at it. The attacks he and his wingman made here resulted in the above listed claims for the 435th FS.

First Lieutenant Donald H. Stott. *Courtesy of Clarence G. Haynes.*

Major Claire A. P. Duffié accounted for Bison Squadron in this report:

"On 16 April 1945, in accordance with F. O. 1997A of the 8th AF, our bombers hit the town and marshalling yards at Landshut, northeast of Munich, Germany. This target was an alternative to the one assigned at Rosenheim, southeast of Munich. Having previously observed many aircraft on the fields both east and west of the town, we had planned prior to takeoff, to strafe these two fields. After bombs away at 1536, I took Bison Squadron, which I was leading, down to look over the situation. There were numerous aircraft at Landshut and six or seven at Ergolding. I made two dive-strafing passes by myself on Landshut to test for flak. The results were nil so I set up a northwest to southeast pattern for three of my six flights, leaving the other three as top cover. The aircraft were parked largely at the edge of a wooded area located along the base of a cliff that was 200-250 feet high. The planes were well camouflaged with nets strung over them and topped by tree branches as well as brush. This situation made it difficult for the pilots to properly assess their claims, most of which were confirmed on the second or subsequent passes.

"The squadron strafed from 1536 to 1635 hours, having interchanged White with Yellow Sections when the former ran low on ammunition. Yellow Section then strafed Ergolding airfield on the west bank of the Isar River. Claims at Landshut A/F are 25-0-0 and at Ergolding, they are 6-0-0. As we prepared to leave, I counted the fires and am certain that the claims will all be verified by assessment of the day's films."

Upon completion of the strafing, the group left the area by squadrons and turned towards home, making L/O in the vicinity of Knokke, Belgium approximately 1850 hrs.

Observations made during the mission included a heavy oil fire producing smoke that rose to 10,000 ft. that was believed to be coming from a large vessel seen eight miles off the coast of Ostend. There were heavy fires spotted that were the result of bombings at Landshut and Regensburg. Seventy-five plus unidentified A/C were located at Eferding airfield. An unidentified P-51 that was bellied in and burning was spotted between Kircham airfield and the Inn River. Flak at Wels, Traun, Linz and Eferding airfields was light, intense and accurate. Flak at Ergolding airfield was light, meager and inaccurate. At Pocking, Kircham and Reichersburg, it was sporadic, light and intense.

Lieutenant Colonel George E. Falkner was along on this trip. The former troop carrier pilot had requested assignment with a fighter group and wound up with the 479th FG/436th FS. He later became the Deputy Group Commander. *Courtesy of Clarence G. Haynes.*

17 April 1945

Eighth AF FO 2007A

No. 349 Tuesday. Maj. Duffié led the group, which consisted of 50 P-51s (10-434th, 18-435th & 22-436th) on an escort to target and withdrawal support for 2nd AD B-24s attacking their 8th AF Mission 957 primary target, a rail junction and rail bridge at Falkenau, Czechoslovakia as well as strafing attacks on German and German-held airfields. Up: 1231 hrs., down: 2045 hrs. with a total of three early returns.

L/F was over Blankenberghe, Belgium at 1311 hrs./14,000 ft. After driving across Germany, R/V with the proper bombers was 20 miles south of Marienberg at 1442 hrs./18,000 ft. Almost at the Czechoslovakian border, the bombers and their escorts turned southwest and into that country. The short trip to Falkenau (now Sokolov) brought the group over the target at 1450 hrs./18,000 ft. Bombing results were noted as excellent and the Little Friends accompanied their Big Friends north and out to the vicinity of Kirchberg where the two parted company so that the Mustangs could return to their designated strafing area to conduct some business from the CAVU skies. The petrol-starved Luftwaffe was being compressed on all sides by the advancing Allied forces. The number of German airfields was being reduced, forcing those remaining in their hands to house increasing quantities of aircraft. The situation made for great strafing harvests as previously noted and as was the case for today. The 434th FS was joined by a flight from the 436th FS. Newcross Squadron was only able to put up ten planes today because six of its A/C were still located at other airfields, having landed there the previous day. Also, another six P-51s were undergoing repairs from yesterday's flak damage. Irregardless, the composite squadron racked up nearly half of the group's total for the day, bringing home a score of 19-0-4. Their targets were Landau and Puchhof. The 435th FS went after an unidentified airfield located about five miles north of Plzen and took care of another 9-0-6. The remainder of the 436th FS went to Budejovice and Karlsbad (Carlsbad) airdromes and brought home the squadron's final scalps of the war, in the form of 14-0-1. The breakdown was as follows:

434th FS

1-0-0	Me 109	Capt. Donald J. Pierce	Landau
0-0-1	Me 109	Capt. Donald J. Pierce	Landau
0-0-1	U/I T/E	Capt. Donald J. Pierce	Landau
1-0-0	Me 109	1st Lt. David L. Born	Puchhof
2-0-0	U/I S/E	1st Lt. David L. Born	Puchhof
1-0-0	U/I S/E	2nd Lt. Donald W. Mastin	Puchhof
2-0-0	Fw 190	2nd Lt. Cecil M. Peacock	Puchhof
2-0-0	Fw 190	Capt. Donald J. Pierce	Puchhof
2-0-0	Me 109	F/O Arthur J. Valluzzi	Puchhof

435th FS

1-0-0	Me 262	1st Lt. Robert J. Baird	Plzen
1-0-0	Fi 156	1st Lt. Clark R. Hoffman	Plzen
2-0-1	Me 262	1st Lt. Clark R. Hoffman	Plzen
0-0-1	U/I E/A	Capt. Verne E. Hooker	Plzen
0-0-1	Me 262	1st Lt. Cecil R. Mathews	Plzen
1-0-0	Me 262	1st Lt. Sylvan R. Routh	Plzen
0-0-1	U/I E/A	1st Lt. George M. Salter, Jr.	Plzen
1-0-0	Me 262	2nd Lt. Floyd W. Salze	Plzen
1-0-0	Me 262	1st Lt. Edward H. Sims	Plzen
2-0-0	Me 262	Capt. Theo J. Sowerby	Plzen
0-0-1	Me 262	1st Lt. Donald W. Thorn	Plzen
0-0-1	U/I E/A	1st Lt. Donald W. Thorn	Plzen

436th FS with 434th FS

1-0-0	Fi 156	1st Lt. Ernest J. Hopcroft	Landau
1-0-0	Fw 190	1st Lt. Ernest J. Hopcroft	Puchhof
1-0-0	Me 109	1st Lt. Ernest J. Hopcroft	Puchhof
0-0-1	U/I S/E	1st Lt. Ernest J. Hopcroft	Puchhof
0-0-1	Fw 190	1st Lt. Charles S. Kreger	Puchhof
2-0-0	Fw 190	2nd Lt. Richard C. J. Palson	Puchhof
2-0-0	Me 109	2nd Lt. Richard C. J. Palson	Puchhof
1-0-0	Me 109	Capt. Presson S. Shane	Puchhof

436th FS

1-0-0	U/I E/A	1st Lt. Charles H. Darling	Karlsbad
1-0-0	Fw 190	Maj. Claire A. P. Duffié	Karlsbad
2-0-0	Ju 87	Maj. Claire A. P. Duffié	Karlsbad
2-0-0	Fi 156	1st Lt. Charles B. Elmgren	Karlsbad
1-0-0	U/I E/A	1st Lt. Charles B. Elmgren	Karlsbad
1-0-0	U/I S/E	Lt. Col. George E. Falkner	Karlsbad
1-0-0	Ju 87	2nd Lt. Pasquale J. Romano	Karlsbad
1-0-0	U/I S/E	2nd Lt. Pasquale J. Romano	Karlsbad
1-0-0	U/I S/E	1st Lt. Alfred J. Smigel	Karlsbad
0-0-1	U/I E/A	1st Lt. Alfred J. Smigel	Karlsbad
1-0-0	Fw 190	1st Lt. George H. Witzel	Karlsbad
1-0-0	U/I E/A	1st Lt. George H. Witzel	Karlsbad
1-0-0	Fw 189	1st Lt. Kenneth J. Hansen	Budejovice

Captain Donald J. Pierce gave this report on the day's strafing:

"On 17 April, we were on a bomber escort to Falkenau. We gave close support through the target area and back to friendly territory, breaking away there when bandits were reported. None found, we dropped down to 10,000 feet and went back looking for targets of opportunity.

"We checked various airfields for parked E/A as we went along. Bison Squadron hit the A/D at Karlsbad, but Bison Leader said his squadron could handle the field alone, so we went on. As we approached the grass field at Landau from the west, I had nine P-51s with me; five from Newcross Squadron and four from Bison. I took my flight in on a dive-strafing pass from west to east, starting the dive at about 6,000 feet to test the flak defense. First

Lieutenant David L. Born flying L2-Z, The Impatient Virgin. *Courtesy of David L. Born.*

Lt. Kreger, who was leading the Bison flight, circled at 6,000 feet to spot flak, the likes of which wasn't too bad. On this first pass, I hit an Me 109, which burned nicely. After we pulled up, Lt. Kreger took his flight down from west to east. A Fi 156 was hit and set on fire by First Lt. Ernest J. Hopcroft on this pass. I took my flight down again, this time from south to north. I got some strikes on an Me 109 and an unidentified twin-engine aircraft, but neither caught fire. By this time, the flak was getting a good deal heavier, so we moved on.

"Upon arriving at Puchhof A/D we circled twice at 6,000 feet before spotting any E/A. The planes were all well dispersed and camouflaged. I made a dive-strafing pass from south to north, getting strikes on an Me 109 and setting it on fire. I spotted another A/C in amongst the trees on the northeast corner of the field as I pulled up. Bison Flight made a dive-strafing pass from south to north and after they pulled up, I went down again, this time from northeast to southwest, hitting the A/C that I had spotted. No flak was observed on any of the three passes, so I called for a left-hand traffic pattern from south to north and we worked the field over. Each of us made eight to ten passes. After I finished firing, I climbed above the field to count the fires. I counted 17 individual fires, two of which were large ones in the areas where several more A/C were parked. All of the E/A burned readily and appeared to be fully serviceable.

"At the critique held after the mission, the existence and location of every aircraft spotted was confirmed either by the number of fires in the area or by actual confirmation by wingmen, with the exception of one claimed by Second Lt. Richard C. J. Palson. It could not be established whether there were two or just one E/A in a location that he hit. If there were two and Lt. Palson's combat film shows the destruction of four E/A, then he should be awarded a total of five E/A destroyed. If his film shows only three destroyed, then he should be awarded four destroyed. Note that one of the E/A destroyed by Lt. Palson was almost completely hidden in the woods and undoubtedly will not be seen in the film, but its destruction was confirmed by actual sighting of the fire."

First Lieutenant Charles S. Kreger appended that report, giving this statement:

"I was leading the Bison Flight on the above engagement. I saw the fires from two aircraft claimed destroyed on Landau A/D, by Captain Pierce and Lieutenant Hopcroft. After I had run out of ammunition strafing Puchhof, I circled the field and counted fires. My count agrees with that of Capt. Pierce. I confirm the destruction of all the E/A plotted on the diagram drawn up to show the claims. The exception is the one claimed by Lt. Palson as noted above by Capt. Pierce. In addition, I confirm the destruction of an Me 109 by Flight Officer Arthur J. Valluzzi. The A/C was almost inside a hangar and may not show on his film."

David (Dave) L. Born, in a conversation during 1999, recalled his part in the strafing attacks. He stated:

"The airfield at Puchhof was well camouflaged and we were not even sure there were any planes there until we got down very low. Then someone spotted the tail of one plane sticking out from under some camouflage. When we started strafing, I went down on the deck and got an Me 109 that was parked in what looked like a low, open-fronted farmer's shed. As we circled the area a few times, something below struck me as odd. There were two open fields located side-by-side that were separated by a little wooded strip that ran between them. Now, that in itself was not curious, but the fact that there was a road that ran into the wooded area and there appeared to be one continuing out, but I couldn't see where they met. In other words, I couldn't see the entire road. The center portion seemed to be so thickly wooded that you couldn't see through it to the ground. I became suspicious and so I made a strafing run on that thick portion of the woods. I couldn't see that I had done anything, but my wingman, who was following me, said there were three aircraft parked under the thick covering and further stated that I had gotten two of them. He claimed the other." Dave said with a chuckle, "Half the planes that I'm credited with, I never saw."

Captain Theo J. Sowerby described Lakeside Squadron's attack:

"Lakeside and Newcross Squadrons left Bison Squadron at the airfield they were strafing and set out on a course of 110 degrees. After about 15 minutes, I called in a landing strip on our left and told Newcross Leader I was going to check on it. It was a newly built runway, running 270 degrees and located about five miles north of Plzen. The runway was unfinished and no buildings were observed.

"I called for my flight (White Flight) to make a dive-strafing pass. The flight consisted of First Lieutenants Larry J. Cano, Edward H. Sims, Cecil R. Mathews and me. On this pass I shot up one Me 262 just to the north of the east end of the runway. I claim this A/C as destroyed. Yellow Flight, which consisted of First Lieutenants Clark R. Hoffman, Sylvan R. Routh, George M. Salter and Donald W. Thorn, called in flak guns, which they then dove on. White Flight made the next pass. It was to the east and I shot up another Me 262, which caught fire and exploded as I was firing at it. This plane was one of a group of three at the west end of the runway. White and Yellow Flights, plus Blue Flight, which was made up of Captain Verne E. Hooker and Lieutenants George R. Dettenmeyer, Floyd W. Salze and Frederick F. Shriner, then made a left-hand pattern and pretty well cleaned up the field. First Lieutenant Robert J. Baird also claimed a damaged Me 262 during this time.

"I got some machine gun fire from a marshalling yard to the south of the field on one of my orbits. Flak at this field was both light and heavy, meager and fairly accurate.

"Approximately 1545 hours, about fifteen minutes after we began, we pulled off and set a course of 125 degrees, heading towards Strakonice. Arriving there, we saw the airfield had about 40 plus A/C, but also lots of flak. The gunners opened up while we were still at 6,000 feet so we left the field alone. We then went over to Regensburg, but some other outfit had already started four or five fires on the field there and it looked pretty well clobbered. We set a course of zero-degrees north and didn't find any more fields so we turned for home at 1630 hours."

Major Claire A. P. Duffié for the 436th FS:

"On 17 April 1945, in accordance with 8th AF FO 2007A, I was leading the 479th Fighter Group on a bomber escort mission to Falkenau, Czechoslovakia. After leaving the bombers, we sought airfields within our strafing area. Approaching Karlsbad A/D, I made two dive-strafing passes from 10,000 feet to check for flak. There was no reaction, so I set up a pattern from northeast to southwest with my White Section, leaving Yellow Section as top cover and releasing Lakeside and Newcross Squadrons to search for other airdromes. Many passes were made on Karlsbad from 1515 to 1545 hours. At the south end of the field were two hangars. The westernmost one had at least five aircraft in it at the time of the first pass. The doors were open at that time, but were closed later. After five pilots had made passes at this hangar, the entire building was seen to be burning violently and the steel roof melted and collapsed. Five aircraft are claimed in this hangar. The easternmost hangar had two trainers parked in it and they were hit from low level. The burning aircraft inside set this hangar afire also. A total of 14-0-0 miscellaneous aircraft are claimed here as well as 2-0-0 hangars."

First Lieutenant Kenneth J. Hansen on his solo strafing run:

"After leaving the bombers we had been escorting, we drove back in towards our assigned strafing area. I was leading Yellow Section of Bison Squadron and as White Section had previously hit Karlsbad A/F, I was given permission to dive-strafe Budejovice A/D as we approached it from the west. The field looked well defended with flak so I dive-strafed it alone, from west to east, breaking to the south. I started my pass from 7,000 feet, recovering at 2,000 feet. I observed hits on a Fw 189 on the south perimeter of the field and it was seen to burn by my wingman, First Lieutenant Frank G. Beatty, Jr. The flak was very intense, so we left the field."

The squadrons made their way back across the continent and L/O was in the vicinity of Ostend approximately 2000 hrs./ 5,000 ft.

Observations made during the mission included a notation that nervous gunners in the bombers fired on the fighters at R/ V and, of course, the question was asked; were the bombers aware that fighters were to R/V? The lead box of B-24s dropped three bombs in the vicinity of Tachau. The bombing results were excellent with both the railroad tracks and the railroad bridge being well-clobbered. Twenty to twenty-five A/C were dispersed over the field at Straubing A/D. There were also ten light flak positions in the area and on a hangar there. There were two or three machine gun positions in the hangar area to the south of the field at Landau A/D as well as a 20mm position in the barracks area to the north. There were an estimated three hundred plus, that's right, three zero zero plus, assorted enemy aircraft at Budejovice A/F. The field seemed fully operational, too. Ten fires were spotted on the A/D south of Klatovy. There was no activity on the A/F at Stirakonice. There was still smoke and fire in the water eight miles north of Ostend, the same location as was reported the day before. Flak was light, intense and accurate at Tremosa A/D, Straubing A/D and Budejovice A/D. Flak at Landau A/D was light, moderate and accurate. It was light, meager and accurate at Karlsbad. Fifty cal. fire was coming from the marshalling yard at Plzen.

18 April 1945

Eighth AF FO 2017A

No. 350 Wednesday. Capt. Hooker led the group, which consisted of 50 P-51s (14-434th, 18-435th & 18-436th) on a penetration to target and withdrawal escort for 2nd AD B-24s attacking their 8th AF Mission 959 primary target, the marshalling yard at Passau, Germany, as well as strafing attacks on German and German-held airfields. Up: 1115 hrs., down: 1755 hrs. with one early return.

L/F was over Ostend, Belgium at 1154 hrs./14,000 ft. Crossing Belgium and passing eastward into Germany, the group R/V'd with their assigned B-24s in the area north of (Schwäbisch) Hall at 1309 hrs./20,000 ft. Accompanying the bombers the rest of the way across Germany to Passau, right on the Austrian border, the Big Friends bombed visually from the CAVU skies, releasing their loads on the target with good to excellent results. The attack at 1405 hrs./22,000 ft. produced many fires and heavy black smoke. Turning back and heading towards home, the group broke escort near Weissenburg at 1445 hrs./20,000 ft. and turned back once again to strafe the Luftwaffe's airfields by squadrons. The 434th FS first picked the A/F at Ingolstadt, but found the red-nosed P-47s of the 56th FG already there and working over the field when the squadron arrived at 1510 hrs. Looking the action over from 10,000 feet, Newcross picked out four Ju 88s located on the southeast corner of the airfield and made two dive-strafing passes from 8-3,000 feet, destroying one and leaving another smoking.

Seeking other targets, Newcross Squadron drove northwest to Ottingen, arriving there at 1545 hrs. Observing from above at 8,000 feet, the squadron saw six or eight serviceable A/C amidst the wreckage caused by previous attacks. The field was dive-strafed to test for flak and when only scattered light AA and small arms fire was received, four or five minimum-altitude passes were made, destroying six and damaging another. The squadron left six fires on the field when they departed for Deiningen A/F. Arriving there at 1610 hours, the field was dive-strafed to test for flak. Only one machine gun plus some small arms were firing; so once again, the squadron went down after the grounded German Air Force. They worked the field over, destroying four and damaging one, but had to pull up due to the single machine gun. The gun crew was very accurate in their shooting and well hidden, as they could not be found and silenced.

After leaving the bombers, Lakeside Squadron went back to Mühldorf and strafed Mettenheim A/F there for a tally of 1-0-5. The field was loaded with A/C and flak so not much time was spent there. The squadron left at 1610 hrs.

The 436th FS returned to stooge around the Landshut, Ingolstadt and Neuburg areas again. Ingolstadt was dive-strafed, but the flak was bad and the squadron was discouraged from further attempts. Moving on to Neuburg, Bison Squadron lost their leader, Captain Jay C. Malone, to flak. He had made

Three Newcross Squadron P-51s, L2-H, L2-Y and L2-C, make their way back home through clear skies. *Courtesy of David L. Born.*

one dive-strafing pass to test for flak and was making his second when he was hit by light flak and went straight in and exploded. That soured the Bison gang on that field and they left what appeared to be a flak trap behind. The claims were as follows:

434th FS

1-0-0	Ju 88	1st Lt. Gail E. Jacobson	Ingolstadt
1-0-0	Me 109	1st Lt. Clifford W. Bowers	Ottingen
1-0-0	Me 110	1st Lt. Clifford W. Bowers	Ottingen
0-0-1	U/I T/E	1st Lt. Clifford W. Bowers	Ottingen
1-0-0	Fw 190	1st Lt. Gail E. Jacobson	Ottingen
1-0-0	Ju 88	1st Lt. Gail E. Jacobson	Ottingen
1-0-0	Fw 190	2nd Lt. George H. Looney	Ottingen
1-0-0	Ju 88	1st Lt. Jerome K. Nagel	Ottingen
1-0-0	U/I T/E	1st Lt. Clifford W. Bowers	Deiningen
1-0-1	Me 109	2nd Lt. Elidio E. Monaco	Deiningen
1-0-0	Fw 190	1st Lt. Jerome K. Nagel	Deiningen
1-0-0	Me 109	1st Lt. Jerome K. Nagel	Deiningen

435th FS

0-0-1	U/I S/E	1st Lt. William M. Barsky	Mettenheim
0-0-2	U/I T/E	Capt. Verne E. Hooker	Mettenheim
1-0-0	U/I T/E	1st Lt. James H. Koerber	Mettenheim
0-0-1	U/I T/E	1st Lt. Edward H. Sims	Mettenheim
0-0-1	U/I S/E	1st Lt. Elmer A. Splittstoesser	Mettenheim

436th FS

0-0-1	Ju 88	Capt. Jay C. Malone	Neuburg

Starting with the 434th's leader, First Lieutenant Gail E. Jacobson, these are the strafing reports:

"On 18 April, I was leading the squadron on a bomber escort mission to Passau, Germany. After escorting the bombers through the target and back to friendly territory, we took up a heading of 120 degrees and dropped down to 8,000 feet in order to look for targets of opportunity. As we approached Ingolstadt A/D from the northeast, I saw several red-nosed P-47s working the field over. They were either dive-strafing or dive-bombing as I observed several explosions on the field. I saw 40-50 assorted E/A dispersed in the woods to the east and southeast of the field and since the P-47s were not working that end, I went down in a dive-strafing pass from south to north, testing for flak. We [Jacobson and a wingman] started our dive at about 6,000 feet and pulled out around 1,000 feet. Only one 20mm position was spotted, but I wasn't satisfied that it was the only one, so I made another dive-strafing pass the same as before, firing at a Ju 88 parked near the edge of the woods, then pulling through the flak position. As I climbed away, I saw the Ju 88 burst into flames. On this last pass, four more light guns opened up, so we moved on.

"I checked Neuburg A/D from 8,000 feet, but the flak there was much too rough. I started to take the formation back in, but decided that our gas was a little low, so I took up a heading of 305 degrees. About 20 minutes later, while at 8,000 feet, we went over Ottingen A/D. The field was pretty well beat up, but I could see eight serviceable A/C among the burned out hulks. I made a pass from south to north, firing into the buildings area and pulling out at about 1,000 feet. I didn't receive any flak other than some small arms fire, so a left-hand traffic pattern from north to south was set up. At this time, I had five P-51s still with me. We made a total of five to six minimum altitude passes on the field. On my first pass, I set a Ju 88 on fire that was parked near a service building. On my second pass, I set a Fw 190 on fire that was parked on the taxiway located on the southeast side of the field. I made three or four more passes, but couldn't get any more aircraft to burn. As I was just about out of ammunition by then, I pulled up and circled the field at 5,000 feet while the rest of the flight made a few more passes. While I was circling, I counted six separate and distinct fires from burning aircraft.

"On Deiningen airfield to the south, I spotted eight to ten A/C dispersed in some trees located to the southeast of the field itself. I let the other four P-51s go down to strafe and they made four or five passes down on the deck from north to south, setting four A/C on fire. I counted the fires as I circled above. At that point, we began to get low on gasoline, so I called them back up and we came home."

First Lieutenant Clifford W. Bowers. *Courtesy of David L. Born.*

First Lieutenant Clifford W. Bowers:

"I was flying as fifth man in Lt. Jabcobson's flight during the above actions. As we pulled away from each of the fields, I looked back and counted the fires. I counted six fires on Ottingen airfield and four on Deiningen."

Second Lieutenant Elidio E. Monaco:

"I was flying as White Four in Lt. Jacobson's flight during the above-described engagements. I followed Lt. Jacobson down on his dive-strafing pass on Ingolstadt airdrome and saw the Ju 88 he shot at burst into flames. I confirm his claim of one Ju 88 destroyed on Ingolstadt airdrome."

Captain Verne E. Hooker:

"I was leading Lakeside Squadron. We had taken our bombers out from their target, broke from them and returned back to Pocking A/F for a look-see. We made two or three passes, but everything was pretty well burned out. We did receive some light flak there though. We then proceeded on to Mettenheim A/F, where I took White Flight and made one dive-strafing pass. I looked down as

> I rolled out and saw some hits. My tail end Charlie was the only one who got flak on that pass. I then called on my radio and said I would make one more pass by myself and told the rest of the flight to spot for flak. I damaged another plane on this pass. The flak, however, was too intense, so we left and set course for home. There was one fire on the field when we left."

Captain Carl V. Ernst, concerning the loss of Captain Jay C. Malone from the 436th FS:

> "Bison Leader dive-strafed the south end of Neuburg A/D, passing from north to south. He picked up a little flak from the south side. At 1530 hours, he called over the radio that he was going to test the field for flak again. This time he made his pass from northeast to southwest, coming down over a wooded area at the north end of the field. He got some strikes on a Ju 88 and was at about 400 feet when the whole wooded area lit up with flak and he was hit. The aircraft rolled over, hit the ground and exploded."

Captain Frederick M. Mead, concerning the loss of Captain Jay C. Malone:

> "Captain Malone went down on a dive strafing pass from northeast to southwest, damaging a Ju 88. At approximately 400 feet, he was hit by light fire (20mm, .50 cal. and small arms) which tore his left wing flap and elevator off. I also saw his canopy come off and at that moment he called: 'Bison Leader here, I am hit.' The aircraft then turned over on its back, crashed into the ground and exploded."

The strafing done, the squadrons returned homeward, making L/O over Ostend around 1720 hrs.

Observations made during the mission included: The marshalling yards and locks at Passau were well hit with one big oil fire still burning 45 minutes after the strike. A B-24 from the 466th BG was seen to have its number two engine shut down and propeller feathered. The bomber was at 16,000 ft. in the vicinity of Crailsheim and heading homeward. The same A/C was seen later at 1615 hrs./13,000 ft. in the vicinity of Liège, Belgium and appeared to be still okay. The marshalling yard southwest of Ingolstadt had a twenty-car train with no engine. It was made up of oil cars and flat cars carrying what appeared to be six to eight foot long sections of concrete

Lieutenant Elidio E. Monaco and two unidentified crew members. *Courtesy of Clarence G. Haynes.*

viaducts. In addition, the yard was loaded with miscellaneous freight cars. There were 75 military trucks driving bumper to bumper, heading towards Landshut on a highway northwest of the town. A train marked with red crosses was headed south, about ten miles from that town. The airfield at Neuburg had ten to fifteen Me 262s dispersed on the field's northwest perimeter and approximately ten more east of the hangar area. Six Ju 88s and six to eight Me 109s were also there and looked to be poorly camouflaged. There was one lone Fw 189 parked on the southeast corner of the field. Forty to fifty Ju 88s and He 111s were parked on the field and in the wooded area that extended from the east to southeast portion of the airdrome at Ingolstadt. It appeared that burned out A/C were being camouflaged to appear as serviceable planes in order to set up a flak trap at Lichtenau airfield. At Mühldorf, there was what looked like an underground hangar located in a wooded area southwest of the airfield. In addition, there were over a hundred A/C sitting around the field. Flak over Neuburg and Mühldorf was light, intense and accurate. It was light, moderate to intense and accurate at Ingolstadt. At Pocking, it was light, intense and inaccurate. At Ottingen, flak was light, moderate and accurate on the deck. At Deiningen, it was light, meager and accurate.

19 April 1945

Eighth AF FO 2024A

No. 351 & 352 Thursday. The group was divided into two forces, A and B groups, both freelance patrols to the Brandenburg, Germany area in support of 8th AF Mission 961.

Capt. Pierce led A group, which consisted of 26 P-51s (16-434th & 10-436th). Up: 0759 hrs., down: 1339 hrs. with one early return. Capt. Anderson led B group, which consisted of 26 P-51s (18-435th & 8-436th). Up: 0802 hrs., down: 1350 hrs. with two early returns.

A group made L/F ten miles south of Ijmuiden, Holland at 0855 hrs./17,000 ft. They arrived in the Brandenburg area at 1010 hrs./20,000 ft. and patrolled from there to Leipzig at 20-27,000 ft. The group started home at 1125 hrs. and made L/O ten miles north of The Hague, Holland at 1250 hrs./9,000 ft. The whole patrol was absolutely uneventful.

B group made L/F near Ijmuiden at 0854 hrs./18,000 ft. and arrived at Brandenburg at 1003 hrs./22,000 ft. From there, they turned north heading to Oranienburg, then northwest to Neuruppin and south back to twelve miles south of Brandenburg. There they R/V'd with two boxes of 1st AD B-17s at 1025 hrs./26,000 ft. The group escorted the bombers through their targets south of Berlin where sky markers went down at 1050 and 1101 hrs. The CAVU weather there permitted observation of extensive damage to a marshalling yard and large oil fires resultant from the attacks. The group broke from the B-17s north of Gotha at 1105 hrs./26,000 ft. and made L/O north of The Hague at 1306 hrs./13,000 ft.

Observations made during the mission included; first and most telling, was the note that the group had "50-yard line seats for the front line activity." Smoke was seen coming from a series of objects both along the southern edge of Berlin and heading north on the western side of the city. It was believed to be marking the trails of the Russian advance. There were large fires at Ruhland and Magdeburg. Two A/C, identified as MiG-3s, almost spun out wagging their wings in their anxiety to be recognized. It was noted that the planes appeared to be "handy little crates". Nuthouse reported Sunhat (364th FG) in a minor engagement, but the only bogies called out was the group itself. Flak over the unidentified targets south of Berlin was heavy, intense and accurate.

20 April 1945

Eighth AF FO 2039A

No. 353 Friday. The group was divided into two forces, A and B groups, both penetration to target and withdrawal escorts for a CW of 2nd AD B-24s attacking their 8th AF Mission 962 primary target at Schwandorf, Germany. Maj. Duffié led A group, which consisted of 40 P-51s (18-434th & 22-436th).

These two P-51s, L2-H and L2-Y from the 434th FS are returning home after a mission. *Courtesy of David L. Born.*

Up: 0913 hrs., down: 1435 hrs. with no early returns. Capt. Sowerby led B group, which consisted of 21 P-51s from the 435th FS. Up: 0916 hrs., down: 1456 hrs. with one early return.

A group made L/F in the area of Ostend, Belgium at 0958 hrs./15,000 ft. R/V with their proper bombers was in Germany, near Weisbaden at 1045 hrs./23,000 ft. The Big Friends were taken through their target where bombs away was at 1143 hrs./22,000 ft. The bombing results appeared to be excellent. Returning, the escorts broke from the bombers ten miles northeast of Koblenz at 1300 hrs./12,000 ft. L/O was south of Walcheren Island, Holland at 1345 hrs./9,000 ft.

B group made L/F in the same area of Belgium at 0959 hrs./14,000 ft. and R/V'd with their B-24s south of Weisbaden at 1045 hrs./16,000 ft. The bombers were escorted to the target and back out to breakaway west of Weisbaden at 1300 hrs./12,000 ft. L/O was near Knokke, Belgium at 1345 hrs./3,000 ft. They also reported the bombing as excellent.

Me 262s were reported in the target area at 1142 hours, but it was also reported that none were seen.

Observations made during the mission included: The combat wing being escorted was in very poor formation and very indifferent on the radio. There was a large oil fire with smoke rising to 15,000 ft. on the Danube River, between Straubing and Plattling. A train consisting of 75 plus goods wagons, 30 of which were camouflaged, was seen in the target area. The train's engine had no steam up. No flak was reported.

The date of 21 April 1945 was a sad occasion for the men of two AAF stations. On this Sunday date, the 467th Bomb Group (H) stationed at Rackheath was enjoying the second day of celebrating the group's 200th Mission Party. The B-24 group had laid on an air circus to conclude the weekend-long festivities. Two fighter groups from the 65th Fighter Wing were scheduled to participate in the afternoon show. The appointed time of 1300 hours arrived and P-47 Thunderbolts from the 56th Fighter Group as well as their accompanying P-51 Mustangs from the 479th Fighter Group began their show for the bomber boys. During the performance, First Lieutenant Robert C. Young, recently assigned to the 436th FS and who was in the area on a familiarization flight, tacked onto the 479th FG planes as they flew through their routine. Previously, Lt. Young had been a bomber pilot with the 328th Bomb Squadron/93rd Bomb Group (H). Having recently completed his tour, he volunteered to join a fighter group and fly a tour with them. Assigned to the 479th, he was learning to fly the P-51. As the Mustangs began buzzing past the audience, they were flying low and inverted. Lt. Young had joined the flight from the rear and as the 51s passed under a 50-foot high radio antenna that was strung in front of the airfield's control tower, he lost control of his aircraft. The fighter crashed and Lt. Young was killed. That put a damper on the afternoon's program and the celebration, which was to include a big party featuring a band and free beer in the main hangar later, was canceled.

25 April 1945

Eighth AF FO 2084A

No. 354 & 355 Wednesday. The group was divided into two forces, A and B groups, both penetration to target and withdrawal escorts for a CW of 2nd AD B-24s attacking their 8th AF Mission 968 primary targets, a marshalling yard and an electrical power station at Traunstein, Germany. Col. Riddle led A group, which consisted of 30 P-51s (18-435th & 12-436th). Up: 0759 hrs., down: 1400 hrs. with no early returns. Maj. Olds led B group, which consisted of 27 P-51s (18-434th & 9-436th). Up: 0806 hrs., down: 1353 hrs. with one early return.

These were the last missions the 479th Fighter Group flew during the war. Their job was an escort of the heavies on the last 8th Air Force bombing mission of the war.

Both A and B groups gave close support with similar timings. L/F was near Ostend, Belgium at 0840 hrs./12,000 ft. Having crossed into the air above Germany, R/V with their assigned bombers was over the Rhine River, north of Mannheim at 0940 hrs./22,000 ft. At 1048 hours, the group was at 26,000 feet and approaching Hallein on the German/Austrian border. They were two minutes ahead of the bombers and off to their left. Salzburg, Austria was to their right. At this point, Col. Riddle spotted a twin-tail, twin-engine bogie headed across his nose towards the target. When he approached to identify the stranger, the bogie went into a diving right turn in an effort to evade him. As Col. Riddle pulled inside of the bogie's turn, he was able to observe white square markings with some sort of insignia within the square. Moments later, not only did the bogie open fire at him from a top gun turret, but very heavy, intense and accurate flak began exploding around him. Now down to about 18,000 feet, Col. Riddle sensed a flak trap. He dropped his wing tanks, set his gunsight for an Me 410 and crossed to directly behind the bogie from his previous four o'clock position. The bogie continued firing and Col. Riddle returned fire. Both the Colonel and his wingman, Captain William C. Anderson from Lakeside Squadron, overshot the bogie. As they were passing the unidentified A/C, they noted Russian markings and immediately broke off the engagement. By this time, the flight was approaching Mond Lake, east of Salzburg. The Russian

L2-K, The Yakima Chief, named and flown by Lieutenant Harold L. Stotts. *Courtesy of Frederick C. Hayner.*

plane had headed eastward at 10,000 ft. His left engine was smoking, but he was flying straight and level apparently under control. The fight lasted about two minutes and during that time, the bogie gave no recognition signals. Both P-51s received damage, Col. Riddle from the Russian's gunfire and Capt. Anderson from flak. Col. Riddle arrived back at Wattisham with his coolant pouring all over the ground. Positive identification of the Russian A/C was not possible, but it was believed to be either a Pe-2 or a Yak-4.

Escort was provided through the targets where the CAVU skies permitted bombing results that were called excellent. Two boxes of B-24s hit the marshalling yard and a third hit the power station and electrical lines. Newcross Squadron broke away at 1055 hours, during the run on the target, to chase an Ar 234 off to the southeast and gained the distinction of being credited with destroying the last German fighter downed by an 8th AF pilot during the war. That squadron then swept the immediate area up to Nauburg without results. Returning, the fighters stayed with the Big Friends until the vicinity of Mannheim, where they broke away at 1208 hrs./ 12,000 ft. L/O was over Walcheren Island, Holland at 1308 hrs./9,000 ft.

First Lieutenant Hilton O. Thompson from the 434th Fighter Squadron gave the following report of his engagement and destruction of the Ar 234:

> "I was flying Newcross Blue Three position on a bomber escort mission to Traunstein, Germany. At the target, we started a 360-degree turn and during the first quarter of the turn, I sighted a bogie flying in an easterly direction about 2,000 feet above and almost directly over me. We were flying at 24,000 feet at this time. I broke from the turn with my wingman and a spare and started climbing beneath the bogie, trying to identify it. I recognized the A/C as an enemy Ar 234 and my identification was confirmed by Newcross Blue Four and the one Newcross Spare that had followed us from the group. The jet turned to a southeasterly direction and I closed to 800 yards at his level. Ranging with my K-14 sight, I fired two short bursts and observed hits around his left engine. Then I began closing rapidly from seven o'clock astern and fired several more bursts from 600 to 300 yards, observing strikes along the entire left side of the A/C's fuselage which caused many pieces to fly off. At 200 yards I pulled to the right and watched the jet spiral down at about a 40-degree angle. Lieutenant Harold L. Stotts who was the Newcross Spare with me, then fired on the E/A getting repeated strikes. The jet pilot bailed out between 10,000 and 8,000 feet. I believe the jet crashed in the vicinity of Berchtesgaden, Germany. I claim one Ar 234 destroyed in the air."

First Lieutenant Harold L. Stotts, confirmed the Ar 234 as destroyed:

> "I was flying Newcross Spare in the above engagement. As I was flying off Blue Flight's wing, I broke with Blue Three and Four and saw the bogie they were after. On closer inspection, I saw it was an Ar 234. I followed Lt. Thompson as he pressed his attack and observed strikes on the left side of the jet. When I got within 800 to 600 yards, I opened fire, but saw no strikes. Lt. Thompson closed to within 500 yards and I observed many strikes as he fired from this distance. Several parts flew off and the Ar 234 started to trail smoke and began a 45-degree dive. Lt. Thompson broke off and although the jet was definitely headed down, I closed in and fired again, observing strikes and additional pieces flying off of it. The Ar 234 went down in a loose spiral dive and at less than 10,000 feet, the pilot bailed out and his chute opened. I confirm First Lt. Hilton O. Thompson's claim of one Ar 234 destroyed in the air."

As an interesting note, the guns from Lt. Thompson's P-51 were later removed and were sent to Eighth Air Force Headquarters, to be presented to Army Air Force Commanding General H. Hap Arnold. The six .50 cal. Browning machine guns had been used to fire upon and bring down the last German aircraft claimed by the Eighth during the war.

Observations made during the mission included this note: "The bomber formation was excellent and for once, it was easy to cover." One B-24 identified as Vinegrove 2-1, asked for help and was given an escort from the target to Mannheim. The bomber had its left inboard engine shut down and the prop feathered. At 1245 hours, three chutes were seen to come from a B-17 flying 20 miles northwest of Crailsheim. The B-17 continued on course northward from there. Enemy aircraft seen during the mission were listed as thirty unidentified, twin-engine A/C on the airfield at Schleissheim, an unknown quantity of E/A parked at Munich and eleven unidentified E/A parked at Nauburg. There were no E/A seen at Salzburg. Fifteen B-26s were seen to bomb the area south of Ingolstadt at 1126 hrs. They seemed to make a perfect bombing pattern with all hits looking to be on target. Debris was thrown 2,000 feet in the air. Ground fires with much white smoke were spotted 15 miles west of Ingolstadt and extending to Donauwörth. There was a ground explosion that raised smoke to 8,000 feet at 1117 hours, 15 miles southeast of Ingolstadt. What was believed to be Allied troops and fires were observed along the eastern bank of the Danube River, from Regensburg and points westward. A column of trucks, also believed to be Allied, was headed into Regensburg from the west. A large fire located in the vicinity of Klatovy was noted. Flak 50 miles north of Salzburg was heavy, moderate and accurate. At Traunstein, it was heavy, meager and inaccurate. In the vicinity of Hallein, the flak was heavy, intense and accurate.

For Riddle's Raiders, the war was over and VE Day was just about upon them. The group had been in combat for almost eleven months after becoming operational at AAF Station F-377, Wattisham Airfield, Suffolk County, England. Shortly after VE Day arrived, and for the first time since the group became operational, the ammunition was removed from the aircraft on the field.

434th FS armorers Corporal Raymond A. Martinez and Corporal Herbert Taylor loading .50 cal. ammunition for the guns on the right wing of a P-51. *Courtesy of Loetta Taylor (Kennedy).*

436th FS armorers Corporal Stanley E. Wayne and Private First Class Louis D. Guernsey examining a .50 cal. machine gun. *Carroll C. Sprague Collection, courtesy of the East Essex Aviation Society.*

436th FS armorers Corporal William R. Holtman and Sergeant William E. Shaw. *Carroll C. Sprague Collection, courtesy of the East Essex Aviation Society.*

434th FS Technical Sergeant Louis E. Kirby is putting fuel into the fuselage tank on a P-51. *Courtesy of David L. Born.*

Captain William H. Pickering by Edith, a Lakeside ship. *Courtesy of Robert H. Horman.*

First Lieutenant William H. Daudistel, armorer Corporal Herbert Taylor and crew chief Staff Sergeant Carrol P. Perkins by their 434th FS P-51. The aircraft had the distinction of having Mickey's Mustang painted on the right side of its nose and The Impatient Virgin painted on its left side. The plane also had The Impatient Virgin painted on the left side of its canopy rail and a small box lettered with the pilot and crew's names painted on the left side of its nose. *Courtesy of Herbert Taylor.*

Below: 434th FS mission take off – the pilot of L2-W and his wingman are lined up and awaiting the flagman's wave to start their roll. © *2000 Elmo Sears, courtesy of Elmo Sears.*

Bottom: The 434th FS pilot of L2-B has begun his take off roll. © *2000 Elmo Sears, courtesy of Elmo Sears.*

CHAPTER SIXTEEN

FINIS 1945

May 1945

The month of May started on a sour note for on 4 May, First Lieutenant Anthony J. Scordino from the 436th FS was killed during training. While diving in his P-51 during a practice dive-bombing mission, one of the plane's wings came off and man as well as machine crashed into the channel. Unfortunately, death was not about to take a holiday from the group.

On the plus side, the month brought V-E Day on the eighth after which there was great rejoicing by all. That day, after Winston Churchill announced the end of hostilities in Europe over the radio, Colonel Kyle L. Riddle, the 479th FG's commanding officer, addressed the men of the station. His main purpose in doing so was to compliment the officers and enlisted men upon their good work during the past year in the ETO. Each of the squadrons also received talks by their respective commanding officers. Throughout it all, church bells from all the little surrounding churches could be heard wildly ringing in the distance. Their sound had not been heard since the war began. In the celebration of it all though, many of the men relaxed in their quarters or played in the sun. Few people were on pass as most were restricted to the station because the brass was trying to contain any excess youthful jubilation from getting out of hand. However, on most of the military installations, the joy was tempered by the realization that the job of ending the war still raging in the Pacific continued and that many of the officers and enlisted men of AAF faced the possibility of service in that theater of war. (In fact, within a short time, three P-47s arrived at Wattisham and one was assigned to each of the squadrons for the purpose of training ground crews on the various aspects of that aircraft should the men someday be called upon to service the Republic-built fighter.) That evening, the Rocker Club, the Little Wheels Club and the Red Cross Aero Club, all held open houses.

Charles B. Elmgren, then a First Lieutenant and pilot with the 436th FS, was one of the few off base when the V-E Day announcement came. He recently told of what occurred during that time:

> "It happened that another pilot from the squadron, First Lieutenant Ernest J. Hopcroft, was in the teletype room when a message came through announcing that the war would officially end in three days. The message was labeled Top Secret and signed by General Ike Eisenhower. Lt. Hopcroft gathered myself and one other flyer from our squadron, First Lieutenant Presson S. Shane, and we three went to our squadron C.O., Major Claire A.P. Duffié to inform him of the news and to ask for leave time. [The military had been forewarned that the V-E Day announcement was coming and that all personnel would be restricted to base for a period of time. Only those already on pass or leave would be allowed off base.] Maj. Duffié inquired as to where we wanted to go and we told him Scotland. He requested that we keep 'mum' about it and he would likely go also. We respected that and didn't tell a soul.
>
> "The next morning, the group's B-26, which had been converted to carry passengers, was on the flight line ready to go. We loaded in along with several others and headed for Glasgow, Scotland. The plane's pilot was Maj. Duffié and I believe the copilot was Maj. Robin Olds. I don't

One of the P-47s that arrived at Wattisham. This one came from the 5th ERS (Emergency Rescue Squadron). *Courtesy of David L. Born.*

suppose that either of them had ever flown it. [Actually Maj. Olds had experience in the plane, having acquired it for the group and flown it a number of times. This was unknown to Lt. Elmgren at the time though.] Looking back now, I felt it was probably my most dangerous flight. At any rate, after landing at Glasgow, Lt.'s Hopcroft, Shane and I caught a train up to Aberfoyle a small resort village. We spent a few days at the Bailie Nicol Jarvie Hotel, the local of Scott's novel, 'Rob Roy'.

"Winston Churchill's announcement on V-E Day resulted in a celebration that evening in the village square. It seemed as though all of the local people were there and they hung an effigy of Hitler from a light pole during the festivities. There was live music and we three timid American airmen learned to dance the Highland Fling with the Scottish Lassies."

The CBI (China-Burma-India) Theater of Operations became a topic of conversation as well as attention and during the next week, serious orientation and instructional classes dealing with subjects of importance such as living, existing and fighting in the South Pacific. Training films were shown and lectures were given to all. The pilots began attending regular recognition classes on Japanese aircraft, military vehicles and ships. It began to look like that would be the group's next port of call. A return to the rifle range in late May added to that belief. The men had not fired their weapons on the station's range for the past six months and were certainly rusty in both their aim and

434th FS Armament Officer Captain Themis N. Anastos (center) and his armorers are celebrating at this party. *Courtesy of David L. Born.*

434th FS Adjutant, Chief Warrant Officer Herbert Plemens and squadron S-2, Captain Donald D. Horton are seen with a couple of English ladies during this party. *Courtesy of David L. Born.*

later the disassembly, cleaning and re-assembly of their firearms.

To maintain the high moral and physical fitness of the men, a required physical training program was instituted and began during the middle of the month. A minimum of two hours of athletics five days a week were to be engaged in and organized sports such as volleyball, softball, basketball, football and tennis were begun. Attendance schedules were set up assigning the men to specific time periods and rosters were kept for the purpose of accounting each man's weekly exercise. As they evolved, some of the sports became quite competitive.

Leslie L. Heuman, who was a part of the 434th FS's communications section, played ball and remembered those times:

The group's baseball team. *Courtesy of Harold L. Stotts.*

> "After the war in Europe ended, Colonel Kyle Riddle organized a station baseball team. I played right field and caught some. We practiced two to three hours every day and played other teams, sometimes touring to their airfields and sometimes at home when the opposing team came to Wattisham. When we went to other bases, we rode in army 6x6 trucks, but we had it made. We enlisted men didn't have to pull any duties, we just played ball. We also moved from our barracks building to quarters above the Rocker Club where we each had private rooms during this time.
>
> "Toward the end of our playing time that summer, we were engaged in a contest for the 2nd Air Division championship. The winning team, in addition to the honor of being the best, was to be awarded the prize of an all-expense paid trip to Belfast, Ireland. The championship was to be played at our airfield so the day of the big game, we got up early in the morning to prepare the ball diamond for the afternoon's game. Wouldn't you know it, a little while after we were done, it began to pour down rain! When it stopped, the ground was all wet. Col. Riddle called up the base fuel dump and ordered a tanker of aviation gasoline to be brought to the playing field. When it arrived, we sprayed gas all over the grounds and put a match to it. After the gas all burned off, the ground was dry. We went to work again and raked the diamond back into shape. After we limed the lines, we were ready for the game once more. About 3:00, the opposing team arrived and we began to play. We no sooner got started than another rainstorm came through. When the rain stopped, Col. Riddle ordered another tanker of gasoline brought to the playing field. We put the fuel down on the ground once more and lit it. This time, the smoke drew the attention of the fire department at Hitcham and they came over to investigate. All was well though; the ground had dried and we began to prepare the ball diamond for the third time that day. When it was ready, the game resumed. At the conclusion of the baseball game, we had won the championship. Our prize, in addition to the trip, was a small medal awarded to each of us by the Special Services branch at our base.
>
> "After I came home, I continued playing ball and in 1991, I was voted into the Softball Hall of Fame. I had played the game my whole life."

Colonel Kyle Riddle with his winning ball team. Baseball teams in the ZOI donated all the uniforms, and as a consequence few matched. *Carroll C. Sprague Collection, courtesy of the East Essex Aviation Society.*

A 446th BG/707th BS B-24, one of the bombers that arrived at Wattisham to take the men on a tour of war-torn Germany. *Courtesy of Raymond Niekamp.*

One of the groups from the 434th FS who went on a Trolley tour over Germany. *Courtesy of David L. Born.*

The Eighth Air Force started what was affectionately known as "Trolley Trips" over the war-torn continent. The three air divisions, now freed from the grind of constant bombing missions, utilized some of their heavy bombers to take groups of men up on sight seeing trips into Germany. That meant Second Air Division B-24 Liberators flew into the airfields such as Wattisham and took the AAF ground-borne troops up into the air. The trips, which began the first week of May and continued for several weeks, were intended as a holiday gesture, but they also allowed the men to personally witness the destruction that was brought to the enemy's lands through Allied airpower. The devastation was well noted by those who had not seen it before.

Probably the single most item of interest to all concerned though was the "Point System" for discharge. Discussion among the enlisted men was especially full after the showing of a training film that explained the future disposition of the ground, service and air forces. Realizing the importance of battle participation awards, members of most service organizations voiced their displeasure with the allotment of the honors and considered themselves discriminated against in favor of the fighter group. Few members of the group would benefit from the system when all was said and done because of the shortness of time the group had spent in the ETO. Many would be amongst the last to leave for home, spending the better part of 1945, still in England.

Old faces began showing up at Wattisham as the surviving pilots who had gone down during the previous days of conflict returned to the 479th FG for a look see, to share their stories and await transportation home. Colonel Hubert Zemke passed through for a brief visit. From the 434th FS, Major Frank J. Keller, Captain James M. Hollingsworth, First Lieutenants Ossie J, Huval, Ronald L. Maley, Tom D. Neely and Albert S.J. Tucker, Jr. all stopped by during the month. Some stayed on assuming post-war duties with the squadron. The 435th FS heard from Captain Calvin J. Butler and Lieutenant Rayne B. Fairchild. Captain Richard G. Candelaria (promoted shortly after he became a POW) returned and went back to work with

This special ops, B-24 was another of the bombers utilized for the "Trolley Missions". The all-black aircraft sported three small domes under that portion of its belly below the cockpit. These clear plastic covers housed aerials for the "Carpet" jamming transmitter the aircraft carried. *Courtesy of David L. Born.*

his squadron. Lieutenant Carl B. Jarrell did not return, but made contact via direct correspondence. The 436th FS saw or heard from Lieutenants Albert R. DiPaola, Barrett B. Eskell, Fred A. Moser, Louis K. Nesselbush, and Thomas J. O'Holleran.

The various service sections began winding down to a peacetime pace, while others such as the Chemical Section figurative closed shop when it began dismantling its gas defense installations. Flying time was cut in half, but the squadrons still participated in training missions and some cross-country flights.

Interestingly enough, a shortage of food began to become a problem at the airfield and a campaign against waste was begun.

As the month closed, Americans everywhere observed Memorial Day. It was an appropriate time for them to remember the men who had given more then their share to help preserve the freedom their country and others enjoyed and continue to enjoy even to this day. May God bless them and continue to favor us all with His countenance.

The group had a Martin B-26G Marauder, Serial Number 43-34226, squadron code T. It had been previously used by the 654th BS for night photographic work. Painted jet black on its undersides and OD on its topsides, the medium bomber was named Liberty Run while at Wattisham. Allen J. Moon recalled a story in which the plane played a part:

Captain Richard G. Candelaria, back from POW status. *Carroll C. Sprague Collection, courtesy of the East Essex Aviation Society.*

The B-26 Marauder named Liberty Run that was used for the above flight as well as many other trips about. *Courtesy of David L. Born.*

> "During the latter days of the war, our base was enhanced with a Martin B-26 Marauder in which I had the pleasure of serving as the radio operator when it was being flown. The converted bomber was utilized by a select few pilots for the purpose of taking pilots on leave, requisitioning spirits for the officer's club and in fact was once pressed into service to take Red Cross girls on leave. It was a mission of the latter that Major Robin Olds arranged to Langford Lodge, Lockheed's facility in Northern Ireland. The air depot was near Belfast, the leave site the women had chosen. Ready to depart, Major Olds noted a look of dismay on the young women's faces. They were dejected at the thought of an hour-long bus ride into Belfast from where they would be landing. The ladies assured Major Olds that a Royal Navy airfield was located right in Belfast. A check with the Air Ministry confirmed the airfield's existence, but telephone calls for information on the field were discouraging as no information could be found concerning its current usage or adaptability for our B-26. Major Olds, who was having some doubts about the Royal Navy field, warned the girls of the possibility that we still might have to go on into of our original destination at Langford Lodge. The gals still looked dejected, but brightened somewhat when Robin assured them 'We would look it over.'
>
> "We took off and a short time later we were nearing Belfast. We began picking up airspeed in a shallow dive and in making a low pass across the Royal Navy airfield; we zipped past its tower a bit lower than the guardrail on the roof. The mixture of control tower warnings and threats we heard did not intimidate Major Olds. He in fact took one more look at the runway by means of another fast pass that left the grass waving. A long 'airline approach' resulted in our entering final approach and crossing over the barrier fence, full flaps down and at near-stalling speed. We sat down on the very beginning of the runway and

This sign was painted by the 434th FS painter Staff Sergeant Frederick C. Hayner and placed in front of the low building that the 434th used for their ready room, S-2, etc. It shows the squadron's crew chiefs and the victories that their airplanes had accumulated during the war. *Courtesy of the Wings of Freedom Museum.*

with lots of screeching brakes, slowed enough for a fast turnoff. We then casually taxied up to the tower where the precious cargo was unloaded. Robin was modest in accommodating their wishes for a short commute into Belfast. With cheery faces beaming, they waved at us and thanked him profusely.

"We shut the hatch and taxied to the end of the runway where Robin very methodically ran up the engines several times, checking the mags. He held the brakes, turned to me and said 'Moon, we got it in, but I don't know how in the hell we are going to get it out!' When we started our take off roll, our savior of the girls travel time was cool, calculating and determined to use every inch of the runway. We built up airspeed and finally lifted off near the end of the field. The landing gear came up immediately, then the flaps were bled off. We made it! I would have flown down to look at the fires of hell with him because I knew he could get us back."

Robin Olds told just how the group acquired the Martin B-26 Marauder:

On the last day of May, Bison pilot Lieutenant Presson S. Shane, while at the controls of 9B-N, over ran Lieutenant Richard P. Thrall in 9B-C-. Amazingly, no one was injured, but it is a safe bet that Lt. Thrall was more than in need of some "medicinal spirits" afterwards! That was the end of two 436th FS birds, My Best Bett and Bruiser. *Courtesy of George E. Falkner.*

"One day I was up in the tower with Major William [Bill] Hugill, the senior ATC [Senior Flying Control Officer] at Wattisham. We watched as a B-26 landed on the field and taxied up to the tower. The aircraft parked below, shut down and the crew got out. Pretty soon the pilot came up to us and asked who wanted to sign for the plane. I looked at Bill, he looked at me and I said: 'I will!' It was all very curious, but the bird would make a wonderful hack. I signed and then the pilot asked for someone to take him and his crew back to their base. I had flown twin-engine P-38s, so I had some basis of experience with the twin-engine bomber. After boarding the plane, I was given a quick check out on the controls, then we took off. I watched the pilot as he flew us back to his base and landed. Once there, the crew got off and walked away, leaving me on my own. Since I had observed things like take off and landing speeds, and the controls bore some resemblance to those of the P-38, I headed the bomber down the runway, got it off the ground and headed home with our new ship."

At some point, the growing number of aircraft accidents at the field had led Major Robin Olds to draw up this cartoon. *Courtesy of George E. Falkner.*

June 1945

June was the first month of non-operational activity for the 479th Fighter group and its attached units since the group left the United States. That said, the records indicate well over 3,000 hours of training flights having taken place during the month. Involving simulated combat, gunnery and bombing missions, the practice was all in preparation for the Pacific. During the course of that, only three accidents occurred, none of which involved pilot injury.

Most of the month was spent readying the entire group for redeployment and training films as well as lectures became staples for the month. While life in the ETO did not exactly correspond to the routine of Training Command in the ZOI, there were many points of similarity what with standing reveille, drill, work call and the like. The pilots got a break from the tedium when they began learning to fly the P-47 Thunderbolts the group had been given. They thus became qualified to pilot both that heavy radial engine fighter as well as their sleeker inline engine stallions. Some of the old timers with P-38 experience could claim that additional credit for their repertoires.

Last minute recommendations for awards were rushed through and returning former POW pilots filed some encounter reports for addition enemy aircraft that they had destroyed.

About half of the group's Mustangs were flown off the station, destined for storage and later possible use in other theaters of war or sale to allied countries. Those that remained had a greater number of hours than the maximum 100 hours used as the cut off for those birds destined for storage. (As a side note, the last P-51 that 434th FS C.O. Robin Olds flew in combat, Scat VII, was one of those low hour planes that went into storage. The plane escaped the fate of a salvage axe and after its military career was finished, ultimately came into the possession of Jim and Carol Shuttleworth of Huntington, Indiana who lovingly and painstakingly restored the warbird to its former glory and colors during the 1990s. The award winning aircraft was hangared at the Wings of Freedom Museum on the grounds of the Huntington Municipal Airport where the well-maintained ex-fighter occasionally took to the air in the capable hands of Jim or his son, John to relive its heritage once more. Unfortunately, both Jim and the Mustang were lost in an accident on a beautiful, sunny day February 20, 2003.) The group received a small quantity of war weary P-51Bs in exchange for those given up, but the number of planes the group had was diminishing. An example of this is the 434th FS. From a high of about 30 P-51s assigned to the squadron at the end of the war, it was down to only 14 P-51Ds and five P-51Bs by months end.

434th FS P-51 L2-Z, The Impatient Virgin bellied in near Wattisham. Lieutenant Clarence L. Waters made the wheels-up landing was the result of running out of fuel and the plane went to the scrap yard. L2-Z had just gotten a new wing and engine. *Courtesy of George E. Falkner.*

In this photo of the hardstands where the 434th FS's A and B Flights were located, 23 P-51s can be seen parked. *Courtesy of Harold L. Stotts.*

Fewer aircraft and less flying time meant less maintenance and the records show that there were only five engine changes for the month verses a record high of 52 in one month during the offensive over the continent. The ground crews began to find themselves with time on their hands as their workweek slowed to a mere 60 hours per week. For some, the additional slack time was utilized to explore the countryside on their cycles while for others; the time was spent pub-crawling.

These two lovely ladies are behind the bar at Saracen's Head Pub in Ipswich. *Carroll C. Sprague Collection, courtesy of the East Essex Aviation Society.*

A relaxation of Flying Regulations permitted up to four pilots and the planes they were flying, to remain overnight at a location during cross-country flights. This of course provided the opportunity for pilots to visit with friends at other air bases. Captain Clarence (Buck) G. Haynes from the 434th FS took a flight to Northern Ireland during mid-month and from all accounts, they tried to eat the place out of rations. Capt. Haynes returned to Wattisham with six steaks, which he prepared himself at the squadron's snack bar. There was much drooling done by the onlookers.

Mid month also was the focus of a training or "conditioning" hike for the 434th FS. The entire squadron fell out with field packs for the exercise. While meant to simulate combat conditions with full gear stowed away in the packs, many of the men "fudged" a bit and lightened their loads. In the spirit of the times and occasion, the officers looked the other way for the most part, regarding the packs. Former Master Sergeant Alvin (Al) R. Willhite, one of the squadron's aircraft inspectors, remembers that march and a humorous story that came out of it:

> "During the summer of 1945, the war was over and everyone was biding time until we could return home. All of the men had time on their hands and I suppose we needed things to do in order to keep us fit as soldiers. So once more, physical training, drills, inspections and the like became a part of our army routine. One of the things

that soldiers always seem to do is march and hike and so we had to do some hiking. Before each outing, we had to check our bulletin board to see what equipment we needed to take with us, how it was to be packed and carried. For this one, we were to wear all of our equipment and be marched just as we had done during training. Tech Sergeant Clifton M. Greene, who was one of our airplane mechanics, decided it was unnecessary for him to carry all the things listed. He got some small cardboard boxes, wrapped them with a few of the articles of clothing we were required to have and put it all in his back pack. His load thusly lightened, he was ready to go. Having finished his preparations early, he went to the Red Cross Aero Club for a quick cup of coffee. His barracks mates decided to play a little trick on T/Sgt. Greene and replaced his light load with some bricks that they got from a pile outside the barracks building. The T/Sergeant got back just in time to grab his equipment and get to formation before the hike.

"From formation, we broke down into our squads and headed out. During the hike I overheard T/Sgt. Greene commenting about how heavy his pack seemed to be getting and how sorry he felt for all the other suckers carrying their full loads. Major Robin Olds was our Squadron C.O. then. He was leading us and sometime during the march, someone had let him in on the joke. Maj. Olds decided the men needed a laugh at T/Sgt. Greene's expense so when we had returned to the base, he called the squadron to order. Very straight-faced, he told the men that for the benefit of the lower ranking enlisted men among them, he would have an experienced, upper ranking non-com show them how to properly display the equipment they had just carried. Then he called for T/Sgt. Greene to step forward and show the men how to properly display the equipment they were supposed to have with them. I was standing beside T/Sgt. Green and said 'That's got to be you Cliff.' Poor old T/Sgt. Greene just stood there making a little funny noise with his mouth. He finally stepped forward, put his pack on the ground close to Maj. Olds, kneeled down and slowly started to unbuckle the straps. Then he looked up at the Major. Maj. Olds said something like 'Speed it up Sergeant; the whole squadron is waiting.' T/Sgt. Greene finally reached into his pack and then felt the bricks. He pulled one out, drew it back and looked at Maj. Olds like he was going to hit him with it. Maj. Olds said, 'Sergeant, don't you hit me with that brick, I didn't put it in your pack.' Then he yelled out: 'SQUADRON DISMISSED!' I couldn't help but feeling sorry for T/Sgt. Green that day."

Captain Clarence G. Haynes by his Rabid Rebel. This aircraft was the second Rebel he flew and is shown post-war. Note that the carburetor filtered air intake on the side of the aircraft's nose has been deleted. There was an intake for air on each side and both have been replaced with a sheet metal panel, leaving only the chin scoop for ram air. *Courtesy of Clarence G. Haynes.*

The 435th FS finally began receiving their new squadron insignia patches during middle of the month and there was a scramble to get them sewed on the various permitted articles of clothing.

Good weather held for a period and the station held a Field Day on Sunday 17 June. Both officers and enlisted men participated in the various track and field sporting events, which included a three-legged race and a bicycle race. Major Robin Olds, Major Donald J. Pierce and Captain Richard D. Creighton from the 434th FS plus Major William C. Anderson, C.O. of the 435th FS put on an air show to add to the day's festivities. Maj. Pierce enlivened the proceedings by making a spectacular forced landing when his engine went out over the field. Fortunately, the Major was not injured in the landing. The evening meal was served picnic style on the wide expanse of grass within the perimeter of the flying field. Included were fried chicken and ice cream. The meal was followed by a baseball game. Dancing and beer at the Officer's Club, the NCO Rocker Club and the Red Cross Aero Club wound up a very enjoyable day for all.

There were changes in command and authority outside of the fighter group as about the middle of the month, it, along with its parent 65th Fighter Wing ceased to be a part of the disbanding Second Air division. In turn, the wing along with its fighter groups became a part of the Third Air Division.

The training continued through out the month and a revision of the group's battle star awards brought many men closer to leaving for the ZOI. This of course set off another tirade from the service groups who were not affected by the increase in awards. Finally, on the 26th, Colonel Riddle announced that tentatively, the group was scheduled to be heading home sometime during the month of September.

Men with higher numbers of "points" were transferred to other groups going home sooner and men from other groups with lower "points" were transferred into the 479th. Many of the men went to the 100th Bomb Group, which was quite a change for them.

Probably culprits all: front – Master Sergeant Jack E. Gowan, Technical Sergeant Harold L. Greenlee and Master Sergeant James W. Smart. Back – Master Sergeant Alvin R. Willhite, Technical Sergeant William M. Morgan and Technical Sergeant Clifton M. Greene. *Courtesy of James W. Smart.*

July 1945

The individual days were still dragging with each seeming to be an eternity as the men of the 479th Fighter Group watched and waited for the time that they would ship out to home. Rumors, transfers, training, inspections and increasing amounts of time to accomplish nothing were the activities for the period. Sporting events were still popular with the men, however. The pilots and armament sections became concerned with the possibility of learning the intricacies of a rocket firing P-47 and a new technique in aerial gunnery, which utilized Royal Navy gliders for targets, became possibilities. Nothing came of the rocket firing and the gliders met with mishap. Men were slowly being dropped from the roster as they were sent to other units or in some cases, directly to the Pacific Theater. Personnel replaced them to a degree from other groups as they also wound down or left.

The pilots of the group were taking advantage of the dwindling number of aircraft the group had left to fly. Cross-country flights were being made to all points of the compass, even Germany. Several members were added to the engineering staff for the purpose of taking care of some captured German aircraft the group was to receive, but there is no mention in the group's records of that ever happening. They were put to work in the line working on P-51s. During this time Wattisham began receiving aircraft from fighter groups leaving for the ZOI. These in turn were ferried to the various depots for storage or salvage. Robin Olds told of an experience he called a horror story during that time:

> "Those of us left during this time and who had previously flown P-38s, were pressed into service ferrying brand new birds from a depot in England to Langford Lodge just outside Belfast, Northern Ireland. The only one I took over had a total of nineteen hours on it and even smelled new like a new car. After landing at the depot, I was signing over the forms to some character when a truck drove up and a bunch of scruffy-looking civilians unloaded some gear near the plane. They proceeded to cut the ship's tail booms off with torches. I blew a gasket, left in anger and refused to ferry any more of those beauties to their fate. At least the low-time 51s taken to Liverpool

First Lieutenant David L. Born from the 434th FS was caught taking a nap in the grass. *Courtesy of David L. Born.*

Left: This P-51 did not come home. Belonging to the 434th FS, L2-K, the Yakima Chief had an engine failure and had to be bellied in. The pilot, Lieutenant Francis C. Schiess put her in about a half-mile northeast of Wattisham on this date. *Courtesy of George E. Falkner.* Right: The Yakima Chief back at Wattisham after being recovered. Lieutenant Schiess is standing on her wing, looking kind of downcast. *Courtesy of David L. Born.*

were crated up and sent back to the states. My bird Scat VII, the last P-51 that I flew during the war, was one of the lucky ones. It had fewer than 100 hours on it and came home."

On 19 July, the 434th FS lost a member of the squadron when First Lieutenant Hilton O. Thompson crashed into the channel while on a training mission. His former roommate, Harold L. (Lyle) Stotts wrote of that tragic loss in 1999. He stated:

"When the war was over, several of us got into a discussion regarding the most effective way to drop a bomb from a fighter plane and have the greatest likelihood of striking a target. Hilton and I argued that a vertical descent prior to releasing the bomb was the most effective while others maintained that a glide angle attack prior to releasing the bomb was just as effective. To test the opposing viewpoints, a target was set up in the channel. Hilton and I would make the vertical run and Lieutenants Ralph M. Lulay and Albert S.J. Tucker, Jr. would make the glide run. I do not recall whether the other two made their runs or not, but I do know that I preceded Hilton. My hairy dive on the target was followed by a recovery that pulled a bushel of Gs. When I had gained a little altitude, I looked down at the target and witnessed a huge displacement of water that could only mean that a plane had gone in. It was Hilton. No one witnessed whether he waited too long to pull out or if a wing had come off. We were subsequently informed that the P-51 was not to engage in such dives. Was it possible that the plane was not stressed for that maneuver? I don't know, but in any case, it was a sad loss due to youthful foolishness."

Lt. Thompson was an experienced fighter pilot and to him had gone the credit of destroying the last enemy plane shot down by the Eighth.

August 1945

The days still dragged! The month seemed like one of the most hectic in the group's history as men came into the group and others left at, both at a seemingly preposterous rate. The 436th FS alone transferred in ten officers and 150 enlisted men while six officers and 128 men were transferred out. Those persons who weren't busy with regular duties and cleaning up the station, were enjoying or bemoaning, depending upon how many points one had, the enormous amount of spare time at hand. Preparations for the voyage home, the taking of passes and getting a few more hours of sack time was becoming more the order of the day. One of the big events of the month was to

First Lieutenant Hilton O. Thompson. *Courtesy of Clarence G. Haynes.*

be a decoration of awards ceremony. After much marching and practicing for the long-awaited event, the awarding was done inside in as much as the countryside was drenched in "English Dew" that day.

Clifford (Cliff) W. Bowers was one of the remaining pilots in the 434th FS at this point. A former First Lieutenant at that point, Cliff remembered the times:

> "Aircraft from many groups were being dumped off at Wattisham and the planes were setting around the airfield by the dozens. All of the pilots from those groups had been shipped home, leaving those of us who were relatively latecomers to 'clean up the mess'. Those of us left at Wattisham had the duty of ferrying the war-weary birds to Liverpool where they were to be scrapped. Always greedy for flying time and the half-base flying pay, we had fun flying them there. Most of the time, we would be flown back to the base in B-24s.
>
> "Finally all the planes were gone with the exception of our UC-64 Noorduyn Norseman. Jerome (Jerry) Nagel and I needed four hours of flying time so we decided to take the old girl and get going. It was late in the day and a storm was brewing. As we flew around, it became dark rather quickly – no moon and no stars, just overcast. We never should have taken off because we could only find one parachute and forced landings at night aren't the kind of things that allow one to grow to a ripe old age. When we found our way back to our field, we discovered that our landing lights wouldn't work and the radio receiver went out. In addition to those things, we knew that our left front tire was worn through the first layer of cording. Jerry had never flown the Norseman before, so it fell upon me to make the landing since I had some previous experience in it. On our final approach, I leveled off three times thinking that I was ready to land. No soap! By the fourth time, I was ready to go around again when the wheels squeaked slightly and we were down. 'Good job!' Jerry said. Little did he know how much luck I packed around."

Captain Harold M. Jenkins from the 434th FS had to set L2-M, The Onley Genevieve II down near Apramont, France when his engine failed over the continent. The accident occurred the second day of the month and was one of the very last the 479th FG suffered. *Courtesy of George E. Falkner.*

The biggest event was of course V-J Day. The victory over Japan was celebrated by all with the usual liquid refreshments, much whooping and hollering as well as the expenditure of no small amount of flares and other pyrotechnics. Now the rumors really began to fly as the group looked toward the announced September ship date.

These are some of the many P-51s that went through Wattisham during the summer of 1945. Mustangs from the 356th FG and 359th FG can be seen in this picture. *Courtesy of Frederick C. Hayner.*

September 1945

Men moved in and men moved out during the month and it appeared even more hectic than the previous month if that were possible. The days seemed like weeks and the weeks seemed like months. Again, using the 436th FS as an example, the squadron gained four officers and 265 enlisted men while it lost 32 officers and 305 enlisted men. Most of the old faces were by now gone including almost all of the pilots. Wattisham and the 479th FG was becoming a shell of its former self as men were transferred to other fighter and bomber groups, service groups, the occupational air force or to holding stations as they awaited shipment home. The ship date for the 479th FG as a whole was moved back to November but by and large most of the group's former members had left by now. The group strength was by now down to approximately 20% of what it had come into the ETO with.

October 1945

The month of October was uneventful with the exception of numerous personnel changes and a further reduction in the group's strength.

November/December 1945

The readiness date for shipment of the group home was finally set for 28 November and the actual embarkation date occurred during the first week of December.

The last contingent from Army Air Force Station F-377; Wattisham, England arrived home during December and the men of the 479th FG proceeded to their respective separation centers for demobilization. The group was deactivated that same month at Camp Kilmer, New Jersey. Thus ends the World War II history of Riddle's Raiders, the 479th Fighter Group.

OOPS! This AT-6 (42-84586) formerly belonging to the 4th SAD at Hitcham was assigned to the 479th FG during the summer of 1945. As pictured, the North American Aviation built trainer became involved in what was probably the last accident for the group during its time in England. On the morning of 4 December 1945, a day that began with a fog that coated the surrounding area with frost, Lieutenant Charles H. Philbrick II was set to return to the states. He had been a Bison Squadron pilot, but had received his orders that would return him to the ZOI the next day. Before leaving the group however, he had wanted to get his monthly flying hours in to qualify for flight pay. Instead, he suffered the embarrassment of upending the pictured plane during an early morning take off. The runway he was using that day had a slight dip in it and just as he reached its beginning during his roll, he felt the trainer about ready to lift off. It in fact had begun to fly, but only because of its forward momentum and because the runway surface fell away from its wheels as it began passing over the dip. Believing the plane to be airborne, Lt. Philbrick eased back on the control stick and immediately began applying its wheel brakes, preparatory to retracting its landing gear. Misfortune stepped in and the aircraft quickly settled toward the ground and hit the rising portion of the dip, brakes on. With its wheel brakes having slowed or stopped tire rotation, when the Texan touched down again the bird pivoted on them, pitched up on its nose and began to slide down the frost-covered runway in that attitude. Lt. Philbrick, flung forward in his seat, his feet still on the rudder pedals holding the brakes, found himself pressing even harder on the brakes as his weight forced him down on the pedals. The frost on the runway allowed the plane to slide some distance before it finally came to rest, its nose and wheels badly abraded from the concrete runway. Lt. Philbrick escaped any wrath and exited Wattisham the following day. © *Eugene E. Sears, courtesy of Elmo Sears.*

A member of the ground crew is seated in the cockpit of Chug-A-Lug, a 436th FS P-51 flown by Lieutenant Alfred J. Smigel. *Courtesy of John J. Sipek.*

Left: One of the 434th FS auxiliary aircraft – this one is a Fairchild UC-61. *Courtesy of David L. Born.*

This truck from the 435th FS somehow caught fire and is now seen as a crewman plays a stream of water on the fire in an attempt to extinguish it. *Courtesy of David L. Born.*

First Lieutenant William H. (Hank) Daudistel did his part in keeping a good relationship with his English hosts. Here he is explaining some point about a Mustang's landing gear to some young English lads. *Courtesy of David L. Born.*

The armorer, First Lieutenant Robert H. Horman and the plane's crew chief Technical Sergeant Charlton N. Harman are pictured on their 435th FS ship, Lady Jean. *Courtesy of Robert H. Horman.*

The station's Glee Club traveled into Germany, giving performances there during the month of July in 1945. Part of the Glee Club went over in the B-26, Liberty Run. *Courtesy of Lewis J. West.*

The Glee Club came back from Germany in this B-17. *Courtesy of Lewis J. West.*

Right: 436th FS armorer Corporal Stanley Kellett in one of the Bison Squadron's P-51s, 9B-Q, which became a two-place conversion. *Courtesy of Stanley Kellett.*

Above left: Brothers Clarence G. and James H. Koerber are shown standing by a C-47 that belonged to the 354th FG, a 9th AF outfit that became stationed in Germany after the war. James, a 435th FS pilot, had flown over to the continent for a visit with his brother who was a pilot assigned to the 354th FG. At the time, both were First Lieutenants in the AAF and both flew P-51 Mustangs. *Courtesy of James H. Koerber.* Above: The brothers as youngsters in 1927. Even then they both were flyers at heart. *Courtesy of James H. Koerber.*

Left: First Lieutenant James H. Koerber and his crew chief Staff Sergeant Harold J. Fox by their 435th FS P-51, Betty Jean. Note that the carburetor air intakes have been deleted on this aircraft. *Courtesy of James H. Koerber.*

First Lieutenant Robert I. Bromschwig is posed near the front of the station's BOQ. *Courtesy of Robert I. Bromschwig.*

436th FS pilot First Lieutenant Bernard R. (Robert) Kleinman. *Courtesy of the 436th Fighter Squadron Association.*

Liberty Run, the Martin B-26 Marauder that the group inherited. © *Eugene E. Sears, courtesy of Elmo Sears.*

An AT-6 that belonged to the group. Notice that the aircraft is trimmed in colors representative of the group's three squadrons. © *Eugene E. Sears, courtesy of Elmo Sears.*

First Lieutenant Clifford W. Bowers by another of the 434th FS's UC-61s. *Courtesy of David L. Born.*

L2-H, one of the P-47s that were assigned to the 434th FS takes to the air during a nice sunny day. Life was good. *Courtesy of Robert I. Bromschwig.*

A 435th FS P-51. Note one of the airfield's tannoy's located on a pole just right of the plane. *Courtesy of Robert I. Bromschwig.*

L2-L Kraut Knocker, the 434th FS ship that Lieutenant Robert I. Bromschwig named and flew. *Courtesy of Robert I. Bromschwig.*

Some of the many aircraft that went through Wattisham during post-war downsizing. F-5s from the 7th PG, P-47s from the 56th FG and P-51s from other fighter groups can be seen in this photo. *Courtesy of Robert I. Bromschwig.*

Captain Gail E. Jacobson is standing beside a 434th FS Fairchild UC-61. © *Eugene E. Sears, courtesy of Elmo Sears.*

First Lieutenant David L. Born is seated in Just Born, a 434th FS P-51 as his crew chief, Technical Sergeant John E. Gilchrist looks at the photographer. *Courtesy of David L. Born.*

Major Robin Olds is seated in one of the 434th FS's war-weary P-51Bs. *Courtesy of David L. Born.*

A Noorduyn UC-64 that was used by all three squadrons. Note the three squadron colors represented on the aircraft. © *Eugene E. Sears, courtesy of Elmo Sears.*

Two men from the 436th FS, communications chief Master Sergeant Albert H. Morgenstern and Corporal Biagio Valente are seen in front of their communications building. *Carroll C. Sprague Collection, courtesy of the East Essex Aviation Society.*

Lieutenants Lauri A. Hendrickson and Jerome (Jerry) K. Nagel are seated in J2-Q, a 435th FS P-51B conversion. Nicknamed "Double Bubble", the war-weary aircraft sported a yellow overall finish with black trim. © *2000 Elmo Sears, courtesy of Elmo Sears.*

L2-B Beautiful Jan, the P-51 that Lieutenant Eugene H. Wendt named and flew. *Courtesy of David L. Born.*

L2-3, a war-weary P-51B that was assigned to the 434th FS. *Courtesy of David L. Born.*

A full view of Double Bubble. *Courtesy of 435th Fighter Squadron.*

Some more of the 436th FS communications men, in the front row: Staff Sergeant Charles K. Pruyne, Corporal Biagio Valente, Sergeant Vincent B. Stolz and Corporal Lester G. Kronberg. In the back row are Sergeant Hinton J. Dillard Staff Sergeant Raymond Niekamp and Corporal Charles Pasternack. *Courtesy of Raymond Niekamp.*

First Lieutenant Dalton F. Tommie is seated on the wing of Ruffles, a 434th FS P-51. *Courtesy of Harold L. Stotts.*

Wedding bells rang in overseas for James Manwell and his English bride. *Carroll C. Sprague Collection, courtesy of the East Essex Aviation Society.*

Crew chief Corporal Wilfred D. Lessard is pointing at his Pauline, a 434th P-51. *Courtesy of Victor R. Plassenthal.*

First Lieutenant David L. Born and "man's best friend" are seen in the doorway of the BOQ. *Courtesy of David L. Born.*

Mr. and Mrs. James Manwell cutting the cake at their wedding reception. *Carroll C. Sprague Collection, courtesy of the East Essex Aviation Society.*

Another G.I. wedding in England, this one for 434th FS Corporal Thomas Speirs and his new bride, both flanked by their Best Man and Maid of Honor. That's Corporal Lewis J. (Jack) West performing the duties of Best Man during the October wedding. The Brides Maid is unknown. *Courtesy of Lewis J. West.*

434th FS munitions workers, front row: Corporal George R. Smith, Sergeant Wayne W. Wright, Corporal Harold I. Surridge and Corporal Joseph M. Streit. Rear: Corporal Lyle D. White, Private First Class Carl H. Homan and Sergeant Ralph A. Bottorff, a sheet metal man. *Courtesy of Loetta Taylor (Kennedy).*

Outdoor maintenance was much nicer when the weather was pleasant as is shown in this photo taken on a 434th FS hardstand. *Courtesy of Harold L. Stotts.*

434th FS First Lieutenant David L. Born in one of the P-47 training aircraft. He really liked the P-47. *Courtesy of David L. Born.*

Left: 434th FS First Lieutenant Clifford W. Bowers beside a P-47 that came to the group from the 5th ERS. *Courtesy of David L. Born.*

434th FS First Lieutenant Robert I. Bromschwig in the same P-47. *Courtesy of David L. Born.*

435th FS crew chief Staff Sergeant Harder J. Lind, Major William Anderson and armorer Corporal John P. Clodfelter by their P-51, Jane. Again, note that the carburetor filtered air intakes have been deleted. Note also the attachment points for rockets under the plane's wing. *Courtesy of Carol Donaldson.*

436th FS aircraft mechanics Sergeant James R. (Ralph) Helms and Sergeant Kenneth H. McCoy are examining an engine part. *Courtesy of James R. Helms.*

436th FS Sergeant John J. Sipek, a propeller mechanic, is seated on the wing of a 435th FS P-51. *Courtesy of John J. Sipek.*

First Lieutenant Clifford W. Bowers flying his 434th FS Skunk Chaser. *Courtesy of David L. Born.*

436th FS pilot Lieutenant Charles S. Kreger is seated in a Bison Squadron P-51. *Courtesy of the 436th Fighter Squadron Association.*

When the B-24s arrived at Wattisham, of course everyone had to look them over, especially the fighter pilots who had flown so many escorts for the Big Friends. First Lieutenant Clifford W. Bowers is under the left wing of one named My Lorraine. *Courtesy of David L. Born.*

First Lieutenant David L. Born appears to be holding up the tail of a B-24. He said he wasn't, but it certainly looks that way. *Courtesy of David L. Born.*

The "front office" of one of the visiting Big Friends. *Courtesy of David L. Born.*

434th FS Lieutenant Donald A. Van Waes and Technical Sergeant Victor R. Plassenthal. *Courtesy of Victor R. Plassenthal.*

435th FS pilot First Lieutenant Edward H. Sims. *Courtesy of Edward H. Sims.*

Lieutenant Harold J. Hagerman from the 434th FS is flying the B-26 Liberty Run. *Courtesy of David L. Born.*

First Lieutenant Kenneth J. Hansen, a 436th FS pilot is seated in one of the newer P-47s. Those are 434th FS ships immediately behind him and further in the background, hangars two and three can be seen. *Courtesy of Kenneth J. Hansen.*

The 434th FS occupied the left wing, ground floor in the BOQ. The warmer weather saw many windows open for ventilation. Consequently, heads were always hanging out to talk to those passing by. Here Lieutenants Roy M. Rossel and Hilton O. Thompson must have gotten the photographer's attention and he snapped their picture. *Courtesy of David L. Born.*

An A-20 that was assigned to the 4th SAD at nearby Hitcham. Note the clouds above. *Courtesy of Eugene W. Bailey.*

This P-47N came to the 434th FS courtesy of the 56th FG where it had served as mount to 62nd FS pilot Michael J. Jackson. *Courtesy of Clarence G. Haynes.*

436th FS CO, Major Claire A. P. Duffié and his crew chief Technical Sergeant Don M. Blachly by their P-51, one of a line named Give 'em Hell For H. L. The H. L. refers to Helen Louise. *Courtesy of the Wings of Freedom Museum.*

Definitely a couple of "good ole boys" – from the 434th FS, Master Sergeants James W. Smart and Jack E. Gowan. *Courtesy of James W. Smart.*

A 436th FS P-51 sits parked on its hardstand in the summer sun. One of the ground crew's belly tank shacks can be seen in the background just off the aircraft's right wing tip. Unfortunately it cannot be seen in this picture without magnification, but there is also a good-sized tree house present about mid-way up in the tall tree to the right of the photo. Post war left the men with time on their hands. *Carroll C. Sprague Collection, courtesy of the East Essex Aviation Society.*

434th FS P-51 L2-V, setting in the sun on a lovely day. *Courtesy of David L. Born.*

434th FS P-51 L2-Y, Just Born. *Courtesy of David L. Born.*

Left: 436th FS P-51 9B-G, Poontang II. First Lieutenant Ernest J. Hopcroft flew the original Poontang, a P-51B that was lost while being flown by another pilot. Lt. Hopcroft then received a P-51D that he named Daisy after his dog. The aircraft pictured was a new bird, having been received from BAD 2 at the end of June. Painted to represent Lt. Hopcroft's first Mustang, it was eventually sold to Sweden. *Carroll C. Sprague Collection, courtesy of the East Essex Aviation Society.* Right: 434th FS P-51 L2-D, Rabid Rebel. *Courtesy of Clarence G. Haynes.*

This photo of the 434th FS's L2-M, The Onley Genevieve II and L2-K, The Yakima Chief was taken during better times, obviously before they each had been wrecked. The two aircraft are in flight with L2-J. *Courtesy of Harold L. Stotts.*

434th FS P-51s parked around their hardstand. Note the "putt-putt" electric starter trolley cart, the parts wash tank and the stack of paper belly tanks in the foreground. *Courtesy of Harold L. Stotts.*

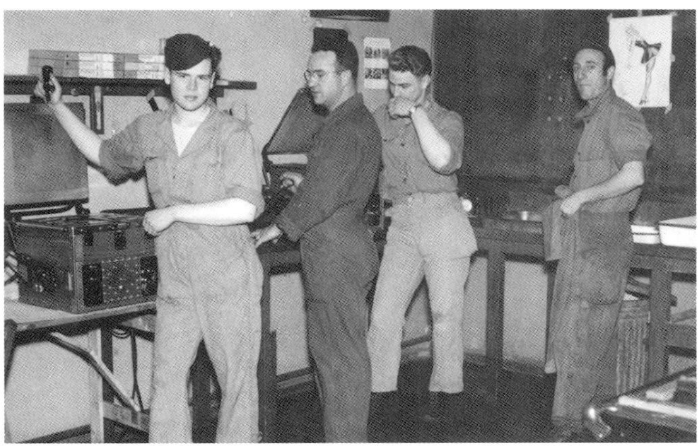

These are some of the men Corporal Sprague worked with as seen in the base photo lab: Donald Wadsworth, Earle Gerding, Raymond Lundgren and Burton Bradford. *Carroll C. Sprague Collection, courtesy of the East Essex Aviation Society.*

Corporal Carroll C. Sprague, the 436th FS photographer whose many photos are found within this book. His is a tragic story. In 1946, shortly after having returned to the U. S. and receiving his discharge from the army, he re-enlisted in the army where he became a photographer assigned to the Stars and Stripes Newspaper. He rose to the rank of sergeant and was ready to receive his second discharge during November of 1948. Unfortunately he was killed in a B-17 crash during a rescue mission near Digne, France on 30 January 1948. His personal photographs survived in a scrapbook he had put together and serve to preserve both his memory and that of the 479th FG. *Carroll C. Sprague Collection, courtesy of the East Essex Aviation Society.*

Communications men Staff Sergeant Raymond Niekamp, Staff Sergeant Charles K. Pruyne and Technical Sergeant John P. Starr, Jr. by one of the 436th FS P-51s, Bessie Lee. *Courtesy of Raymond Niekamp.*

Two captured Me 163s are being looked over by men of the 479th FG, post-war. The train carrying them had stopped near Wattisham. *Courtesy of James R. Helms.*

The destruction war had brought to the people of Europe is seen in this photo taken of a town located along the section of Rhine River between Wuppertal and Düsseldorf. Nearly the whole town lies in rubble. *Eugene H. Wendt courtesy of Stephen Decker.*

A view of Cologne and its once beautiful cathedral shows the loss and ruin. *Eugene H. Wendt courtesy of Stephen Decker.*

This picture provides a closer view of the devastation brought by the war. *Courtesy of Harold L. Stotts.*

The tranquility of this rural scene near Wattisham was photographed during the summer of 1945. The war was over, peace was at hand and the photo provides a fitting image with which to close this book. *Courtesy of Raymond Niekamp.*

BOOK CLOSING

by Coburn T. Palmer

THE FOUR-SOME FAMILY

First Lieutenants William H. (Hank) Daudistel, David (Dave) L. Born, Coburn (Cobie) T. Palmer and Clifford (Cliff) W. Bowers. First Lieutenant Robert (Bob) I. Bromschwig, another of the Hearts players, probably took the photo. *Courtesy of David L. Born.*

The sounds of roaring Mustangs now
No longer fills the air.
The "Spam-Cans" were their nicknames,
Their silver wings tipped square.
But Dave was there and Bud was there,
With little Hank they flew,
But all I ever did was sit
And watch the heavens blue.
Yes, blue they were those skies above,
When not smeared o'er with gray.
But "Seagulls Walking" snow or sleet,
My friends flew every day.

At night, though, it was gayer.
We gathered in a room,
Much famed for daring pin-ups
Of starlets in full bloom.
The four of us played endless "Hearts",
A wicked game it's true.
(You pass the cards and get the queen,
And pretty soon you're through.)

What power has a deck of cards
Against a World War II?
A shallow pastime, most would say,
And I suppose it's true.
But something made us very close,
'Twas not alone the game.
We found that out too soon, in fact,
When V-E finally came.
The "Peace" arrived and broke us up,
And scattered us afar.
We hadn't thought about that much
When we were in the war.

Oh, let the "Hearts" which made our gang
A four-some family,
Keep Short-Small, Dave and Bud and I
Like brothers constantly.
Cobie

Lieutenant Coburn T. Palmer and Sergeant Charles C. Claybaugh are loading parachutes. *Courtesy of Clarence G. Haynes.*

First Lieutenant Coburn (Cobie) T. Palmer was the 434th Fighter Squadron's Personal Equipment Officer. He wrote this mid- to late-1945. Short-Small was First Lieutenant William Hank Daudistel's nickname. Dave was First Lieutenant David L. Born and Bud was First Lieutenant Clifford W. Bowers.

APPENDICES

Appendix 1 Commanding Officers 453
Appendix 2 Group and Squadron Aircraft Identifications 454
Appendix 3 Group and Squadron Insignia 455
Appendix 4 Pilots and Dates of Service 459
Appendix 5 Aircraft and Pilots 463
Appendix 6 Victories 470
Appendix 7 Pilots Lost 477
Appendix 8 Crew Chiefs 479

APPENDIX 1

COMMANDING OFFICERS

479th Fighter Group

Name	*From*	*To*
Lt. Col. Leo F. Dusard, Jr.	15 Oct 43	11 Nov 43
Maj. Francis J. Pope	11 Nov 43	26 Dec 43
Lt. Col. Kyle L. Riddle	26 Dec 43	10 Aug 44
Col. Hubert Zemke	12 Aug 44	30 Oct 44
Col. Kyle L. Riddle	30 Oct 44	Late 1945

434th Fighter Squadron

Name	*From*	*To*
Maj. Joseph A. Shalmistras	15 Oct 43	17 Jan 44
Lt. Col. James H. Herren	17 Jan 44	30 Oct 44
Lt. Col. Arthur F. Jeffrey	1 Nov 44	25 Mar 45
Maj. Robin Olds	25 Mar 45	Aug 45
Maj. Donald J. Pierce	Aug 45	Late 45

435th Fighter Squadron

Name	*From*	*To*
Lt. Col. John G. Glover	15 Oct 43	23 Nov 44
Maj. Herbert H. Jordan	23 Nov 44	5 Apr 45
Maj. William C. Anderson	5 Apr 45	Late 45

436th Fighter Squadron

Name	*From*	*To*
Capt. William R. Walker	15 Oct 43	25 May 44
Maj. John D. Monahan	26 May 44	1 Aug 44
Maj. John A. Sullivan	1 Aug 44	5 Dec 44
Maj. Jules D. Biscayart	5 Dec 44	31 Dec 44
Ma. Claire A. P. Duffié	31 Dec 44	9 Nov 45

APPENDIX 2

GROUP AND SQUADRON AIRCRAFT IDENTIFICATIONS

434th FS: L2
435th FS: J2
436th FS: 9B

The P-38's that the 479th Fighter Group operated were a mixture of olive drab (OD) over neutral gray and natural metal finish (NMF) aircraft. The twin-engine fighters bore no specific group markings and in many cases the OD planes were hand-me-downs from other P-38 groups. Hence, they were a mixed bag of coloration in the beginning. The P-38's were identified according to squadron through the use of large geometric symbols painted on the outsides of the two vertical tail surfaces. White symbols were applied to OD aircraft and black symbols were applied to NMF aircraft. The 434th FS was assigned a circle, the 435th FS a triangle and the 436th FS, a square. In addition, large letters (A through Z) painted in the appropriate color on the two inside vertical tail surfaces identified individual aircraft. In the case of duplicate aircraft letters, a bar was added after the letter or in some cases, under the letter. After August 1944, the geometric symbols system was replaced by squadron colors applied to the rudder surfaces of the aircraft vertical tail surfaces. The 434th FS was red, the 435th FS was yellow and the 436th FS was black. In some cases, squadron codes and the aircraft's individual identification code letter were applied to the outside of the plane's twin tail booms.

When the group converted over to P-51's, the group's identification became the plain NMF spinner and nose already existent on each aircraft. The system of identifying each squadron by means of rudder colors was retained, although for a short time, rudders identifying aircraft belonging to the 436th FS were covered by a large black and white checkered pattern. That, however, was soon replaced with a solid black color that corresponded to the other two squadron's rudder coloration. In addition, each aircraft bore its squadron identification and individual aircraft identification letters, one on each side of the national "star and bar" insignia painted on the rearward portion of the aircraft's fuselage. Again, in the case of duplicate aircraft letters, a bar was added after the letter or in some cases, under the letter.

A peculiarity of the 479th Fighter Group was its maddening habit of eradicating the aircraft serial number from the vertical tail surfaces. This endured until nearly war's end.

The radio call signs used by the 479th FG were as follows:

Wattisham – Heater
Group – Highway
434th FS – Newcross
435th FS – Lakeside
436th FS – Bison

APPENDIX 3

GROUP AND SQUADRON INSIGNIA

479th Fighter Group Insignia

Created during the first few months of 1945, the group insignia was not approved at that time. The significance of the insignia is as follows: There are four colored shafts extending outward from the center of the shield. The single white shaft represents the headquarters of the group, while the three remaining colors represent the three fighter squadrons. (Note these three colors were individually applied on the rudder surfaces of the group's aircraft for the purpose of squadron identification.) The dagger surmounted on the shafts expresses the unity of the group as set forth in the motto "Icimus ut Unum", as inscribed in Latin and meaning, "We Strike as One". *Courtesy of the Air Force Historical Research Agency.*

434th Fighter Squadron Insignia

The original, approved insignia created by an unknown artist at the Training Aids Division located at the Santa Ana Army Air Base, Santa Ana, California. The insignia, suited for the P-38s the 479th FG would be flying, was created there through the efforts of Sergeants Frederick C. Hayner and Frederic A. Richmond, both of whom had been transferred to the newly-formed squadron from the 332nd FS/329th FG. Approved 7 July 1944, the squadron color, red was used for the devils. They are symbolic of the impression that the squadron's aircraft will have on the enemy. *Courtesy of the Air Force Historical Research Agency.*

The second, unapproved insignia popularly used when the group transitioned from P-38s to P-51s. The insignia was the creation of Captain Robin Olds, a member of the squadron. The significance of the insignia is as follows: The knave denotes youth and agressiveness. The heart denotes devotion to duty. The stallion, rouge, couped and looking right and left, denotes the roaming spirit and eternal vigilance. The blue diaginal stripe denotes a change. The motto "Tutor et Ultor", inscribed in Latin, means "To Protect and Avenge". *Courtesy of the Air Force Historical Research Agency.*

435th Fighter Squadron Insignia

The first squadron patch was to consist of Bugs Bunny riding a winged cannon that had two bolts of lightning replacing the usual P-38 twin-booms. The design was drawn up and forwarded through official channels for approval. It is unknown what happened to the submission.

The second, unapproved squadron patch was created and drawn by cartoonist Leon Schlesinger of Warner Bros. Cartoons, Inc., Hollywood, California. It was developed at the request of squadron member Captain Albert M. Myers while the squadron was training at Oxnard, California. The significance of the insignia is that it portrays the type of aircraft then in use by the squadron. *Courtesy of the Air Force Historical Research Agency.*

Lieutenant Billy C. Means, a pilot who served with the 435th FS, was responsible for the approved insignia. Accepted 20 March 1945, it had been redrawn from a previous submission, which showed a black hawk grasping a machine gun in each of its claws and standing on a white cloud, placed upon a light blue shield bearing stars. The change occurred because the shield was reserved for group coats of arms, and also because several insignias depicting birds clutching machine guns by their feet had already been approved. The insignia is a portrayal of the prowess and striking power of the squadron's aircraft and the ability of its pilots to seek out and destroy the enemy. *Courtesy of the Air Force Historical Research Agency.*

The possibility exists that there was another design in consideration for the 435th FS's insignia. A photo, as reproduced here, shows another insignia found on display behind the BOQ Club bar. It was mounted on the wall along with the other two squadron's insignia. However, no one that the author has contacted remembers anything about the unknown caricature depicting Bugs Bunny riding a bucking Mustang. *Courtesy of George D. Hendrix.*

434th Fighter Squadron Insignia

Lieutenant Hans J. Grasshoff, a pilot who served with the 436th FS, designed the original and only squadron insignia. The approved caricature shows an angry black cat with wings on its shoulders and hind legs. Holding a bolt of lightning in its forepaws, the feline is superimposed upon a blue background representative of the squadron's branch of service. The ferocious winged cat depicts the fighting spirit of the squadron and the bolt of lightning represents the swiftness and speed with which they strike. *Courtesy of the Air Force Historical Research Agency.*

The 436th FS insignia as it normally appeared and was worn as a patch is shown here. *Courtesy of the Air Force Historical Research Agency and the author.*

PILOTS AND DATE OF SERVICE

434th Fighter Squadron

Name	*Start*	*End*	*Note*
Atwater, John S.	Jan 45	EOW	
Born, David L.	Oct 44	EOW	
Bouchier, James E.	Oct 44	EOW	
Bowers, Clifford W.	Oct 44	EOW	
Bromschwig, Robert I.	Oct 44	EOW	
Bronaugh, Edward D.	Jan 45	EOW	
Brown, Philip A.	Sep 44	EOW	
Butler, Calvin J.	*Jan 44	May 44	to 435FS
Canella, Keith E.	*Oct 43	Jun 44	KIA
Creighton, Richard D.	Sep 44	EOW	
Daudistel, William H.	Oct 44	EOW	
Denny, Jack S.	May 44	Jul 44	EVD
Donnell, John C., Jr.	Sep 44	Feb 45	KIA
Drake, Walter M.	May 44	Nov 44	
Duffié, Claire A. P.	*Oct 43	Oct 44	
Fleming, James E., Jr.	May 44	Aug 44	KIA
Gates, William M.	Nov 44	Apr 45	
Gavrys, Thomas A.	Jul 44	Sep 44	MIA
Gleason, George W.	May 44	Mar 45	
Golden, John T.	Sep 44	Apr 45	POW
Granville, Chester W.	*Jan 44	Jan 44	to 435FS
Grdenich, Frank	*Jan 44	Jun 44	KIA
Grenning, Harold F.	*Jan 44	Nov 44	
Grossenbacher, Jack G.	*Oct 43	Jul 44	KIA
Hagerman, Harold J.	Mar 45	EOW	
Hansen, John W.	*Jan 44	Nov 44	
Harper, Flamm D.	*Jan 44	Jul 44	EVD
Harris, Elbert N.	Nov 44	Mar 45	POW
Haas, Jene A.	*Jan 44	Jul 44	POW
Haynes, Clarence G.	Sep 44	EOW	
Hehn, William H.	*Jan 44	Nov 44	
Helding, Arnold G.	*Jan 44	Jan 45	
Hendrickson, Lauri, A.	Nov 44	EOW	
Hendrickson, Robert H.	*Jan 44	Nov 44	
Hendrix, George D.	*Jan 44	Nov 44	
Herren, James M., Jr.	*Dec 43	Oct 44	KIA
Hollingsworth, James M.	Jul 44	Dec 44	POW
Hollis, Dewey H.	Nov 44	Dec 44	KIT
Hollister, Berkley E.	*Jan 44	Dec 44	
Holmes, Douglas I.	Sep 44	Oct 44	POW
Hurtig, Edward L.	Sep 44	Dec 44	KIA
Huval, Ossie J.	Nov 44	Apr 45	POW
Ilsley, Dwight F.	Jun 44	Jun 44	KIA
Jacobson, Gail E.	Sep 44	EOW	
Jeffrey, Arthur F.	*Oct 43	Apr 45	
Jenkins, Harold M.	Sep 44	EOW	
Keller, Frank J.	May 44	Aug 44	POW
Kline, Robert B.	Sep 44	EOW	
Krauss, Harold F., Jr.	Jan 45	Apr 45	KIA
Kuentzel, Ward A.	*Apr 44	Jun 44	KIA
Lindley, Glenn D.	Jul 44	Oct 44	to 2nd SF
Little, Harry E.	Jul 44	Sep 44	POW
Looney, George H.	Jan 45	EOW	
Lulay, Ralph M.	Apr 45	EOW	
Lunstrum, Richard M.	Jun 44	EOW	
Lutz, Leroy	*Feb 44	Jun 44	KIA
Magill, Robert T.	Apr 45	EOW	
Maley, Ronald L.	Jul 44	Dec 44	POW
Manning, Phillip W.	Jul 44	Aug 44	KIA
Marlowe, Wendell H.	Sep 44	Dec 44	KIA
Mastin, Donald W.	Jan 45	EOW	
Mathews, Harold E.	Jun 44	Dec 44	
McArthur, Marden L.	Jul 44	Jul 44	KIA
McChrystal, Richard G.	Jun 44	Mar 45	
McDaniel, Walter R.	Apr 45	EOW	
Monaco, Elidio E.	Jan 45	EOW	
Morrow, John W.	Jul 44	EOW	
Munson, Robert L.	Jan 45	EOW	
Murphy, Calvin J., Jr.	Jul 44	Sep 44	KIA
Murr, John N.	Jul 44	Mar 45	
Nagel, Jerome K.	Sep 44	EOW	
Neely, Tom D.	Jun 44	Dec 44	POW
Neumann, Walter A.	Jun 44	Dec 44	KIA
Olds, Robin	*Feb 44	EOW	
Ohligschlager, James K.	*Feb 44	Jun 44	POW
Olson, Richard L.	Apr 45	EOW	
Olson, Thomas C.	*Jan 44	Dec 44	
Pavlock, Quentin S.	*Feb 44	Oct 44	Killed
Peacock, Cecil M.	Jan 45	EOW	
Pease, Roscoe I.	Mar 45	EOW	

Peterson, Carl L.	*Feb 44	Nov 44	
Pfund, Robert F.	Feb 45	EOW	
Pierce, Donald J.	Feb 45	EOW	
Plazibat, John A.	Jan 45	EOW	
Proctor, Clayton F.	Jun 44	Jul 44	KIA
Redwood, Robert K.	Jan 45	EOW	
Rodgers, William H.	Jul 44	Sep 44	MIA
Rollins, William A.	Apr 45	EOW	
Rossel, Roy M.	Dec 44	EOW	
Sands, Thurman E.	Dec 44	Jan 45	KIT
Schiess, Francis C.	Dec 44	EOW	
Sears, Eugene E.	Sep 44	EOW	
Simpson, Richard G.	Jul 44	EOW	
Stott, Donald H.	Dec 44	Apr 45	KIA
Stotts, Harold L.	Dec 44	EOW	
Stroop, Joseph E.	*		S-3
Taylor, Frank M.	Jan 45	Apr 45	POW
Thompson, Hilton O.	Dec 44	Jul 45	**MIA
Tipps, John T.	May 44	Oct 44	
Tommie, Dalton F.	Dec 44	EOW	
Tucker, Albert S. J., Jr.	*Feb 44	Jun 44	POW
Turner, Hiram G., Jr.	*Oct 43	Aug 44	POW
Valuzzi, Arthur J.	Jan 45	EOW	
Van Waes, Donald A.	Apr 45	EOW	
Wallace, James L.	*Jan 44	Aug 44	KIA
Waters, Clarence L.	Jan 45	EOW	
Wendt, Eugene H.	Aug 44	EOW	
White, Joseph L.	Apr 45	EOW	
Wigton, William L.	Feb 45	EOW	
Williams, Bailey A.	*Feb 44	Dec 44	

435th Fighter Squadron

Name	*Start*	*End*	*Note*
Anderson, William C.	Apr 45	EOW	
Baird, Robert J.	Sep 44	EOW	
Barsky, William M.	Sep 44	EOW	
Benoit, Norman R.	Jun 44	Feb 45	
Butler, Calvin J.	May 44	Jun 44	POW
Butler, Nelson W.	Jun 44	Mar 45	
Candelaria, Richard G.	Sep 44	Apr 45	POW
Cano, Larry J.	Sep 44	EOW	
Carter, Raymond S.	*Oct 43	Sep 44	KIA
Clarke, William D.	Nov 44	Dec 44	KIA
Coursey, Richard R.	*Feb 44	Nov 44	
Courtney, John J., Jr.	*Oct 43	Aug 44	EVD
Detlefsen, Heinz W.	May 44	Nov 44	KIA
Dettenmayer, George R.	Feb 45	EOW	
Doolittle, Gordon L.	May 44	Feb 45	
Ervin, Ivan A.	Jun 44	Sep 44	KIT
Evanenko, Alexander	May 44	Jul 44	MIA
Fairchild, Rayne B.	*Jan 44	Jul 44	POW
Ford, Everett P.	May 44	Sep 44	KIT
Friend, Ray K.	Jun 44	Mar 45	
Frost, Russell B.	Mar 45	EOW	
Gates, William M.	*Oct 43	Nov 44	to 434FS
Glover, John G.	*Oct 43	Oct 44	
Gorian, Martin G.	*Jan 44	Nov 44	
Gossard, Philip D.	*Jan 44	Dec 44	
Granville, Chester W.	*Jan 44	Sep 44	MIA
Green, Robert D.	*Oct 43	Feb 44	to 479HQ
Gross, Burton S.	*Jan 44	Jun 44	KIA
Gunn, William B.	May 44	Nov 44	
Hanlon, Bernard L.	Nov 44	EOW	
Harrell, John W., Jr.	Aug 44	Mar 45	to 479HQ
Hart, Frederick L.	Sep 44	EOW	
Heathman, Charles E.	Nov 44	EOW	
Hendrickson, Robert H.	*Jan 44	Jan 44	to 434FS
Hill, Glen W.	Nov 44	EOW	
Hoffman, Clark R.	Nov 44	EOW	
Hooker, Verne E.	*Jan 44	EOW	
Horman, Robert H.	Nov 44	EOW	
Horne, Leland K.	*Jan 44	Jun 44	MIA
Hymans, Robert B.	Nov 44	Dec 44	KIT
Jarrell, Carl B.	Nov 44	Feb 45	POW
Johnson, Francis R.	*Oct 43	Nov 44	
Jones, Robert L.	Apr 45	EOW	
Jordan, Herbert R.	Sep 44	Apr 45	
Keefe, Lawrence A.	Sep 44	EOW	
Keller, Frank J.	*Mar 44	May 44	to 434FS
King, David E.	Sep 44	EOW	
Knofczynski, Joseph J.	Sep 44	EOW	
Koerber, James H.	Sep 44	EOW	
Maier, William F.	*Jan 44	Nov 44	
Manson, Edward L.	Feb 45	EOW	
Matthews, Allen E.	Mar 45	EOW	
Matthews, Cecil R.	*Jan 44	Dec 44	
Maule, Donald L.	*Jan 44	Nov 44	
McCann, John P.	*Jan 44	Dec 44	
McClure, Donald D.	*Feb 44	Jun 44	MIA
McKay, William B.	*Jan 44	Jul 44	KIA
Means, Billy C.	Jul 44	Apr 45	
Miller, John H.	Jul 44	Oct 44	to 2nd SF
Monsell, Charles F., Jr.	Jun 44	Dec 44	
Moore, Carl W.	Jun 44	Aug 44	KIA
Morris, Louis E.	Jul 44	Feb 45	
Muller, Wilbert	*Jan 44	Nov 44	
Nicholson, Thomas S.	Feb 45	EOW	
Park, David C.	Feb 45	EOW	
Peterson, Charles H.	Apr 45	EOW	
Petterson, Lewis P.	*Feb 44	Dec 44	
Pickering, William H.	*Jan 44	Dec 44	
Pigg, Robert N.	*Feb 44	Dec 44	KIA
Powers, Thomas A.	Feb 45	EOW	
Prevosti, Mario V.	Jan 45	Sep 45	
Ralston, Robert E.	Feb 45	EOW	
Ricker, James E.	Apr 45	EOW	
Rock, Norbert W.	Sep 44	Feb 45	**MIA
Rogers, John R.	Dec 44	EOW	
Rossman, George P.	Dec 44	Mar 45	to 2nd SF
Rourke, William B., Jr.	Dec 44	EOW	
Routh, Sylvan R.	Dec 44	EOW	
Rudat, Wallace A.	Dec 44	EOW	
Salter, George M., Jr.	Oct 44	EOW	
Salze, Floyd W.	Dec 44	EOW	
Sawyer, Douglas E.	Apr 45	EOW	
Schoonover, George F.	Dec 44	EOW	
Shewfelt, Ray L.	Sep 44	Jan 45	to 2nd SF
Shriner, Frederick F.	*Feb 44	Feb 45	

Sims, Edward H.	Dec 44	EOW	
Smith, Howard C.	Jul 44	Feb 45	
Smith, Thomas V.	Jun 44	Nov 44	POW
Sowerby, Theo J.	Jul 44	EOW	
Splittstoesser, Elmer A.	Dec 44	EOW	
Stage, Lawrence Jr.	Jan 45	EOW	
Sullivan, John A.	Jun 44	Jul 44	to 436FS
Sykes, George K.	*Oct 43	Sep 44	EVD
Thompson, Roland H.	Dec 44	EOW	
Thorn, Donald W.	Sep 44	EOW	
Trabucco, Thomas F.	Sep 44	Mar 45	KIA
Uhley, Charles R.	Apr 45	EOW	
Waller, Charles S.	*Feb 44	Nov 44	
Watkins, Donald B., Jr.	Apr 45	EOW	
Wendt, Eugene H.	Jul 44	Aug 44	to 434FS
Whitmer, Lewis W., Jr.	Apr 45	EOW	
Williams, George F.	Jan 45	EOW	
Zuchowski, Stephen H.	*Feb 44	Nov 44	

436th Fighter Squadron

Name	*Start*	*End*	*Note*
Anderson, William C.	Feb 45	Apr 45	to 435FS
Archibald, John M.	Jan 45	EOW	
Beatty, Frank G., Jr.	Mar 45	Jul 45	
Biscayart, Jules D.	*Oct 43	Dec 44	
Burgess, Warren H.	Jan 45	EOW	
Darling, Charles H.	Oct 44	Jul 45	
Derby, Stanley E.	Oct 44	Apr 45	
DiPaola, Albert R.	Oct 44	Feb 45	POW
Duffié, Claire A. P.	Dec 44	EOW	
Dunn, Donald A.	May 44	Oct 44	
Early, John H. III	Oct 44	Jul 45	
Elmgren, Charles B.	Oct 44	Jul 45	
Ernst, Carl V.	Sep 44	EOW	
Eskell, Barrett B.	Oct 44	Dec 44	POW
Falkner, George E.	Apr 45	EOW	
Fillipow, Edwin J.	May 44	Nov 44	
Frolking, James E.	May 44	Oct 44	EVD
Galloway, Thomas T.	*Oct 43	Jul 44	KIA
Glenn, John G.	*Jan 44	Oct 44	
Granger, Jesse V.	May 44	Nov 44	
Grasshoff, Hans J.	*Jan 44	Dec 44	
Greenwood, Travis M.	*Jan 44	Oct 44	
Hansen, Kenneth J.	Oct 44	EOW	
Harrell, John W., Jr.	*Oct 43	Aug 44	to 435FS
Hartman, Elmer	Jul 44	Aug 44	Killed
Hartnett, Vincent C.	*Jan 44	Nov 44	
Hedenberg, John W.	*Jan 44	Oct 44	
Henry, Price E.	*Jan 44	Oct 44	
Henry, Raymond E.	Nov 44	Nov 45	
Hightower, Howard G.	*Jan 44	Oct 44	
Hopcroft, Ernest J.	Nov 44	Jun 45	
Hoversten, Herman C.	*Jan 44	Nov 44	
Howard, William N.	*Jan 44	Aug 44	EVD
Huycke, Andre E.	*Jan 44	Dec 44	
Johnson, Clarence O.	*Nov 43	Aug 44	
Jordan, Herbert H.	Aug 44	Sep 44	to 435FS
Joseph, George	Sep 44	Mar 45	
Kelly, William D.	Nov 44	EOW	
Kemper, Neil W.	Jul 44	Jul 44	EVD
King, Benjamin H.	*Nov 43	Aug 44	to 359FG
King, Raymond E.	Nov 44	Jan 45	KIA
Kleinman, Bernard R.	Sep 44	EOW	
Kreger, Charles S.	Sep 44	Jul 45	
Lewin, Edwin C.	May 44	Dec 44	
Long, Sylvester F.	Jan 45	EOW	
Malone, Jay C.	Sep 44	Apr 45	KIA
Massey, Alton A.	Jan 45	EOW	
McKeown, Arthur J.	Jan 45	Jul 45	
McLaurin, Grover G., Jr.	Oct 44	EOW	
Mead, Frederick M.	Jun 44	Apr 45	
Melton, Allen B.	Apr 45	EOW	
Merritt, William J.	Feb 45	EOW	
Mickey, Melvin S.	Jul 44	Feb 45	
Monahan, John D.	*Oct 43	Aug 44	
Moore, Clifford J., Jr.	*Nov 43	Mar 45	
Morris, Jesse F.	Jan 45	EOW	
Morton, Richard C.	Feb 45	EOW	
Moser, Fred A., Jr.	Jul 44	Aug 44	POW
Mosier, Arlett G., Jr.	Jun 44	EOW	
Mulvany, Gerold M.	Jun 44	Mar 45	
Myers, Thomas E.	Jul 44	EOW	
Nesslebush, Louis K.	*Feb 44	Jun 44	POW
Ogron, Zeymour	Jun 44	Nov 44	
O'Holleran, Thomas J.	Jun 44	Aug 44	POW
Olson, Marvin A.	Apr 45	EOW	
Orrick, Thomas H.	Jun 44	Sep 44	to 2nd SF
Palson, Richard C., Jr.	Jan 45	EOW	
Philbrick, Charles H. II	Jan 45	Nov 45	
Pleiman, Herbert P.	Apr 45	EOW	
Plunk, Henry P.	Jun 44	EOW	
Proffatt, Victor J.	May 45	EOW	
Pulchinski, Edwin J.	Feb 45	EOW	
Race, Francis E.	Jan 45	EOW	
Rawley, Walter N., Jr.	Feb 45	EOW	
Red, Douglas L.	Sep 44	Dec 44	MIA
Romano, Pasquale J.	Dec 44	Nov 45	
Rosness, Joseph H.	*Feb 44	Nov 44	
Schoen, Charles F., Jr.	Dec 44	Feb 45	KIA
Schuck, John R.	Sep 44	EOW	
Scordino, Anthony J.	Dec 44	May 45	KIT
Shane, Presson, S.	Jan 45	Jul 45	
Sherer, Carl W.	Dec 44	EOW	
Shonborn, Paul J.	Dec 44	Jul 45	
Smigal, Alfred J.	Dec 44	EOW	
Smith, Lewis C.	Dec 44	Mar 45	KIA
Spencer, Richard S., Jr.	*Jan 44	Dec 44	
Spillane, James E., Jr.	*Jan 44	Jun 44	Killed
Steele, Marion W.	Sep 44	Nov 44	MIA
Steph, Walter B.	Sep 44	Apr 45	
Straub, George	*Jan 44	Oct 44	
Struby, Joseph R.	*Jan 44	Dec 44	
Sullivan, John A.	Jul 44	Dec 44	MIA
Teeter, Robert R.	*Jan 44	Jul 44	Killed
Thompson, Thomas H.	Sep 44	EOW	
Thornton, William E.	EOW	Aug 45	
Thrall, Richard P.	Dec 44	EOW	
Uhley, Charles R.	Apr 45	Apr 45	to 435FS

Upsall, Richard H., Jr.	Apr 45	EOW	
Vassuer, Peter C.	Sep 44	Feb 45	MIA
Walker, William R.	*Oct 43	May 44	KIT
Walsh, George W.	Apr 45	EOW	
Ward, James J.	Apr 45	EOW	
West, Eric F.	Apr 45	Jul 45	
Wilkins, John K., Jr.	Sep 44	Jan 45	to 2nd SF
Witzel, George H.	Oct 44	Oct 45	
Wolski, Victor C.	*Jan 44	Oct 44	
Young, Robert C.	Mar 45	Apr 45	KIT
Zellman, Fred	Oct 44	EOW	

HQ 479th Fighter Group

Name	***Start***	***End***	***Note***
Green, Robert D.	Feb 44	Jul 44	KIA
Hollingsworth, James M.	Sep 44	Nov 44	to 434FS
Riddle, Kyle L.	*Dec 43	EOW	
Stoops, Edward F.	*Oct 43		
Woods, Sidney S.	*Mar 44	Sep 44	to 4th FG
Zemke, Hubert	Aug 44	Oct 44	POW

* Original pilot to squadron
** Lost in Wash/North Sea during training
Notice how the alphabet played such a part in the assignment of replacement pilots.

APPENDIX 5

AIRCRAFT AND PILOTS

434th Fighter Squadron

Pilot	*A/C*	*Aircraft Name*	*Sqdrn*	*A/C ID*	*Ser. No.*	*Comments*
	AT-6		434		42-84587	Training/hack, damaged in landing accident 14-5-45, pilot: Bronaugh, Edward D., damaged durin take off 20-7-45, pilot: Kline, Robert B., both at Wattisham
	B-26	Liberty Run	434		43-34226	Hack
	C-61		434		41-4603	Hack
	C-64		434		44-70286	Hack, damaged in a ground loop/Wattisham 30-7-45, pilot: Maley, Ronald L.
Born, David L.	P-51	Just Born	434	L2-Y	44-14393	Damaged in landing accident/Wattisham 12-7-45, pilot: Schiess, Francis C., salvaged at later, formerly FLAT TOP JR., pilot: Grenning, Harold F., Jr.
Bowers, Clifford W.	P-51	Skunk Chaser	434	L2-N	44-14373	Salvaged at war's end, formerly TEDDY # 4, pilot: Williams, Bailey A.
Bromschwig, Robert I.	P-51	Kraut Knocker	434	L2-T	44-14423	Recoded L2-T, damaged during taxiing after landing/Wattisham, 1-3-45, pilot: unk, formerly BOOMERANG JR., pilot: Jeffrey, Arthur F.
Bromschwig, Robert I.	P-51	Kraut Knocker	434	L2-L	44-14423	Recoded L2-L after 1-3-45 taxiing accident repairs, destroyed in belly landing 2 mi. NW of Hadleigh, ENG, engine failure 28-5-45, pilot: Bouchier, James E., salvaged 31-5-45
Bromschwig, Robert I.	P-51	Kraut Knocker	434	L2-L	44-15381	A/C was previously Creighton, Richard D.'s "Super Wabbit"
Canella, Keith E.	P-38	Sweet Mary	434	L2-K	43-28731	NMF, lost due to enemy aa fire 22-6-44, pilot: Canella, Keith E. KIA/FRA, MACR # 6108, name applied L & R
Creighton, Richard D.	P-51	"Super Wabbit"	434	L2-L	44-15381	Salvaged at war's end, picture of Superman-like rabbit wearing a cape, to right of name, nose art painted by Eugene E. Sears, one of three a/c he painted
Daudistel, William H.	P-51	The Impatient Virgin	434	L2-Z	44-63175	Damaged in belly landing Wattisham 4-6-45, pilot: Waters, Clarence L., to Swiss AF post war, The Impatient Virgin on L side of nose & canopy rail, Mickey's Mustang on R side of nose
Donnell, John C., Jr.	P-51	PIN UP GIRL/ Muriel of Troy	434	L2-V	44-14651	Lost due enemy aa fire 14-2-45, pilot: Donnell, John C., Jr. KIA/GER, MACR # 12332, formerly flown by Berkley E. Hollister, Varga Girl added by Donnell, PIN UP GIRL & Varga art on L. side, Muriel of Troy (artist F. Hayner's wife and hometown) on Rt.
Drake, Walter M.	P-38		434	L2-I		OD/gray, squadron code per pilot-always remembered "I" for Invasion
Drake, Walter M.	P-51	Margie	434	L2-I	44-14288	Lost due to unknown cause 29-11-44
Duffié, Claire A. P.	P-38	Give'm Hell- For H.L.	434	L2-A	43-28474	NMF, H.L. refers to Helen Louise, transferred to 367th FG
Duffié, Claire A. P.	P-51	Givem HELL For H.L.	434	L2-A-	44-14355	Lost due to crash landing/Martlesham Heath, ENG 27-9-44, pilot: Duffie, C.A.P., a/c had a painted band encircling the fuselage between code L2-A and bar, after A, before bar, H.L. refers to Helen Louise
Gates, William M.	P-51	Swanee Jr.	434	L2-I	44-15325	Recoded L2-B and reassigned to Marlowe, W. H. who was KIA this a/c
Gavrys, Thomas A.	P-51	[MISS FORTUNE]	434	L2-G	44-14138	Lost forming up in bad weather 21-9-44, pilot: Gavrys, Thomas A. MIA/N. Sea, MACR # 9152
Gleason, George W.	P-38		434	L2-H		NMF
Gleason, George W.	P-51	HOT TODDY	434	L2-H	44-14740	Lost due to enemy aa fire 16-4-45, pilot: Taylor, Frank M. POW/GER, MACR #14118, named for wife Todd
Golden, John T.	P-51	[JUNIOR]	434	L2-G	44-14856	Lost due to enemy aa fire 16-4-45, pilot: Golden, John T. POW/GER, MACR #14117
Grdenich, Frank	P-38		434	L2-T	43-28456	Lost in dive/mid-air collision with Kuentzel, Ward A. 19-6-44, pilot: Grdenich, Frank KIA/FRA, MACR #5959, Kuentzel a/c rolled over onto Grdenich a/c & cut off empenage
Grenning, Harold F.	P-38	No Guts ?	434	L2-Y	43-28651	NMF, damaged while taxiing into position for mission take off, right brake failed causing a/c to go into a ditch/Wattisham 15-7-44, pilot: McArthur, Marden L., salvaged, Grenning's first P-38, question mark is part of the name
Grenning, Harold F.	P-38	NO NAME APPLIED	434	L2-Y		NMF, per pilot: a/c was an almost new P-38L w/gun camera mounted in bomb shackle, few like it at Wattisham
Grenning, Harold F.	P-51	FLAT TOP, JR.	434	L2-Y	44-14393	Named for the Chester Gould "Dick Tracy" comics strip character
Harper, Flamm D.	P-38	Mary Anna	434			OD/gray, per pilot: named after wife Mary and daughter Dee Anna, nude between Mary and Anna
Harris, Elbert N.	P-51	MARY/GEORGIA ANN	434	L2-A	44-63189	Lost due to engine failure/Germany 3-3-45, pilot:Harris, Elbert N. POW/GER, MACR #12881,MARY on L side of nose, GEORGIA ANN on R side of nose
Haynes, Clarence G.	P-51	Rabid REBEL	434	L2-D	44-72297	Returned to US 16-7-45, picture of Donald Duck's face to left of a/c name
Haynes, Clarence G.	P-51	Rabid REBEL	434	L2-D		Crash landed/ENG, pilot: Donnell, John C., Jr., picture of Donald Duck's face to right of a/c name
Hehn, William H.	P-38	Rumboogie	434	L2-X	43-28443	NMF, named by crew chief T/Sgt. Stanovich, Milan J. who's nicknamed was "Boogie"
Hehn, William H.	P-51	Rumboogie JR.	434	L2-X	44-14596	Lost due to enemy aa fire 23-12-44, pilot: Neely, Tom D. POW/GER, MACR #11072, named by crew chief T/Sgt Stanovich, Milan J.
Helding, Arnold G.	P-38	LUCKY LADY	434	L2-L	43-28714	NMF, lost due to enemy aa fire 22-6-44, pilot: Lutz, Leroy KIA/FRA, MACR #6106, name applied L & R
Helding, Arnold G.	P-51	Lil' Trouble !	434	L2-Q	44-13864	Crash landing/ENG 16-4-45, pilot: Tommie, Dalton F., salvaged
Hendrickson, Laurie A.	P-51	Miss Georgia Carol	434	L2-X	44-11761	Two names: Miss Georgia Carol on a/c's nose (by crew chief T/Sgt. Stanovich, Milan J.)/ THE FLYING DUTCHMAN (by pilot) on both sides of canopy rail, salvaged at war's end
Hendrickson, Robert H.	P-51	[MY JEANNE]	434	L2-E		
Hendrix, George D.	P-38	TARZANA	434			OD/gray, per pilot, name applied L & R

Herren, James M., Jr.	P-38	TOUCHÉ	434	L2-A	42-68008	NMF, renamed after received, per crew chief: Plassenthal, Victor R., a/c was originally named Snafuperman before being turned over to squadron – any connection to Tony LeVier?
Herren, James M., Jr.	P-51	TOUCHÉ	434	L2-A	44-14396	Lost due to weather 30-10-44, pilot: Herren, James M., Jr. KIA/GER, MACR #10422, devils face artwork from original 434FS insignia to right of name
Hollingsworth, James M.	P-38	NO NAME APPLIED	434			Per son
Hollingsworth, James M.	P-51	NO NAME APPLIED	434	L2-A	44-14892	Lost due to being rammed from behind by E/A 25-12-44, pilot: Hollingsworth, James M. POW/GER, MACR #11177
Hollister, Berkley E.	P-38	LITTLE Edris	434	L2-V	42-68029	OD/gray, lost due to enemy aa fire 5-7-44, pilot: Proctor, Clayton F. KIA/FRA, MACR #6691
Hollister, Berkley E.	P-38	NO NAME APPLIED	434			NMF
Hollister, Berkley E.	P-51	PIN UP GIRL	434	L2-V	44-14651	Reassigned 6-12-44 to Donnell, John C., Jr. who was KIA this a/c
Hurtig, Edward L.	P-51		434	L2-M	44-14416	Lost due to unk cause 25-12-44, pilot: Hurtig, Edward L. KIA/GER, MACR #11175
Huval, Ossie J.	P-51	THE FLYING FRENCHMAN	434	L2-A	44-12156	Lost due to enemy aa fire 13-4-45, pilot: Huval, Ossie J. POW/GER, MACR #14120
Jacobson, Gail E.	P-51	Burn'n Bernie	434	L2-P	44-15380	Damaged in landing accident/Wattisham 25-12-44, pilot: Jacobson, Gail E., lost due to wing collapse while practising dive bombing/ENG 19-7-45, pilot: Thompson, Hilton O. killed, nose art painted by Eugene E. Sears, one of three a/c he painted
Jeffrey, Arthur F.	P-38	BOOMERANG	434	L2-O	42-104425	NMF, lost due to enemy aa fire 6-9-44, pilot: Murphy, Calvin J., Jr. KIA/GER, MACR #8566
Jeffrey, Arthur F.	P-51	BOOMERANG "JR."	434	L2-O	44-11674	Recoded L2-I and reassigned to Thompson, Hilton O. who was killed in this a/c
Jeffrey, Arthur F.	P-51	BOOMERANG JR.	434	L2-O	44-14423	Recoded L2-T and reassigned to Bromschwig, Robert I.
Keller, Frank J.	P-38	[HILO HATTIE]	434	L2-D	42-104140	Damaged in landing accident/Wattisham 27-7-44, pilot: Helding, Arnold G., salvaged
Keller, Frank J.	P-38	[HILO HATTIE]	434	L2-I	43-28377	NMF, lost due to enemy aa fire 9-8-44, pilot: Keller, Frank J. POW/GER, MACR #7785, name applied L & R
Kline, Robert B.	P-51	The Onley Genevieve	434	L2-M	44-11764	Lost due to enemy aa fire - bellied in 13-4-45, pilot: Kline, Robert B. EVD/GER, name on canopy rail salvaged,
Kline, Robert B.	P-51	The ONLEY Genevieve IV	434	L2-M	44-14395	Damaged in belly landing due to engine failure/FR 2-8-45, pilot: Jenkins, Harold M., name on canopy rail
Krauss, Harold F., Jr.	P-51	[LITTLE DROOPY]	434	L2-F	44-14929	Lost due to unk cause (poss enemy aa fire) 16-4-45, pilot: Krauss, Harold F., Jr. KIA/died of wounds, in allied territory, MACR #14116
Kuentzel, Ward A.	P-38		434	L2-N	42-104427	Lost in dive/mid-air collision with wingman Grdenich, Frank 19-6-44, pilot: Kuentzel, Ward A. KIA/FRA, MACR #5960, cause unk - possibly Anoxia
Lunstrum, Richard M.	P-38		434			OD/gray
Lunstrum, Richard M.	P-51	SATAN'S AGENT	434	L2-J	44-14381	Lost due to forced landing/FRA 6-1-45, name applied on the a/c nose and both sides of canopy on rails
Maley, Ronald L.	P-51	TOMMY TROJAN	434	L2-T	44-11214	Lost due to enemy aa fire 5-12-44, pilot: Maley, Ronald L. POW/GER, MACR #10807
Marlowe, Wendell H.	P-51	PEREGRINE JR.	434	L2-F	44-14225	Salvaged 31-10-44, reason: wing stress following 30-10-44 mission
Marlowe, Wendell H.	P-51	Swanee Jr.	434	L2-B	44-15325	Lost due to unk cause 25-12-44, pilot: Marlowe, Wendell H. KIA/GER, MACR #11178
Matthews, Harold E.	P-51	Tenacious Torchy	434	L2-C	44-14845	Salvaged due to battle damage
McChrystal, Richard G.	P-51	[PRETTY BARBARA]	434			
Morrow, John W.	P-38	SHOO SHOO BABY	434	L2-S		NMF, name plus musical notes on nose
Morrow, John W.	P-51	CACTUS Jack	434	L2-R	44-15086	Damaged while under tow 2-3-45, struck by pilot: Paulson, Richard C.J. taxiing 9B-A (44-14591), later transferred to 436th FS, salvaged 4-3-45, cactus and mountains artwork
Murphy, Calvin J., Jr.	P-38		434	L2-O	42-104426	Transferred to 367th FG
Murr, John N.	P-51	Little WILDFIRE	434	L2-K	44-14523	Reassigned 18-11-44 to Stotts, Harold L., damaged in landing accident/Wattisham 6-3-45, pilot: Murr, John N.
Nagel, Jerome K.	P-51	The BRAT	434	L2-L	44-15370	
Neely, Tom D.	P-51	"Hi-Baller"	434	L2-Z		Per Fred Hayner (squadron painter)
Neumann, Walter A.	P-51	Buzzin' Texan	434	L2-U	44-14592	Lost due to unk enemy action 5-12-44, pilot: Neuman, Walter A. KIA/GER, MACR #10805
Olds, Robin	P-38	SCAT	434	L2-W		OD/gray per Fred Hayner the squadron painter
Olds, Robin	P-38	SCAT II	434	L2-W	43-28707	NMF, destroyed in belly landing and fire due to engine failure during takeoff/Wattisham 5-7-44, pilot: Peterson, Carl L.
Olds, Robin	P-38	SCAT III	434	L2-W	43-28341	NMF, lost due to enemy aa fire 10-8-44, pilot: Fleming, James E., Jr. KIA/FRA, MACR # 7622
Olds, Robin	P-38	SCAT IV	434	L2-W		
Olds, Robin	P-51	SCAT # 5	434	L2-W	44-14426	Damaged due to forced landing, out of gas 27-12-44, pilot: Morrow, John W., salvaged
Olds, Robin	P-51	SCAT VI	434	L2-W	44-11746	Per R. Olds, a/c declared war-weary due to battle damage suffered 13-4-45
Olds, Robin	P-51	SCAT VII	434	L2-W	44-72922	Returned to US, destroyed in crash 20-2-03, pilot: Shuttleworth, James J. killed, existed as a two place conversion belonging to Shuttleworth and painted as Scat VII
Olson, Thomas C.	P-38	LELAH MAY/ The SLUGGER	434			NMF, LELAH MAY on L side nose, The SLUGGER on R side nose
Olson, Thomas C.	P-51	LELAH MAY/ The SLUGGER	434	L2-G-	44-14212	Crashed due to engine failure/RAF Ipswich 3-1-45, pilot: Nagel, Jerome K., LELAH MAY on L side nose, The SLUGGER on R side nose, salvaged
Pavlock, Quentin S.	P-38		434	L2-G	43-28528	
Pavlock, Quentin S.	P-51		434	L2-G	44-14616	Destroyed - a/c failed to leave ground during take off/Wattisham 2-10-44, pilot: Pavlock, Quentin S. killed
Pierce, Donald J.	P-51	Setonia No.3	434	L2-R	44-72336	To Swiss AF 13-3-48, presentation a/c from Seton Hall Preparatory School War Loan Drive (third of three bought). Miss SARA M on canopy rail for CC T. O'Grady.
Rodgers, William H.	P-51		434	L2-L	44-14324	Lost due to unk cause 27-9-44, pilot: Rodgers, William H. MIA/N. Sea, MACR #9247
Sears, Eugene E.	P-51	**American MAID**	434	L2-U	44-15317	Salvaged at war's end, **American MAID** on both sides, nose art painted by Eugene E. Sears, one of three a/c he painted
Simpson, Richard G.	P-51	NO NAME APPLIED	434		44-14623	
Stott, Donald H.	P-51	SHOO SHOO BABY	434	L2-S	44-14629	Lost due to unk cause 16-4-45, pilot: Stott, Donald H. KIA/GER, MACR #14119, name plus musical notes artwork
Stotts, Harold L.	P-51	The YAKIMA Chief	434	L2-K	44-14523	Damaged due to engine failure/crash landing/half mile NE Wattisham 17-7-45, pilot: Schiess Francis C., name plus an indian chief's head in feathered head dress artwork, salvaged
Thompson, Hilton O.	P-51	Speedball	434	L2-I	44-11674	Formerly L2-O, BOOMERANG "JR." flown by Jeffrey, Arthur F., transferred to 355th FG
Tipps, John T.	P-38	THE ZANEIS WILDCAT	434	L2-R		NMF, named for his school (Zaneis) and football team (Wildcats) undefeated in 1939
Tipps, John T.	P-51	The WILDCAT	434	L2-R	44-14311	Lost due to allied aa fire 19-10-44, pilot: Gleason, George W. bailed out/FR
Tucker, Albert S. J., Jr.	P-38		434	L2-B	43-28349	Lost due to enemy aa fire 22-6-44, pilot: Tucker, Albert S. J., Jr. POW/FRA, MACR #5966
Turner, Hiram G. Jr.	P-38	ELBOW DOTTIE II	434	L2-H	43-28378	NMF, reassigned (pilot POW), name plus full beer (English-dark) mug sliding down a bar left of name artwork, later transferred to 474th FG
Turner, Hiram G. Jr.	P-38	ELBOW DOTTIE	434			NMF
Wallace, James L.	P-38	SLEEPY TIME GAL	434	L2-Z	44-23169	NMF, lost due to enemy aa fire 15-8-44, pilot: Wallace, James L. KIA/HOL, MACR # 8121, name applied L & R plus Varga girl artwork
Wendt, Eugene H.	P-51	Beautiful Jan	434	L2-B	44-14391	To Free French AF 19-8-45, named after his wife Jan
Williams, Bailey A.	P-38	[TEDDIE]	434	L2-N	42-67264	Lost due to enemy a/c 26-9-44, pilot: Little, Harry E. POW/GER, MACR #9249
Williams, Bailey A.	P-51	TEDDIE # 4	434	L2-N	44-14373	Damaged in landing accident/Wattisham 10-11-44, pilot: Denny, Jack S., reassigned to Bowers, Clifford W.
	P-38		434	L2-R	42-67296	Lost due to enemy aa fire 18-8-44, pilot: Manning, Phillip W. KIA/FRA, MACR #8118

Pilot	A/C	Aircraft Name	Sqdrn	A/C ID	Ser. No.	Comments
	P-38		434	L2-F	42-67472	Crashed mechanical failure 8-9-44, salvaged
	P-38		434	L2-P	42-67732	Lost due to enemy a/c 6-7-44, pilot: Haas, Jene A. POW/BEL, MACR #6788
	P-38		434	L2-P	42-67822	Damaged in landing accident/Wattisham 26-8-44, pilot: Williams, Bailey A., this was a piggy-back P-38, transferred to 370th FG
	P-38		434	L2-B	42-67865	Lost due to enemy aa fire 27-7-44, pilot: McArthur, Marden L. KIA/FRA, MACR #7573
	P-38		434	L2-H	42-67915	Damaged in taxi accident 25-7-44, pilot: Neumann, Walter A., salvaged
	P-38		434	L2-V	42-68147	Lost due to flying through explosion debris during straffing run 15-7-44, pilot: Harper, Flamm D. EVD/FRA, MACR # 6780
	P-38		434	L2-G	42-104258	Lost due to enemy aa fire 22-6-44, pilot: Ilsley, Dwight F. KIA/FRA, MACR #5970
	P-38		434	L2-A	43-28367	Lost due to enemy aa fire 4-7-44, pilot: Denny, Jack S. EVD/FRA, MACR #6692
	P-38		434	L2-U	43-28376	Lost due to enemy aa fire 15-8-44, pilot: Turner, Hiram G., Jr. POW/HOL, MACR # 8120
	P-38		434	L2-N	43-28416	Lost due to unk cause 12-8-44, pilot: Little, Harry E. survived bail out over channel/ENG
	P-38		434		43-28454	NMF, destroyed due to pilot error in crash at Wattisham 24-5-44, pilot: Canella, Keith E. was buzzing the field too low and failed to pull up for the rise in ground at the runway, both props hit the ground, crashed into Hitcham hangar
	P-38		434	L2-M	43-28465	
	P-38		434		43-28483	NMF, Droop Snoot
	P-38		434	L2-G	43-28647	Lost due to enemy aa fire 21-7-44, pilot: Grossenbacher, Jack G. KIA/GER, MACR #6829
	P-38		434	L2-E	43-28701	
	P-38		434	L2-Q	43-28705	NMF, destroyed in belly landing 5-7-44
	P-38		434	L2-Q	43-28729	Lost due to mid-air collision with 44-23175 flown by Grdenich, Frank 17-6-44, pilot: Ohligschlager, James K. POW/FRA, MACR #5958
	P-38		434	L2-L	43-28731	Recoded to L2-K
	P-38		434	L2-S	44-23175	Damaged in mid-air collision with 43-28729 flown by Ohligschlager, James K. 17-6-44, pilot: Grdenich, Frank
	P-38		434		44-23489	OD/gray, Droop Snoot
	P-47		434	L2-F	42-75855	Former 5th ERS 5F-A
	P-47	Teddy	434	L2-Y	44-21117	Former 56th FG/62nd FS LM-J, P-47M named Teddy by 56th FG pilot: Michael J. Jackson
	P-47		434	L2-H		NMF
	P-51		434	L2-2	42-102999	Damaged in landing accident/Wattisham 8-6-45, pilot: Monaco, Elidio E.
	P-51		434		42-106925	Destroyed in crash/Wattisham 22-2-45, high speed stall @ 1000 ft., pilot: Peacock, Cecil M.
	P-51		434		43-6393	Struck train engine at Haughley Junction N of Stowmarket, ENG and crashed 4-1-45, pilot: Sands, Thurman E. killed/ENG, War-Weary
	P-51		434	L2-3	43-6772	Destroyed in training crash unk cause/Hundon, ENG 13-12-44, pilot: Hollis, Dewey H. killed/ENG, War-Weary
	P-51		434	L2-3	43-7040	Damaged in taxi accident 10-4-45, pilot: Pease, Roscoe I., Jr., War-Weary
	P-51		434	L2-2	43-12150	Lost due to belly landing/Leiston, ENG - out of gas 25-2-45, pilot: Plazibat, John A., War-Weary
	P-51		434	L2-K	44-11215	
	P-51		434		44-12150	Crashed/Wattisham 25-2-45, pilot: Plazibat, John A., salvaged 8-4-45
	P-51	LAURA JO	434	L2-F	44-13843	
	P-51		434	L2-D	44-13880	Crashed - belly landing due to engine failure/Wattisham 15-11-44, pilot: Olson, Thomas C., salvaged
	P-51	Pretty Jeanie	434		44-14232	Salvaged due to battle damage 11-4-45
	P-51		434	L2-F-	44-14333	Transferred to 435th FS
	P-51		434	L2-F	44-14396	Recoded and reassigned
	P-51		434	L2-S	44-14396	Recoded and reassigned to Herren, James M., Jr. who was KIA this a/c
	P-51		434	L2-J	44-14502	Damaged due to belly landing 6 mi SE Ipswich, ENG, engine failure 28-9-44, pilot: Hendrix, George D.
	P-51	[KATYDID]	434	L2-R-	44-14574	Transferred to 436th FS
	P-51		434		44-14604	Destroyed in crash - structural failure/Mendelsham, ENG 9-12-44, pilot: Neely, Tom D. bailed out
	P-51	[PAULINE]	434	L2-S	44-14627	Lost due to weather 30-10-44, pilot: Holmes, Douglas I. POW/GER, MACR #10421
	P-51	My Janet	434	L2-A-	44-14645	Transferred to 436th FS
	P-51	Pauline	434	L2-S	44-14846	
	P-51		434	L2-B	44-14931	Salvaged at war's end
	P-51		434	L2-D	44-14989	Lost due to prior enemy aa fire and weather 19-10-44, pilot: Tipps, John T. bailed out EVD/BEL
	P-51		434	L2-T-	44-15???	
	P-51		434		44-15376	Lost due to friendly aa fire 25-12-44, pilot: Bouchier, James E. survived bail out/BEL
	P-51		434		44-15377	Damaged in belly landing due to engine failure/4 mi. N of Maidston, ENG 27-2-45, pilot: Wendt, Eugene H., salvaged
	P-51		434		44-70286	Damaged due to ground loop/Wattisham 30-7-45, pilot: Maley, Ronald L.
	P-51		434	L2-G	44-72826	Damaged in landing accident (a/c nosed up) 1-5-45, pilot: White, Joseph L., Jr., a/c had 34.45 hrs. total time
	P-51		434	L2-T	44-??9?2	
	P-51		434	L2-B	44-??754	
	P-51		434	L2-V	44-72???	
	P-51	WIDOW - MAKER	434	L2-F		

435th Fighter Squadron

Pilot	*A/C*	*Aircraft Name*	*Sqdrn*	*A/C ID*	*Ser. No.*	*Comments*
	AT-6		435		42-84586	Training/hack, transferred from 4th SAD, damaged in take off accident/Wattisham 4-12-45, pilot: Philbrick Charles H. II
Anderson, William C.	P-51	Jane	435			
Baird, Robert J.	P-51	[APPLE KNOCKER]	435	J2-H	44-14392	Salvaged at war's end, from Benoit, Norman R.
Barsky, William M.	P-51	ROARIN' ROSE	435	J2-G	44-14263	Salvaged at war's end
Benoit, Norman R.	P-51	VICTORY QUEEN	435	J2-H	44-14392	Reassigned to Baird, Robert J.
Butler, Calvin J.	P-38	NO NAME APPLIED	435	J2-F	44-23168	Lost due to enemy aa fire 17-6-44, pilot: Butler, Calvin J. POW/FRA, MACR #5965
Butler, Nelson W.	P-51	NO NAME APPLIED	435	J2-H	44-14417	Transferred from 78th FG (HL-A), salvaged 19-1-45 due to taxiing accident at RAF Southend, pilot: Rourke, William B., Jr.
Candelaria, Richard G.	P-51	my Pride 'n Joy	435	J2-K	44-11755	Lost due to enemy aa fire 13-4-45, pilot: Candelaria, Richard G. POW/GER, MACR #13904, a/c named by crew chief T/Sgt. Muller, Leslie A.
Cano, Larry J.	P-51	"Fast Company"	435	J2-F	44-14341	Salvaged at war's end
Carter, Raymond S.	P-38	[SAN ANGELO, TEX]	435	J2-N	44-23177	Lost due to enemy aa fire 5-9-44, pilot: Carter, Raymond S. KIA/GER, MACR #8565
Coursey, Richard R.	P-38	Schab???	435			OD/gray
Courtney, John J.	P-51	ROARIN' ROSE	435	J2-J	44-14263	Recoded and reassigned to Barsky, William M.
Detlefsen, Heinz W.	P-51		435		44-14294	Lost due to mid-air collision with Smith, Thomas V. 8-11-44, pilot: Detlefsen, Heinz W. KIA/GER, MACR #10424

Doolittle, Gordon L.	P-38	[MUGS]	435			Per pilot
Doolittle, Gordon L.	P-51	MUGS	435	J2-P	44-14406	A/C name has a foaming beer mug painted on each side of it, salvaged at war's end
Friend, Ray K.	P-51	"SWEET EL"	435	J2-B	44-14378	Transferred
Friend, Ray K.	P-51	SWEET EL II	435	J2-J	44-63236	Destroyed in belly landing due to engine cutting out and inoperable landing gear/Wattisham 31-3-45, pilot: Salze, Floyd W., salvaged 1946
Gates, William M.	P-38	Swanee Jr.	435	J2-B	43-28476	NMF
Glover, John G.	P-51	[TUSCON]	435	J2-V	44-11162	Damaged while taking off/Wattisham 8-11-44, pilot: Baird, Robert J., a/c struck takeoff aborted 44-14333, pilot: Muller, Wilbert, salvaged due to landing accident/Wattisham 20-4-45, pilot: Hoffman, Clark R.
Gossard, Phillip D.	P-38	Ruth	435	J2-O	43-28648	NMF
Gossard, Phillip D.	P-51	V for 'VAL'	435	J2-O	44-14354	Damaged in ground loop/Wattisham 2-12-44, pilot: Gossard Philip D., salvaged at war's end
Granville, Chester W.	P-38	DOSSIE	435			NMF
Hill, Glen W.	P-51	DARLIN FRAN	435	J2-S	44-15338	Reassigned from Maier, William F.
Hooker, Verne E.	P-51		435	J2-N	44-14827	Salvaged at war's end
Hooker, Verne E.	P-51		435	J2-H	44-73138	Salvaged 31-3-46
Horman, Robert H.	P-51	Lady JEAN	435	J2-A	44-62249	
Jordan, Herbert R.	P-51	HUN-NEE	435	J2-Q		Crash landed at 9th AF base/Aachen, GER after flak hit, pilot:Jordan Herbert R.
Keefe, Lawrence A.	P-51	BUTCH	435	J2-D	44-11176	Named after a high school girlfriend
King, David E.	P-51	[CADYDID]	435			Per pilot, named for wife Carolyne whose nickname was "Cady"
Koerber, James H.	P-51	Betty Jean	435	J2-E	44-15470	Per pilot, named for wife
Maier, William F.	P-38	NO NAME APPLIED	435			NMF
Maier, William F.	P-51	DARLIN FRAN	435	J2-S	44-15338	Reassigned to Hill, Glen W.
Maule, Donald L.	P-38	NO NAME APPLIED	435			NMF
McCann, John P.	P-38	[JERRY]	435			OD/gray
McCann, John P.	P-51	"Jerry"	435		44-143??	
Monsell, Charles F., Jr.	P-38	"My Buddy"	435			NMF
Monsell, Charles F., Jr.	P-51	My Buddy	435	J2-D		
Muller, Wilbert	P-38	NO NAME APPLIED	435			OD/gray
Nicholson, Thomas S.	P-51		435	J2-B-	44-15228	Damaged in landing accident/Wattisham 31-3-45, pilot: Nicholson, Thomas S., salvaged at war's end
Petterson, Lewis P.	P-38	NO NAME APPLIED	435			NMF
Pickering, William H.	P-38	???HG GAL	435			OD/gray, the name is over a picture of woman's head all of which is superimposed upon a painted circle
Pickering, William H.	P-51	RUFF HUSTLER	435		44-14708	
Pigg, Robert N.	P-51		435		44-14344	Lost due to engine failure 12-12-44, pilot: Pigg, Robert N. KIA/BEL, pilot reportedly bailed out of a/c but was struck by a B-26 while descending
Ricker, James E.	P-38	Pretty ???	435			OD/gray, name written in script - high on nose
Rock, Norbert W.	P-51	Little CHEVY	435	J2-Z	44-14304	A/C reassigned to Edward H. Sims after original pilot was lost, per Sims: a/c was named after original pilot's wife, damaged in mid-air coll/Wash 9-7-45, pilot: Salze, Floyd W.
	P-51	[LITTLE GEORGE]	435	J2-M	44-14333	Transferred from 434th FS, damaged in take off accident/Wattisham 8-11-44, pilot: Muller, Wilbert, a/c was struck by 44-11162, pilot: Baird, Robert J.
Rogers, John R.	P-51	[LITTLE GEORGE]	435	J2-Q	44-14333	Recoded, damaged in landing accident due to battle damage/Wattisham 24-3-45, pilot: Rogers, John R., salvaged
Rossman, George P.	P-51	[LITTLE JEAN]	435	J2-A	44-11163	Salvaged at war's end
Rudat, Wallace A.	P-51	LITTLE JOAN	435	J2-B	44-14345	Damaged in landing accident/Wattisham 9-2-45, brakes locked causing a/c to skid, pitch up on nose and slide, pilot: Hoffman, Clark R.
Salze, Floyd W.	P-51	"BIRMINGHAM KID"	435			Pilot was from Birmingham, AL.
Schoonover, George F.	P-51	[LUCKY MARK]	435	J2-W	44-14366	Salvaged at war's end, former pilot: Smith, Howard C.
Shewfelt, Ray L.	P-51		435	J2-P-		
Shriner, Frederick F.	P-38	*SEE COMMENTS*	435			[FORBIDDEN FOR THE FAINT OF HEART]
Shriner, Frederick F.	P-51	REBELLIOUS REBEL	435			
Sims, Edward H.	P-51	[THE UNINVITED]	435	J2-Z	44-14304	A/C was renamed per pilot, later damaged in taxi accident/Wattisham 27-7-45, pilot: Thompson, Roland H., salvaged later
Smith, Howard C.	P-51		435	J2-W	44-14366	Reassigned 28-2-45 to Schoonover, George F.
Sowerby, Theo J.	P-51		435	J2-U	44-63217	Damaged in take off accident & crash landing/Wattisham 28-1-45, pilot: Sowerby, Theo J., salvaged later due to battle damage
Sykes, George K.	P-38	NO NAME APPLIED	435			NMF
Sykes, George K.	P-51	[SUGAR KAYNE]	435		44-14424	Lost due to enemy aa fire 17-9-44, pilot: Sykes, George K. EVD/HOL, MACR #9013, named for wife
Trabucco, Thomas F.	P-51	[DOTTY]	435	J2-A-	44-15374	Lost due to unk cause 1-3-45, pilot: Trabucco, Thomas F. KIA/GER, MACR #12837, Dotty - blue in yellow frames plus green, red, yellow & orange 3 inch dots
Zuchowski, Stephen H.	P-51	Lady Jayne no. II	435		44-14320	
	P-38		435		42-67424	OD/gray
	P-38		435	J2-L-	42-68098	Crash landed 5 mi NE of Friston, ENG 26-8-44, pilot: Monsell, Charles F., salvaged due to battle damage
	P-38		435		42-68161	Lost due to mid-air collision with McClure, D. D. 19-6-44, pilot: Horne, Leland K. MIA/FRA, MACR #5968
	P-38		435		42-68189	Lost due to mid-air collision with Horne, L. K. 19-6-44, pilot: McClure, Donald D. MIA/FRA, MACR #5969
	P-38		435	J2-S	42-104147	Damaged in taxiing accident/Wattisham 20-7-44, pilot: Wendt, Eugene H.
	P-38	[SHORT???]	435		42-104287	
	P-38		435		42-104416	Lost due to unk cause during strafing run 27-6-44, pilot: Gross, Burton S. KIA/FRA, MACR #6557
	P-38		435	J2-C	42-104420	Damaged in landing accident/Wattisham 3-6-44, pilot: McCann, John P., salvaged
	P-38		435	J2-N	43-28268	Damaged in landing accident 28-7-44, pilot: Waller, Charles S., salvaged
	P-38		435		43-28426	Lost due to striking tree while straffing truck 8-8-44, pilot: Courtney, John J., Jr. EVD/FRA, MACR #7786
	P-38		435		43-28467	Lost due to enemy aa fire 4-7-44, pilot: Green, Robert D. KIA/FRA, MACR #6789
	P-38		435		43-28472	Lost due to enemy aa fire 5-8-44, pilot: Moore, Carl W. KIA/GER, MACR #7425
	P-38		435		43-28550	Damaged in belly landing/RAF Deanland, ENG due to electrical failure 10-6-44, pilot: McKay, William B., salvaged
	P-38		435	J2-R	43-28716	Lost over channel due to enemy a/c 24-7-44, pilot: Evanenko, Alexander MIA/ENG, MACR #7572
	P-38		435		44-23160	Lost due to enemy aa fire 27-7-44, pilot: McKay, William B. KIA/FRA, MACR #7575
	P-38		435		44-23484	Lost due to enemy aa fire 4-7-44, pilot: Fairchild, Rayne B. POW/FRA, MACR #6693
	P-47		435		42-22476	A/C assigned for training, damaged in landing accident/Wattisham 12-7-45, pilot: Park, David C.
	P-51		435	J2-N	43-6496	
	P-51		435	J2-Q	43-6865	Two place conversion, yellow paint overall with black trim, nicknamed Double Bubble due to two Malcolm hoods used
	P-51		435	J2-Z	43-6875	Salvaged at war's end
	P-51		435	J2-7	43-7157	Lost due to unk cause 12-12-44, pilot: Hymans, Robert B. MIA/ channel, MACR #11304, recovered 1998

Pilot	A/C	Aircraft Name	Sqdrn	A/C ID	Ser. No.	Comments
	P-51	[TOMMIE]	435	J2-X	43-12408	War-Weary, salvaged at war's end
	P-51	[SQUIRREL]	435	J2-T	44-11346	Salvaged at war's end
	P-51		435	J2-T	44-14246	Damaged in belly landing due to engine failure/Wattisham 27-12-44, pilot: Thorn, Donald W., salvaged
	P-51		435	J2-Q	44-14255	Destroyed in belly landing after taking off - engine failure/1/2 mi. N of Bildeston ENG 20-9-44, pilot: Sowerby, Theo J.
	P-51		435		44-14264	Lost due to battle damage, pilot had to belly land/HOL 18-11-44, pilot: Muller, Wilbert
	P-51		435	J2-R-	44-14295	Lost on training mission, found destroyed in crash /10 mi. NE Dundalk IRE 14-9-45, weather related, pilot: Ervin, Ivan A. killed, see Granville, Chester W.
	P-51		435	J2-E	44-14308	Damaged in taxiing accident/Wattisham15-10-44, pilot: Rock Norbert W.
	P-51	NOBODY'S BABY	435	J2-B	44-14345	A/C reassigned & renamed, damaged in take off accident/Wattisham 24-2-45, pilot: Salter, George M. Jr., salvaged at war's end
	P-51		435		44-14364	Lost due to enemy a/c 9-2-45, pilot: Jarrell, Carl B. POW/GER, MACR #12174
	P-51	Edith	435	J2-Y	44-14371	Salvaged at war's end
	P-51		435		44-14405	Destroyed in practice flight crash - failed to pull out of a dive/1 mi. NW of Lavenham ENG 9-9-44, pilot: Ford, Everett P. killed
	P-51		435	J2-J	44-14436	Salvaged, non-battle damage 19-6-45
	P-51		435	J2-C	44-14437	Lost on training mission, unk cause 14-9-44, weather related, pilot: Granville, Chester W. MIA/Irish Sea, MACR #9248, see Ervin, Ivan A.
	P-51		435		44-14589	Lost due to mid-air collision with Detlefsen, Heinz W. 8-11-44, pilot: Smith, Thomas V. POW/GER, MACR #10419
	P-51		435	J2-H	44-14840	Lost due to structural failure 5-2-45, pilot: Rock, Norbert W. killed practicing dive bombing/The Wash (10 mi. N of Sherringham, ENG)
	P-51		435		44-14850	Damaged in landing accident/Wattisham 27-12-44, pilot: Sowerby, Theo J., salvaged due to battle damage
	P-51		435	J2-J	44-15236	Unk
	P-51		435	J2-X	44-15335	Damaged in landing accident/Wattisham 1-5-45, pilot: Williams, George E. and damaged in taxi accident due to blown tail wheel/Wattisham 15-5-45, pilot: Candelaria, Richard G., later transfered to 355th FG
	P-51		435		44-15497	Crashed due to engine failure/Merville, FRA (1 1/2 mi. SE B-53) 27-1-45, pilot: Thorn, Donald W. bailed out
	P-51	Shoo Shoo BABY!	435	J2-S	44-63???	Aircraft name was prefaced with a treble cleft sign
	P-51		435		44-72395	To Swedish AF 24-3-47
	P-51		435	J2-N	44-72627	To Swiss AF post war
	P-51		435	J2-V	44-72802	Salvaged at war's end
	P-51		435	J2-K	44-73137	Transferred to 354th FG
	P-51	HELL-UN	435	J2-L		Name on both sides

436th Fighter Squadron

Pilot	*A/C*	*Aircraft Name*	*Sqdrn*	*A/C ID*	*Ser. No.*	*Comments*
	AT-6		436			Training/hack
Burgess, Warren H.	P-51	[LADY KAY]	436	9B-W	44-14813	Damaged in landing accident/Wattisham 15-10-44, pilot: Burgess, Warren M., possibly reassigned to Morris, Jessie F.
Darling, Charles H.	P-51	Dottie Mae	436		44-14280	Name changed from Bottleneck to Dottie Mae by Darling, salvaged at war's end
Derby, Stanley E.	P-51	[AZUCA CRUZ]	436			Per pilot, since his crew chief was Mexican, his girlfriend's nickname Sugar, *Azuca* in Spanish, was applied on the a/c. *Cruz*, meaning cross, was added by the CC. Therefore, *Azuca Cruz* is Sugar Cross.
DiPaola, Albert R.	P-51	[JAYBEE PRINCESS]	436			Per pilot
Duffié, Claire A. P.	P-51	Give'em Hell For H.L.Jr.	436	9B-A	44-14645	Salvaged at war's end, H.L. refers to Helen Louise
Duffié, Claire A. P.	P-51	Give'em Hell For H.L.Jr.	436	9B-A	44-72516	Rec'd from BAD 2 8-4-45, also named Give 'em Hell for H.L. 2, H.L. refers to Helen Louise, reassigned to Morton Richard C., renamed
Dunn, Donald A.	P-38	[DING HAO]	436			Per pilot
Dunn, Donald A.	P-51	DING HAO II	436		44-14767	Damaged taxiing to take off under frosty conditions 10-12-44, pilot: Darling Charles H. ran into 44-14607 pilot: Kreger, Charles S., damaged in forced landing/FR 13-1-45, salvaged due to battle damage
Elmgren, Charles B.	P-51	NO NAME APPLIED	436	9B-P	44-11739	No name per pilot, lost due to 4th FG a/c crossfire while strafing airfield 22-2-45, pilot: Vassuer, Peter C. MIA/GER, MACR #12672
Ernst, Carl V.	P-51	AKIN ASSAM DRAGON	436	9B-C-		
Fillipow, Edwin J.	P-51	Daisy Mae	436		44-14559	Named by crew chief, reassigned 00-11-44 to Red, Douglas L. who was MIA this a/c
Frolking, James E.	P-38	NO NAME APPLIED	436			
Frolking, James E.	P-51	NO NAME APPLIED	436	9B-N	44-14577	Lost due to enemy aa fire 7-10-44, pilot: Frolking, James E. EVD/HOL, MACR #9271, per pilot: a/c was brand new with only a few hrs on it; flown two missions
Glenn, John G.	P-51	LAGUNA GOONA	436			
Grasshoff, Hans J.	P-38	ZIPPIE	436	9B-J	43-28529	Destroyed by take off accident/Wattisham 26-8-44, pilot: Fillipow, Edward J.
Grasshoff, Hans J.	P-51	Little ZIPPIE	436	9B-C	44-14574	Reassigned 00-10-44 to King, Raymond E. who was KIA this a/c
Greenwood, Travis M.	P-38	NO NAME APPLIED	436			Per pilot
Greenwood, Travis M.	P-51	NO NAME APPLIED	436			Per pilot
Hansen, Kenneth J.	P-51	[JEANNE]	436	9B-D	44-15412	Formerly flown by Wolski, Victor C., lost due to enemy aa fire 22-2-45, pilot: Di Paola, Albert R. POW/GER, MACR #12692
Harrell, John W., Jr.	P-38	[PEACEMAKER]	436			Per squadron records
Hartnett, Vincent C.	P-38	[MERRILY ANN]	436		43-28418	Per squadron records
Hedenberg, John W.	P-38	Pretty Gal	436	9B-S	42-67???	OD/gray
Hedenberg, John W.	P-51	NO NAME APPLIED	436	9B-S		Per pilot
Henry, Raymond E.	P-51	King's Queen	436	9B-F	44-14534	
Hightower, Howard G.	P-38	Calamity Flo	436		43-28477	NMF, salvaged 2-8-44
Hightower, Howard G.	P-51	[CALAMITY FLO]	436	9B-T		
Hopcroft, Ernest J.	P-51	Poontang II	436	9B-G	44-72431	Received from BAD 2 29-3-45, to Swedish AF post war
Hoversten, Herman E.	P-38	the Virgin	436		44-23152	NMF
Howard, William N.	P-38	[MARION]	436		42-104407	Lost due to enemy aa fire 28-8-44, pilot: Howard, William N. EVD/FRA, MACR #8321
Huycke, Andre E.	P-38	[MY BEST BETT]	436		43-28406	Damaged due to enemy aa fire, belly landed at Wattisham 17-8-44, pilot: Hedenberg, John W., salvaged
Huycke, Andre E.	P-51	My Best Bett #4	436	9B-C-	44-14607	Destroyed taxiing to take off under frosty conditions 10-12-44, pilot: Kreger, Charles S., a/c 44-14767 and pilot: Darling, Charles H. a/c 44-14607 hit each other
Huycke, Andre E.	P-51	My Best Bett	436	9B-C-	44-63192	Named for wife Betty, reassigned to Mosier, Arlett G. Jr., damaged in landing accident/Ridgewell (Station 167) ENG 11-1-45 and ground loop/Wattisham 3-2-45, pilot both times: Mosier

Johnson, Clarence O.	P-38	[BULA B III]	436	9B-R	43-28697	Credited with group's first air kill 22-6-44, pilot: Johnson, Clarence O.
King, Benjamin H.	P-38	[MATILDA II]	436			Named after pilot's mother
King, Raymond E.	P-51	Little ZIPPIE	436	9B-C	44-14574	Lost due to engine failure 13-1-45, pilot: King, Raymond E. ditched in N. Sea near Clacton, died from exposure
Kleinman, Bernard R.	P-51	[LADY KAY]	436	9B-W	44-14813	Per pilot: a/c named after wife, damaged in landing accident/Wattisham 15-10-44, pilot: Joseph, George, a/c only had 16.55 hours
Kreger, Charles S.	P-51	BESSIE LEE	436			
Lewin, Edward C.	P-51	Scotty IV	436	9B-G		
Massey, Alton A.	P-51	Mimi's Pride	436	9B-H		Per pilot
McKeown, Arthur J.	P-51		436		44-14594	Formerly flown by Shonborn, Paul J., reassigned 00-7-45, salvaged post war
McLaurin, G. G.	P-51	MAC'S HACK	436	9B-Z		
Mead, Frederick M.	P-51		436		44-14576	Lost due to engine failure 11-3-45, pilot: Smith, Lewis C. bailed out over N. Sea 30 mi. E. of Lowestoft, died from exposure within 30 min.
Meyers, Thomas E.	P-51	AS-CEND Charlie	436	9B-3	44-14613	Damaged in mid-air collision/10 mi. NW of Ipswich 11-6-45, pilot: Hopcroft, Ernest J., collided w/44-13902, salvaged later
Monahan, John D.	P-38	Scotty II	436			Per pilot, original Scotty was flown in Alutiens prior to joining the squadron, named for wife to be whose last name was Scott
Moore, Clifford J., Jr	P-38	[THE UNINVITED]	436			NMF, per Axt, Kenneth D. (Armorer)
Moore, Clifford J., Jr	P-51	"The UNINVITED II"	436	9B-A	44-14591	After landing, a/c was damaged when taxied into 44-15086 being towed/Wattisham 2-3-45, repaired, damaged in taxi accident again/Wattisham 12-3-45, salvaged, pilot both occasions: Paulson, Richard C.J.
Morris, Jesse F.	P-51	[LADY KAY]	436	9B-W	44-14813	Damaged in landing accidents/Wattisham 15-10-44, pilot: Joseph, George, 7-3-45, pilot: Burgess, Warren M., later lost due to unk cause 26-3-45, pilot: Morris, Jesse F. bailed out over channel
Morton, Richard C.	P-51	Lady Kay III	436	9B-A	44-72516	To Italian AF post war
Moser, Fred A., Jr.	P-38	NO NAME APPLIED	436			Per wife
Mosier, Arlett G., Jr.	P-38	TIGER LILLY	436	9B-D	42-104397	OD/gray, lost due to enemy aa fire 2-8-44, pilot: Moser, Fred A., Jr. POW/BEL, MACR #7738
Mosier, Arlett G., Jr.	P-51	My Best Bett	436	9B-C-	44-63192	Reassigned to Thrall, Richard P.
Mulvany, Gerold M.	P-38	JERRY	436			NMF
Mulvany, Gerold M.	P-51	BOTTLENECK	436		44-14280	Name on both sides, later reassigned to Darling, Charles H., renamed Dottie Mae, salvaged at war's end
Nesselbush, Louis K.	P-38	[RABBLE ROUSER]	436	9B-N	42-67452	Lost due to engine failure/fire 20-6-44, pilot: Nesselbush, Louis K. POW/GER, MACR #5967 a/c received with name already applied
Plunk, Henry P.	P-51	Ambrosia	436	9B-O	44-14532	
Red, Douglas L.	P-51	Daisy Mae	436		44-14559	Lost due to unk cause (poss enemy a/c) 25-12-44, pilot: Red, Douglas L. MIA/GER, MACR #11176
Schoen, Charles F., Jr.	P-51	DEAREST MINE	436	9B-N	44-14583	Lost due to enemy aa fire 28-2-45, pilot: Schoen, Charles F., Jr. KIA/GER, MACR #12792
Shane, Presson S.	P-51	JAYHAWK	436			
Shonborn, Paul J.	P-51	Smoky City Fireball	436	9B-E	44-14594	Damaged in landing accident/Wattisham 22-3-45, pilot: McKeown, Arthur J., reassigned 00-7-45 to McKeown, Arthur J., salvaged later
Smigel, Albert J.	P-51	CHUG-A-LUG	436	9B-U	44-14750	Damaged in landing accident/Wattisham 14-3-45, pilot: Scordino, Anthony J., salvaged at war's end
Spencer, Richard S., Jr.	P-38	Muz's "Mighty Molecule"	436	9B-G	43-28641	NMF, damaged in take off accident/Wattisham 14-8-44, pilot: Spencer Richard S. Jr., salvaged
Spencer, Richard S., Jr.	P-51	"Muz's Mighty Molecule III"	436	9B-F		
Steph, Walter B.	P-51	THE OKLAHOMA KID	436	9B-I		Pilot was from Oklahoma
Struby, Joseph R.	P-51	Little Hemorrhoid	436	9B-E	44-14583	Recoded and reassigned to Schoen, Charles F., Jr. who was KIA this a/c
Sullivan, John A.	P-51	[CAROL II & III]	436	9B-A	44-14636	Lost due to unk cause 5-12-44, pilot: Sullivan, John A. MIA/North Sea, MACR #11305
Thompson, Thomas H.	P-51	Weezy	436	9B-R		Squadron ID letter per pilot. Named and lettered by pilot for wife Louise. Pilot was a F/O, made a flight leader and promoted to Lt. by C.A.P. Duffie
Thrall, Richard P.	P-51	My Best Bett	436	9B C-	44-63192	Destroyed in landing accident/Wattisham 31-5-45, pilot: Thrall, Richard P., a/c was run over by 44-15742, pilot: Shane, Presson S.
Walker, William R.	P-38	NO NAME APPLIED	436	9B-A	42-67261	OD/Gray, lost due to engine failure NW of Rattlesden (Station 126) ENG during a training exercise 25-5-44, pilot: Walker, William R. killed/ENG
Wilkins, John K., Jr.	P-51	[LI'L EXTERMI-NATOR]	436		44-14517	Lost due to mid-air collision with wingman Kreger, Charles S. 5-12-44, pilot: Eskell, Barrett B. POW/GER, MACR #10806
Witzel, George H.	P-51	Bruiser	436	9B-N	44-15742	Damaged in landing accident/Wattisham 31-5-45, pilot: Shane, Presson S., a/c ran up and over 44-63192, pilot: Thrall, Richard P., salvaged 1-4-46
Wolski, Victor C.	P-51		436	9B-D	44-15412	Reassigned to Hansen, Kenneth J.
	P-38		436	9B-R	42-67973	OD/gray, damaged in taxi accident 26-5-44, pilot: Spillane, James E. Jr.
	P-38		436		42-104327	NMF, crew chief was T/Sgt. Steele, Stanley L.
	P-38		436		43-28419	Lost due to mid-air collision with Kemper, Neil W. 24-7-44, pilot: Galloway, Thomas T. KIA/FRA, MACR # 7576
	P-38		436		43-28432	Lost due to enemy aa fire 14-8-44, pilot: O'Holleran, Thomas J. POW/FRA, MACR #8119
	P-38		436	9B-D	43-28459	Destroyed in take off accident, nose wheel collapsed causing a/c to flip on its back and burn/Wattisham 4-8-44, pilot: Hartman, Elmer killed
	P-38	"Polly"	436		43-28462	NMF
	P-38		436		43-28533	NMF, damaged in belly landing/Wattisham, hydraulic failure due to battle damage 4-7-44, pilot: Orrick, Thomas H., salvaged
	P-38		436	9B-X	43-28636	Destroyed in crash – engine failed during take off/Wattisham 28-7-44, pilot: Teeter, Robert R. killed
	P-38		436		43-28646	Damaged in belly landing/Burlywood/Pethem near Canterbury, ENG, out of gas 15-7-44, pilot: Mead, Frederick M., salvaged
	P-38		436	9B-Q	43-28655	Destroyed, failed to pull out of a maneuver while rat-racing with a 353rd FG P-47, crashed near Raydon (Station 157) ENG 9-6-44, pilot: Spillane, James E. Jr., Killed/ENG
	P-38		436	9B-D-	43-28712	Damaged in take off accident/Wattisham 14-8-44, pilot: Hartnett, Vincent C.
	P-38		436		44-23172	Lost due to mid-air collision with Galloway, Thomas T. 24-7-44, pilot: Kemper, Neil W. EVD/FRA, MACR #7596
	P-51		436		43-12184	4th SAD (Hitcham) installed a bubble canopy 10-2-45, salvaged at war's end
	P-51		436		43-12444	War-Weary, transferred in, saw combat with squadron 24-3-45, DS in FRA 1-4-45, salvaged at war's end
	P-51	RUTH	436	9B-3	43-12451	Damaged in taxi accident/Wattisham 4-1-45, pilot: Rossman, George P. War-Weary, salvaged
	P-51		436		43-12460	4th SAD (Hitcham) installed a bubble canopy 9-2-45, destroyed as the result of a mid-air collision/ENG 12-6-45
	P-51		436		43-24799	Destroyed in compressibility crash/ Wattisham - Doughty's farm 9-2-45, pilot: Shane, Presson S. sucessfully bailed out
	P-51		436		44-11157	Lost due to battle damage, bellied in/BELG 24-12-44, pilot: Early, John H. III
	P-51		436		44-11201	Ditched in North Sea - out of gas 6-11-44, pilot: Steele, Marion W. killed
	P-51		436		44-11228	Salvaged at war's end

	P-51	Little "Vic"	436	9B-A	44-11591	
	P-51		436		44-11749	Lost during training, a/c lost wing & spun in/The Wash (Admiralty Point Range) 4-5-45, pilot: Scordino, Anthony J. killed
	P-51		436		44-12117	Salvaged at war's end
	P-51		436	9B-Q	44-13341	Two place conversion, salvaged for unk reason
	P-51		436		44-13344	Lost due to belly landing south of Charleroi, Belg. 14-10-44, pilot: Dunn, Donald A.
	P-51		436	9B-K	44-13902	Forced landing/FRA 10-4-45, damaged in mid-air collision/10 mi. NW Ipswich, ENG 11-6-45 pilot: Olson, Marvin A., collided w/ 44-14613, salvaged later
	P-51		436	9B-D	44-14382	Destroyed in taxi accident/Wattisham 29-12-44, pilot: Derby, Stanley E., hit by a/c 44-15429, pilot: Witzel, George H., a/c only had 29.55 hrs. total time
	P-51		436		44-14544	Damaged due to ground loop/Wattisham 16-1-45, salvaged
	P-51		436		44-14553	Crash landed in channel 7-10-44, pilot: Wolski, Victor C.
	P-51		436		44-14567	Salvaged at war's end
	P-51		436		44-14570	
	P-51		436		44-14571	Lost due to unk cause while on training mission 22-4-45, pilot: Young, Robert C. killed/Rackheath (Station 145) ENG, pilot joined airshow there and crashed while flying low & inverted
	P-51		436	9B-C	44-14578	Destroyed in landing accident/Wattisham 12-3-45, pilot: Mead, Frederick M., run over by 44-14591, pilot: Palson, Richard C.J.
	P-51		436	9B-F	44-14583	Recoded and reassigned to Struby, Joseph R.
	P-51	[DAISEY MAE]	436		44-14601	Reassigned
	P-51	[QUEENIE-EL DIABLO]	436		44-14601	Lost due to enemy aa fire 18-4-45, pilot: Malone, Jay C. KIA/GER, MACR #14127
	P-51		436		44-14624	Destroyed in taxi accident 4-1-45, pilot: Thrall, Richard A.
	P-51		436		44-14788	Salvaged at war's end
	P-51		436		44-14915	Damaged in crash landing/Wattisham (crashed into hanger and burned) 19-2-45, pilot: Morton, Richard C.
	P-51		436		44-15010	Destroyed in crash/Wattisham 17-1-45, cause unknown, pilot bailed out
	P-51	[SCOTTY III]	436	9B-G	44-15057	Destroyed in landing accident/Wattisham 6-11-44, pilot: Spencer, Richard S. Jr., a/c only had 38.35 hrs. total time, one of the original P-51's to sq.
	P-51		436		44-15086	Damaged in taxi accident/Wattisham 2-3-45, pilot: Palson, Richard C.J., salvaged
	P-51		436	9B-E-	44-15429	Damaged in taxi accident/Wattisham 29-12-44, pilot: Witzel, George H., hit 44-14382, pilot: Derby, Stanley E., 44-15429 only had 59.35 hrs. total time, salvaged
	P-51		436		44-15533	Damaged in landing accident/Wattisham 25-1-45, salvaged at war's end
	P-51		436		44-15553	Battle damage 28-2-45, salvaged at war's end
	P-51		436	9B-S	44-15662	Destroyed in crash/W of Ipswich, ENG 2-4-45, pilot: Sherer, Carl W. bailed out
	P-51		436		44-62420	Received 14-3-45
	P-51		436		44-64069	Received from BAD 2 3-26-45, salvaged 13-12-46
	P-51		436		44-72420	
	P-51		436		44-72519	Salvaged at war's end
	P-51		436		44-72714	Received from BAD 2 1-7-45, salvaged 16-7-46
	P-51		436	9B-C	44-72751	Received from BAD 2 3-4-45, destroyed in crash, a/c stalled out/Wattisham 22-5-45, pilot: Rawley, Walter M. Jr.
	P-51		436	9B-D	44-72950	Received from BAD 2 15-4-45, to Italian AF post war
	P-51		436		44-72981	Received from BAD 2 23-4-45, to Swiss AF post war
	P-51		436		44-73295	Received from BAD 2 29-4-45, to Italian AF post war
	P-51	Rosita	436	9B-F		Name in small letters on right side, left side unk. could be Raymond E. Henry's King's Queen
	P-51		436	9B-4		Listed in squadron armament records
Riddle, Kyle L.	P-38	NO NAME APPLIED	HQ	J2-Q	44-23171	NMF, lost due to enemy aa fire 10-8-44, pilot: Riddle, Kyle L. EVD/FRA, MACR #7621
Riddle, Kyle L.	P-51	NO NAME APPLIED	HQ	J2-R	44-14327	Salvaged at war's end
Woods, Sidney S.	P-38	NO NAME APPLIED	HQ	L2-M	43-28465	
Woods, Sidney S.	P-51	NO NAME APPLIED	HQ	L2-M	44-14416	Reassigned to and later lost due to unk cause 25-12-44, pilot: Hurtig, Edward L. KIA/GER MACR # 11175
Zemke, Hubert	P-38	NO NAME APPLIED	HQ	J2-Z	43-28832	NMF, transferred to 474th FG
Zemke, Hubert	P-51	NO NAME APPLIED	HQ	9B-Z	44-14351	Lost due to weather 30-10-44, pilot: Zemke, Hubert POW/GER, MACR #10423
	P-38		Unk		43-28474	Transferred to 367th FG
	P-38		Unk		42-104324	Damaged in collision with parked a/c at Metfield (Station 366) ENG 21-6-44, salvaged
	P-38		Unk		43-28640	NMF
	P-51		Unk	??-X	42-106866	
	P-51		Unk		44-11562	Crashed/ENG 27-12-44
	P-51		Unk		44-14394	Lost due to unk cause 29-11-44
	P-51		Unk		44-15542	Salvaged at war's end
	P-51		Unk		44-62236	Damaged in belly landing 31-3-45, salvaged
	P-51	[PEGASUS]	Unk		44-72419	To Swedish AF post war

Notes:

This list is representative of the 479th Fighter Group's aircraft. It is not complete in that it does not present all of the planes assigned to the group. The list probably contains by far the majority of those assigned to the 434th Fighter Squadron. Those shown as belonging to the 436th Fighter Squadron comprise the next most complete listing. The 435th Fighter Squadron is the least complete. In addition to the fighter aircraft the group utilized, there were at various times at least four P-47's, a B-26 Marauder, several AT-6's, an AT-23, a UC-61, and a UC-64A assigned.

An attempt has been made to represent the A/C names as they appeared on the airplane, viz. small letters for small and caps for large. If the A/C name is known, but no photographic evidence has been found to depict its format, the name is shown in capital letters and enclosed within brackets. Where there was no name applied to the A/C, it is noted as such. Blank spaces denote unknown.

During the war, it was the general policy of the 479th Fighter Group to remove or paint over the serial numbers usually found on aircraft tail surfaces. This was probably done by the group for security purposes, but the practice was not something widely done within the 8th Air Force. As a consequence, this identification is missing from many of the group's aircraft found on the list above. Those that are listed were found by thorough and painstaking examination of many photographs as well as diligent searches of the group's records.

The P-38's utilized by the 479th Fighter Group were a mixed lot of both OD/Gray (olive drab over gray) and NMF (natural metal finish). All of the group's P-51's were NMF.

APPENDIX 6

VICTORIES

434th Fighter Squadron — Air: 93.5-7-22, Ground: 127.5-0-59

Name	*Sqdrn*	*KIA*	*Date*	*Air*	*Grnd*	*E/A*	*A/C*	*Shared*	*Decorations*
Born, David L.	434		14-2-45	1-0-0		Me 109	P-51		AM 8 OLC
			17-3-45		1-0-0	Me 109	P-51		
			17-3-45		2-0-0	U/I	P-51		
Bowers, Clifford W.	434		1-1-45	.5-0-0		Fw 190	P-51	K. L. Riddle	AM 9 OLC
			23-2-45		.5-0-0	B-17	P-51	G. W. Gleason	
			13-4-45		.5-0-1	U/I	P-51	434 pilots	
			18-4-45		1-0-0	Me 109	P-51		
			18-4-45		1-0-0	Me 110	P-51		
			18-4-45		1-0-1	U/I	P-51		
Bromschwig, Robert I.	434		1-1-45	0-0-1		Fw 190	P-51		AM 4 OLC
			31-3-45	0-0-1		Me 262	P-51		
Brown, Philip A.	434		25-12-44	1-1-0		Fw 190	P-51		AM 8 OLC
			20-2-45		.5-0-0	He 111	P-51	D. J. Pierce	
			20-2-45		0-0-.5	He 111	P-51	D. J. Pierce	
			13-4-45		.5-0-1	U/I	P-51	434 pilots	
			16-4-45		1-0-0	U/I	P-51		
Creighton, Richard D.	434		25-12-44	1-0-0		Fw 190	P-51		AM 9 OLC, DFC
			9-2-45	1-0-0		Me 109	P-51		
			9-2-45	0-1-0		Fw 190	P-51		
			13-4-45		.5-0-2	U/I	P-51	434 pilots	
Daudistel, William H.	434		14-2-45	1-0-0		Me 109	P-51		AM 4 OLC
Donnell, John C., Jr.	434	X	2-11-44	1-0-0		Me 109	P-51		AM 3 OLC
			9-2-45	0-0-2		Me 109	P-51		
Drake, Walter M.	434		18-8-44		1-0-0	Fw 190	P-38		AM 5 OLC, DFC
			18-8-44		2-0-0	Ju 88	P-38		
			26-9-44	1-0-0		Me 109	P-38		
Duffié, Claire A. P.	434/436		18-8-44		1-0-0	Ju 88	P-38		AM 17 OLC, SS 1 OLC, DFC
			18-8-44		.5-0-0	Ju 88	P-38	R .K. Friend	
			25-8-44	2-0-0		Me 109	P-38		
			26-9-44	1-0-2		Me 109	P-38		
Gleason, George W.	434		18-8-44		1-0-1	Fw 190	P-38		AM 17 OLC, DFC 1 OLC
			18-8-44		.5-0-0	He 111	P-38	C. F. Monsell	
			18-8-44		.5-0-0	He 111	P-38	C. F. Monsell	
			18-8-44		.5-0-0	Ju 88	P-38	H. W. Detlefsen	
			26-9-44	3-0-1		Me 109	P-38		
			28-9-44	1-0-0		Fw 190	P-51		
			28-9-44	1-0-0		Me 109	P-51		
			23-12-44	2-0-1		Fw 190	P-51		
			25-12-44	3-0-0		Fw 190	P-51		
			9-2-45	1-0-0		Fw 190	P-51		
			9-2-45	1-0-0		Me 109	P-51		
			23-2-45		.5-0-0	B-17	P-51	C. W. Bowers	
Golden, John T.	434		14-2-45	1-0-0		Me 109	P-51		AM 10 OLC, DFC
			20-2-45		1-0-0	He 111	P-51		

			20-2-45		.5-0-0	He 111	P-51	R .B. Kline	
			20-2-45		0-0-.5	Fw 190	P-51	R. B. Kline	
			13-4-45		.5-0-2	U/I	P-51	434 pilots	
			16-4-45		3-0-0	U/I	P-51		
Grenning, Harold F.	434		18-8-44		1-0-0	He 111	P-38		AM 7 OLC, DFC
			18-8-44		1-0-2	Ju 88	P-38		
			26-9-44	1-0-0		Me 109	P-38		
Hansen, John W.	434		15-8-44	1-0-0		Me 109	P-38		AM 10 OLC, DFC
			15-8-44		2-0-1	Me 109	P-38		
			15-8-44		0-0-1	U/I	P-38		
			18-8-44		1-0-1	He 111	P-38		
			18-8-44		1-0-0	Ju 88	P-38		
			26-9-44	1-0-1		Me 109	P-38		
Hehn, William H.	434		9-8-44		2-0-0	HE 111	P-38		AM 6 OLC, DFC
			9-8-44		0-0-1	Ju 52	P-38		
Helding, Arnold G.	434		25-12-44	1-0-0		Fw 190	P-51		AM 6 OLC
Hendrickson, Lauri A.	434		13-4-45		1-0-0	Fw 190	P-51		
Hendrickson, Robert H.	434		18-8-44		2-0-1	Ju 88	P-38		AM 8 OLC, DFC
			28-8-44		0-0-1	U/I	P-38		
			5-9-44		2-0-0	Do 217	P-38		
Hendrix, George D.	434		9-8-44		1-0-0	Ju 88	P-38		AM 7 OLC, DFC
			12-8-44	1-0-0		Ju 88	P-38		
			15-8-44		1-0-2	Me 109	P-38		
			18-8-44		0-0-1	Ju 88	P-38		
			6-10-44	0-0-1		Fw 190	P-51		
Herren, James M., Jr.	434	X	18-8-44		1-0-0	He 111	P-38		AM 8 OLC, DFC
			18-8-44		1-0-0	Ju 52	P-38		
			26-9-44	3-0-0		Me 109	P-38		
			28-9-44	1-0-0		Me 109	P-51		
Hollingsworth, James M.	434		28-8-44		1-0-0	Do 217	P-38		AM 12 OLC, DFC
			5-9-44		2-0-0	Do 217	P-38		
			5-9-44		4-0-0	Me 410	P-38		
			25-12-44	0-1-1		Me 109	P-51		
Hollister, Berkley E.	434		25-8-44	2-0-0		Me 109	P-38		AM 8 OLC, DFC
			5-9-44		2-0-0	Ju 88	P-38		
			5-12-44	0-1-0		Fw 190	P-51		
Huval, Ossie J.	434		21-2-45		1-0-0	He 111	P-51		AM 5 OLC
			31-4-45		.5-0-1	U/I	P-51	434 pilots	
Jacobson, Gail E.	434		5-12-44	2-0-0		Fw 190	P-51		AM 7 OLC, DFC
			23-12-44	1-0-0		Fw 190	P-51		
			25-12-44	0-1-0		Me 109	P-51		
			21-2-45		1-0-0	He 111	P-51		
			19-3-45	.5-0-0		Fw 190	P-51	F. M. Taylor	
			7-4-45	1-0-0		Me 109	P-51		
			16-4-45		2-0-1	Fw 190	P-51		
			16-4-45		0-0-1	Ju 88	P-51		
			18-4-45		2-0-0	Ju 88	P-51		
			18-4-45		1-0-0	Fw 190	P-51		
Jeffrey, Arthur F.	434		5-7-44	1-0-0		Fw 200	P-38		AM 16 OLC, DFC 1 OLC, SS
			29-7-44	1-0-0		Me 163	P-38		
			15-8-44	1-0-0		Me 109	P-38		
			28-8-44	1-0-0		Ju 52	P-38		
			7-10-44	1-0-0		Me 109	P-51		
			2-11-44	1-0-0		Me 109	P-51		
			5-12-44	3-0-1		Fw 190	P-51		
			23-12-44	3-0-0		Me 109	P-51		
			25-12-44	1-0-0		Me 109	P-51		
			14-2-45	1-0-1		Me 109	P-51		
Jenkins, Harold M., Jr.	434		25-12-44	1-0-0		Fw 190	P-51		AM 7 OLC, DFC
Keller, Frank J.	435/434		31-5-44		1-0-0	Ju 88	P-38		AM 3 OLC, DFC
			9-8-44		1-0-0	Fw 200	P-38		
			9-8-44		0-0-.5	He 111	P-38	T .D. Neely	
Kline, Robert B.	434		28-9-44	0-0-1		Me 109	P-51		AM 9 OLC, DFC
			20-2-45		2-0-0	Do 217	P-51		
			20-2-45		.5-0-0	He 111	P-51	J. T. Golden	
			20-2-45		0-0-.5	Fw 190	P-51	J. T. Golden	
			13-4-45		.5-0-1	U/I	P-51	434 pilots	
Little, Harry E.	434		18-8-44		.5-0-0	He 111	P-38	G. K. Sykes	AM 3 OLC
			18-8-44		1-0-0	Ju 88	P-38		
			18-8-44		0-0-2	He 111	P-38		
Looney, George H.	434		18-4-45		1-0-0	Fw 190	P-51		AM 1 OLC

Lunstrum, Richard M.	434		28-9-44	1-0-0		Fw 190	P-51		AM 8 OLC, DFC
Maley, Ronald L.	434		18-8-44		0-0-1	Fw 190	P-38		AM 5 OLC
			18-8-44		0-0-2	He 111	P-38		
			10-9-44		0-0-1	He 111	P-38		
			26-9-44	1-0-0		Me 109	P-38		
			5-12-44	0-1-0		Fw 190	P-51		
Marlowe, Wendell H.	434	X	6-11-44		.5-0-0	Fw 190	P-51	T. C. Olson	AM 1 OLC
Mastin, Donald W.	434		17-4-45		1-0-0	U/I	P-51		AM 2 OLC
Mathews, Harold E.	434		9-8-44		1-0-0	Fw 200	P-38		AM 10 OLC, DFC
			5-9-44		1-0-0	Ju 88	P-38		
			10-9-44		0-0-1	He 111	P-38		
			5-12-44	1-0-0		Fw 190	P-51		
McChrystal, Richard G.	434		26-9-44	1-0-1		Me 109	P-38		AM 10 OLC, DFC
			5-12-44	1-0-1		Me 109	P-51		
			14-2-45	1-0-0		Me 109	P-51		
Monaco, Elidio E.	434		18-4-45		1-0-1	Me 109	P-51		AM 2 OLC
Morrow, John W.	434		5-9-44		1-0-0	Me 109	P-38		AM 9 OLC, DFC
			26-9-44	1-0-0		Me 109	P-38		
Munson, Robert L.	434		7-4-45	1-0-0		Me 109	P-51		AM 3 OLC
			16-4-45		2-0-1	Fw 190	P-51		
Murphy, Calvin J., Jr.	434	X	15-8-44		1-0-1	Me 109	P-38		AM 4 OLC
			18-8-44		1-0-0	Fw 190	P-38		
			18-8-44		0-0-1	Ju 88	P-38		
			5-9-44		1-0-0	Me 410	P-38		
Murr, John N.	434		5-9-44		3-0-0	Me 110	P-38		AM 11 OLC, DFC
			26-9-44	1-0-0		Me 109	P-38		
			25-12-44	1-1-1		Fw 190	P-51		
Nagel, Jerome K.	434		7-4-45	1-0-0		Me 109	P-51		AM 11 OLC, DFC
			13-4-45		1-0-0	Ju 88	P-51		
			18-4-45		1-0-0	Fw 190	P-51		
			18-4-45		1-0-0	Ju 88	P-51		
			18-4-45		1-0-0	Me 109	P-51		
Neely, Tom, D.	434		3-8-44		0-0-0	B-24	P-38	435 + 436 pilots	AM 11 OLC, DFC
			9-8-44		1-0-0	He 111	P-38		
			9-8-44		0-0-.5	He 111	P-38	F. J. Keller	
			5-9-44		1-0-0	Ju 88	P-38		
			5-9-44		2-0-0	Me 110	P-38		
			23-12-44	2-0-0		Fw 190	P-51		
Olds, Robin	434		14-8-44	2-0-0		Fw 190	P-38		AM 27 OLC, DFC 1 OLC, SS 1 OLC
			18-8-44		1-0-0	He 111	P-38		
			18-8-44		2-0-0	Ju 88	P-38		
			25-8-44	3-0-0		Me 109	P-38		
			6-10-44	1-0-0		Fw 190	P-51		
			9-2-45	1-0-0		Me 109	P-51		
			14-2-45	2-0-0		Me 109	P-51		
			14-2-45	1-0-0		Fw 190	P-51		
			20-2-45		1-0-0	Do 217	P-51		
			20-2-45		1-0-0	Fw 190	P-51		
			19-3-45	1-0-0		Fw 190	P-51		
			19-3-45	1-0-0		Me 109	P-51		
			7-4-45	1-0-0		Me 109	P-51		
			7-4-45	0-0-1		Me 262	P-51		
			13-4-45		1-0-0	Ar 234	P-51		
			13-4-45		0-0-1	Me 410	P-51		
			16-4-45		1-0-0	He 177	P-51		
			16-4-45		2-0-0	Ju 87	P-51		
			16-4-45		1-0-0	Me 109	P-51		
			16-4-45		1-0-0	Me 110	P-51		
Olson, Thomas C.	434		18-8-44		.5-0-0	Fw 190	P-38	T. J. Sowerby	AM 14 OLC, DFC
			18-8-44		1-0-1	He 111	P-38		
			18-8-44		.5-0-0	He 111	P-38	N. W. Butler	
			18-8-44		1-0-0	Ju 88	P-38		
			18-8-44		1-0-0	Me 109	P-38		
			28-8-44	1-0-0		Fw 190	P-38		
			28-8-44		0-0-1	Me 109	P-38		
			5-9-44		4-0-0	Do 217	P-38		
			5-9-44		1-0-0	Me 110	P-38		
			6-11-44		.5-0-0	Fw 190	P-51	W. H. Marlowe	
			27-11-44		0-0-1	Me 410	P-51		
Pavlock, Quentin S.	434	X	27-7-44		0-0-.5	Ju 88	P-38	W. H. Rodgers	AM 4 OLC, DFC
			15-8-44	1-0-0		Me 109	P-38		

			26-9-44	2-0-0		Me 109	P-38		
			26-9-44	1-0-0		Fw 190	P-38		
Peacock, Cecil M.	434		17-4-45		2-0-0	Fw 190	P-51		AM 2 OLC
Peterson, Carl I.	434		18-8-44		1-0-0	Ju 52	P-38		AM
Pierce, Donald J.	434		14-2-45	0-0-2		Me 109	P-51		AM 13 OLC, DFC
			20-2-45		.5-0-0	He 111	P-51	P. A. Brown	
			20-2-45		0-0-.5	He 111	P-51	P. A. Brown	
			13-4-45		1-0-0	Ar 234	P-51		
			13-4-45		0-0-1	Ju 88	P-51		
			16-4-45		1-0-0	Fw 190	P-51		
			16-4-45		1-0-0	Ju 88	P-51		
			16-4-45		2-0-2	Me 109	P-51		
			17-4-45		2-0-0	Fw 190	P-51		
			17-4-45		1-0-1	Me 109	P-51		
			17-4-45		0-0-1	U/I	P-51		
Plazibat, John A.	434		16-4-45		1-0-0	Fw 190	P-51		AM 2 OLC
Rodgers, William H.	434	X	27-7-44		0-0-.5	Ju 88	P-38	Q. S. Pavlock	
			18-8-44		0-0-4	Ju 88	P-38		
Rossel, Roy M., Jr.	434		13-4-45		1-0-0	Ar 234	P-51		AM 3 OLC
Sears, Eugene E.	434		25-12-44	1-0-0		Me 109	P-51		AM 8 OLC, DFC
			20-2-45		1-0-0	Do 217	P-51		
Simpson, Richard G.	434		13-4-45		.5-0-2	U/I	P-51	434 pilots	AM 6 OLC, DFC, PH
Stott, Donald H.	434	X	16-4-45		1-0-0	U/I	P-51		AM 3 OLC
Stotts, Harold L.	434		16-4-45		1-0-1	Ju 88	P-51		AM 3 OLC
Taylor, Frank M.	434		19-3-45	.5-0-0		Fw 190	P-51	G. E. Jacobson	AM 1 OLC
			13-4-45		.5-0-2	U/I	P-51	434 pilots	
Thompson, Hilton O.	434	X	7-4-45	1-0-0		Me 262	P-51		AM 4 OLC
			25-4-45	1-0-0		Ar 234	P-51		
Tipps, John T.	434		6-7-44	1-0-0		Me 109	P-38		AM 5 OLC, DFC
			5-9-44		1-0-0	Do 217	P-38		
Tommie, Dalton F.	434		16-4-45		0-0-1	Fw 190	P-51		AM 3 OLC
			16-4-45		0-0-1	Me 109	P-51		
Valluzzi, Arthur J.	434		17-4-45		2-0-0	Me 109	P-51		AM 2 OLC
Wendt, Eugene H.	434		28-9-44	0-0-1		Fw 190	P-38		AM 10 OLC, DFC
			9-2-45	1-0-1		Me 109	P-51		
			14-2-45	2-0-0		Me 109	P-51		
			25-3-45	1-0-0		Me 262	P-51		
Williams, Bailey A.	434		5-7-44		0-0-1	Ju 88	P-38		AM 6 OLC, DFC
			5-9-44		2-0-0	Do 217	P-38		

435th Fighter Squadron — Air: 33.5-5-9, Ground: 36-0-46

Name	*Sqdrn*	*KIA*	*Date*	*Air*	*Grnd*	*E/A*	*A/C*	*Shared*	*Decorations*
Baird, Robert J.	435		17-4-45		1-0-0	Me 262	P-51		AM 7 OLC
Barsky, William M.	435		18-4-45		0-0-1	U/I	P-51		AM 6 OLC, DFC
Benoit, Norman R.	435		7-10-44	.5-0-0		Me 109	P-51	H. Zemke	AM 7 OLC
			5-12-44		0-0-1	Me 262	P-51		
			6-12-44		0-0-1	He 111	P-51		
			25-12-44	1-0-1		Me 109	P-51		
			21-1-45		0-0-1	Ju 88	P-51		
			21-1-45		0-0-1	Me 262	P-51		
			9-2-45	1-0-0		Fw 190	P-51		
Butler, Nelson W.	435		18-8-44		.5-0-0	He 111	P-38	V. E. Hooker	AM 7 OLC
			18-8-44		.5-0-0	He 111	P-38	T. C. Olson	
			26-9-44	2-0-0		Me 109	P-51		
			24-12-44	1-0-0		Fw 190	P-51		
Candelaria, Richard G.	435		5-12-44	2-0-0		Fw 190	P-51		AM 8 OLC, SS
			3-3-45		0-0-3	Me 109	P-51		
			7-4-45	4-0-0		Me 109	P-51		
			7-4-45	0-1-0		Me 262	P-51		
Carter, Raymond S.	435	X	5-8-44	1-1-0		Me 109	P-38		AM 3 OLC, DFC
Coursey, Richard R.	435		26-9-44	1-0-0		Me 109	P-51		AM 5 OLC, DFC
Detlefsen, Heinz W.	435	X	18-8-44		.5-0-0	Ju 88	P-38	G. W. Gleason	AM 4 OLC, DFC
			18-8-44		0-0-1	He 111	P-38		
Doolittle, Gordon L.	435		5-12-44	1-1-1		Fw 190	P-51		AM 5 OLC, DFC
			9-2-45	1-0-0		Me 109	P-51		
Friend, Ray K.	435		18-8-44		.5-0-0	Ju 88	P-38	C. A. P. Duffié	AM 6 OLC, DFC
			18-8-44		0-0-3	He 111	P-38		
			26-9-44	1-0-1		Me 109	P-51		
Frost, Russell B.	435		16-4-45		0-0-2	U/I	P-51		
Gates, William M.	435/434		3-8-44		.33-0-0	B-24	P-38	434 + 436 pilots	AM 6 OLC
Gorian, Martin G.	435		26-9-44	1-0-0		Me 109	P-51		AM 5 OLC, DFC
Gossard, Philip D.	435		18-8-44		1-0-0	He 111	P-38		AM 6 OLC, DFC

Name	Sqdrn	KIA	Date	Air	Grnd	E/A	A/C	Shared	Decorations
			5-12-44	1-0-0		Fw 190	P-51		
Granville, Chester W.	435	X	18-8-44		1-0-0	He 111	P-38		AM 3 OLC
			18-8-44		1-0-0	Ju 88	P-38		
Harrell, John W., Jr.	436/435		27-11-44	0-0-1		Fw 190	P-51		AM 5 OLC, DFC
			25-12-44	1-0-0		Me 109	P-51		
Hart, Frederick L.	435		5-12-44	0-1-0		Fw 190	P-51		AM 4 OLC
Hoffman, Clark R.	435		17-4-45		1-0-0	Fi 156	P-51		AM 7 OLC
			17-4-45		2-0-1	Me 262	P-51		
Hooker, Verne E.	435		18-8-44		.5-0-0	He 111	P-38	N. W. Butler	AM 12 OLC, DFC 1 OLC
			18-8-44		.5-0-0	He 111	P-38	C. F. Monsell	
			18-8-44		0-0-1	Ju 88	P-38		
			5-9-44		0-0-1	He 111	P-38		
			7-4-45	1-0-0		Me 109	P-51		
			7-4-45	1-0-0		Me 262	P-51		
			13-4-45		2-0-1	Ju 88	P-51		
			16-4-45		1-0-0	U/I	P-51		
			16-4-45		0-0-1	Me 109	P-51		
			17-4-45		0-0-1	U/I	P-51		
			18-4-45		0-0-2	U/I	P-51		
Jordan, Herbert R.	435		14-1-45	1-0-0		Me 109	P-51		AM 10 OLC
			9-2-45	1-0-0		Fw 190	P-51		
King, David E.	435		9-2-45	1-0-0		Me 109	P-51		AM 7 OLC
Koerber, James H.	435		18-4-45		1-0-0	U/I	P-51		AM 7 OLC
Mathews, Cecil R.	435		17-4-45		0-0-1	Me 262	P-51		AM 4 OLC, DFC
Maule, Donald L.	435		18-8-44		1-0-0	He 111	P-38		AM 5 OLC, DFC
Means, Billy C.	435		5-12-44	1-0-0		Me 109	P-51		AM 6 OLC
			3-3-45		0-0-1	Me 109	P-51		
Monsell, Charles E., Jr.	435		18-8-44		.5-0-0	He 111	P-38	G. W. Gleason	AM 6 OLC
			18-8-44		.5-0-0	He 111	P-38	G. W. Gleason	
			18-8-44		.5-0-0	He 111	P-38	V. E. Hooker	
			9-26-44	1-0-0		Me 109	P-51		
Muller, Wilbert	435		18-8-44		0-0-2	Ju 88	P-38		AM 4 OLC, DFC
Petterson, Lewis P.	435		27-11-44	1-0-0		Fw 190	P-51		AM 5 OLC, DFC
Pickering, William H.	435		26-9-44	2-0-0		Me 109	P-51		AM 6 OLC, DFC
Pigg, Robert N.	434/435	X	18-8-44		1-0-4	He 111	P-38		AM 6 OLC
			18-8-44		1-0-1	Ju 88	P-38		
Rogers, John R.	435		9-2-45	1-0-1		Me 109	P-51		AM 3 OLC
Rourke, William B., Jr.	435		13-4-45		1-0-2	Ju 88	P-51		AM 3 OLC
Routh, Sylvan R.	435		17-4-45		1-0-0	Me 262	P-51		AM 4 OLC
Salter, George M., Jr.	435		17-4-45		0-0-1	U/I	P-51		AM 4 OLC
Salze, Floyd W.	435		25-3-45	0-0-1		Me 262	P-51		AM 3 OLC
			17-4-45		1-0-0	Me 262	P-51		
Shriner, Frederick F.	435		9-2-45	0-1-0		Me 109	P-51		AM 4 OLC
Sims, Edward H.	435		21-1-45		0-0-1	Ju 52	P-51		AM 4 OLC
			4-4-45	0-0-1		Me 262	P-51		
			17-4-45		1-0-0	Me 262	P-51		
			18-4-45		0-0-1	U/I	P-51		
Smith, Howard C.	435		18-8-44		4-0-0	He 111	P-38		AM 6 OLC, DFC
Sowerby, Theodore J.	435		18-8-44		.5-0-0	Fw 190	P-38	T. C. Olson	AM 15 OLC, DFC
			18-8-44		1-0-1	Ju 88	P-38		
			18-8-44		0-0-2	He 111	P-38		
			26-11-44	1-0-0		Fw 190	P-51		
			25-12-44	1-0-0		Fw 190	P-51		
			21-1-45		1-0-0	Ju 52	P-51		
			21-1-45		1-0-0	Ju 88	P-51		
			13-4-45		1-0-4	Ju 88	P-51		
			17-4-45		2-0-0	Me 262	P-51		
Splittstoesser, Elmer A.	435		18-4-45		0-0-1	U/I	P-51		AM 3 OLC
Sullivan, John A.	435/436	X	24-7-44	0-0-1		Me 109	P-38		AM 7 OLC
Sykes, George K.	435		5-8-44	1-0-1		Me 109	P-38		AM 3 OLC, DFC
			18-8-44		1-0-0	He 111	P-38		
			18-8-44		.5-0-0	He 111	P-38	H. E. Little	
Thorn, Donald W.	435		17-4-45		0-0-1	Me 262	P-51		AM 6 OLC
			17-4-45		0-0-1	U/I	P-51		

436th Fighter Squadron — Air: 24-0-6, Ground: 111.5-0-63

Name	*Sqdrn*	*KIA*	*Date*	*Air*	*Grnd*	*E/A*	*A/C*	*Shared*	*Decorations*
Anderson, William C.	436/435		22-2-45		1-0-0	He 111	P-51		AM 9 OLC, DFC
Archibald, John M.	436		13-4-45		1-0-0	Fw 190	P-51		AM 2 OLC
			13-4-45		0-0-1	Me 110	P-51		
Biscayart, Jules D.	436		28-9-44	2-0-0		Fw 190	P-38		AM 6 OLC, SS, DFC

Darling, Charles H.	436		22-2-45		0-0-2	Ju 88	P-51		AM 9 OLC
			13-4-45		2-0-0	Fw 190	P-51		
			13-4-45		0-0-1	Me 110	P-51		
			13-4-45		0-0-1	U/I	P-51		
			16-4-45		1-0-0	He 111	P-51		
			17-4-45		1-0-0	U/I	P-51		
DiPaola, Albert R.	436		22-2-45		0-0-1	Fw 190	P-51		AM 2 OLC
Duffié, Claire A. P.	434/436		22-2-45		1-0-1	Ju 88	P-51		AM 17 OLC, SS 1 OLC, DFC
			22-2-45		0-0-2	U/I	P-51		
			16-4-45		4-0-0	Fw 190	P-51		
			17-4-45		1-0-0	Fw 190	P-51		
			17-4-45		2-0-0	Ju 87	P-51		
Dunn, Donald A.	436		28-9-44	3-0-0		Fw 190	P-38		AM 7 OLC, DFC
Early, John H., III	436		13-4-45		1-0-0	Fw 190	P-51		AM 5 OLC
			13-4-45		1-0-0	Me 110	P-51		
			13-4-45		0-0-1	Me 410	P-51		
Elmgren, Charles B.	436		16-4-45		4-0-0	Fw 190	P-51		AM 8 OLC, DFC
			17-4-45		2-0-0	Fi 156	P-51		
			17-4-45		1-0-0	U/I	P-51		
Ernst, Carl V.	436		23-12-44	1-0-0		Fw 190	P-51		AM 5 OLC
			16-4-45		1-0-0	He 111	P-51		
Falkner, George E.	436		17-4-45		1-0-0	U/I	P-51		BS, AM 20 OLC, DFC, CdeG, RS
Fillipow, Edwin J.	436		5-9-44		0-0-2	Fw 190	P-38		AM 4 OLC, DFC, PH
Frolking, James E.	436		5-9-44		1-0-1	Fw 190	P-38		AM 4 OLC, DFC
			28-9-44	0-0-1		Fw 190	P-38		
Granger, Jesse V.	436		5-9-44		2-0-0	Fw 190	P-38		AM 3 OLC, DFC
Grasshoff, Hans J.	436		24-7-44	.5-0-0		Me 109	P-38	H. P. Plunk	AM 8 OLC
			8-8-44	0-0-1		Me 109	P-38		
			5-9-44		4-0-1	Fw 190	P-38		
			26-9-44	1-0-0		Me 109	P-38		
			27-11-44	1-0-0		Fw 190	P-51		
Greenwood, Travis M.	436		5-9-44		2-0-1	Do 217	P-38		AM 4 OLC, DFC
Hansen, Kenneth J.	436		13-4-45		3-0-0	Fw 190	P-51		AM 8 OLC
			13-4-45		1-0-0	Me 110	P-51		
			17-4-45		1-0-0	FW 189	P-51		
Hartnett, Vincent C.	436		5-9-44		2-0-1	Fw 190	P-38		AM 6 OLC, DFC
Hedenberg, John W.	436		5-9-44		1-0-1	Do 217	P-38		AM 5 OLC, DFC
Henry, Raymond E.	436		22-2-45		1-0-0	Ju 88	P-51		AM 4 OLC, DFC
			22-2-45		0-0-1	He 111	P-51		
			16-4-45		3-0-0	Fw 190	P-51		
Hightower, Howard G.	436		28-9-44	0-0-1		Fw 190	P-38		AM 4 OLC, DFC
Hopcroft, Ernest J.	436		22-2-45		0-0-1	He 111	P-51		AM 11 OLC
			13-4-45		1-0-0	Me 109	P-51		
			13-4-45		2-0-0	Me 410	P-51		
			16-4-45		1-0-0	He 111	P-51		
			17-4-45		1-0-0	Fi 156	P-51		
			17-4-45		1-0-0	Fw 190	P-51		
			17-4-45		1-0-0	Me 109	P-51		
			17-4-45		0-0-1	U/I	P-51		
Huycke, Andre E.	436		5-9-44		1-0-1	He 111	P-38		AM 8 OLC, DFC
			5-9-44		0-0-1	Do 217	P-38		
			23-12-44	1-0-0		Fw 190	P-51		
Johnson, Clarence O.	436		22-6-44	1-0-0		Fi 156	P-38		AM 18 OLC, DFC
Kleinman, Bernard R.	436		13-4-45		1-0-0	Fw 190	P-51		AM 9 OLC, DFC
			13-4-45		1-0-0	Me 110	P-51		
Kreger, Charles S.	436		17-4-45		0-0-1	Fw 190	P-51		AM 5 OLC
Lewin, Edward C.	436		5-9-44		1-0-0	Fi 156	P-38		AM 8 OLC, DFC
			5-9-44		2-0-0	Fw 190	P-38		
			5-9-44		0-0-2	U/I	P-38		
			23-12-44	1-0-0		Fw 190	P-51		
Long, Sylvester F.	436		13-4-45		2-0-0	Fw 190	P-51		AM 3 OLC
Malone, Jay C.	436	X	21-2-45		0-0-1	Ju 188	P-51		AM 6 OLC, DFC
			22-2-45		0-0-1	Ju 88	P-51		
			13-4-45		2-0-2	Fw 190	P-51		
			13-4-45		1-0-0	Me 110	P-51		
			13-4-45		0-0-1	Me 410	P-51		
			16-4-45		1-0-0	Fw 190	P-51		
McLaurin, Grover G., Jr.	436		16-4-45		2-0-0	Fw 190	P-51		AM 5 OLC
Mickey, Melvin S.	436		5-8-44	1-0-0		Me 109	P-38		AM 3 OLC
Moore, Clifford J., Jr.	436		5-8-44	1-0-0		Me 109	P-38		AM 7 OLC, DFC

Name	Sqdrn	KIA	Date	Air	Grnd	E/A	A/C	Shared	Decorations
			5-9-44		1-0-0	U/I	P-38		
			5-9-44		0-0-2	Fw 190	P-38		
			22-2-45		0-0-1	Ju 52	P-51		
Mulvany, Gerald M.	436		3-8-44		.33-0-0	B-24	P-38	T. E. Myers +	AM 8 OLC, DFC
			5-9-44		2-0-1	Fw 190	P-38		
			26-9-44	1-0-0		Me 109	P-38		
Myers, Thomas E.	436		3-8-44		.33-0-0	B-24	P-38	G. M. Mulvany +	AM 10 OLC
			6-10-44	1-0-0		Me 109	P-51		
			5-12-44	.5-0-0		Fw 190	P-51	P. C. Vasseur	
			5-12-44	0-0-1		Me 109	P-51		
Ogron, Zeymour	436		5-9-44		0-0-3	Fw 190	P-38		AM 5 OLC
Palson, Richard C. Jr.	436		13-4-45		2-0-1	He 111	P-51		AM 9 OLC, DFC
			13-4-45		0-0-1	Fw 190	P-51		
			16-4-45		2-0-0	Fw 190	P-51		
			17-4-45		2-0-0	Fw 190	P-51		
			17-4-45		2-0-0	Me 109	P-51		
Philbrick, Charles H., II	436		13-4-45		1-0-0	Fw 190	P-51		AM 5 OLC
			13-4-45		1-0-3	Me 109	P-51		
			13-4-45		0-0-1	U/I	P-51		
			16-4-45		1-0-0	Me 109	P-51		
Plunk, Henry P.	436		24-7-44	.5-0-0		Me 109	P-38	H. J. Grasshoff	AM 5 OLC, DFC
Rawley, Walter N., Jr.	436		16-4-45		1-0-0	Fw 190	P-51		AM 1 OLC
Romano, Pasquale J.	436		17-4-45		1-0-0	Ju 87	P-51		AM 5 OLC
			17-4-45		1-0-0	U/I	P-51		
Rosness, Joseph H.	436		5-9-44		0-0-2	Do 217	P-38		AM 4 OLC, DFC
			5-9-44		0-0-1	Fw 190	P-38		
Scordino, Anthony J.	436	X	22-2-45		1-0-0	Ju 88	P-51		AM 2 OLC
			22-2-45		0-0-2	He 111	P-51		
Shane, Presson S.	436		13-4-45		1-0-0	Me 410	P-51		AM 6 OLC
			13-4-45		1-0-0	U/I	P-51		
			13-4-45		0-0-1	Me 109	P-51		
			16-4-45		2-0-0	Fw 190	P-51		
			17-4-45		1-0-0	Me 109	P-51		
Smigel, Alfred J.	436		22-2-45		1-0-0	He 111	P-51		AM 5 OLC
			22-2-45		0-0-2	Ju 88	P-51		
			16-4-45		2-0-0	Fw 190	P-51		
			16-4-45		1-0-0	Me 109	P-51		
			17-4-45		1-0-1	U/I	P-51		
Spencer, Richard S., Jr.	436		25-12-44	2-0-0		Fw 190	P-51		AM 8 OLC, DFC
Steph, Walter B.	436		13-4-45		1-0-0	Fw 190	P-51		AM 8 OLC, DFC
			13-4-45		0-0-1	Me 109	P-51		
			16-4-45		1-0-0	Me 109	P-51		
Straub, George	436		28-9-44	1-0-1		Fw 190	P-38		AM 5 OLC, DFC
Struby, Joseph R.	436		23-12-44	1-0-0		Fw 190	P-51		AM 7 OLC, DFC
Sullivan, John A.	435/436	X	5-9-44		1-0-4	Do 217	P-38		AM 7 OLC
			5-9-44		0-0-1	He 111	P-38		
Thompson, Thomas H.	436		16-4-45		1-0-0	He 111	P-51		AM 6 OLC
Vassuer, Peter C.	436	X	5-12-44	.5-0-0		Fw 190	P-51	T. E. Myers	AM 4 OLC
Witzel, George H.	436		21-2-45		0-0-1	Ju 188	P-51		AM 9 OLC, DFC
			13-4-45		2-0-1	Fw 190	P-51		
			13-4-45		0-0-1	Me 110	P-51		
			16-4-45		3-0-0	Fw 190	P-51		
			17-4-45		1-0-0	Fw 190	P-51		
			17-4-45		1-0-0	U/I	P-51		
Wolski, Victor	436		5-9-44		2-0-1	Fw 190	P-38		AM 4 OLC
			28-9-44	3-0-1		Fw 190	P-38		
Zellman, Fred	436		13-4-45		1-0-1	Me 109	P-51		AM 7 OLC
			13-4-45		1-0-0	Me 410	P-51		

479th Fighter Group Headquarters — Air: 4-0-2, Ground: 1-0-0

Name	*Sqdrn*	*KIA*	*Date*	*Air*	*Grnd*	*E/A*	*A/C*	*Shared*	*Decorations*
Riddle, Kyle L.	HQ		5-12-44	1-0-1		Fw 190	P-51		AM 8 OLC, DFC, CdeG, SS
			1-1-45	.5-0-0		Fw 190	P-51	C. W. Bowers	
Woods, Sidney S.	HQ		5-9-44		1-0-0	Ju 88	P-38		AM 6 OLC, DFC 1 OLC, DSC
Zemke, Hubert	HQ		26-9-44	2-0-1		Me 109	P-51		AM 3 OLC, SS, DFC 6 OLC, BDFG
			7-10-44	.5-0-0		Me 109	P-51	N. R. Benoit	

APPENDIX 7

PILOTS LOST

D/M/Yr	*Time*	*MACR*	*Pilot*	*Status*	*How*	*Loc*	*ABMC*	*Sqdrn*	*A/C*	*A/C ID*	*Ser No*
28-9-43			Brooks, W. H.	Killed	UNK	USA		UNK	P-47		
13-11-43			Stansbury, Charles D.	Killed	AUTO	USA		436	—	—	—
22-12-43			Dyess, William E.	Killed	TOA	USA		HQ	P-38		
12-3-44			Twyman, Robert C.	Killed	TRN	USA		HQ	P-38		
24-3-44			Henderson, William E.	Killed	TRN	USA		436	P-38		
25-5-44			Walker, William R.	Killed	TRN	Eng.		436	P-38	9B-A	42-67261
9-6-44			Spillane, James E., Jr.	Killed	1	Eng.		436	P-38	9B-Q	43-28655
17-6-44	2030	5965	Butler, Calvin J.	POW	EAA	Fr.		435	P-38	J2-F	44-23168
17-6-44	2030	5958	Ohligschlager, James K.	POW	MAC	Fr.		434	P-38	L2-Q	43-28729
19-6-44	0920	5959	Grdenich, Frank	KIA	MAC	Fr.		434	P-38	L2-T	43-28456
19-6-44	0920	5960	Kuentzel, Ward A.	KIA	MAC	Fr.		434	P-38	L2-N	42-104427
19-6-44	0935	5968	Horne, Leland K.	MIA	MAC	Fr.	RH	435	P-38		42-68161
19-6-44	0935	5969	McClure, Donald D.	MIA	MAC	Fr.	NO	435	P-38		42-68189
20-6-44	1035	5967	Nesselbush, Louis K.	POW	MF	Ger.		436	P-38	9B-N	42-67452
22-6-44	1445	6108	Canella, Keith E.	KIA	EAA	Fr.	EP	434	P-38	L2-K	43-28731
22-6-44	1445	5970	Ilsley, Dwight F.	KIA	EAA	Fr.	EP	434	P-38	L2-G	42-104258
22-6-44	1445	6106	Lutz, Leroy	KIA	EAA	Fr.		434	P-38	L2-L	43-28714
22-6-44	1500	5966	Tucker, Albert S. J., Jr.	POW	EAA	Fr.		434	P-38	L2-B	43-28349
27-6-44	2020	6557	Gross, Burton S.	KIA	UNK	Fr.		435	P-38		42-104416
4-7-44	0845	6693	Fairchild, Rayne B.	POW	EAA	Fr.		435	P-38		44-23484
4-7-44	0850	6789	Green, Robert D.	KIA	EAA	Fr.	NO	435	P-38		43-28467
4-7-44	1925	6692	Denny, Jack S.	EVD	EAA	Fr.		434	P-38	L2-A	43-28367
5-7-44	0900	6691	Proctor, Clayton F.	KIA	EAA	Fr.	EP	434	P-38	L2-V	42-68029
6-7-44	0900	6788	Hass, Jene A.	POW	EAC	Fr.		434	P-38	L2-P	42-67732
15-7-44	1908	6780	Harper, Flamm D.	EVD	2	Fr.		434	P-38	L2-V	42-68147
21-7-44	1130	6829	Grossenbacher, Jack G.	KIA	EAA	Ger.		434	P-38	L2-G	43-28647
24-7-44	1300	7576	Galloway, Thomas T.	KIA	MAC	Fr.		436	P-38		43-28419
24-7-44	1300	7596	Kemper, Neil W.	EVD	MAC	Fr.		436	P-38		44-23172
24-7-44	1343	7572	Evanenko, Alexander	MIA	EAC	Chan.	CA	435	P-38	J2-R	43-28716
27-7-44	1905	7573	McArthur, Marden L.	KIA	EAA	Fr.		434	P-38	L2-B	42-67865
27-7-44	1955	7575	McKay, William B.	KIA	EAA	Fr.		435	P-38		44-23160
28-7-44			Teeter, Robert R.	KILLED	TOA	Eng.	CA	436	P-38	9B-X	43-28636
2-8-44	1850	7738	Moser, Fred A., Jr.	POW	EAA	Belg.		436	P-38	9B-D	42-104397
4-8-44			Hartman Elmer	KILLED	TOA	Eng.		436	P-38	9B-D	43-28459
5-8-44	1155	7425	Moore, Carl W.	KIA	EAA	Ger.	AR	435	P-38		43-28472
8-8-44	1350	7786	Courtney, John J., Jr.	EVD	3	Fr.		435	P-38		43-28426
9-8-44	1145	7785	Keller, Frank J.	POW	EAA	Ger.		434	P-38	L2-I	43-28377
10-8-44	1040	7621	Riddle, Kyle L.	EVD	EAA	Fr.		HQ	P-38	J2-Q	44-23171
10-8-44	1045	7622	Fleming, James E., Jr.	KIA	EAA	Fr.	EP	434	P-38	L2-W	43-28341
14-8-44	0600	8119	O'Holleran, Thomas J.	POW	EAA	Fr.		436	P-38		43-28432
15-8-44	1315	8120	Turner, Hiram G., Jr.	POW	EAA	Neth.		434	P-38	L2-U	43-28376
15-8-44	1315	8121	Wallace, James L.	KIA	EAA	Neth.		434	P-38	L2-Z	44-23169
18-8-44	1700	8118	Manning, Philip W.	KIA	EAA	Fr.	LO	434	P-38	L2-R	42-67296
28-8-44	1005	8321	Howard, William N.	EVD	EAA	Fr.		436	P-38		42-104407
5-9-44	1830	8565	Carter, Raymond S.	KIA	EAA	Ger.		435	P-38	J2-N	44-23177
6-9-44	1320	8566	Murphy, Calvin J., Jr.	KIA	EAA	Ger.		434	P-38	L2-O	42-104425
9-9-44			Ford, Everett P.	KILLED	TRN	Eng.		435	P-51		44-14405
14-9-44			Ervin, Ivan A.	KILLED	TRN	Eire		435	P-51	J2-R-	44-14295
14-9-44	1515	9248	Granville, Chester W.	MIA	TRN	Eire	CA	435	P-51	J2-C	44-14437
17-9-44	1245	9013	Sykes, George K.	EVD	EAA	Neth.		435	P-51		44-14424
21-9-44	1240	9152	Gavrys, Thomas A.	MIA	UNK	Chan.	CA	434	P-51	L2-G	44-14138
26-9-44	1630	9249	Little, Harry E.	POW	EAC	Ger.		434	P-38	L2-N	42-67264
27-9-44	0755	9247	Rodgers, William H.	MIA	UNK	Chan.	CA	434	P-51	L2-L	44-14324

2-10-44			Pavlock, Quentin S.	KILLED	TOA	Eng.		434	P-51	L2-G	44-14616
7-10-44	1630	9271	Frolking, James E.	EVD	EAA	Neth.		436	P-51	9B-N	44-14577
30-10-44	1310	10423	Zemke, Hubert	POW	WEA	Ger.		HQ	P-51	9B-Z	44-14351
30-10-44	1315	10422	Herren, James M., Jr.	KIA	WEA	Ger.	AR	434	P-51	L2-A	44-14396
30-10-44	1315	10421	Holmes, Douglas I.	POW	WEA	Ger.		434	P-51	L2-S	44-14627
6-11-44			Steele, Marion W.	MIA	OOG	N. Sea	CA	436	P-51		44-11201
8-11-44	1250	10424	Detlefsen, Heinz W.	KIA	MAC	Ger.	NE	435	P-51		44-14294
8-11-44	1250	10419	Smith, Thomas V.	POW	MAC	Ger.		435	P-51		44-14589
5-12-44	1030	10806	Eskell, Barrett B.	POW	MAC	Ger.		436	P-51		44-14517
5-12-44	1100	10807	Maley, Ronald L.	POW	EAA	Ger.		434	P-51	L2-T	44-11214
5-12-44	1100	10805	Neumann, Walter A.	KIA	UNK	Ger.		434	P-51	L2-U	44-14592
5-12-44	1330	11305	Sullivan, John A.	MIA	MF	N. Sea	NE	436	P-51	9B-A	44-14636
10-12-44			Clarke, William D.	KIA	UNK	Fr.	EP	435	P-51		Unk
12-12-44	1200	11304	Hymans, Robert B.*	MIA	UNK	Eng.	CA	435	P-51	J2-7	43-7157
12-12-44			Pigg, Robert N.	KIA	MF	Belg.		435	P-51		44-14344
13-12-44			Hollis, Dewey H.	KILLED	TRN	Eng.		434	P-51		43-6772
23-12-44	1500	11072	Neely, Tom D.	POW	EAA	Ger.		434	P-51	L2-X	44-14596
25-12-44	1200	11177	Hollingsworth, James M.	POW	UNK	Ger.		434	P-51	L2-A	44-14892
25-12-44	1200	11175	Hurtig, Edward L.	KIA	UNK	Ger.	LU	434	P-51	L2-M	44-14416
25-12-44	1200	11178	Marlowe, Wendell H.	KIA	UNK	Ger.		434	P-51	L2-B	44-15325
25-12-44	1210	11176	Red, Douglas L.	MIA	UNK	Ger.	CA	436	P-51		44-14559
4-1-45			Sands, Thurman E.	KILLED	TRN	Eng.		434	P-51		43-6393
13-1-45			King, Raymond E.	KIA	MF	Chan.		436	P-51	9B-C	44-14574
5-2-45			Rock, Norbert W.	MIA	TRN	Eng.	CA	435	P-51	J2-H	44-14840
9-2-45	1215	12174	Jarrell, Carl B.	POW	EAC	Ger.		435	P-51		44-14364
14-2-45	1240	12332	Donnell, John C., Jr.	KIA	EAA	Ger.		434	P-51	L2-V	44-14651
22-2-45	1345	12672	Vassuer, Peter C.	MIA	FAC	Ger.	HC	436	P-51	9B-P	44-11739
22-2-45	1330	12692	DiPaola, Albert R.	POW	EAA	Ger.		436	P-51	9B-D	44-15412
28-2-45	1405	12792	Schoen, Charles F., Jr.	KIA	EAA	Ger.	LO	436	P-51	9B-N	44-14583
1-3-45	1400	12837	Trabucco, Thomas F.	KIA	UNK	Ger.		435	P-51	J2-A-	44-15374
3-3-45	1115	12881	Harris, Elbert N.	POW	MF	Ger.		434	P-51	L2-A	44-63189
11-3-45			Smith, Lewis C.	KIA	MF	N. Sea		436	P-51		44-14576
13-4-45	1630	13904	Candelaria, Richard G.	POW	EAA	Ger.		435	P-51	J2-K	44-11755
13-4-45	1830	14120	Huval, Ossie J.	POW	EAA	Ger.		434	P-51	L2-A	44-12156
16-4-45	UNK	14117	Golden, John T.	POW	EAA	Ger.		434	P-51	L2-G	44-14856
16-4-45	UNK	14116	Krauss, Harold F., Jr.	KIA	EAA	Neth.	NE	434	P-51	L2-F	44-14929
16-4-45	UNK	14119	Stott, Donald H.	KIA	UNK	Ger.		434	P-51	L2-S	44-14629
16-4-45	UNK	14118	Taylor, Frank M.	POW	EAA	Ger.		434	P-51	L2-H	44-14740
18-4-45	1530	14127	Malone, Jay C.	KIA	EAA	Ger.	AR	436	P-51		44-14601
20-4-45			Young, Robert C.	KILLED	TRN	Eng.		436	P-51		44-14571
4-5-45			Scordino, Anthony J.	KILLED	TRN	Eng.		436	P-51		44-11749
19-7-45			Thompson, Hilton O.	MIA	TRN	Eng.	CA	434	P-51	L2-I	44-11674

*Found in the mud flats off the Essex Coast of England 1998
UNK = Unknown cause
AUTO = Automobile accident
TOA = Takeoff accident
TRN = Training accident
EAA = Enemy anti-aircraft fire
MAC = Mid-air collision
MF = Mechanical failure
EAC = Enemy aircraft fire
1 A/C crashed rat racing at Raydon
2 A/C damaged by debris from exploding target
3 A/C struck a tree while strafing a truck
WEA = Weather conditions
OOG = Out of gas - ditched in water
FAC = Friendly aircraft fire
FAA = Friendly anti-aircraft fire
ABMC = American Battle Monuments Commission
ABMC cemetery/memorial
AR = Ardennes (Belg.)
CA = Cambridge (Eng.)
EP = Epinal (Fr.)
HC = Henri-Chapelle (Belg.)
LO = Lorraine (Fr.)
LU = Luxembourg (Lux.)
NE = Netherlands (Neth.)
NO = Normandy (Fr.)
RH = Rhone (Fr.)

APPENDIX 8

CREW CHIEFS

434th Fighter Squadron
Line Chief – Gowen, Jack E.

Flight	*Crew Chief*	*Asst.Crew Chief*	*Pilots*
A Flight	Flight Chief - Greenlee, Harold L.		Flight Ldr. - Duffié, C. A. P.
	Bargainnier, Obe H.		
	Hicks, Earl L.		
	Ingram, Dean J.		
	Lessard, Wilfred D.		Mathews, H. E.
	Pilcavage, Joseph J.	Daggett, A. A.	Duffié, C. A. P.
	Plassenthal, Victor R.	Marhefky, Regis P.	Herren, J. M.
	Robitz, Henry J.		Hendrix, G. D., Haynes, C. G.
	Skelly, David J.		Tucker, A. S. J.
B Flight	Flight Chief - Greene, Clifton M.		Flight Ldr. - Grossenbacher, Pavlock, Drake,
	Baker, Norval D.		Keller, F. J., Drake, W. M.
	Coakley, Stephen O.		Stotts, H. L.
	Davis, Wilmer D.		Murr, J. N.
	Frankovich, John J.		Golden, J. T.
	Johnson, Neuman L.		
	Perdue, Alfred M.	Coakley, Stephen O.	Gleason, G. W.
	Slaton, Loy C.	Larson, Alworth D.	Olson, T. C.
	Wendt, John E.	Trimble, Mondell G.	Hass, J. A., Lunstrum, R. M., Simpson, R. G.
C Flight	Flight Chief - Haas, William A.		Flight Ldr. - Jeffrey, A. F.
	Atteberry, John B.		Canella, K. E., Helding, A. G.
	Corder, Maxey O.		Stott, D. H.
	Drais, Elsworth Jr.		Jacobson, G. E.
	Flynn, Cullie D.		Tipps, J.T.
	Gaddis, Clifford E.	Wolf, Marvin	Woods, S. S., Kline, R. B.
	Hummel, Nevoy C.	Schust, Warren D.	Jeffrey, A. F.
	Kirby, Louis E.		Bowers, C. W.
D Flight	Flight Chief - Smart, James W.		Flight Ldr. - Turner, H. G.
	Dornbos, Neil		Bromschwig, R. I.
	Gilchrist, John E.	Purdy, Guy M.	Grenning, H. F., Born, D. L.
	O'Grady, Thomas J.	Dorsey, Lewis C.	Hollister, B. E., Pierce, D. J.
	Perkins, Carrol P.		Wallace, J. L., Daudistel, W. H.
	Schafer, Eugene H.	Atwell, Alfred H.	Turner, H. G., Neumann, W. A., Sears, E. E.
	Stanovich, Milan J.	Lepkoski, Peter P.	Hehn, W. H., Hurtig, E. L.
	Wold, Glen A.	Ayers, Carl O.	Olds, R.

435th Fighter Squadron*
Line Chief – Unknown

Flight	*Crew Chief*	*Asst.Crew Chief*	*Pilots*
Flight	Flight Chief - Ginn, Cornelius B.		Candelaria, R. G.
	Flight Chief - Hudson, Robert H.		
	Flight Chief - Lemons, Robert K.		Monsell, C. F.
	Flight Chief - McVaigh, Ralph V.		
	Bailly, Raymond G.		Doolittle, G. L.
	Crabtree, Howard C.		
	Deetjen, Johnny M.		

Druecke, Russell H.		Monsell, C. F., Pigg, R. N.
Fox, Harold J.		Pickering, W. H., Koerber J. H.
Fox, Robert T.		Sykes, G. K.
Grant, James L.		Glover, J. G.
Gunter, Curtis B.		Matthews, C. R.
Harman, Carlton N.		McCann, J. P., Horman, R. H.
Hewitt, Cleve G.		Friend, R. K.
Johnson, Allen M.		Gates, W. M., Ricker, J. E.
Kerekes, Frank S.		
Leachman, Harlan W.		Riddle, K. L., Zemke H.
Ledlie, William A.		Coursey, R. R.
Miller, George A.		
Mock, Wilbur J.		Sowerby, T. J.
Muller, Leslie A.		
Pederson, Leslie A.		Maier, W. F., Sims, E. H.
Potts, Victor E.	Alexis, John D.	Hooker, V. E., Knofczynski, J. J.
Pryzbyla, Anthony F.		Gates, W. M.
Ramsey, Woodrow W.		
Samples, William M.		Gossard, P. D., King D. E.
Schmelzer, Raymond A.		Detlefsen, H. W.
Singleton, Charles E.		Gunn, W. B.
Stamer, Edward H.		
Thompson, Alfred		Muller, W.
Wilson, Henry W.		

436th Fighter Squadron

Line Chief – Johnson, Harrison B.

Flight	***Crew Chief***	***Asst.Crew Chief***	***Pilots***
A Flight	Flight Chief - Pruett, Jack L.		Flight Ldr. - King, B. H.
	DeVito, Thomas P.	Menzione, John	Henry, R. E., Steph, W. B.
	Doyle, Walter J.		Shoneborn, P. J.
	Newton, Oren C.		Romano, P. J.
	Richardson, J.T.	Haynes, Thomas E.	Huycke, A. E., Hightower, H. G.,
	Sanborn, Everett A.	Winn, O.	Mosier, A. G. Jr., Thrall, R. P.
	Virgin, Harold E.	Akin, Edward L.	Galloway, T., Struby, J. Massey, A.
B Flight	Flight Chief - Venezia, Eugene V.		Flight Ldr. - Harrell, J. W.
	Blachly, Don M.		Duffié, C. A. P., Kleinman, R. B.
	Hoxie, David A.		
	Hoskins, Leonard A.		
	Lindbeck, Spencer W.		
	Pantoja, Nicholas Y.		
	Robere, Raymond A.		McLaurin, G. G.
	Standiford, James H.		Harrell,
	Steele, Stanley L.		Mulvany, G. M., Darling, C. H.
C Flight	Flight Chief - Lindbeck, Spencer W.		Flight Ldr. - Biscayart, J. D.
	Evjen, Gordon E. T.		Fillipow, E. J., Elmgren, C. B.
	Green, Herbert R.	Helms, J. Ralph	Nesselbush, L. K., Plunk, H. P.,
	Hansen, Vernon A.		
	LaVelle, Olin F.	Harper, Duncan M.	Greenwood T. M.
	O'Neneske, Robert S.		
	Shoemaker, Kenneth G.		Steph, W. B.
	Taydus, Stanley M.	Axt, Kenneth D.	Moore, C. J.
	Trombly, Harold F.		
	Watkins, Frank W.	Wyman, Robert E.	Hedenberg, J. W., Wilkins, J. K., Sherer, C. W.
D Flight	Flight Chief - Babb, Lloyd W.		Flight Ldr. - Johnson, C. O.
	Hofstra, Roger F.		Schuck, J. R.
	Holloway, Jessie M.		
	Kessler, William		
	Kortis, Louis	Dasta, Thomas J.	Hoversten, H. E., Early, J. H. III
	Marlar, Clarence O.		Thompson, T. H.
	McCloskey, Robert E.		Witzel, G. H.
	Paulson, Kenneth W.		Wolski, V. C., Hansen, K. J.
	Walker, Martin E.		Grasshoff, H. J.

*The determination of which crew chief served with what flight is unknown at this time for the 435th FS.

434th FS P-38, serial number 43-28714, Lucky Lady flown by Lieutenant Arnold G. Helding. The aircraft is shown as it would have appeared immediately following the commencement of D-Day, marked with invasion stripes on upper and lower wing surfaces as well as around both tail booms.

435th FS P-38, serial number 43-28476, Swanee Jr. flown by Captain William M. Gates. The aircraft is shown marked with invasion stripes only on the lower wing surfaces and lower tail booms, as it would have appeared during mid-summer 1944.

436th FS P-38, serial number 43-28641, Muz's Mighty Molecule flown by Lieutenant Richard S. Spencer, Jr. The aircraft is shown marked with invasion stripes only on the lower wing surfaces and lower tail booms, as it would have appeared during mid-summer 1944.

HQ/435th FS P-51, serial number 44-14327, flown by Colonel Kyle L. Riddle. The only artwork on the A/C was a black rectangle stenciled with the pilot's and the crew chief's (Technical Sergeant Harlan W. Leachman) names. Note the camera port aft of the radiator shutter.

434th FS P-51, serial number 44-14651, Pin Up Girl as flown by Lieutenant John C. Donnell, Jr. The aircraft also bore the name Muriel of Troy on right side of its nose. That name was put there by squadron painter Staff Sergeant Frederick C. Hayner. He was from Troy, New York as was his wife, Muriel. The kills registered below the aircraft's canopy are from her previous pilot, Lieutenant Berkley E. Hollister who also had named her.

434th FS P-51, serial number 44-14740, Hot Toddy flown by Lieutenant George W. Gleason. Named for his wife Todd, the aircraft soldiered with the 479th FG from its conversion to Mustangs until almost war's end, when it was lost 16 April 1945.

434th FS P-51, serial number 44-14212, Lelah May flown by Lieutenant Thomas C. Olson. Named for Lt. Olson's mother, the aircraft also bore the name The Slugger on the right side of its nose. The victory markings represent the ten and a half (one air and nine and a half ground) Lt. Olson was credited with. The Slugger went down for the count 3 January 1945 when she was bellied in near Ipswich, England after her engine failed.

434th FS P-51, serial number 44-63175, The Impatient Virgin flown by Lieutenant William H. Daudistel. Probably the most decorated aircraft of the group in terms of artwork, L2-Z carried a lot of Staff Sergeant Frederick C. Hayner's paint on her. In addition to The Impatient Virgin name on her left side nose, she bore a block giving the name of the pilot, crew chief (Staff Sergeant Carrol P. Perkins) and armorer (Corporal Herbert Taylor). The canopy rail was lettered with The Impatient Virgin name again and the name Mickey's Mustang was located on the right side of her nose. Staff Sergeant Perkins was responsible for all of the naming.

435th FS P-51, serial number 44-14378, "Sweet El" flown by Lieutenant Ray K. Friend. The black rectangle below the windshield was stenciled with the pilot's name as well as that of the crew chief Technical Sergeant Cleve G. Hewitt and armorer Corporal John D. McDuffie.

435th FS P-51, serial number 44-14354, V for 'Val' flown by Lieutenant Philip D. Gossard.

435th FS P-51, serial number 44-14392, Victory Queen as flown by Lieutenant Norman R. Benoit.

435th FS P-51, serial number 44-62249, Lady Jean flown by Lieutenant Robert H. Horman. Note that the side air intake for the Merlin engine's carburetor has been covered over.

436th FG P-51, serial number 44-14574, Little Zippie as flown by Lieutenant Hans J. Grasshoff.

436th FS P-51, serial number 44-72431, Poontang II as illustrated, is shown as it existed very shortly after the war's end. This aircraft was representative of Poontang, an earlier P-51 flown by Lieutenant Ernest J. Hopcroft.

436th FS P-51, serial number 44-63192, My Best Bett as flown by Lieutenant Arlett G. Mosier, Jr.

436th FS P-51, serial number 44-14645, Give 'em Hell for H.L. Jr. flown by Captain Claire A.P. Duffié. The H. L. stood for Helen Louise. One of several P-51's named by Captain Duffié, 9B-A had in addition to her name, a black painted block which listed the pilot's name as C.A.P. Duffié, the crew chief as T/Sgt. Blachly (Don M. Blachly) and the armorer as Sgt. Hansen (Boyd A. Hanson).

BIBLIOGRAPHY

Archer, Robert D., *USAAF Aircraft Markings and Camouflage 1941 – 1947*. Atglen, PA: Schiffer Publishing Ltd., 1997.

Barbas, Bernd, *Aircraft of the Luftwaffe Fighter Aces II*. Atglen, PA: Schiffer Publishing Ltd., 1995.

Bodie, Warren M., *The Lockheed P-38 Lightning*. Hiawassee, GA: Widewing Publications, 1991.

Butcher, Geoffrey, *Next To A Letter From Home*. Edinburgh EH1 3UG: Mainstream Publishing Company (Edinburgh), Ltd., 1986.

Butler, Calvin J., *The Struggle*. Unpublished manuscript, no date given.

Caldwell, Donald, *The JG 26 War Diary*. London, England: Grub Street, 1998.

Davis, Richard G. *Carl A. Spaatz and the Air War in Europe*. Washington, DC: Smithsonian Institution Press, no date given.

Delve, Ken, *D-Day The Air Battle*. London, England: Arms & Armour Press division of the Cassell Group, 1994.

Dillon, Carrol F., *A Domain of Heroes*. Sarasota, FL: Palm Island Press, 1995.

Doolittle, General James H. "Jimmy" with Carroll V. Glines, *I Could Never Be So Lucky Again*. Atglen, PA: Schiffer Publishing Ltd., 1995.

Drake, Walter M., *Personal Experiences from the 479th FG, 434th Fighter Squadron*. Unpublished manuscript, no date given.

Foreman, John and S.E. Harvey, *The Messerschmitt Me 262 Combat Diary*. Rev. ed. Walton-on-Thames, England: Air Research Publications, 1995.

Foreman, John, *Over the Beaches*. Walton-on-Thames, England: Air Research Publications, 1994.

Freeman, Roger A. with David Osborne, *The B-17 Flying Fortress Story*. London, England: Arms & Armour Press division of the Cassell Group, 1998.

Freeman, Roger A., *Airfields of the Eighth Then and Now*, 6th ed. London, England: Battle of Britain Prints International Ltd., 1992.

Freeman, Roger A., *The American Airman in Europe*. Osceola, WI: Motorbooks International, Publishers and Wholesalers Inc., 1991.

Freeman, Roger A., *The Mighty Eighth War Manual*. Osceola, WI: Motorbooks International, Publishers and Wholesalers Inc., 1993.

Freeman, Roger A., *The Mighty Eighth Warpaint & Heraldry*. London, England: Arms & Armour Press, 1997.

Freeman, Roger A., *The Mighty Eighth*. Osceola, WI: Motorbooks International, Publishers and Wholesalers Inc., 1991.

Freeman, Roger A., *The Ninth Air Force in Colour*. London, England: Arms & Armour Press, 1995.

Freeman, Roger A., with Alan Crouchman and Vic Maslen. *The Mighty Eighth War Diary*. Osceola, WI: Motorbooks International, Publishers and Wholesalers Inc., 1993.

Freeman, Roger A., *Zemke's Wolf Pack*. New York, NY: ORION division of Crown Publishers, 1988.

Frolking, James E., *Down in the Dutch Islands*. Unpublished manuscript, 1999.

Green, Michael and Gladys Green, *Patton Operation Cobra and Beyond*. Osceola, WI: Motorbooks International, Publishers and Wholesalers Inc., 1998.

Green, William, *Famous Fighters of the Second World War*. New York, NY: Hanover House, 1958-1960. 4 vols.

Gurney, Gene, *Five Down and Glory*. Ed. by Mark P. Friedlander, Jr. New York, NY: Ballantine Books, Inc., 1958.

Hammel, Eric, *Air War Europa Chronology*. Pacifica, CA: Pacifica Press, 1994.

Hedenberg, John W., *Reminiscences: 479th Fighter Group, Wattisham, 1944*. Unpublished manuscript, 1983 & 1996.

Hellström, Leif, *J26 Mustang*. Stockholm, Sweden: Gummerus Printing, 1989.

Langewiesche, Wolfgang, *Stick and Rudder*. New York, NY: Whittlesey House division of the McGraw-Hill Book Company, Inc., 1944.

Le Strange, Richard and James R. Brown, *Century Bombers The story of the Bloody Hundredth*. Diss, England: The 100th Bomb Group Memorial Museum, 1989.

MacDonald, Charles B., *A Time for Trumpets*. New York, NY: William Morrow and Company, Inc., 1985.

McLaren, David R., *Beware the Thunderbolt!* Atglen, PA: Schiffer Publishing Ltd., 1994.

Mondey, David, *The Concise Guide to American Aircraft of World War II*. Edison, NJ: Chartwell Books, Inc., division of Book Sales, Inc., 1994.

Morgan, Janalee J., *Life and Times in the 434th*. Unpublished manuscript by daughter-in-law of Wm. M. Morgan, 1998.

Müller, Werner, *German FLAK in World War II*, translated Ed Force. Atglen, PA: Schiffer Publishing Ltd., 1998.

No Author listed, *479th Fighter Group*. Publisher unknown, 1946.

No Author listed, *Pilot's Information File 1944*. Atglen, PA: Schiffer Publishing Ltd., 1995.

No Author listed, *The Times Atlas of the World*. 7th ed. New York, NY: Times Books division of Random House, Inc., 1988.

Noah, Joe and Samuel L. Sox, Jr., *George Preddy Top Mustang Ace*. Osceola, WI: Motorbooks International, Publishers and Wholesalers Inc., 1991.

Olynyk, Frank, *Stars & Bars, A tribute to the American Fighter Ace 1920-1973*. London, England: Grub Street, 1995.

Parker, Danny S., *To Win the Winter Sky, The Air War Over the Ardennes, 1944-1945*. Conshohocken, PA: Combined Publishing, 1994.

Parton, James, *"Air Force Spoken Here" General Ira Eaker and the Command of the Air*. Bethesda, MD: Adler & Adler, Publishers, Inc., 1986.

Persico, Joseph E., *Roosevelt's Secret War*. New York, NY: Random House, Inc., 2001.

Prien, Jochen, *Jagdgeschwader 53, A History of the "Pik As" Geschwader, January 1944 - May 1945*. Atglen, PA: Schiffer Publishing Ltd., 1998.

Schaefer, Vincent J. and John A. Day, *A Field Guide to the Atmosphere*. New York, NY: Peterson Field Guide division of the Houghton Mifflin Company, 1981.

Snelling, Steve, *Over Here, The Americans in Norfolk during World War Two*. Derby, England: The Breedon Books Publishing Company Limited, 1996.

Speer, Frank E., *The Debden Warbirds, The 4th Fighter Group in World War II*. Atglen, PA: Schiffer Publishing Ltd., 1999.

Thole, Lou, *Forgotten Fields of America*. Missoula, MT: Pictorial Histories Publishing Co., Inc., 1996 and 1999. 2 vols.

Toliver, Raymond F., *The Interrogator*. Atglen, PA: Schiffer Publishing Ltd., 1997.

Van Sickle, Neil D., BG, USAF, editor. *Modern Airmanship*. Princeton, NJ: D. Van Nostrand Company, Inc., 1959.

Varnedoe, W.W., editor, *History of the 385th Bomb Group (H)*. St. Petersburg, FL: Southern Heritage Press, 1995.

White, Graham, *Allied Aircraft Piston Engines of World War II*. Warrendale, PA: Society of Automotive Engineers, Inc., 1995.

Whiting, Charles, *Massacre at Malmédy*. London, England: Transworld Publishers Ltd., 1972.

Wood, Tony and Bill Gunston, *Hitler's Luftwaffe*. New York, NY: Crescent Books division of Crown Publishers, Inc., 1979.

Zijlstra Gerrit, *Diary of an Air War*. Austin, TX: Eakin Press, 1994.

INDEX

Akin, Edward L., 290, 381
Alexis, John D., 384
Anastos, Themis N., 20, 79, 424
Anderson, William C., 286, 330, 417, 431, 444
Archibald, John M., 397
Atteberry, John B., 274, 289
Atwater, John S., 361
Auton, Jesse, 116, 263, 421
Axt, Kenneth D., 97
Ayers, Carl O., 286

Baird, Robert J., 277, 314, 373, 409
Bardotz, Stephen J., 300
Barsky, William M., 218, 369, 389, 390, 391, 413
Beatty, Frank G., Jr., 412
Benoit, Norman R., 122, 123, 209, 210, 218, 250, 252, 258, 276, 277, 278, 281, 300, 310, 314, 315
Berryman, Henry S., 420
Biernet, Lucien, 250
Biscayart, Jules D., 23, 82, 84, 98, 179, 195, 205, 206, 241, 242
Blachly, Don M., 447
Bloom, Alfred Jr., 287
Born, David L., 47, 53, 217, 242, 269, 279, 317, 318, 319, 324, 327, 375, 408, 410, 432, 440, 442, 443, 445, 451
Bottenus, William R., Jr., 305, 342
Bouchier, James E., 279, 280, 407
Bowers, Clifford W., 47, 265, 269, 270, 275, 287, 288, 289, 338, 374, 382, 400, 413, 414, 434, 438, 443, 444, 445, 451
Bradford, Burton, 449
Bragman, Melvin, 163
Brickson, Kermit A., 339
Broadstone Chester W., 150, 248, 304
Bromschwig, Robert I., 248, 275, 288, 289, 322, 343, 373, 385, 437, 439, 444, 451
Brooks, W. H., 14
Brown, Philip A., 266, 273, 278, 328, 355, 400, 405, 406
Brown, Thomas R., 16, 19, 70, 375
Busch, Donald P., 312
Butler, Calvin J., 64, 335, 426
Butler, Nelson W., 168, 185, 189, 270, 308
Butler, Theodore R., Jr., 347

Campbell, Edwin R., 124
Candelaria, Richard G., 256, 344, 347, 388, 389, 390, 400, 426, 427
Canella, Keith E., 16, 30, 31, 74
Cano, Larry J., 247, 257, 281, 297, 411
Capers, Frank W., Jr., 342
Carter, Raymond S., 122, 123, 168
Chapin, John D., 303
Chevallier, Joane, 227
Chism, Joseph C., 285
Clark, Angus W., 181, 227
Clark, Jack M., 24, 392, 393
Clarke, William D., 261
Claybaugh, Charles C., 225, 451
Cleous, Orie W., 172
Clodfelter, John P., 106, 163, 444
Coakley, Stephen O., 61, 348
Cooper, Theodore E., 308
Corder, Maxey O., 167, 286
Cornelius, Frank J., 142
Coursey, Richard R., 185
Courtney, John J., Jr., 16, 19, 127
Creighton, Richard D., 218, 219, 221, 274, 310, 312, 313, 323, 324, 328, 400, 403, 431
Culbertson, William S., 60, 73, 205

Darling, Charles H., 235, 236, 251, 261, 330, 364, 397, 402, 405, 409
Dasta, Thomas J., 85
Daudistel, William H., 266, 267, 298, 317, 322, 358, 396, 422, 436, 451
Denny, Jack S., 90
Derby, Stanley E., 245, 272, 283
Detlefsen, Heinz W., 236, 237
Dettenmayer,George R., 411
Dewey, Ralph E., 143
Diaz, Joe, 268
Dieujenio, James P., 285
Dillard, Hinton J., 442
Dillon, James B., 82, 375
DiPaola, Albert R., 251, 278, 331, 332, 427
Donnell, John C., Jr., 232, 241, 306, 310, 324, 343
Doolittle, Gordon L., 234, 256, 302, 310, 313
Dorsey, Lewis C., 92
Doyle, Walter J., 290
Drais, Elsworth Jr., 359
Drake, Walter M., 121, 148, 152, 153, 185, 189, 194, 221, 222, 225, 246
Duffié, Claire A. P., 16, 120, 152, 153, 162, 166, 167, 168, 182, 185, 193 ,194, 287, 295, 298, 331, 405, 407, 409, 411, 421, 421, 423, 447
Dunn, Donald A., 117, 195, 196, 197, 224, 226
Dusard, Leo F., 14
Dussling, Bernard P., 265
Dvorak, John L., 138
Dyess, William E., 15

Early, John H. III, 272, 397
Ellis, Paul E., 163
Elmgren, Charles B., 286, 405, 409, 423
Ernst, Carl V., 267, 268, 405, 415
Ervin, Ivan A., 112, 178
Eskell, Barrett B., 252, 427
Evanenko, Alexander, 109
Evjen, Gordon E.T., 242

Fairchild, Rayne B., 64, 89, 426
Falco, Charles, 180
Falkner, George E., 408, 409
Ferguson, William M., 342
Fillipow, Edwin J., 117, 165, 215, 226, 242
Fleming, James E., Jr., 103, 131
Flynn, Cullie D., 93, 219
Ford, Everett P., 89, 117, 172
Foster John D., 249
Fox, Harold J., 124, 437
Friend, Ray K., 147, 179, 183, 185, 190, 218, 271, 278, 305, 314
Frolking, James E., 8, 85, 130, 144, 165, 195, 197, 210, 211
Frost, Russell B., 405, 407

Galloway, Thomas T., 19, 20, 24, 62, 94, 109
Gates, William M., 109, 133, 159, 218, 255, 256, 272
Gavrys, Thomas A., 182
Gerding, Earle, 449
Gilchrist, John E., 82, 375, 440
Gleason, George W., 60, 61, 100, 131, 139, 141, 147, 185, 186, 187, 193, 194, 218, 220, 263, 273, 310, 337, 338, 382
Glenn, John G., 23, 117, 211, 225
Glover, John G., 64, 109, 183
Golden, John T., 317, 320, 328, 400, 404, 406
Gorian, Martin G., 24, 185, 218
Gossard, Philip D., 106, 249, 257
Gowan, Jack E., 41, 133, 249, 432, 447
Granger, Jesse V., 169, 195
Granville, Chester W., 21, 178
Grasshoff, Hans J., 83, 85, 110, 128, 165, 185, 191, 244, 245, 268, 269, 272
Grdenich, Frank, 64, 69
Green, Herbert R., 206
Green, Robert D., 89
Greene, Clifton M., 133, 420, 431, 432
Greenlee, Harold L., 41, 133, 249, 420, 432
Greenwood, Travis M., 23, 169, 170, 173, 225, 226
Grenning, Harold F., 25, 82, 105, 120, 135, 149, 150, 185, 215, 217, 247
Gross, Burton S., 83
Grossenbacher, Jack G., 16, 90, 108
Guernsey, Louis D., 300, 419
Gunn, William B., 183

Haas, Jene A., 93
Haas, William A., 19, 286
Hagerman, Harold J., 446
Hamilton, James E., 204
Hansen, John W., 127, 140, 185, 188, 189, 250
Hansen, Kenneth J., 332, 333, 398, 409, 411, 446
Harman, Carlton N., 374, 436
Harper, Duncan M., 420
Harper, Flamm D., 32, 59, 85, 100
Harrell, John W., Jr., 245, 247, 276, 300, 301
Harris, Elbert N., 263, 347
Hart, Frederick L., 242, 257, 328
Hartman, Elmer, 121
Hartnett, Vincent C., 165
Hayner, Frederick C., 43, 56, 57, 77, 79, 217, 250, 306, 324, 325, 428
Haynes, Clarence G., 202, 279, 280, 354, 369, 379, 380, 406, 430, 431
Heathman, Charles E., 347, 370, 389, 390, 391
Hedenberg, John W., 32, 33, 35, 55, 56, 59, 61, 70, 80, 82, 84, 85, 104, 130, 131, 134, 142, 144, 150, 169, 170, 173, 174, 176, 202, 207, 208, 218
Hehn, William H., 20, 128, 129, 247
Helding, Arnold G., 77, 78247, 274, 288, 289
Helms, J. Ralph , 444
Hendrickson, Lauri, A., 397, 399, 421, 440
Hendrickson, Robert H., 157, 164, 167
Hendrix, George D., 25, 59, 60, 129, 133, 134, 140, 182, 197, 207
Henry, Price E., 83, 220
Henry, Raymond E., 331, 377, 405
Hernandez, John M., 285
Herren, James M., Jr., 16, 17, 24, 122, 147, 162, 185 186, 187, 193, 209, 221, 223, 224
Heuman, Leslie L., 425
Hewitt, Cleve G., 305
Hicks, Earl L., 16, 20, 249, 347
Hightower, Howard G., 57, 62, 119, 134, 195, 197
Hill, Glen W., 262, 376
Hoffman, Clark R., 271, 339, 409, 411
Hofstra, Roger F., 268
Hollingsworth, James M., 133, 157, 164, 166, 167, 260, 278, 279, 280, 426
Hollis, Dewey H., 263
Hollister, Berkley E., 20, 34, 73, 75, 76, 77, 78, 92, 136, 152, 154, 164, 240, 241, 242, 249, 255, 256, 259, 287, 306, 324
Holmes, Douglas I., 215, 221, 224
Holtman, William R., 419
Hooker, Verne E., 70, 146, 168, 356, 383, 384, 388, 390, 397, 401, 405, 407, 409, 411, 413, 414
Hopcroft, Ernest J., 331, 341, 398, 405, 409, 410, 423, 448
Horman, Robert H., 262, 315, 326, 349, 436
Horne, Leland K., 70
Horton, Donald D., 15, 16, 424
Hoversten, Herman C., 45, 83, 85
Howard, William N., 157
Hugill, William, 205, 428
Hummel, Nevoy C., 254, 306
Hurtig, Edward L., 218, 219, 240, 278, 279
Huval, Ossie J., 265, 317, 329, 338, 400, 403, 426
Huycke, Andre E., 144, 164, 173, 220, 241, 268, 269
Hymans, Robert B., 262

Ilsley, Dwight F., 74

Jacobson, Gail E., 218, 221, 224, 253, 254, 265, 275, 321, 329, 359, 360, 386, 387, 404, 413, 414, 440
Jarrell, Carl B., 315, 427
Jeffrey, Arthur F., 92, 113, 140, 157, 171, 209, 247, 253, 254, 264, 272, 282, 317
Jenkins, Harold M., 221, 224, 276, 278, 322, 403, 434
Johnson, Clarence O., 16, 17, 57, 62, 73
Jordan, Herbert R., 164, 166, 262, 297, 310, 312, 313, 344, 345, 383
Joseph, George, 257, 258, 291

Kaufman, Stanley, 163
Keefe, Lawrence A., 290
Keller, Frank J., 34, 75, 128, 129, 426
Kellett, Stanley, 26, 40, 198, 199, 241, 294, 304, 436
Kelly, Carl E., 242
Kemper, Neil W., 109
King, David E., 218, 258, 310, 313, 389, 390
King, Raymond E., 295, 296
Kirby, Louis E., 270, 419
Kleinman, Bernard R., 272, 398, 438
Kline, Robert B., 193, 194, 255, 328, 329, 400, 403
Knofczynski, Joseph J., 245
Koerber, James H., 218, 293, 413, 437
Kortis, Louis, 85
Krauss, Harold F., Jr., 406, 407
Kreger, Charles S., 252, 261, 409, 410, 444
Kronberg, Lester G., 180, 442
Kuentzel, Ward A., 69

Landreth, Gerald R., 22, 25
Lanning, Clayton J., 377
Larson, Alworth D., 158
LaVelle, Olin F., 420
Leachman, Harlan W., 233
Lemke, Jack E., 16, 80
Lessard, Wilfred D., 420, 442
Lewin, Edwin C., 165, 241, 266, 269
Lewis Earle L., 249
Lind, Harder J., 444
Linduska, Frank P., 24
Little, Harry E., 133, 134, 185, 189
Long, Sylvester F., 398
Looney, George H., 386, 413
Lowell, John H., 31, 32
Lulay, Ralph M., 433
Lundgren, Raymond, 449
Lundstrom, Ernest S., 224
Lunstrum, Richard M., 63, 193, 194, 224, 349, 395

Lutz, Leroy, 74, 76, 77, 78, 79

Maier, William F., 218
Maley, Ronald L., 150, 172, 185, 239, 252, 426
Malone, Jay C., 286, 329, 398, 401, 405, 412, 413, 415
Manning, Phillip W., 148, 150
Manwell, James, 442
Marhefky, Regis P., 377
Marlar, Clarence O., 298, 342, 376
Marlowe, Wendell H., 234, 235, 261, 278, 279
Martinez, Raymond A., 348, 419
Massey, Alton A., 246, 380, 381
Massimino, Bart, 127
Mastin, Donald W., 408
Mathews, Harold E., 77, 78, 83, 129, 164, 173, 255, 266, 267, 269
Matthews, Cecil R., 409, 411
McArthur, Marden L., 100, 111
McCann, John P., 185
McChrystal, Richard G., 69, 185, 186, 254, 317, 323
McClure, Donald D., 22, 70
McCoy, Kenneth H., 444
McCredie, James G., 285
McDuffie, John D., 305
McElhinney, William T., 15, 162
McKay, William B., 112
McLaurin, Grover G., Jr., 405
Mead, Frederick M., 104, 173, 354, 415
Means, Billy C., 190, 243, 257, 262, 313, 347
Mickey, Melvin S., 124, 169, 170
Miller, Glenn, 110
Monaco, Elidio E., 413, 414
Monahan, John D., 16, 24
Monsell, Charles F., Jr., 147, 159, 185, 190, 218
Moon, Allen J., 25, 26, 27, 62, 70, 88, 89, 427
Moore, Carl W., 123, 124
Moore, Clifford J., Jr., 15, 97, 124, 165, 286, 331, 332
Morgan, William M., 27, 41, 133, 239, 420, 432
Morganstern, Albert H., 440
Morris, Jesse F., 371
Morris, Louis E., 182
Morrow, John W., 140, 167, 168, 185, 187, 246, 282, 305, 354
Moser, Fred A., Jr., 119, 427
Mosier, Arlett G., Jr., 128, 138, 173, 225, 226, 286, 345, 395, 420
Moyer, George W., 248
Muller, Wilbert, 168, 240
Mulvany, Gerold M., 94, 165, 169, 175, 185, 191, 197, 215, 269, 270
Munson, Robert L., 386, 387, 404
Murphy, Calvin J., Jr., 140, 154, 167, 171
Murr, John N., 164, 185, 189, 239, 240, 266, 274, 278
Myers, Albert M., 525
Myers, Thomas E., 174, 207, 226, 241, 257, 258, 268

Nagel, Jerome K., 291, 386, 387, 388, 397, 413, 434, 440
Neely, Tom D., 128, 129, 164, 259, 266, 267, 426
Nesslebush, Louis K., 70, 427
Neumann, Walter A., 152, 154, 171, 188, 253
Niekamp, Raymond, 48, 180, 442, 450
Nolan, Harper H., 223

Ochoa, Adolfo, 355, 420
O'Grady, Thomas J., 92, 240, 249, 375
Ogron, Zeymour, 165, 175, 176
Ohligschlager, James K., 64, 68
O'Holleran, Thomas J., 119, 138, 427
Olds, Robin, 17, 21, 43, 54, 75, 91, 99, 100, 119, 138, 147, 148, 152, 155, 182, 207, 241, 263, 310, 314, 317, 320, 322, 328, 358, 359, 361, 365, 377, 384, 386, 397, 398, 399, 404, 406, 423, 427, 429, 431, 432, 440
Olson, Thomas C., 147, 148, 157, 158, 164, 167, 188, 234, 245
O'Malley, Thomas E., 97, 374
Orrick, Thomas H., 91, 166
Ortega, Philip, 40

Pagano, Daniel F., 248
Palmer, Coburn T., 451
Palson, Richard C., Jr, 398, 405, 409, 410
Pasternack, Charles, 40, 442
Pastor, Herbert, 252
Paulson, Kenneth W., 354
Pavlock, Quentin S., 74, 92, 111, 140, 141, 154, 185, 187, 190, 202
Peacock, Cecil M., 337, 408
Pence, H. A., 250
Perdue, Alfred M., 61
Perkins, Carrol P., 422
Peterson, Carl L., 22, 91
Petterson, Lewis P., 244
Pfund, Robert F., 202
Philbrick, Charles H. II, 30, 398, 405, 435
Pickering, William H., 188, 190, 191, 218, 422
Piepenburg, Ralph N., 377
Pierce, Donald J., 317, 318, 328, 375, 397, 399, 404, 408, 409, 431
Pigg, Robert N., 9, 147, 178, 261, 262
Pillsbury, Evan S. II, 30
Plassenthal, Victor R. , 249, 265, 445
Plazibat, John A., 404, 406
Plemens, Herbert, 24, 424
Plunk, Henry P., 110, 175, 205, 206
Pope, Francis J., 14, 15
Potts, Victor E., 384
Prevosti, Mario V., 365, 421
Proctor, Clayton F., 92
Pruyne, Charles K., 127, 442, 450
Purdy, Guy M., 82, 375

Rawley, Walter N., Jr., 405
Red, Douglas L., 251, 278, 286
Richards, Thomas W., 374
Richardson, J.T., 106
Riddle, Kyle L., 15, 25, 30, 33, 57, 65, 116, 130, 131, 205, 224, 233, 243, 271, 288, 298, 353, 405, 417, 421, 423, 425, 432
Robertson, Ray L., 402
Robitz, Henry J., 60, 133, 377
Rock, Norbert W., 281, 309
Rodgers, William H., 111, 181, 182, 192
Rogers, John R., 310, 314
Romano, Pasquale J., 409
Rosness, Joseph H., 169
Rossel, Roy M., 385, 397, 398, 446
Rossman, George P., 292
Rourke, William B., Jr., 397, 401
Routh, Sylvan R., 390, 391, 409, 411
Rudat, Wallace A., 394, 421
Ryan, Richard F., 294

Salter, George M., Jr., 257, 281, 409, 411
Salze, Floyd W., 342, 370, 371, 389, 390, 409, 411
Samples, William M., 106, 249
Sanborn, Everett A., 138
Sands, Thurman E., 291, 292
Schiess, Francis C., 299, 407, 433
Schlaffman, Herbert J., 19
Schneider, Joseph F., 15, 16, 20, 248, 304
Schoen, Charles F., Jr., 341
Schuck, John R., 268, 286
Scordino, Anthony J., 331, 423
Sears, Eugene E., 218, 219, 276, 306, 328, 376
Shane, Presson, S., 398, 405, 409, 423, 428
Shaw, William E., 41, 419
Sherer, Carl W., 331, 332, 378, 379
Shewfelt, Ray L., 306
Shoemaker, Kenneth G., 402
Shonborn, Paul J., 403
Shriner, Frederick F., 310, 411
Shurmistras, Joseph J., 14, 16
Silver, Frank R., 162
Simpson, Richard G., 108, 115, 134, 171, 347, 358, 400
Sims, Edward H., 300, 301, 309, 328, 409, 411, 413, 446
Sipek, John J., 250, 444
Skelly, David J., 420

Slaton, Loy C., 158
Smart, James W., 19, 21, 105, 217, 286, 432, 447
Smigal, Alfred J., 331, 405, 409
Smith, Howard C., 147, 182, 247
Smith, Lewis C., 353
Smith, Thomas V., 236, 237, 335
Sowerby, Theo J., 146, 180, 243, 277, 278, 300, 301, 397, 400, 401, 409, 411
Speirs, Thomas, 443
Spencer, Richard S., Jr., 144, 199, 226, 241, 251, 277
Spillane, James E., Jr., 58, 61
Splittstoesser, Elmer A., 413
Sprague, Carroll C., 228, 449
Standiford, James H., 296
Stanovich, Milan J., 128, 201, 202, 247, 399
Starr, John P., Jr., 450
Steele, Marion W., 236
Steele, Stanley L., 124, 191, 402
Stenten, William F., 162
Steph, Walter B., 357, 398, 402, 405
Stoltz, Vincent B., 442
Stoops, Edward F., Jr., 16, 93, 225
Stott, Donald H., 406, 407
Stotts, Harold L., 347, 348, 404, 405, 417, 418, 433
Straub, George, 57, 62, 195, 197, 202
Struby, Joseph R., 158, 241, 268, 269, 290
Sullivan, John A., 109, 169, 170, 258
Surges, Clarence M., 17, 27, 181, 227
Susong, Denver T., 249
Sykes, George K., 16, 123, 124, 147, 179

Taydus, Stanley M., 97
Taylor, Frank M., 359, 360, 382, 400, 406, 407
Taylor, Herbert, 419, 422
Teeter, Robert R., 82, 85, 112
Thompson, Hilton O., 323, 355, 384, 385, 418, 433, 446
Thompson, Thomas H., 298, 342, 376, 405
Thorn, Donald W., 194, 278, 409, 411
Thrall, Richard P., 292, 428
Tinker, Edward A., 113, 359
Tipps, John T., 69, 79, 81, 93, 131, 164, 218, 219
Tommie, Dalton F., 318, 320, 375, 404, 406, 442
Trabucco, Thomas F., 344, 345
Trimble, Mondell G., 136
Tucker, Albert S. J., Jr., 74, 77, 426, 433
Turner, Hiram G., Jr., 15, 16, 82, 96, 140, 141
Tyman, Robert C., 22

Valente, Biagio, 440, 442
Valuzzi, Arthur J., 408, 410
Van Waes, Donald A., 445
Vassuer, Peter C., 257, 258, 331, 332
Venezia, Eugene V., 192
Virgin, Harold E., 381

Wadsworth, Donald, 449
Walker, William R., 15, 31
Wallace, James L., 20, 140, 141, 142
Ward, Earl D., 124
Warth, Aloysius G., 51, 303
Waters, Clarence L., 360, 361, 373, 429
Watkins, Frank W., 33, 208
Wayne, Stanley E., 419
Wendt, Eugene H., 193, 194, 304, 310, 311, 317, 318, 338, 350, 369, 370, 441
Wendt, John E., 136, 224, 347
Werner, Edward R., 225
West, Lewis J., 303, 443
White, Marshall F., 342
Wiley, Roy A., Jr., 24, 26
Wilkins, John K., Jr., 267, 305
Willhite, Alvin R., 27, 74, 133, 306, 420, 430, 432
Williams, Bailey A., 64, 86, 92, 93, 141, 164, 258, 259
Williams, George F., 389
Winn, Ora, 138
Withrow, Carl F., 374
Witzel, George H., 272, 283, 329, 398, 405, 409
Wold, Glen A., 54, 55, 154, 399
Wolski, Victor C., 57, 62, 165, 195, 196, 210, 211, 212, 225
Woods, Sidney S., 30, 117, 122, 162, 163, 164, 173, 234, 335
Wyman, Robert E.,

Young, Robert C., 417

Zellman, Fred, 268, 296, 329, 398
Zemke, Hubert, 132, 146, 147, 150, 173, 176, 182, 185, 190, 201, 209, 219, 220, 221, 226, 315, 354, 426
Zuchowski, Stephen H., 133, 159, 225

Also from the Publisher

Beware the Thunderbolt!
The 56th Fighter Group in World War II
David R. McLaren/Foreword by Hub Zemke

The story of the 56th Fighter Group in a chronological narrative of their combat missions. Composed of heroic pilots that aggressively took the air war into the enemy heartland in 1943, the "Wolfpack's" P-47 Thunderbolt contrails crossed high in the upper stratosphere as they escorted heavy bomber missions, or fell upon the enemy on the ground as their pilots destroyed over 1000 Luftwaffe aircraft. Also coupled with their post-war history of innovative Mustang missions to Alaska, and the first trans-Atlantic jet fighter missions in the P-80 Shooting Star.
Size: 81/2"x11" • over 250 color and b/w photographs • 208 pp.
ISBN: 0-88740-660-2 • hard cover • $39.95

The 79th Fighter Group Over Tunisia, Sicily, and Italy in World War II
Don Woerpel

The men of the 79th Fighter Group on the "forgotten" Mediterranean front in WWII – who they were, what they did, and also shows how the war on the ground influenced their war in the air. The 79th spent much of its tour with the RAF's Desert Air Force in Tunisia, Sicily, and the "other side" of Italy – providing readers with an inside look at battles generally not well known to the American public – and also took part in the battle for Rome and the invasion of southern France.
Size: 81/2"x11" • 200+ b/w photographs, color profiles • 264 pp.
ISBN: 0-7643-1322-3 • hard cover • $45.00

Kearby's Thunderbolts
The 348th Fighter Group in World War II
John C. Stanaway

The 348th Fighter Group was the most successful P-47 Thunderbolt unit in the Pacific. Medal of Honor recipient Colonel Neel Kearby took an aircraft that was generally despised in the southwest Pacific and made it into the terror of the skies over such formidable targets as Wewak on New Guinea, and Cape Gloucester on New Britain. Ending the war in P-51 Mustangs, the 348th ranged over the Japanese homeland – completing their impressive record and honor, and the drive begun by the illustrious Kearby.
Size: 81/2"x11" • 350+ b/w photographs, 12 color profiles • 224 pp.
ISBN: 0-7643-0248-5 • hard cover • $45.00

The 350th Fighter Group in the Mediterranean Campaign
2 November 1942 to 2 May 1945

This facsimile reprint of the actual 350th Fighter Group war book appears here in a new quality edition. The 350th Fighter Group flew against the Luftwaffe during the Moroccan, Tunisian, Sicilian, and Italian campaigns in P-39s and P-47s.
Size: 9"x12" • over 90 b/w photographs, map • 80 pp.
ISBN: 0-7643-0220-5 • soft cover • $19.95

The 356th Fighter Group in World War II
in Action over Europe with the P-47 and P-51
Kent D. Miller

This 9th Air Force unit spent over two years in England, occupying the airfield at Martlesham Heath, Suffolk. Originally flying P-47 Thunderbolts and later switching to P-51 Mustangs, the 356th dispatched its aircraft on 407 missions across the Channel. Between October 15, 1943, and the final mission on May 7, 1945, the 356th was credited with destroying 277 enemy planes. As the principle of bomber escort was strictly adhered to by the 356th's leaders, pilots of the group often had to pass up opportunities to engage enemy fighters and increase their scores. While this fact helped earn the 356th a reputation as being a "hard luck" outfit, due to their low victory to loss ratio, the gratitude and praise from the bomber crews more than offset this misnomer.
Size: 81/2"x11" • over 450 b/w photographs, color aircraft profiles • 336 pp.
ISBN: 0-7643-1768-7 • hard cover • $49.95

Yellowjackets!
The 361st Fighter Group in World War II
P-51 Mustangs over Germany
Paul B. Cora

A narrative history of a combat unit attached to the U.S. 8th Air Force in the ETO from December 1943 through the end of the war in Europe. More than a narrow unit history, Yellowjackets! places the experiences of the Group's personnel in perspective with the larger context of the war, and also presents the human side, speaking, at times, from the intensely personal standpoint of the pilots and personnel.
Size: 81/2"x11" • over 130 b/w & color photographs, color aircraft profiles • 152 pp.
ISBN: 0-7643-1466-1 • hard cover • $39.95

The 363rd Fighter Group in World War II
in Action over Germany with the P-51 Mustang
Kent D. Miller

The 363rd Fighter Group was the third P-51 Mustang equipped unit to enter combat in the ETO during the Second World War. Over the years, very little has been written about the 363rd, primarily because it flew as a pure fighter unit for only seven months. Disbanded to become a Tactical Recon Group, the 363rd did not amass a large victory total compared to other 8th and 9th Air Force units, and as such has not warranted the attention of historians or the general public. This history is intended to shed light on the achievements of the 363rd for the period it flew escort and ground support missions over Europe. The day-to-day operations are interspersed with quotes from the group and squadron diaries, and supplemented by an exhaustive appendix to give the reader a look into the combat activities of this little known Army Air Force organization.
Size: 81/2"x11" • over 220 black and white photographs, color aircraft profiles • 192 pp.
ISBN: 0-7643-1629-X • hard cover • $49.95

The 370th Fighter Group in World War II
in Action over Europe with the P-38 and P-51
Jay Jones

The history of the 370th Fighter Group in WWII, conveyed in the words and photos of the veterans. The 370th was organized in 1943 to fly the P-47 Thunderbolt. When the group arrived in England in early 1944, they were assigned to the 9th Air Force and converted to fly P-38 Lightnings. They were involved in every major Allied offensive from D-Day onward. The group supported Operation Cobra, flew missions over the Falaise Gap, and flew cover over Operation Market Garden. On missions after the weather cleared, the men could actually watch from the base as their planes made dive-bombing runs on German armored columns. The group converted to P-51 Mustangs in March 1945, just in time for cover missions during Operation Varsity, the Rhine River crossing. This is one of the most thorough and comprehensive group histories written and is a must for veterans, their families, and enthusiasts.
Size: 81/2"x11" • over 700 black and white and color photographs, color aircraft profiles • 448 pp.
ISBN: 0-7643-1779-2 • hard cover • $59.95

The Debden Warbirds
The 4th Fighter Group in World War II
Frank E. Speer

The P-51 Mustangs of the 4th Fighter Group were the first to escort bombers over Berlin during World War II, the first to escort bombers from England to Russia, and at war's end ranked first in the number of enemy aircraft destroyed (over 1,000). This authentic account, gleaned from the Squadron and Tower Diaries, is enhanced by dozens of combat reports and personal accounts from pilots and crews whose day-to-day encounters are faithfully recorded
Size: 81/2"x11" • over 170 b/w and color photographs • 224 pp.
ISBN: 0-7643-0725-8 • hard cover • $45.00